Frommer's®

Hong Kong

11th Edition, with Macau

by Beth Reiber

WILEY

Wiley Publishing, Inc

Published by:

WILEY PUBLISHING, INC.

111 River St.
Hoboken, NJ 07030-5774

ISBN 978-0-470-87633-6 (paper); 978-1-118-01983-2 (ebk); 978-1-118-01929-0 (ebk); 978-1-118-01984-9 (ebk)

Editor: Lorraine Festa, with Linda Barth
Production Editor: Michael Brumitt
Cartographer: Roberta Stockwell
Photo Editor: Richard Fox
Production by Wiley Indianapolis Composition Services

Front Cover Photo: View of Hong Kong and the Central skyline from Victoria Peak ©Gavin Hellier / Robert Harding Picture Library Ltd. / Alamy Images
Back Cover Photo: Fisherman selling his fresh catch, Sai Kung, New Territories ©Michael Coyne / Lonely Planet Images

For information on our other products and services or to obtain technical support, please contact our Customer Care Department within the U.S. at 877/762-2974, outside the U.S. at 317/572-3993 or fax 317/572-4002.

Wiley also publishes its books in a variety of electronic formats. Some content that appears in print may not be available in electronic formats.

Manufactured in the United States of America

5   4   3   2   1

CONTENTS

LIST OF MAPS

ABOUT THE AUTHOR

Long before she could read, **Beth Reiber** spent hours pouring over her grandparents' latest *National Geographic* magazines. After living four years in Germany as a university student and then as a freelance travel writer selling to major U.S. newspapers like the *Los Angeles Times* and *The Washington Post,* followed by a stint in Tokyo as editor of the *Far East Traveler,* she authored several Frommer's guides, including *Frommer's Japan* and *Frommer's Tokyo.* She also contributes to *Frommer's China* and *Frommer's USA,* and writes a blog for the Japan National Tourist Organization's website at www.japantravelinfo.com. When not on the road, she resides in Lawrence, Kansas, with her two sons, a dog, and a cat in an 1890 Victorian home.

ACKNOWLEDGMENTS

I would like to thank some very special people who graciously extended their help in the preparation of this book: Lillibeth Bishop, Diana Budiman, Gloria Yam, and Mayee Tang of the Hong Kong Tourism Board; and João H. Rodrigues and Teresa Costa Gomes of the Macau Government Tourist Office. A special thanks goes to Carole Klein for her gracious hospitality over the years and infectious enthusiasm for her adopted town; to Jack Graham for being such a great travel partner; and to my sons, Matthias and Johannes, for putting up with my long absences ever since they can remember.

—Beth Reiber

HOW TO CONTACT US

In researching this book, we discovered many wonderful places—hotels, restaurants, shops, and more. We're sure you'll find others. Please tell us about them, so we can share the information with your fellow travelers in upcoming editions. If you were disappointed with a recommendation, we'd love to know that, too. Please write to:

Frommer's Hong Kong, 11th Edition
Wiley Publishing, Inc. • 111 River St. • Hoboken, NJ 07030-5774
frommersfeedback@wiley.com

AN ADDITIONAL NOTE

Please be advised that travel information is subject to change at any time—and this is especially true of prices. We therefore suggest that you write or call ahead for confirmation when making your travel plans. The authors, editors, and publisher cannot be held responsible for the experiences of readers while traveling. Your safety is important to us, however, so we encourage you to stay alert and be aware of your surroundings. Keep a close eye on cameras, purses, and wallets, all favorite targets of thieves and pickpockets.

FROMMER'S STAR RATINGS, ICONS & ABBREVIATIONS

Every hotel, restaurant, and attraction listing in this guide has been ranked for quality, value, service, amenities, and special features using a **star-rating system.** In country, state, and regional guides, we also rate towns and regions to help you narrow down your choices and budget your time accordingly. Hotels and restaurants are rated on a scale of zero (recommended) to three stars (exceptional). Attractions, shopping, nightlife, towns, and regions are rated according to the following scale: zero stars (recommended), one star (highly recommended), two stars (very highly recommended), and three stars (must-see).

In addition to the star-rating system, we also use **seven feature icons** that point you to the great deals, in-the-know advice, and unique experiences that separate travelers from tourists. Throughout the book, look for:

special finds—those places only insiders know about

fun facts—details that make travelers more informed and their trips more fun

kids—best bets for kids and advice for the whole family

special moments—those experiences that memories are made of

overrated—places or experiences not worth your time or money

insider tips—great ways to save time and money

great values—where to get the best deals

The following **abbreviations** are used for credit cards:

AE	American Express	**DISC**	Discover	**V**	Visa
DC	Diners Club	**MC**	MasterCard		

TRAVEL RESOURCES AT FROMMERS.COM

Frommer's travel resources don't end with this guide. Frommer's website, **www.frommers. com,** has travel information on more than 4,000 destinations. We update features regularly, giving you access to the most current trip-planning information and the best airfare, lodging, and car-rental bargains. You can also listen to podcasts, connect with other Frommers. com members through our active-reader forums, share your travel photos, read blogs from guidebook editors and fellow travelers, and much more.

THE BEST OF HONG KONG

Hong Kong is such a feast for the senses it reminds me of a movie set. Maybe I'm an incurable romantic, but when I stand at the railing of the famous Star Ferry as it glides across the harbor, ride a rickety old tram as it winds its way across Hong Kong Island, or marvel at the stunning views afforded from atop Victoria Peak, I can't help but think I must have somehow landed in the middle of an epic drama where the past has melted into the present. So many images float by—wooden boats bobbing up and down in the harbor beside huge ocean liners; crumbling tenements next to ultramodern high-rises; squalid alleys behind luxury hotels; elderly people pushing wheelbarrows as Rolls-Royces glide by; market vendors selling chicken feet and dried squid while talking on cellphones.

In fact, one of the most striking characteristics of Hong Kong is this interweaving of seeming contradictions and the interplay of the exotic and the technically advanced. There are as many skyscrapers here as you're likely to see anywhere, but they're built with bamboo scaffolding and in accordance with the principles of feng shui. Historic trams rumble through Central, while below ground is one of the most efficient subways in the world, complete with the world's first "contactless" tickets, cards that can be waved over a scanner without even taking them out of your purse or wallet. The city has some of the best and most sophisticated restaurants in the world, but it also has *dai pai dong,* street-side food stalls. Hong Kong is home to one of the world's largest shopping malls, but lively makeshift street markets are virtually everywhere.

The more you search for in Hong Kong, the more you'll find. Before long, you, too, may find yourself swept up in the drama.

THE most UNFORGETTABLE TRAVEL EXPERIENCES

○ **Observing a Chinese Festival:** Hong Kong celebrates with several colorful festivals throughout the year, featuring everything from dragon boat races to celebrations honoring Tin Hau, goddess of the sea. Cantonese opera, performed on temporary stages, is also common at Chinese festivals. See "Hong Kong Calendar of Events" in chapter 3.

THE BEST OF HONG KONG | The Most Unforgettable Travel Experiences

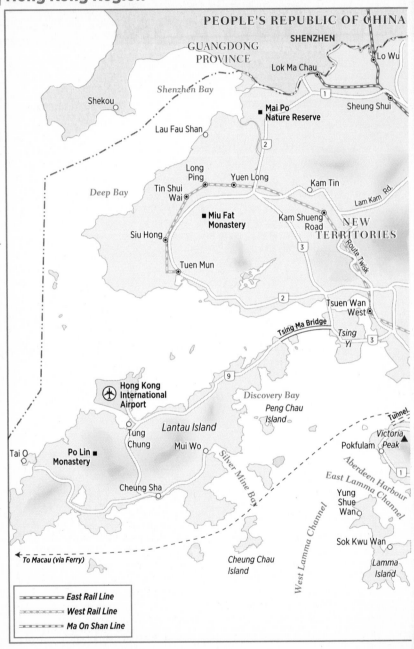

PEOPLE'S REPUBLIC OF CHINA

SHENZHEN

GUANGDONG PROVINCE

Lo Wu

Lok Ma Chau

Shenzhen Bay

1

Sheung Shui

Shekou

Mai Po Nature Reserve

Lau Fau Shan

2

Deep Bay

Long Ping

Yuen Long

Kam Tin

Tin Shui Wai

Lam Kam Rd.

Miu Fat Monastery

Kam Shueng Road

NEW TERRITORIES

Siu Hong

3

Route Twisk

Tuen Mun

2

Tsuen Wan West

Tsing Ma Bridge

Tsing Yi

3

9

Hong Kong International Airport

Discovery Bay

Peng Chau Island

Tunnel

Victoria Peak

Pokfulam

1

Lantau Island

Tung Chung

Mui Wo

Aberdeen Harbour

Tai O

Po Lin Monastery

Silver Mine Bay

East Lamma Channel

Yung Shue Wan

Cheung Sha

Sok Kwu Wan

West Lamma Channel

Lamma Island

← To Macau (via Ferry)

Cheung Chau Island

East Rail Line

West Rail Line

Ma On Shan Line

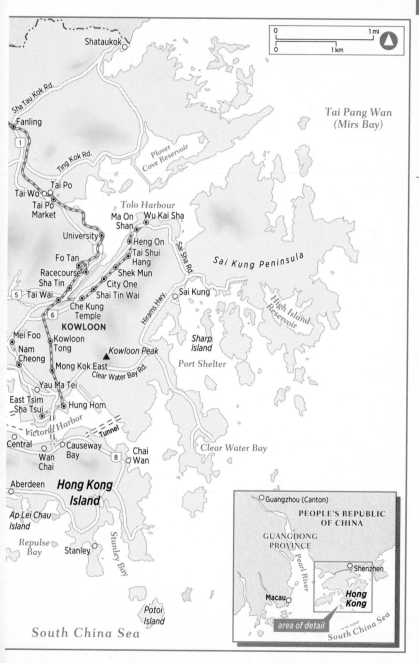

Shataukok

Sha Tau Kok Rd.

Fanling

Ting Kok Rd.

Plover Cove Reservoir

Tai Pang Wan (Mirs Bay)

Tai Po

Tai Wo

Tai Po Market

Tolo Harbour

Ma On Shan

Wu Kai Sha

University

Sai Kung Peninsula

Sai Sha Rd.

Fo Tan

Heng On

Tai Shui Hang

Racecourse

Shek Mun

Sha Tin

City One

Tai Wai

Shai Tin Wai

Sai Kung

High Island Reservoir

Che Kung Temple

Hirams Hwy.

KOWLOON

Mei Foo

Kowloon Tong

Kowloon Peak

Sharp Island

Port Shelter

Nam Cheong

Mong Kok East

Clear Water Bay Rd.

Yau Ma Tei

East Tsim Sha Tsui

Hung Hom

Victoria Harbor

Tunnel

Clear Water Bay

Central

Causeway Bay

Chai Wan

Wan Chai

Aberdeen

Hong Kong Island

Ap Lei Chau Island

Repulse Bay

Stanley

Stanley Bay

South China Sea

Potoi Island

Guangzhou (Canton)

PEOPLE'S REPUBLIC OF CHINA

GUANGDONG PROVINCE

Pearl River

Shenzhen

Macau

Hong Kong

area of detail

South China Sea

0   1 mi
0   1 km

- **Riding the Star Ferry:** The subway between Kowloon and Hong Kong Island may be quicker, but it doesn't hold a candle to the historic Star Ferry, offering one of the most dramatic—and cheapest—5-minute boat rides in the world. The trip is a good reminder that Hong Kong, with its breathtaking skyline, is dominated by water, with one of the world's busiest harbors. See p. 41.

- **Gazing upon Hong Kong from Victoria Peak:** You don't know Hong Kong until you've seen it from here. Take the funicular to Victoria Peak, famous for its views of Central, Victoria Harbour, South China Sea, Kowloon, and undulating hills beyond, followed by a 1-hour circular hike and a meal with a view. Don't miss the nighttime view, one of the most spectacular and romantic in the world. See p. 254.

- **Listening to the World's Largest Professional Chinese Orchestra:** Established 30 years ago, the 80-member Hong Kong Chinese Orchestra is the world's largest, playing traditional and modern Chinese instruments in orchestrations that combine Chinese and Western musical elements. See p. 242.

- **Celebrating Sundown with a Cocktail:** Many hotel lounges offer spectacular views of the city as well as live music. As the sun disappears, watch the city explode in neon. See "Bars, Pubs & Lounges" in chapter 10, beginning on p. 246, for venues with especially good views.

- **Partying until Dawn in Lan Kwai Fong:** It's standing room only at bars and pubs in Central's most famous nightlife district, where the action spills out onto the street and continues until dawn. Other burgeoning nightlife districts include SoHo, Knutsford Terrace, and Wan Chai. See chapter 10.

- **Paying Respects at the Big Buddha:** Laze on the open aft deck during the 50-minute ferry ride to Lantau Island (and enjoy great views of the harbor and skyline along the way), followed by a hair-raising bus ride over lush hills to see the world's largest, seated, outdoor bronze Buddha, located at the Po Lin Monastery. Complete your pilgrimage with a vegetarian meal at the monastery and a visit to Ngong Ping Village with its shopping and Walking with Buddha museum, and then make your return trip via cable car offering more great views. See the "Lantau" section of chapter 11, beginning on p. 267.

- **Zipping over to Macau:** Macau, for centuries a Portuguese outpost until it was handed back to the Chinese in 1999, is just an hour away by jetfoil and offers a fascinating blend of Chinese and Mediterranean lifestyles, evident in its spicy Macanese cuisine, colorful architecture, temples, churches, and many special-interest museums. It's also famous for its Las Vegas–style casinos. Although you can "do" Macau in a day, I strongly urge you to spend at least a couple days here. See chapter 12.

THE best SPLURGE HOTELS

- **InterContinental Hong Kong,** 18 Salisbury Rd., Tsim Sha Tsui (© **800/327-0200** in the U.S., or 852/2721 1211): No hotel lobby boasts a better view of Victoria Harbour and Hong Kong Island than the light-infused lobby of this standout property, right at water's edge in Tsim Sha Tsui. State-of-the-art rooms (most with harbor views), a spa renowned for its anti–jet lag and healing treatments, restaurants that are as fun as they are excellent, and free tai chi and yoga classes make this one of the city's top choices. See p. 80.

- **The Peninsula Hong Kong,** Salisbury Road, Tsim Sha Tsui (© 866/382-8388 in the U.S., or 852/2920 2888): The grand old dame of Hong Kong, this historic hotel, built in 1928, exudes elegance and colonial splendor, with one of the most famous, ornate lobbies in town—a must for afternoon tea. A tower with a top-floor restaurant designed by Philippe Starck, a state-of-the-art spa, classes ranging from cooking to tai chi, Hong Kong's most venerable restaurants, and outstanding service assure this historic hotel a top rating despite newer and more glamorous competitors. See p. 81.
- **Island Shangri-La Hong Kong,** Pacific Place, Central (© 866/565-5050 in the U.S., or 852/2877 3838): There's no mistaking you're anywhere but Asia in Hong Kong Island's tallest hotel, adorned with lush Tai Ping carpets, artistic flower arrangements, and more than 500 paintings, including the world's largest Chinese landscape painting. Spacious rooms combine Asian touches (like Chinese lacquerware TV cabinets) with up-to-date technology (like LCD TVs and DVD players), but the top-floor French restaurant opts for old-world charm as it wows with one of the best dining views in Hong Kong. See p. 87.
- **Mandarin Oriental, Hong Kong,** 5 Connaught Rd., Central (© 800/526-6566 in the U.S., or 852/2522 0111): This is one of Hong Kong's oldest yet newest hotels, first opened in 1963 but recently renovated from top to bottom. Travelers returning for repeat stays will find familiarity in the Captain's Bar, the Chinnery, Clipper's Lounge, and Mandarin Grill, all back by popular demand, but new are the spa with a 1930s Shanghai ambience, restaurants serving French and international cuisine, and luxuriously remodeled rooms with great sitting rooms where the balconies used to be. See p. 83.

THE best MODERATELY PRICED HOTELS

- **Eaton Hotel,** 380 Nathan Rd., Kowloon (© 800/588-9141 in the U.S., or 852/2782 1818): This efficient hotel goes the extra mile, with free daily guided tours of the nearby Temple Street Night Market, free tai chi classes, a rooftop pool, free Internet service in its cafe, and impressive efforts at being green. See p. 89.
- **The Luxe Manor,** 39 Kimberley Rd., Tsim Sha Tsui (© 852/3763 8888): This boutique hotel is like no other, with a whimsical decor that resembles a stage setting for *Alice in Wonderland*—but designed by Salvador Dalí. Unusually shaped furniture, faux fireplaces, and other fun touches make a stay here totally out of the ordinary. See p. 92.
- **The Mira Hong Kong,** 118–130 Nathan Rd., Tsim Sha Tsui (© 852/2368 1111): Style-conscious IT junkies should make a beeline for this übercool hotel, which makes life interesting with its colorful decor, 40-inch TVs that double as computers, and personal mobile phones you can take with you anywhere in Hong Kong. See p. 93.
- **Lan Kwai Fong Hotel @ Kau U Fong,** 3 Kau U Fong, Central (© 852/3650 0000): I love this boutique hotel for several reasons, including its chic Chinese decor and its lively location in the Western District near Graham Street Market. See p. 95.

○ **Bishop Lei International House,** 4 Robinson Rd., Mid-Levels (℃ **852/2868 0828**): There's nothing fancy about this hotel, but I love its location near the Central–Mid-Levels Escalator in a residential neighborhood, its outstanding views from otherwise standard rooms, its coffee shop with an outdoor terrace, and its outdoor pool. A great choice for expat wannabes. See p. 95.

○ **JIA Hong Kong,** 1–5 Irving St., Causeway Bay (℃ **852/3196 9000**): Designed by Philippe Starck, this boutique hotel is Hong Kong's hippest, with 54 stylish rooms complete with kitchenettes and entertainment centers. Guests also enjoy a host of freebies, including free local calls, free Internet access, free breakfast and cocktail hour, free access to a nearby gym, and—for long-staying guests—a free massage. See p. 97.

○ **Lanson Place Boutique Hotel & Residences,** 133 Leighton Rd., Causeway Bay (℃ **852/3477 6888**): This JIA competitor offers much of the same at slightly lower prices, including upbeat, contemporary rooms with kitchenettes (and a welcoming basket of goodies), large LCD TVs, and DVD players (there's a free DVD library on premise). See p. 97.

THE most UNFORGETTABLE DINING EXPERIENCES

○ **Eating Your Way Through China:** There's no better place in the world to sample regional Chinese cuisine than Hong Kong, where you can eat everything from the ubiquitous Cantonese food to Sichuan, Shanghainese, Hunanese, Beijing, Chiu Chow, and Pekingese dishes. See chapter 6.

○ **Stuffing Yourself at a Buffet Spread:** If you have a big appetite or like variety in your meals, the best Hong Kong bargain is the all-you-can-eat buffet spread. Almost all hotels offer buffet lunches and dinners; other restaurants may feature buffets for lunch. Most offer an assortment of international fare, from Japanese sushi and Chinese dishes to pasta and carveries. See chapter 6.

○ **Dining with a View:** Enjoy Chinese or Western cuisine at one of Hong Kong's many restaurants that offer spectacular views of either Kowloon (with its glowing neon lights) or Hong Kong Island (with its skyscrapers and Victoria Peak). In fact, Hong Kong boasts so many restaurants with views, the dilemma will be in the choosing. The absolute winners? Those atop Victoria Peak. See "Around Hong Kong Island" in chapter 6, beginning on p. 154.

○ **Dining on Dim Sum:** Nothing conveys a sense of Chinese life more vividly than a visit to a crowded, lively Cantonese restaurant for breakfast or lunch, when you can feast on spring rolls, steamed dumplings, and other goodies served in bamboo steamers. See the "Dim Sum" section in chapter 6, beginning on p. 157, for more on Hong Kong's dim sum restaurants.

○ **Taking High Tea at a Posh Hotel:** The British rulers may be gone, but their legacy lives on in the afternoon tea. Virtually all upper-class hotels offer afternoon tea, but my favorites are those offered by the Peninsula Hong Kong and InterContinental Hong Kong. Come for afternoon tea, nibble on finger sandwiches, and gaze away. See p. 162.

○ **Relaxing at an Open-Air Seafood Restaurant:** Get rid of stress by relaxing over a meal of fresh seafood at one of Hong Kong's rural waterfront seafood restaurants. My favorite place is Lamma island. See p. 274.

THE best THINGS TO DO FOR FREE (OR ALMOST FREE)

o **Expand Your Horizons at Hong Kong's Museums:** A Museum Pass allowing entry to seven major museums, covering everything from Chinese art and Hong Kong's history to space, science, and cultural life in the New Territories, costs just HK$30. Or, go on Wednesday, when admission to these same museums is absolutely free. For more information on Hong Kong's museums, see chapter 7.

o **Explore Hong Kong's Parks:** Hong Kong's parks are destinations in themselves, offering a wide range of free activities and attractions. Among the most unique are Kowloon Walled City Park, once a no-man's land of slums and now a Chinese garden; Kowloon Park, with free kung fu demonstrations and a small arts fair on Sundays; and Hong Kong Park, with a huge aviary and the Flagstaff House Museum of Tea Ware. For descriptions of Hong Kong's many parks, see chapter 7.

o **"Meet the People":** Learn about pearls, feng shui (geomancy), Cantonese opera, Chinese medicine, Chinese tea, and other cultural traditions on free, 1-hour tours and lectures given by local experts. Inexpensive harbor cruises are also available aboard an authentic junk. To learn more about the Hong Kong Tourism Board's "Meet the People" program, stop by an HKTB Visitor Centre for the *Cultural Kaleidoscope* brochure (or access it online at www.discoverhongkong.com by clicking on "Things to Do"), which outlines the current free offerings. See p. 187.

o **Get Up Early to Watch Tai Chi:** Before breakfast, head to one of Hong Kong's many parks to watch people going through the slow, graceful motions of tai chi. For the best viewing, go to Kowloon Park, Hong Kong Park, Victoria Park, or the Zoological and Botanical Gardens (see "Parks & Gardens" in chapter 7, beginning on p. 180, for more on these parks and gardens). You can even participate in free practice sessions, held three mornings a week on the Tsim Sha Tsui waterfront promenade. See p. 190.

o **Explore the Western District:** Produce, bolts of cloth, live snakes, ginseng, dried seafood, Chinese herbs and medicines, a historic temple, a museum dedicated to Chinese and Western medicine, and antiques and collectibles are just some of the things you'll see while strolling through one of Hong Kong's most fascinating neighborhoods. See p. 61.

o **Stroll Tsim Sha Tsui's Waterfront:** A pedestrian promenade stretches from the Star Ferry eastward along the Sha Tsui and Tsim Sha Tsui East waterfront, providing close-up views of the harbor and Hong Kong Island with its skyscrapers. After dark, this is a wonderful romantic stroll, with the lights of Hong Kong Island shimmering across the water. *A bonus:* Every evening at 8pm, Hong Kong puts on a spectacular laser-and-light show projected from skyscrapers on both sides of the harbor. The best place to see this colorful extravaganza? On the Tsim Sha Tsui waterfront. See p. 255.

o **Get Cultured at the Hong Kong Cultural Centre:** Free family shows two Saturdays a month, which may feature Chinese dance, a magic show, or music, the monthly Thursday Happy Hour spotlighting local groups performing Chinese classical music and other acts, and occasional free outdoor concerts are great entertainment at a price that can't be beat. See p. 244.

o **Imbibe at Happy Hour at a British Pub:** To save money engaged in our favorite sport (we are talking darts here, aren't we?), end a busy day of sightseeing and shopping by rubbing elbows with Hong Kong's working population as they take advantage of happy-hour prices in British pubs throughout the city. Most pubs and bars offer a happy hour that can stretch on for hours, with two drinks for the price of one or drinks at reduced prices. See "Bars, Pubs & Lounges" section of chapter 10, beginning on p. 246, for more on Hong Kong's pubs and bars.

THE best SHOPPING EXPERIENCES

o **Looking for Chinese Souvenirs:** Hong Kong has some great Chinese emporiums, selling vases, vase stands, porcelain figurines, chinaware, calligraphy brushes, bird cages, jade, jewelry, silk jackets, furniture, teas, and various Chinese crafts and products. See chapter 9.

o **Browsing Antiques Shops on Hollywood Road:** Whether you have thousands of dollars to spend on Ming dynasty heirlooms or just a couple of bucks for a snuff bottle, there's something for everyone in the dozens of antiques shops lining this famous Hong Kong Island road and from outdoor vendor stalls on nearby Cat Street. A sightseeing bonus is Man Mo Temple (p. 178), Hong Kong's oldest temple, on Hollywood Road. See p. 224 and the "Antiques & Collectibles" section of chapter 9, beginning on p. 224.

o **Window-Shopping on Nathan Road:** Open-fronted clothing boutiques, jewelry stores, camera shops, tailors, tourists from around the world, international cuisine, huge neon signs, and whirling traffic combine to make this boulevard Hong Kong's most famous shopping street. See p. 223.

o **Feeling Groovy at Shanghai Tang:** This 1930s-style Chinese department store is oh-so-chic, with lime green and fuchsia jackets, 1930s reproduction home decor, and more. The shopping bag that comes with your purchase is a bonus—just way too cool—and the shop's free postcards are also pretty fab. See p. 228.

o **Bargaining at a Street Market:** Hong Kong has more street markets than you can shake a stick at, located on both sides of the harbor and in operation from morning to night. Most famous is Temple Street Night Market, where you can shop for casual clothing, music, toys, and accessories; enjoy a meal at a *dai pai dong* (roadside food stall); watch amateur street musicians; and have your fortune told. See p. 236.

o **Bargain Hunting in Stanley:** Stall after stall of casual wear, silk clothing, tennis shoes, accessories, and souvenirs and crafts imported from China make this a shopper's paradise. And after a day of bargaining, I like to recuperate in one of Stanley's trendy yet casual restaurants. See p. 235.

o **Getting Mall-ed:** Hong Kong is famous for its shopping malls, and with good reason. Ranging from humongous affairs like Harbour City to chic, high-end complexes like ifc mall, shopping malls are great escapes on humid or rainy days and offer everything from clothing and toys to electronics and antiques. See "Megamalls & Shopping Centers" in chapter 9, beginning on p. 237.

o **Visiting a Tailor:** Nothing beats the satisfaction of having something custom-made to fit you perfectly. If this is your dream, make a trek to a tailor one of your first priorities so that you'll have time for several fittings. See p. 238.

THE best ACTIVITIES FOR FAMILIES

- **Running Free in Hong Kong's City Parks:** Hong Kong's parks are great destinations for families. Children can swim or explore playgrounds at Kowloon Park (including one with restored fortifications and cannon emplacements), see jaguars and monkeys at the Zoological and Botanical Gardens, and walk through an aviary at Hong Kong Park. See p. 180, 182, and 182.
- **Cavorting with Mickey at Hong Kong Disneyland:** The smallest of the world's Disney properties but undergoing expansion, Hong Kong Disneyland has the usual attractions, high-powered shows, and fireworks extravaganzas, as well as the world's only Fantasy Gardens, where kids can meet famous Disney characters. A must for families crossing all Disney properties off their to-do list. See p. 183.
- **Regressing to Childhood at Ocean Park:** Southeast Asia's largest oceanarium and fun park boasts one of the world's longest and fastest roller coasters among its many thrill rides. Plus, there's a great cable-car ride with breathtaking views of the South China Sea and playgrounds just for kids. If it's wildlife you're wild about, you'll find the world's largest reef aquarium, a shark tank, a fascinating collection of weird and wonderful goldfish, an aviary, pandas, a dolphin show, and much, much more. A must for kids of all ages. See p. 183.
- **Heading to the Beach:** Life's a beach at a number of Hong Kong Island destinations, but families can make an excursion out of it and take a ferry (kids love that!) to one of the outlying islands like Cheung Chau or Lamma, where there are beaches with lifeguards, changing rooms, and showers. See p. 190, 269, and 272.

THE best OFFBEAT EXPERIENCES

- **Taking a Tram:** Ride a double-decker tram from one end of Hong Kong Island to the other for an unparalleled view of life in the crowded city as you pass skyscrapers, street markets, traditional Chinese shops, and department stores. See p. 169.
- **Hopping Aboard the Central–Mid-Levels Escalator:** Hop aboard the world's longest covered people mover as it snakes its way uphill in a series of escalators. You can hop off at one of 29 exits to enjoy a drink or meal at one of the many establishments along its link, or take it to the top on a 20-minute ride. See p. 174.
- **Having Your Fortune Told:** Want to know about your future love life, marriage, family, or career? Consult one of Hong Kong's many fortunetellers; those who speak English can be found at Man Mo Temple in the Western District, Wong Tai Sin temple, and the Tin Hau Temple near the Temple Street Night Market. See p. 178, 178, and 236, respectively.
- **Hearing the Birds Sing at Yuen Po Street Bird Garden:** See pampered birds at this unusual garden, brought by their owners so they can sing and communicate with other birds on their daily outing. Vendors sell exotic birds, wooden bird cages, porcelain bird dishes, and other paraphernalia. See p. 181.
- **Escaping to the New Territories:** The New Territories are a vast area stretching from the densely populated Kowloon to the Chinese border. About half of Hong Kong's population is housed here in huge satellite towns, but pockets of rural life

and preserved country parks remain. One of the best things to do is follow a self-guided hike that will take you past traditional Chinese homes, temples, and other buildings in a small village. Nature lovers should head to Geopark with its geological wonders. See the section "The New Territories," in chapter 11.

o **Hiking Across Lamma:** An excursion to this outlying island will do your soul good. Start with the 35-minute ferry trip, followed by a 90-minute hike across the island, perhaps some swimming at a beach, and finally a meal of fresh seafood at an open-air waterfront restaurant. See the "Lamma" section of chapter 11, beginning on p. 272.

HONG KONG
IN DEPTH

With a population of seven million and a total land area less than half the size of Luxembourg (or Rhode Island), Hong Kong is one of the most densely populated areas in the world. The best place to appreciate this is atop Victoria Peak, where you can feast your eyes on Hong Kong's famous harbor and, as far as the eye can see, high-rise apartments and office buildings. If Hong Kong were a vast plain, it would be as ugly as Tokyo. But it's saved by undulating mountain peaks, which cover virtually all of Hong Kong and provide dramatic background to the cityscape and coastal areas. Indeed, viewed from Victoria Peak or the Tsim Sha Tsui waterfront, Hong Kong is one of the most beautiful cities in the world.

Hong Kong offers visitors something highly unique—the chance to experience a vibrant Chinese city without sacrificing the comforts of home. To be sure, much of Hong Kong's Western fabric comes from the legacy left by the British, who ruled the colony until 1997, when it was handed back to China as a Special Administrative Region (thus the SAR abbreviation you'll see there and throughout this book). British influence is still evident everywhere, from Hong Kong's school system to its free-market economy, from its rugby teams to its double-decker buses, and from the English pubs and tea in the afternoon to (my favorite) orderly queues. But though the city was molded by the British, it has always been, at heart, Chinese, with Chinese medicine shops, street vendors, lively dim sum restaurants, old men taking their caged birds for walks, and colorful festivals.

It's this juxtaposition of the past and present, and the extreme differences between street life and the high life, that has fueled my love affair with Hong Kong for more than 20 years. Ancient temples stand alongside some of the world's tallest skyscrapers; quaint villages slumber on the fringes of densely packed satellite towns; colorful traditional festivals share the stage with highbrow entertainment. I can eat dim sum for breakfast, cross Victoria Harbour on the historic Star Ferry, hike through a tropical landscape, scout for souvenirs at a street market, get a massage at a state-of-the-art spa, and zip over to Macau for a Macanese meal—all in 1 day. Hong Kong's talent at constantly reinventing itself never ceases to amaze me; the promise of boundless possibilities draws me back again and again.

Hong Kong was founded as a place to conduct business and to trade, and it continues to serve that purpose both aggressively and successfully.

Hong Kong is the "Wall Street of Asia," with banking, international insurance, advertising, and publishing among its biggest industries. Hong Kong boasts the world's 13th-largest trading economy and is one of the world's leading exporters of toys, garments, and watches. Little wonder, then, that as a duty-free port, Hong Kong attracts approximately 29 million visitors a year, making tourism one of its leading industries.

This chapter highlights how Hong Kong came to be the way it is today, providing, I hope, some insight for the experiences you will surely have of your own.

HONG KONG TODAY

Even though the 1997 handover is now long past, the most common question I get about Hong Kong is: "How much has Hong Kong changed?"

If it hadn't dominated the news, I doubt the average tourist would even notice there'd been a handover. Entry formalities for most nationalities remain unchanged. English remains an official language, and the Hong Kong dollar, pegged to the U.S. dollar, remains legal tender. Scores of lanes, roads, and sites are still named after Hong Kong's former governors, and Queen Victoria's statue still graces Victoria Park. In hotels, restaurants, and shops that cater to tourists, it's business as usual.

The most visible difference after the handover was the immediate replacement of the Union Jack and colonial Hong Kong flag with China's starred flag and the new Hong Kong Special Administrative Region's flag emblazoned with the bauhinia flower. In addition, new coins bearing the bauhinia were minted (the old coins with the queen's head remain valid but have been snapped up by collectors) and new stamps were issued. The words "Royal" and "ER" (Elizabeth Regina) disappeared throughout Hong Kong, along with royal crests, crowns, and coats of arms. The police sported new badges.

Otherwise, today, as before the handover, you'll see ducks hanging by their necks in restaurant windows, bamboo scaffolding, Chinese characters on huge neon signs, wooden fishing boats, shrines to the kitchen god, fortunetellers, temples, and laundry fluttering from bamboo poles; you'll still hear the click-clack of mah-jongg tiles and the complexities of Cantonese. All these sensory experiences create an atmosphere that has always been undeniably Chinese.

As for the British population, although it noticeably declined after the handover and has since increased, the number of U.K. residents was never huge anyway (less than 2% before the handover). Yet the British presence loomed understandably larger when Hong Kong was a colony. In other words, the biggest change since the handover, in my opinion, is that Hong Kong seems more Chinese, with more in common with Shanghai and Shenzhen across the Chinese border than with its former colonizer. Hong Kong is overwhelmingly Chinese—some 95% of its residents are Chinese, more than half of whom were born in Hong Kong. Most Hong Kong residents (referred to as Hongkongers in the local press) are Cantonese from southern China, the area just beyond Hong Kong's border—hence, Cantonese is the most widely spoken language of the region. But the Chinese themselves are a diverse people, and today Hongkongers hail from different parts of China, with the city's many Chinese restaurants specializing in Cantonese, Sichuan, Chiu Chow, Pekingese, Shanghainese, and other regional foods serving as delicious testaments to the city's diversity.

Of course, Hong Kong has more links now—financially and emotionally—with mainland China than it ever had in the past. Tourists from Europe, North America, and Japan are now outnumbered by visitors from mainland China, especially since

CHINESE medicine FOR WHAT ails YOU

For most minor ailments, many Chinese are more likely to pay a visit to their neighborhood medicine store than see a doctor. Most traditional medicine stores cater solely to the practice of Chinese herbal medicine, with some cures dating back 2,000 years. The medicinal stock, however, includes much more than roots and plants. Take a look inside one of Hong Kong's many medicinal shops and you'll find a bewildering array of jars and drawers containing everything from ginseng and deer's horn to fossilized bones and animal teeth. Deer's horn is said to be effective against fever; bones, teeth, and seashells are used as tranquilizers and cures for insomnia. In prescribing treatment, herbalists take into account the patient's overall mental and physical well-being in the belief that disease and illness are caused by an imbalance in bodily forces. In contrast to Western medicine, treatment is often preventive rather than remedial. Visitors particularly interested in traditional Chinese medicine will want to visit the **Hong Kong Museum of Medical Sciences** (p. 174).

Acupuncture is also alive and well in Hong Kong. With a history in China that goes back 4,000 years, acupuncture is based on 365 pressure points, which in turn act upon certain organs; slender, stainless-steel needles are used, which vary in length from 1.3 to 25cm (½–10 in.). Most acupuncturists also use moxa (dried mugwort), a slow-burning herb that applies gentle heat. I'm also a fan of foot reflexology, a treatment in which various pressure points in the foot—each one corresponding to a specific organ or body part such as the kidney, brain, or colon, for example—are massaged to promote health.

the 2003 introduction of relaxed travel laws that eliminated the requirement that they visit Hong Kong only in tour groups. Today, mainland Chinese make up more than half of all visitor arrivals into Hong Kong. And whereas they used to seem like poor cousins in awe of the big city, today they are just as likely to be affluent and shopping for designer goods, while Hongkongers travel to the mainland looking for bargains.

Perhaps most striking about Hong Kong since the handover is that it suffers from an identity crisis: What should be its role in a greater China? Long serving as the manufacturing liaison between China and the rest of the world, Hong Kong is now challenged by a dazzling, dynamic, confident Shanghai. Hong Kong manufacturers have moved across the border to Shenzhen to take advantage of lower production costs. Guangzhou threatens to take over Hong Kong's role as a transportation hub. Pollution, primarily from rapid industrial development in the Pearl River Delta and increased traffic, has reached an all-time high, threatening not only the health of its citizens but also Hong Kong's status as a major tourist destination. Even diminutive Macau, touted as Asia's Las Vegas, now challenges Hong Kong's historic role as the region's number-one tourist destination.

All these issues—worsening pollution, the high cost of living in Hong Kong compared to China, a growing tendency for foreign companies to base their workers on the mainland, and the lure of job opportunities in Macau—have led to a decline of professionals living in Hong Kong, both foreign and Chinese.

But if you ask me, Hong Kong isn't going to fade away as a global capital any time soon. Although it, too, is impacted by international events like the economic downturn and swine flu, its economy seems stable, recording more visitors in 2010 than in 2009, fewer bankruptcies, lower unemployment, and climbing housing prices. It seems increasingly clear that Hong Kong's future lies as a financial center, no longer in the position of the low-cost manufacturing base it once was. Several of Hong Kong's major attractions, including Hong Kong Disneyland and Ocean Park, are in the midst of huge expansions, and hotels in all price categories continue to make their debut.

I'm heartened, too, by a new generation of Hongkongers who show a heightened awareness for social issues that were largely ignored by the older generation—indicative, perhaps, of greater freedoms since the handover but also of a greater global awareness. These issues include concerns for the environment, Hong Kong's cultural and architectural heritage, education, and social equity. Grass-roots movements are growing to fight pollution (http://cleartheair.org.hk and www.hongkongcan.org), protect Victoria Harbour from excessive land reclamation (www.harbourprotection.org and www.friendsoftheharbour.org), and even to save the Central Street Market on Graham Street from developers (www.savethestreetmarket.hk) and the Tsim Sha Tsui bus terminal from being turned into a piazza (www.ourbusterminal.org). Hopefully, growing public sentiment will curb the unbridled development that has ruled Hong Kong in the past and nudge it toward being a model city for the rest of China.

Still, no one can predict the future, as Hong Kong has always been a city in transformation. The Hong Kong I am writing about now is not the same city that existed just a few short years ago and is not the Hong Kong you'll probably experience when you go there. Changes occur at a dizzying pace: Relatively new buildings are torn down to make way for even newer, shinier skyscrapers; whole neighborhoods are obliterated in the name of progress; reclaimed land is taken from an ever-shrinking harbor; and traditional villages are replaced with satellite towns. Hong Kong's city skyline has surged upward and outward so dramatically since my first visit in 1983, it sometimes seems like decades must have elapsed each time I see it anew. Change is commonplace, and yet it's hard not to lament the loss of familiar things that suddenly vanish; it's harder still not to brood over what's likely to come.

DATELINE

4,000–1,500 B.C.	Early settlers of Asian Mongoloid stock spread throughout south China, including Hong Kong, leaving behind Neolithic artifacts ranging from pottery and stone tools to burial grounds.
221 B.C.	Hong Kong becomes part of the Chinese empire with unification of China by the first emperor of Qin.
960–1500s	Pirates roam the seas around Hong Kong; Han Chinese settle in what is now the New Territories.
1514	Portuguese traders establish a base in southern China.
1839	The Chinese emperor attempts to abolish the opium trade and destroys the British opium stockpile; the Royal Navy retaliates by firing on Chinese war junks, starting the first Opium War.
1841	British naval Capt. Charles Elliot lands at Possession Point on Hong Kong Island, raises the British flag, and declares himself governor.
1842	The first Opium War ends in the Treaty of Nanking, ceding Hong Kong Island to Britain in perpetuity.

LOOKING BACK AT HONG KONG

Although some people might erroneously believe that Hong Kong's history began after the British took control of the island in 1842, it actually began millennia before that. Stone, bronze, and iron artifacts indicate that Hong Kong Island has been inhabited for at least 6,000 years, and more than 100 Neolithic and Bronze Age sites have been identified throughout the territory, including a 5,000-year-old kiln unearthed on Lantau Island, 4,000-year-old burial grounds, a 2,000-year-old brick tomb, and Neolithic rock carvings.

Early Settlers

Although the area now called Hong Kong became part of the Chinese empire some 2,230 years ago during the Qin dynasty, it was not until after the 12th century that the area became widely settled. Foremost were settler families, known as the Five Great Clans, who built walled cities complete with moats and gatehouses to protect their homes against roving pirates. First to arrive was the Tang clan, who built at least five walled villages and maintained imperial connections with Beijing for 800 years, until the end of the 19th century. Several of these walled villages remain, along with study halls where members of the Tang clan studied for exams that would gain them coveted entrance into the Imperial Civil Service; you can visit these and other historic buildings built by the Tang clan by walking the Lung Yeuk Tau and the Ping Shan heritage trails (p. 261 and 265 in chapter 11). The other four clans were the Hau, Pang, Liu, and Man.

The clans were joined by the Tanka people, who lived their whole lives on boats anchored in sheltered bays throughout the territory and were employed as pearl divers in Tolo Harbour; and by the Hoklos, another seafaring people who established coastal fishing villages. They were followed by the Hakka, primarily farmers who cultivated rice, pineapples, and tea. Garrison troops were stationed at Tuen Mun and Tai Po

---

1846 Hong Kong's population is 24,000. First horse races held at Happy Valley.

1856 Chinese officials searching for pirates arrest the crew of a British ship, prompting the second Opium War, which ends in 1858.

1860 Victorious in the second Opium War and seeking a foothold on the mainland, Britain forces China to cede Kowloon Peninsula and Stonecutters Island to the British in perpetuity in the First Convention of Peking. Population reaches 94,000.

1888 The Victoria Peak Tram is completed, reducing the journey to the Peak from 3 hours to 8 minutes.

1898 With the signing of the Second Convention of Peking, the New Territories are leased to Britain for 99 years, for which Britain pays nothing.

1900 Hong Kong's population is 263,000.

1904 The street tramway system is constructed along the waterfront on Hong Kong Island.

continues

(now major satellite towns in the New Territories) to guard the pearls harvested from Tolo Harbour by Tanka divers, while forts to guard against invasion were constructed at Tung Chung and other coastal regions. By the end of the 19th century, as many as 100,000 people resided in what is now the New Territories.

Tea & Opium

Hong Kong's modern history, however, begins a mere 170 years ago, under conditions that were far less than honorable. During the 1800s, the British were extremely eager to obtain Chinese silk and tea. Tea had become Britain's national drink, but the only place it was grown was China, from which it was being imported to England in huge quantities. The British tried to engage the Chinese in trade, but the Chinese were not interested in anything offered—only silver bullion would do. The Chinese also forbade the British to enter their kingdom, with the exception of a small trading depot in Canton.

But then the British hit upon a commodity that proved irresistible—opium. Grown in India and exported by the British East India Company, this powerful drug enslaved everyone from poor peasants to the nobility, and before long, China was being drained of silver, traded to support a drug habit. The Chinese emperor, fearful of the damage being wreaked on Chinese society and alarmed by his country's loss of silver, declared a ban on opium imports in the 1830s. The British simply ignored the ban, smuggling their illegal cargo up the Pearl River. In 1839, with opium now India's largest export, the Chinese confiscated the British opium stockpiles in Canton and destroyed them. The British responded by declaring war and then winning the struggle. As a result of this first Opium War, waged until 1842, China was forced to open new ports for trade, agree to an exorbitant cash indemnity for the loss of the destroyed opium, and cede Hong Kong Island in perpetuity to the British in a treaty China never recognized. Not only was this Treaty of Nanking demoralizing to the Chinese, but it also ensured that their country would remain open to the curse of opium. And although opium was the cause of the war, it was never even mentioned in the Treaty of Nanking.

1911 The Manchu dynasty is overthrown by Sun Yat-sen's Nationalist revolution; refugees flood into Hong Kong.	**1945** The British resume control of Hong Kong following World War II. Hong Kong's prewar population of 1.6 million now stands at 600,000.
1938 Japan seizes Canton; Hong Kong becomes an arms-smuggling route for the Nationalist forces, now under Chiang Kai-shek; 500,000 Chinese refugees flee into Hong Kong.	**1949** Mao declares the founding of the People's Republic; a subsequent flood of refugees to Hong Kong causes the Communist government to seal the Chinese–Hong Kong border.
1941 Japanese forces occupy Hong Kong and begin deporting residents to the mainland to ease food and housing shortages.	**1950** Mass influx of refugees continues following the fall of Shanghai to the Communists. Population of Hong Kong reaches two million.

Please Don't Pass the Bread

In 1857, a popular but disgruntled Chinese baker, Cheong Ah Lum, was accused of adding arsenic to his bread, poisoning nearly 300 Europeans in retaliation for the Opium Wars. He was acquitted but was deported to China.

Following the second Opium War, waged from 1856 to 1858 as the British sought more trading ports and pushed for the legalization of the opium trade, the tip of Kowloon Peninsula and Stonecutters Island were added to the colony in 1860. In 1898, Britain decided it needed more land for defense and dictated a lease for the New Territories (despite the 100,000 Chinese living there) and more than 200 outlying islands, for 99 years, until 1997. The only piece of land the British didn't acquire was a Chinese fort, constructed in 1847 to defend Kowloon after the British takeover of Hong Kong Island (today the site is the Kowloon Walled City Park; see p. 180).

The Promised Land

When the British took control of Hong Kong Island in 1842, some 7,000 Chinese lived on the island in farming and fishing communities. Although Hong Kong had a deep and protected harbor, no one, including the Chinese, was much interested in the island itself, and many in the British government considered its acquisition an embarrassing mistake. No sooner had the island been settled than a typhoon tore through the settlement. Repairs were demolished only 5 days later by another tropical storm. Fever and fire followed, and the weather grew so oppressive and humid that the colony seemed to be enveloped in a giant steam bath.

Yet, while the number of headstones in the hillside cemetery multiplied, so too did the number of the living, especially as word spread of the fortunes being made by merchants who had established trading houses for the booming trade in silk, tea, spices, and opium. Soon after the turn of the 20th century, the population had

1953 Following a huge fire in a squatter camp, Hong Kong begins an ambitious public housing program to house its still-growing population of refugees.

1966 A fare increase on the Star Ferry prompts clashes between Chinese and the police.

1967 The Cultural Revolution in China leads to pro-Communist riots in Hong Kong; 51 people are killed, and hundreds more are wounded or arrested in the fighting.

1972 First cross-harbor tunnel opens.

1979 Establishment of Hong Kong's Mass Transit Railway subway system. Hong Kong governor Sir Murray MacLehose goes to Beijing for the first Sino-British discussions on the return of Hong Kong to Chinese rule.

1981 British Parliament downgrades Hong Kong passports to prevent an exodus of Hong Kong Chinese to the United Kingdom.

continues

A barren Island, with hardly a House upon it.
—Lord Palmerston, Britain's Foreign Secretary, in a letter to Hong Kong's first British administrator, Sir Charles Elliot, 1841

swelled to 300,000. British families lived along the waterfront and called it Victoria (now the Central District), slowly moving up toward the cooler temperatures of Victoria Peak (still home of stately mansions, Victoria Peak is one of Hong Kong's main attractions; p. 168). The Chinese, barred from occupying the Peak and other European-only neighborhoods, resided in a shantytown farther west, now called the Western District. Conditions were so appalling that when the bubonic plague struck in 1894, it raged for almost 30 years, claiming more than 20,000 lives (the Pathological Institute, established to combat the plague, now houses the Hong Kong Museum of Medical Sciences; p. 174).

Hong Kong's growth in the 20th century was no less astonishing in terms of both trade and population. In 1900, approximately 11,000 ships pulled into Hong Kong harbor; just a decade later, the number had doubled. In 1911, the overthrow of the Manchu dynasty in China sent a flood of refugees into Hong Kong, followed, in 1938, by an additional 500,000 immigrants. Another mass influx of Chinese refugees arrived after the fall of Shanghai to the Communists in 1950. From this last wave of immigrants, including many Shanghai industrialists, emerged the beginnings of Hong Kong's now-famous textile industry. Throughout the 1950s, Hong Kong grew as a manufacturing and industrial center for electronics, watches, and other low-priced goods. By 1956, Hong Kong's population stood at 2.5 million.

Change, Unrest & the Last of the British

As a British colony, Hong Kong was administered by a governor appointed by the queen. There were no free elections, and the Legislative Council, Hong Kong's main governing body (popularly referred to as LegCo), was also appointed. As 1997 drew

1984 China and Britain sign the Joint Declaration for the handover of Hong Kong to China in 1997.

1989 Events at Tiananmen Square in Beijing send shock waves through Hong Kong. Some 80,000 demonstrators brave a typhoon in support of the pro-democracy uprising.

1997 Britain transfers Hong Kong to Communist China, ending 156 years of British rule. Hong Kong's first outbreak of avian flu at the end of the year, killing six people, prompts the new government to order the slaughter of 1.3 million chickens.

2003 An outbreak in Hong Kong of severe acute respiratory syndrome (SARS) spreads around the globe, infecting more than 8,000 people and delivering a shocking blow to Hong Kong's economy.

2007 Hong Kong becomes mostly smoke-free, including its restaurants; bars and nightclubs join the smoking ban in 2009. China announces it will allow Hong Kong to directly elect its chief executive in 2017 and all its Legislative Council (LegCo) members in 2020.

nearer, marking the end of the 99-year lease on the New Territories, it soon became clear that China had no intention of renewing the lease or renegotiating a treaty it had never recognized in the first place.

Finally, after more than 20 rounds of talks and meetings, Britain's Prime Minister Margaret Thatcher signed the Sino-British Joint Declaration of 1984, agreeing to transfer all of Hong Kong to Chinese Communist rule on June 30, 1997. China declared Hong Kong a Special Administrative Region, granting it special privileges under a "one country, two systems" policy that guaranteed Hong Kong's capitalist lifestyle and social system for at least 50 years after 1997. Under provisions set forth in the Sino-British Joint Declaration and in Hong Kong's constitution, the Basic Law, Hong Kong would remain largely self-governing, and its people would retain rights to their property, to freedom of speech, and to travel freely in and out of Hong Kong. Throughout the negotiations, however, Hong Kong's residents were never consulted.

Then came the events of June 1989 in Tiananmen Square, in which hundreds of students and demonstrators were attacked by Chinese authorities in a brutal move to quash the pro-democracy movement. China's response to the uprising sent shock waves through Hong Kong and led to rounds of angry protest.

Those who could emigrate did so, primarily to Australia, Canada, and the United States; at its height, more than 1,000 people were emigrating each week. After all, nearly half of Hong Kong's Chinese are refugees from the mainland, and as one Hong Kong Chinese told me, his family fled to escape Communist rule, so why should he stay after 1997? Most of Hong Kong's Chinese, however, remained confident (or at least hopeful) that China realized it had more to gain by keeping Hong Kong as it was. In a move that angered Communist China, Hong Kong Chinese were granted more political autonomy during the last few years

2010 LegCo, in a compromise between Beijing and pan-democrats pushing for universal suffrage for the 2012 elections, votes to increase LegCo membership from 60 to 70 and to expand the election committee for the chief executive from 800 to 1,200. Legislators also pass Hong Kong's first-ever minimum wage law.

of the colony's existence than in all the preceding 150 years, including various demo-cratic reforms such as elections for the Legislative Council. Some early emigrants began returning to Hong Kong, confident they could do better in their native country and willing to wait to see how life might change under the Chinese. Except now they had a safety net: foreign passports.

On June 30, 1997, the last British governor of Hong Kong, Chris Patten, sailed out of Hong Kong, 4,000 Chinese troops marched in, and Tung Chee-hwa, appointed by the Chinese government, became the new chief executive of the Special Administra-tive Region (SAR). Mainland China celebrated the event as the end of more than 100 years of shame. On July 1, it dissolved Hong Kong's elected Legislative Council and replaced it with a handpicked Provisional Legislature until a new Legislative Council, with both elected and appointed members, could be formed.

After the Handover

Hong Kong's first elections under Chinese rule, in 1998, allowed for one-third of the 60-member legislature to be elected by direct popular vote, with the Democrats—Hong Kong's largest party—winning the most seats (although full suffrage, with a fully elected legislature and chief executive, is declared a goal in the Basic Law, it has no timetable). Meanwhile, like the rest of Asia, Hong Kong was hit hard by economic recession, made worse by manufacturers moving across the Chinese border into Shenzhen to take advantage of cheaper land prices and cheaper wages.

After the handover, the SAR began allowing 150 mainland Chinese to migrate to Hong Kong every day—more than 54,000 a year. In January 1999, Hong Kong's Court of Final Appeal ruled that the Basic Law also granted automatic Hong Kong residency to any mainland Chinese with one Hong Kong parent, even if that parent gained residency after the child was born. However, fearing an explosion of unplanned population growth, with an estimated 1.6 million additional qualified immigrants potentially pouring in from the mainland, coupled with increased unemployment, Tung Chee-hwa asked Beijing to review the immigration ruling, a move interpreted by critics as a threat to the judicial independence of the SAR. China responded by overturning the immigration judgment issued by Hong Kong's highest court and pro-viding a narrower interpretation of the Basic Law, thereby cutting the number of potential new immigrants over the next decade from 1.6 million to about 200,000. Only mainland children who were born *after* a parent received legal resident status were given a "right of abode." In January 2002, Hong Kong's Court of Final Appeal affirmed the Chinese government's reversal of its earlier ruling and ordered 7,300 "unlawful migrants" to leave the SAR. Only 3,000 complied; the remaining 4,300 were forcibly removed to the mainland by police.

A bigger rift in Hong Kong–Beijing relations came in 2003, when an anti-subver-sion bill was introduced by Tung Chee-hwa's Beijing-backed administration. The measure—meant to outlaw subversion, sedition, treason, the theft of state secrets, and other crimes against the state—brought more than 500,000 protesters to Hong Kong's streets on July 1, 2003, making it the SAR's largest protest since the Tianan-men Square massacre. Tung Chee-hwa withdrew the bill, but another blow to Hong Kong democracy came in 2004, when Beijing ruled against a public election for Hong Kong's chief executive in 2007 and declared that there would be no universal suffrage for the Legislative Council election slated for 2008. Hong Kong's pro-democracy leaders responded that Hong Kong's autonomy had been violated, with the core prin-cipals of the Basic Law and the 1984 Sino-British Joint Declaration—that Hong

SARS & Avian Flu

While no one can be certain that new outbreaks of SARS and avian flu will never happen (the last outbreaks for both in Hong Kong occurred in 2003), Hong Kong is ready. The temperatures of all passengers passing through border controls—at the Hong Kong airport, the border checkpoint between Hong Kong and mainland China, and ferry terminals serving Macau and beyond—are thermally scanned for fever, and hand sanitizers are strategically placed throughout Hong Kong. See "Medical Requirements," under "Entry Requirements" in chapter 3, for more information.

Kong would be ruled by the people of Hong Kong—replaced by a Beijing dictatorship. In September 2004, elections for the 60-member Legislative Council allowed an increase in the number of elected members from 24 to 30; the remaining 50% were elected by functional constituencies, consisting mostly of special-interest groups with ties to Beijing.

The biggest news to garner international attention during this time, however, was not Hong Kong's long struggle for autonomy, but rather its role in the eruption of a mysterious, flulike illness in 2003. Spreading from a Hong Kong hotel, severe acute respiratory syndrome (SARS) infected more than 8,000 people in 29 countries over the next few months, killing more than 700 of them. In Hong Kong, which together with China suffered the most, the illness sickened 1,775 people and claimed almost 300 lives. Needless to say, SARS was a major blow to Hong Kong's economy, reducing the city to a tourist ghost town and costing it $4 to $6 billion in retail trade and business. Unemployment hit 8.7%, the highest since the statistic was first recorded in 1981. To encourage tourism and boost the local economy, Hong Kong turned to action film star Jackie Chan as its international spokesperson.

In March 2005, Tung Chee-hwa, Hong Kong's only leader since the handover, unexpectedly announced his resignation, citing ill health and igniting rumors that Beijing had forced his exit in an effort to curb Hong Kong's growing discontent and resultant push for greater democracy. Donald Tsang Yam-kuen, a career civil servant educated at Harvard and backed by Beijing, was chosen to finish out Tung's remaining 2 years of office and in 2007 was selected for an additional 5-year term. In 2007, China finally announced it would allow Hong Kong to directly elect its own leader in 2017 and all its lawmakers by 2020 (but gave no road map for elections in 2012 and 2016). More than 20 years after the handover, Hong Kong would finally be a democracy.

THE LAY OF THE LAND

The Hong Kong SAR, with a population of just over seven million, is located at the southeastern tip of the People's Republic of China, some 2,000km (1,240 miles) south of Beijing; it lies just south of the Tropic of Cancer at about the same latitude as Mexico City, the Bahamas, and Hawaii. Some people who have never been to Asia may think of Hong Kong as an island—and they'd be right if it were 1842. But not long after the colony was first established on Hong Kong Island, the British felt the need to expand, which they did by acquiring more land across Victoria Harbour on the Chinese mainland. Today, Hong Kong Island is just a small part of the SAR, which covers 1,100 sq. km (425 sq. miles) and measures 49km (30 miles) north to south and 73km (45 miles) east to west—much of it mountainous.

Hong Kong, comprising 18 administrative districts, can be divided into four distinct geographic areas: Hong Kong Island, Kowloon Peninsula, the New Territories, and the outlying islands. On **Hong Kong Island** are the Central District (Hong Kong's main financial and business district and usually referred to simply as Central), the Western District, Wan Chai, and Causeway Bay, all on the island's north side. Hong Kong Island is the home to such major attractions as Hong Kong Park, Victoria Peak, Stanley Market, Ocean Park, Aberdeen, the Zoological and Botanical gardens, Lan Kwai Fong nightlife district, several shopping malls, and Hollywood Road with its many antique shops.

Across Victoria Harbour, at the tip of **Kowloon Peninsula,** is Tsim Sha Tsui and its many hotels, restaurants, museums, and shops, as well as Tsim Sha Tsui East, and the Yau Ma Tei and Mong Kok districts.

The **New Territories** cover by far the largest area, stretching north of Kowloon all the way to the Chinese border. Once a vast area of peaceful little villages, fields, and duck farms, the New Territories in the past few decades have witnessed a remarkable mushrooming of vast satellite towns with huge public-housing projects. Sha Tin, with a population of more than 700,000 and home to one of Hong Kong's two horse-racing tracks, is the largest; in all, the New Territories house approximately half of the SAR's population, mostly in virtual "cities" that can number in the hundreds of thousands. And yet, much of the New Territories remains open and uninhabited. Close to 70% of Hong Kong's total landmass is rural, with 23 country parks and 14 nature reserves accounting for more than 40% of Hong Kong's land area. One of the most pristine regions is Sai Kung, which, together with the northeast New Territories, is home to the new Geopark.

As for Hong Kong's 260 **outlying islands,** most are barren and uninhabited; those that aren't lend themselves to excellent exploration into Hong Kong's past. Lantau, Lamma, and Cheung Chau are three of the region's best known and most easily accessible islands, where a gentler, slower, and more peaceful life prevails. Lantau, boasting the world's largest seated bronze Buddha (located near a monastery noted for its vegetarian meals), is the most popular destination, accessible by ferry and cable car. Lamma is famous for its open-air waterfront seafood restaurants, beaches, pleasant hiking trails, and expat community, while Cheung Chau makes for a pleasant half-day excursion with its lively traditional village, boat population, and beach.

HONG KONG'S ARCHITECTURE

Historic Architecture

If you never ventured much beyond the waterfronts of Victoria Harbour, you might easily believe that Hong Kong is nothing more than chrome-and-glass skyscrapers, huge housing projects, shopping malls, and miles of glowing neon signs heralding countless open-fronted shops.

But Hong Kong was inhabited long before the British arrived, and some precolonial Chinese architecture still survives in the hinterlands. Several rural villages boast buildings and temples with fine woodcarving and are examples of centuries-old Chinese craftsmanship. Especially fascinating are the walled villages in the **New Territories,** a few of which are still inhabited, and one has been meticulously restored and turned into a museum of traditional lifestyles (p. 264 in chapter 11). These villages were built

FENG SHUI: IN balance WITH nature

Feng shui, which translates literally as "wind water," is an ancient method of divination in which harmony is achieved with the spirits of nature. Virtually every Hong Kong Chinese believes that before a house or building can be erected, a tree chopped down, or a boulder moved, a geomancer must be called in to make certain that the spirits inhabiting the place aren't disturbed. The geomancer, who uses a compasslike device as an aid, determines the alignment of walls, doors, desks, and even beds, so as not to provoke the anger of the spirits residing there. He does this by achieving a balance among the eight elements of nature—heaven, earth, hills, wind, fire, thunder, rain, and ocean. Also considered are the spirits of yin (male-active) and yang (female-passive) forces that control our world.

Even non-Chinese-owned companies in Hong Kong comply with feng shui principles, if only to appease their Chinese employees. But it doesn't hurt to be safe; tales abound of ill luck befalling those working or living inside buildings that ignored the needs of resident spirits.

Because facing the water is considered excellent feng shui, when the Regent Hotel (now the InterContinental) was constructed, it incorporated a huge glass window overlooking the harbor, which served the dual purpose of allowing the mythical nine Kowloon dragons to pass through the building on their way to the harbor to bathe. The next best thing, if you can't look out over water, is to bring the water inside, which is why many offices, shops, and restaurants have aquariums. Another way to deflect evil influences is to hang a small, eight-sided mirror outside your window. Other Chinese touches are incorporated into modern architecture—the HSBC bank (formerly the Hongkong and Shanghai Bank), for example, is guarded by a pair of bronze lions, protecting its occupants.

from the 14th through the 17th centuries by clan families to protect themselves from roving bandits, invaders, and even wild tigers. A few of the clans' ancestral halls, study halls, homes, and courtyard mansions also survive; these are best seen on walks along the **Lung Yeuk Tau** and **Ping Shan Heritage Trails** in the New Territories (also in chapter 11).

Also surviving are some of Hong Kong's temples, most famous of which is **Man Mo** on Hollywood Road, built in the 1840s and dedicated to the gods of literature and war (p. 178). Not quite as old but surrounded by a colorful street market is the **Man Mo Temple** in Tai Po (p. 260). Remains of old forts and garrison towns erected by the Chinese government during the Ming and Qing dynasties include foundation remnants in what is now the **Kowloon Walled City Park** (p. 180).

Some colonial architecture also remains. Early Western-style buildings, with their long verandas and wooden shutters, were built with local materials and designed to accommodate the colony's humid climate. The **Flagstaff House,** in Hong Kong Park, is the oldest surviving colonial-style building, constructed in 1846 and now home to a museum of tea ware (p. 173). The **former Supreme Court** in Central features Greco-Victorian columns and Chinese wood-beam eaves. Today it houses the Legislative Council chamber but will become home to the Court of Final Appeals at the end of 2011. Other imposing colonial buildings on Hong Kong Island include the **former French Mission Building, St. John's Cathedral,** the

Western Market, and the **Central Police Station** (see "Walking Tour 1" and "Walking Tour 2" in chapter 8 for more information on these buildings).

On the Kowloon side, one of Hong Kong's most familiar landmarks is the 1921 **clock tower** next to the Star Ferry terminus at Tsim Sha Tsui; it is all that remains of the old railway station that once linked the colony with China and beyond. The **Hong Kong Observatory,** on a banyan-covered hill above Tsim Sha Tsui, is a handsome two-story structure with arched windows and long verandas. Built in 1883, it continues to monitor Hong Kong's weather but is closed to the public (you can catch a glimpse of it behind iron gates). The most imposing colonial structure in Tsim Sha Tsui, however, is undoubtedly the **former Marine Police Headquarters,** occupying a commanding position overlooking the harbor. It has been renovated into 1881 Heritage, an imposing complex housing trendy shops, restaurants, and a small boutique hotel.

Contemporary Architecture

Construction in Hong Kong has been going on at such a frenzied pace that if you haven't been here in 20 years (or even 10), you probably won't recognize the skylines on both sides of the harbor. One of the first major changes to the skyline was the extension of the **Hong Kong Convention and Exhibition Centre** on reclaimed land on the Wan Chai waterfront, boasting the world's largest plate-glass window at the time and a three-tiered roof said to resemble a gull's wings in flight. The 78-story **Central Plaza,** located near the Wan Chai waterfront, boasts an Art Deco style with eye-catching nighttime lighting that changes color with each quarter-hour, thereby giving the time. The **HSBC** bank, designed by British architect Norman Foster, features entire floors suspended from steel masts and a 48m-tall (157-ft.) sun scoop on the roof that uses 480 mirrors to reflect sunlight down into the bank's atrium and public plaza. Atop Victoria Peak is the **Peak Tower,** topped by a crescent-shaped bowl not unlike a wok. But Hong Kong Island's tallest building is the 88-story **Two IFC (International Finance Centre)** tower beside Hong Kong station, which at 415m (1,362 ft.) was the fourth-tallest building in the world at its completion in 2003.

All of Hong Kong's present skyscrapers will soon be eclipsed by **Union Square,** in West Kowloon next to Kowloon Station. The massive 1.1-million-square-meter (12-million-sq.-ft.) development will include three 75-story residential towers, the Elements shopping mall, and Hong Kong's new tallest building (International Commerce Center) housing the world's highest elevated hotel (a Ritz-Carlton, opened Dec 2010) on the 102nd to 118th floors.

Even though Hong Kong's structures are Western, they are built using bamboo scaffolding and constructed according to ancient Chinese beliefs, especially the 3,000-year-old Taoist principle of feng shui that allows humankind to live in peace with the environment and nature, ensuring good luck, prosperity, wealth, health, and happiness. Even today, most office and apartment buildings in Hong Kong have been laid out in accordance to feng shui principles (see "Feng Shui: In Balance with Nature," above).

No discussion of Hong Kong's buildings would be complete without a mention of its most prevalent structures: housing for its seven million inhabitants. Because of Hong Kong's dense population and limited land space, with more than 43,000 people per sq. km (⅔ sq. mile) in Kowloon, Hong Kong has long been saddled with acute housing deficiencies. Just a few decades ago, in an area called Mong Kok in northwestern Kowloon, an astounding 652,910 people were packed in per square mile. One house designed for 12 people had 459 living in it, including 104 people who shared one room and four people who lived on the roof.

After 1953, when a huge fire left more than 50,000 squatters homeless, Hong Kong pursued one of the world's most ambitious housing projects, with the aim of providing every Hong Kong family with a home of its own. By 1993, half of Hong Kong's population lived in government-subsidized public housing, a higher proportion than anywhere else in the world (today, that number stands at about 29%, as new housing is constructed by the private sector).

Most housing estates are clustered in the New Territories, in a forest of high-rises that leaves foreign visitors aghast. Each apartment building is at least 30 stories tall, containing about 1,000 apartments and 3,000 to 4,000 residents. Seven or eight apartment buildings comprise an estate, which is like a small town with its own name, shopping center, recreational and sports facilities, playgrounds, schools, and social services. A typical subsidized apartment is indescribably small by Western standards—approximately 23 sq. m (248 sq. ft.), with a single window. It consists of a combination living room/bedroom, a kitchen nook, and bathroom, and is typically shared by a couple with one or two children. According to government figures, every household in Hong Kong has at least one TV; many have one for each member of the household, even if the house consists of only one or two rooms. More than 70% of households also have computers connected to the Internet.

But as cramped, unimaginative, and sterile as these housing projects may seem, they're a vast improvement over the way much of the population used to live and the way Hong Kong's poorest live even to this day. An estimated 100,000 live in flats that have been divided into "cage homes," tiered bunk beds encircled by wire mesh. As many as 30 occupants may inhabit a single flat.

Because of Hong Kong's land value, even families who can afford private housing often live in what would be considered cramped quarters in the West. One young woman told me she lived in Tsim Sha Tsui in a 46-sq.-m (495-sq.-ft.) flat, which she shared with four other members of her family. At the other end of the extreme, of course, are Hong Kong's wealthy class, many with villas nestled on hills on Hong Kong Island or luxury apartments in ritzy developments like Discovery Bay on Lantau Island.

HONG KONG IN POPULAR CULTURE: BOOKS & FILM

Books

If you want to read about Hong Kong before setting out on your trip, good places to start are *A Concise History of Hong Kong* by John Carroll (Rowman & Littlefield, 2007) or *A Modern History of Hong Kong* by Steve Tsang (I.B. Tauris, 2007), both of which give a thorough historical account of the colony's ignoble beginnings through the 1997 handover. I love looking at pictures of old Hong Kong, and especially fascinating is Nigel Cameron's *An Illustrated History of Hong Kong* (Oxford University Press, 1991), with photographs that show Hong Kong of yore and vividly illustrate how much the city has changed. An even more thorough pictorial history is presented in *Old Hong Kong* (FormAsia Books Ltd., 2002), edited by Trea Wiltshire and covering Hong Kong from 1860 through the June 1997 handover.

Life in the infamous Walled City is the subject of Greg Girard and Ian Lambot's *City of Darkness: Life in Kowloon Walled City* (Watermark Publications, 2003), complete with photographs of a life now vanished. Even though it's dated, one of my favorite books is Jan Morris's *Hong Kong* (Vintage, 1997), which traces the evolution of the British colony from its birth during the Opium Wars to just before the handover. This book gives a unique perspective on the workings of the former colony and imparts an astonishing wealth of information.

For an intimate view of Hong Kong, try *Hong Kong: Borrowed Place, Borrowed Time* (Praeger, 1968) by Richard Hughes, a foreign correspondent who lived in Hong Kong for several decades and was said to have been the inspiration for several characters in John Le Carré's novels. *Gweilo: Memories of a Hong Kong Childhood* (Bantam, 2005), written by Martin Booth just before he died, is a poignant memoir of growing up in Hong Kong in the 1950s. Enjoying unrestricted freedom, Booth as a child even entered the notorious Kowloon Walled City. An interesting counterpart, this time from the Chinese point of view during the same period, is *Diamond Hill* (Blacksmith Books, 2009), about author Feng Chi-shun's teenage years growing up in a Hong Kong squatter village.

A great accompaniment to any guidebook is *Travelers' Tales Hong Kong* (Travelers' Tales, 2000), an anthology edited by James O'Reilly and filled with personal accounts and essays by well-known writers about life in Hong Kong, including those by Jan Morris, Bruce Chatwin, and Paul Theroux. *Hong Kong: Somewhere Between Heaven and Earth* (Oxford University Press, 1996), edited by Barbara-Sue White, is a collection of poems, short stories, novel excerpts, letters, speeches, and diaries with ties to Hong Kong, written by both Chinese and people of other nationalities from all walks of life—soldiers, doctors, politicians, writers, and others, from Queen Victoria to Jules Verne and ranging from historical accounts dating from the Song dynasty to modern times.

Fictional accounts that depict the character of Hong Kong are the classics: Richard Mason's *The World of Suzie Wong* (Signet, 1957) and Han Suyin's *A Many-Splendored Thing* (Little Brown, 1952), an autobiographical account of life in Hong Kong shortly after the Chinese revolution in the late 1940s and early 1950s. James Clavell's *Tai-Pan* (Atheneum, 1966) is a novel about Hong Kong's beginnings; *Noble House* (Delacorte Press, 1981) is its sequel. John Le Carré's *The Honourable Schoolboy* (G. K. Hall, 1977) details the activities of George Smiley, acting head of the British Secret Service in Hong Kong. *The Monkey King*, by Timothy Mo (Paddleless Press, 2000), is a hilarious account of a Macau native who marries into a dysfunctional Cantonese family in 1950s Hong Kong. *Fragrant Harbor* (Penguin, 2003) by John Lanchester is a historical novel that brings to life Hong Kong from the 1930s to the present, as seen through the eyes of an Englishman in love with a Chinese woman and spying for the Empire during the Japanese occupation. In *The Train to Lo Wu* (Dial Press, 2006), author Jess Row gives food for thought in seven short stories about dysfunctional foreigners and Chinese struggling to make sense of life in today's Hong Kong. Janice Y. K. Lee's gripping love story, *The Piano Teacher* (Viking, 2009), takes place during a tumultuous time in Hong Kong's history—before, during, and after Japanese occupation—and skillfully shows what people will endure to survive.

Films

Several classic novels, described above, were made into movies, including *The World of Suzie Wong* (1960), shot mainly in Wan Chai and starring William Holden and

Nancy Kwan (I love the movie for its shots of old Hong Kong, as well as for tackling interracial relationships); *Love Is a Many Splendored Thing* (1955), also starring Holden and considered the first Hollywood film to put Hong Kong on the international movie map; and *Tai Pan* (1986), shot entirely on location in Hong Kong, Macau, and the Pearl River Delta.

Popular movies shot in Hong Kong have included three films in the 007 series: *You Only Live Twice* (1967), *The Man with the Golden Gun* (1974), and *Die Another Day* (2002). Other movies with scenes shot in Hong Kong include *Around the World in 80 Days* (1956), *A Countess from Hong Kong* (1967), *Lara Croft Tomb Raider: The Cradle of Life* (2003), *The Hitchhiker's Guide to the Galaxy* (2005), *Fantastic Four: Rise of the Silver Surfer* (2007), and *The Dark Knight* (2008).

Enter the Dragon (1973), starring Bruce Lee, introduced martial arts to the Western world and began Hong Kong's long tradition of kung fu movies. Jackie Chan, who has long served as an ambassador for Hong Kong tourism, directed and starred in *Police Story* (1985), in which the actor performed his own stunts in many memorable large-scale action scenes. Chan returns to Hong Kong in scenes appearing in *Rush Hour 2* (2001).

As for local filmmakers, probably none is as internationally known as Hong Kong director Wong Kar-wai, who first hit the international radar with his *Chungking Express* (1994), which follows the lives of two cops in Hong Kong and the mysterious women they fall in love with. *In the Mood for Love* (2000), set in 1960s Hong Kong, is a slow-paced film about a man and a woman who rent rooms next to each other. It doesn't provide any views of Hong Kong, but it's worth seeing just for the various cheongsams (Chinese-style dresses) worn by actress Maggie Cheung.

Infernal Affairs (2002), directed by Andrew Lau and Alan Mak, is a crime thriller about a police officer who infiltrates a triad crime gang and a triad member who infiltrates the police department. Its success spawned two more films and was remade in 2006 by Martin Scorsese as *The Departed*, which went on to receive four Academy Awards. More recent movies include *Bodyguards and Assassins* (2009), directed by Teddy Chan and set in 1905 Hong Kong when Sun Yat-sen came to the colony to plot an overthrow of the Qing government; and *Echoes of the Rainbow*, directed by Alex Law, about a boy growing up in Sheung Wan in the 1960s (the movie inspired a grass-roots effort to save a row of tenements used in the film).

PLANNING YOUR TRIP TO HONG KONG

3

Much of the anxiety associated with travel comes from a fear of the unknown—not knowing what to expect can give even seasoned travelers butterflies. This chapter will help you prepare for your trip to Hong Kong—but don't stop here. Reading through the other chapters before leaving will also help you in your planning. Just learning that Hong Kong has hiking trails and beaches, for example, may prompt you to pack your hiking boots or swimsuit. In any case, Hong Kong doesn't require the advance preparations that some other Asian destinations require, such as visas for most nationalities or inoculations. However, keep in mind that information given here may change during the lifetime of this book. For additional help in planning your trip and for more on-the-ground resources in Hong Kong, see "Fast Facts: Hong Kong & Macau," in chapter 13.

WHEN TO GO

Hong Kong's peak tourist season used to be in spring and fall, but now tourists come to Hong Kong virtually year-round, especially from neighboring mainland China. It's best, therefore, to make hotel reservations well in advance, particularly if you're arriving during the Chinese New Year, one of the festivals described below, or during the two peak vacation periods for mainland Chinese (the so-called "Golden Weeks" beginning May 1 and Oct 1). In addition, major conventions and trade fairs can also tie up the city's best hotels, particularly in spring (Mar–Apr) and autumn (Oct–Nov); check www.discoverhongkong.com for an updated calendar. If you're on a budget, keep in mind that many Hong Kong hotels offer package deals and cheaper rates in summer and winter.

Climate

Because of its subtropical location, Hong Kong's weather is generally mild in winter and uncomfortably hot and humid in summer, with an average annual rainfall of 2.3m (89 in.). The most pleasant time of year is late September through early December, when skies are clear and sunny, temperatures are around 70° to 78°F (21°–26°C), and the humidity drops to 70%. January and February are the coldest months, when temperatures can drop to 50°F (10°C) but usually hover around 60°F (16°C). You'll want a jacket during this time.

UNDERSTANDING THE DELUGE: TROPICAL storm WARNINGS

It's not likely you'll experience a tropical storm during your stay in Hong Kong, but if you do, consider it part of your Asian experience. Called typhoons (after the Cantonese *dai fung,* which translates as "big wind") and cyclones in this part of the world and called hurricanes in the West, these severe tropical storms can vent their fury from May to November but are especially prevalent in September. There's no need to worry that a storm may sneak up on you unaware—storms are tracked and monitored and are rated according to their strength. Their approach dominates local news, but even if you don't read the newspapers or listen to the evening news, you'll see other telltale signs of a coming typhoon—Mass Transit Railway (MTR) stations, hotel lobbies, and businesses post notices, and shopkeepers cover their windows with storm shutters.

Whenever a severe tropical rainstorm or typhoon is approaching Hong Kong, an alert is broadcast continuously on TV and the radio to keep you informed of the storm's movements. To keep people better informed of the severity of a storm, a system of numbers has been developed that begins at Typhoon Signal No. 1, continues to Typhoon Signal No. 3, and then jumps to Typhoon Signal No. 8 and up. (The numbers in between were dropped when the long range proved too confusing.)

Typhoon Signal No. 1 goes up when a tropical storm that could escalate into a typhoon has moved within an 800km (497-mile) radius of Hong Kong. Although public transportation and organized tours and outdoor activities continue as scheduled, this signal indicates that the public should be on alert. Most locals, however, are rather indifferent to a No. 1, especially since this condition can last for several days, with little physical indication of an approaching storm.

Typhoon Signal No. 3 is given when the winds have escalated, accompanied, perhaps, by heavy rains. By this time, organized guided tours and harbor cruises have generally been suspended. Visitors should check with authorities before venturing on day trips to the outlying islands or Macau. Some businesses may close, as employees head for home while public transportation is still running.

Typhoon Signal No. 8 indicates that the gale has reached Hong Kong. Banks, offices, museums, and most shops and restaurants close, and road, ferry, rail, and air transport is suspended. Never take a Signal No. 8 lightly, but rather, remain in your hotel and celebrate with a typhoon party, which is pretty much what everyone else does. There's nothing like a tropical storm to set the adrenaline running. The last time a No. 10 typhoon reached Hong Kong (with hurricane force wind reaching sustained speeds of upwards from 118 km/73 miles per hour) was in 1999.

Full details of Hong Kong's typhoon warning system can be found in the local telephone directory. For information during a storm, listen to TV or radio broadcasts or call the Hong Kong Observatory at ✆ **852/2835 1473** or check its website at www.hko.gov.hk.

In spring (Mar–May), the temperature can range between 64° and 81°F (18°–27°C) and the humidity rises to about 85%, with fog and rain fairly common. That means you'll need a raincoat and the cloud-enveloped Victoria Peak won't provide much of a view. By May, it can also be quite hot and muggy.

By summer (late May to mid-Sept), temperatures are often between 89° and 99°F (32°–37°C), humidity can be 90% or more, and there's little or no relief, even at night. If you're visiting the SAR this time of year, you'd be prudent to carry a hat, sunblock, sunglasses, and plenty of bottled water with you wherever you go. You'll also want a light jacket for air-conditioned rooms and an umbrella. This is when Hong Kong receives the most rain; it's also typhoon season. However, Hong Kong has a very good advance-warning system (see box, above).

Hong Kong's Average Monthly Temperatures & Days of Rain

	JAN	FEB	MAR	APR	MAY	JUNE	JULY	AUG	SEPT	OCT	NOV	DEC
TEMP. (C°)	16	16	19	22	26	28	29	29	28	25	21	18
TEMP. (F°)	61	61	66	72	79	80	84	84	80	77	70	64
DAYS OF RAIN	5.6	9.4	10.4	11.6	15.4	18.7	17.7	17.4	14.8	8.1	5.6	4.2

Holidays

Hong Kong has 17 public holidays a year, including some of the festivals described below. The majority are Chinese and are therefore celebrated according to the lunar calendar, with different dates each year (for a rundown of Hong Kong's 2011 holidays, see "Fast Facts: Hong Kong & Macau" in chapter 13; for 2012 lunar holidays, which had not yet been determined when this book went to press, go to www.lcsd.gov.hk/en/home.php). Because most shops, restaurants, and attractions remain open except during the Chinese New Year, the holidays should not cause any inconvenience to visitors. Banks, however, are closed.

Hong Kong Calendar of Events

If you're lucky, your trip might coincide with one of Hong Kong's colorful festivals. The only festival that shops and offices close for is the Chinese New Year, though some in Tsim Sha Tsui remain open to cater to tourists.

Below are the most popular events, including Chinese festivals and festivals of the arts. For additional information on all of these events the **Hong Kong Tourism Board** (**HKTB;** ☎ **852/2508 1234** in Hong Kong; www.discoverhongkong.com) can provide detailed information on where events are being staged and how to get there. For several of the festivals, HKTB even offers organized tours, which are one of the best ways to secure front-row seats without battling the crowds.

For an exhaustive list of events beyond those listed here, check http://events.frommers.com, where you'll find a searchable, up-to-the-minute roster of what's happening in cities all over the world.

JANUARY/FEBRUARY

Chinese New Year. The most important Chinese holiday, this is a 3-day affair, a time for visiting friends and relatives, settling debts, doing a thorough housecleaning, consulting fortunetellers, and worshipping ancestors. Strips of red paper with greetings of wealth, good fortune, and longevity are pasted on doors, and families visit temples. Most shops (except those in tourist areas) close down for at least 2 or 3 days; streets and building facades are decorated with elaborate light displays; flower markets sell peach trees, chrysanthemums, and other good-luck flowers; a colorful parade winds its way along the waterfront, usually on the first day; and a dazzling display of fireworks lights up the harbor, usually on the second day of the holiday. Because this festival is largely a family affair (much like the Christian Christmas), it holds little interest for the tourist. In fact, if you're planning a side trip into China, this would be the worst time to go, since all routes to the mainland are clogged with Hong Kong Chinese returning home to visit relatives. Late January or early February (Feb 3–5, 2011).

FEBRUARY/MARCH

Hong Kong Arts Festival. This is a month-long celebration with performances by world-renowned orchestras, pop and jazz ensembles, and opera, dance, and theater companies (including experimental theater and Chinese operas); and with ethnic music and art exhibitions. For a schedule of events, venues, and ticket information, call ✆ **852/2824 2430** or HKTB at ✆ **852/2508 1234,** or visit the website www.hk.artsfestival.org. February/March (Feb 17–Mar 27, 2011).

MARCH

Hong Kong Sevens Rugby Tournament, Hong Kong Stadium. Known as "the Sevens," this is one of Hong Kong's most popular, and one of Asia's largest, sporting events, with more than 20 teams from around the world competing for the Cup Championship. Tickets (priced at HK$880 for a 3-day pass) are often sold out. For more information, contact the Hong Kong Rugby Football Union at ✆ **852/2504 8311** or check the websites www.hkrugby.com or www.hksevens.com.hk. Fourth weekend in March.

MARCH/APRIL

Ching Ming Festival, all Chinese cemeteries (especially in Aberdeen, Happy Valley, Chai Wan, and Cheung Chau island). A Confucian festival to honor the dead, observed by sweeping ancestral graves, burning incense, offering food and flowers, and picnicking among the graves. Contact HKTB at ✆ **852/2508 1234.** Fourth or fifth day of the Third Moon, March/April (Apr 5, 2011).

Hong Kong International Film Festival, Hong Kong Arts Centre, Hong Kong Cultural Centre, City Hall, and other venues around town. More than 250 films from more than 50 countries are featured at this 2-week event, including new releases, documentaries, and archival films. Tickets for most events cost HK$60. For more information, call ✆ **852/2970 3300,** or check www.hkiff.org.hk. Two weeks in March/April.

APRIL

Tin Hau Festival, all Tin Hau temples, especially in Joss House Bay (Sai Kung) and Tai Shu Ha (Yuen Long). This colorful festival celebrates the birth of Tin Hau, goddess of the sea and Hong Kong's most popular deity among fishing folk. The celebration stems from a legendary fisherman's daughter who could supposedly calm stormy seas and protect fishermen. To pay her tribute, fishing boats are decorated with colorful flags, parades and lion dances fill the streets, and family shrines are carried to shore to be blessed by Taoist priests. A similar festival is held at A-Ma Temple in Macau. Contact HKTB, which organizes special tours of the events, at ✆ **852/2508 1234.** Twenty-third day of the Third Moon, usually in April (Apr 25, 2011).

APRIL/MAY

Cheung Chau Bun Festival, Pak Tai Temple, Cheung Chau island. Unique to Hong Kong, this weeklong affair is thought to appease restless ghosts and spirits. Originally held to placate the unfortunate souls of those murdered by pirates, it features a street parade of lions and dragons and Chinese opera, as well as floats with children seemingly suspended in the air, held up by cleverly concealed wires. The end of the festival is heralded by three bun-covered scaffolds erected in front of the Pak Tai Temple, with selected contestants scrambling up them to retrieve the buns, which supposedly bring good luck to those who receive them. HKTB organizes tours of the parade; call ✆ **852/2508 1234.** Usually late April or early May (May 10, 2011).

Buddha's Birthday, Buddhist temples throughout Hong Kong. Worshippers flock to pay respect to Siddhartha, founder of Buddhism, and to bathe Buddha statues. The Po Lin Monastery on Lantau Island is one of the most popular destinations on this day. Contact the HKTB at ✆ **852/2508 1234.** Ninth day of the Fourth Moon, usually either in April or May (May 10, 2011).

Dragon Boat Races (Tuen Ng Festival). Races of long, narrow, gaily painted boats are powered by 20 to 22 oarsmen who row to the beat of drums. The races originated in ancient China, where legend held that an imperial advisor drowned himself in a Hunan river to protest government corruption. His faithful followers, wishing to recover his body, supposedly raced out into the river in boats, beating their paddles on the surface of the water and throwing rice to distract sea creatures from his body. Tai O, on Lantau, holds a religious ceremony, featuring dragon boats carrying deities to four temples and residents burning paper offerings. Otherwise, qualifying heats for the races are held in Aberdeen, Sai Kung, Cheung Chau, and Lantau, with final races on the main day best seen from Stanley Beach. For a front-row seat, contact HKTB at ✆ **852/2508 1234** for special race-day tours. Fifth day of the Fifth Moon (June 6, 2011).

AUGUST

Yue Lan Festival (Festival of the Hungry Ghosts). Released from the underworld, ghosts are believed to roam the earth for 1 lunar month each year. Religious ceremonies and offerings of food and paper replicas of life's necessities are burned to appease the spirits of discontented ghosts (those who were murdered, died without proper funeral rites, or are without descendants to care for them), in an attempt to prevent the unhappy souls from seeking vengeance on humans. Popular venues are King George V Memorial Park in Kowloon and Moreton Terrace Playground in Causeway Bay. Contact HKTB at ✆ **852/2508 1234** for more information. Fourteenth day of the Seventh Moon (Aug 14, 2011).

Mid-Autumn Festival, Victoria Park, Kowloon Park, and Victoria Peak. Held in early autumn, this major festival (sometimes referred to as the Moon Festival) celebrates the harvest and the brightest moon of the year. In honor of the event, local people light lanterns in the shapes of fish, flowers, and even ships and planes; gaze at the moon; and eat mooncakes (sweet rolls with sesame seeds, duck eggs, and ground lotus seeds). The mooncakes commemorate the 14th-century uprising against the Mongols, when written messages calling for the revolt were concealed in cakes smuggled to the rebels. Today the Urban Council organizes lantern carnivals in parks on both Hong Kong Island and Kowloon, where you can join the Chinese for strolls among hundreds of lanterns, making this one of Hong Kong's most charming and picturesque festivals. In addition, don't miss the dragon fire dance in Causeway Bay's Tai Hang district. Contact HKTB at ✆ **852/2807 1234.** Fifteenth day of the Eighth Moon, either in September or October (Sept 12, 2011).

OCTOBER

Chung Yueng Festival, all Chinese cemeteries. The second time of year when ancestral graves are swept and offerings are made. It's also a popular hiking day. Ninth day of the Ninth Moon (Oct 5, 2011).

Wine and Dine Festival, West Kowloon Promenade. Food vendors set up booths along the promenade, allowing visitors to sample award-winning local dishes and wine from around the world. Four days at the end of October.

ENTRY REQUIREMENTS

Passports

For information on how to get a passport, go to "Passports" in chapter 13 (p. 329).

Visas

The only document most tourists need to enter the Hong Kong Special Administrative Region (SAR) is a passport, valid for at least 1 month beyond the planned departure date from Hong Kong. Americans, Australians, New Zealanders, Canadians, and other British Commonwealth citizens can stay for 90 days without a visa, while citizens of the United Kingdom can stay for 180 days without a visa. Immigration officers may also ask arriving visitors for proof of onward travel or a return ticket (unless they are in transit to mainland China or Macau) and proof that they have adequate funds for their stay in Hong Kong (generally, a confirmed hotel reservation and a credit card will suffice).

Once in Hong Kong, visitors must carry photo identification at all times, such as a passport or driver's license. Safeguard your passport in an inconspicuous, inaccessible place like a money belt. If you lose it, visit the nearest consulate of your native country as soon as possible for a replacement. As an extra safety precaution, it's a good idea to photocopy your passport; keep a copy separate from your passport, such as in your luggage, and give a copy to family or friends at home.

If you plan to make an excursion to **mainland China,** you'll need a visa, which can be obtained easily in Hong Kong. Applications require one photo and generally take 3 working days to process. Your passport must have at least 6 months validity beyond your planned date of departure (see "China," in chapter 11 on p. 275 for information on obtaining a visa to China).

Customs

Visitors 18 and older are allowed to bring into the SAR duty-free a 1-liter (34-oz.) bottle of alcohol and 19 cigarettes (or 1 cigar or 25 grams of tobacco). For more information, go to www.customs.gov.hk.

WHAT YOU CAN TAKE HOME FROM HONG KONG

For information on what you're allowed to bring home, contact one of the following agencies:

U.S. CITIZENS: U.S. Customs & Border Protection (CBP), 1300 Pennsylvania Ave. NW, Washington, DC 20229 (✆ **877/287-8667;** www.cbp.gov).

CANADIAN CITIZENS: Canada Border Services Agency, Ottawa, Ontario, K1A 0L8 (✆ **800/461-9999** in Canada, or 204/983-3500; www.cbsa-asfc.gc.ca).

U.K. CITIZENS: HM Customs & Excise, Crownhill Court, Tailyour Road, Plymouth, PL6 5BZ (✆ **0845/010-9000;** from outside the U.K., 020/8929-0152; www. hmce.gov.uk).

AUSTRALIAN CITIZENS: Australian Customs Service, Customs House, 5 Constitution Ave., Canberra City, ACT 2601 (✆ **1300/363-263;** from outside Australia, 612/6275-6666; www.customs.gov.au).

NEW ZEALAND CITIZENS: New Zealand Customs, The Customhouse, 17–21 Whitmore St., Box 2218, Wellington, 6140 (✆ **04/473-6099** or 0800/428-786; www.customs.govt.nz).

Medical Requirements

No shots or inoculations are required for Hong Kong, but the temperature of all arriving passengers is taken upon entering customs; if you have a fever, you may be quarantined as a protection against H1N1 or avian flu. In addition, you will need proof of a vaccination against cholera if you have been in an infected area during the 14 days preceding your arrival. For information on SARS, see "Staying Healthy" (p. 47).

GETTING THERE & GETTING AROUND

Getting to Hong Kong

With dozens of airlines and half a dozen cruise lines serving Hong Kong from around the world, it's certainly not difficult to get there. Your itinerary, the amount of time you have, and your pocketbook will probably dictate how you travel. Below are some pointers to get you headed in the right direction.

BY PLANE

Because the flight to Hong Kong International Airport (HKG) is such a long one (almost 16 hr. from Chicago, 12 hr. from London, and 9 hr. from Sydney), you may wish to splurge for a roomier seat and upgraded service, including special counters for check-in, private lounges at the airport, and better meals, as well as a higher ticket price when choosing your carrier. You should also consider a mileage program, because this round-trip flight will earn you a lot of miles.

Cathay Pacific, Hong Kong's flagship airline, offers the most flights, with connections from North America, the United Kingdom, and Australia. Dragonair is a Hong Kong–based airline that serves many cities in Asia. Likewise, sister airlines Hong Kong Airlines and Hong Kong Express are both based in Hong Kong and service some 30 cities in Asia.

To find out what other airlines fly into Hong Kong, as well as contact information, see p. 332 in chapter 13.

ARRIVING AT HONG KONG INTERNATIONAL AIRPORT

No one who ever flew into Hong Kong's former Kai Tak Airport could likely forget the experience of landing in one of the world's most densely populated cities. The runway extended out into the bay, past apartments so close you could almost reach out and touch the laundry fluttering from the bamboo poles.

But Kai Tak, which ranked as the world's third-busiest airport in 1996, was retired in 1998. Taking its place is **Hong Kong International Airport** (✆ **852/2181 8888;** www.hongkongairport.com), more than four times the size of Kai Tak when it opened and now consisting of two terminals. Situated just north of Lantau Island on reclaimed land, about 32km (20 miles) from Hong Kong's central business district, the state-of-the-art airport is one of the world's most user-friendly.

Regardless of which terminal you arrive at, after Customs you'll find yourself in the arrivals hall. One of the first things you should do is stop by one of three **Hong Kong Tourism Board (HKTB)** Visitor Centres, where you can pick up maps, sightseeing brochures, and a wealth of other information, as well as get directions to your hotel. They're open daily from 7am to 11pm. The computers at **iCyberLink** provide access to www.discoverhongkong.com 24 hours a day.

Also in the arrivals hall is the counter of the **Hong Kong Hotels Association** (✆ **852/2383 8380** or 852/2769 8822; www.hkha.com.hk), where you can book a room in one of its 100-some member hotels without paying a service fee; it's open daily from 7am to midnight. You won't find any rock-bottom prices here, but they can book rooms in several low-priced lodgings.

If you plan on traveling to Macau sometime during your stay in Hong Kong, stop by the **Macau tourist information counter,** in the arrivals lobby of Terminal 1, at AO6; it's open daily from 9am to 1pm, 1:45 to 6pm, and 6:45 to 10pm. However, if you are traveling directly to Macau from Hong Kong International Airport via the Ferry Transfer service, *do not pass through immigration*. Rather, follow the signs FER-RIES TO MAINLAND/MACAU to the ferry ticketing counter, where you can purchase ferry tickets and proceed directly to the ferry pier (see chapter 12, "Macau," for more information).

You can **exchange money** at the arrivals hall, but because the rate here is rather unfavorable, it's best to exchange only what you need to get into town—about US$50 should do it.

If you need to leave luggage at the airport, a **luggage-storage counter** is located on the departure floor. Other facilities include a post office, a medical center, shops, and restaurants. Wi-Fi is available free throughout the entire airport.

Getting into Town from the Airport

The quickest way to get to downtown Hong Kong is via the sleek **Airport Express Line** (✆ 852/2881 8888; www.mtr.com.hk), which you'll spot straight ahead of you after passing Customs and entering the arrivals hall. Trains run every 12 minutes between 5:50am and 1:15am and take 20 minutes to reach Kowloon Station (off Jordan Rd. and accessible to hotels in Tsim Sha Tsui and Yau Ma Tei) and 24 minutes to reach Hong Kong Station, on Hong Kong Island in the Central District. From both Kowloon and Hong Kong stations, free Airport Express Shuttle Bus service transfers passengers to most major hotels, departing every 12 to 20 minutes between 6:12am and 11:12pm (see www.mtr.com.hk for a list of hotels served). Otherwise, taxis are readily available from both stations.

Fares for the Airport Express are HK$90 to Kowloon and HK$100 to Central; round-trip tickets are HK$160 and HK$180, respectively. Or, if you're in Hong Kong fewer than 14 days, consider purchasing the tourist-only Airport Express Travel Pass for HK$300, which includes round-trip fare from and to the airport and allows unlimited travel by public transportation for 3 days; one-way airport travel plus the 3 days unlimited public transportation will only set you back HK$220. See "Getting Around" below for more information and other ticket options.

In addition to the Airport Express train, dedicated airport buses connect the airport with major downtown Hong Kong areas. Easiest if you have lots of luggage is the **Airport Hotelink** (✆ 852/3193 9333; www.trans-island.com.hk), which provides door-to-door service between the airport and 100-some hotels. Tickets, available at counter B01 near exit B of the arrival hall, cost HK$130 to Kowloon and HK$150 to Hong Kong Island, with buses departing every 30 to 60 minutes. It takes about 30 to 40 minutes to reach Tsim Sha Tsui, depending on the traffic.

Slower and cheaper, with more stops along major streets near hotels, are **Cityflyer** buses operated by Citybus (✆ 852/2873 0818; www.nwstbus.com.hk) and city buses operated by Long Win (✆ 852/2745 4466; www.kmb.hk), both with ticket counters in the arrivals hall (if you pay onboard, you must have exact fare or use an Octopus card; p. 37). Most important for tourists are bus A21, which travels through Mong Kok, Yau Ma Tei, Jordan, and down Nathan Road through Tsim Sha Tsui on its way to Hung Hom Station; and A11, which travels to Hong Kong Island, with stops in Central, Wan Chai, Causeway Bay, and North Point. Buses depart every 10 to 30 minutes from about 6am to midnight, with fares costing HK$33 to Kowloon and HK$40 to Central and Causeway Bay. There's also night bus service, with N21 traveling to Tsim Sha Tsui and N11 traveling to Hong Kong Island.

The easiest way to travel from the airport, of course, is to simply jump in a **taxi,** since taxis are quite cheap in Hong Kong but expensive for the long haul from the

PLANNING YOUR TRIP TO HONG KONG

Getting There & Getting Around

airport. Depending on traffic and your final destination, a taxi to Tsim Sha Tsui costs approximately HK$300 and takes 30 to 45 minutes, while a taxi to the Central District will cost about HK$365 and will take 35 to 50 minutes. An extra luggage charge of HK$5 applies to each piece of baggage.

Departing from the Airport

Passengers flying Cathay Pacific, Continental, Delta, United, Virgin Atlantic, and many other airlines are offered the extra benefit of being allowed to check in for return flights at one of two satellite train stations—at Hong Kong Station in Central and at Kowloon Station, both served by the Airport Express Line (see above) and subway lines. Both allow you advance check-in any time from 24 hours to 90 minutes before your flight: You'll get your boarding pass, and your bags will be transferred to the airport. In addition, a left-luggage service is available at both stations, daily 6am to 1am and useful if your flight is later in the day and you want to do some sightseeing before heading for the airport. Rates per piece of luggage weighing up to 30kg (66 lbs.) are HK$40 for up to 3 hours and HK$55 for 3 to 24 hours.

If you travel directly to the airport and go through check-in there, plan on arriving about 2 hours before departure of your flight.

A final note about departing: Travelers may not bring sharp objects (knives, cutters, scissors, razor blades, household cutlery) in their carry-on but may pack them in checked bags. Also, gels, aerosols, and liquids in carry-on baggage are limited to containers not more than 100ml (3 oz.) and must fit into one quart-size clear plastic bag; otherwise, check it or it will be confiscated.

BY TRAIN

It's unlikely you'll arrive in the SAR by train, unless, of course, you're traveling via China. The Beijing-Kowloon Intercity Through Train provides a direct link between the two cities in approximately 24 hours. One-way tickets cost HK$1,191 for a bed in a deluxe, two-bed cabin, HK$934 for a "soft bed" in a four-bed cabin, and HK$574 for a "hard bed" in a six-bed cabin. Service is also available from Shanghai in about 19 hours (HK$508–HK$1,039 one-way) and from Guangzhou (formerly Canton; HK$190–HK$230 one-way) and taking less than 2 hours.

The end terminus for train travel to Hong Kong is Hung Hom in Kowloon, with Mass Transit Railway (MTR) service onward to East Tsim Sha Tsui Station with its many underground passageways to area hotels.

BY BOAT

Some 30 international cruise ships make Hong Kong a port of call each year. The SAR's main docking facility for cruise liners is Ocean Terminal, located in the heart of Tsim Sha Tsui and part of a massive shopping complex which includes 700 shops and 50 restaurants. Just a stone's throw away is the Star Ferry with service to Hong Kong Island. To accommodate growing demand, another cruise terminal is planned for the former Kai Tak airport runway, with a scheduled opening in 2013.

Extensive ferry service from neighboring Guangdong Province, across the border in mainland China, is offered by the **Chu Kong Passenger Transport Co.** (© 852/2858 3876; www.cksp.com.hk). Ferries from Nan Hai (port of call for Guangzhou), Zhu Hai, Shantou, Sanbu, and a dozen other cities arrive at the China HK Ferry Terminal in Tsim Sha Tsui.

TurboJET (© 852/2859 3333; www.turbojet.com.hk) operates jetfoil service from Macau and Shenzhen to the Hong Kong Macau Ferry Terminal on Hong Kong

Island, with MTR connection to the rest of the city. A limited number of jetfoils also go to the China HK Ferry Terminal in Tsim Sha Tsui.

BY BUS

The CTS Express Coach, a branch of the China Travel Service (℅ **852/3604 0118;** http://ctsbus.hkcts.com), operates an extensive fleet of cross-boundary buses that travel some 90 routes between Hong Kong, Macau, and destinations in Shenzhen and Guangdong, with numerous departures daily. Buses from Guangzhou to Wan Chai MTR station, for example, cost HK$80 one-way.

Getting Around

If you've just been to Tokyo or Bangkok, Hong Kong will probably bring a rush of relief. For one thing, English is everywhere—on street signs, on buses, and in the subways. In addition, almost 1,000 pink and blue directional signs posted on streets and intersections throughout Hong Kong point to attractions and points of interest (signs in rural areas are green). The city of Hong Kong is so compact, and its public transportation system so efficient and extensive, that it's no problem at all zipping from Tsim Sha Tsui to Causeway Bay or vice versa for a meal or some shopping. Even the novice traveler should have no problem getting around. Transportation is also extremely cheap. Just remember that cars drive on the left side of the street, English style, so North Americans need to be careful when stepping off the curb (luckily for most of us, warnings painted on the street at many major intersections remind pedestrians which direction to look).

BY PUBLIC TRANSPORTATION

Each mode of transportation in the SAR—bus, ferry, tram, and train/subway—has its own fare system and thus requires a new ticket each time you transfer from one mode of transport to another. If you're going to be in Hong Kong for a few days, however, you'll find it much more convenient to travel with the **Octopus.** This electronic smart card allows users to hop on and off trains, trams, subways, buses, and ferries without worrying about purchasing tickets each time or fumbling for exact change. Sold at Customer Service Centres at all MTR stations (including the airport) and some ferry piers, the Octopus costs a minimum of HK$150, including a HK$50 refundable deposit (minus a HK$7 handling fee if returned within 3 months), and can be reloaded in HK$50 and HK$100 increments. Children and seniors pay HK$70 for the card, including deposit.

Exact Change, Please

Keep in mind that transportation on buses and trams requires the **exact fare,** so be certain to have lots of loose change with you wherever you go. Even though ferries and subways will give change, you'll find it more convenient if you have exact change, especially during rush hours.

Alternatively, several other stored-value tickets are available for non–Hong Kong residents who will be in Hong Kong fewer than 14 days. The Airport Express Travel Pass, for example, is good for 3 days of unlimited travel: The HK$300 card includes a round-trip from and to the airport on the Airport Express Line; the HK$220 card includes one trip from or to the airport. There's also a Tourist Day Pass, allowing 1 day of MTR travel (except the Airport Express, MTR buses, which travel betweens stations, and first class on the East Rail) for HK$55.

To use the Octopus, simply sweep the card across a special pad at the entry gate (you'll notice that most commuters don't even bother removing the card from their wallets or purses); the fare is automatically deducted. The Octopus is valid for all MTR lines (including those serving the New Territories), the Airport Express Line (which runs between the airport and Kowloon and Central), all trams (including the Peak Tram), buses, some minibuses, the Star Ferry, and ferries to outlying islands. In addition, the Octopus can be used for purchases at all 7-Eleven, Circle K, and Metro Store convenience stores; fast-food chains like KFC, Starbucks, and McDonald's; some vending machines; and even to make phone calls at Pacific Century Cyber Works (PCCW) public telephones. At the end of your Hong Kong stay, be sure to turn in the Octopus card for a refund of your deposit (minus a HK$7 handling fee) and any unused value stored in the card. For information, call the Octopus hot line at ℂ **852/2266 2222** or check its website at www.octopus.com.hk.

By Train & Subway

The Star Ferry and trams are so popular and at times so crowded that it's hard to imagine what they must have been like before Hong Kong's subway system was constructed to relieve the human crunch. Hong Kong's **Mass Transit Railway (MTR)** is modern, efficient, clean, and easy to use, and it's also much faster than the older modes of transportation (and sometimes even taxis). Take note, however, that there are no public toilets at any of the stations or on the trains, and that smoking, drinking, and eating are prohibited. The MTR operates daily from 6am to about midnight or 1am, depending on the line and station. For general inquiries, call the MTR 24-hour hot line at ℂ **852/2881 8888** or check its website at www.mtr.com.hk.

Built primarily to transport commuters in the New Territories to and from work and running under the harbor to link Kowloon with Hong Kong Island, the MTR serves about 3.7 million passengers a day. You'll probably want to avoid rush hours, unless you want to know what it feels like to be a sardine in a can.

ROUTES   The 11 train and subway lines are color coded. When you ride the train the name of the next station is displayed above each compartment door and announced in English, so you shouldn't have any problem finding your way around. Stations are named for the areas they serve: Go to Central MTR station if you're looking for an address in the Central District, or to Mong Kok MTR station if you're looking for a place in Mong Kok, Kowloon. Probably the most important line for tourists is the **red-coded Tsuen Wan Line,** which starts in Central on Hong Kong Island, goes underneath Victoria Harbour to Tsim Sha Tsui, and then runs north the length of Nathan Road, with stops at Jordan, Yau Ma Tei, and Mong Kok stations before heading northwest to the satellite town of Tsuen Wan in the New Territories. The **blue-coded Island Line,** with 14 stations, operates on the north side of Hong Kong Island from Sheung Wan (where you'll find the Macau Ferry Pier) east to Chai Wan, passing through Central, Wan Chai, and Causeway Bay.

Three other lines, used mainly by commuters, are the **Kwun Tong Line,** which arches from Yau Ma Tei eastward to the New Territories; the **Tseung Kwan O Line,** which runs from North Point on Hong Kong Island and then goes under the harbor before connecting with the Kwun Tong Line; and the **Tung Chung Line,** which mirrors the Airport Express Line as it runs from Hong Kong Station in Central to Kowloon Station and onward to Tung Chung on Lantau Island. The **Disney Resort Line** branches off the Tung Chung Line to Disneyland. The **Airport Express Line** also serves airport passengers, running between Hong Kong Station in Central and Hong Kong International Airport, with a stop at Kowloon Station.

In 2007, the former Kowloon-Canton Railway (KCR), which operated four rail lines in the New Territories as well as through train service to mainland China, merged with MTR to form one vast network of rail service extending from Central on Hong Kong Island through the New Territories. Most useful for visitors is the **East Rail,** which travels from Hung Hom Station in Kowloon up to Sheung Shui in the New Territories. That is, Sheung Shui is where you must get off if you don't have a visa to go onward to China. If you do have a visa, you can continue to the border station of Lo Wu and travel onward all the way through China—and even Russia and Europe if you want to, ending up in London. This line has two different kinds of trains: the express through-train to Guangzhou, Shanghai, and Beijing; and the local commuter service for those going to towns in the New Territories.

If you're taking the East Rail commuter train, you'll make stops at Mong Kok East, Kowloon Tong, Tai Wai, Sha Tin, Fo Tan, Racecourse (on horse-racing days only), University, Tai Po Market, Tai Wo, and Fanling before reaching Sheung Shui. The whole trip from East Tsim Sha Tsui to Sheung Shui takes only 38 minutes, so it's the easiest and fastest way to see part of the New Territories. It's also convenient, with trains running every 3 to 8 minutes. Connecting to East Rail at Tai Wai Station is the **Ma On Shan Rail,** useful for visiting Che Kung Temple.

Serving the western part of the New Territories is the **West Rail,** which links East Tsim Sha Tsui Station in Kowloon with Tuen Mun in the northwestern part of the New Territories in 30 minutes. Extending from the western end of the West Rail is a feeder **Light Rail** transit system, useful for visiting Hong Kong Wetland Park.

FARES   Single, one-way tickets start at HK$4 for most lines and increase according to the distance traveled, but the most expensive ride is the trip underneath the harbor, which costs HK$8.50 from Tsim Sha Tsui to Central (still cheap, but outrageous when compared to the Star Ferry's fare of HK$2.50 for first class). Fares for seniors 65 and older and children ages 3 to 11 start at HK$3. Fares are indicated by inputting your destination on a touch screen above all vending machines, which accept HK$10, HK$5, HK$2, HK$1, and HK50¢ coins, as well as HK$500, HK$100, HK$20, and HK$10 notes, and give back change.

Even if you're traveling long distances, transportation is fairly cheap in Hong Kong. From Hung Hom to Sheung Shui in the New Territories, for example, it costs HK$8.50 for ordinary (second) class and HK$17 for first class for the 38-minute trip.

Your ticket is plastic, the size of a credit card, and you feed it into a slot at the turnstile. It disappears and then shoots up at the other end of the turnstile. *Be sure to save your ticket*—at the end of your journey, you will again insert it into the turnstile (only this time you won't get it back unless it's an Octopus). Because these tickets are used again and again and have a magnetized strip, be careful not to bend or damage them.

As mentioned above, if you think you're going to be doing a lot of traveling on public transportation, consider buying the Octopus, which not only saves you from having to buy another ticket each time you ride but also provides a slight discount. Numerous transportation passes are also available just for tourists.

By Bus

Hong Kong buses are a delight—especially the British-style double-deckers. They're good for traveling to places where other forms of public transport don't go, such as to the southern part of Hong Kong Island like Stanley, around Lantau, or up into parts of Kowloon and the New Territories. Bus numbers containing an "X" are for express buses, with limited stops. Depending on the route, buses run daily from about 6am to midnight, with fares ranging from HK$1.20 to HK$45; the fare is halved for children 11 and under and seniors 66 and over. *You must have the exact fare,* which you deposit into a box as you get on. Make sure, therefore, that you always carry a lot of spare change, or buy an Octopus card. Although final destinations are clearly displayed in English on the front of the bus, drivers often don't speak English, so you may want to have someone at your hotel write down your destination in Chinese, particularly if you're traveling in the New Territories. And with the exception of congested areas like Central or Tsim Sha Tsui where queues of people wait at the stop, you must flag down a bus to make it stop, especially in the New Territories or on an island. If you don't wave your arm, it will just go barreling past. When on board, be sure to push the signal button for your stop.

Hong Kong's buses are operated by two companies: **New World First Bus(NWFB)/ Citybus** (© 852/2136 8888 for NWFB, © 852/2873 0818 for Citybus; www. nwst.com.hk) and **Kowloon Motor Bus** (**KMB; © 852/2745 4466;** www.kmb. com.hk), which collectively cover Hong Kong Island, Kowloon, and the New Territories. The **New Lantao Bus Co.** (© 852/2984 9848; www.newlantaobus.com) operates on Lantau Island.

The two major bus terminals are located at or near both ends of the Star Ferry. On Hong Kong Island, most buses depart from Exchange Square in the Central District or from bus stops in front of the Central Ferry Piers. Some buses also depart from Admiralty Station. In Kowloon, buses depart from in front of the Star Ferry concourse in Tsim Sha Tsui.

The HKTB has individual leaflets for Hong Kong Island, Kowloon, and the New Territories that show bus routes to most of the major tourist spots, indicating where you can catch buses, their frequency and fares, and where to get off. Keep in mind that buses can get very crowded at rush hours and that some buses look pretty ancient—which can make the winding trip to Stanley in a double-decker bus a bone-rattling and exciting experience.

Alternatively, there are two companies offering hop-on/hop-off service aboard double-decker buses traveling to key attractions. The **Big Bus Company** (© 852/ **2723 2108;** www.bigbustours.com) operates routes along north Hong Kong Island from Central and Lan Kwai Fong through Wan Chai to Causeway Bay; from Central to Stanley; and around Kowloon. Cost of a ticket, which includes a ride on the Star Ferry and the Peak Tram to and from Victoria Peak, is HK$320 for 24 hours or HK$420 for 48 hours (children pay HK$200 and HK$300, respectively). Buses run every 30 minutes from 9:30 or 10am to 6pm (buses to Stanley run less frequently). People purchasing the 48-hour ticket can also board a 7pm evening bus to Kowloon's night market.

Rickshaw Sightseeing Bus (© 852/2136 8888; www.rickshawbus.com) operates two routes on north Hong Kong Island departing every 30 minutes from the Central Ferry Piers. The Heritage Route, running daily from 10am to 6pm, is convenient for sightseeing in the Western District and includes Man Mo Temple, Ladder Street, and the Dr. Sun Yat-sen Museum. The Metropolis Route, running daily from 10:15am to 9:45pm, travels to Wan Chai and Causeway Bay. A day ticket covering both routes costs HK$50; the fare for a single journey is HK$8.70. Children and seniors pay half fare.

Tickets for both companies can be purchased on board the bus.

By Tram

Tram lines are found only on Hong Kong Island. Established in 1904 along what used to be the waterfront, these are narrow, double-decker affairs that clank their way 16km (10 miles) in a straight line slowly along the northern edge of the island from Kennedy Town in the west to Shau Kei Wan in the east, with one branch making a detour to Happy Valley. Passing through the Western District, Central District, Wan Chai, and Causeway Bay on Des Voeux Road, Queensway Road, and Hennessy Road, they can't be beat for atmosphere and are easy to ride since most of them travel only on one line (those branching off to Happy Valley are clearly marked). In the zeal to modernize Central, it's a wonder that these trams have survived at all. Ever since the advent of the subway, there's been talk of getting rid of them, but this has raised a storm of protest. Comprising the largest fleet of double-decker trams in the world, they are easily one of the most nostalgic forms of transportation in Hong Kong.

Enter the trams from the back and go immediately up the winding stairs to the top deck. The best seats are those in the front row, where you have an unparalleled view of Hong Kong: laundry hanging from second-story windows, signs swinging over the street, markets twisting down side alleys, crowded sidewalks, and people darting in front of the tram you'd swear wouldn't make it. Riding the tram is one of the cheapest ways of touring Hong Kong Island's northern side, and the fare is the same no matter how far you go. Once you've had enough, simply go downstairs to the front of the tram and deposit the exact fare of HK$2 into a little tin box next to the bus driver as you exit. If you don't have the exact amount, don't panic—no one will arrest you for overpaying a few cents. Children and seniors pay HK$1. You can also use the Octopus card. Trams run daily from about 6am to midnight. More information is available at © **852/2548 7102** or www.hktramways.com.

In addition to the old-fashioned trams, the **Peak Tram** (© **852/2522 0922**; www.thepeak.com.hk) is a funicular that transports passengers to one of Hong Kong's star attractions: Victoria Peak and its incomparable views. Its lower terminus is on Garden Road in Central, which you can reach via the 15C shuttle bus departing from the Central Ferry Piers at 15- to 20-minute intervals daily from 10am to 11:45pm and costing HK$4.25. The tram itself runs every 10 to 15 minutes from 7am to midnight, with round-trip tickets costing HK$36 for adults, HK$16 for seniors and children. You can also use an Octopus card.

By Star Ferry

A trip across Victoria Harbour on one of the white-and-green ferries of the **Star Ferry Company** (© **852/2367 7065**; www.starferry.com.hk) is one of the most celebrated rides in the world. Carrying passengers back and forth between Hong Kong Island and Kowloon ever since 1898, these boats have come to symbolize Hong Kong itself and are almost always featured in travel articles on Hong Kong Island. They all incorporate the word "star" in their names, like *Night Star, Twinkling Star,* or *Meridien Star.*

The Star Ferry is very easy to ride. Simply use your Octopus card or buy a token for the ancient-looking turnstile, follow the crowd in front of you down the ramp, walk over the gangway, and find a seat on one of the polished wooden benches. A whistle will blow, a man in a sailor uniform will haul up the gangway, and you're off, dodging fishing boats, tugboats, and barges as you make your way across the harbor. Businesspeople who live in Hong Kong are easy to spot (they're usually buried behind their newspapers); visitors, on the other hand, tend to crowd around the railing, cameras in hand.

The whole trip is much too short, about 7 minutes total from loading pier to unloading dock, with the ride across the harbor taking about 5 minutes. But that 5-minute ride is one of the best in the world, and it's also one of the cheapest. It costs only HK$2 Monday to Friday and HK$2.40 weekends and holidays for ordinary (second) class (seniors 66 and over can ride ordinary class for free; children pay reduced fares). If you really want to splurge, first class costs HK$2.50 Monday to Friday and HK$3 weekends and holidays. First class is located on the upper deck, and it has its own entryway and gangway (follow the signs in the ferry concourse); if it's raining or cold, first class is preferable because of the glass windows in the bow. Otherwise I find ordinary class much more colorful and entertaining because it's the one the locals use and the view of the harbor is often better.

Star Ferries ply the waters daily from 6:30am to 11:30pm between Hong Kong Island's Central District and the tip of Kowloon's Tsim Sha Tsui. Ferries depart every 6 to 8 minutes, except for early in the morning or late at night, when they leave every 10 to 12 minutes.

By Other Ferries

Besides the Star Ferry, many other ferries run to other parts of the city. Ferries from the Central District, for example, also go back and forth to Kowloon's Hung Hom from about 7am to 8pm Monday through Friday; 7am to 7pm Saturday, Sunday, and holidays for HK$6.30. From Wan Chai, ferry service to Tsim Sha Tsui runs from 7:30am to 11pm and costs HK$2.50 Monday to Friday and HK$3 Saturday, Sunday, and holidays. Ferries from Wan Chai to Hung Hom run from about 7am to 7 or 8pm and cost HK$6.30.

In addition to ferries crossing the harbor between Kowloon and Hong Kong Island, a large fleet serves the many outlying islands and points north of Kowloon. If you want to go to one of the outlying islands, you'll find that most of these ferries depart from the Central Ferry Piers (home also to the Star Ferry) in Central. The latest schedules and fares are available from the Hong Kong Tourism Board. One thing to keep in mind is that on the weekends the fares are higher and the ferries can be unbelievably crowded with locals who want to escape the city, so it's best to travel on a weekday. Even so, the most you'll ever pay for a ferry, even on deluxe class on a weekend, is HK$37. You can use the Octopus card. See chapter 11, "Side Trips from Hong Kong," for more information on ferries to specific islands.

BY TAXI

REGULAR TAXI   As a rule, taxi drivers in Hong Kong are strictly controlled and are fairly honest. If they're free to pick up passengers, a red FOR HIRE flag will be raised in the windshield during the day and a lighted TAXI sign will be on the roof at night. You can hail them from the street, though there are some restricted areas, especially in Central. In addition, taxis are not allowed to stop on roads with a single yellow line between 7am and 7pm; they are not allowed to stop at all on roads with a double yellow line on the edge of the road. Probably the easiest places to pick up a taxi are on side streets, at a taxi stand (located at all bus terminals), or at a hotel. Taxis are generally abundant anytime except when it's raining, during rush hour (about 5–8pm), during shift change (usually around 4pm), and on horse-racing days from September to May. Because many drivers do not speak English, it's a good idea to have your destination written in Chinese. Passengers are required by law to wear seatbelts.

Taxis on Hong Kong Island and Kowloon are red. Fares start at HK$18 for the first 2km (1¼ miles), and then are HK$1.50 for each additional 200m (about 656 ft.).

Waiting time, incorporated in the meter, is HK$1.50 per minute, luggage costs an extra HK$5 per piece, and taxis ordered by phone also add a HK$5 surcharge. Extra charges to pay for the driver's return trip are also permitted for trips through harbor tunnels and Aberdeen Tunnel. Note, too, the additional charge per bird or animal you might want to bring with you in the taxi! For a tip, simply round up to the nearest dollar or add HK$1 to the fare for short journeys; for longer rides, round up to the nearest HK$5. Although taxi drivers can service both sides of Victoria Harbour, they tend to stick to a certain neighborhood and often aren't familiar with anything outside their area.

Taxis in the New Territories are green, with fares starting at HK$15 at flag-fall. They cover only the New Territories and are not allowed to transport you back into Kowloon. Taxis on Lantau are blue and start at HK$13.

If you have a complaint about a taxi driver, call the taxi complaint hot line (*©* **852/2889 9999**), but make sure you have the taxi's license number. The driver's name, photograph, and car number are displayed on the dashboard. Better yet, ask for a receipt, which has the taxi number on it and will also help you track down lost items left behind.

MINIBUSES These small, 16-passenger buses are the poor person's taxis. Although they are quite useful for the locals, they're a bit confusing for tourists. For one thing, though the destination may be written in both Chinese and English, you almost need a magnifying glass to read the English, and by then the vehicle has probably already whizzed by. Even if you can read the English, you may not know the bus's route or where it's going.

The two types of vehicles are distinguishable by color. The green-and-yellow public "light buses" (though also called minibuses) follow fixed routes, have numbers, and charge fixed rates ranging from HK$2 to HK$23, depending on the distance. They also require the exact fare as you enter, or you can use an Octopus card. The most useful ones on Hong Kong Island are probably those that depart from the Star Ferry concourse for Bowen Road and Ocean Park, as well as those that travel from Central's Lung Wui Road to Victoria Peak or from Causeway Bay to Stanley.

The red-and-yellow minibuses are a lot more confusing and shouldn't be used by anyone not familiar with Hong Kong, because they have no fixed route and will stop when you hail them from the street (except for some restricted areas in Central). However, they're useful for traveling along Nathan Road or between Central and Causeway Bay. Fares range from HK$2 to HK$23, depending on the distance and demand (higher fares are charged on rainy days, race days, or cross-harbor trips), and you pay as you exit. Just yell when you want to get off.

BY CAR

Rental cars are not advisable in Hong Kong and hardly anyone uses them, even businesspeople. For one thing, nothing is so far away that you can't get there easily, quickly, and cheaply by taxi or public transport. In addition, there probably won't be any place to park once you get to your destination. If you want a chauffeur-driven car, most major hotels have their own private fleet—you can even rent a limousine. If you're still determined to rent a car or plan to take a driving tour of the New Territories (you are not allowed to enter mainland China), car-rental agencies—such as Avis and Hertz—have branches here, along with a couple of dozen local firms. Your hotel concierge should be able to make arrangements. A valid driver's license is required, and, remember, traffic flows on the left-hand side of the street.

ON FOOT

One of the great things about Hong Kong is that you can explore virtually the entire city proper on foot, with directional signage posted seemingly everywhere directing you to tourist attractions. You can walk from the Central District all the way through Wan Chai to Causeway Bay in about an hour or so, while the half-hour walk up Nathan Road to Yau Ma Tei is a colorful experience I recommend to all visitors. Unfortunately, land reclamation has been carried out so ambitiously, it may even be possible one day to walk from Hong Kong Island to Kowloon.

In the Central District, mazes of covered, elevated walkways separate pedestrians from traffic, and connect office buildings, shopping complexes, and hotels. In fact, some roads have no pedestrians because they're all using overhead passageways. These walkways can be confusing, though signs direct pedestrians to major buildings. Tourists will probably find streets easier to navigate if using a map, but walkways are convenient when it rains and are safer, since the walkways keep pedestrians safe from traffic. I was able to pick up a handy "Walkway System in Central" folding map at the Hong Kong Planning and Infrastructure Exhibition Gallery (p. 176), but I can't guarantee it will still be available when you get there.

An interesting "people mover" is the free Central–Mid-Levels Escalator between Central on Des Voeux Road Central and the Mid-Levels on Victoria Peak. It's a series of moving walkways and escalators that snake their way through the Central District up the steep slope of the Peak. Constructed in the hope of alleviating traffic congestion for commuters who live in the Mid-Levels (about halfway up the Peak), the combination escalator/walkway has a total length of just less than .8km (½ mile) and transports approximately 27,000 people a day, moving downward in the morning until 10am and then reversing uphill the rest of the day to accommodate those returning home. The escalator has many entrances/exits, so commuters can get on and off as they like.

MONEY & COSTS

THE VALUE OF THE HONG KONG DOLLAR VS. OTHER POPULAR CURRENCIES

HK$	US$	Can$	UK£	Euro (€)	Aus$	NZ$
HK$10	US$1.29	C$1.31	86p	€.96	A$1.40	NZ$1.82

Frommer's lists exact prices in the local currency. The currency conversions quoted above were correct at press time. However, rates fluctuate, so before departing consult a currency exchange website such as **www.oanda.com/convert/classic** to check up-to-the-minute rates.

According to figures released by the Hong Kong Tourism Board, the average per capita spending of overnight visitors to Hong Kong is HK$5,700 per day on hotels, meals, shopping, and entertainment (frugal travelers, of course, can experience Hong Kong on much less). While Hong Kong may seem expensive compared to many other Asian cities, bargains abound, especially when it comes to off-season hotel rates, meals at local Chinese restaurants, public transportation, and museum admissions. In addition, because the Hong Kong dollar is pegged to U.S. currency, a falling U.S.

WHAT THINGS COST IN HONG KONG	HK$
Airport Express Line from airport to Kowloon Station	90
MTR subway ride from Tsim Sha Tsui to Central	8.50
Local telephone call (per 5 min.)	1
Double room at the Peninsula (deluxe)	4,200 and up
Double room at the Luxe Manor (moderate)	2,400 and up
Double room at the Salisbury YMCA (inexpensive)	1,080
Lunch for one at Watermark (moderate)	148
Lunch for one at Chilli Fagara (inexpensive)	78
Dinner for one, without drinks, at Nobu (deluxe)	250–820
Dinner for one, without drinks, at café TOO (moderate)	438
Dinner for one, without drinks, at Nomads (inexpensive)	178
Glass of beer or cup of coffee	30
Admission to the Hong Kong Museum of History	10

dollar doesn't impact the cost of travel for Americans in Hong Kong compared to, say, Europe with the euro.

Currency

The basic unit of currency is the **Hong Kong dollar (HK$),** which is divided into 100 cents. Since 1983, when negotiations between Britain and China concerning Hong Kong's future sent public confidence and the value of the Hong Kong dollar into a nose dive, the Hong Kong dollar has been officially pegged to the U.S. dollar at a rate of 7.8 (which means that US$1 equals HK$7.80), giving the Hong Kong currency greater stability.

Three banks, the Hongkong and Shanghai Banking Corporation (HSBC), the Bank of China, and the Standard Chartered Bank, all issue their own colorful notes, in denominations of HK$10, HK$20, HK$50, HK$100, HK$500, and HK$1,000. The government also issues a HK$10 note. As for coins, they're issued by the government in bronze for HK10¢, HK20¢, and HK50¢ pieces; in silver for HK$1, HK$2, and HK$5; and in nickel and bronze for HK$10.

Throughout the SAR, you'll see the dollar sign ("$"), which refers to Hong Kong dollars, not U.S. dollars. To prevent confusion, this guide identifies Hong Kong dollars with the symbol "HK$." Although the official conversion rate is currently pegged at 7.8, you'll receive slightly less at banks, hotels, and currency exchange offices.

When exchanging money in Hong Kong, you'll get the best rate at banks. The exchange rate can vary among banks, however, so it may pay to shop around if you're exchanging a large amount. In addition, most banks also charge commission, which can differ depending on whether you're exchanging cash or traveler's checks (a slightly higher commission is charged for traveler's checks, usually around HK$10 more). A check during my last visit revealed commissions ranging from HK$40 for cash at a Wing Lung Bank to HK$60 for traveler's checks at a Hang Seng Bank. On the other hand, the exchange rate is usually slightly better for traveler's checks than for cash. Others may not charge commission but have less favorable exchange rates.

Ask your hotel where the closest **Hang Seng Bank** (www.hangseng.com) or **Wing Lung Bank** (www.winglungbank.com) is, since I find these generally have favorable rates and lower commissions. The main bank of Wing Lung is at 45 Des Voeux Rd. Central in the Central District (© **852/2826 8333**), with a convenient Tsim Sha Tsui branch at 4 Carnarvon Rd. (© **852/2369 9255**). Hang Seng has a convenient location next to Kowloon Hotel at 4 Hankow Rd., Tsim Sha Tsui (© **852/2198 0575**).

Hotels give a slightly less favorable exchange rate but are convenient because they're open at night and on weekends. Money changers are found in the tourist areas, especially along Nathan Road in Tsim Sha Tsui. Avoid them if you can. They often charge a commission or a "changing fee," or give a much lower rate. Check exactly how much you'll get in return before handing over your money. If you exchange money at Hong Kong International Airport, change only what you need to get into town—US$50 should be enough—because the exchange rate here is lower than what you'll get at banks in town.

I always carry two credit cards (in case there happens to be a problem with one of them), cash, and, for additional safety, traveler's checks.

ATMs

The best way to get cash away from home is from an ATM (automated teller machine). There are ATMs throughout Hong Kong, making a credit or debit card the most convenient way to obtain cash since it eliminates the hassle of exchanging money only during banking hours. Be sure you know your four-digit personal identification number (PIN) and daily withdrawal limit before you depart. *Note:* Remember that many banks impose a fee every time you use a card at another bank's ATM, and that fee can be higher for international transactions than for domestic ones. In addition, the bank from which you withdraw cash may charge its own fee. For international withdrawal fees, ask your bank.

Holders of MasterCard (using the Cirrus network) and Visa (using PLUS) can use ATMs at the airport and various convenient locations around the city, including the Star Ferry concourses in Kowloon and Central, all major MTR (subway) stations, and major banks such as the HSBC and Hang Seng Bank (which have 24-hr. machines). American Express cardholders should look for Aeon ATMs, located at MTR Stations, Circle K convenience stores, and other places around town (Visa and MasterCard holders can also use Aeon ATMs).

Credit Cards

Credit cards are a safe way to carry money, provide a convenient record of all your expenses, and generally offer relatively good exchange rates. You can withdraw cash advances from your credit cards at banks or ATMs, provided you know your four-digit PIN. Beware of hidden credit card fees while traveling. Check with your credit or debit card issuer to see what fees, if any, will be charged for overseas transactions. Recent reform legislation in the U.S., for example, has curbed some exploitative lending practices. But many banks have responded by increasing fees in other areas, including fees for customers who use credit and debit cards while out of the country—even if those charges were made in U.S. dollars. Fees can amount to 3% or more of the purchase price. Check with your bank before departing to avoid any surprise charges on your statement.

Although many of the smaller shops in Hong Kong will give better prices if you pay in cash with local currency, most shops accept international credit cards, but some of the smaller ones do not. Look for credit card signs displayed on the front door or near the cash register. Readily accepted credit cards include American Express, Visa, and MasterCard. Note, however, that shops have to pay an extra fee for transactions that take place with a credit card—and they will try to pass on that expense to you. Keep this in mind if you're bargaining (see "The Shopping Scene," in chapter 9), and make sure the shopkeeper knows whether you're going to pay with cash or plastic. All major hotels and better restaurants accept credit cards, but budget restaurants often don't. If you do pay with a credit card, check to make sure that "HK" appears before the dollar sign in the total amount.

STAYING HEALTHY

The two major health concerns for travelers to Hong Kong in the past have been **SARS** and **avian flu.** At press time, however, neither has posed a threat for some time for those going to the SAR (yes, its name is an unfortunate coincidence). Hong Kong culled its entire poultry population several times after the first reported bird flu outbreak in 1997 (the last reported human case of avian flu in Hong Kong was in 2003), and importation of poultry from mainland China is immediately halted whenever any outbreaks occur there. In 2008, a ban on stocking live chickens overnight in Hong Kong's wet markets went into effect; that, together with a growing preference to shop in supermarkets for packaged meats, has greatly reduced the risk of another outbreak in Hong Kong.

As for SARS, there have been no major occurrences since the 2003 outbreak sickened 1,755 people in Hong Kong and killed 299 of them. However, because of other threats such as H1N1, Hong Kong monitors all passengers arriving by air, boat, and train by taking their temperatures with a thermal scan. Passengers with pneumonia or fever, as well as those arriving from infected areas, are kept under close monitoring or isolation. To avoid being unnecessarily detained, don't travel with a fever. As an extra precaution, you might wish to have a flu shot before departing for Hong Kong.

Healthy Travels to You

The following government websites offer up-to-date health-related travel advice.

○**Australia:** www.smartraveller.gov.au
○**Canada:** www.hc-sc.gc.ca/index_e.html
○**U.K.:** www.nhs.uk/healthcareabroad/pages/healthcareabroad.aspx
○**U.S.:** www.cdc.gov/travel

Once in Hong Kong, you'll notice dispensers for hand sanitizers virtually everywhere, including restrooms, shops, hotels, and other public places; because good hygiene is the best defense against infectious disease, wash your hands as often as you can.

The United States **Centers for Disease Control and Prevention** (✆ **800/311-3435;** www.cdc.gov) provides up-to-date information on health hazards by region or country—including the latest outbreaks of avian flu—and offers tips on food safety.

Health issues are also monitored by Hong Kong's **Department of Health** (✆ **852/2961 8989;** www.dh.gov.hk).

Prescriptions can be filled at Hong Kong pharmacies *only if they're issued by a local doctor.* To avoid the hassle, be sure to bring more prescriptions than you think you'll need, clearly labeled in their original packages, and pack prescription medications in your carry-on luggage. It's also a good idea to carry copies of your prescriptions in case you run out, including generic names in case a local pharmacist is unfamiliar with the brand name. Over-the-counter items are easy to obtain, though name brands may be different from those back home, and some ingredients allowed elsewhere may be forbidden in Hong Kong (and vice versa).

If you're traveling during the hot and humid summer months, limit your exposure to the sun, especially during the first few days of your trip and particularly from 11am to 2pm. Use a sunscreen with a high protection factor. To avoid dehydration, you should also carry a water bottle, especially when hiking.

Another concern when hiking in the New Territories or the islands is snakes. I've never seen one, but of Hong Kong's 49 native species, 9 are venomous.

If you have a respiratory illness, be forewarned that air pollution in Hong Kong has increased significantly in recent years, due mainly to growing manufacturing across the border and increased vehicular traffic. In addition to checking daily air quality reports in the *South China Morning Post,* you can also check the government's Environmental Protection Department website at www.epd-asg.gov.hk/eindex.php for the current and next day's forecast of the air pollution index.

Generally, you're safe eating anywhere in Hong Kong, even at roadside food stalls. Stay clear of local oysters and shellfish, however, and remember that many restaurants outside the major hotels and tourist areas use MSG in their dishes as a matter of course, especially fast-food restaurants and Chinese kitchens that import products from the mainland (some health experts, however, debunk the widely held Western belief that MSG can cause numbness, weakness, or other ailments). Water is safe to drink except in rural areas, where you should drink bottled water. Nonetheless, most upper-end and many medium-range hotels offer free bottled water in their guest rooms.

What to Do If You Get Sick Away from Home

Hong Kong has many Western-trained physicians. If you get sick, you may want to contact the concierge at your hotel—some upper-range hotels have in-house doctors or clinics. Otherwise, your embassy in Hong Kong can provide a list of area doctors who speak English (p. 326). If you still can't find a doctor who can help you right away, try the local hospital. Many have walk-in-clinics for cases that are not life threatening. Doctors and hospitals generally do not accept credit cards and require immediate cash payment for health services. If, on the other hand, you end up in the emergency room of a hospital, you're required to pay a set fee of HK$570 for its services, but if you cannot pay immediately you will be billed. See "Fast Facts: Hong Kong & Macau" in chapter 13 for a list of Hong Kong hospitals and emergency numbers; for Macau hospitals, see chapter 12.

CRIME & SAFETY

Hong Kong is relatively safe for the visitor, especially if you use common sense and stick to such well-traveled nighttime areas as Tsim Sha Tsui, Lan Kwai Fong, Wan

Chai, or Causeway Bay. On the other hand, the main thing you must guard against is pickpockets. They often work in groups to pick men's pockets or slit open a woman's purse, quickly taking the valuables and then relaying them on to accomplices who disappear in the crowd. Favored places are exactly those places where tourists are likely to be, namely Tsim Sha Tsui, Central, Causeway Bay, and Wan Chai. You should also be on guard on crowded public conveyances such as the MTR and in public markets.

It's best to hike in groups of two or more as isolated cases of hikers being robbed in country parks and Victoria Peak have been known to occur.

To be on the safe side, keep your valuables in your in-room safe or hotel's safe-deposit box. If you need to carry your passport or large amounts of money, conceal everything in a money belt.

SPECIALIZED TRAVEL RESOURCES

LGBT Travelers

A vibrant, if not readily apparent, gay and lesbian community of expats and Chinese lives in Hong Kong. Discrimination is not a serious issue here, though, as in most places, you may encounter some less-than-open-minded people. Hong Kong has only a handful of openly gay establishments, concentrated mostly in the Lan Kwai Fong/SoHo nightlife districts, but several clubs have regular gay or lesbian nights. The monthly gay guide *DS Magazine* (www.dimsum-hk.com), is distributed free to clubs, bars, and other venues and has an events calendar. South Bay, a beach on the south end of Hong Kong Island, is popular with gays.

See p. 252 for recommended gay bars in Hong Kong. For more gay and lesbian travel resources, visit Frommers.com.

Travelers with Disabilities

Hong Kong can be a nightmare for travelers with disabilities. City sidewalks—especially in Central and Kowloon—can be so jam-packed that getting around on crutches or in a wheelchair is exceedingly difficult. Moreover, to cross busy thoroughfares it's often necessary to climb stairs to a pedestrian bridge. Also, most shops are a step or two up from the street, due to flooding during rainstorms.

As for transportation, taxis are probably the most convenient mode of transportation, especially since they can load and unload passengers with disabilities in restricted zones under certain conditions and do not charge extra for carrying wheelchairs and crutches. Otherwise, the MTR (subway) has wheelchair access (elevators, ramps, or other aids) at major stations, as well as tactile pathways leading to platforms and exits for the visually impaired. Ferries are accessible to wheelchair users on the lower deck, and approximately 40% of buses are wheelchair accessible. More information on transportation accessibility is available from the **Transport Department,** Floor 41, Immigration Tower, 7 Gloucester Rd., Wan Chai (**℃ 852/2804 2600;** www.td.gov.hk), which publishes a booklet called *A Guide to Public Transport for People with Disabilities*, which can also be downloaded online (www.td.gov.hk/mini_site/people_with_disabilities). Another good source is the **Hong Kong Society for Rehabilitation** (**℃ 852/2817 6277;** www.rehabsociety.org.hk), which provides information on wheelchair accessibility not only for public transport services in Hong

TIPS FOR THE business TRAVELER TO HONG KONG

○ **Bring plenty of business cards.** They are exchanged constantly, and you'll be highly suspect without them (if you run out, hotel business centers can arrange to have new ones printed within 24 hr.). When presenting your card, hold it out with both hands, turned so that the receiver can read it. Chinese names are written with the family name first, followed by the given name and then the middle name.

○ **Use formal names for addressing business associates** unless told to do otherwise; you'll find that many Hong Kong Chinese used to dealing with foreigners have adopted a Western first name.

○ **Shaking hands is appropriate** for greetings and introductions.

○ **Business attire**—a suit and tie for men; blazers/jackets with skirts or pantsuits for women—is worn throughout the year, even in summer (though women can get away without wearing blazers or jackets in the summer).

○ **Avoid the Chinese New Year,** as all of Hong Kong shuts down for at least 3 days; based on the lunar calendar, it falls between late January and mid-February.

○ **Entertainment** is an integral part of conducting business in Hong Kong, whether it's a meal in which the host orders the food and serves his or her guests, an evening at the racetracks, or a round of golf.

○ If an invitation is extended, it is understood that **the host will treat.** Do not insist on paying; this will only embarrass your host. Accept graciously and promise to pick up the tab next time around.

Kong but also for attractions, hotels, malls, and performing venues. It also provides a link to the Transport Department's guide at www.accessguide.hk.

Family Travel

Hong Kong is a great place for older kids, since many of the attractions are geared toward them and even offer discounts for children, sometimes as much as 50%. Public transportation is half price for children. As for very young children, keep in mind that there are many stairs to climb, particularly in Central with its elevated walkways, and in subway stations, making child backpack carriers easier than strollers. Also, young children may not be welcome at finer restaurants.

Many hotels allow children under a certain age (usually 11 and under but occasionally up to 18) to stay free of charge in their parent's room. Generally, only one child is allowed, or there's a maximum limit of three people per room, and no extra charge *only* when no extra bed is required. Baby cots are usually free of charge, and many hotels also offer babysitting for a hefty fee.

To locate those accommodations, restaurants, and attractions that are particularly kid-friendly, refer to the "Kids" icon throughout this guide. For lists of kid-friendly hotels and restaurants, see p. 85 and 136, respectively. "Especially for Kids" on p. 184 describes attractions and activities geared toward children.

Single Travelers

You shouldn't have any problems as a single traveler to Hong Kong. Nearly every time I come here, I travel alone. The biggest problem is one of expense, since many hotels charge the same regardless of whether it's for single or double occupancy. The other problem is Chinese food—it's best when enjoyed with a group. Try fixed-price meals or all-you-can-eat buffets when dining alone, or join one of the organized tours where meals are often included.

Female travelers may also want to check out the website **Journeywoman** (www. journeywoman.com), a "real-life" women's travel information network where you can sign up for a free e-mail newsletter and get advice on everything from etiquette and dress to safety. They have a special section called "GirlTalk Hong Kong," which carries tips on accommodations, restaurants, shopping, things to do, what to wear, and details of venues where solo female travelers will feel at home, submitted by women who have traveled to Hong Kong.

Senior Travel

Seniors receive half-price admission to most museums in Hong Kong. In addition, seniors can ride the cross-harbor ferry free of charge and receive reduced fares for ferries to the outlying islands, the trams (including the Peak Tram), and the subway system. Some discounts are available to seniors 61 and older, others for seniors 66 and older. In any case, seniors should carry identification for proof of age and should keep in mind that there are many stairs to climb in Hong Kong, including overhead pedestrian bridges and in subway stations. Remember that it is *very* hot and humid in summer.

Student Travel

Students receive a slight discount to most museums in Hong Kong, but major attractions like Ocean Park do not offer discounts. Your best bet is to bring along an **International Student Identity Card (ISIC)** together with your university student ID and show them both at museum ticket windows. For information on the card and where and how to obtain one, check the website www.isic.org.

RESPONSIBLE TOURISM

Hong Kong may be crowded, but it's remarkably clean compared to many other major Asian cities. That said, Hong Kong's most pressing environmental concern is air pollution, which has gotten progressively worse over the years, fueled largely by factories just over the border in mainland China and local vehicular traffic. In fact, pollution is sometimes so bad, that even a cloudless day can't guarantee that views will be good from atop Victoria Peak. The euphemism used in weather reports is "haziness." To learn more about grassroots efforts to improve the air, check out the websites www. cleartheair.org.hk and www.hongkongcan.org.

In any case, to ensure that you're not contributing to the global problem, try to choose a nonstop flight to Hong Kong, since it generally requires less fuel than an indirect flight that stops and takes off again. Try to fly during the day—some scientists estimate that nighttime flights are twice as harmful to the environment. And pack light—each 15 pounds of luggage on a 5,000-mile flight adds up to 50 pounds of carbon dioxide emitted.

RESOURCES FOR responsible TRAVEL

In addition to the resources for Hong Kong listed above, the following websites provide valuable wide-ranging information on sustainable travel.

o **Responsible Travel** (www. responsibletravel.com) is a great source of sustainable travel ideas; the site is run by a spokesperson for ethical tourism in the travel industry. **Sustainable Travel International** (www. sustainabletravelinternational.org) promotes ethical tourism practices and manages an extensive directory of sustainable properties and tour operators around the world.

o **Carbonfund** (www.carbonfund. org), **TerraPass** (www.terrapass. org), and **Cool Climate** (http:// coolclimate.berkeley.edu) provide

info on "carbon offsetting," or offsetting the greenhouse gas emitted during flights.

o **Greenhotels** (www.greenhotels. com) recommends green-rated member hotels around the world that fulfill the company's stringent environmental requirements. **Environmentally Friendly Hotels** (www.environmentallyfriendly hotels.com) offers more green accommodation ratings.

o **Volunteer International** (www. volunteerinternational.org) has a list of questions to help you determine the intentions and the nature of a volunteer program. For general info on volunteer travel, visit **www.volunteer abroad.org** and **www.idealist. org**.

In Hong Kong, use public transport where possible—Hong Kong's trains, trams, buses, and ferries are more energy-efficient forms of transport than taxis. Even better is to walk; you'll produce zero emissions and stay fit and healthy.

Where you stay during your travels can also have a major environmental impact. To determine the green credentials of a property, ask about trash disposal and recycling, water conservation, and energy use; also question if sustainable materials were used in the construction of the property. Luckily, Hong Kong hotels are becoming increasingly environmentally aware. The InterContinental Grand Stanford (p. 84), for example, has been a pioneer in green management practices; in 2007 it became the first hotel in Hong Kong to install a more efficient and environmentally friendly new hybrid fuel system for hot water and steam that reduces temperatures around the hotel and is equivalent to taking 70 cars a year off the road. The Eaton Hotel (p. 89) not only employs a full-time environmental manager responsible for monitoring environmental and social performance, but also has an in-house green team, recycles everything from plastic bottles and aluminum to office paper, and provides staff community service (it even used old banquet tablecloths to make restaurant place mats). Finally, to do your part, request that your sheets and towels not be changed daily. (Many hotels already have programs like this in place.) Turn off the lights and air-conditioner when you leave your room.

As for dining, try to eat at locally owned and operated restaurants that use produce grown in the area, like Posto Pubblico (p. 142). This contributes to the local economy and cuts down on greenhouse gas emissions by supporting restaurants where the food is not flown or trucked in across long distances. You might also want to patronize restaurants that donate leftover food to food pantries, such as Pret A Manger and restaurants in the Eaton Hotel (p. 147 and 160). And when shopping, keep in mind that you'll pay HK10¢ for each plastic bag you need at supermarkets, convenience stores, and health and beauty stores; to cut down on unnecessary plastic and to save a little money, bring your own bag.

Volunteer travel has become increasingly popular among those who want to venture beyond the standard group-tour experience to learn languages, interact with locals, and make a positive difference while on vacation. The **Hong Kong YWCA,** 1 MacDonnell Rd., Central (𝄐 **852/3476 1340;** www.esmdywca.org.hk), serves as a local clearinghouse for volunteer opportunities under its "News & Events" button. Although directed toward local residents, some of the volunteer opportunities are short term. The website also offers a variety of courses, including classes for Cantonese, Mandarin, and cooking, open to both YWCA members and nonmembers.

Sustainable tourism is conscientious travel. It means being careful with the environments you explore and respecting the communities you visit. To participate in ethical tourism at a local level, your best bet in Hong Kong is in the village of **Tai O** on Lantau Island (p. 268).

SPECIAL-INTEREST ACTIVITIES

The Hong Kong Tourism Board offers a great introduction to local culture through its Cultural Kaleidoscope program called "Meet the People," in which local authorities give free, 1-hour lectures, classes, and seminars on a wide range of subjects from Cantonese opera to tai chi. During the cooler winter months, HKTB arranges free guided excursions to Hong Kong's rural areas. For more information on HKTB's offerings, architectural guided tours, and other special-interest activities, see p. 187. Several Hong Kong hotels, including the InterContinental, the Peninsula, and Four Seasons, also offer cultural experiences for their guests (see p. 80, 81, and 82).

STAYING CONNECTED
Mobile Phones

The three letters that define much of the world's wireless capabilities are GSM (Global System for Mobiles), a big, seamless network that makes for easy cross-border cellphone use throughout dozens of other countries worldwide.

Using your own mobile phone in Hong Kong is easy, as most of the telephone systems used around the world (such as GSM 900/1800/2100, PCS 1800, CDMA, and WCDMA) are operational in Hong Kong. If your cellphone is on a GSM system, and you have a world-capable multiband phone, you can make and receive calls in Hong Kong. Mobile operators in Hong Kong, such as **CSL** (𝄐 **852/2751 0000** or *CSL from a mobile phone logged on to the CSL network; www.hkcsl.com), have roaming agreements with most overseas operators, enabling visitors to use their own phones in Hong Kong. Just call your wireless operator and ask for "international roaming" to be activated on your account. Be sure to cancel any call-forwarding options to avoid extra roaming charges. Unfortunately, per-minute charges can be high, so ask about pricing before you leave.

It is more economical to buy a removable computer memory phone chip (called a **SIM card**), which allows you to make calls at local rates. Cheap, prepaid SIM cards are sold at retailers throughout Hong Kong, including 7-Eleven convenience stores. **CSL** (𝄐 **852/179 179;** http://one2free.hkcsl.com) offers the Power Prepaid SIM

Card for HK$88, with local calls costing HK10¢ a minute and international calls to 30 destinations (including the U.S., Canada, U.K., Australia, and New Zealand) costing HK18¢ a minute to land lines (calls to cellphones cost more). It's sold at **1010 Centres** throughout Hong Kong, including Century Square, 1–13 D'Aguilar St., Central (🕾 **852/2918 1010**), and China Hong Kong Centre, 122–126 Canton Rd., Tsim Sha Tsui (🕾 **852/2910 1010**), as well as 7-Eleven and Circle K convenience stores.

Similarly, **PCCW** (🕾 **852/1000;** www2.pccwmobile.com), another local company, offers a variety of prepaid, rechargeable SIM cards, including cards for HK$48 and HK$78, with local calls costing HK12¢ during peak hours from noon to 9pm and HK6¢ at other times; calls to North America cost HK$1.60 per minute. PCCW's "All-in-1" Communications SIM Card, costing HK$98 but with HK$150 worth of stored value, enables tourists to make local calls for HK30¢ per minute and also provides access to PCCW's Wi-Fi hot spots throughout Hong Kong. A convenient shop is located at 118 Queen's Road Central, Central (🕾 **852/2888 3326**).

Renting a mobile phone is another option. Many upper- and medium-range hotels offer rental phones at their business centers, though it's an expensive convenience (the more expensive the hotel, the more expensive the rental). It's better to rent from a local company. **CSL** (🕾 **852/2883 3938;** http://roam.hkcsl.com/eng/rent/rent. htm) offers phones for HK$35 a day, plus a refundable deposit of up to HK$500. But you must still buy a SIM card as outlined above.

Newspapers & Magazines

The *South China Morning Post* (www.scmp.com) and the *Standard* (www.thestandard. com.hk) are the two local English-language daily newspapers. The *South China Morning Post* is often delivered to guest rooms free or available for purchase at the front desk or hotel kiosk, at newsstands, and bookstores. The *Standard* is free. For a different perspective, you might also want to pick up the *China Daily,* from Beijing (www.chinadaily.com.cn). The *Asian Wall Street Journal, Financial Times, International Herald Tribune,* and *USA Today International* are also available, as are news magazines like *Time* and *Newsweek.*

Telephones

To call Hong Kong: The international country code for Hong Kong is 852. Therefore, to **call Hong Kong:**

1. Dial the international access code: 011 from the U.S.; 00 from the U.K., Ireland, or New Zealand; or 0011 from Australia.
2. Dial the country code: 852.
3. Then dial the number (there is no city code for Hong Kong). So, the whole number you'd dial from the U.S. would be 011-852-0000 0000.

DOMESTIC CALLS: In Hong Kong, local calls made from homes, offices, shops, restaurants, and some hotel lobbies are free, so don't feel shy about asking to use the phone. Otherwise, local calls from public phones, which accept HK$1, HK$2, HK$5, and HK$10 coins, cost HK$1 for each 5 minutes; from hotel rooms, it's about HK$4 to HK$5.

TO MAKE INTERNATIONAL CALLS: To make international calls from Hong Kong, first dial 🕾 **001** (or **0080** or **009,** depending on which competing telephone services you wish to use) and then the country code (U.S. or Canada 1, U.K. 44, Ireland 353, Australia 61, New Zealand 64). Next dial the area code and number.

FOR DIRECTORY ASSISTANCE IN ENGLISH: Dial ✆ **1081** if you're looking for a number inside Hong Kong, or ✆ **10013** for numbers to all other countries.

FOR COLLECT CALLS: To make a collect call from any public or private phone in Hong Kong, dial ✆ **10010.**

TOLL-FREE NUMBERS: Numbers beginning with **800** within Hong Kong are toll-free. However, calling a toll-free number to a foreign country from Hong Kong is not free but rather costs the same as an overseas call.

Most hotels in Hong Kong offer direct dialing. Otherwise, long-distance calls can be made from specially marked International Dialing Direct (IDD) public phones. The most convenient method of making international calls is to use an Octopus card (see "Getting Around," earlier in this chapter). Alternatively, a PCCW Hello Phone-Card, which comes in denominations ranging from HK$50 to HK$500, is available at PCCW shops, and 7-Eleven and Circle K convenience stores. To use it, you have to key in an access number and then the PhoneCard number. You can also charge your telephone call to a major credit card by using one of about 100 credit card phones in major shopping locations.

Internet & E-Mail

WITHOUT YOUR OWN COMPUTER

Most hotels have business centers with computers for Internet access, but they can be expensive (some may be free for hotel guests, however). Cybercafes, though still few and far between, are growing in number. In addition to the suggestions below, check www.cybercafe.com or contact the HKTB.

All Hong Kong libraries have computers with Internet access you can use for free. The **Hong Kong Central Library,** 66 Causeway Rd., Causeway Bay (✆ **852/3150 1234;** www.hkpl.gov.hk), offers free Internet access from its many computers for a maximum of 2 hours. You'll find them on the ground and first floors. To avoid having to wait, you can make a reservation at ✆ **852/2921 0348.**

More convenient, perhaps, is **Cyber Pro Internet Cafe,** located in the Star House across from the Tsim Sha Tsui ferry terminal, next to McDonald's (no phone). Open daily from 10am to 2am, it requires a HK$40 deposit, plus a minimum charge of HK$20 for 1 hour. Four hours cost HK$60. In Yau Ma Tei, there's **Main Street Café,** 380 Nathan Rd. (✆ **852/2782 1818**), with four computers customers can use for free with purchase of a drink. It's open daily 7am to 10pm.

Pacific Coffee (www.pacificcoffee.com) is Hong Kong's largest chain of coffee shops; most locations offer two or more computers that customers can access for free (you'll probably have to wait in line and use is restricted to 15 min. per visit). Locations include Shop 1022 in the ifc mall, above Hong Kong Station in Central (✆ **852/2868 5100**), open Sunday through Thursday from 7am to 11pm and Friday and Saturday from 7am to midnight.

WITH YOUR OWN COMPUTER

More and more hotels, cafes, and public areas are signing on as Wi-Fi "hot spots." In Hong Kong, accessibility begins at its airport, where passengers with laptops have free Wi-Fi access from virtually anywhere in the terminal.

All upper-range and medium-priced hotels in Hong Kong are equipped with either high-speed dataports or Wi-Fi connections that allow guests to use laptop computers. In some hotels, Internet access is available upon purchase of an Internet access card for about HK$100, valid for anywhere from 100 minutes to unlimited use for 5 days, depending on the hotel (in general, the more expensive the hotel, the more expensive its Internet rates). Other hotels charge a flat rate per day, with HK$120 for 24 hours the prevailing rate. Luckily, a growing percentage of hotels offer it for free (check individual hotel listings in chapter 5 for Internet information or call your hotel in advance to see what your options are).

Hong Kong's electricity uses 220 volts and 50 cycles compared to the U.S. 110 volts and 60 cycles, but most laptop computers nowadays are equipped to deal with both. However, you'll need a prong adapter. Upper-end hotels have built-in adapters that accept foreign (including U.S.) prongs; otherwise, housekeeping can probably lend you one for free. For moderate and budget hotels, you might need a **connection kit** of the right power and—for wired connections—a spare phone cord and a spare Ethernet network cable—or find out whether your hotel supplies them to guests.

Otherwise, there are lots of places outside your hotel where you can access Wi-Fi free of charge. In an impressive effort to make Hong Kong a wireless city, the government offers free wireless Internet access services at approximately 380 hot spots throughout the SAR, including public libraries, sports and recreational centers, major parks, some tourist attractions, and government buildings and offices, including Victoria Park in Causeway Bay, and the Tsim Sha Tsui waterfront promenade and Kowloon Park in Tsim Sha Tsui. You can pick up a brochure outlining how to hook up at various places around town, including HKTB Visitor Centres and public museums like the **Hong Kong Heritage Discovery Centre** in Kowloon Park. For more information, call the GovWiFi help desk at © **852/186 111** or check the website www. gov.hk/wifi.

Finally, lots of cafes, bars, and restaurants offer wireless, including Starbucks, Pacific Coffee, Delifrance, and KFC, with locations throughout Hong Kong, though you may have to pay for the service. Ask your hotel concierge for the nearest location.

SUGGESTED HONG KONG ITINERARIES

Hong Kong offers enough diversions to occupy a lifetime—just ask anyone who lives here. But there are definite highlights, sights that no one should miss, and because transportation is so efficient, you can see quite a bit in just a day or two. If your time in Hong Kong is limited, my suggested itineraries below can make the most of it by guiding you to the best the city has to offer, coordinating sightseeing with dining and evening plans. Be sure, however, to slow down every once in awhile to soak in the atmosphere of Hong Kong street life. And keep in mind that some attractions are closed 1 day of the week, so plan accordingly.

4

GETTING TO KNOW HONG KONG

City Layout

Hong Kong, at the mouth of the Pearl River facing the South China Sea and with busy Victoria Harbour at its center, comprises Hong Kong Island, Kowloon Peninsula, the New Territories, and as many as 260 outlying islands. Most visitors, however, spend the majority of their time in Kowloon and on Hong Kong Island, simply because this is where most of the hotels, restaurants, museums, shops, markets, and bars are located in the Hong Kong Special Administrative Region (SAR). If your time is limited, this is also where I recommend you spend your first 2 days, following the first two itineraries outlined later.

Hong Kong Island, the territory's second-largest island, is where the British first landed and established its colony (Hong Kong's biggest island, Lantau, is the destination of my third itinerary). Covering some 80 sq. km (31 sq. miles), Hong Kong Island is home to some one million residents, most of whom live on its northern edge. The most famous district in Hong Kong is the Central District, home to the SAR's banking and commercial sectors, with the Western District, Wan Chai, and Causeway Bay spreading on both sides and served by a tram line and underground railway network. At Hong Kong Island's southern end, facing the South China Sea, is Stanley, famous for its market and laid-back waterfront; Aberdeen, home to a boat population; and Ocean Park, with its aquariums and thrill rides.

North across Victoria Harbour, linked by ferry, MTR, and cross-harbor tunnels, is Kowloon Peninsula. Kowloon gets its name from *gau lung,* which means "nine dragons." Legend has it that about 800 years ago, a boy emperor named Ping counted eight hills here and remarked that there must be eight resident dragons, since dragons were known to inhabit hills. (The ninth "dragon" was the emperor himself.)

Today the hills of Kowloon provide a dramatic backdrop for one of the world's most stunning cityscapes. Kowloon Peninsula is generally considered the area south of these hills, which means it also encompasses a very small part of the New Territories. However, "Kowloon" is most often used to describe its southernmost tip, the 12 sq. km (4⅔ sq. miles) that were ceded to Britain "in perpetuity" in 1860. Its northern border is Boundary Street, which separates it from the New Territories; included in this area are the districts Tsim Sha Tsui, Tsim Sha Tsui East, Yau Ma Tei, and Mong Kok. Once open countryside, Kowloon has practically disappeared under the dense spread of hotels, shops, restaurants, housing and industrial projects, and land reclamation.

Main Arteries & Streets

Hong Kong Island's Central District is larger now than it was originally, thanks to massive land reclamation. **Queen's Road,** now several blocks inland, used to mark the waterfront, as did **Des Voeux Road** and **Connaught Road** in subsequent years. Today they serve as busy thoroughfares through Central, since the steep incline up Victoria Peak follows close on their heels. From the Central District, **Hennessy, Lockhart, Jaffe,** and **Gloucester** roads lead east through Wan Chai to Causeway Bay.

It wasn't until 1972 that the first **cross-harbor tunnel** was built, connecting Causeway Bay on Hong Kong Island with Tsim Sha Tsui East in Kowloon. In 1989 a second tunnel was completed under Victoria Harbour; a third tunnel was completed in conjunction with the Hong Kong International Airport.

On the Kowloon side, the most important artery is **Nathan Road,** which runs from the harbor north up the spine of Kowloon Peninsula and is lined with hotels, restaurants, and shops. **Salisbury Road** runs east and west at the tip of Tsim Sha Tsui from the Star Ferry through Tsim Sha Tsui East along the waterfront. Also on the waterfront is the **Tsim Sha Tsui Promenade,** affording great views of Hong Kong Island and home to Hong Kong's own Avenue of the Stars.

Finding an Address

With a good map, you should have no problem finding an address. Streets are labeled in English (though signs are sometimes lacking in more congested areas like the Western District and Yau Ma Tei) and building numbers progress consecutively. For the most part, streets that run east to west (such as Des Voeux Rd. Central, Hennessy Rd., Lockhart Rd., and Salisbury Rd.) all have the even-numbered buildings on the north side of the street and the odd-numbered ones on the south. From Central, roads running through Wan Chai all the way west to Causeway Bay start with the lowest numbers near Central, with the highest-numbered buildings ending at Causeway Bay. On Nathan Road, Kowloon's most important thoroughfare, the lowest-numbered buildings are at the southern tip near the harbor; the numbers increase consecutively, with the evens on the east and the odds to the west.

Remember that the floors inside buildings follow the British system of numbering. What Americans call the first floor, therefore, is called the ground floor in Hong

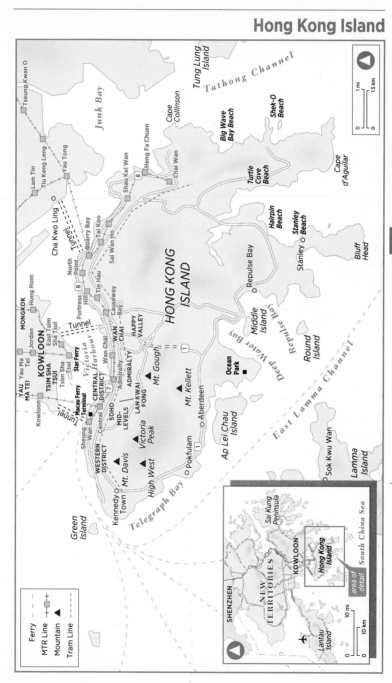

Kong; the American second floor is numbered the first floor. In addition, if you're trying to find a specific office or factory outlet in a big building, it's useful to know that number 714 means it's on the seventh floor in Room 14, while 2312 means Room 12 on the 23rd floor.

Street Maps

You can get a free map of the SAR from the Hong Kong Tourism Board (HKTB; see "Fast Facts: Hong Kong & Macau," in chapter 13 for contact information and local offices). The map should be adequate for locating most hotels, restaurants, sights, shops, and bars mentioned in this book. Free giveaway maps are also available at most hotels. If you want to explore Hong Kong in more detail, you can purchase an entire book with maps of the city region and areas in the New Territories called *Hong Kong Guidebook* (Universal Publications, Ltd; www.up.com.hk), available at bookstores, but you probably won't need this unless you're writing a guide book. Online, electronic maps are available at www.ypmap.com and www.centamap.com.

The Neighborhoods in Brief

HONG KONG ISLAND

CENTRAL DISTRICT This is where the story of Hong Kong begins. A small port and community were established here, on the north end of the island, by the British in the 1840s. Named "Victoria" in honor of the British queen, the community quickly grew into one of Asia's most important financial and business districts, with godowns (waterfront warehouses) lining the harbor. Today the area known as the Central District—but usually referred to simply as "Central"—remains Hong Kong's nerve center for banking, business, and administration. If there is a heart of Hong Kong, it surely lies here, but a few traces of its colonial past remain.

The Central District's glass and steel high-rises represent some of Hong Kong's most innovative architecture, including some of the SAR's most posh hotels, priciest shopping centers, and office buildings. Restaurants and bars here cater to Hong Kong's white-collar workers, primarily in the nightlife districts known as Lan Kwai Fong and SoHo. Although hotel choices in Central are limited to the upper range, staying here makes you feel like a resident yourself, as you rub elbows with the well-dressed professional crowds. Yet Central is also packed with traditional Chinese restaurants, an outdoor market, and the neon signs of family-run businesses. Trams—certainly one of

Hong Kong's most endearing sights—chug their way straight through Central. The neighborhood even has oases of greenery at Chater Garden; the Zoological and Botanical Gardens; and Hong Kong Park, with its museum of tea ware housed in Hong Kong's oldest colonial-age building. By the way, that construction mess you see along the harbor is being transformed into a new Central waterfront that will contain public spaces and office buildings.

LAN KWAI FONG Named after an L-shaped street in Central, this is Hong Kong's premier nightlife and entertainment district, occupying not only Lan Kwai Fong but also neighboring streets like D'Aguilar, Wyndham, and other hillside streets. Filled with restaurants and bars in all price categories, it's a melting pot for people mostly in their 20s and 30s, from expat bankers and chuppies (Chinese yuppies) to Chinese nouveau riche and backpackers. The action—whether it's in a bar with live music and standing room only or in the streets packed with revelers—continues till dawn.

VICTORIA PEAK Hong Kong's most famous mountaintop, Victoria Peak has long been Hong Kong's most exclusive address, ringed by gated villas. Cooler than the steamy streets of Central below, Victoria Peak, often called simply the Peak, was the exclusive domain of the British and other

Europeans—even nannies had to have the governor's permission to go there, and the only way up was by sedan carried by coolies or by hiking. Today, the Peak is much more easily accessible thanks to the Peak Tram, and it affords Hong Kong's best views of Central, Victoria Harbour, and Kowloon. Also on the Peak are shops, restaurants, and multimillion-dollar mansions, glimpses of which can be had on a circular 1-hour walk around the Peak. Check the weather, however, before making the trek—hazy skies can render views disappointing, if nonexistent.

MID-LEVELS   Located above Central on the slope of Victoria Peak, the Mid-Levels has long been a popular residential area for Hong Kong's yuppies and expatriate community. Its swank apartment buildings, grand sweeping views, lush vegetation, and slightly cooler temperatures make it a much-sought-after address. To serve the army of white-collar workers who commute down to Central every day, the world's longest escalator links the Mid-Levels with Central, an ambitious project with 20-some escalators and moving sidewalks (all free) stretching a half-mile (board and exit as you wish).

SOHO   This dining and nightlife district, flanking the Central–Mid-Levels Escalator, is popular with area residents and those seeking a quieter, saner alternative to the crowds of Lan Kwai Fong. Dubbed SoHo for the region "south of Hollywood Road," it's an ever-growing neighborhood of cafe-bars and intimate restaurants specializing in ethnic and innovative cuisine, making it one of the most exciting destinations on Hong Kong's culinary and nightlife map. Most establishments center on Elgin, Shelley, and Staunton streets. North of Hollywood Road, referred to as **NoHo,** also boasts a growing number of bars and restaurants.

WESTERN   DISTRICT   Located west of Central, the Western District was the traditional commercial center for Chinese businesses. Spreading over a large area that includes Sai Ying Pun, Sheung Wan, and Kennedy Town, it's a fascinating neighborhood of Chinese shops and enterprises and is one of the oldest, most traditional areas on Hong Kong Island. I've spent days wandering its narrow streets and inspecting shops selling traditional herbs, ginseng, medicines, dried fish, antiques, and other Chinese products. Unfortunately, modernization has taken its toll, and more of the old Western District seems to vanish every year, replaced by new high-rises and other developments.

SHEUNG WAN   This neighborhood in the Western District, bordered by Victoria Harbour to the north, Central to the east, Sai Ying Pun to the west, and the Mid-Levels to the south, is home to an MTR station (Sheung Wan station) and the Macau Ferry Terminal. This is where the British landed, in 1842, on what is now called Possession Street. Sheung Wan is most famous, however, for Hollywood Road and its many antiques and curio shops, Ladder Street with its grueling staircase, and Man Mo Temple, one of Hong Kong's oldest temples.

ADMIRALTY   Actually part of the Central District, Admiralty is located just below Hong Kong Park, centered around an MTR subway station of the same name. It consists primarily of tall office buildings and Pacific Place, a classy shopping complex flanked by four deluxe hotels. On the waterfront is Tamar, former home of the British naval station, now being redeveloped as new government headquarters.

WAN CHAI   Located east of Central, few places on Hong Kong Island have changed as dramatically or noticeably as Wan Chai in recent decades. Notorious after World War II for its sleazy bars, tattoo parlors, and sailors on shore leave looking for a good time, it also served as a popular destination for American servicemen on R&R during the Vietnam War. Richard Mason's 1957 novel *The World of Suzie Wong* takes place in this bygone era of Wan Chai. Although a somewhat raunchy nightlife remains along Lockhart, Jaffe, and Luard roads, most of Wan Chai has slowly become respectable (and almost unrecognizable) over the past few decades, with the addition of mostly business-style hotels, more high-rises, the Hong Kong Arts Centre, the Academy for Performing Arts, and the huge Hong Kong Convention and Exhibition Centre, a familiar sight on the waterfront with its curved roof and glass facade. Near the convention center is Star Ferry service to Tsim Sha Tsui.

CAUSEWAY BAY   Just east of Wan Chai, this is a popular shopping destination for locals. The whole area was once a bay, until land reclamation turned the water into soil decades ago. Now it's a busy area of department stores; clothing and accessory boutiques; street markets; the Times Square shopping complex; and restaurants. On its eastern perimeter is the large Victoria Park.

HAPPY VALLEY   Once a swampland, Happy Valley's main claim to fame is its racetrack, built in 1846—the oldest racetrack in Asia outside of China.

ABERDEEN   On the south side of Hong Kong Island, Aberdeen was once a fishing village but is now studded with high-rises and housing projects. However, it is still known for its hundreds of sampans, junks, boat people, and huge floating restaurant. Just to the east, in Deep Water Bay, is Ocean Park, with its impressive aquarium and amusement rides.

STANLEY   Once a fishing village, Stanley is now a lively center for its market selling everything from silk suits to name-brand shoes, casual wear, and souvenirs. It's located on the quiet south side of Hong Kong Island with a popular public beach, a Chinese and expat neighborhood, a maritime museum, and trendy restaurants strung along a waterfront promenade.

KOWLOON PENINSULA

TSIM SHA TSUI   At the southern tip of Kowloon Peninsula is Tsim Sha Tsui (also spelled "Tsimshatsui"), which, after Central, rates as Hong Kong's most important area for tourists. This is where most visitors stay and spend their money, since it has the greatest concentration of hotels, restaurants, and shops. In fact, some Hongkongers avoid Tsim Sha Tsui like the plague, calling it the "tourist ghetto." On the other hand, it does boast a cultural center, a great art museum, Kowloon Park, one of the world's largest shopping malls, a nice selection of international restaurants, a jumping nightlife, and Nathan Road, appropriately nicknamed the "golden mile of shopping."

TSIM SHA TSUI EAST   Not surprisingly, this neighborhood is east of Tsim Sha Tsui. Built entirely on reclaimed land, the area has become increasingly important, home to a rash of expensive hotels, shopping and restaurant complexes, and science and history museums. Its East Tsim Sha Tsui Station, connected to Tsim Sha Tsui MTR Station via underground passageway, provides direct train service to Hung Hom Station and onward to mainland China.

JORDAN & YAU MA TEI   If you get on the subway in Tsim Sha Tsui and ride two stations to the north (or walk for about 25 min. straight up Nathan Rd.), you'll reach the Yau Ma Tei district (also spelled "Yaumatei"). In between Tsim Sha Tsui and Yau Ma Tei is Jordan. Like the Western District, Jordan and Yau Ma Tei are very Chinese, with an interesting produce market, jade market, and the fascinating Temple Street Night Market. Several modestly priced hotels are located here, making this a good alternative to tourist-oriented Tsim Sha Tsui.

MONG KOK   On Kowloon Peninsula north of Yau Ma Tei, Mong Kok is a residential and industrial area, home of the Bird Market, the Ladies' Market on Tung Choi Street, and countless shops catering to Chinese. Its northern border, Boundary Street, marks the beginning of the New Territories.

THE BEST OF HONG KONG IN 1 DAY

If you only have 1 day to spend in Hong Kong, I feel for you. Seeing the top sights of Hong Kong in 1 day requires an early start, discipline, and a bit of stamina. *Start: Star Ferry or MTR to Tsim Sha Tsui.*

1 Tsim Sha Tsui Promenade

Start the day with an early morning stroll along the Tsim Sha Tsui Promenade, from which you have a great view of the harbor with its boat traffic and Hong Kong Island. At its eastern end is the Avenue of Stars, with handprints and statues of celebrities like Jackie Chan. If it's Monday, Wednesday, or Friday, you could join a free 1-hour lesson in tai chi, conducted at 8am in the Hong Kong Museum of Art's Sculpture Court near the promenade. See p. 212.

2 Serenade Chinese Restaurant 🍴 ★★

Located in the Hong Kong Cultural Centre, next to the Star Ferry, this is my top choice for dim sum with a view of Victoria Harbour. It opens daily at 8am. On Salisbury Road (✆ 852/2722 0932). See p. 158.

3 Hong Kong Museum of Art ★★★

Beside the Cultural Centre is this impressive museum housing Hong Kong's best collection of Chinese antiquities and fine art, including bronzes, paintings, and ceramics, shown on a rotating basis. Its relatively small size makes it easy to see in an hour or less; I also like the Victoria Harbour views from its windows. It's closed Thursday, and open the rest of the week from 10am to 6pm (Sat to 8pm). See p. 170.

4 Chinese Arts & Crafts ★★

For one-stop shopping, this two-story Chinese emporium in the Star House, across from the Star Ferry, is Hong Kong's best upscale chain for high-quality jade, jewelry, Chinese clothing, embroidered tablecloths, antiques, rosewood furniture, and more. See p. 228.

5 Star Ferry

No visit to Hong Kong would be complete without at least one trip across Victoria Harbour aboard one of the famous Star Ferries, which have been plying the waters between Hong Kong Island and Kowloon since 1898. The 5-minute trip (have your camera ready!) will deposit you at the Central Ferry Piers, where other ferries depart for the outlying islands. See p. 41.

Take the open-top shuttle bus no. 15C from the Star Ferry to the Peak Tram Station.

6 Victoria Peak

Board the Peak Tram, which began operations in 1888, for its 8-minute climb up Victoria Peak, where you'll be rewarded with fantastic views from Hong Kong Island's tallest hill if the weather is clear. Peak Tower has an observation platform with 360-degree panoramic views. If you have the time and energy, walk the 1-hour stroll around the Peak. See p. 154.

The Best of Hong Kong in 1 Day

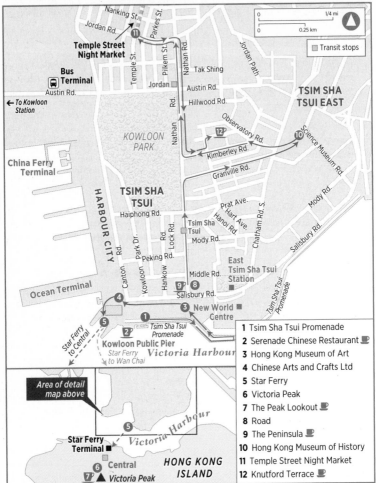

1 Tsim Sha Tsui Promenade
2 Serenade Chinese Restaurant ☕
3 Hong Kong Museum of Art
4 Chinese Arts and Crafts Ltd
5 Star Ferry
6 Victoria Peak
7 The Peak Lookout ☕
8 Road
9 The Peninsula ☕
10 Hong Kong Museum of History
11 Temple Street Night Market
12 Knutford Terrace ☕

7 The Peak Lookout ☕ ★★

Set in a former tram station across from Peak Tower, this restaurant is a delightful setting for American, Chinese, Indian, Japanese, and Southeast Asian fare, especially if the weather is nice and you can sit on its outdoor terrace surrounded by lush greenery. Other good choices abound in Peak Tower and Peak Galleria across the street. Located at 121 Peak Rd. ℂ 852/2849 1000). See p. 154.

Take the Peak Tram back to Central and walk 10 minutes to the Central MTR station, where you should board the subway for Tsim Sha Tsui Station.

8 Nathan Road

Nicknamed the "Golden Mile of Shopping" for its endless string of shops selling electronics, jewelry, clothing, and a million other goods, this is Kowloon's most famous street. See p. 212.

9 The Peninsula 🍵 ★★★

Hong Kong's most famous spot for afternoon tea—and people-watching—is the ornate lobby of the venerable Peninsula, built in 1928. A string quartet serenades as you feast on scones, finger sandwiches, pastries, and fine teas, served daily from 2 to 7pm. Located on the corner of Nathan and Salisbury roads. (852/2315 3146. See p. 162.

10 Hong Kong Museum of History ★★★

For a quick course in Hong Kong's history, from its days as a small fishing village through its years as a British colony, this museum is a must-see. Open Wednesday to Monday 10am to 6pm (until 7pm Sun and holidays). See p. 171.

11 Temple Street Night Market ★★

Hong Kong's most famous night market exudes a festive atmosphere, with its outdoor stalls selling everything from Chinese souvenirs to clothing and accessories, plus its fortunetellers and street opera singers. The market opens daily at 4pm, but the real action doesn't get underway until 7pm.

12 Knutsford Terrace 🍵

This pedestrian alley, north of Kimberley Road, is lined with open-fronted bars and restaurants, including Tutto Bene ★, offering Italian fare ((852/2316 2116), and All Night Long, a bar with live music ((852/2367 9489). See p. 129 and 246, respectively.

THE BEST OF HONG KONG IN 2 DAYS

After a full day following the "The Best of Hong Kong in 1 Day," you'll continue packing in the activities for Day 2 as well. *Start: MTR or Star Ferry to Central.*

1 Shanghai Tang ★★★

This classy shop revolutionized traditional Chinese clothing with mod cheongsams, Chinese jackets, and other fashionable wear in eye-popping colors. It also sells home accessories, purses, and funky goods. See p. 228.

2 Li Yuen Street East & Li Yuen Street West

These two parallel pedestrian lanes between Queen's Road Central and Des Voeux Road Central are packed with stalls selling clothing and accessories, both Western and Chinese. See p. 235.

3 Western District

West of Central, this colorful neighborhood features traditional Chinese shops selling ginseng, herbal medicine, preserved foods, and funeral goods. The area is concentrated on Wing Lok Street, Des Voeux Road, and Queen's Road West. For a more thorough tour of this area, see the walking tour starting on p. 199.

The Best of Hong Kong in 2 Days

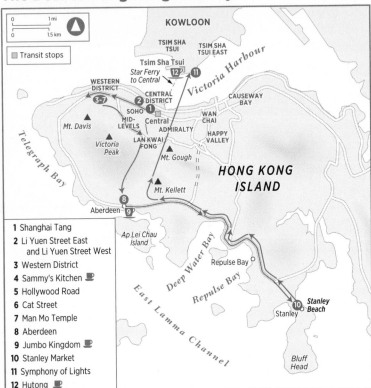

1 Shanghai Tang
2 Li Yuen Street East and Li Yuen Street West
3 Western District
4 Sammy's Kitchen
5 Hollywood Road
6 Cat Street
7 Man Mo Temple
8 Aberdeen
9 Jumbo Kingdom
10 Stanley Market
11 Symphony of Lights
12 Hutong

4 Sammy's Kitchen

It's nothing fancy, but this family-owned restaurant—one of the few serving Western food in the Western District—has been dishing out inexpensive Western and Chinese fare since 1970. A throwback to older days in both decor and atmosphere, it's also good for breakfast, lunch, or simply a refreshing drink. It's located at 204–206 Queen's Rd. W. ☎ 852/ 2548 8400. See p. 157.

5 Hollywood Road

This long street stretching through the Western District to Central is lined with shops selling high-end Chinese antiques and furniture, as well as curio stores selling snuff bottles, old postcards, and bric-a-brac. See p. 224.

6 Cat Street

A pedestrian lane parallel to Hollywood Road, it's lined with street vendors and shops selling antiques, junk, and reproductions. See p. 206 and 224.

7 Man Mo Temple ★

Located on Hollywood Road and dating back to the 1840s, Hong Kong Island's oldest temple makes for a picturesque and peaceful stop. See p. 178.

Take a taxi to Aberdeen's waterfront promenade, on the south side of Hong Kong Island.

8 Aberdeen

Although now surrounded by high-rises, Aberdeen is still known for its fishing fleet of modern boats and traditional junks, many inhabited by boat people who have lived on the sea for generations. If you wish, you can take a sampan tour for an up-close view. See p. 175.

9 Jumbo Kingdom 💻 ★

Take the free shuttle boat from Aberdeen's waterfront promenade to Jumbo Kingdom (𝓒 852/2553 9111), a colorful floating restaurant where you can feast on dim sum and Cantonese fare. Alternatively, try Jumbo's Top Deck restaurant ★★ (𝓒 852/2553 3331), featuring alfresco dining and an international seafood menu. See p. 156.

Catch bus no. 73 or take a taxi to:

10 Stanley Market ★★

This market is great for both Western and Chinese clothing for the whole family, as well as traditional Chinese souvenirs, making it a fun, laid-back destination. See p. 235.

Take bus no. 973 to Kowloon.

11 "Symphony of Lights"

Guinness World Records rates this the world's largest permanent light-and-sound show, where every evening at 8pm more than 40 buildings on both sides of the harbor put on a light-and-laser show. The best vantage point is on the Tsim Sha Tsui Promenade. See p. 255.

12 Hutong 💻 ★★★

Breathtaking views, a dramatic setting, and innovative northern Chinese cuisine make this one of Hong Kong's most talked-about restaurants—so make reservations as early as possible. Located on the 28th floor at 1 Peking Rd. 𝓒 852/3428 8342. See p. 124.

THE BEST OF HONG KONG IN 3 DAYS

While you could spend a third day—and even a fourth and a fifth—visiting more attractions and soaking up Hong Kong's lively street life (see the suggested walking tours in chapter 8), visitors with limited time in Hong Kong should consider an excursion to Lantau, home of a giant outdoor Buddha and adjoining monastery offering vegetarian lunches. ***Start:*** *Central Ferry Piers.*

1 Ferry to Lantau

Though you can now reach Lantau via MTR followed by cable car, I recommend this old-fashioned method of transportation on your outbound journey; from the outdoor deck in deluxe class you're treated to great views. Aim for the 8:30am ferry departure to Mui Wo (9am on Sun). See p. 266.

The Best of Hong Kong in 3 Days

1 Ferry to Lantau
2 Bus to Ngong Ping Plateau
3 Giant Buddha
4 Wisdom Path
5 Po Lin Monastery 🍴
6 Ngong Ping Village
7 Ngong Ping Skyrail
8 Citygate
9 Lan Kwai Fong 🍴

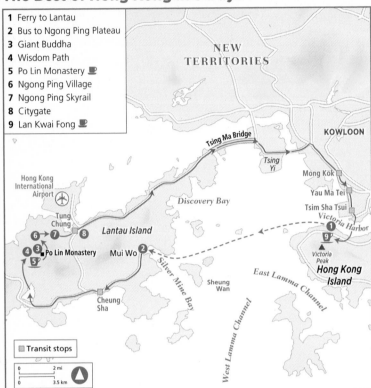

2 Bus to Ngong Ping Plateau

Bus no. 2 from Silvermine Bay (Mui Wo in Chinese) hurtles around hair-raising curves through lush countryside on its 45-minute trip to Ngong Ping. See p. 267.

3 Giant Buddha

Built in 1993, this is the world's largest seated outdoor bronze Buddha. Climb 260-some steps to the viewing platform for sweeping views from Ngong Ping Plateau, 738m (2,420 ft.) above sea level. See p. 268.

4 Wisdom Path

Large wooden pillars, placed in the form of a figure eight to symbolize infinity, display the Heart Sutra, a centuries-old prayer revered by Confucians, Buddhists, and Taoists alike. See p. 268.

5 Po Lin Monastery ★★

Dining at this monastery was a draw long before the Giant Buddha and other attractions arrived. Choose from two fixed-price vegetarian meals, served daily 11:30am to 4:30pm.

Don't miss the monastery's ornate temple, which houses three bronze statues of Buddha representing the past, present, and future. ℂ 852/2985 5248. See p. 269.

6 Ngong Ping Village

Ngong Ping's newest attraction features Walking with Buddha, a multimedia experience relating Siddhartha's path to enlightenment, and Monkey's Tale Theatre, which presents the parable of a selfish monkey who learns a lesson about sharing and kindness; restaurants and shops can also be found. See p. 269.

7 Ngong Ping Skyrail

This cable car travels 5.7km (3½ miles) in about 25 minutes, providing panoramic views of Lantau, the South China Sea, even the airport. See p. 267.

8 Citygate

The cable car deposits you at Tung Chung, where you'll find Hong Kong's only outlet mall offering discounts on international name brands. See p. 234.

Take the MTR to Central's Hong Kong Station.

9 Lan Kwai Fong ☕

It's a party scene every night in Lan Kwai Fong, Hong Kong's most famous nightlife district. Bars and restaurants beckon with open facades, and the action invariably spills onto the streets. See chapters 6 and 10 for recommendations on where to eat and drink.

4

SUGGESTED HONG KONG ITINERARIES

The Best of Hong Kong in 3 Days

WHERE TO STAY

While the previous decade saw a decline in tourism in Hong Kong—due to events like the September 11, 2001, terrorist attacks in the United States, the 2003 outbreak of severe acute respiratory syndrome (SARS), and the 2009 global recession—the new decade shows promise of a rebound, with a healthy influx of visitors and an impressive list of new hotels. The face of the tourist industry, however, has changed. Whereas long-distance visitors, particularly from North America and Europe, used to account for the greater share of Hong Kong's tourism industry, regional tourism now fuels the surge in growth—thanks to a huge influx of mainland Chinese who, because of relaxed visa regulations, are filling Hong Kong's hotels in ever-increasing numbers. A never-ending parade of conventions, trade fairs, and other events also contributes to Hong Kong's healthy tourism industry.

5

Hotel occupancy in Hong Kong now stands around 85%, with increased demand causing room rates to rise. Hotels are not cheap in the SAR, especially when compared with those in many other Asian cities. Rather, prices are similar to what you'd pay in major U.S. and European cities, and while US$200 might get you the best room in town in Topeka, Kansas, in Hong Kong it will get you a small, undistinguished box not unlike a highway motel room. In other words, except for the cost of getting to Hong Kong, your biggest expenditure is going to be for a place to stay.

Still, bargains can be found, especially online and at hotel websites. Upper-end hotels may offer special packages, including weekend getaways, off-season incentives, and upgrades, while lower-end hotels may offer special promotional rates in the off season. Some hotels offer "early bird" discounts if you book a month or two in advance; others may throw in extras, such as breakfast or airport transfers, in package deals.

In any case, you should always book rooms well in advance, especially if you have a particular hotel, location, or price category in mind. The SAR's biggest hotel crunches traditionally occur twice a year, during Hong Kong's most clement weather: in March through May (April is the busiest month) and again in October and November. In addition, major trade fairs at Hong Kong's convention center can wreak havoc on travelers who arrive without reservations—all of Hong Kong's hotels will be fully booked. Unsurprisingly, prices are highest during peak season and major trade fairs. While bargains are abundant during the off seasons,

Where to Stay in Kowloon

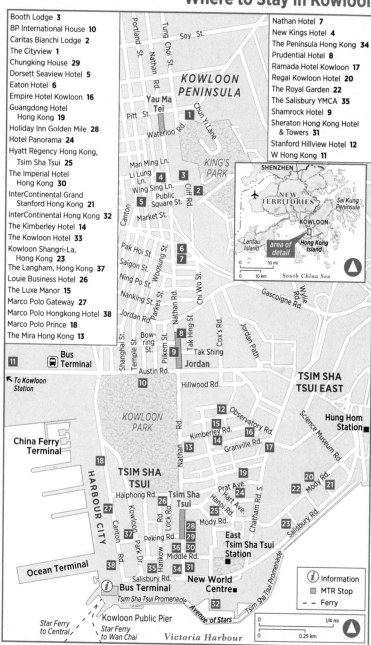

Booth Lodge **3**
BP International House **10**
Caritas Bianchi Lodge **2**
The Cityview **1**
Chungking House **29**
Dorsett Seaview Hotel **5**
Eaton Hotel **6**
Empire Hotel Kowloon **16**
Guangdong Hotel
  Hong Kong **19**
Holiday Inn Golden Mile **28**
Hotel Panorama **24**
Hyatt Regency Hong Kong,
  Tsim Sha Tsui **25**
The Imperial Hotel
  Hong Kong **30**
InterContinental Grand
  Stanford Hong Kong **21**
InterContinental Hong Kong **32**
The Kimberley Hotel **14**
The Kowloon Hotel **33**
Kowloon Shangri-La,
  Hong Kong **23**
The Langham, Hong Kong **37**
Louie Business Hotel **26**
The Luxe Manor **15**
Marco Polo Gateway **27**
Marco Polo Hongkong Hotel **38**
Marco Polo Prince **18**
The Mira Hong Kong **13**

Nathan Hotel **7**
New Kings Hotel **4**
The Peninsula Hong Kong **34**
Prudential Hotel **8**
Ramada Hotel Kowloon **17**
Regal Kowloon Hotel **20**
The Royal Garden **22**
The Salisbury YMCA **35**
Shamrock Hotel **9**
Sheraton Hong Kong Hotel
  & Towers **31**
Stanford Hillview Hotel **12**
W Hong Kong **11**

5

WHERE TO STAY

71

many hotels use their published rack rates (the ones I give later) during peak season and major trade fairs.

As for trends in the hotel industry, Hong Kong's biggest markets nowadays are business travelers and tourists from mainland China. This translates into crowded elevators and lobbies in the moderately priced hotels that Chinese frequent. On the other end of the spectrum are the recent influx of a new niche—boutique hotels offering a more intimate atmosphere and unique decor that's a distinct departure from cookie-cutter hotels. Hotels have also improved services and in-room amenities, so that standard features in even inexpensive rooms are likely to include hair dryers, room safes, minibars or refrigerators you can stock yourself, hot-water kettles with free tea and coffee, Internet access or Wi-Fi (occasionally free but most often for a daily fee of about HK$100–HK$160), and cable and/or satellite TVs with in-house pay movies. Nonsmoking floors are common in all hotels except for rock-bottom guest houses. Most hotels also have tour desks or can book tours for you through the concierge or front desk.

Unless otherwise stated, all hotels in this book have air-conditioning (a must in Hong Kong), private bathroom (most with tub/shower combinations, though many of the newer moderately priced hotels are going shower only), and telephones with international direct dialing. Room service (either 24 hr. or until the wee hours of the morning), babysitting, and same-day laundry service are available in moderate to very expensive hotels, as are Western and Asian restaurants and business centers providing Internet access (usually for a fee). Many also offer health clubs with fitness rooms and swimming pools, almost always free for hotel guests. A growing number of upper-range hotels have also added full-range spas.

Some hotels differentiate among their guests, charging health-club or in-room Internet fees, for example, for those who book through a travel agent or the hotel's website but not for those who pay rack rates (the maximum quoted rates). Guests booking through discount websites may also receive fewer amenities. Note that while many hotels allow children under a specific age (usually 11 and under) to room free with parents, restrictions apply. Some allow only one child, while others allow a maximum of three people in a room. Almost all charge extra if an extra bed is required.

It's nearly impossible to predict what might happen over the next few decades, let alone the next few years. In 1985, Hong Kong had a sparse 18,180 hotel rooms. Today that number has swelled to almost 60,000, with more on the way. Only one thing is certain: If the tourists continue to pour into Hong Kong, hotels will happily continue to raise their rates.

BEST HOTEL BETS

Choosing a favorite hotel in Hong Kong can be a bit overwhelming, if not impossible, because the choices are so vast and competition is steep. Few cities offer such a large number of first-rate hotels, and few places can compete with the service that has made the Hong Kong hotel industry legendary. With apologies to the rest, here are my personal favorites. For my picks on the best splurge and moderately priced hotels, see chapter 1.

o **Best Historic Hotel:** This category has no competition: **The Peninsula Hong Kong,** Salisbury Road, Tsim Sha Tsui (© **866/382-8388** in the U.S, or 852/2920 2888), Hong Kong's oldest hotel, has long been the grand old hotel of Hong Kong.

Where to Stay in the Central District

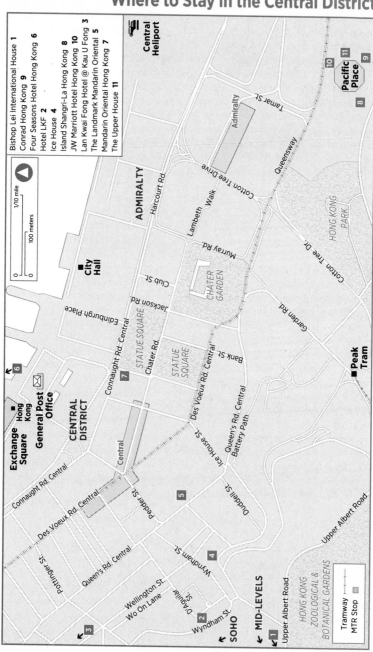

Bishop Lei International House **1**
Conrad Hong Kong **9**
Four Seasons Hotel Hong Kong **6**
Hotel LKF **2**
Ice House **4**
Island Shangri-La Hong Kong **8**
JW Marriott Hotel Hong Kong **10**
Lan Kwai Fong Hotel @ Kau U Fong **3**
The Landmark Mandarin Oriental **5**
Mandarin Oriental Hong Kong **7**
The Upper House **11**

Built in 1928 and boasting the most ornate lobby in Hong Kong, it retains the atmosphere of a colonial past, even down to its restaurants, Gaddi's and the Verandah, both of which have changed little over the decades. Its 1993 tower addition, with high-tech rooms and a trendy rooftop restaurant, only adds to the general aura. See p. 81.

- **Best for Business Executives:** If work brings you to Central, there's no better location than the **Mandarin Oriental, Hong Kong,** 5 Connaught Rd., Central (© **800/526-6566** in the U.S., or 852/2522 0111), Central's landmark hotel since 1963. It offers all the services road warriors have come to expect, from Wi-Fi and good work stations in its spacious rooms (some with the extra bonus of harbor views) to facilities that run the gamut from a health club and spa to restaurants good for clinching that business deal. The MTR, Star Ferry, and express train to the airport are just minutes from the hotel's front door, and for busy executives looking for a convenient place to chill, Chater Garden is just across Statue Square. See p. 83.

- **Best for IT Junkies:** New in 2009, the **Mira Hong Kong,** 118–130 Nathan Rd., Tsim Sha Tsui (© **852/2368 1111**), boasts the most high-tech rooms in town with 40-inch, wall-mounted TVs that double as computers, allowing you to go online or stream Internet radio. You can also use your own stuff, plugging your iPod to the Bose dock or using the hotel's Wi-Fi with your laptop for free. There are even mobile phones in your room you can take with you anywhere in Hong Kong. An engaging, knowledgeable staff makes sure you stay connected not only with the world at large, but with the world right outside hotel doors. See p. 93.

- **Best Trendy Hotel:** Design guru Philippe Starck is the mastermind behind **JIA Hong Kong,** 1–5 Irving St., Causeway Bay (© **852/3196 9000**), a 57-room boutique hotel featuring whimsical furniture in its lobby but minimalist, high-tech decor and gadgetry in its guest rooms. A slew of freebies (continental breakfast and evening cocktails); rooms divided into distinct living, dining, and working areas complete with kitchens; and access to a couple of Hong Kong's hottest clubs make this a shoo-in for fashion-conscious travelers ready to burrow in. See p. 97.

- **Best Budget Hotel:** The overwhelming number-one choice in this category has long been the **Salisbury YMCA,** Salisbury Road, Tsim Sha Tsui (© **852/2268 7000**), with a fantastic location right next to the prestigious (and very expensive) Peninsula and just a short walk from the Star Ferry. Rooms are simple but offer virtually everything (from satellite TVs to Wi-Fi and coffeemakers); some even have stunning harbor views. Throw in two inexpensive restaurants, a health club, and laundry facilities, and you have more than enough to satisfy budget-minded vacationers who don't want to sacrifice location or convenience. See p. 101.

- **Best for Long Stays:** Travelers who can score accommodations at **Ice House,** 38 Ice House St., Central (© **852/2836 7333**), might find themselves wishing they could stay even longer due to its convenient location in Central near Lan Kwai Fong, smart-looking rooms with kitchenettes, and competitive prices. There's no gym, but you'll get plenty of exercise walking to its uphill location. See p. 102.

- **Best Health Club:** Most of Hong Kong's deluxe hotels boast state-of-the-art health clubs, but what I like most about the club at the **InterContinental Hong Kong,** 18 Salisbury Rd., Tsim Sha Tsui (© **800/327-0200** in the U.S., or 852/2721 1211), is that it's open 24 hours a day, so you can work out when it fits your schedule. You can also relax in the outdoor, filled-to-the-brim horizonless Jacuzzi that gives the illusion of flowing into the harbor, and a state-of-the-art spa that observes

Where to Stay in Causeway Bay & Wan Chai

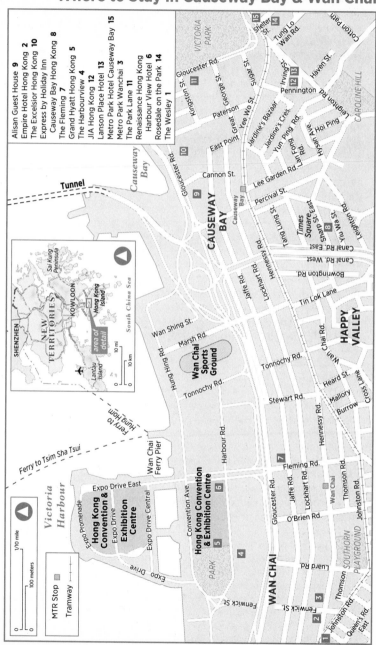

Alisan Guest House **9**
Empire Hotel Hong Kong **2**
The Excelsior Hong Kong **10**
Express by Holiday Inn
  Causeway Bay Hong Kong **8**
The Fleming **7**
Grand Hyatt Hong Kong **5**
The Harbourview **4**
JIA Hong Kong **12**
Lanson Place Hotel **13**
Metro Park Hotel Causeway Bay **15**
Metro Park Wanchai **3**
The Park Lane **11**
Renaissance Hong Kong
  Harbour View Hotel **6**
Rosedale on the Park **14**
The Wesley **1**

architectural rules for feng shui and specializes in jet-lag relief and Oriental treatments. And to top it off, this hotel even offers free tai chi and yoga classes for its guests. See p. 80.

- **Best Hotel Pool:** The **Grand Hyatt Hong Kong,** 1 Harbour Rd., Wan Chai (✆ **800/233-1234** in the U.S., or 852/2588 1234), and **Renaissance Harbour View Hotel Hong Kong,** 1 Harbour Rd., Wan Chai (✆ **800/228-9290** in the U.S., or 852/2802 8888), share one of Hong Kong's largest outdoor pools, surrounded by a lush, landscaped garden and with views of the harbor. See p. 83 and 88.

- **Best Spa:** Spas are big business in Hong Kong, with many of the city's top hotels now offering a myriad of spa treatments. The Spa at **Four Seasons Hotel Hong Kong,** 8 Finance St., Central (✆ **800/819-5053** in the U.S., or 852/3196 8888), exceeds the rest with treatments that begin with hydrotherapy—including a Finnish sauna, an amethyst crystal steam room with mother-of-pearl-covered seating, a fountain that rains crushed ice flakes, and hot tubs—and continue in one of 18 treatment rooms. For the ultimate splurge, spring for one of the VIP suites, where after your massage you'll retire to your own jet bath overlooking the harbor. As far as I'm concerned, it doesn't get any better than this. See p. 294.

- **Best Views:** Most of Hong Kong's deluxe hotels boast harbor views, making this category the most competitive. However, in my opinion, the best harbor views are from the Kowloon side, where you can feast your eyes not only on the boats plying the water but also on Hong Kong Island with its stunning architecture, Victoria Peak, and, at night, the shimmering of neon lights and laser-light extravaganza of Hong Kong's nightly "Symphony of Lights." And no Tsim Sha Tsui hotel is as close to the water as the **InterContinental Hong Kong** (see address and telephone above), built right over the harbor; as many as 70% of its rooms command sweeping views of the water and boast floor-to-ceiling and wall-to-wall windows, making the most of one of the world's most breathtaking city views. See p. 80.

- **Best for Art Lovers:** The Island Shangri-La Hong Kong, Pacific Place, Central (✆ **800/565-5050** in the U.S., or 852/2877 3838), is a gorgeous hotel with more than 700 Viennese chandeliers, lush Tai Ping carpets, flower arrangements, and more than 700 paintings and artworks. But the clincher is the 16-story-high Chinese painting in the hotel atrium, drawn by 40 artists from Beijing and believed to be the largest landscape painting in the world. See p. 87.

- **Best for Expat Wannabes:** Mid-Levels has long been a favorite residential area for expats living and working in Hong Kong. **Bishop Lei International House,** 4 Robinson Rd., Mid-Levels (✆ **852/2868 0828**), is located about halfway up Victoria Peak, with great views from its smallish rooms. Nearby, ethnic restaurants and neighborhood bars abound, but for a real taste of Mid-Levels living, travel the escalator that local residents use to get to and from their jobs in Central. See p. 95.

 A Romantic Getaway

If you're planning a romantic getaway, go to Macau, where the **Westin Resort Macau,** Estrada de Hac Sa on Colôane Island (✆ **800/WESTIN-1** [800/937-8461]), has the perfect and most idyllic setting with large rooms (each with private terrace) overlooking the sea, landscaped grounds, indoor and outdoor pools, an 18-hole golf course, spa, and a nearby beach for moonlit walks. See p. 298.

SELECTING HOTELS

No one area in this compact city is really a more convenient location than any other. Public transportation is efficient and easy to use, and the attractions are spread throughout the city. However, most visitors do stay in **Tsim Sha Tsui,** on the Kowloon side, simply because that's where you'll find the greatest concentration of hotels, as well as shops and restaurants. Business travelers often prefer the **Central District,** while those attending events at the convention center usually opt for hotels strung along the waterfront of **Wan Chai** and **Causeway Bay.** **Yau Ma Tei** and **Mong Kok,** situated on the Kowloon Peninsula north of Tsim Sha Tsui, are great places to stay if you want to be surrounded by Chinese stores and locals, with hardly a souvenir shop in sight. See "The Neighborhoods in Brief," beginning on p. 60, for more information on these neighborhoods.

The hotel prices listed in this book are the rack rates, which you might end up paying if you come during peak season (Chinese New Year, Mar–May, Oct–Nov). Otherwise, you can probably get a room for much, much less. It's *imperative,* therefore, to shop around and ask about special packages, upgrades, or promotional fares when making reservations, particularly in the off season. Although I've included toll-free numbers for the United States and Canada for many of the listings later, I also recommend contacting the hotels directly to inquire about rates and special deals, and checking hotel websites for deals that might be offered only through the Internet.

Generally speaking, the price of a room in Hong Kong depends upon its view and height rather than upon its size. Not surprisingly, the best and most expensive rooms are those with a sweeping view of Victoria Harbour, as well as those on the higher floors. Is a harbor view worth it? Emphatically, yes. Hong Kong's harbor, with watercraft activity ranging from cruise ships and barges to fishing boats and the Star Ferry, is one of the most fascinating in the world; the city's high-rises and mountains are icing on the cake. Waking in the morning and opening your curtains to this famous scene is a thrill. Hotels know it, which is why they charge an arm and a leg for the privilege. A few moderately and inexpensively priced accommodations offer harbor views, though these, too, represent their most expensive rooms.

In any case, don't be shy about asking what price categories are available and what the differences are among them. Keep in mind that the difference in price between a room facing inland and a room facing the harbor can be staggering, with various price categories in between. For example "partial" or "side" harbor views means you can glimpse the harbor looking sideways from your window or between tall buildings. Double rooms that range from HK$2,000 to HK$3,000, for example, may include five different categories, beginning with a "standard" room on a lower floor facing inland and then increasing in cost to those on upper floors facing inland, those with side harbor views, those on lower floors facing the harbor, and, most expensive, "deluxe" rooms on higher floors with full harbor views. To save money, consider requesting the highest room available in the category you choose. If "standard" rooms, for example, run up to the eighth floor and deluxe rooms are on floors 9 to 20, ask for a standard room on floor 8, where you might just have a bit of a view. If you decide to spring for a full harbor view, be sure to ask for it when making your reservation, and request the highest floor available.

For moderately priced or inexpensive lodgings, few of which offer any kind of view at all, rates are usually based on height, decor, and sometimes size, and it's prudent

WAYS TO save ON YOUR HOTEL ROOM

The **rack rate** is the maximum rate that a hotel charges for a room. Although a few deluxe hotels stick to their published rack rates year-round and most hotels charge rack rates during peak travel times in spring and autumn and during major fairs and conventions, you can probably strike a better bargain.

○ **Ask about special rates, packages, or other discounts.** Always ask whether a room less expensive than the first one quoted is available. Hong Kong hotels usually have a variety of rates based on room amenities, views, and other factors. If the hotel won't budge on price, ask whether special privileges or amenities can be thrown in, such as free breakfast. In addition, hotels often offer packages that include breakfasts, airport transfers, and other services that are cheaper than buying separately.

○ **Dial direct.** When booking a room, compare the rates offered by the hotel's local line with that of the toll-free number. A hotel makes nothing on a room that stays empty, so the local hotel reservation desk may be willing to offer a special rate unavailable elsewhere.

○ **Book online.** Many hotels offer Internet-only discounts on their own websites. Cheaper rates are also available through room suppliers on the Internet. In addition to the well-known online travel booking sites Travelocity, Expedia, and Orbitz, other good shopping grounds for hotels are www.asia hotels.com, www.asiarooms.com, www.asiatravel.com, and http://info.wotif.com. In any case, make sure you get a confirmation number and make a printout of any online booking transaction.

○ **Remember the law of supply and demand.** Avoid high-season stays whenever you can: Planning your vacation just a week before or after official peak season (generally spring and autumn) can mean big savings. Many hotels offer promotional fares throughout the summer. Business hotels may offer discounts over the weekend, while inexpensive accommodations on Cheung Chau are cheaper on weekdays. Some hotels also offer discounts for reservations made at least a month in advance.

to inquire whether there's a difference in price between twin and double rooms; some hotels charge more for two beds in a room (more sheets to wash, I guess).

You might also be able to save money by spending more—that is, selecting a room on the executive floor. While the "hotel-within-a-hotel" concept usually costs more than a regular room (though note that deluxe harbor-view rooms may cost more than an executive room facing inland), it may more than make up for the price difference with a wide range of privileges and services, which might include express check-in and checkout; use of a private executive lounge serving complimentary breakfasts, snacks, and evening cocktails complete with an appetizer buffet (thereby saving on dinner); complimentary pressing service and/or discounted laundry service; free use of the business center or free in-room Internet connections; and an executive-floor concierge attendant who can take care of such details as restaurant reservations or transportation arrangements. Some hotels have dedicated executive-level floors,

- **Look into group or long-stay discounts.** If you come as part of a large group, you should be able to negotiate a bargain rate, since the hotel can then guarantee occupancy in a number of rooms. Likewise, if you're planning a long stay (at least a week but sometimes a month), you might qualify for a discount.

- **Avoid excess charges.** Find out whether your hotel imposes a surcharge on local and long-distance calls. A pay phone, however inconvenient, may save you money. If a fee is charged for Internet use in your room, ask whether there's free Wi-Fi in the hotel lobby or bar. And don't be tempted by the room's minibar offerings: Most hotels charge through the nose for beer, soda, and snacks. Although many offer one or two complimentary bottles of water, they may charge for extra bottles consumed or for more expensive sparkling brands, so be sure to check before opening the bottle.

- **Consider an executive-level room.** Check the hotel's website for privileges offered for executive-level rooms. These can include everything from free Internet connections in your room or the executive lounge to free breakfasts and evening cocktails complete with an appetizer buffet.

- **Consider a suite.** If you are traveling with your family or another couple, you can pack more people into a suite (which usually comes with a sofa bed), and thereby reduce your per-person rate. Remember that some places charge for extra guests.

- **If traveling with children, try to find a hotel that allows children to stay free in their parent's room.** There's an age limit (usually 11 and under in Hong Kong), there's sometimes a maximum of three people to a room, and children are usually free only if no extra bed is required.

- **Book an efficiency.** A room with a kitchenette allows you to shop for groceries and cook some meals. This is a big money saver, especially for families on long stays.

while others offer executive-level privileges from any room by paying a surcharge. Even some moderately priced hotels now offer executive-level rooms, though it goes without saying that service levels (or the quality of their free buffets) don't compare with those offered by deluxe hotels.

The wide range of prices listed for double/twin rooms in each of the listings reflects the various categories available. In moderately priced and inexpensive lodgings, single rates are also usually available, but more expensive hotels often charge the same for double or single occupancy.

All of Hong Kong's expensive hotels, most of the moderately priced hotels, and many of the inexpensive hotels are members of the **Hong Kong Hotels Association** (HKHA; © 852/2383 8380; www.hkha.com.hk), though not every hotel named in this chapter is. The advantage of staying at a member hotel is that if you have a complaint, you can lodge it directly with the Hong Kong Tourism Board

(HKTB). Furthermore, the HKHA maintains a counter at Hong Kong International Airport where you can reserve a room at one of its member hotels at no extra charge. The hotels in this chapter are arranged first by price and then by geographical location. The categories are based on rates for a double room (excluding service charge) as follows: **Very Expensive,** HK$4,000 and up; **Expensive,** HK$2,600 to HK$4,000; **Moderate,** HK$1,300 to HK$2,600; and **Inexpensive,** less than HK$1,300.

Keep in mind that prices given in this book are for room rack rates only—a 10% service charge will be added to your final bill. Because a 10% increase can really add up, be sure to take it into account when choosing your hotel.

VERY EXPENSIVE

Hong Kong's top hotels are among the best in the world, with unparalleled service, state-of-the-art business, health-club, and often spa facilities, beautifully appointed guest rooms equipped with just about everything you can imagine, some of the city's best restaurants, and usually views of famous Victoria Harbour from their most expensive rooms. They also offer the convenience of a concierge or guest-relations staff, on hand to help with everything from procuring theater tickets to making restaurant and tour reservations. Among other extras are turndown service, 24-hour room service, welcoming tea brought to your room shortly after your arrival, free bottled water, free fruit basket, free newspaper delivered to your room, and many in-room conveniences and amenities, including voice mail, wired and/or Wi-Fi Internet access, and bedside controls that regulate everything from do-not-disturb lights to the opening of the curtains (it's great to wake up in the morning and have the city appear before you with a mere push of a button). Large bathrooms are standard, all with separate shower and tub facilities (useful for couples trying to get ready at the same time), magnifying mirrors, and bathroom scales so you can monitor your weight gain as you eat your way through Hong Kong. Most also offer executive lounges, accessible by staying on designated executive-level floors or, at some hotels, by paying a surcharge (guests staying at any room in the InterContinental, for example, can use the private executive lounge and have special privileges by paying extra).

Kowloon

InterContinental Hong Kong ★★★   Whereas the Peninsula, across the street, is the grand old dame of Hong Kong's hotels, the InterContinental is like its youthful, stylish cousin. Built right on the water's edge, it boasts the best views of Victoria Harbour from Tsim Sha Tsui, making its lobby lounge with soaring windows one of Hong Kong's best for afternoon tea or evening cocktails. Great views are also trademarks of its guest rooms, 70% of which command sweeping vistas of the harbor (the remaining—and less expensive but larger—rooms face the outdoor swimming pool and landscaped sun terrace). Other notable features here are the highly rated restaurants; upscale shopping arcade; state-of-the-art spa with outdoor cabanas and healing treatments (like the popular Jetlag Relief); free tai chi and yoga classes; contemporary rooms with huge walk-in closets adjoining bathrooms (you can shower and get dressed without disturbing another guest in the room); and Wi-Fi that enables guests to access the Internet even from poolside.

18 Salisbury Rd., Tsim Sha Tsui, Kowloon, Hong Kong. © **800/327-0200** in the U.S. and Canada, or 852/2721 1211. Fax 852/2739 4546. www.hongkong-ic.intercontinental.com. 495 units. HK$4,700–HK$6,300 single or double; HK$900 extra per room per night for club lounge privileges; from

HK$6,800 suite. Children 11 and under stay free in parent's room. AE, DC, MC, V. MTR: Tsim Sha Tsui. **Amenities:** 5 restaurants, including SPOON by Alain Ducasse, Yan Toh Heen, Nobu, STEAK HOUSE winebar + grill, and Harbourside (p. 122, 123, 122, 123, and 124); lounge (p. 162 and 247); bar; babysitting; concierge; executive-level rooms; exercise room (24 hr.) and free tai chi and yoga lessons; house doctor; Jacuzzis overlooking Victoria Harbour; landscaped outdoor pool w/underwater music; room service; spa. *In room:* A/C, TV/DVD/CD, hair dryer, minibar, MP3 docking station, Wi-Fi (HK$156 for 24 hr.).

The Peninsula Hong Kong ★★★ This is Hong Kong's most famous hotel, *the* place to stay if you have a penchant for the historical. Built in 1928, it exudes elegance, from its white-gloved doormen and one of the world's largest limousine fleets of Rolls-Royces to its ornate lobby, Hong Kong's foremost spot for afternoon tea and people-watching. Spacious rooms—so wonderfully equipped that even jaded travelers are likely to be impressed—include headphones for both radio and TV; tightly focused bedside reading lights designed to keep sleeping partners happy; telephones and control panels on both sides of gigantic beds; a display panel showing outdoor temperature and humidity; and a box in the closet where attendants place your morning newspaper or take your dirty shoes for complimentary cleaning. Each huge bathroom comes with TV, hands-free phone (which automatically mutes the TV or radio and digitally filters the sound of running water), and two sinks, both with magnifying mirrors. For the culture-minded, there are classes on everything from tai chi and feng shui to cooking; for the travel weary, its spa focuses on the journey to rejuvenation with views of the harbor from its sauna. There are even helicopter rides from the roof. I absolutely love this place.

Salisbury Rd., Tsim Sha Tsui, Kowloon, Hong Kong. © **866/382-8388** in the U.S., or 852/2920 2888. Fax 852/2722 4170. www.peninsula.com. 300 units. HK$4,200–HK$5,800 single or double; from HK$6,800 suite. AE, DC, MC, V. MTR: Tsim Sha Tsui. **Amenities:** 6 restaurants, including Gaddi's, Felix, and Spring Moon (p. 120, 120, and 159); bar; 2 lounges (p. 162 and 248); babysitting; concierge; health club and spa; gorgeous indoor pool w/sun terrace overlooking the harbor; in-house nurse; room service; practice music room w/grand piano. *In room:* A/C, TV/DVD/CD w/free DVD library, fax, hair dryer, minibar, free Wi-Fi.

Central District

Conrad Hong Kong ★★★ The 61-story Conrad is one of a trio of exclusive hotels perched on a hillside above Pacific Place, an upscale shopping center located about halfway between the Central District and Wan Chai. Hong Kong Park is just steps away, and the MTR can be reached without venturing outside. Although the architecture is contemporary (with free Wi-Fi in public spaces), the hotel's classic furnishings and Asian touches throughout soften the modern effect, giving it a cozy atmosphere. Large rooms (from 42 sq. m/452 sq. ft.), which start from the 40th floor, have windows that extend the width of the room, offering views of either the Peak or the harbor (harbor-view rooms cost more, though some so-called "city view" rooms offer a partial harbor view through buildings). On a playful note, bathrooms feature a floating duck or other bath toy for a bit of fun, while a stuffed bear is placed on beds at turndown. A great choice for business or leisure.

Pacific Place, 88 Queensway, Central, Hong Kong. © **800/CONRADS** (800/266-7237) in the U.S. and Canada, or 852/2521 3838. Fax 852/2521 3888. www.conradhotels.com. 513 units. HK$5,000–HK$5,500 single or double; HK$5,800–HK$6,000 executive floor; from HK$6,800 suite. Children 17 and under stay free in parent's room (maximum 3 people per room). AE, DC, MC, V. MTR: Admiralty. **Amenities:** 4 restaurants, including Nicholini's (p. 136); bar; lounge; concierge; house doctor; executive-level rooms; state-of-the-art health club w/sauna, steam room, and Jacuzzi; heated outdoor pool; room service. *In room:* A/C, TV/DVD/CD, hair dryer, Internet (HK$120 for 24 hr.), minibar.

Four Seasons Hotel Hong Kong ★★★ Just a stone's throw from the Central Ferry Piers, ifc mall, and Hong Kong Station, this is a cool urban oasis, buffered from the city's inherent bustle and providing a polished service that rises above even Hong Kong's legendary pampering. It boasts a luxurious spa, outdoor lap and infinity pools with great harbor views, and one of the hottest French restaurants in town. Its rooms are to die for, decorated in either contemporary Western style or a modern take on traditional Chinese design, with either city or harbor views, 42-inch plasma TVs, and spacious bathrooms with two sinks, shower stalls, and deep soaking tubs from which you can operate a small, mounted TV via remote. An executive lounge on the top floor, which any guest can use by paying a daily supplement, boasts fantastic views and even an outside deck. There's no mistaking that this is a Four Seasons, and until a new glam hotel comes along, it's at the top of the pack.

8 Finance St., Central, Hong Kong. ☎ **800/819-5053** in the U.S. and Canada, or 852/3196 8888. Fax 852/3196 8899. www.fourseasons.com/hongkong. 399 units. HK$4,200–HK$5,300 single or double; extra HK$800 single or HK$1,000 double for executive lounge; from HK$8,800 suite. Children 17 and under stay free in parent's room. AE, DC, MC, V. MTR: Central. **Amenities:** 2 restaurants, including Caprice (p. 134); bar; lounge; babysitting; concierge; executive-level rooms; health club and spa w/free tai chi classes; outdoor infinity pool (heated in winter) and lap pool w/underwater music and whirlpool; room service. *In room:* A/C, TV/DVD/CD, hair dryer, minibar, Wi-Fi (HK$160 for 24 hr.).

JW Marriott Hotel Hong Kong ★★★ This 27-story flagship property has completed a recent renovation that elevates it to the tier of Hong Kong's top hotels. Rooms, with right-angled "saw-toothed" windows to maximize views of the harbor or peak, offer unique in-room features, like 42-inch TVs with connections for computers and MP3s (you can even use both at once), BOSE audio systems, and touch-screen smart phones that will inform you of the weather in your next destination and other information. Other hotel features worth noting include a lounge with one of Hong Kong's largest selections of teas (more than 60 varieties), a wine bar with a room devoted to premium wines served in Riedel crystal, free Wi-Fi in public areas, free shoe shines, and a poolside restaurant specializing in sustainable seafood. The hotel is connected to Pacific Place, which abounds in very good restaurants, greatly expanding dining options without having to venture far.

Pacific Place, 88 Queensway, Central, Hong Kong. ☎ **800/228-7014** in the U.S. and Canada, or 852/2810 8366. Fax 852/2845 0737. www.jwmarriotthongkong.com. 602 units. HK$4,200–HK$4,800 single or double; HK$5,400–HK$5,700 executive floor; from HK$7,700 suite. AE, DC, MC, V. MTR: Admiralty. **Amenities:** 5 restaurants; wine bar (p. 245); lounge; babysitting; concierge; executive-level rooms; health club w/sauna and steam room; outdoor heated pool and Jacuzzi; room service. *In room:* A/C, TV/DVD, hair dryer, minibar, MP3 docking station, Wi-Fi (HK$120 for 24 hr.).

The Landmark Mandarin Oriental ★★★ Located atop the Landmark shopping complex and popular with designers who have shops there, this small hotel has a contemporary yet laid-back, refined atmosphere, with lobby seating grouped in a library setting and a stylish bar attracting a well-heeled crowd. Though the nightlife district is within staggering distance, it's hard to imagine guests here taking advantage of it. Rather, the focus is on state-of-the-art guest rooms, which measure 42 or 56 sq. m (452 or 603 sq. ft.); their stunning, glass-walled bathrooms, which take up about a third of the room's space, are what really takes the cake. Big enough to live in, they have two separate vanities and dual sinks, shower stall, TV, and a huge, round tub. Unfortunately, surrounding buildings can make guests feel like they're living in a fish bowl. One unwitting guest closed the sheers upon check-in but forgot to close the block-out drapes during her nighttime bath, discovering her faux pas only the next

If Money's No Object

Hong Kong's largest and most luxurious suite is the five-bedroom, 650-sq.-m (7,000-sq. ft.) Presidential Suite in the InterContinental Hong Kong. A two-story living room, wrap-around terrace, and rooftop infinity pool with Jacuzzi, all with expansive views of Victoria Harbour, are complemented by a dining room, kitchenette, a study, and a private gym with indoor Jacuzzi, steam room, and sauna. A night here will set you back HK$87,000, plus 10% service charge, in case you're considering it.

morning. Though there are no views from this hotel, the same may not be said, perhaps, for office workers across the street.

15 Queen's Rd. Central, the Landmark, Central, Hong Kong. ✆ **800/526-6566** in the U.S. and Canada, or 852/2132 0188. Fax 852/2132 0199. www.mandarinoriental.com. 113 units. HK$5,200–HK$6,800 single or double; from HK$9,300 suite. AE, DC, MC, V. MTR: Central. **Amenities:** Restaurant; bar; babysitting; concierge; health club w/yoga and Pilates studios and spa; indoor pool; room service. *In room:* A/C, TV/DVD, hair dryer, minibar, MP3 docking station, Wi-Fi (HK$160 for 24 hr.).

Mandarin Oriental, Hong Kong ★★★ Opened in 1963, this landmark recently underwent complete renovation, making it a new yet familiar property in the middle of Central (newer properties can only drool over its location). Updates include a spa with a 1930s Shanghai atmosphere and remodeled rooms, but back by popular demand are its retro-gilded lobby, the **Captain's Bar** (p. 249), the Chinnery, and Mandarin Grill. Gone from the rooms are the small balconies, replaced by comfortable sitting areas perfect for that first morning coffee while you peruse the newspaper and gaze out the window. Rooms face either the harbor or inland (those facing the harbor come with binoculars) and feature such standouts as mood lighting, a cupboard beside the front door for receiving newspapers, laundry, or messages so you don't have to open the door, and lighted anti-fog mirrors in the shower. Whatever you do, don't miss a stroll past the cake shop; its fantastic chocolate creations are displayed in glass cases like crown jewels.

5 Connaught Rd., Central, Hong Kong. ✆ **800/526-6566** in the U.S. and Canada, or 852/2522 0111. Fax 852/2810 6190. www.mandarinoriental.com. 502 units (some with showers only). HK$4,500–HK$5,800 single or double; from HK$6,500 suite. AE, DC, MC, V. MTR: Central. **Amenities:** 4 restaurants; 3 bars, including Captain's Bar; lounge; babysitting; concierge; health club and spa; indoor pool w/flume jet for a real workout; room service. *In room:* A/C, TV/DVD/CD, hair dryer, minibar, MP3 docking station, Wi-Fi (HK$160 for 24 hr.).

Causeway Bay & Wan Chai

Grand Hyatt Hong Kong ★★★ ☺ Decorated to resemble the salon of a 1930s Art Deco ocean liner, this hotel literally flaunts space, with huge black granite columns, massive flower arrangements, palm trees, bubbling fountains, and statuettes. It's not the kind of place you want to be seen on a bad hair day. Located on the waterfront adjacent to the Convention Centre and a 5-minute walk from the Wan Chai Star Ferry pier that delivers passengers to Tsim Sha Tsui, it offers smart-looking rooms, some 75% with a full harbor view (the rest overlook Hong Kong's largest outdoor hotel pool and garden). For extra pampering, stay at Plateau, a residential spa with 23 guest rooms (and nine treatment rooms), where you can enjoy a massage, manicure, and a soak in an infinity bathtub without leaving the privacy of your room

5

WHERE TO STAY | Very Expensive

(doubles here start at HK$7,700, including breakfast). I also like the hotel's restaurants, including the Grill, a poolside, landscaped restaurant offering sumptuous buffet spreads and grilled specialties year-round (weather permitting).

1 Harbour Rd., Wan Chai, Hong Kong. © **800/233-1234** in the U.S. and Canada, or 852/2588 1234. Fax 852/2802 0677. www.hongkong.grand.hyatt.com. 549 units. HK$5,000–HK$8,500 single; HK$5,200–HK$8,700 double; from HK$6,800 club executive-floor double; from HK$8,500 suite. Children 11 and under stay free in parent's room (maximum 3 people per room). AE, DC, MC, V. MTR: Wan Chai. **Amenities:** 6 restaurants, including Grissini and One Harbour Road (p. 148); lounge; 2 bars; babysitting; concierge; executive-level rooms; golf-driving range; health club and spa; jogging track; 50m outdoor heated pool (shared w/adjacent Renaissance Hong Kong Harbour View Hotel and open year-round); children's splash pool and playground; room service; 2 outdoor lit tennis courts. *In room:* A/C, TV, hair dryer, minibar, Wi-Fi (HK$160 for 24 hr.).

EXPENSIVE

A few hotels in this category, including some of my favorites, offer almost as much as Hong Kong's very expensive hotels and some even have great views of Victoria Harbour. In this category you can expect a guest-relations/concierge desk, 24-hour room service, swimming pools and/or health clubs or exercise rooms, business centers, same-day laundry service, and comfortable rooms with hair dryers, satellite TVs with in-room movies, voicemail, Internet access, coffee/tea-making facilities, bathroom scales, and usually free bottled water and a welcome basket of fruit. Many also have executive floors for business travelers.

Kowloon

InterContinental Grand Stanford Hong Kong ★★
This hotel gets kudos for being the first hotel in Hong Kong to install a hybrid hot-water fuel system that drastically cuts its carbon dioxide output. The hotel is located right on the waterfront and boasts a lively, high-ceilinged lobby with a cafe perfect for watching the never-ending stream of international guests. I also like the rooftop heated swimming pool, open year-round and affording great views. Rooms are more homey than most, with good bedside lights, plants, lit magnifying mirrors that reveal flaws you never knew you had, and good harbor views through floor-to-ceiling windows in half of the rooms (because of a highway that runs alongside the harbor, request a room on a high floor). If you can't afford a full harbor view, "side harbor views" are almost as good, due to the hotel's undulating V-shaped facade; unfortunately, the windows of the least expensive rooms open rather unceremoniously onto a windowless wall. Probably the biggest drawback is the 10-minute walk to Tsim Sha Tsui, but the InterContinental does offer a free shuttle service.

70 Mody Rd., Tsim Sha Tsui E., Kowloon, Hong Kong. © **800/327-0200** in the U.S. and Canada, or 852/2721 5161. Fax 852/2732 2233. www.hongkong.intercontinental.com. 578 units. HK$3,100–HK$3,800 single or double; HK$700 extra single and HK$900 extra double per night for club lounge privileges; from HK$5,200 suite. Children 11 and under stay free in parent's room. AE, DC, MC, V. MTR: East Tsim Sha Tsui. **Amenities:** 3 restaurants; bar; lounge; babysitting; concierge; executive-level rooms; exercise room; outdoor heated pool; room service; free shuttle service to several locations in Tsim Sha Tsui every 30–45 min; spa (men only). *In room:* A/C, TV/DVD/CD, hair dryer, minibar, Wi-Fi (HK$120 for 24 hr.).

Kowloon Shangri-La, Hong Kong ★★★ 🔥
The Kowloon Shangri-La, on the Tsim Sha Tsui East waterfront and a 5-minute walk to Tsim Sha Tsui (there's also free shuttle service to the Star Ferry), is a popular choice for business travelers, the majority of whom are American. The well-trained staff provides sterling service

FAMILY-friendly HOTELS

BP International House (p. 89) This reasonably priced hotel offers "Family Rooms" with a pair of bunk beds that sleep four for HK$1,450, as well as the convenience of a laundry room. But best of all is the adjacent Kowloon Park with its indoor and outdoor public swimming pools, children's playground, lake with flamingos and other birds, and plenty of romping space for active bodies.

Grand Hyatt Hong Kong/Renaissance Hong Kong Harbour View Hotel (p. 83 and 88) These two hotels share one of Hong Kong's largest outdoor swimming pools, as well as a splash pool for smaller children and a playground. Both hotels also offer babysitting.

Holiday Inn Golden Mile (p. 90) This functional hotel with a great location in Tsim Sha Tsui lets two children 19 and under stay free in parent's room; children 12 and under with two adults can eat for free in hotel restaurants. A rooftop pool, open year-round, and babysitting service clinch the deal for traveling families.

The Salisbury YMCA (p. 101) The overwhelming choice for families in terms of price, facilities, and location (just a short walk to both the Star Ferry and the MTR), this Salisbury Road establishment offers large suites suitable for families, an inexpensive cafeteria serving buffet meals, two indoor swimming pools (including a children's pool), an indoor climbing wall, and a bookstore with a children's corner where tots can try out games and books before parents fork over the cash. Babysitting is also available.

(there's even a technology butler on hand around the clock to iron out laptop snafus), which is probably one reason why repeat guests make up more than 55% of hotel occupancy. The spacious lobby is one of my favorites with its expansive white Carrara marble floor, massive Viennese crystal chandeliers, fountain, and Chinese landscape murals. Rooms are spacious (starting at 42 sq. m/452 sq. ft.) and luxuriously appointed, with ceiling-to-floor bay windows offering either harbor views or rather mundane "garden views" (a popular euphemism for windows that face inland).

64 Mody Rd., Tsim Sha Tsui East, Kowloon, Hong Kong. 866/565-5050 in the U.S., or 852/2721 2111. Fax 852/2723 8686. www.shangri-la.com. 688 units. HK$3,700–HK$4,200 single or double; HK$700 Horizon Club executive-floor supplement; from HK$5,780 suite. Children 11 and under stay free in parent's room. AE, DC, MC, V. MTR: East Tsim Sha Tsui. **Amenities:** 4 restaurants, including Shang Palace for Cantonese (p. 159); tapas bar (p. 248); lounge; babysitting; concierge; house doctor; executive-level rooms; exercise room; Jacuzzi; small indoor pool; room service; sauna; free shuttle service to Tsim Sha Tsui every 45 min. *In room:* A/C, TV/DVD and free DVD library, hair dryer, minibar, MP3 docking station, free Wi-Fi.

The Royal Garden ★★ 📖 The Royal Garden has always been one of my favorites because of its architectural surprises that invite exploration (be sure to explore all restaurant floors). It features a cool, sleek lobby and a 15-story inner atrium, a concept adapted from the traditional Chinese inner garden (and employed here long before it became the standard of some U.S. chains). Plants hang from the balconies ringing the soaring space, glass-enclosed elevators glide up the wall, a piano sits on an island in the middle of a pool, and the sound of rushing water adds freshness and coolness to the atmosphere. Off the lobby is a very interesting martini bar, and its Italian restaurant, **Sabatini** (p. 122), is one of Hong Kong's best. Rooms, the most expensive of which have partial harbor views between two buildings and the cheapest of which face the Regal Kowloon Hotel, are rather small. Although a slight hike to the action of Tsim Sha Tsui, it's close to the railway station with service to the New Territories and China.

69 Mody Rd., Tsim Sha Tsui East, Kowloon, Hong Kong. © **800/223-5652** in the U.S. and Canada, or 852/2721 5215. Fax 852/2369 9976. www.rghk.com.hk. 419 units. HK$3,100–HK$4,100 single or double; HK$4,300–HK$4,600 Crown Club executive floor; from HK$5,000 suite. 1 child 11 and under can stay free in parent's room. AE, DC, MC, V. MTR: East Tsim Sha Tsui. **Amenities:** 7 restaurants, including Sabatini and the Greenery; martini bar; lounge; babysitting; concierge; executive-level rooms; health club w/ sauna; wonderful 25m-long heated rooftop outdoor pool and Jacuzzi; putting green; room service; lighted outdoor tennis court. *In room:* A/C, TV, hair dryer, minibar, Wi-Fi (HK$150 for 24 hr.).

Sheraton Hong Kong Hotel & Towers ★★ The Sheraton has one of the most envied locations in Hong Kong—near the waterfront on the corner of Nathan Road and Salisbury Road—and is an easy walk to the subway and Star Ferry. Its lobby, tucked away on the second floor to discourage foot traffic, has a sleek, contemporary look graced by Asian motifs and subdued lighting, but the front desk is annoyingly high (I have to stand on tippy-toes). The outdoor rooftop swimming pool, heated in winter, is a plus, offering spectacular views and more privacy than pools lower to the ground. Guest rooms range from those facing an inner courtyard (the cheapest) to those facing the harbor with great views even from bathrooms. In between are those that overlook surrounding Tsim Sha Tsui, some of which face Nathan Road and even provide sideways glimpses of the harbor. Still, located between the Peninsula and InterContinental, it plays second fiddle to both in terms of reputation, class—and, luckily, price.

20 Nathan Rd., Tsim Sha Tsui, Kowloon, Hong Kong. © **800/325-3535** in the U.S. and Canada, or 852/2369 1111. Fax 852/2739 8707. www.sheraton.com/hongkong. 782 units. HK$3,000–HK$3,800 single; HK$3,100–HK$3,900 double; HK$4,000–HK$4,800 tower executive-floor double; from HK$5,700 suite. AE, DC, MC, V. MTR: Tsim Sha Tsui. **Amenities:** 4 restaurants, including Japanese restaurant Unkai (p. 123); bar; 3 lounges, including Sky Lounge (p. 248); babysitting; concierge; house doctor; executive-level rooms; health club and spa; outdoor heated rooftop swimming pool and Jacuzzi; room service. *In room:* A/C, TV, hair dryer, Internet (HK$115 for 24 hr.), minibar, MP3 docking station.

W Hong Kong ★★★ 👬 "W" could stand for whimsical in this new property above Kowloon Station that tries its darndest to stand out as the antithesis of standard hotels. It calls its reception desk a "Welcome" desk. Its friendly staff is identifiable by simple "W" badges in place of name tags, and its "Living Room" (aka lobby lounge) overlooking the harbor is upbeat and playful, with funky furniture, colorful pillows, weird statues (yes, that's a humongous mosquito on the wall), coffee books, board games, and a nightly DJ. Its rooftop pool, on the 76th floor, is Hong Kong's highest to date. Elevator hallways, lined with white shelves and an eclectic mix of equally white knickknacks (think alarm clocks, seashells, candelabra, and books) lead to contemporary rooms with all the trimmings, including focused bed lights and bathrooms with separate shower and tub areas; some have harbor views. Unfortunately, attempts at being different can lead to confusion; perhaps you, too, will have a hard time locating the elevator button (hint: look for the picture frame).

1 Austin Rd. West, Kowloon Station, Kowloon, Hong Kong. © **877/946-8357** in the U.S. and Canada, or 852/3717 2222. Fax 852/3717 2888. www.whotels.com/hongkong. 392 units. HK$,3,600–HK$4,300 single or double; from HK$8,000 suite. Children 10 and under stay free in parent's room. AE, DC, MC, V. MTR: Kowloon. **Amenities:** 2 restaurants; lounge; babysitting; concierge; health club and spa; outdoor rooftop swimming pool and Jacuzzi; room service. *In room:* A/C, TV/DVD and free DVD library, hair dryer, minibar, MP3 docking station, Wi-Fi (HK$115 for 24 hr.).

Central District

Hotel LKF ★★ 🎁 If the only thing you want separating you from Hong Kong's biggest nightlife scene is an elevator, this is for you (luckily, keyed elevator access keeps inebriated nonguests from wandering the halls). Located at the top of upward-sloping Lan Kwai Fong (often abbreviated to LKF), this hushed and refined oasis is most noted for its enormous rooms (starting at about 46 sq. m/500 sq. ft.), bigger than most Hong Kong apartments and the kind of place you wouldn't mind being holed up in to nurse a hangover or watch movies on the 62-inch LCD TV. Rooms are also high enough to provide good city views, though only the highest floors have a glimpse of the harbor between buildings. In-room espresso machines and free breakfast help jump-start the day, while complimentary evening cocktails can serve as a launch to another night of pub crawls. Don't confuse this hotel with the Lan Kwai Fong Hotel (p. 95), which isn't in Lan Kwai Fong at all.

33 Wyndham St., Central, Hong Kong. ✆ **800/448-8355** in the U.S. and Canada, or 852/3518 9333. Fax 852/3518 9338. www.hotel-lkf.com.hk. 95 units. HK$3,500–HK$4,800 single or double; from HK$6,000 suite. Rates include continental breakfast buffet. AE, DC, MC, V. MTR: Central. **Amenities:** Restaurant (Azure, p. 137); bar; access to nearby fitness center; room service. *In room:* A/C, satellite TV/DVD, hair dryer, minibar, MP3 docking station, Wi-Fi (HK$150 for 24 hr.).

Island Shangri-La Hong Kong ★★★ 🎁 Hong Kong Island's tallest hotel (measured from sea level) offers the ultimate in extravagance and luxury, rivaling the grand hotels in Paris or London: It's one of my favorite hotels in the world. More than 700 Viennese chandeliers, lush Tai Ping carpets, artistic flower arrangements, and more than 700 paintings and artworks adorn the hotel. A 17-story atrium, which stretches from the 39th to the 56th floors, features a marvelous 16-story-high Chinese painting, drawn by 40 artists from Beijing and believed to be the largest landscape painting in the world. The hotel itself is enhanced by the connecting Pacific Place with its many options in dining; across the street is Hong Kong Park. Guest rooms, all of which ring the atrium and measure 41 sq. m (441 sq. ft.) or more, feature European furnishings with Asian accents and face either the Peak or spectacular Victoria Harbour. Oversize bathrooms are equipped with two sinks and separate tub and shower areas (harbor-view rooms only), bidet, and TVs.

Pacific Place, Supreme Court Rd., Central, Hong Kong. ✆ **866/565-5050** in the U.S., or 852/2877 3838. Fax 852/2521 8742. www.shangri-la.com. 565 units. HK$3,200–HK$3,600 single or double; HK$3,950–HK$4,350 executive floor; from HK$6,500 suite. Children 11 and under stay free in parent's room. AE, DC, MC, V. MTR: Admiralty. **Amenities:** 7 restaurants, including Restaurant Petrus and café TOO (p. 136 and 139); bar; lounge; babysitting; concierge; executive-level rooms; health club and spa w/free yoga classes; indoor/outdoor Jacuzzis; medical clinic; outdoor heated pool; room service; free shuttle to Central and Wan Chai. *In room:* A/C, TV/DVD, fax/printer/scanner, hair dryer, minibar, MP3 docking station, free Wi-Fi.

The Upper House ★★★ 🍃 Unless you arrive by taxi, you might have trouble finding the entrance to this low-key, ultramodern spot located above Pacific Place. Once you do, you'll be greeted not by the traditional front desk (with an eye to conservation, both arrival and departure procedures are paperless) but by a well-trained, multitasking staff offering personalized service that is both intuitive and professional. Rooms, on the 38th to 48th floors, are gigantic by any measure (starting at 68 sq. m/730 sq. ft.), with an L-shaped sofa at the window with views of the harbor or the city, ample-sized desk, espresso machine, a "maxi-bar" designed to hold wine at the perfect temperature as well as free beer, soft drinks, and treats, spacious bathroom, yoga mat (there are free yoga classes every Sun), and—in keeping with the hotel's paperless philosophy—even an iPod loaded with hotel information, games, music, and information on area attractions.

Pacific Place, 88 Queensway, Central, Hong Kong. © **800/323-7500** in the U.S. and Canada, or 852/2918 1838. Fax 852/3968 1200. www.upperhouse.com. 117 units. HK$3,000–HK$3,500 single or double; HK$5,500 suite. AE, DC, MC, V. MTR: Admiralty. **Amenities:** Restaurant; bar (p. 249); lounge; exercise room; room service. *In room:* A/C, TV, hair dryer, minibar, MP3 docking station, free Wi-Fi.

Causeway Bay & Wan Chai

The Excelsior Hong Kong   Located on the waterfront near a lively shopping area, Hong Kong Island's largest hotel belongs to the Mandarin Oriental group of hotels but is more plebian than its sister properties in Central, with correspondingly lower prices. It enjoys a solid reputation and high occupancy rate, including many tour groups, which translates into an overcrowded lobby buzzing with activity, occasional difficulty getting front-desk service, and crowded elevators. On the plus side are nearby Victoria Park, Hong Kong's largest city park and good for joggers; the top-floor restaurant **ToTT's** (p. 150) with its spectacular harbor views; and the hotel's free guided tours to the historic Noon Day Gun across the street, which fires daily at, well, noon. Most rooms are the same small size with the same decor and tend to be crowded. Those that command panoramas of the harbor, with window-side sofas, are the most expensive and largest; slightly cheaper are those with side harbor views or views of the park, while the cheapest face inland toward the city.

281 Gloucester Rd., Causeway Bay, Hong Kong. © **800/526-6566** in the U.S. and Canada, or 852/2894 8888. Fax 852/2895 6459. http://mandarinoriental.com/excelsior. 885 units. HK$2,600–HK$3,400 single or double; HK$3,400–HK$3,800 executive floor; from HK$6,000 suite. 1 child 11 or under stays free in parent's room. AE, DC, MC, V. MTR: Causeway Bay. **Amenities:** 5 restaurants, including ToTT's and Roof Terrace (p. 150); bar; lounge; babysitting; concierge; executive-level rooms; exercise rooms; room service; spa. *In room:* A/C, TV, hair dryer, minibar, Wi-Fi (HK$130 for 24 hr.).

Renaissance Hong Kong Harbour View Hotel ★ ☺   This large, 43-story hotel (and Marriott affiliate) sits beside the Convention and Exhibition Centre on the Wan Chai waterfront, separated from the Grand Hyatt (p. 83) by Hong Kong's largest outdoor hotel swimming pool and a garden with a playground and jogging trail, shared by the two hotels. Just a couple of minutes' walk from the Wan Chai Star Ferry that delivers passengers to Tsim Sha Tsui (but a longer hike to the nearest tram or MTR station), it provides some of the same facilities and advantages as the Hyatt but at a lower price. It caters largely to those attending functions at the convention center, which can make it quite busy, as well as business travelers. More than 65% of the rooms boast outstanding views of the harbor through floor-to-ceiling windows. The rest of the rooms face the pool and garden, which for Hong Kong isn't bad at all.

1 Harbour Rd., Wan Chai, Hong Kong. © **800/228-9290** in the U.S. and Canada, or 852/2802 8888. Fax 852/2802 8833. www.renaissancehotels.com/hkghv. 860 units (most bathrooms have shower only). HK$3,300–HK$4,100 single or double; HK$4,200–HK$4,700 Renaissance Club executive floor; from HK$5,000 suite. AE, DC, MC, V. MTR: Wan Chai. **Amenities:** 3 restaurants; lounge; babysitting; concierge; house doctor; executive-level rooms; exercise room; golf-driving range; Jacuzzi; jogging trail; huge heated outdoor pool; children's splash pool and playground; room service; 2 lighted outdoor tennis courts. *In room:* A/C, TV, hair dryer, Internet (HK$60 per hr.), minibar.

MODERATE

Tour groups have long been a mainstay of tourism in Hong Kong, and you're most likely to encounter them at the moderately priced hotels, which account for the majority of hotels in Hong Kong. (You'll also find groups at large, higher-quality inexpensive hotels.) With increased tourism from mainland China filling rooms in this category, it's imperative to book early. Guest rooms tend to be rather small compared to American hotel rooms, with generally unexciting views, but have such amenities as hair dryers, Internet access or Wi-Fi, minibars or empty fridges you can stock yourself, and instant coffee and sometimes free bottled water, plus room service, bellhops, nonsmoking floors, tour desks, and sometimes a swimming pool and/or fitness room. Because harbor views are usually not available except for some hotels on the Hong Kong Island side, rates are generally based on height/floor number and decor and sometimes on size, though cheapest rooms may face another building in this space-challenged city.

Kowloon

BP International House ★ ☺ The word "House" in the name is misleading, since this is actually a 25-story hotel, with a spacious but utilitarian lobby catering mainly to tour groups, school excursions, and budget-conscious business travelers, which gives it a dormitory-like atmosphere. Located at the north end of Kowloon Park, it's just a stone's throw from the park's indoor and outdoor public swimming pools and a short walk to a playground, making it good for families, too. Guest rooms, located on the 14th to 25th floors, are tiny but spotless, pleasant, and modern, with showers rather than tubs and fold-down vanity mirrors to create more space. Despite the hotel's inland location, some corporate rooms on the top floors offer great views over Kowloon Park of the harbor, the Peak, and the "Symphony of Lights" nightly laser show, as well as such extras like combination tubs/showers, minibars, and hot-water kettles. The very simple "family rooms" are equipped with a pair of bunk beds that sleep four.

8 Austin Rd., Tsim Sha Tsui, Kowloon, Hong Kong. ℂ **800/223-5652** in the U.S. and Canada, or 852/2376 1111. Fax 852/2376 1333. www.bpih.com.hk. 529 units (most bathrooms have showers only). HK$1,350–HK$1,900 single or double; family room HK $1,450; HK$1,900–HK$2,600 corporate room; from HK$3,800 suite. Children 11 and under stay free in parent's room. AE, DC, MC, V. MTR: Jordan. **Amenities:** Restaurant; lounge; babysitting; executive-level rooms. *In room:* A/C, TV, fridge, Wi-Fi (HK$100 for 24 hr.).

The Cityview (formerly YMCA International House) Although still affiliated with the Chinese YMCA of Hong Kong, this hotel has rebranded itself as a city hotel after renovating its rooms and transforming itself into a smart-looking establishment that can rival many of the more expensively priced hotels in terms of facilities. It's located just off Nathan Road, only a minute's walk from the Yau Ma Tei MTR station, but because it's halfway up Kowloon Peninsula far from the action of Tsim Sha Tsui, it has always played second fiddle to the Salisbury YMCA in terms of convenience and views. Otherwise, contemporary-styled rooms are similar to hotel rooms anywhere in the city, with the cheapest rooms equipped with showers instead of tubs. Ask for a room on a top floor, where it's brighter, the decor more upbeat, and you can look out over the city.

23 Waterloo Rd., Yau Ma Tei, Kowloon, Hong Kong. ℂ **852/2783 3888.** Fax 852/2783 3899. www. thecityview.com.hk. 413 units (some bathrooms have shower only). HK$1,380–HK$2,180 single or twin; from HK$2,580 suite. Children 11 and under stay free in parent's room. AE, DC, MC, V. MTR: Yau Ma Tei. **Amenities:** 2 restaurants; lounge; babysitting; 25m indoor pool; sauna; tennis and squash courts. *In room:* A/C, TV, fridge, hair dryer, Wi-Fi (HK$100 for 24 hr.).

Eaton Hotel ★★★ 🛏 This hotel has more class and more facilities than most hotels in its price range, making it one of my top picks. A handsome brick 21-story hotel near the Temple Street Night Market, it features one of the longest hotel escalators I've seen, taking guests straight up to the fourth-floor lobby where a cheerful and efficient staff awaits your arrival. The lobby lounge is bright and airy, with a four-story glass-enclosed atrium that overlooks a garden terrace. Other pluses are the small but nicely done rooftop pool with sunning terrace, free daily tours of the jade and night markets, free tai chi classes, free use of computers in its bar, and **Yat Tung Heen** (p. 160), a Cantonese restaurant serving great dim sum. Also impressive is the hotel's concerted sustainability efforts, including an in-house green team, donations to a food pantry, and staff community service. Guest rooms are small but welcoming, with all the basic creature comforts and then some, including focused bedside reading lights and comfy desk chairs.

380 Nathan Rd., Kowloon, Hong Kong. © **800/588-9141** in the U.S. and Canada, or 852/2782 1818. Fax 852/2782 5563. http://hongkong.eatonhotels.com. 465 units. HK$2,100–HK$2,250 single or double; HK$2,500–HK$2,800 club room; from HK$3,000 suite. AE, DC, MC, V. MTR: Jordan. **Amenities:** 3 restaurants, including Yagura (p. 130) and Yat Tung Heen; bar; lounge; babysitting; concierge; executive-level rooms; exercise room; small outdoor heated pool. In room: A/C, TV, hair dryer, Internet (HK$100 for 24 hr.), minibar, MP3 docking station.

Empire Hotel Kowloon This is a functional hotel in a colorful location close to Knutsford Terrace with its open-air restaurants and the Hong Kong Museum of History. Small rooms, occupying the 8th through 26th floors of a round, hollow, glass-sheathed tower, boast wall-to-wall and floor-to-ceiling windows, though only the highest-priced rooms above the 17th floor have distant harbor views. Glass-topped desks and bowl-shaped basins rise above ordinary hotel furnishings in more deluxe rooms, but the dim, bedside-reading lamps will ruin your eyes. Unlike older Hong Kong hotels, showers here greatly outnumber tubs. The pool is at the bottom of the pitlike tower, rendering it grossly uninviting. Still, this hotel, popular with Japanese guests, compares favorably with Kowloon's other medium-priced accommodations.

62 Kimberley Rd., Tsim Sha Tsui, Kowloon, Hong Kong. © **800/830-6144** in the U.S. and Canada, or 852/2685 3000. Fax 852/2685 3685. www.empirehotel.com.hk. 343 units (most bathrooms have showers only). HK$1,600–HK$2,400 single or double; from HK$3,200 suite. Children 11 and under stay free in parent's room. AE, DC, MC, V. MTR: Tsim Sha Tsui. **Amenities:** Restaurant; bar; babysitting; exercise room; outdoor pool; room service; sauna. In room: A/C, TV, hair dryer, Internet (HK$120 for 24 hr.; Wi-Fi in some rooms), minibar.

Holiday Inn Golden Mile ☺ ✦ Named after the "golden mile of shopping" on Nathan Road, this Holiday Inn has a great location right in the heart of bustling Tsim Sha Tsui. Maybe that's why it's popular with tour groups, mainly from North America and China, which can make the lobby rather crowded and bothersome. However, it's a good bet for families thanks to the pool and the fact that children 12 and under with two adults can eat free in the hotel's restaurants. Rooms, decorated in Ming blue or Oriental red with Chinese-influenced accents on everything from the drapes to the TV cabinets, impart a warm, cozy feeling and are large for Tsim Sha Tsui, featuring either a king-size bed or two double beds. Although rooms boast floor-to-ceiling windows, views are blocked by adjacent buildings; those facing the unsightly Chungking Mansion are glazed (believe me, it's better this way). Those facing Mody Road are brighter but noisier; try to get a room on a high floor. All in all, this is a functional hotel in a convenient location.

50 Nathan Rd., Tsim Sha Tsui, Kowloon, Hong Kong. © **800/465-4329** in the U.S. and Canada, or 852/2369 3111. Fax 852/2369 8016. www.holidayinn.com/hongkong-gldn. 614 units. HK$1,500–HK$2,200 single or double; HK$2,000–HK$2,900 executive club; from HK$3,500 suite. Up to 2 children

19 and under stay free in parent's room. AE, DC, MC, V. MTR: Tsim Sha Tsui. **Amenities:** 4 restaurants; bar; babysitting; concierge; house doctor; executive-level rooms; health club; rooftop pool open year-round; room service; sauna. *In room:* A/C, TV, hair dryer, minibar, Wi-Fi (HK$180 for 24 hr.).

Hotel Panorama ★★ 🍴 This hotel, despite a location several blocks inland, actually does have panoramic views from its guest rooms, on the 7th to 37th floors. While the least expensive rooms, on lower floors, don't offer much to gaze upon (of these, try to get a room on the highest floor facing the harbor [17th], where views are actually quite good); those from the 18th floor and above offer great vistas over surrounding buildings of either the harbor or the city (naturally, the most expensive rooms are at the top). The restaurant is on the 38th floor, while on the roof is the so-called Sky Garden, an expanse of green along with an exercise room. There's a lot to like about this hotel, including its location, tucked away on a side street between Tsim Sha Tsui and Tsim Sha Tsui East, yet it's very convenient to both subway lines and trains to the New Territories and beyond.

8A Hart Ave., Tsim Sha Tsui, Kowloon, Hong Kong. ⓒ 852/3550 0388. Fax 852/3550 0288. www. hotelpanorama.com.hk. 325 units (some bathrooms with showers only). HK$2,400–HK$3,100 single or double; HK$3,800–HK$4,100 platinum executive-floor double; from HK$5,800 suite. Children 11 and under stay free in parent's room. AE, DC, MC, V. MTR: Tsim Sha Tsui. **Amenities:** 2 restaurants; executive-level rooms; exercise room; putting green. *In room:* A/C, TV, hair dryer, Internet (HK$100 for 24 hr.), minibar.

Hyatt Regency Hong Kong, Tsim Sha Tsui 🍴 The Hyatt Regency closed its long-time location on Nathan Road in 2006 but has recently resurfaced here, in a new complex that includes offices and the K11 shopping mall. You're forgiven if you momentarily confuse the colorless reception area, decorated only with a few plants and the front desk, for one of the many office floors, but thankfully guest rooms impart local flavor with black-and-white photographs of the city; pricier rooms even provide harbor views. Probably the most unique room feature is the closet, with sliding doors on opposite sides so that it can be accessed from both the bathroom and the main room. A good location, outdoor pool, and gym make this a practical address in the heart of Tsim Sha Tsui.

18 Hanoi, Tsim Sha Tsui, Kowloon, Hong Kong. ⓒ 800/233-1234 in the U.S. and Canada, or 852/2311 1234. Fax 852/3721 1235. http://hongkong.tsimshatsui.hyatt.com. 381 units. HK$1,450–HK$1,950 single or double; HK$2,050–HK$2,450 executive club; from HK$3,250 suite. Children 11 and under stay free in parent's room. AE, DC, MC, V. MTR: Tsim Sha Tsui. **Amenities:** 3 restaurants; bar; babysitting; concierge; exercise room; outdoor pool w/Jacuzzi; room service. *In room:* A/C, TV, hair dryer, minibar, MP3 docking station, Wi-Fi (HK$150 for 24 hr.).

The Kimberley Hotel The Kimberley, near Knutsford Terrace with its alfresco dining options and about a 15-minute walk from the Star Ferry, opened in 1991 and shows its age, a bit worn around the edges and with outdated decor. It's clearly time for a face-lift, yet it still does a brisk business attracting both the tourist and business trade, including many Japanese and tour groups. A touch screen in the lobby allows guests to check flight information. Rooms, constructed with V-shaped windows that let in more sunlight and allow for more panoramic—though not scenic—views, are very small and plain but come with all the basics. The most expensive rooms are on higher floors and are larger, but still rather small. Suites represent an especially good deal because they occupy the top two floors and are equipped with kitchenettes and a lounging/dining area, making them ideal for long-term guests and families.

28 Kimberley Rd., Tsim Sha Tsui, Kowloon, Hong Kong. ⓒ 800/876-5278 in the U.S., or 852/2723 3888. Fax 852/2723 1318. www.kimberleyhotel.com.hk. 546 units. HK$1,500–HK$2,350 single or double; from

Moderate

HK$2,800 suite. AE, DC, MC, V. MTR: Tsim Sha Tsui. **Amenities:** 3 restaurants; lounge; babysitting; exercise room; golf-driving range; room service; spa. *In room:* A/C, TV, hair dryer, Internet (HK$120 for 24 hr.), minibar.

The Kowloon Hotel This modern, glass-walled structure right behind the Peninsula has a great location just a few minutes' walk from the Star Ferry and MTR. Though it has no recreational facilities of its own, guests can use the pool and health club at the YMCA cater-cornered to the hotel or at its sister Harbour Plaza Metropolis hotel (free shuttle available) at reduced fees. The downside of the hotel: Rooms are minuscule and plagued by traffic noise. Although they have V-shaped bay windows, allowing unobstructed views up and down the street, the Peninsula's tower robs views from all but the most expensive rooms. Recommended only if you don't plan on spending any quality time in your room.

19–21 Nathan Rd., Tsim Sha Tsui, Kowloon, Hong Kong. © **800/223-5652** in the U.S., or 852/2929 2888. Fax 852/2739 9811. www.harbour-plaza.com/klnh. 739 units. HK$1,300–HK$1,650 single or double; HK$1,650–HK$2,000 Harbour Club floor double; from HK$4,000 suite. Children 11 and under stay free in parent's room. AE, DC, MC, V. MTR: Tsim Sha Tsui. **Amenities:** 2 restaurants; bar; babysitting; executive-level rooms; access to nearby YMCA (fee: HK$120) or sister hotel pool and health club (fee: HK$100); room service. *In room:* A/C, TV, hair dryer, minibar, Wi-Fi (HK$120 for 24 hr.).

The Langham, Hong Kong ★★★ ⬧ This affiliate of London's historic Langham Hotel and Hong Kong's only member of the Leading Hotels of the World is conveniently located a couple of blocks inland from the harbor, just a few minutes' walk from the Star Ferry and huge Harbour City shopping complex. Its lobby exudes a classic Italian atmosphere, with chandeliers, marble floor, a hand-painted dome ceiling, and lots of artwork and statues that give it the atmosphere of an art gallery, including glass art by American artist Dale Chihuly and paintings from mainland China. Photos of old Hong Kong adorn corridor walls and rooms. Its restaurants—which include a renowned Cantonese venue, **T'ang Court** (p. 160); an American deli; and a seafood restaurant—are well respected among locals. Contemporary rooms are small but comfortable, with separate shower and tub areas, but unfortunately none of its rooms have harbor views. Take solace in the deep soaking tubs in the Grand Rooms, where you can watch television while you soak.

8 Peking Rd., Tsim Sha Tsui, Kowloon, Hong Kong. © **800/223-6800** in the U.S. and Canada, or 852/2375 1133. Fax 852/2375 6611. http://hongkong.langhamhotels.com. 495 units. HK$1,950–HK$2,750 single or double; HK$700 extra single and HK$900 extra double for club lounge privileges; from HK$3,750 suite. Children 12 and under stay free in parent's room (children not allowed in Grand Rooms). AE, DC, MC, V. MTR: Tsim Sha Tsui. **Amenities:** 4 restaurants, including T'ang Court and Main Street Deli (p. 132); bar; lounge; babysitting; concierge; executive-level rooms; health club; rooftop outdoor pool and Jacuzzi open year-round. *In room:* A/C, TV, hair dryer, minibar, MP3 docking station, Wi-Fi (HK$150 for 24 hr.).

The Luxe Manor ★★★ 🛎 The entrance to this boutique hotel is so discrete, you could walk right by the proverbial looking glass and never know it leads to one of the most whimsical hotels I've seen, with rooms looking like something Salvador Dalí might have dreamed up if asked to design the set for *Alice in Wonderland*. In other words, things are not as they seem: wall-mounted TVs framed like gilded mirrors above faux fireplaces, picture frames framing nothing, and fun furniture such as desks with four different leg shapes. Six suites, each one unique, are even more exaggerated flights of fantasy: The Safari Bedroom, for example, gives the illusion of being inside a tent. Hoteliers the world over, guilty of selling boring rooms, should take lessons here, but visitors will have to decide for themselves if this is the Hong Kong they've come to see.

39 Kimberley Rd., Tsim Sha Tsui, Kowloon, Hong Kong. (☎ **852/3763 8888.** Fax 852/3763 8899. www. theluxemanor.com. 159 units (bathrooms have shower only). HK$2,400–HK$3,000 single or double; from HK$10,000 suite. Children 11 and under stay free in parent's room. AE, DC, MC, V. MTR: Tsim Sha Tsui. **Amenities:** Restaurant; bar (p. 247); exercise room; room service. *In room:* A/C, TV, hair dryer, minibar, free Wi-Fi.

Marco Polo Hongkong Hotel   The best (and most expensive) of three Marco Polo properties lining this street, this hotel is as close as you can get to the Star Ferry and is connected to the largest shopping complex in Asia, Harbour City. In fact, its lobby opens right into the Lane Crawford department store, making for an "only in Hong Kong" surreal experience. Large rooms are mostly so-called "Hollywood" twins (two twin beds pushed together) with a sitting area, large working desks, and walk-in closet. The lowest-price rooms face the small courtyard swimming pool and other guest rooms and can be quite dark, while the most expensive rooms boast unparalleled views of harbor activity, including the ocean liners that dock right next door. Avoid rooms facing Canton Road, which can be noisy. Down the street are the Marco Polo Gateway (☎ **852/2113 0888**) and the Marco Polo Prince (☎ **852/2113 1888**), which are cheaper but with fewer facilities. For my money, I'd rather stay at several of the other hotels listed in this price category than the merely functional Marco Polo brands.

Harbour City, 3 Canton Rd., Tsim Sha Tsui, Kowloon, Hong Kong. (☎ **800/448-8355** in the U.S. and Canada, or 852/2113 0088. Fax 852/2113 0011. www.marcopolohotels.com. 664 units. HK$2,450–HK$3,750 single; HK$2,550–HK$3,850 double; HK$3,400–HK$4,520 Continental Club executive-floor double; from HK$5,000 suite. 1 child 13 and under stays free in parent's room. AE, DC, MC, V. MTR: Tsim Sha Tsui. **Amenities:** 4 restaurants; lounge; babysitting; executive-level rooms; access to nearby health club (fee charged); small heated outdoor pool open year-round; room service; spa. *In room:* A/C, TV, hair dryer, Internet (HK$120 for 24 hr.), minibar.

The Mira Hong Kong ★★★ 🏨   On Nathan Road across from Kowloon Park, the Mira beats them all when it comes to in-room, high-tech convenience, not to mention cool decor and design—a hot choice for style-conscious IT junkies. Fashioned from an older property and therefore faced with structural restrictions, the hotel nevertheless made clever use of what it had—cladding low ceilings, for example, with mirror-like black tiles that give corridors the illusion of being twice their height. Rooms, though small, rise above the ordinary, with vibrant color schemes of red, green, or purple and silver, Arne Jacobsen "Egg Chairs," mood lighting, a seemingly endless choice of pillows, 40-inch LCD TVs that double as computers, Bose sound systems, and—I really like this—personal mobile phones you can take with you anywhere in Hong Kong. Views range from those of the city (the cheapest) and the courtyard garden to those overlooking Kowloon Park (most expensive). But what most impresses me about this hotel is its enthusiastic and personable young staff.

118–130 Nathan Rd., Tsim Sha Tsui, Kowloon, Hong Kong. (☎ **852/2368 1111.** Fax 852/2369 1788. www. themirahotel.com. 492 units. HK$1,700–HK$2,000 single or double; HK$2,300–HK$2,600 Mira Club rooms; from HK$3,400 suite. AE, DC, MC, V. MTR: Tsim Sha Tsui. **Amenities:** 3 restaurants; bar; lounge; health club and spa; indoor pool; room service. *In room:* A/C, TV/DVD/computer, hair dryer, minibar, MP3 docking station, free Wi-Fi.

Prudential Hotel ★   This hotel at the northern end of Tsim Sha Tsui towers 17 stories above a six-level shopping complex and the MTR Jordan station, providing easy and direct access to the rest of Hong Kong. About a 20-minute walk from the Star Ferry and only minutes from the Temple Street Night Market, Jade Market, and a Tin Hau (the goddess of the sea) temple, it offers smartly decorated rooms with sleek furniture, artwork, and window panels that can be pulled shut for complete darkness. Rates are based on height, with the cheapest rooms on lower floors. If possible, avoid those facing the back and nondescript buildings. Deluxe rooms feature floor-to-ceiling bay windows and receive more sunshine. Although the hotel itself has only a coffee shop and a bar, several other restaurants are within the shopping complex. Another plus is the 18m-long rooftop pool.

222 Nathan Rd. (entrance on Tak Shing St.), Tsim Sha Tsui, Kowloon, Hong Kong. © **852/2311 8222.** Fax 852/2311 4760. www.prudentialhotel.com. 432 units. HK$2,200–HK$2,700 single or double; HK$3,100 executive club floor; from HK$4,000 suite. Children 11 and under stay free in parent's room. AE, DC, MC, V. MTR: Jordan. **Amenities:** Restaurant; bar; babysitting; executive-level rooms; exercise room; golf-driving range; outdoor pool; room service. *In room:* A/C, TV, hair dryer, minibar, MP3 docking station, Wi-Fi (HK$120 for 24 hr.).

Ramada Hotel Kowloon   Popular with Asian business travelers, this no-nonsense Chinese-owned hotel offers simple, clean rooms and not much else in terms of facilities or services. Its location on Chatham Road, across the street from the science and history museums, is not as convenient as other business hotels in this category, though it is within walking distance of the MTR (about 6 min.), Star Ferry (about 15 min.), and train station (5 min.). The cheapest rooms, devoid of character, are small and have glazed windows, while the highest-priced rooms face Chatham Road and have the best views but can be noisy. There's nothing exciting about this hotel, but it will suffice if more desirable and convenient properties are full. Another no-frills hotel, the **Ramada Hong Kong Hotel,** is across the harbor with similar prices, at 308 Des Voeux Rd. W., Western District (© **852/3410 3333;** MTR: Sheung Wan), near the Macau Ferry Pier.

73-75 Chatham Rd. S., Tsim Sha Tsui, Kowloon, Hong Kong. © **800/268 8998** in the U.S., or 852/2311 1100. Fax 852/2311 6000. www.ramadahongkong.com. 205 units. HK$1,500–HK$2,300 single or double; from HK$2,800 suite. 1 child 11 and under stays free in parent's room. AE, DC, MC, V. MTR: Tsim Sha Tsui. **Amenities:** Coffee shop; babysitting; room service. *In room:* A/C, TV, hair dryer, minibar, Wi-Fi (HK$120 for 24 hr.).

Regal Kowloon Hotel 🍴   The Regal Kowloon is the most moderately priced of several hotels in Tsim Sha Tsui East. On the down side, its good value translates into a busy lobby and reception desk, though the overworked staff tries to please. Guest rooms are rather middle of the road but perfectly adequate, with the exception of good bedside reading lights. The cheapest rooms face another building, provide no view whatsoever, and tend to be dark. The more expensive rooms are larger and face a garden; some even have a glimpse of the harbor between buildings. Best, of course, are the Regal Club executive rooms, with contemporary furnishings and added services and amenities. In any case, this is a solid choice for guests who would rather sightsee than laze around a pool (and pay for it with higher room rates).

71 Mody Rd., Tsim Sha Tsui East, Kowloon, Hong Kong. © **800/637 7200** in the U.S., or 852/2722 1818. Fax 852/2369 6950. www.regalhotel.com. 600 units. HK$1,800–HK$2,600 single or double; HK$3,300–HK$3,600 Regal Club; from HK$5,500 suite. Children 12 and under stay free in parent's room (maximum 3 people per room). AE, DC, MC, V. MTR: East Tsim Sha Tsui. **Amenities:** 5 restaurants; bar; lounge; babysitting; concierge; executive-level rooms; exercise room; room service. *In room:* A/C, TV, hair dryer, minibar, Wi-Fi (HK$150 for 24 hr.).

Stanford Hillview Hotel ★ 🛍 This small, intimate hotel is near the heart of Tsim Sha Tsui and yet it's a world away, located on top of a hill in the shade of huge banyan trees, next to the Royal Observatory with its colonial building and greenery. Knutsford Terrace, an alley with trendy al fresco bars and restaurants, is just around the corner. Its lobby is quiet and subdued (quite a contrast to most Hong Kong hotels) and its staff is friendly and accommodating. Standard rooms are mostly twins, fairly basic and small with tiny bathrooms. Deluxe accommodations are larger, while so-called upscale Premium rooms are larger still and add DVD players (ask for one facing the observatory). A kitchen is available for long-staying guests only. The Stanford is a very civilized place, but be prepared for the uphill hike to the hotel.

13–17 Observatory Rd., Tsim Sha Tsui, Kowloon, Hong Kong. ⓒ **852/2722 7822.** Fax 852/2723 3718. www.stanfordhillview.com. 177 units (Premium bathrooms have showers only). HK$1,480–HK$2,080 single or double; from HK$2,680 suite. Long-term rates available. AE, DC, MC, V. MTR: Tsim Sha Tsui. **Amenities:** Restaurant; lounge; babysitting; small exercise room; outdoor golf-driving nets; room service; free shuttle to Mong Kong, Hung Hom Station, and China Ferry Terminal in Tsim Sha Tsui. *In room:* A/C, TV, hair dryer, minibar, Wi-Fi (HK$120 for 24 hr.).

Central District

Lan Kwai Fong Hotel @ Kau U Fong ★★★ 🛍 I don't know why this boutique hotel uses Lan Kwai Fong in its name (it's actually in the Western District), but this is one of my top picks, for many reasons. I love its colorful location, surrounded by narrow streets with ma-and-pa shops and only minutes from the Graham Street wet market, Hollywood Road with its antique shops, and SoHo with its many ethnic eateries and bars. The hotel's interior is fun, too, with a hip twist on traditional Chinese decor. Rooms, some with distant harbor views, are decorated in red and gold, with Asian artwork, quirky touches such as Internet cables tucked inside decorative stone turtles, and Chinese-style doors leading to very tiny bathrooms. Standard rooms, too, are small (starting at 19 sq. m/200 sq. ft.), but deluxe rooms are large corner rooms with more windows. My only gripe about this 33-story hotel is that it's a player in the gentrification of the Western District, which is slowly losing its once-distinct Chinese atmosphere. If you can overlook that, this is a great place to stay.

3 Kau U Fong, Central, Hong Kong. ⓒ **852/3650 0000.** Fax 852/3650 0088. www.lankwaifonghotel. com.hk. 162 units (some bathrooms have showers only). HK$2,400–HK$3,800 single or double; from HK$5,800 suite. AE, DC, MC, V. MTR: Sheung Wan. **Amenities:** Restaurant; lounge; babysitting; exercise room; room service; free shuttle bus to Hong Kong Station every 30 min. *In room:* A/C, TV, hair dryer, minibar, Wi-Fi (HK$120 for 24 hr.).

Mid-Levels

Bishop Lei International House ★★ 🛍 If you want to pretend that you live in Hong Kong, in a residential area popular with expats and abounding in charming neighborhood restaurants and bars, call this home. Located at the top of the Central–Mid-Levels Escalator, it's not as convenient as other hotels, but the hotel makes up for its out-of-the-way location with free shuttle service; plus, a half-dozen city buses stop outside its door. Managed by the Catholic Diocese of Hong Kong, it offers tiny standard single and double rooms (with even tinier bathrooms) that have large windows letting in lots of sunshine but, unfortunately, facing inland. If you can, spring for a more expensive room facing the harbor (all twins or suites). Because they're so high up, views are fantastic. Other bonuses include a reading room for relaxation, a coffee shop with an outdoor terrace, and (surprising for a hotel this size) a small pool and exercise room.

4 Robinson Rd., Mid-Levels, Hong Kong. (© **852/2868 0828.** Fax 852/2868 1551. www.bishopleihtl.com. hk. 224 units (most bathrooms have showers only). HK$1,280 single; HK$1,480–HK$2,080 double; from HK$2,480 suite. Long-term packages available. 1 child 11 and under stays free in parent's room. AE, DC, MC, V. Bus: 3B, 12, 12M, 23, 23A, or 40 to Robinson Rd. **Amenities:** Coffee shop; babysitting; small exercise room; small outdoor pool; room service; free shuttle bus to Central, Admiralty, and convention center in Wan Chai every hour or so. *In room:* A/C, TV, hair dryer, minibar, free Wi-Fi.

Causeway Bay & Wan Chai

Empire Hotel Hong Kong ★ 🗝 Nicely situated in the heart of Wan Chai and popular with Mid-Levels business travelers for its convenience to Central and the convention center, this business hotel offers good value, with many of the same amenities, services, and facilities found at higher-priced hotels, including a rooftop outdoor swimming pool. Narrow hallways, however, may prove a challenge to the claustrophobic, and rooms are so small that couples may fight over the lone luggage rack. None of the rooms provide harbor views from their bay windows. Still, they're comfortable and pleasant enough, with wall-mounted LCD TVs (leaving mercifully more desk space).

33 Hennessy Rd., Wan Chai, Hong Kong. (© **800/830-6144** in the U.S. and Canada, or 852/3692 2111. Fax 852/3692 2100. www.empirehotel.com.hk. 360 units. HK$1,600–HK$1,800 single or double; HK$2,400 executive floor; from HK$2,800 suite. Children 11 and under stay free in parent's room. AE, DC, MC, V. MTR: Wan Chai. **Amenities:** Restaurant; lounge; babysitting; concierge; executive-level rooms; exercise room w/sauna; outdoor pool; room service; spa. *In room:* A/C, TV, hair dryer, Internet (HK$120 for 24 hr.), minibar.

The Fleming ★★ 🗝 A great choice for business travelers on a budget, this hotel—which calls itself an "urban lifestyle hotel"—is the first I've come across in Hong Kong that woos female travelers with a dedicated women's floor, offering rooms with fresh flowers, jewelry boxes, furry rugs and pillows (I'm stymied by this choice), leg massage machines, facial steamers, healthier food in the minibar like herbal teas, female-oriented toiletries, and yoga mats. Otherwise, rooms are fairly standard except for good working space with ergonomic chairs and office supplies like paper clips and rubber bands. Executive rooms, most with partial harbor views, and some deluxe rooms are good for long-staying guests because of kitchenettes. With its minimalist lobby sporting an oh-so-cool lime-green reception desk and hosting free nightly cocktails, this business boutique hotel fills a unique niche in Wan Chai, offering JIA wannabes (p. 97) a more economical yet stylish alternative close to the convention center.

41 Fleming Rd., Wan Chai, Hong Kong. (© **852/3607 2288.** Fax 852/3607 2299. www.thefleming.com. hk. 66 units (most bathrooms have shower only). HK$1,880–HK$2,680 single or double; HK$2,980 executive room. Extended stay rates available. AE, DC, MC, V. MTR: Wan Chai. **Amenities:** Restaurant; executive-level rooms; free access to nearby fitness center. *In room:* A/C, TV, hair dryer, minibar, Wi-Fi (HK$120 for 24 hr.).

The Harbourview ★ 🗝 This YMCA occupies a prime spot on the Wan Chai waterfront, right next to the Hong Kong Arts Centre and not far from the convention center. Rooms, all twin or double beds, are rather modish for a YMCA, attracting guests (including many groups) mostly from mainland China and North America. Best of all, more than half the rooms face the harbor with V-shaped windows, making this the cheapest place on Hong Kong Island with great views of Kowloon. Rooms that face inland are even cheaper but face another building. Personally, I prefer the Salisbury YMCA (p. 101) for its facilities and its location, but if you can't get a room there, this is a good alternative.

4 Harbour Rd., Wan Chai, Hong Kong. © **852/2802 0111.** Fax 852/2802 9063. www.theharbourview. com.hk. 320 units (some bathrooms have showers only). HK$1,600–HK$2,000 single or double; HK$2,500–HK$2,800 executive room. 1 child 11 and under stays free in parent's room. AE, DC, MC, V. MTR: Wan Chai. **Amenities:** Restaurant; executive-level rooms; room service. *In room:* A/C, TV, hair dryer, fridge, Wi-Fi (HK$100 for 24 hr.).

JIA Hong Kong ★★★

Travelers who are allergic to ugly hotel rooms should head straight to Hong Kong's first—and still hippest—boutique hotel, designed by Philippe Starck. From the moment guests step into the low-key lobby with its teak-wood floors, white sheer curtains, and whimsical furniture and are greeted by staff in chic Shanghai Tang–designed uniforms, they know this is no ordinary abode. Stylish rooms (35 sq. m/380 sq. ft.), bathed in white and divided into living, dining, and working areas, feature kitchens and home theater units with surround sound. One- and two-bedroom suites are also available. Guests enjoy free local calls, free Wi-Fi, complimentary continental breakfast and cocktail hour, free access to a local gym, and access to both Kee, a private members' club, and the VIP area of Dragon-i (p. 250). I wouldn't be surprised if some people check in and never move out, especially with this incentive: Long-staying guests get a free massage.

1–5 Irving St., Causeway Bay, Hong Kong. © **852/3196 9000.** Fax 852/3196 9001. www.jiahongkong. com. 54 units (all bathrooms have showers only). HK$2,500 single or double; from HK$3,500 suite. Monthly rates available. Rates include continental breakfast. AE, DC, MC, V. MTR: Causeway Bay. **Amenities:** Restaurant; lounge; free access to nearby health club; room service; sun deck. *In room:* A/C, TV w/DVD/CD player, hair dryer, kitchen, free Wi-Fi.

Lanson Place Hotel ★★★ 🎁

Following close on JIA's heels (and just down the street), this laid-back boutique hotel caters to long-staying guests with upbeat, contemporary rooms. Ranging in size from 35 to 55 sq. m (380–590 sq. ft.), with one-and two-bedroom residences also available, they come with fully stocked kitchenettes complete with a small welcome basket of goodies (coffee, popcorn, soup, bottled water, and so on), home theater systems (you can checkout DVDs for free at the reception desk), and free use of a cellphone during your stay in Hong Kong (on a request basis). The best views are over Victoria Park, while the cheapest rooms face other buildings. While in-house facilities are limited, this is a perfect home-away-from-home for weary road warriors, and the staff, who run operations from sit-down desks rather than the usual front desk, couldn't be nicer.

133 Leighton Rd., Causeway Bay, Hong Kong. © **852/3477 6888.** Fax 852/3477 6999. www.lanson place.com. 194 units (all bathrooms have showers only). HK$2,500–HK$3,800 single or double; from HK$4,800 suite. Weekly/monthly rates available. Children 11 and under stay free in parent's room. AE, DC, MC, V. MTR: Causeway Bay. **Amenities:** Bar; small gym; free shuttle service to Wan Chai and Central. *In room:* A/C, TV w/DVD/CD player w/free DVD library, hair dryer, kitchenette, MP3 docking station, Wi-Fi (HK$140 for 24 hr.).

Metro Park Hotel Causeway Bay ★★ 🏷

Although not as centrally located as my other picks in Causeway Bay, this hotel has some compelling advantages that put it near the top of the list (and in any case, the MTR and tram lines are just outside the door, and the hotel provides a free shuttle bus to nearby shopping districts). It's cheerier and more colorful than most hotels, with a contemporary and fun design that extends through the lobby and into the rooms, the most expensive of which have great views over Victoria Park to the harbor (ask for a room on the 18th floor) and the cheapest of which face another building. In addition, it has all the facilities most travelers need, including a rooftop pool complete with great views and a China Travel

5

WHERE TO STAY

Moderate

Service office for those needing mainland visas. Unfortunately, bathrooms are small with limited counter space.

More convenient is sister hotel **Metro Park Wanchai,** 41–49 Hennessy Rd., Wan Chai (✆ **852/2861 1166;** MTR: Wan Chai), which offers smaller but slightly cheaper rooms but no other facilities.

148 Tung Lo Wan Rd., Causeway Bay, Hong Kong. ✆ **800/223-5652** in the U.S. and Canada, or 852/2600 1000. Fax 852/2600 1111. www.metroparkhotel.com. 266 units (most bathrooms have shower only; executive rooms have tub/showers). HK$900 single; HK$1,900–HK$2,300 double; from HK$3,500 executive room or suite. 1 child 11 and under stays free in parent's room. AE, DC, MC, V. MTR: Tin Hau. **Amenities:** Restaurant; bar; executive-level rooms; exercise room w/sauna; Jacuzzi; outdoor pool; room service; free shuttle to Wan Chai (hourly or less) and Causeway Bay (evenings only). *In room:* A/C, TV, hair dryer, free Internet, minibar.

The Park Lane ★   Although it's inland, I've always liked the location of this hotel—across from huge Victoria Park and close to many restaurants, shops, and department stores. Be sure to book at least one meal at the top-floor Riva, with sweeping views of Victoria Park and the harbor. The hotel coffee shop runs 24 hours on weekends, a rarity in Hong Kong. Rooms are all the same adequate size but vary in price according to floor level, decor, and view—the best are those facing Victoria Park (where you can watch people practicing tai chi in the morning), with the harbor beyond. Standard rooms, on the other hand, have uninspiring views and are rather ordinary, while the best are deluxe rooms with fun, contemporary furnishings like glass-topped desks and coffee tables and bowl-shaped glass sinks. On the downside, the lobby gets a lot of street traffic from area shoppers, making it difficult to attract individual attention from the overworked staff.

310 Gloucester Rd., Causeway Bay, Hong Kong. ✆ **800/223-5652** in the U.S. and Canada, or 852/2293 8888. Fax 852/2576 7853. www.parklane.com.hk. 810 units. HK$2,000–HK$3,800 single or double; HK$4,200–HK$5,200 Premier Club executive rooms; from HK$6,200 suite. Children 11 and under stay free in parent's room (maximum 3 persons per room). AE, DC, MC, V. MTR: Causeway Bay. **Amenities:** 2 restaurants; bar; lounge; babysitting; concierge; executive-level rooms; health club; medical clinic; room service. *In room:* A/C, TV, hair dryer, minibar, Wi-Fi (HK$120 for 24 hr.).

Rosedale on the Park ★ 🎣   Although overshadowed by savvier, newer hotels in Causeway Bay, this is still a solid choice for its targeted corporate accounts, for which it sweetens the deal with complimentary Wi-Fi, cordless phones, in-house mobile phones that allow you to receive calls if you're out of your room (but inside the hotel), free bottled water, and a lounge with computers you can use for free with the purchase of a drink. Only 13 rooms on each floor give it a more intimate atmosphere than the city's many huge hotels. Rooms are minuscule but have everything you need, though note that the least expensive "superior" rooms are on lower floors and face another building. Some rooms on the 31st-floor executive level have side views of the harbor (you have to be standing at the window to see it), but the best deal is a junior suite, with microwave and kitchen utensils, a good bet for long-staying guests.

8 Shelter St., Causeway Bay, Hong Kong. ✆ **852/2127 8888.** Fax 852/2127 3333. www.rosedale.com. hk. 274 units. HK$1,580–HK$1,880 single or double; HK$2,080 executive room; from HK$2,380 suite. Weekly and monthly rates available. Children 11 and under stay free in parent's room. AE, DC, MC, V. MTR: Causeway Bay. **Amenities:** Restaurant; lounge; babysitting; executive-level rooms; small fitness room; room service; free shuttle bus to convention center during major trade fairs. *In room:* A/C, TV, hair dryer, minibar, free Wi-Fi.

INEXPENSIVE

Unfortunately, Hong Kong has more expensive hotels than it does budget properties. Hotels in this category generally offer small, functional rooms with a bathroom and air-conditioning but usually have few services or facilities. Always inquire whether there's a difference in price between rooms with twin beds and those with double beds. If possible, try to *see* a room before committing yourself, since some may be better than others in terms of traffic noise, view, condition, and size. You shouldn't have any problems with the inexpensive hotels recommended here, though larger ones are often filled with tour groups.

Kowloon

Booth Lodge ★★ 🏠 About a 30-minute walk to the Star Ferry but close to the Jade Market, Temple Street Night Market, Ladies' Market, and MTR station, Booth Lodge is located just off Nathan Road on the seventh floor of the Salvation Army building. It has a comfortable lobby and an adjacent coffee shop offering reasonably priced buffets with Chinese, Japanese, and Western selections, but best is the restaurant's outdoor brick terrace overlooking a wooded hillside, where buffet barbecues are held in peak season. Rooms, all twins or doubles and either standard rooms or larger deluxe rooms, are all nonsmoking and spotlessly clean with a small window. Some face the madness of Nathan Road, but those facing the hillside are quieter. If you're looking for inexpensive yet reliable lodging in a convenient location, this is a good bet. A bonus: Local telephone calls are free, and there's a lobby computer you can use for free.

11 Wing Sing Lane, Yau Ma Tei, Kowloon, Hong Kong. © **852/2771 9266.** Fax 852/2385 1140. http:// boothlodge.salvation.org.hk. 53 units. HK$620–HK$1,500 single or double. Rates include buffet breakfast. AE, MC, V. MTR: Yau Ma Tei. **Amenities:** Coffee shop. *In room:* A/C, TV, fridge, hair dryer, Wi-Fi (HK$20 for 2 hr.).

Caritas Bianchi Lodge ⚓ Just down the street from Booth Lodge (see above) and also convenient to the jade and night markets and MTR station, this hotel is not as homey as Booth Lodge and has as much personality as a college dormitory. However, most of the year it charges less than the rack rates listed below, making it a bargain that can't be beat. Most of its very simple rooms, with large desks and closets, face toward the back of the hotel, offering a view of a wooded cliff and a small park, certainly a nicer vista than most hotels can boast. Try to get a room on a higher floor. This establishment, under management of the Roman Catholic Church's social welfare bureau and popular with long-staying guests for its monthly rates, is a good choice for single travelers, including women.

4 Cliff Rd., Yau Ma Tei, Kowloon, Hong Kong. © **852/2388 1111.** Fax 852/2770 6669. www.caritas-chs. org.hk/eng/bianchi_lodge.asp. 90 units. HK$920 single; HK$1,020–HK$1,400 double. Rates include buffet breakfast. Monthly rates available. AE, DC, MC, V. MTR: Yau Ma Tei. **Amenities:** Restaurant; room service. *In room:* A/C, TV, free Internet, minibar.

Dorsett Seaview Hotel This 19-story hotel looks slightly out of place amid the hustle and bustle of this Chinese neighborhood, near a famous Tin Hau (goddess of the sea) Temple and Temple Street's famous Night Market. Catering to visitors from the mainland and Southeast Asia, it has a tiny lobby (often packed) and a cafe on the top floor with views of a harbor (not the famous Victoria Harbour, but a working harbor nonetheless). Narrow corridors lead to tiny rooms; they remind me of a Japanese business hotel, functional and clean but so small you can almost reach out and touch all four walls. Because rooms lack the convenience of a desk or large closet space, there's virtually no place to unpack or put your luggage. As for those Night Market bargains you just purchased, you'll have to either stow them under your bed or sleep with them. The Dorsett is all about its superb, colorful location.

268 Shanghai St., Yau Ma Tei, Kowloon, Hong Kong. © **852/2782 0882.** Fax 852/2781 8800. www. dorsettseaview.com.hk. 268 units (some bathrooms have showers only). HK$880–HK$1,280 single; HK$1,280–HK$1,580 double; from HK$2,400 suite. AE, DC, MC, V. MTR: Yau Ma Tei. **Amenities:** Restaurant; babysitting; free shuttle service hourly to Kowloon Station. *In room:* A/C, TV, hair dryer, Internet (HK$100 for 24 hr.), minibar.

Guangdong Hotel Hong Kong ★   The Guangdong is part of a mainland Chinese hotel chain and was once plagued by Asian tour groups but now caters to individual travelers. It's located in the heart of Tsim Sha Tsui, about a 10-minute walk from the Star Ferry and only minutes from the Tsim Sha Tsui MTR station. Its lobby is spare but upbeat, with an illuminated glass wall behind the reception desk and Picasso-esque masks adorning one wall. Its rooms are very small but clean and pleasant enough, with room rates based primarily on floor level. None of the rooms here offer views, however. If you want to be away from the din of traffic, splurge for a larger deluxe room on a higher floor. Better yet are executive-floor rooms, which reflect either Japanese or European influences in their design and decor.

18 Prat Ave., Tsim Sha Tsui, Kowloon, Hong Kong. © **852/3410 8888.** Fax 852/2721 1137. www.gdh hotels.com. 245 units. HK$1,280–HK$1,780 single or double; HK$1,880–HK$1,980 executive floor; from HK$2,380 suite. 2 children 11 and under stay free in parent's room. AE, DC, MC, V. MTR: Tsim Sha Tsui. **Amenities:** 2 restaurants; babysitting; executive-level rooms; small fitness room; room service. *In room:* A/C, TV, hair dryer, minibar, Wi-Fi (HK$120 for 24 hr.).

The Imperial Hotel Hong Kong   Location, location, location—that's the best thing this hotel has going for it. It's located right on Nathan Road between the Sheraton and Holiday Inn and near the MTR station. Otherwise, it doesn't offer much in terms of service, though a slow renovation is bringing rooms up to par, adding double-paned windows to cut down on noisy street traffic, duvet-covered beds, and remodeled bathrooms with showers instead of tubs. Its cheaper rooms face the back of Chungking Mansion, notorious for its cheap rooms and garbage piled up below, apparently tossed unconcernedly from the windows above. You won't know this, however, as glazed windows now hide the formerly enlightening view. It's an improvement with a price: Rooms tend to be gloomy and claustrophobic and the cheapest are quite small. If you can, spring for a deluxe room that faces Nathan Road, which tends to be noisier but is brighter and has a city view. Because of its cheap prices, this hotel attracts a mixed international clientele, many of whom look like they wish they were elsewhere.

30–34 Nathan Rd., Tsim Sha Tsui, Kowloon, Hong Kong. © **852/2366 2201.** Fax 852/2311 2360. www. imperialhotel.com.hk. 225 units (most bathrooms have showers only). HK$950–HK$1,700 single; HK$1,100–HK$1,850 double. 1 child 11 and under stays free in parent's room. AE, DC, MC, V. MTR: Tsim Sha Tsui. **Amenities:** Restaurant; Irish pub (p. 247). *In room:* A/C, TV, hair dryer, minibar, Wi-Fi (HK$120 for 24 hr.).

Nathan Hotel   More than 40 years old, this hotel underwent a massive overhaul a few years back, adding contemporary furniture, artwork by a local artist, an inviting rooftop bar with outdoor seating, and a Starbucks. Remaining, luckily, is one of the property's best features—large rooms and bathrooms, dating from an era when land was less expensive. Choose from three levels of service: nicely done standard rooms on lower floors, executive rooms for business travelers, and larger, chic Nathan club rooms from the 9th to 13th floors offering 42-inch TVs, DVD players, free Internet, and a private lounge. The hotel attracts business travelers from mainland China and other Asian countries, though its location near the Temple Street Night Market and Jordan MTR station make it a good choice for leisure travelers as well. It's located north of Tsim Sha Tsui, about a 20-minute walk from the Star Ferry.

378 Nathan Rd. (main entrance on Pak Hoi St.), Yau Ma Tei, Kowloon, Hong Kong. ⓒ **852/2388 5141.** Fax 852/2770 4262. www.nathanhotel.com. 189 units (club rooms have showers only). HK$1,080–HK$1,680 single or double; from HK$2,280 club floor. Children 11 and under stay free in parent's room. AE, DC, MC, V. MTR: Jordan. **Amenities:** Restaurant; rooftop bar; Starbucks; babysitting; executive-level rooms; exercise room; room service. In room: A/C, TV, hair dryer, Internet (HK$50 per 24 hr.).

New Kings Hotel 🗡 This property could do with some updating. Still, its low rates (it usually offers discounts on its rack rates, so be sure to ask when making a reservation) and interesting location near the jade and night markets and a Tin Hau (goddess of the sea) temple make it recommendable. Otherwise, it doesn't have any facilities, its tiny rooms are rather plain and dark, and the tiled bathrooms lack counter space. There are only six rooms on each floor, a good thing since corridors are barely wide enough for one person. Expect to wait for the hotel's one elevator. This is a good choice only for budget travelers on the go, since you probably wouldn't want to spend more time here than necessary.

473 Nathan Rd. (entrance on Wing Sing Lane), Yau Ma Tei, Kowloon, Hong Kong. ⓒ **852/2780 1281.** Fax 852/2782 1833. www.kingsdenathan.com. 72 units. HK$550–HK$600 single; HK$650–HK$75 double. AE, MC, V. MTR: Yau Ma Tei. In room: A/C, TV, fridge, free Wi-Fi.

The Salisbury YMCA ★★★ ☺ For decades the number-one choice among low-cost accommodations, this YMCA right next to the Peninsula hotel near the waterfront and Star Ferry offers Tsim Sha Tsui's cheapest rooms with harbor views. Great for families are its inexpensive restaurants and sports facility boasting two indoor swimming pools (a lap pool and a children's pool, free for hotel guests except those in dormitory), a gym, squash courts, and indoor climbing wall (fees charged). Rooms vary from 17 singles (none with harbor view) and more than 250 doubles and twins (the most expensive provide great harbor views), to suites with and without harbor views that are great for families. Although simple in decor, these carpeted rooms are on a par with those at more expensively priced hotels in terms of in-room amenities. For budget travelers, dormitory-style rooms are available only to visitors who have been in Hong Kong fewer than 7 days. Obviously it's quite popular, so book in advance, especially for peak times.

Salisbury Rd., Tsim Sha Tsui, Kowloon, Hong Kong. ⓒ **852/2268 7000** (852/2268 7888 for reservations). Fax 852/2739 9315. www.ymcahk.org.hk. 363 units. HK$980 single; HK$1,080–HK$1,330 double; from HK$1,800 suite. Dormitory bed HK$240. AE, DC, MC, V. MTR: Tsim Sha Tsui. **Amenities:** 2 restaurants, including the Salisbury (review, p. 133); babysitting; badminton; climbing wall; exercise room; Jacuzzi; coin-op laundry; 2 indoor pools; room service; sauna; 2 squash courts. In room: A/C, TV, hair dryer, minibar, Wi-Fi (HK$40 for 4 hr.).

Shamrock Hotel A pioneer member of HKHA and catering mainly to visitors from China, the Shamrock was built in the early 1950s and, despite lobby renovations that added marble floors and artwork from Beijing, I don't think it's changed much since then, including the half dozen or so small chandeliers hanging from the ceiling. The guest rooms are unexciting, clean, simple, and small, though high ceilings (with the ubiquitous small chandeliers) give the rooms something of a spacious feeling. Avoid the cheapest room without windows—Dracula might feel at home, but you might want to spring for some sunshine, though deluxe rooms facing Nathan Road are also noisier. It's about a 20-minute walk from the Star Ferry, just north of Kowloon Park and not far from the Temple Street Night Market.

223 Nathan Rd., Yau Ma Tei, Kowloon, Hong Kong. © **852/2735 2271.** Fax 852/2736 7354. www. shamrockhotel.com.hk. 158 units. HK$1,250–HK$2,200 single or double; from HK$3,000 suite. Children 11 and under stay free in parent's room. AE, DC, MC, V. MTR: Jordan. **Amenities:** 2 restaurants; babysitting; room service. *In room:* A/C, TV, hair dryer, Internet (HK$80 for 24 hr.), minibar.

Central District

Ice House ★★★ 👔 This is a great place to stay if you can get in, and that's a big if due to its small size, excellent location near Lan Kwai Fong, serviced rooms/apartments with kitchenettes, reasonable prices, and high demand for monthly rates that keep it at high occupancy—so book early. Smart-looking rooms, measuring 23 to 32 sq. m (250–344 sq. ft.), have queen-size beds, maid service (except Sun and holidays; bed linen is changed weekly), 24-hour security, a dedicated phone line with your own personal number and free local calls, and generous desk space. If you're coming to Hong Kong to work, don't need the services and facilities of a hotel, and don't want to spend a fortune, this is a top pick. One drawback: It's a killer walk uphill from Central.

38 Ice House St., Central, Hong Kong. © **852/2836 7333.** Fax 852/2801 0355. www.icehouse.com.hk. 64 units (bathrooms have showers only). HK$1,000–HK$1,800 single or double. Monthly rates available. AE, DC, MC, V. MTR: Central. *In room:* A/C, TV, hair dryer, free Internet, kitchenette.

Causeway Bay & Wan Chai

Holiday Inn Express Causeway Bay Hong Kong ★ 🍴 Targeting budget business travelers in town for only a night or two, this is a bare-bones, do-it-yourself kind of place located across from Times Square, with luggage carts instead of bellboys and even a designated ironing room. That said, it does offer a few perks, including free breakfast, free Wi-Fi in the lobby, and a computer corner with free Internet access. It also houses a China Travel Service office, which can arrange visas, transportation, and package tours to China. Its rooms, all measuring 24 sq. m (258 sq. ft.) and priced the same (the range below reflects low to peak seasons), feature contemporary furnishings (including sofa beds) and good reading lamps. Since prices are the same, try to get one of the 15 rooms on the highest floors that have partial harbor views between buildings.

33 Sharp St. E., Causeway Bay, Hong Kong. © **888/465-4329** in the U.S. and Canada, or 852/3558 6688. Fax 852/3558 6633. www.hiexpress.com. 282 units (bathrooms have showers only). HK$1,000–HK$1,500 single or double. Rates include breakfast buffet. AE, DC, MC, V. MTR: Causeway Bay. **Amenities:** 4 restaurants; access to nearby fitness club (fee charged). *In room:* A/C, TV, fridge, hair dryer, free Internet.

The Wesley I like this hotel for its location: on the tramline and only a few minutes' walk from the Pacific Place shopping center. Otherwise, its lobby, devoid of furniture, looks like someone tried to make it hip, with an odd mixture of oversized fake flowers and other objects hanging on the wall. Facilities and services are also limited, and all rooms are minuscule. Rates are based on bed configurations, floor level, and, to a small degree, room size: The cheaper rooms are on lower floors and are furnished with twin beds; the most expensive are slightly larger, with king-size beds and a small sitting area. Rooms facing the front of the hotel are noisier. The

bathrooms are only large enough for one person, and the closets aren't tall e₁.
hang dresses. Even its "business center" is the size of a closet.

22 Hennessy Rd., Wan Chai, Hong Kong. ☎ **852/2866 6688.** Fax 852/2866 6633. www.hanglung.c
251 units. HK$1,150–HK$2,000 single or double. Monthly rates available. AE, DC, MC, V. MTR: Admiral
or Wan Chai. **Amenities:** Restaurant; babysitting. *In room:* A/C, TV, fridge, hair dryer, Internet (HK$80
for 24 hr.).

ROCK-BOTTOM RATES

Budget travelers can find cheap accommodations in Hong Kong, but they generally
come with a price. One way to save money is to stay outside the heavily touristed areas
outlined earlier (Kowloon, Central, Wan Chai, Causeway Bay), though keep in mind
you'll have a longer commute. Hong Kong also abounds in so-called "guesthouses" (see
below), but you'll have few creature comforts other than a bed and small bathroom.

Hotels & Other Choices

B&B Cheung Chau   For some cheap R & R, take the ferry to Cheung Chau (see
chapter 11, "Side Trips from Hong Kong") and walk 2 minutes inland, where you'll
find this charming, nonsmoking B&B, just a stone's throw from Tung Wan Beach.
Tiny rooms are nonetheless modern, though note that some do not have a window (a
glass wall separating the shower from the room, on the other hand, provides its own
distraction). Rates are higher on weekends (reflected in the range below) and higher
still during school and public holidays. Incidentally, renting rooms to tourists is big
business in Cheung Chau; you'll find makeshift stands set up outside the ferry terminal, where locals stand ready to show you photos of their rooms, but unlike this place,
they may not speak English. The biggest drawback to staying here, of course, is the
ferry ride, but it's a more pleasant commute than a 30-minute subway ride.

12-14 Tung Wan Rd., Cheung Chau, Hong Kong. ☎ **852/2986 9990.** Fax 852/2986 9980. www.
bbcheungchau.com.hk. 18 units (bathrooms have showers only). HK$420–HK$820 single or double.
Rates include breakfast. No credit cards. *In room:* A/C, TV, hair dryer, free Wi-Fi.

Hotel Ibis Hong Kong North Point ♦   North Point, on Hong Kong Island three
MTR stations past Causeway Bay, has several hotels, including this one across from
the bus terminal and just a couple minutes' walk from the subway. Rooms are tiny,
only 12 to 13 sq. m (129–140 sq. ft.), but of all my rock-bottom recommendations
this one is the most mainstream. Rooms on higher floors even have views of the
harbor, though rooms facing the back are quieter.

138 Java Rd., North Point, Hong Kong. ☎ **852/2588 1111.** Fax 852/2588 1123. www.ibishotel.com. 275
units (bathrooms have showers only). HK$450–HK$700 single or double. AE, DC, MC, V. MTR: North
Point. **Amenities:** Restaurant; bar. *In room:* A/C, TV, fridge, hair dryer, Wi-Fi (HK$40 for 3 hr.).

Louie Business Hotel   You have to walk up the stairs to the second-floor reception area, but an elevator delivers you to higher floors from there. With a good location across from Kowloon Park, the nonsmoking hotel—actually, it seems more like a
guesthouse—offers a variety of clean, basic rooms, ranging from windowless (the
cheapest) rooms to those on higher floors overlooking the park. It's an adequate and
conveniently located choice; don't expect more.

49-50 Haiphong Rd., Tsim Sha Tsui, Hong Kong. ☎ **852/2311 1366.** Fax 852/2311 2166. louiebusiness
hotel@hotmail.com. 41 units (bathrooms have showers only). HK$400–HK$450 single; HK$500–
HK$700 double; HK$750–HK$850 triple. MC, V. MTR: Tsim Sha Tsui. *In room:* A/C, TV, fridge, hair dryer,
free Internet.

...st accommodations aren't hotels and aren't recommended for visi-
...anliness and comfort. Rather, these accommodations, usually
...attract a young backpacking crowd, many of whom are traveling
...are interested only in a bed at the lowest price. They also attract
...rs, mostly men from Asia, Africa, and the Middle East. At any rate, some guesthouses offer rooms with a private bathroom; others are nothing more than rooms filled
with bunk beds. Of Hong Kong's rock-bottom establishments, none is more notorious
than **Chungking Mansion,** an inspiration for the Wong Kar-Wai film *Chungking
Express.* Although it occupies a prime spot at 40 Nathan Rd., between the Holiday Inn
Golden Mile and the Sheraton in Tsim Sha Tsui, Chungking Mansion is easy to overlook; there's no big sign heralding its existence. In fact, its ground floor is one huge
maze of inexpensive shops and stalls. But above all those shops are five towering concrete blocks, each served by its own tiny elevator and known collectively as Chungking
Mansion. Inside are hundreds of little businesses, apartments, guesthouses, eateries,
and sweatshops. Some of the guesthouses are passable; many are not. But while most
guesthouses were once borderline squalor, today many have cleaned up their act in a
bid for the tourists' dollars. Still, Chungking is not the kind of place you'd want to
recommend to anyone uninitiated in the seamier side of travel. The views from many
room windows are more insightful than some guests might like—the backside of the
building and mountains of trash down below. Even worse are the ancient-looking tiny
elevators filled to capacity with human cargo; you might want to stick to the stairs. In
any case, sometimes the elevators don't work at all, making it a long hike up the dozen
flights of stairs to the top floors. But the most compelling argument for avoiding Chungking Mansion is one of safety: It could be a towering inferno waiting to happen.
However, for some budget travelers, it's a viable alternative to Hong Kong's high-priced
hotels. And you certainly can't beat it for location.

If you insist on staying here, see my review for the Chunking House (see below).
Chungking Mansion contains approximately 100 guesthouses, divided into five separate tower blocks, from A Block to E Block. For the less daring, A Block is the best,
since its elevator is closest to the front entrance of the building. The other elevators
are farther back in the shopping arcade, which can be a little disconcerting at night
when the shops are all closed and the corridors are deserted. I recommend that you
begin your search in Block A. I also recommend that you stay on lower floors. But no
matter what the block, never leave any valuables in your room.

Alisan Guest House ★   If Chungking Mansion is your idea of a horror house, this
guesthouse on the other side of the harbor is a good alternative. Located in a typical
residential building (where the front door is locked and there's an entryway attendant
and security cameras), it's owned by English-speaking Tommy Hou, who spends
about 15 minutes with each of his mostly Western guests to give advice on sightseeing
in Hong Kong. Rooms, scattered on several floors (and also with security cameras in
corridors), are small but clean. The best rooms are the triples located on the third
floor. However, though these rooms face the harbor, they also look out onto a busy
highway, making them slightly noisy. Single rooms are mostly without windows. Mr.
Hou offers free tea, a communal microwave and fridge, and use of his office computer to check e-mail.

Flat A, 5th floor, Hoi To Court, 275 Gloucester Rd. (entrance on Cannon St.), Causeway, Hong Kong.
© **852/2838 0762** or 852/2574 8066. Fax 852/2838 4351. http://home.hkstar.com/~alisangh. 21 units

(bathrooms have showers only). HK$300–HK$350 single; HK$380–HK$450 double; HK$480–HK$550 triple. Rates 10% higher in peak season. MC, V (cash preferred; 7% higher if paying by credit cards). MTR: Causeway Bay. *In room:* A/C, TV, free Wi-Fi.

Chungking House This is the best-known guesthouse in Chungking Mansion, due primarily to its location in A Block, with front desks and lobbies on both the fourth and fifth floors. Rooms are dreary, dark, and depressing, with ancient tiled bathrooms, though recent renovations have helped spruce up things a bit (ask for a "deluxe" room facing Nathan Road; though noisier, they are brighter and thus a tad more cheerful).

A Block, 4th and 5th floors, Chungking Mansion, 40 Nathan Rd., Tsim Sha Tsui, Kowloon, Hong Kong. *©* **852/2739 1600.** Fax 852/2721 3570. www.chungkinghouse.com. 75 units (bathrooms have showers only). HK$200–HK$275 single; HK$250–HK$500 double. No credit cards. MTR: Tsim Sha Tsui. **Amenities:** Wi-Fi (free, in lobby). *In room:* A/C, TV.

Youth Hostels & Dormitory Beds

If you don't mind giving up your privacy, the cheapest accommodations in town are the dormitory beds available at the **Salisbury YMCA** (p. 101) for HK$240. Otherwise, Hong Kong's hostels—there are seven of them on the islands and territories—offer the cheapest rates around. However, most are not conveniently located—indeed, some require a ferry ride and/or a 45-minute hike from the nearest bus stop, as they are located in country parks.

If you don't have a youth hostel card, you can still stay at a youth hostel by paying an extra HK$30 per night. After 6 nights, nonmembers are eligible for member status and subsequently pay overnight charges at members' rates. It's cheaper for the long haul, however, to purchase Youth Hostels Association (YHA) membership for HK$130, available at any youth hostel. Note that children 4 and under are not allowed at Hong Kong's youth hostels. For more information, contact the **Hong Kong Youth Hostels Association** (*©* 852/2788 1638; www.yha.org.hk). Bookings can be made through the website, and credit cards are accepted.

The most conveniently located youth hostel is the 169-bed **Jockey Club Mt. Davis Youth Hostel,** on top of Mt. Davis on Hong Kong Island (*©* **852/2817 5715**), with fantastic panoramic views. It charges youth hostel members HK$110 per night for a dormitory bed for those 18 and over (younger guests get a discount). There are also a few private rooms, with a double costing HK$340. Facilities include a communal kitchen, free Wi-Fi, and coin-op laundry room. To reach it, take the free hostel shuttle bus, which departs from the Macau Ferry Terminal (MTR: Sheung Wan) seven times daily (check the website for specific times). A taxi from Central costs approximately HK$80. The hostel itself is open daily from 7am to 11pm, but check-in starts at 3pm.

Other hostels are on outlying islands and in the New Territories; most charge HK$65 for dormitory beds for those 18 and older. Check-in is from 4pm. There are kitchens and washing facilities, as well as campsites. Since these hostels are not easily accessible, they are recommended only for the adventurous traveler. Of these, the **Hong Kong Bank Foundation S.G. Davis Hostel,** on Lantau Island about a 10-minute walk from the Po Lin Monastery with its giant Buddha (*©* **852/2985 5610**), is the easiest to reach from the airport.

WHERE TO EAT

Shopping is big in Hong Kong, but I'd rate dining right up there with it. I love topping off a shopping expedition to Stanley Market with a meal and drink atop the Jumbo floating restaurant in Aberdeen; ending a hike across Lamma island with an alfresco seafood meal; or splurging on a first-rate dinner at a top-floor restaurant with dreamy views of Hong Kong's stunning skyline. What better way to start the day than sharing a table for dim sum at a noisy Cantonese restaurant, unless it's Sunday brunch at the Verandah in Repulse Bay?

And you don't have to spend a lot of money to dine well. Hong Kong is literally riddled with hole-in-the-wall noodle shops, reasonably priced buffet restaurants, and upscale restaurants offering very good lunch specials.

In other words, dining is one of *the* things to do in Hong Kong. Half the population dines in the city's estimated 11,000 eateries every day. Not only is the food excellent, but the range of culinary possibilities is nothing short of staggering. Hong Kong also has what may well be the greatest concentration of Chinese restaurants in the world. In a few short days, you can take a culinary tour of virtually every major region of China, dining on Cantonese, Sichuan, Shanghainese, Pekingese, Chiu Chow, and other Chinese specialties. Some restaurants are huge, bustling, family affairs, countless others are mere holes in the wall, and a few of the trendiest are Shanghai chic, remakes of 1930s salons and opium dens, or strikingly modern affairs with sweeping views of the city.

Back in the 1980s, Hong Kong's most well known, exclusive restaurants, both Chinese and Western, were located primarily in hotels. In a welcoming trend that began near the end of the last century, however, enterprising and talented chefs began opening establishments in ever-greater numbers, often in modest but imaginative surroundings. A cluster of these restaurants even created a whole new dining enclave, located on the steep hill alongside the Central–Mid-Levels Escalator. Dubbed "SoHo" for the region "south of Hollywood Road," it blossomed into an ever-expanding dining and nightlife district, making it Hong Kong's most exciting culinary scene.

Today, what began as a trickle in SoHo has now engulfed virtually all of Hong Kong. Restaurants stretch from the Lan Kwai Fong nightlife district all the way to SoHo and beyond. Knutsford Terrace, an alley in Tsim Sha Tsui, features one packed venue after another offering alfresco dining. And with Hong Kong's never-ending land reclamation and development, you can expect more restaurants to have opened before you finish reading this book—even local foodies have trouble keeping up.

Unfortunately, the small-time entrepreneurs who served as catalysts for today's culinary explosion probably wouldn't make it in today's competitive climate, at least not in SoHo or any other place where rents have risen dramatically. Instead, Hong Kong's restaurant business is mostly a group thing, with most trendy newcomers part of a well-marketed chain.

On the other hand, there has never been as many dining possibilities as there are now, with French, Italian, American, Mexican, Indian, Korean, Vietnamese, Japanese, Thai, and other ethnic eateries available even in far-flung parts of Hong Kong. Other welcome trends are the inclusion of vegetarian and healthy foods on many menus and the growing popularity of crossover, East-meets-West fusion cuisine, which capitalizes on ingredients and flavors from both sides of the Pacific Rim. And of course, hotel restaurants remain among the best in town, from legendary classics to innovative cutting edge.

I'm convinced that you can eat as well in Hong Kong as in any other city in the world. And no matter where you eat or how much you spend, it's sure to be an adventure of the senses. Little wonder, then, that a common greeting among Chinese in Hong Kong translates literally as "Have you eaten?" In Hong Kong, eating is the most important order of the day.

The restaurants in this chapter are grouped first according to location and then according to price. In Kowloon, restaurants are concentrated in hotels, in shopping malls, and along Nathan Road and its side streets, such as Knutsford Terrace with its many alfresco eateries. Central District caters to area office workers with a wide range of restaurants in ifc mall and Pacific Place and to night revelers in the Lan Kwai Fong nightlife district and SoHo (South of Hollywood Road), with many more restaurants sprinkled in between. Wan Chai, home to both a convention center and the city's raunchiest nightlife (think strip shows), offers a wide range of restaurants catering to diverse crowds, while the nearby Causeway Bay's dining scene centers in and around Times Square shopping center. The most striking views are from restaurants atop Victoria Peak, while Stanley, with its market and laid-back beachfront restaurants, seems like a different part of the world altogether.

As for pricing, you can expect restaurants in the **Very Expensive** category ($$$$) to cost more than HK$800 per person for dinner without drinks (some restaurants average HK$1,200 or more), while in the **Expensive** category ($$$), meals average HK$500 to HK$800.

Moderate restaurants ($$) serve dinners ranging mostly from HK$250 to HK$500, while **Inexpensive** restaurants ($) offer meals for less than HK$250. Keep in mind, however, that these are only guidelines. Some dishes (such as steaks or seafood like lobster) can easily make your meal more expensive than the calculations above.

I should add that many Chinese restaurants often have very long menus, sometimes listing more than 100 dishes. The most expensive dishes will invariably be such delicacies as bird's nest (bird's nest is a real nest, created by glutinous secretions of small swifts or swallows to build their nests), shark's fin, or abalone, for which the sky's the limit. In specifying price ranges for "main courses" under each Chinese establishment, I excluded these delicacies, as well as inexpensive rice and noodle dishes which are considered side dishes (except, of course, in specialized noodle shops). In most cases, therefore, "main courses" refers to meat and vegetable combinations.

WAYS TO save ON YOUR HONG KONG MEALS

Wherever you decide to eat, remember that a 10% service charge will be added to your food-and-beverage bill (see p. 329 in chapter 13 for more information on tipping in Hong Kong). There is no tax, however. You can save a few Hong Kong dollars when eating out by keeping the following tips in mind:

o **Eat your big meal at lunch.** Most Asian (excluding Chinese) and Western restaurants offer special set (fixed-price) lunches that are much cheaper than evening meals; their menus often include an appetizer, main course, and a side dish. Don't neglect expensive restaurants just because you assume they're out of your price range. If you feel like splurging, lunch is the way to go. For example, you can eat lunch at Gaddi's (one of Hong Kong's most famous restaurants; p. 120) for HK$428 per person, including a glass of wine (dinner would be at least double that). Note, however, that set lunches may not be available on Sundays or holidays or may cost more on weekends.

o **Jump on the buffet bandwagon.** Buffet spreads are another great Hong Kong tradition and bargain. I find the quality is generally much, much better than what you typically find in the West. Even the priciest hotels offer buffets (witness the Island Shangri-La's café TOO, p. 139), and a big part of their popularity is the variety, from sushi to roast beef to noodles to fresh seafood. Almost all hotels offer buffets for breakfast, lunch, and dinner; independent restaurants are more likely to feature buffets at lunch (some allow you to choose your main dish from a menu, complemented with buffets for appetizers and desserts). There are always reduced prices for children; the Salisbury and the Spice Market also give discounts to seniors (p. 133 and 128).

o **Eat an early or late dinner to take advantage of special prices.** A few

The usual lunch hour in the SAR is from 1 to 2pm, when thousands of office workers pour into the city's more popular restaurants. Try to eat before or after the lunch rush, especially in Central, unless you plan on an expensive restaurant or have a reservation.

Unless stated otherwise, the open hours given later are exactly that—the hours a restaurant remains physically open but not necessarily the hours it serves food. The last orders are almost always taken at least a half-hour before closing. Restaurants that are open for lunch from noon to 3pm, for example, will probably stop taking orders at 2:30pm. To avoid disappointment, call beforehand to make a reservation or arrive well ahead of closing time.

As for dress codes, unless otherwise stated, most upper-end restaurants have long done away with the jacket-and-tie requirement (those that do have a jacket requirement often have a loaner on hand). Rather, "smart casual" or business casual is nowadays appropriate for most of the fancier places, meaning that men should wear long-sleeved shirts and that jeans, sport shoes, shorts, and flip-flops are inappropriate. Keep in mind that because many restaurants are air-conditioned, you might wish to bring a light jacket.

restaurants offer early bird or late-night specials. If you dine before 7pm at trendy Felix (p. 120), for example, a three-course meal costs only HK$448 as opposed to the HK$1,000 or more you could spend for dinner a la carte. At the Spice Market (p. 128), come for the weekend tea-time buffet from 3:15 to 5:15pm, where you can fill up on finger food and pastries for only HK$148 and then eat a light dinner or skip it altogether. At the Greenery (p. 126), a light supper buffet is available Thursday to Saturday from 10:15pm for HK$198, less than half the usual dinner buffet price.

o **If you want to imbibe, stick with tea.** Hong Kong abolished import duties on wine and beer in 2008, making drinks with a meal even more enjoyable (in early 2007, the duty on wine was an astonishing 80%). That, coupled with a growing appreciative audience among young Hong Kong Chinese, has led to a much larger selection than ever before. Still, to keep prices down, stick to tea or try one of the two most popular and less expensive brands of beer: **San Miguel** (Filipino) and **Tsingtao** (Chinese). And speaking of beer, many bars and pubs mentioned in chapter 10, "Hong Kong After Dark," also serve food.

o **Go the dim sum route.** Dim sum, served mainly in Cantonese restaurants, is another way to economize on breakfast or lunch. Dim sum are usually served three or four to a basket or plate; three baskets are usually filling enough for me, which means I can have breakfast or lunch for less than HK$120. Some restaurants even discount their dim sum before or after the peak dining times or on weekdays. If you don't want tea, be sure to say so. Otherwise, it will be brought to your table automatically and generally costs HK$10 and up.

All of Hong Kong's restaurants went nonsmoking in 2007, prompting those that could to open outdoor terraces for smokers (bars became nonsmoking in 2009).

Finally, in addition to the restaurant recommendations below, HKTB maintains a program called Quality Tourism Services (QTS), in which member restaurants adhere to stringent guidelines designed to help visitors find restaurants they can trust. A list of QTS restaurants is available on the HKTB website, www.discoverhongkong.com; restaurants that qualify also display a QTS decal.

BEST RESTAURANT BETS

I'm convinced Hong Kong has some of the best restaurants in the world—which makes it extremely difficult to choose the best of the best. Nevertheless, the following are my personal favorites.

o **Best Spot for a Romantic Dinner:** With views of Hong Kong's fabled harbor, great service, and French cuisine, **Caprice,** Four Seasons Hotel Hong Kong, 8 Finance St., Central (© **852/3196 8860**), sets the mood for a special evening à deux. You'll want to linger for some time here, savoring the innovative dishes, the gorgeous setting, the view, and each other. See p. 134.

- **Best Spot for a Business Lunch: Nicholini's,** in the Conrad Hotel, Pacific Place, Central (☎ 852/2521 3838, ext. 8210), serves what some claim is the best Italian food in town, including weekday set lunches that are dependably good yet won't blow your expense account. Its atmosphere is both highbrow and relaxed, giving it a winning combination for clinching those business deals. See p. 136.

- **Best Spot for a Celebration:** An elegant, colonial-age setting, attentive service, dependably good French haute cuisine, an extensive wine list, and a long history make **Gaddi's** at the Peninsula Hong Kong, Salisbury Road, Tsim Sha Tsui (☎ 852/2315 3171), a natural for a splurge, special celebration, or memorable place to pop the question. See p. 120.

- **Best Decor:** Designed by Philippe Starck, the avant-garde **Felix,** in the Peninsula Hong Kong, Salisbury Road, Tsim Sha Tsui (☎ 852/2315 3188), manages to hold its own despite competing newcomers. In addition to providing Hong Kong's most unusual, innovative setting, the restaurant offers stunning views, one of the world's smallest discos, and slightly exhibitionist bathrooms. Wear your trendiest duds—you, too, will be part of the display. See p. 120.

- **Best View:** In a town famous for its views, you might as well go to the very top, where the curved facade of **Cafe Deco,** Peak Galleria, Victoria Peak (☎ 852/2849 5111), offers Hong Kong's best panorama, plus moderately priced—though occasionally mediocre—international cuisine. Reserve a harbor-view window seat a couple of weeks in advance; what you're really paying for here is the unparalleled view. See p. 154.

- **Best Chinese Hot Spot:** Make reservations early for **Hutong,** on the 28th floor of an office building at 1 Peking Rd., Tsim Sha Tsui (☎ 852/3428 8342). It's as hip as a Chinese restaurant can be, with great views over Hong Kong, a dark interior with splashes of red lighting, and innovative northern Chinese cuisine. See p. 124.

- **Best Fusion:** Gregarious Chef Nobu is conquering the world with his modern Japanese cuisine; witness **NOBU InterContinental Hong Kong,** Salisbury Rd., Tsim Sha Tsui (☎ 852/2313 2323), with its outstanding Japanese/American/Latin-influenced dishes, great interior design, and fabulous harbor views. See p. 122.

- **Best Dim Sum Experience:** The quaint ceiling fans, spittoons, and wooden booths evoke a 1930s ambience at **Luk Yu Tea House,** 24–26 Stanley St., Central (☎ 852/2523 5464). First opened in 1933, it's one of Hong Kong's oldest restaurants, famous for its dim sum and filled daily with regular customers. It's hard to find an empty seat here but worth the effort. See p. 161. For a less touristy, completely down-home alternative, **Lin Heung Tea House,** 160–164 Wellington, Central (☎ 852/2544 4556), has been serving dim sum from trolleys at its humble abode for more than 80 years. See p. 161.

- **Best Suzie Wong–Era Relic:** There's no better dive for pretending you're in a B-grade 1950s movie than the **Mido Café,** 63 Temple St., Yau Ma Tei (☎ 852/2384 6402), a time capsule of the era with its antique cash register, ceiling fans, hard booths, and own interpretations of Western and Chinese food. See p. 133.

- **Best Vegetarian:** With its informal atmosphere, wood furnishings, and health-foods store, **Life,** 10 Shelley St. in SoHo (☎ 852/2810 9777), is a lifesaver for those in search of organic, vegetarian fare, including salads, quiche, noodle and pasta dishes, daily specials, and power drinks. See p. 146.

- **Best Buffet Spread:** Lots of hotels offer buffets, but none can match the sheer extravagance and chic atmosphere of **café TOO,** Island Shangri-La Hong Kong, Supreme Court Road, Central (✆ **852/2820 8571**). Overlooking the greenery of Hong Kong Park and sporting a hip, contemporary look, it features open kitchens and seven "stations" of food presentations spread throughout the restaurant, thus eliminating the assembly-line atmosphere inherent in most buffet restaurants. The danger? The temptation to try every delectable dish on display. See p. 139.

- **Best Outdoor Dining:** Atop Victoria Peak, away from the constant drone of Hong Kong's traffic, is the delightful **Peak Lookout,** 121 Peak Rd., Victoria Peak (✆ **852/2849 1000**), which serves international cuisine. From an outdoor terrace surrounded by lush foliage, you can actually hear the birds sing. Some tables provide views of Hong Kong Island's southern coast. See p. 154.

- **Best Takeout:** Whether you're after hearty, meaty meals or vegetarian curries, there's a little something for everyone at the combination health-food store/cafeteria **Three Sixty,** with locations in the Landmark, Central (✆ **852/2111 4880**), and Elements, 1 Austin Rd. W., Kowloon (✆ **852/2196 8066**). See p. 147.

- **Best Place to Chill Out:** If the stress of travel and the noise and crowds of Hong Kong have pushed you to the breaking point, take the free shuttle boat to Aberdeen's Jumbo Kingdom floating restaurant, where **Top Deck, at the Jumbo** (✆ **852/2553 3331**) offers great seafood, comfy sofa seating, and alfresco dining with views of surrounding Aberdeen. See p. 156.

- **Best Afternoon Tea:** For that most British institution, no place is more famous than the golden-age and unparalleled **Lobby** of the Peninsula Hong Kong, Salisbury Road, Tsim Sha Tsui (✆ **852/2315 3146**), where you can nibble on delicate finger sandwiches and scones, watch the parade of people, and listen to live classical music being played from an upstairs balcony. See p. 162.

A TASTE OF HONG KONG
Meals & Dining Customs

Traditionally speaking, Chinese restaurants tend to be noisy and crowded affairs, the patrons much more interested in food than in decor. They range from simple diners where the only adornment is likely to be the Formica atop the tables, to very elaborate affairs with Chinese lanterns, splashes of red and gold, and painted screens. In the 1980s, a new kind of Chinese restaurant exploded onto the scene: trendy, chic, and minimalist, many in Art Deco style, and catering to Hong Kong's young and upwardly mobile. More recent years have witnessed a return to the nostalgic, with restaurants designed in Shanghai chic of the 1930s.

In any case, Chinese restaurants are places for social gatherings; because Hong Kong apartments are usually too small to entertain friends and family, the whole gang simply heads for their favorite restaurant. The Chinese, therefore, usually dine in large groups; the more, the merrier. You'll typically encounter these big groups at dinner, the main meal of the day. In smaller restaurants, sharing a table is a common practice, so if your party is small and a bigger group shows up, you may be asked to share your space or move to another table. As for ordering, the basic rule is to order one dish per person, plus one extra dish or a soup, with all dishes placed in the center of the table and shared by everyone. The more people in your party, therefore, the more dishes are ordered and the more fun you'll have. Dishes usually come in two or three different sizes, so ask your waiter which size is sufficient for your group.

Because most Chinese restaurants cater to groups and Chinese food is best enjoyed if there are a variety of dishes, lone diners are at a distinct disadvantage when it comes to Chinese cuisine. A few restaurants make life easier by offering fixed-price course menus, but they're usually for parties of two people or more. An alternative is to dine at hotel buffets that offer Chinese and international dishes.

You shouldn't have any problem ordering, since many Chinese restaurants have English menus. If you want to be correct about it, though, a well-balanced meal should contain the five basic tastes of Chinese cuisine—acid, hot, bitter, sweet, and salty. The texture should vary as well, ranging from crisp and tender to dry and saucy. The proper order is to begin with a cold dish, followed by dishes of fish or seafood, meat (pork, beef, or poultry), vegetables, soup, and noodles or rice. Some dishes are steamed, while others may be fried, boiled, or roasted. Many of the dishes are accompanied by sauces, typically soy sauce, chili sauce, and hot mustard.

At a Chinese restaurant, the beginning of your meal is usually heralded by a round of hot towels, a wonderful custom you'll soon grow addicted to and wish would be adopted by restaurants in your home country. Your eating utensils, of course, will be chopsticks, which have been around for 3,000 years and are perfect for picking up bite-size morsels. If you're eating rice, pick up the bowl and scoop the rice directly into your mouth with your chopsticks.

Keep in mind, however, that several superstitions are associated with chopsticks. If, for example, you find an uneven pair at your table setting, it means you are going to miss a boat, plane, or train. Dropping chopsticks means you will have bad luck; laying them across each other is also considered a bad omen, except in dim sum restaurants where your waiter may cross them to show that your bill has been settled. You can do the same to signal the waiter that you've finished your meal and wish to pay the bill. When dining in a group, avoid ordering seven dishes, since seven dishes are considered food for ghosts, not humans.

As for dining etiquette, it's considered perfectly acceptable to slurp soup, since this indicates an appreciation of the food and also helps cool the soup so it doesn't burn the tongue. Toothpicks are also acceptable for use at the table during and after meals; they can even be used to spear foods too slippery or elusive for chopsticks, such as button mushrooms and jellyfish slices. As in most Asian countries, good toothpick manners call for covering your mouth with one hand while you dislodge food particles from your teeth.

A final custom you may see in Chinese restaurants is that of finger tapping: Customers often tap three fingers on the table twice as a sign of thanks to the person pouring the tea.

The Cuisine

Chinese cooking has evolved over the course of several thousand years, dictated often by a population too numerous to feed. The prospect of famine meant that nothing should be wasted, and the scarcity of fuel meant that food should be cooked as economically as possible; thus, it was chopped into small pieces and quickly stir-fried. Food needed to be as fresh as possible to avoid spoiling. Among the many regional Chinese cuisines, the most common ones found in Hong Kong are from Canton, Beijing (or Peking), Shanghai, Sichuan, and Chiu Chow (Swatow).

Of course, many other dishes and styles of cuisine besides those outlined below are found throughout China and in Hong Kong. It's said that the Chinese will eat anything that swims, flies, or crawls; although that may not be entirely true, if you're adventurous enough, you may want to try such delicacies as snake soup, pig's brain, chicken feet (served as dim sum or in soups), bird's-nest soup (derived from the saliva of swallows), Shanghai freshwater hairy crabs (available only in autumn), tiny rice birds that are roasted and eaten whole, and eel heads simmered with Chinese herbs. One of the more common—albeit strange—items found on most Chinese menus is *bèche-de-mer,* which translates as sea cucumber but which is actually nothing more than a sea slug, prized as a low-cholesterol food.

Dim sum and *congee,* a thick rice porridge, are the preferred Chinese breakfast (which is why some Cantonese restaurants open as early as 6 or 7am), but Western choices like scrambled eggs and bacon are also readily available in hotel restaurants and buffets.

Words of warning: According to government authorities, you're safe eating anywhere in the SAR, except when it comes to hawkers (food carts), which have pretty much disappeared from the Hong Kong scene anyway and were largely unlicensed. In addition, don't eat local oysters—there have been too many instances of oyster poisoning. Eat oysters only if they're imported from, say, Australia. The good restaurants will clearly stipulate on the menu that their oysters are imported. Some expats, warning of cholera, also steer clear of local shellfish and fish caught from local waters. Nowadays, restaurants catering largely to tourists offer fresh seafood caught outside Hong Kong's waters.

Hong Kong was also ravaged by several outbreaks of avian flu beginning in 1997 (6 out of 18 people infected in 1997 died), resulting in mass poultry cullings. Vigilance by local authorities has prevented any recent outbreaks in the SAR, and importation from mainland China ceases during outbreaks there. I still eat chicken in Hong Kong, but whether you choose to is up to you.

Watch your reaction to monosodium glutamate (MSG), which is used to enhance the flavor in Chinese cooking. Some people react strongly to this salt, reporting bouts of nausea, headaches, and a bloated feeling. Fortunately, an awareness of the detrimental side effects of MSG has long prompted most Chinese upper- and medium-range restaurants, especially those in hotels, to stop using it altogether. However, Chinese fast food is likely to be full of MSG, as are dishes prepared using products imported from China, where MSG is used as a matter of course.

CANTONESE FOOD

The majority of Chinese restaurants in Hong Kong are Cantonese; this is not surprising since most Hong Kong Chinese are originally from Canton Province (now called Guangdong). It's also the most common style of Chinese cooking around the world and probably the one with which you're most familiar. Among Chinese, Cantonese cuisine is considered the finest, and many Chinese emperors employed Cantonese chefs in their kitchens.

Cantonese food, which is noted for fast cooking at high temperatures (usually either steamed or stir-fried), is known for its fresh, delicate flavors. Little oil and few spices are used so that the natural flavors of the various ingredients prevail, and the Cantonese are sticklers for freshness (traditionalists may shop twice a day at the market). If you're concerned about cholesterol, Cantonese food is preferable. On the other hand, those with active taste buds may find it rather bland.

Because the Cantonese eat so much seafood, the obvious choice in a Cantonese restaurant is fish. Cantonese restaurants specializing in seafood always have tanks with live fish, with the price determined by the current market price for a *tael* (a tael

> XO sauce, first introduced in Hong Kong by the Peninsula hotel, is a spicy condiment made from a secret recipe incorporating, among other things, Hunan ham, scallops, and Chinese spices. It's so good, you may want to bring a bottle home with you; check hotel gift stores or the food emporiums **city'super** or **Three Sixty** (p. 229 and 147).

is a Chinese unit of measurement approximately equal to 1.2 oz.). I love steamed whole fish prepared with fresh ginger and spring onions, but equally good are slices of garoupa (a reef fish popular in Southeast Asia), pomfret, red mullet, sole, and bream. It's considered bad luck to turn a fish over on your plate (it represents a boat capsizing), so the proper thing to do is to eat the top part of the fish, lift the spine in the air and then extract the bottom layer of meat with your chopsticks. Other popular seafood choices include shrimp and prawns, abalone, squid, scallops, crab, and sea cucumber. Shark's-fin soup is an expensive delicacy, but many consider it a culinary no-no due to the culling of sharks expressly for their fins.

Other Cantonese specialties include roast goose (delicious when dipped in plum sauce), duck, and pigeon; pan-fried lemon chicken; stir-fried minced quail and bamboo shoots rolled in lettuce and eaten with the fingers; *congee* (thick rice porridge); crab meat; sweet corn soup; and sweet-and-sour pork.

A popular Cantonese dish is dim sum, which means "light snack" but whose Chinese characters literally translate as "to touch the heart." Dating back to the 10th century, dim sum is eaten for breakfast and lunch and with afternoon tea; in Hong Kong it is especially popular for Sunday family outings. It consists primarily of finely chopped meat, seafood, and vegetables wrapped in thin dough and then steamed, fried, boiled, or braised. Dim sum can range from steamed dumplings to meatballs, fried spring rolls, and spareribs.

Many Cantonese restaurants offer dim sum from about 7:30am until 4pm, traditionally served from trolleys wheeled between the tables but nowadays more likely to be offered from a written menu. There are nearly 100 different kinds of dim sum, but some of my favorites are *shiu mai* (steamed minced pork dumplings), *har gau* (steamed shrimp dumplings), *cha siu bau* (barbecued pork buns), *au yuk* (steamed minced beef balls), *fun gwor* (steamed rice-flour dumplings filled with pork, shrimp, and bamboo shoots), and *tsuen guen* (deep-fried spring rolls filled with shredded pork, chicken, mushrooms, bamboo shoots, and bean sprouts). A serving of dim sum usually consists of two to four pieces on a plate and averages about HK$20 to HK$40 per plate, though at fine restaurants, particularly in hotels, the prices can be much higher. Your bill is calculated at the end of the meal by the number of plates on your table or, more common nowadays, by a card marked each time you order a dish.

Because I can usually manage only three dishes, dim sum is one of the cheapest meals in Hong Kong and is also the best when dining alone. I often have dim sum for breakfast with lots of tea (the actual term is *yum cha,* traditionally meant as an early breakfast of dim sum and Chinese tea). But it's more than just the price that draws me to traditional dim sum restaurants—they are noisy, chaotic, and the perfect place to soak in the local atmosphere, read a newspaper, or gossip. No one should go to Hong Kong without visiting a dim sum restaurant at least once.

For a light snack or late-night meal, try *congee,* which is a rice porridge popular for breakfast and usually topped with a meat, fish, or vegetable. Many of Hong Kong's countless, cheapest restaurants specialize in *congee,* as well as noodles in soup, the most famous of which is probably *wun tun meen,* noodle soup with shrimp dumplings.

PEKINGESE FOOD

Many Pekingese dishes originated in the imperial courts of the emperors and empresses and were served at elaborate banquets. This theatrical flamboyance is still evident today in the theatrical pulling of Pekingese noodles and the smashing of the clay around "beggar's chicken." Because of its northern source, the food of Peking (or Beijing) tends to be rather substantial (to keep the body warm), and it is richer than Cantonese food. Liberal amounts of peppers, garlic, ginger, leeks, and coriander are used. Noodles and dumplings are more common than rice, and roasting is the preferred method of cooking.

Most famous among Peking-style dishes is Peking duck (or Beijing duck), but unfortunately, a minimum of six people is usually required for this elaborate dish. The most prized part is the crisp skin, which comes from air-drying the bird and then coating it with a mixture of syrup and soy sauce before roasting. It's served by wrapping the crisp skin and meat in thin pancakes together with spring onion, radish, and sweet plum sauce.

Another popular dish prepared with fanfare is beggar's chicken: A whole chicken is stuffed with mushrooms, pickled Chinese cabbage, herbs, and onions, wrapped in lotus leaves, sealed in clay, and then baked all day. The guest of honor usually breaks open the hard clay with a mallet, revealing a tender feast more fit for a king than a beggar.

For do-it-yourself dining, try the Mongolian hot pot, where diners gather around a common pot in a scene reminiscent of campfires on the Mongolian steppes. One version calls for wafer-thin slices of meat, usually mutton, to be dipped in a clear stock and then eaten with a spicy sauce. Another variety calls for a sizzling griddle, over which thin-sliced meat, cabbage, bean sprouts, onions, and other vegetables are barbecued in a matter of seconds.

SHANGHAINESE FOOD

A big, bustling city, Shanghai incorporates the food of several surrounding regions and cities, making it the most diverse cuisine in China. Because of the cold winters in Shanghai, its food is heavier, richer, sweeter, and oilier than Cantonese or Pekingese food, seasoned with sugar, soy sauce, and Shaoxing wine. In addition, because of hot summers, which can spoil food quickly, specialties include pickled or preserved vegetables, fish, shrimp, and mushrooms. Some dishes are rather heavy on the garlic, and portions tend to be enormous. The dishes are often stewed, braised, or fried.

The most popular Shanghainese delicacy in Hong Kong is freshwater hairy crab (a crab with long, hairy-looking legs), flown in from Shanghai in autumn, steamed, and eaten with the hands. Other Shanghainese dishes include "yellow fish" (usually marinated in wine lees), braised eel with huge chunks of garlic, "drunken chicken" (chicken marinated in Chinese wine), sautéed shrimp in spicy tomato sauce over crispy rice, and sautéed shredded beef and green pepper. As for the famous 100-year-old egg (also called 1,000-year-old egg), it's actually only several months old, with a limey, pickled-ginger taste. Breads, noodles, and dumplings are favored over rice in this region's cuisine.

SICHUAN FOOD

This is my favorite Chinese cuisine, because it's the spiciest, hottest, and most fiery style of cooking. The fact that its spiciness recalls Thailand, India, and Malaysia is no coincidence, since this huge province shares a border with Burma and Tibet.

The culprit is the Sichuan chili, fried to release its explosiveness. Seasoning also includes chili-bean paste, peppercorns, garlic, ginger, coriander, fennel, star anise, and other spices. Foods are simmered and smoked rather than stir-fried. The most famous Sichuan (also called Szechuan) dish is smoked duck, which is seasoned with peppercorns, ginger, cinnamon, orange peel, and coriander; marinated in rice wine; then steamed; and then smoked over a charcoal fire of camphor wood and tea leaves.

Other specialties include pan-fried prawns in spicy sauce, sour-and-peppery soup, sautéed diced chicken in chili-bean sauce, and dry-fried spicy string beans. Most Sichuan menus indicate which dishes are spicy.

CHIU CHOW FOOD

Chiu Chow refers to the people, dialect, and food of the Swatow area of eastern Guangdong province. Chiu Chow chefs pride themselves on their talents for vegetable carvings—those incredible birds, flowers, and other adornments that are a part of every Chiu Chow banquet.

Influenced by Cantonese cooking, Chiu Chow food is rich in protein, light, and tasty. Seafood, ducks, and geese are favorites, while sauces, often sweet and using tangerine or sweet beans for flavor, are liberally applied. A meal begins with a cup of *tiet kwun yum* tea, popularly called Iron Buddha and probably the world's strongest and most bitter tea. It's supposed to cleanse the system and stimulate the taste buds. Drink some of this stuff and you'll be humming for hours.

Two very expensive Chiu Chow delicacies are shark's fin and bird's nests. Other common menu items include steamed lobster, deep-fried shrimp balls, sautéed slices of whelk, fried goose blood, goose doused in soy sauce, stuffed eel wrapped in pickled cabbage, and crispy fried *chuenjew* leaves, which literally melt in the mouth. While not greasy, the food does favor strong, earthy tastes.

Drinks

Tea is often provided regardless of whether you ask for it, usually at a charge of around HK$10 to HK$20. Grown in China for more than 2,000 years, tea is believed to help clear the palate and aid digestion. There are three main types: green or unfermented tea; black *bo lay* fermented tea (the most popular in Hong Kong); and oolong, or semifermented tea. These three teas can be further subdivided into a wide variety of specific types, with taste varying according to the region, climate, and soil. If you want free refills, simply cock the lid of the teapot half open and someone will come around to refill it. Afterward, tap three fingers on the table twice as a sign of thanks.

If you want something a bit stronger than tea, choose a **Chinese wine.** Although some Chinese red and white wines are made from grapes, most Chinese wines aren't really wines in the Western sense of the word. Rather, they are spirits distilled from rice, millet, and other grains, as well as from herbs and flowers. Popular Chinese wines include *siu hing,* a mild rice wine that resembles a medium-dry sherry, which goes well with all kinds of Chinese food and is best served warm; *go leung* and *mao toi,* fiery drinks made from millet with a 70% alcohol content; and *ng ka pay,* a sweet herbal wine favored for its medicinal properties, especially against rheumatism. These wines can be cheap or expensive, depending on what you order.

As for **beer**, there's Tsingtao from mainland China, first brewed years ago by Germans and made from sparkling mineral water. San Miguel is also very popular. One thing to keep in mind, however, is that excess drinking is frowned upon by the Chinese, especially the older generation, who often don't drink anything stronger than tea in restaurants. In fact, one waiter told me that Westerners spend much more in restaurants than Chinese simply because Westerners drink alcoholic beverages. Hong Kong's young, affluent generation, however, has developed a growing appreciation for imported wine, though it's rare to find a good international wine list at Chinese restaurants outside of hotels and the trendiest of restaurants.

RESTAURANTS BY CUISINE

AFTERNOON TEA
See "Afternoon Tea," on p. 162

AMERICAN
California Pizza Kitchen (Tsim Sha Tsui, Mong Kok, Causeway Bay, $, p. 131)

Dan Ryan's Chicago Grill ★ (Central, Tsim Sha Tsui, $$, p. 126)

The Flying Pan (Central, Wan Chai, $, p. 145)

Main Street Deli ★★ (Tsim Sha Tsui, $, p. 132)

ASIAN
Nomads ★ (Tsim Sha Tsui, $, p. 133)

The Spice Market (Tsim Sha Tsui, $$, p. 128)

AUSTRALIAN
Wooloomooloo Steakhouse ★ (Tsim Sha Tsui East, Kowloon, Central, Wan Chai, $$, p. 130)

BRITISH
The Pawn ★★ (Wan Chai, $$, p. 150)

BUFFET
café TOO ★★★ (Central, $$, p. 139)

The Greenery (Tsim Sha Tsui East, $$, p. 126)

Harbourside ★★ (Tsim Sha Tsui, $$$, p. 124)

Nomads ★ (Tsim Sha Tsui, $, p. 133)

The Salisbury (Tsim Sha Tsui, $, p. 133)

The Spice Market (Tsim Sha Tsui, $$, p. 128)

CANTONESE
Fook Lam Moon ★★★ (Tsim Sha Tsui, Wan Chai, $$$, p. 158)

Jade Garden (Tsim Sha Tsui, Mong Kok, Causeway Bay, $$, p. 127)

Jumbo Kingdom ★ (Aberdeen, $$, p. 156)

One Harbour Road ★★ (Wan Chai, $$$, p. 148)

Shang Palace ★★ (Tsim Sha Tsui East, $$$, p. 159)

The Square ★ (Central, $$, p. 161)

Super Star Seafood Restaurant ★ (Tsim Sha Tsui, Central, Wan Chai, Causeway Bay, $$, p. 128)

T'ang Court ★★ (Tsim Sha Tsui, $$$, p. 125)

Tsui Hang Village Restaurant (Tsim Sha Tsui, Central, $$, p. 129)

Yan Toh Heen ★★★ (Tsim Sha Tsui, $$$$, p. 160)

Yung Kee ★★ (Central, $$, p. 144)

Zen ★★ (Central, $$, p. 144)

CHINESE (VARIED)
Bo Innovation ★★ (Wan Chai, $$$$, p. 147)

Chinese Kitchen (Tsim Sha Tsui, $, p. 131)

Heaven on Earth (Tsim Sha Tsui, Central, $, p. 146)

Mido Café (Yau Ma Tei, $, p. 133)

Tsui Wah ★ (Tsim Sha Tsui, Yau Ma Tei, Central, Causeway Bay, $, p. 153)

KEY TO ABBREVIATIONS:
$$$$** = Very Expensive   **$$$** = Expensive   **$$** = Moderate   **$ = Inexpensive

CHIU CHOW

Chiuchow Garden (Central, $$, p. 139)
City Chiuchow Restaurant (Tsim Sha Tsui East, $$, p. 158)
Golden Island Bird's Nest Chiu Chau Restaurant (Tsim Sha Tsui, $$, p. 126)

CONTINENTAL

Azure ★★ (Central, $$$, p. 137)
Jimmy's Kitchen ★ (Tsim Sha Tsui, Central, $$, p. 141)
Pearl on the Peak ★ (Victoria Peak, $$$, p. 154)
Post 97 ★ (Central, $$, p. 141)
Sammy's Kitchen (Western District, $, p. 157)
The Verandah ★★★ (Repulse Bay, $$$, p. 155)
Watermark ★★ (Central, $$, p. 143)

DIM SUM

See "Dim Sum," on p. 157

FRENCH

Caprice ★★★ (Central, $$$$, p. 134)
The French Window ★★★ (Central, $$$$, p. 134)
Gaddi's ★★★ (Tsim Sha Tsui, $$$$, p. 120)
The Press Room ★★ (Central, $$, p. 142)
Restaurant Petrus ★★★ (Central, $$$$, p. 136)
SPOON by Alain Ducasse ★★★ (Tsim Sha Tsui, $$$$, p. 122)

FUSION

Felix ★★★ (Tsim Sha Tsui, $$$$, p. 120)
ToTT's and Roof Terrace ★★★ (Causeway Bay, $$$, p. 150)

HUNANESE

Hunan Garden ★★ (Central, Causeway Bay, $$$, p. 140)

INDIAN

Gaylord ★★ (Tsim Sha Tsui, $$, p. 126)
Khana Khazana (Wan Chai, $, p. 152)
Koh-I-Noor ★ (Tsim Sha Tsui, Central, $, p. 132)
Spice (Tsim Sha Tsui, $$, p. 127)

INTERNATIONAL

Cafe Deco ★ (Victoria Peak, $$, p. 154)
café TOO ★★★ (Central, $$, p. 139)
The Greenery (Tsim Sha Tsui East, $$, p. 126)
Harbourside ★★ (Tsim Sha Tsui, $$$, p. 124)
Lucy's ★ (Stanley, $$, p. 155)
The Peak Lookout ★★ (Victoria Peak, $$, p. 154)
Pearl on the Peak ★ (Victoria Peak, $$$, p. 154)
The Salisbury (Tsim Sha Tsui, $, p. 133)
Three Sixty ★ (Central, Kowloon, $, p. 147)
Top Deck, at the Jumbo ★★ (Aberdeen, $$, p. 156)
ToTT's and Roof Terrace ★★★ (Causeway Bay, $$$, p. 150)
Tsui Wah ★ (Tsim Sha Tsui, Yau Ma Tei, Central, Causeway Bay, $, p. 153)
Wildfire (Stanley, Tsim Sha Tsui, Kowloon, Causeway Bay, $, p. 156)

ITALIAN

Bistecca Italian Steak House ★ (Central, $$, p. 138)
Fat Angelo's (Tsim Sha Tsui, Central, Wan Chai, Causeway Bay, $, p. 131)
Gaia Ristorante ★ (Central, $$$, p. 137)
Grappa's ★ (Central, $$, p. 140)
Grissini ★★★ (Wan Chai, $$$$, p. 148)
Isola ★★ (Central, $$, p. 141)
Nicholini's ★★★ (Central, $$$$, p. 136)
Posto Pubblico ★ (Central, $$, p. 142)
Sabatini ★★★ (Tsim Sha Tsui East, $$$$, p. 122)
Spaghetti House (Tsim Sha Tsui, Yau Ma Tei, Mong Kok, Central, Wan Chai, Causeway Bay, $, p. 133)
Tutto Bene ★ (Tsim Sha Tsui, $$, p. 129)
Va Bene ★★ (Central, $$$, p. 137)

JAPANESE

Genki Sushi (Tsim Sha Tsui East, Yau Ma Tei, Mong Kong, Central, Wan Chai, $, p. 132)
Kiku (Central, $$, p. 141)
NOBU InterContinental Hong Kong ★★★ (Tsim Sha Tsui, $$$$, p. 122)

Tokio Joe ★ (Central, $$, p. 143)
Unkai ★★ (Tsim Sha Tsui, $$$$, p. 123)
Wasabisabi ★★ (Causeway Bay, $$, p. 151)
Yagura ★ (Tsim Sha Tsui, $$, p. 130)
Zuma ★★★ (Central, $$$, p. 138)

KOREAN
Sorabol ★ (Tsim Sha Tsui, Causeway Bay, $, p. 153)

LIGHT FARE
Café O ★ (Central, Wan Chai, $, p. 152)
Main Street Deli ★★ (Tsim Sha Tsui, $, p. 132)
Pret A Manger (Central, Wan Chai, $, p. 147)
Three Sixty ★ (Central, Kowloon, $, p. 147)

MALAYSIAN
Spice (Tsim Sha Tsui, $$, p. 127)

MEXICAN
¡Caramba! (Central, $, p. 145)

NEPALESE
Nepal (Central, $, p. 146)

NORTHERN CHINESE
Hutong ★★★ (Tsim Sha Tsui, $$$, p. 124)
Yun Fu ★ (Central, $$, p. 144)

PEKINGESE
American Restaurant (Wan Chai, $, p. 151)
Peking Garden ★ (Tsim Sha Tsui, Central, $$, p. 127)
Spring Deer Restaurant ★ (Tsim Sha Tsui, $$, p. 128)

PIZZA
Café O ★ (Central, Wan Chai, $, p. 152)
California Pizza Kitchen (Tsim Sha Tsui, Mong Kok, Causeway Bay, $, p. 131)
PizzaExpress (Tsim Sha Tsui, Central, Wan Chai, Stanley, $, p. 147)
Spaghetti House (Tsim Sha Tsui, Yau Ma Tei, Mong Kok, Central, Wan Chai, Causeway Bay, $, p. 133)
Wildfire (Stanley, Tsim Sha Tsui, Kowloon, Causeway Bay, $, p. 156)

SEAFOOD
Dot Cod Seafood Restaurant & Oyster Bar (Central, $$, p. 139)
Harbourside ★★ (Tsim Sha Tsui, $$$, p. 124)
Super Star Seafood Restaurant ★ (Tsim Sha Tsui, Central, Wan Chai, Causeway Bay, $$, p. 128)
Top Deck, at the Jumbo ★★ (Aberdeen, $$, p. 156)

SHANGHAINESE
Shanghai Garden (Central, $$, p. 142)
Wu Kong ★★ (Tsim Sha Tsui, Causeway Bay, $$, p. 130)

SICHUAN
Chilli Fagara ★ (Central, $, p. 145)
Red Pepper ★★ (Causeway Bay, $$, p. 151)
Shui Hu Ju (Central, $$, p. 143)

STEAK
Bistecca Italian Steak House ★ (Central, $$, p. 138)
STEAK HOUSE winebar + grill ★★★ (Tsim Sha Tsui, $$$$, p. 123)
Wooloomooloo Steakhouse ★ (Tsim Sha Tsui East, Kowloon, Central, Wan Chai, $$, p. 130)

THAI
Chili Club (Wan Chai, $, p. 152)
Simply Thai (Causeway Bay, Mong Kok, Sha Tin, $, p. 152)
Spice (Tsim Sha Tsui, $$, p. 127)

VEGETARIAN
Khana Khazana (Wan Chai, $, p. 152)
Life ★ (Central, $, p. 146)

VIETNAMESE
Indochine 1929 ★★ (Central, $$, p. 140)

WESTERN
Mido Café (Yau Ma Tei, $, p. 133)

KOWLOON

Very Expensive

Felix ★★★ FUSION   Located on the Peninsula Hong Kong's top floor, this strikingly avant-garde restaurant was designed by Philippe Starck. Your first hint that Felix is not your ordinary dining experience begins with the elevator's wavy walls, which suggest a voyage to the world beyond, and continues inside the restaurant with its glass facades that curve seductively to reveal stunning views and its two eye-catching zinc cylinders that resemble gigantic snails and contain a cocoon-cozy bar and what may be one of the world's tiniest discos (spiraling staircases also lead to bars on top). The menu, featuring Pacific Rim ingredients brought together in contemporary East-meets-West combinations, rarely disappoints. You might start with Dungeness crab cake served with avocado and jalapeño remoulade, followed by the seared ahi tuna served with crispy chorizo and cauliflower. You can save a bundle by dining before 7pm on the early bird, three-course dinner for HK$448, which includes a glass of wine. You can also come just for a drink, though note that the dress code is smart casual (no flip-flops or shorts allowed).

In the Peninsula Hong Kong, Salisbury Rd., Tsim Sha Tsui. ⓒ **852/2315 3188.** www.peninsula.com. Reservations required. Children 11 and under not allowed. Main courses HK$320–HK$680; set dinner HK$788. AE, DC, MC, V. Daily 6pm–1:30am (last order 10:30pm). MTR: Tsim Sha Tsui.

Gaddi's ★★★ FRENCH   Opened in 1953, Gaddi's was once considered the best European restaurant in Hong Kong. Although that reputation has long been challenged by other superb restaurants, Gaddi's is still a legend, the epitome of old Hong Kong. Also located in the Peninsula, Gaddi's atmosphere, intended to evoke the hotel's original 1928 neoclassical architecture, is that of an elegant European dining room blended with the best of Asia, with crystal-and-silver chandeliers from Paris, Tai Ping carpet, and a Chinese coromandel screen dating from 1670. The food is French haute cuisine at its finest, classically French but with inventive, European influences, with past dishes on the changing menu including slow-cooked Bresse chicken with roasted leg, artichokes, and black truffles. The wine cellar, with a collection of rare vintages, is among the best in Hong Kong—but who could blame you if you get carried away and splurge on champagne? There's live, discreet music at night and a small dance floor.

In the Peninsula Hong Kong, Salisbury Rd., Tsim Sha Tsui. ⓒ **852/2315 3171.** www.peninsula.com. Reservations recommended for lunch, required for dinner. Jacket required for men at dinner. Children

---

 Dining Behind the Scenes

If you've ever wondered what a kitchen is like during the hustle and bustle of meal times, you have your chance to experience it firsthand by participating in Gaddi's Chef's Table at the Peninsula Hong Kong. Seating only four (with a minimum of two people), it offers a fascinating front-row view of Gaddi's kitchen in action, a tour of the Peninsula's massive kitchens, and includes a 3-course lunch for HK$728 or a 5- or 10-course dinner for HK$1,688 and HK$2,388 per person. For Chinese food enthusiasts, a similar dining experience is offered by the Peninsula's Spring Moon Chef's Table. For reservations, contact the Peninsula Hong Kong at ⓒ 852/2920 2888 or by e-mail at dining.pen@peninsula.com.

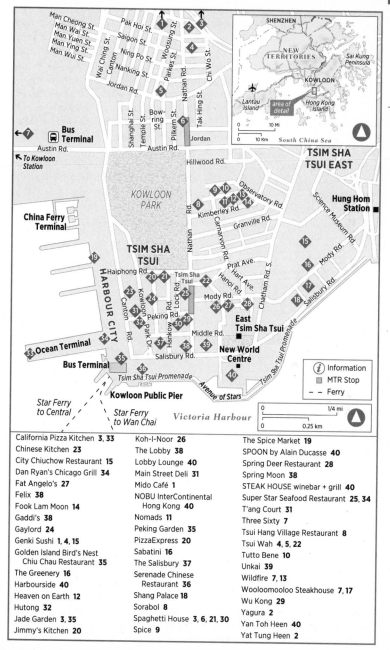

11 and under not allowed except Sun and holidays. Main courses HK$640–HK$720; set dinner HK$1,388; set lunch HK$428. AE, DC, MC, V. Daily noon–2:30pm and 7–10:30pm (last order). MTR: Tsim Sha Tsui.

NOBU InterContinental Hong Kong ★★★ MODERN JAPANESE Where isn't there a NOBU these days? Opened in 2006 as the 17th venue in Nobuyuki Matsuhisa's culinary empire, this one offers fabulous harbor views and a sleek design that utilizes wood, bamboo, sea urchin spines, black river rocks, and other natural materials in a thoroughly modern way. The yuzu-and-piña martini (pineapple vodka, fresh pineapple purée, and yuzu juice) makes an apt introduction to the unique pairing of Japanese, American, and Latin cuisines (Chef Nobu, as everyone calls him, has lived in Japan, Peru, and the United States). Sushi, sashimi, and tempura are listed on the long menu, along with such intriguing choices as yellowtail sashimi with jalapeño, Chilean sea bass with dried miso, and Wagyu beef strip loin with wasabi salsa. If making a choice is too daunting, order the *omakase,* the chef's recommended dinner starting at HK$888. Despite the huge wine selection, this cuisine goes great with sake; the knowledgeable staff is happy to make recommendations based on what you've ordered.

In the InterContinental Hong Kong, Salisbury Rd., Tsim Sha Tsui. ✆ **852/2313 2323.** www.hongkong-ic. intercontinental.com. Reservations required. Main courses HK$250–HK$820; set lunches HK$130– HK$588. AE, DC, MC, V. Daily noon–2:30pm and 6–11pm (last order). MTR: Tsim Sha Tsui.

Sabatini ★★★ 🍴 ITALIAN In 1954, three Sabatini brothers opened their first restaurant in Rome; their success in Italy led them to open branches in Tokyo and Hong Kong. The dining hall is rustic and cozy yet refined, with a terra-cotta tile floor, wooden ceiling, and traditional Roman murals, giving it a more casual ambience than most hotel Italian restaurants in the same price range. The menu is a faithful replica of the original Roman fare, with liberal doses of olive oil, garlic, and peppers and featuring such popular dishes as chargrilled lamb, and Dover sole with *prosecco* and artichokes. The antipasti buffet is so delicious it's tempting to fill up just on its selections, but you will want to leave room for a sinful finale from the bountiful dessert trolley. The list of mostly Italian wines is seemingly endless. Evenings feature live music; lunch is popular for its reasonable set menus. The service is cheerful and polished.

In the Royal Garden hotel, 69 Mody Rd., Tsim Sha Tsui East. ✆ **852/2733 2000.** www.rghk.com.hk. Reservations required. Main courses HK$388–HK$788; set lunches HK$218–HK$398; Sun/holiday buffet HK$498. AE, DC, MC, V. Daily noon–2:30pm and 6–11pm. MTR: Tsim Sha Tsui.

SPOON by Alain Ducasse ★★★ MODERN FRENCH Dinner at this seductive venue is more than a meal—it's an experience. From the moment you walk past the restaurant's "wine cellar," with approximately 3,000 bottles of both new- and old-world selections, you know that this is a place of superlatives. The focal point of the dining room is the ceiling, where 550 hand-blown Murano glass spoons are lined up like a landing strip, directing one's attention from above to the open kitchen and to the stunning harbor view just beyond the massive windows. The restaurant is so low and close to the water that dining here is almost like being on a junk—albeit a very luxurious one. From the innovative cuisine, created by chef-restaurateur Alain Ducasse, you might opt for the delectable steamed duck foie gras, followed, perhaps, by pan-seared tuna with satay sauce and vegetables or the beef tenderloin and foie gras cooked in brioche. Alternatively, your entire group may opt for the Spoon Experience, a tasting menu costing HK$888 per person for five courses.

In the InterContinental Hong Kong, Salisbury Rd., Tsim Sha Tsui. 852/2313 2323. www.hongkong-ic.intercontinental.com. Reservations required. Main courses HK$350–HK$680; Sun lunch HK$558, including champagne and wine. AE, DC, MC, V. Sun noon–2:30pm; daily 6–11pm. MTR: Tsim Sha Tsui.

STEAK HOUSE winebar + grill ★★★ STEAK Not only is the food great, but dining here is fun! Start your meal with a trip through one of Hong Kong's most extensive salad bars, featuring 24 different vegetables, 6 homemade salad dressings, and 11 condiments. Follow it with a filet mignon, Australian or Japanese Wagyu beef, a New York strip, or other meat (including nonbeef choices) imported from around the world, cooked on Hong Kong's only charcoal grill. You then get to choose your gourmet steak knife (10 options, from Japan, France, Germany, and other parts of the globe), your mustard (from a dozen homemade varieties), sauce (eight of them), and salt (from a selection of rock salts from around the world). Even though the restaurant has no view, to be truthful I barely noticed, because I was so absorbed in making my many selections, including—need I add?—wine from the winebar's 450 offerings.

In the Hotel InterContinental Hong Kong, Salisbury Rd., Tsim Sha Tsui. 852/2313 2323. www.hongkong-ic.intercontinental.com. Reservations required. Main courses HK$330–HK$1,380; Sun lunch HK$598. AE, DC, MC, V. Sun noon–2:30pm; daily 6pm–midnight. MTR: Tsim Sha Tsui.

Unkai ★★ JAPANESE Located in the Sheraton Hong Kong, this is the Hong Kong branch of a well-known group of restaurants in Japan, serving excellent and authentic traditional Japanese cuisine and catering to discerning Japanese, who make up a large proportion of the Sheraton's guests. True to Japanese form, the contemporary, hip elegance of the restaurant is subtly understated, an aesthetic that is also carried into the food presentation. Foremost, of course, are the *kaiseki* courses, artfully arranged dishes that change according to the season. There are also counters for tempura, *teppanyaki* (grilled foods), and sushi. Because ordering a la carte can be expensive and bewildering due to the many choices, order a set meal (called a "course" on the menu) or come for lunch, when you have a choice of many set meals, including sushi, tempura, and *teppanyaki* courses and *obento* lunch boxes. The sake offerings are extensive.

In the Sheraton Hong Kong Hotel & Towers. 20 Nathan Rd., Tsim Sha Tsui. 852/2369 1111, ext. 3087. www.starwoodhotels.com. Reservations recommended. *Kaiseki* set meals HK$500–HK$795; *teppanyaki* set meals HK$800–HK$1,200; set lunches HK$200–HK$490. AE, DC, MC, V. Daily noon–2:30pm and 6:30–10:30pm. MTR: Tsim Sha Tsui.

Yan Toh Heen ★★★ CANTONESE Keeping true to the restaurant's name that translates loosely to "elegant dining establishment to enjoy the beautiful view," this great restaurant envelopes diners in a sophisticated, hushed environment, with large windows that treat diners to a view of famous Victoria Harbour. The decor emphasizes the beauty of stark simplicity, with bonsai trees and flower arrangements that change with the lunar calendar; the restaurant is famous for its beautiful jade table settings (each setting is valued at approximately HK$8,000!). Dishes include traditional Cantonese preparations as well as imaginative creations that border on Chinese nouvelle cuisine and healthy variations of authentic Cantonese delicacies. The menu changes with each lunar month but always includes seafood, the restaurant's signature barbecued suckling pig, Peking duck (HK$680; advance orders required), and crispy Lung Kong chicken. The restaurant is also known for its dim sum.

In the InterContinental Hong Kong, 18 Salisbury Rd., Tsim Sha Tsui. 852/2313 2323. www.hongkong-ic.intercontinental.com. Reservations recommended (request a window seat). Main dishes HK$165–HK$420; set dinner HK$988. AE, DC, MC, V. Mon–Sat noon–2:30pm; Sun 11:30am–3pm; daily 6–11pm. MTR: Tsim Sha Tsui.

Expensive

Fook Lam Moon ★★★ CANTONESE   Upon entering this restaurant (look for the shrine to the kitchen god at the entrance), you immediately feel as if you've stepped back a couple of decades to a Hong Kong that has all but vanished. The decor is outdated and, unless you're a regular, waiters can be indifferent. Yet for almost 40 years this has remained *the* place to go for exotic dishes, including shark's fin (the obvious number-one choice, with 12 different renditions listed on the menu), bird's nest, and abalone, as well as more down-to-earth dishes such as fried crispy chicken and pan-fried lobster bars. The spicy XO sauce on every table is a great condiment, though the fresh ingredients speak for themselves. If you're not careful, you could end up spending a small fortune, but whatever you order it's apt to be memorable. Indeed, some Hong Kong old-timers swear this restaurant serves the best Cantonese food in the world.

Another branch, located in Wan Chai at 35–45 Johnston Rd. (© **852/2866 0663**; MTR: Wan Chai), keeps the same hours.

53-59 Kimberley Rd., Tsim Sha Tsui. © **852/2366 0286.** www.fooklammoon-grp.com. Reservations recommended for dinner. Main dishes (excluding exotic dishes) HK$150–HK$380. AE, DC, MC, V. Mon-Sat 11:30am–3pm; Sun 11am–3pm; daily 6–11pm. MTR: Tsim Sha Tsui.

Harbourside ★★ INTERNATIONAL/SEAFOOD/BUFFET   This bright and airy informal dining hall is the InterContinental's all-day "casual" restaurant, but if you go for the very tempting dinner buffet—it's hard to resist—you'll pay a pretty penny for the privilege of chowing down on fish, shrimp, sushi, and other seafood, along with pastas, pizzas, and salads. Included in the dining experience are views of people strolling along the waterfront Avenue of Stars promenade and chefs bustling about in an open kitchen. You can, however, eat more cheaply by coming for the lunch buffet or ordering a la carte, with selections ranging from burgers, pizza, and steaks to Asian and Western dishes. Harbourside even has a health-conscious menu, with specific dishes designed to help aid against diabetes, hypertension, heart disease, and a lack of antioxidants.

In the InterContinental Hong Kong, Salisbury Rd., Tsim Sha Tsui. © **852/2313 2323.** www.hongkong-ic. intercontinental.com. Reservations recommended. Main courses HK$180–HK$430; dinner buffet HK$588; lunch buffet HK$268 Mon–Fri, HK$288 Sat; Sun champagne brunch HK$638. AE, DC, MC, V. Daily 6am–midnight. MTR: Tsim Sha Tsui.

Hutong ★★★ 🍴 NORTHERN CHINESE   A *hutong* is an ancient alley or lane, once common in Beijing's courtyard neighborhoods but now quickly disappearing. This stunning restaurant, however, is located on the 28th floor of a strikingly modern high-rise about as far from a real *hutong* as one can get, but it's to be commended for its down-to-earth yet dramatic setting, with red lanterns providing the only splash of color against a dark, muted interior, and windows providing fantastic views of Hong Kong. The cuisine, which is northern Chinese in origin but uses new ingredients and combinations to create its own trademark dishes, is so enticing it's hard to know what to recommend. I love the drunken raw crab (an appetizer marinated 3 days in Chinese wine), scallops tossed with pomelo segments, the crispy deboned lamb ribs, and crispy soft-shelled crab with Sichuan red chili. Even the pig throat–and-leek salad is a whole lot better than it sounds, especially when you wash it down with chilled lichee wine with a touch of soda. Note that there's a minimum charge of HK$300 per person, but you won't have trouble meeting the minimum at this pricey but great venue.

1 Peking Rd. (28th floor), Tsim Sha Tsui. ℂ **852/3428 8342.** www.hutong.com.hk. Reservations required for dinner. Main dishes HK$138–HK$468. AE, DC, MC, V. Daily noon–3pm and 6–11pm. MTR: Tsim Sha Tsui.

Shang Palace ★★ CANTONESE   While most Chinese restaurants have ditched time-honored red and gold for a more contemporary look, this remains one of Hong Kong's most traditionally and elaborately decorated restaurants, with walls of carved red lacquerware and Chinese lanterns hanging from the ceiling. If your experience of Chinese food is limited to chop suey, this is a comfortable and memorable place to get acquainted with it, though you also can't go wrong if you're a Chinese-food connoisseur. The dinner menu changes with the seasons and is quite extensive, with an emphasis on fresh seafood (plucked from a tank in the kitchen), but also serving chicken, duck (including Peking duck), pigeon, beef, and pork, Cantonese-style. Recommendations include the deep-fried crispy chicken, or the sparerib casserole cooked in a clay pot and doused with homemade sweet-and-sour sauce with Chinese wine. Expect to spend about HK$700 per person for a royal feast. Lunch is more economical and always includes a dozen or more varieties of dim sum.

In the Kowloon Shangri-La, 64 Mody Rd., Tsim Sha Tsui East. ℂ **852/2733 8754.** www.shangri-la.com. Reservations recommended. Main dishes HK$125–HK$370. AE, DC, MC, V. Mon–Sat noon–3pm; Sun and holidays 10:30am–3pm; daily 6:30–11pm. MTR: Tsim Sha Tsui.

T'ang Court ★★ CANTONESE   Jackie Chan and a host of other celebrities have dined here, testament to this restaurant's award-winning cuisine famous for its original take on classic Cantonese fare. Named after the T'ang Dynasty, often characterized as the Golden Age in Chinese history, this hotel restaurant is richly decorated in burgundy and gold, with velvet curtains, contemporary sculptures, and generously spaced tables. Faced with an extensive menu of interesting choices, you might opt for one of the signature dishes like crispy salty chicken; stir-fried lobster with spring onion, red onion, and shallots; or sautéed prawns and crab roe with golden-fried pork and crab meat puffs. If the sky's the limit, you can also dine on bird's nest and abalone, but on the other end of the spectrum are the set meals and the dim sum lunch (both good for lone diners).

In the Langham, 8 Peking Rd., Tsim Sha Tsui. ℂ **852/2375 1133,** ext. 2250. http://hongkong.langham hotels.com. Reservations recommended. Main dishes HK$190–HK$380; set dinner HK$450. AE, DC, MC, V. Mon–Fri noon–3pm; Sat–Sun and holidays 11am–3pm; daily 6–11pm. MTR: Tsim Sha Tsui.

Moderate

A good standby for Continental cuisine is the Tsim Sha Tsui branch of **Jimmy's Kitchen,** covered in the Central District dining section (p. 141).

City Chiuchow Restaurant CHIU CHOW   A longtime favorite for Chiu Chow food, this spacious restaurant overlooks a plaza leading down to a major promenade in Tsim Sha Tsui East. Seating 500, it features a big tank with unwitting fish swimming about, soon to end up on the chopping block. Famous dishes here include honey-flavored smoked duck breast; sliced spicy goose; stir-fried pickled olive, minced pork, and French beans; Chiuchow superior hot pot; and seafood dishes, including lobster. I particularly recommend the cold sliced lobster in a special honey sauce—it's not on the menu but it's available year-round. Dim sum is also served. And don't forget to try the Iron Buddha tea, a specialty of Chiuchow's, a tea that is so strong it will knock your socks off—and may keep you awake all night.

East Ocean Centre, 98 Granville Rd., Tsim Sha Tsui East. ℂ **852/2723 6226.** Main dishes HK$68–HK$120. AE, DC, MC, V. Daily 11am–11pm. MTR: Tsim Sha Tsui.

Dan Ryan's Chicago Grill ★ ☺ AMERICAN

Located in the huge Ocean Terminal complex at its southernmost end, where cruise ships dock, this casual restaurant serves real American food, with portions big enough to satisfy a hungry cowboy. The decor is Anywhere, USA, but with a difference—it offers views of the famous harbor from a few select barstool seats. The lunch menu is substantial, including such classic American favorites as Buffalo chicken wings, nachos, potato skins, New England clam chowder, barbecued ribs, steaks, spaghetti, lasagna, great hamburgers (a hit with kids, as is the children's menu), and large deli sandwiches, as well as weekday lunch specials beginning at HK$85. The dinner menu is confined mainly to barbecued steaks, chops, fish, and pasta. Admittedly, most dishes here are a bit pricey, but if you're hankering for the real thing you might consider it a lifesaver. You can also come just for a drink at its bar, and English-language newspapers are available for customer perusal.

Another Dan Ryan's is in Pacific Place in Admiralty, 88 Queensway (ℂ **852/2845 4600;** MTR: Admiralty), open the same hours.

200 Ocean Terminal, Harbour City, Tsim Sha Tsui. ℂ **852/2735 6111.** www.windy-city.com.hk/dans/index.html. Main courses HK$98–HK$288 before 6pm, HK$118–HK$398 after 6pm. AE, DC, MC, V. Mon–Fri 11am–midnight; Sat–Sun and holidays 10am–midnight. MTR: Tsim Sha Tsui.

Gaylord ★★ 🗡 INDIAN

This long-established, first-floor restaurant in the heart of Tsim Sha Tsui is classy and comfortable, with private booths, overstuffed sofas, and live music most evenings. It's popular for its authentic North Indian classics, including tandoori, lamb curry cooked in North Indian spices and herbs, chicken cooked in a fiery vindaloo curry, prawns with green pepper and spices, and fish with potatoes and tomatoes. You can also choose from a dozen vegetarian dishes; the lunchtime buffet, served Monday to Friday (except holidays) until 2:30pm, is a winner.

23–25 Ashley Rd., Tsim Sha Tsui. ℂ **852/2376 1001.** www.chiram.com.hk. Main dishes HK$98–HK$178; set dinners (2-person minimum) HK$168–HK$238; lunch buffet Mon–Fri HK$98; set lunches HK$48–HK$58. AE, DC, MC, V. Daily noon–3pm and 6–11pm. MTR: Tsim Sha Tsui.

Golden Island Bird's Nest Chiu Chau Restaurant CHIU CHOW

This Chiu Chow restaurant, traditionally decorated but without views, is conveniently located right in front of the Star Ferry terminus. This was Hong Kong's first restaurant to offer bird's nest as a specialty; it's prepared 14 ways, available as a soup, entree, and even dessert. Although the prices for this dish have risen dramatically over the years, here it costs around HK$380—expensive, but less than what you'd pay elsewhere. Anyway, you might want to try at least one bird's-nest dish, along with such Chiu Chow preparations as oyster omelets, prawn balls, or roast soy goose, topping it all off with a thimble-size cup of Chiu Chow tea, which is believed to aid in digestion.

Star House (2nd floor), 3 Salisbury Rd., Tsim Sha Tsui. ℂ **852/2736 6228.** Main dishes HK$70–HK$180 (not including bird's nest dishes). AE, DC, MC, V. Mon–Sat 11:30am–2:30pm; Sun and holidays 11am–2:30pm; daily 5:30–10:30pm. MTR: Tsim Sha Tsui.

The Greenery INTERNATIONAL/BUFFET

If you're looking for a quick, filling feast in Tsim Sha Tsui East, look no farther than the buffets offered in this popular, airy restaurant, located in the 15-story atrium of the Royal Garden hotel. The sounds of piano music (evenings only), a waterfall, and multitudes of hungry diners make eating a rather noisy affair, but the food is good and varied, ranging from Chinese and Japanese to Western fare, from salads and vegetables to ribs and seafood, and an efficient staff keeps water glasses filled and used plates whisked away. Bargain-seeking night owls take note: A lighter supper buffet is available Thursday to Saturday evenings from 10:15pm for HK$198.

In the Royal Garden, 69 Mody Rd., Tsim Sha Tsui East. (✆ **852/2733 2030.** www.rghk.com.hk. Lunch buffet HK$235 Mon–Fri, HK$275 Sat–Sun and holidays; dinner buffet HK$428 Mon–Thurs, HK$458 Fri–Sun and holidays. AE, DC, MC, V. Mon–Fri noon–2:30pm; Sat–Sun and holidays noon–3pm; Sun–Wed 6:30–10pm; Thurs–Sat 6:30–9:45pm and 10:15pm–12:15am. MTR: Tsim Sha Tsui.

Jade Garden CANTONESE   Jade Garden is part of a chain of restaurants owned by the Maxim's Group, a company that has long been wildly successful throughout Hong Kong and is popular with large Chinese families; other establishments in the group include Sichuan Garden, Shanghai Garden, Chiuchow Garden, and Peking Garden, which has a branch in Star House, in front of the Star Ferry. Because it has been welcoming foreigners for decades, Jade Garden is the place to go if you don't know much about Chinese food. A plus is the view of the old KCR clock tower and harbor afforded by some of the window-side tables. Dim sum is available for lunch from an English menu. If you'd rather come for dinner, you might consider drunken shrimp boiled in Chinese rice wine, deep-fried boneless chicken with lemon sauce, or stir-fried minced pigeon served with lettuce leaves.

Other Jade Garden locations are at Grand Century Place, Level 8, 193 Prince Edward Rd. W., Mong Kok (✆ **852/2628 9668;** MTR: Mong Kok), open daily 7:30am to 4pm and 5:30 to 11:30pm; and two locations in Causeway Bay, 463–483 Lockhart Rd. (✆ **852/2573 9339**) and 1 Hysan Ave. (✆ **852/2577 9332**), both open daily from 7:30am to midnight (MTR: Causeway Bay).

Star House (4th floor), 3 Salisbury Rd., Tsim Sha Tsui. (✆ **852/2730 6888.** www.maxims.com.hk/en. Main dishes HK$98–HK$198. AE, DC, MC, V. Mon–Sat 11am–11:30pm; Sun and holidays 10am–11:30pm. MTR: Tsim Sha Tsui.

Peking Garden ★ PEKINGESE   Another member of the well-known Maxim's Group of restaurants, elegant Peking Garden specializes in Pekingese and northern Chinese dishes, including stir-fried Pekingese noodles with shredded pork, deep-fried Mandarin fish with black vinegar sauce, braised prawns in red-wine sauce, Hunan ham with lotus seed in honey sauce, and beggar's chicken (HK$320; order it 24 hr. in advance). Try to be here during the nightly presentation of handmade noodles at 8 or 8:30pm. It's located in the Star House right in front of the Star Ferry, with harbor views.

You'll find branches in the first and second basements of Alexandra House, 16–20 Chater Rd., Central (✆ **852/2526 6456;** MTR: Central), open daily 11am to 3pm and 6 to 11pm; and in Pacific Place, 88 Queensway, Central (✆ **852/2845 8452;** MTR: Admiralty), open daily 11:30am to 11:30pm.

Star House (3rd floor), 3 Salisbury Rd., Tsim Sha Tsui. (✆ **852/2735 8211.** www.maxims.com.hk/en. Main dishes HK$90–HK$195. AE, DC, MC, V. Mon–Sat 11:30am–3pm; Sun and holidays 11am–3pm; daily 5:30–11pm. MTR: Tsim Sha Tsui.

Spice INDIAN/THAI/MALAYSIAN   This dark, cozy restaurant, with candle-lit tables, stands out from the others on Knutsford Terrace (a tiny narrow lane known for its bars and restaurants) for two reasons: It has no outdoor terrace (which is regret-table) and it is an independent, meaning it doesn't belong to any restaurant conglomer-ation (which is remarkable). In addition, its Indian and Thai chefs have created a menu that's a modern take on Indian, Thai, and Malaysian cuisine (no beef or pork is served), with standouts including the Thai soups, tandoori black cod tikka (marinated and then baked in a tandoori oven), tandoori roasted chicken in tomato curry, jumbo prawns with chili, and Malay lamb Randang (braised with galangal, lemon grass, and lime). A good choice for a quiet, romantic meal.

1 Knutsford Terrace, Tsim Sha Tsui. © **852/2191 9880.** Main dishes HK$78–HK$168; lunch buffet Mon-Fri HK$78. MC, V. Mon-Fri noon-3pm and 6-11pm; Sat-Sun and holidays 11am-11:30pm. MTR: Tsim Sha Tsui.

The Spice Market 🍴 ASIAN/BUFFET   Accessible from both the Marco Polo Prince hotel and the third floor of Harbour City shopping mall, this dark and cozy restaurant specializes in buffets offering diners a culinary adventure throughout Asia. On offer are Chinese noodles; Indian curries; Japanese sushi; and Chinese, Thai, Vietnamese, and Singaporean favorites. Included are steamed fish, satays, Mongolian stir-fried noodles, tandoori, *congee*, dim sum, soups, salads, appetizers, and desserts. True to its name, some of the foods are spicy, but others lack pizzazz, probably due to international palates unaccustomed to fiery cuisine. While none of the dishes are outstanding, most of them are good; with so many choices, you'll probably end up eating more than you should. The best deal: Saturday, Sunday, and holidays from 3:15 to 5:15pm, when the tea-time buffet costs only HK$148 per person. In addition to the usual children's prices, seniors also get a discount.

In the Marco Polo Prince, 23 Canton Rd., Tsim Sha Tsui. © **852/2113 6046.** www.marcopolohotels.com. Lunch buffet HK$168 Mon-Fri, HK$188 Sat-Sun and holidays; dinner buffet HK$318 Sun-Thurs, HK$358 Fri-Sat and holidays. AE, DC, MC, V. Mon-Fri noon-2:30pm; Sat-Sun and holidays noon-2:30pm and 3:15-5:15pm; daily 6:30-9:30pm. MTR: Tsim Sha Tsui.

Spring Deer Restaurant ★ 🍴 PEKINGESE   A longtime favorite in Hong Kong, this 40-some-year-old restaurant offers excellent Pekingese food at reasonable prices. Spring Deer is cheerful and very accessible to foreigners, but don't expect anything fancy; it's just a long, brightly lit dining hall packed with groups of loyal fans (I don't think they've remodeled since they opened). This restaurant is famous for its specialty—honey-glazed Peking duck, which costs HK$280 and is good for two to four persons. Because you'll probably have to wait 40 minutes for the duck if you order it during peak time (7:30–9:30pm), it's best to arrive either before or after the rush. Chicken dishes are also well liked, including the deep-fried chicken and walnuts in soy sauce, and the handmade noodles are excellent. Other recommendations include the hot-and-sour soup, freshwater shrimp, and stewed ham and cabbage. Most dishes come in three sizes, with the small dishes suitable for two people. Unfortunately, because Spring Deer is crowded with groups, the lone diner is apt to be neglected in the shuffle; it's best to come here only if there are at least two of you.

42 Mody Rd., Tsim Sha Tsui. © **852/2366 4012.** Reservations required. Small dishes HK$65–HK$90. AE, MC, V. Daily 11:30am-3pm and 6-11pm. MTR: Tsim Sha Tsui.

Super Star Seafood Restaurant ★ CANTONESE/SEAFOOD   Walk past the tank filled with sea creatures up to this lively Cantonese restaurant on the first floor. It's very popular with local Chinese, many of whom consider it one of Hong Kong's top Cantonese restaurants. Its menu, with pictures of major dishes, emphasizes fresh seafood, though the menu does offer other dishes (including, oddly enough, Wagyu beef). Recommended are the steamed lobster with garlic, stewed crab with Chinese wine, drunken shrimp in wine, giant scallops, stir-fried assorted mushrooms, and Royal Crab (available June–Sept). Otherwise, prices for live seafood vary with the season and depend on the size of the creature you desire. If you want a specific fish or something else in the tank, be sure to ask the price first. Stone fish is popular with the Chinese and is the restaurant's specialty. It's a rather ugly fish, expensive, and poisonous to boot if not prepared correctly. If this is what you want, you'll have to wait an hour for it to cook, though you can alternatively order a quicker, cheaper option, like the stone fish *potage* (soup) or stone fish fried roll. Dim sum is served until 4:30pm.

Super Star has many branches, including: Tsim Sha Tsui's Harbour City (4th floor), 21 Canton Rd. (✆ **852/2628 0336**; MTR: Tsim Sha Tsui); in Central at 19–27 Wyndham St. (✆ **852/2628 0826**; MTR: Central); in Wan Chai on the first floor of the Shui On Centre, 8 Harbour Rd. (✆ **852/2628 0989**; MTR: Wan Chai); and in Causeway Bay on the 10th floor of Times Square, 1 Matheson St. (✆ **852/ 2628 0886**; MTR: Causeway Bay). Call for individual open hours.

83-97 Nathan Rd., Tsim Sha Tsui. ✆ **852/2628 0339**. www.superstargroup.com.hk. Main dishes HK$88–HK$368. AE, DC, MC, V. Daily 7:30am–11pm. MTR: Tsim Sha Tsui.

Tsui Hang Village Restaurant CANTONESE   Tsui Hang is named after the home village of Dr. Sun Yat-sen (a Chinese revolutionary leader and statesman who lived from 1866–1925). Located across the street from the Mira hotel, on the ground floor of a shopping complex called Miramar Plaza, it's a windowless, bright (a bit too bright) and characterless place, but people clearly don't come here for the atmosphere. Rather, Tsui Hang is renowned for its own Cantonese original creations, but also serves traditional, home-style Chinese cooking. You might wish to start with the shredded chicken marinated with ground chili and oil or the honey-glazed barbecue pork, followed by roasted baby pigeon or the pan-fried rack of lamb with maple syrup. Dim sum is also available until 5pm.

Another Tsui Hang Village is in Central on the second floor of the New World Tower, 16–18 Queen's Rd., Central (✆ **852/2524 2012**; MTR: Central), open Monday through Friday from 11am to 3pm and 5:30 to 11:30pm, Saturday from 11am to 11:30pm, and Sunday and holidays from 10am to 11:30pm.

Miramar Shopping Centre G11, 132-134 Nathan Rd., Tsim Sha Tsui. ✆ **852/2376 2882**. www.miramar-group.com. Main dishes HK$98–HK$240; set lunch HK$298. AE, DC, MC, V. Mon-Sat 11:30am-11:30pm; Sun and holidays 10am-11:30pm. MTR: Tsim Sha Tsui.

Tutto Bene ★ ITALIAN   This is one of the oldest restaurants on Knutsford Terrace (since 1992); if the weather's pleasant, request a table on the lovely outdoor patio. Although prices seem a bit high for this neck of the woods (about HK$400 per person without drinks), the imaginative Italian food, spiced with Asian ingredients, has clearly won over a faithful clientele. Bread, served with roasted garlic, pesto, and a tomato-based cream cheese, is brought swiftly to your table, but you might want to complement it with a starter like the buffalo mozzarella with fresh tomatoes and basil dressing, or portobello mushroom caps. The antipasto platter is so huge that two can share. My personal entree favorites are the cannelloni with minced beef and spinach, and the grilled tiger prawns with shiitake mushrooms and Italian parsley butter (though the daily specials are not to be overlooked). This is a good, reliable choice for Italian food, especially if you wish to dine alfresco in Tsim Sha Tsui.

7 Knutsford Terrace, Tsim Sha Tsui. ✆ **852/2316 2116**. www.mhihk.com. Reservations recommended. Pasta HK$148–HK$248; main dishes HK$208–HK$268; set lunches HK$88–HK$128. AE, DC, MC, V. Daily noon-3pm and 6pm-1am. MTR: Tsim Sha Tsui.

Wooloomooloo Steakhouse ★ AUSTRALIAN/STEAK Wooloomooloo, is an aboriginal word originally meaning "kangaroo" or "burial place," but that's a far cry from this restaurant in Kowloon's newest luxury mall located at Kowloon Station. Consisting of two dining areas, including a "sidewalk" venue that opens onto the mall, it specializes in Australian grain-fed beef, aged for 26 days and ranging from filet mignon and rib-eye to sirloin steak, served with a choice of au jus or peppercorn, mushroom, or red-wine sauce. Freshly shucked oysters, tiger prawns, pan-seared chicken breast, and pasta are also available. During lunch time, sandwiches and burgers round out the menu.

Additional branches, all with the same open hours as below, are located in the Tsim Sha Tsui Centre, 66 Mody Rd., Tsim Sha Tsui East (✆ **852/2722 7050;** MTR: Tsim Sha Tsui); 29 Wyndham St., Central (✆ **852/2894 8010;** MTR: Central); and, with breathtaking views of the harbor and city from the 31st floor and rooftop of the Hennessey, at 256 Hennessy Rd., Wan Chai (✆ **852/2893 6960**).

Shop 2100, Elements, 1 Austin Rd., Kowloon. ✆ **852/2736 9771.** www.wooloo-mooloo.com. Main dishes HK$155–HK$550; set dinner HK$280; set lunches (Mon–Sat) HK$88–HK$138; Sun brunch HK$185. AE, DC, MC, V. Daily 11:45am–11pm. MTR: Kowloon.

Wu Kong ★★ SHANGHAINESE This basement restaurant, in the heart of Tsim Sha Tsui just off Nathan Road, is often packed with locals who come for the good food at excellent prices. More upscale than many Shanghainese restaurants, with its stark-white walls and tank of colorful fish in the foyer, it serves a variety of shark's fin dishes, as well as cold pigeon in wine sauce (its signature appetizer), braised shredded eels, braised eggplant with hot garlic meat sauce, Peking duck, and crispy duck. If you've had your fill of the more readily available and popular Cantonese and Sichuan food and are ready to experiment with other types of Chinese cuisine, this is an excellent place to start.

Another branch is located on the 13th floor of Food Forum, Times Square, 1 Matheson St., Causeway Bay (✆ **852/2506 1018;** MTR: Causeway Bay), open daily from 11:45am to 3pm and 5:45 to 11:30pm.

27 Nathan Rd. (entrance on Peking Rd.), Tsim Sha Tsui. ✆ **852/2366 7244.** www.wukong.com.hk. Main dishes HK$60–HK$200. AE, DC, MC, V. Daily 11:30am–11:15pm (last order). MTR: Tsim Sha Tsui.

Yagura ★ JAPANESE This *izakaya* (Japanese-style pub) is convenient if you're visiting nearby Temple Street Night Market. Casual yet hip, with dark wooden beams reminiscent of Japanese farmhouses, latticed screens, and an entire wall lined with sake bottles (including the restaurant's own private label), Yagura is divided into a general seating area plus a sushi counter. You can, however, order whatever you like no matter where you sit, allowing you to design your own meal. You might, for example, wish to start with sushi rolls (the Wagyu foie gras roll is a pricey but excellent choice), progress to prawn or sweet potato tempura, and finish up with noodles or one of the *robatayaki* (grilled) dishes, like grilled Wagyu beef with teriyaki or garlic soy sauce. Because the purpose of an *izakaya* is to socialize with friends, it's common to order one or two dishes at a time rather than the whole meal at once, making it a good choice for both a snack with drinks or a relaxed, drawn-out meal.

380 Nathan Rd. (below the Eaton Hotel), Tsim Sha Tsui. ✆ **852/2710 1010.** www.yagura.com.hk. Sushi rolls HK$68–HK$198; main dishes HK$88–HK$428; set dinners HK$148–HK$328; set lunches HK$78–HK$148. AE, DC, MC, V. Daily noon–3pm and 6pm–midnight. MTR: Jordan.

Inexpensive

These restaurants have branches in Kowloon: **PizzaExpress** (p. 147); **Heaven on Earth** (p. 146), offering Shanghainese, Sichuan, and Taiwanese food; **Sorabol** (p. 153), a Korean restaurant; **Three Sixty** (p. 147), a grocery store and cafeteria specializing in organic food; **Tsui Wah** (p. 153), a quick-service chain serving Chinese dishes and international fare; and **Wildfire** (p. 156), for pizza.

California Pizza Kitchen PIZZA/AMERICAN   This Beverly Hills transplant is known for its gourmet pizzas with unusual toppings, like the Thai chicken with chicken marinated in a spicy peanut-ginger and sesame sauce, mozzarella, green onions, bean sprouts, julienne carrots, cilantro, and roasted peanuts; and the Peking duck with roasted duck breast, mozzarella, soy-glazed shiitake mushrooms, crispy wontons, slivered green onions and ginger hoisin sauce. More than two dozen pizzas are listed on the menu, and I'd like to try all of them. You can also choose from a lengthy list of pastas, as well as salads and sandwiches. Although this location, at the far end of LCX (a department store catering to teenagers), is quite a hike, it has a great view of the bay and cruise ships docked at the terminal.

Other branches are on the 13th floor of Times Square in Causeway Bay (© 852/3102 9132; MTR: Causeway Bay) and near Ladies' Market at 56 Dundas St., Mong Kok (© 852/2374 0032; MTR: Mong Kok), with same hours as below.

Ocean Terminal, Level 3 LCX, Tsim Sha Tsui. © **852/3102 0375.** www.cpk.com. Pizzas HK$72–HK$112. AE, DC, MC, V. Daily 11:30am–11pm. MTR: Tsim Sha Tsui.

Chinese Kitchen VARIED CHINESE   This all-purpose Chinese-style diner is a large, brightly lit room, with round stools gathered around round tables and with what can only be called Chinese elevator music. It lists more than 150 items on the menu, including Taiwan beef noodles, Taiwan chicken with chrysanthemum, boneless Hainan chicken, roasted goose, mandarin fish in chili and aniseed sauce, stir-fried bean curd, and minced pork in chili sauce. It's popular with locals looking for a quick, cheap meal, but it also lures tourists with an English menu posted outside the door. The food isn't great, but it will do for a fast fix.

78 Canton Rd., Tsim Sha Tsui. © **852/2926 3088.** Main dishes HK$48–HK$128. MC, V. Daily 8am–midnight. MTR: Tsim Sha Tsui.

Fat Angelo's ITALIAN   With its checkered tablecloths, black-and-white family photographs, and other decor reminiscent of a new-world Italian restaurant from the first half of the 20th century, this local chain offers good value with its hearty, American renditions of Italian food, including pastas ranging from traditional spaghetti marinara to fettuccine with salmon, and main courses like rosemary roasted chicken, grilled salmon with pesto, and eggplant Parmesan, all of which come with salad and homemade bread. The emphasis here is on quantity, not quality, though the food isn't bad. And they really pack 'em in; this place is bustling, loud, and slightly chaotic, making it sometimes hard to flag down your server. Still, it makes for a fun outing with a group.

Three branches are on the other side of the harbor, at 49A–C Elgin St., Central (© **852/2973 6808;** MTR: Central); Wu Chung House, 213 Queen's Rd. E., Wan Chai (© **852/2126 7020;** MTR: Wan Chai); and in the Elizabeth House, 250 Gloucester Rd., in Causeway Bay (© **852/2574 6263;** MTR: Causeway Bay). All are open daily noon to midnight.

The Pinnacle (basement), 8 Minden Ave., Tsim Sha Tsui. ℂ **852/2730 4788.** www.fatangelos.com. Reservations recommended. Pastas HK$98–HK$148; main dishes HK$118–HK$238. AE, DC, MC, V. Daily noon–midnight. MTR: Tsim Sha Tsui.

Genki Sushi JAPANESE   Taking advantage of Hong Kong's surge in popularity of everything Japanese, this simple and always-crowded establishment offers plates of sushi, which circle around the counter via a conveyor belt. Customers seated at the counter simply reach out and take whatever they want. The color-coded plates vary in price and include traditional selections such as tuna and shrimp sushi, along with California handrolls and more unusual combinations such as corn sushi and crab salad sushi. During lunch and dinner, a line of customers is often waiting at the door (when I don't want to wait, I go straight inside and order takeout). While the food is too generic to pass in Japan, this place is as good as it gets for rock-bottom sushi prices in Hong Kong.

Other branches can be found in Shop G102 on the ground floor of Chuang's London Plaza, 219 Nathan Rd., Yau Ma Tei (ℂ **852/2736 0019;** MTR: Jordan); Shop 6, Level 4A in Langham Place, 555 Shanghai St., Mong Kok (ℂ **852/3514 4223;** MTR: Mong Kok); on the ground floor of the Far East Finance Centre, 16 Harcourt Rd., Central (ℂ **852/2865 2933;** MTR: Admiralty); Shop G05, Great Eagle Centre, 23 Harbour Rd., Wan Chai (ℂ **852/2511 8084;** MTR: Wan Chai); and Shop A, on the ground floor of the CRE Building, 303 Hennessy Rd., Wan Chai (ℂ **852/2802 7018;** MTR: Wan Chai); all are open daily 11:30am to 11:30pm.

Shops G7-9, East Ocean Centre, 98 Granville Rd., Tsim Sha Tsui East. ℂ **852/2722 6689.** Main dishes HK$9–HK$35. AE, DC, MC, V. Daily 11:30am–11:30pm. MTR: Tsim Sha Tsui.

Koh-I-Noor ★ INDIAN   Don't let the dinginess of the Peninsula Apartments building deter you from trying this restaurant. Located up on the first floor, it's modern and clean, with spotless tablecloths and a pleasant pink color scheme. What's more, service is prompt and courteous and the food is great and reasonably priced; the specialties here are North Indian tandoori and fresh seafood. The restaurant is especially proud of its king prawns, but they also make fine chicken, lamb, and vegetable curries. My favorites on the menu include the samosas, crab with coconut, and the Gosht vindaloo, a spicy mix of lamb and potatoes; mashed eggplant with onions and tomatoes; *palak paneer* (Indian cottage cheese with spinach); and garlic-flavored nan (Indian flat bread) or nan stuffed with cheese, potatoes, or other ingredients. All of it is good and recommendable.

Another branch is on the other side of the harbor in the Lan Kwai Fong nightlife district, on the first floor of the California Entertainment Building, 34 D'Aguilar St., Central (ℂ **852/2877 9706;** MTR: Central), open Monday through Saturday from noon to 2:30pm and daily from 6 to 11pm.

Peninsula Apartments, 16C Mody Rd., Tsim Sha Tsui. ℂ **852/2368 3065.** www.lankwaifong.com. Curries HK$75–HK$100; tandoori HK$80–HK$135; lunch buffet (Mon–Fri) HK$58 for vegetarian, HK$75 with meat. AE, DC, MC, V. Daily 11:30am–2:30pm and 6–11:30pm. MTR: Tsim Sha Tsui.

Main Street Deli ★★ 🏛 AMERICAN/LIGHT FARE   Hong Kong's first traditional New York–style deli comes as close as you can get to the real thing—its chef was trained at the 2nd Avenue Deli in the Big Apple and the authentic ingredients are flown in from New York. The tiled floor, open kitchen, deli case, strung sausages, and wood furniture add to the ambience, but the chandeliers left over from a previous restaurant seem woefully out of place. Still, serious deli lovers will find plenty to love, including latkes, matzo ball soup, salads, pizza, pastas, burgers, all-day breakfasts, and a large selection of three-decker and hot deli sandwiches, including a Reuben, the restaurant's signature sandwich (if you're counting carbs, order the Naked Reuben, which comes without bread). This is a lifesaver for those in desperate need of Western comfort food. Portions are so generous that the restaurant has instituted the doggy bag, a previously unknown concept in Hong Kong. Try to save room for the cheesecake.

In the Langham, 8 Peking Rd., Tsim Sha Tsui. ✆ **852/2375 1133**, ext. 7883. http://hongkong.langham hotels.com. Main dishes HK$128–HK$358; set meal HK$228. AE, DC, MC, V. Sun–Thurs 10am–10pm; Fri–Sat 10am–11pm. MTR: Tsim Sha Tsui.

Mido Café 🏠 VARIED CHINESE/WESTERN   I'm not sure how to classify the food here, but that's beside the point. This retro diner, open since 1950, is a time capsule with its antique cash register, mosaic tiled walls, ceiling fans, hard booths, and windows overlooking the Tin Hau Temple across the street (head upstairs to the second level for the best views and ambience). The varied Chinese dishes and Chinese versions of Western fare is so-so, ranging from pork chops and curry chicken with rice to fried noodles with sliced pork. The cashier couldn't be more indifferent, and the kitchen and bathroom wouldn't meet U.S. regulations (a local Chinese friend dismissed the Mido as being too low class for foreigners). Still, this old-timer is unique in fast-changing Hong Kong. No wonder it's been used in countless movies.

63 Temple St., Yau Ma Tei. ✆ **852/2384 6402.** Main dishes HK$45–HK$110. No credit cards. Daily 8:30am–9:30pm (last order). MTR: Yau Ma Tei.

Nomads ★ 🏠 ASIAN/BUFFET   This very popular Mongolian restaurant allows diners to select their own raw ingredients for one-dish meals and pizzas prepared by short-order cooks. All-you-can-eat lunches and dinners offer vegetables, meats, seafood, sauces, noodles, rice, and spices, spread buffet-style along a counter together with salads, and dessert. Sheepskin-draped chairs, rawhide lampshades, animal skins, and tribal weaponry hung on walls transport this restaurant straight into the Mongolia of our fantasies, making dining here not only cheap but fun.

55 Kimberley Rd., Tsim Sha Tsui. ✆ **852/2722 0733.** www.igors.com. Lunch buffet HK$68 Mon–Fri, HK$80 Sat–Sun and holidays; dinner buffet HK$178. AE, DC, MC, V. Daily noon–2:30pm and 6:30–10:30pm. MTR: Tsim Sha Tsui.

The Salisbury 🏊 INTERNATIONAL/BUFFET   One of the cheapest places for a filling meal in Tsim Sha Tsui is the YMCA's main restaurant, a bright and cheerful dining hall on the fourth floor of the south tower. It serves both Western and Asian food, with an a la carte menu offering sandwiches, pastas, and Asian dishes. Best, however, are the lunch and dinner buffets. The lunch buffet includes a roast-beef wagon, as well as other meat dishes, soups, salads, and desserts, while the dinner buffet includes many more entrees plus one soda or beer. A rare plus for seniors: They get a discount off the lunch buffet. While the food won't win any culinary awards, there's enough variety that probably all can find something they like. And if the prices here are too high, a cheaper ground-floor cafeteria, the Mall Cafe, offers sandwiches and daily specials.

In the Salisbury YMCA, 41 Salisbury Rd., Tsim Sha Tsui. ✆ **852/2268 7818.** www.ymcahk.org.hk. Lunch buffet HK$115; Sun brunch buffet HK$158; dinner buffet HK$228 Mon–Thurs, HK$258 Fri–Sun. AE, DC, MC, V. Mon–Sat noon–2:30pm; Sun 11:30am–2:30pm; daily 6:15–9:30pm. MTR: Tsim Sha Tsui.

Spaghetti House 😊 PIZZA/ITALIAN   The Spaghetti House chain already has 24 branches throughout Hong Kong—and there will probably be more by the time you read this. They're popular with families, young Chinese couples on dates, and foreigners who have had their fill of Chinese food and crave something familiar but cheap. Spaghetti and pizza cooked American style or with Asian ingredients are the specialties here, and the decor and atmosphere resemble those of an American pizza parlor. Choose from more than two dozen varieties of spaghetti with both Western and Asian toppings, as well as pizzas (in two sizes). Although the food is only average in quality, the quantity makes up for it; most orders can be taken out.

Branches include 38 Haiphong Rd., Tsim Sha Tsui (© 852/2376 1015; MTR: Tsim Sha Tsui); 221 Nathan Rd., Yau Ma Tei (© 852/2377 2005; MTR: Jordan); 594 Nathan Rd., Mong Kok (© 852/2388 4379; MTR: Mong Kok); Admiralty Centre, 18 Harcourt Rd., Central (© 852/2866 1522; MTR: Admiralty); China Overseas Building, 139 Hennessy Rd., Wan Chai (© 852/2529 0901; MTR: Wan Chai); 314 Hennessy Rd., Wan Chai (© 852/2972 2143; MTR: Wan Chai or Causeway Bay); and Matheson Centre, 3–5 Matheson St., Causeway Bay (© 852/ 2234 0605; MTR: Causeway Bay). All are open daily 11am to 11pm or later.

57 Peking Rd., Tsim Sha Tsui. © **852/2367 1683.** www.spaghettihouse.com. Individual-size pizza and pasta HK$64–HK$158. AE, DC, MC, V. Daily 11am–11:30pm. MTR: Tsim Sha Tsui.

CENTRAL DISTRICT

Very Expensive

Caprice ★★★ FRENCH Ensconced in the sleek Four Seasons Hotel Hong Kong, this is one of *the* places to dine in Hong Kong, and deservedly so. (Need I add that reservations are a must?) Caprice garners high marks for its innovative take on French classics and its gorgeous setting. A glowing catwalk lends a celebrity feel upon entering the dining room, which mirrors the cuisine's contemporary/classic theme with portraits of women that combine an Art Nouveau style with Chinese influences, shimmering custom-made chandeliers, an open kitchen, and dramatic views of Victoria Harbour. The knowledgeable staff is happy to make recommendations from the menu, orchestrated around the seasons and drawing inspiration from provincial France. You might, for example, opt for the langoustine ravioli with veal sweetbreads and chanterelle mushrooms in a delicate shellfish bisque, followed by Kagoshima beef or roast Bresse chicken with morel mushrooms.

In the Four Seasons Hotel Hong Kong, 8 Finance St., Central. © **852/3196 8860.** www.fourseasons. com/hongkong. Reservations required. Main courses HK$400–HK$770. AE, DC, MC, V. Daily noon– 2:30pm and 6-10:30pm. MTR: Central.

The French Window ★★★ FRENCH You're not sure what to expect when walking through this restaurant's slightly industrial-looking long and narrow entry (it's supposed to emote the dim hallway of a French chateau), but there's no mistaking you're in Hong Kong when you reach the dining room with its fantastic harbor views and contemporary, sleek setting. But it's the cuisine that really wows, with creative interpretations of classic French dishes that are presented so beautifully they're like works of art. Luckily, the food tastes as good as it looks, with fresh ingredients from around the world on the seasonal menu, which always includes variations of steak, seafood, and dishes like pan-seared lamb tenderloin. You can easily spend a fortune here—*if* you can snag a reservation.

Shop 3101, Podium Level 3, ifc mall, Central. © **852/2393 3812.** www.thefrenchwindow.hk. Reservations required. Main courses HK$400–HK$490; set dinners HK$800–HK$1,480; set lunch HK$590. AE, DC, MC, V. Mon-Sat noon-2:30pm; Sun and holidays 11:30am-3:30pm; daily 6-10pm. MTR: Central or Hong Kong.

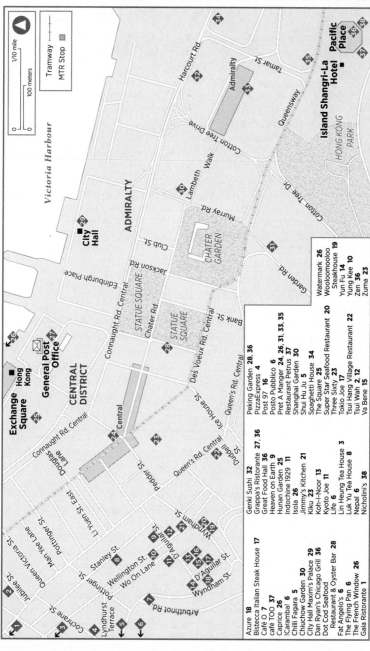

Tramway
MTR Stop

Victoria Harbour

ADMIRALTY

CHATER GARDEN

STATUE SQUARE

CENTRAL DISTRICT

Island Shangri-La Hotel

Pacific Place

HONG KONG PARK

Azure **18**
Bistecca Italian Steak House **17**
Café O **7**
café TOO **37**
Caprice **26**
ICarambal **6**
Chilli Fagara **5**
Chiuchow Garden **30**
City Hall Maxim's Palace **29**
Dan Ryan's Chicago Grill **36**
Dot Cod Seafood
  Restaurant & Oyster Bar **28**
Fat Angelo's **6**
The Flying Pan **6**
The French Window **26**
Gaia Ristorante **1**

Genki Sushi **32**
Grappa's Ristorante **27, 36**
Great Food Hall **36**
Heaven on Earth **9**
Hunan Garden **25**
Indochine 1929 **11**
Isola **26**
Jimmy's Kitchen **21**
Kiku **23**
Koh-I-Noor **13**
Kyoto Joe **11**
Life **6**
Lin Heung Tea House **3**
Luk Yu Tea House **8**
Nepal **6**
Nicholini's **38**

Peking Garden **28, 36**
PizzaExpress **4**
Post 97 **16**
Posto Pubblico **6**
Pret A Manger **24, 26, 31, 33, 35**
Restaurant Petrus **37**
Shanghai Garden **30**
Shui Hu Ju **5**
Spaghetti House **34**
The Square **25**
Super Star Seafood Restaurant **20**
Three Sixty **23**
Tokio Joe **17**
Tsui Hang Village Restaurant **22**
Tsui Wah **2, 12**
Va Bene **15**

Watermark **26**
Wooloomooloo
  Steakhouse **19**
Yun Fu **14**
Yung Kee **10**
Zen **36**
Zuma **23**

Cafe Deco (p. 154) If the spectacular views of Hong Kong don't hold your kids' attention at this solid international eatery, the children's play corner will.

Dan Ryan's Chicago Grill (p. 126) These two restaurant/bars serve some of the best burgers in town, as well as huge deli sandwiches. There are plenty of other American dishes, and a children's menu as well.

The Flying Pan (p. 145) If *congee* (rice porridge) is not your kid's idea of breakfast, this restaurant specializing in American breakfasts offers lots of familiar Western choices, including a children's menu offering French toast, waffles, and grilled cheese sandwiches.

Spaghetti House (p. 133) Locations all over town and low prices make this family chain a winner. The menu is filled with two dozen different kinds of spaghetti, as well as a wide range of pizza.

Top Deck, at the Jumbo (p. 156) A short shuttle by boat through Aberdeen Harbour should catch any child's attention, but this alfresco seafood restaurant on top of a huge floating restaurant follows through with a children's menu and, during Sunday brunch, a play corner, allowing parents to relax as they soak in the views and feast on everything from salmon and sushi to steaks and curries.

Wildfire (p. 156) Before heading to Stanley Beach, take the family to this restaurant on the top floor of the historic Murray House, with dreamy views of the South China Sea from its outside terrace, a play area for children, and handcrafted pizzas, salads, pastas, and main dishes like barbecue pork ribs at reasonable prices.

Nicholini's ★★★ ITALIAN Most of Hong Kong's Italian restaurants seem to fall into one of two categories—highbrow and sophisticated, or rustic and trattoria-like. This one is a bit of both, combining elegance and lightheartedness in keeping with the Conrad Hotel's overall playful style. The dining room bathes patrons in soothing colors of gold; if you're a fan of Murano glass, be sure to check out the collection spread throughout the restaurant. The cuisine is northern Italian, combined with inventiveness—some claim it's the best Italian restaurant in Hong Kong. Entrees range from roasted sea bass with herbs to veal shank *osso buco* in a vegetable orange-flavored sauce served with saffron risotto. Pasta—like the popular angel hair pasta with Maine lobster, fresh tomato, and basil—is available as either a side dish or a main course. For dessert, the Chef's Special Dessert Sampler solves the dilemma for those who want it all. The extensive wine list features mainly Italian selections, and the service is beyond reproach . . . too bad there's no view.

In the Conrad Hong Kong, Pacific Place, 88 Queensway Rd., Central. ℰ **852/2521 3838,** ext. 8210. www. conradhotels.com. Reservations recommended. Main courses HK$358–HK$788; set dinners HK$618–HK$828; set lunches Mon–Fri HK$328–HK$418; Sun brunch HK$638. AE, DC, MC, V. Mon–Fri noon–3pm; Sun 11am–3pm; daily 6:30–11pm. MTR: Central.

Restaurant Petrus ★★★ 👖 FRENCH Simply put, the views from this 56th-floor restaurant are breathtaking. In fact, it is probably the best of any hotel restaurant on the Hong Kong side; the only place with a better view is atop Victoria Peak. If you can bear to take your eyes off the windows, you'll find the restaurant decorated like a French castle, with the obligatory crystal chandeliers, black marble and gilded columns, thick draperies, Impressionist paintings, murals gracing dome-shaped ceilings, and a harpist playing softly in the background. The traditional haute cuisine is spiced sparingly to complement the dishes' natural aroma and flavor. The menu changes often but has included such intriguing choices as sautéed frog legs and veal sweetbread in a watercress sauce or poached salmon with garlic, black olives, and artichokes. As expected, the wine list—particularly bordeaux—is among the best in Hong Kong, if not the world, with 12,000 bottles in stock. With the impressive blend of great views, refined ambience, excellent cuisine, tables spaced far enough apart for intimacy, and professional staff, this restaurant is a top choice for a splurge, romantic dinner, or special celebration.

In the Island Shangri-La (56th floor), Pacific Place, Supreme Court Rd., Central. © **852/2820 8590.** www.shangri-la.com. Reservations recommended. Jacket required for dinner. Main courses HK$390–HK$980; set dinner HK$1,280; set lunches HK$368–HK$428. AE, DC, MC, V. Daily noon–3pm and 6:30–11pm. MTR: Admiralty.

Expensive

Azure ★★ CONTINENTAL   Lan Kwai Fong isn't exactly known for sophisticated dining, but this alluring venue rises above it—literally. Located on the top two floors of the Hotel LKF, it offers city views from its lofty perch. On the 29th floor is a casual bar with a pool table and free canapés daily from 5:30 to 8:30pm, while a white, winding staircase gives dramatic entrance to the tall-ceilinged restaurant one floor up, decorated in cool blue colors accented by deep-blue water goblets on all the tables. The menu is an innovative twist on classic European cuisine, with artfully presented dishes. It's hard to resist the six-layer blue crab salad, with its layers of blue crab, avocado, smoked salmon, crispy pancetta, tomato, mesclun greens, and Dijon vinaigrette, which you might follow with lobster fettucini with black truffle and then Australian lamb chop. Take note that a DJ spinning hip-hop takes over from 10:30pm to 3am Thursday to Saturday, making this just one of many LKF hip venues.

LKF Hotel, 29th floor, 33 Wyndham St., Central. © **852/3518 9330.** www.azure.hk. Reservations required. Main dishes HK$218–HK$688; set dinners HK$380–HK$570; set lunch Mon–Fri HK$158. AE, DC, MC, V. Daily 11:30am–2:30pm and 6:30–11pm (last order). MTR: Central.

Gaia Ristorante ★ 👪 ITALIAN   If you can't beat 'em, join 'em. That's the way I feel about all the new construction encroaching on the quaint Western District. This restaurant, ensconced in the colossal Grand Millennium Plaza building on the border between the Central and Western districts, has won me over with a great terrace, surrounded by lush trees and bushes that create the illusion of dining in a park. The contemporary interior is also inviting, with glass windows overlooking the terrace and a blindingly red bar off to one side. And the menu is the perfect accompaniment. Temptations include wafer-thin Roman-style pizzas, homemade pasta tossed in a Sangiovese-marinated rabbit stew ragout, or the veal with shaved black truffle. I also love coming for lunch, when the set meal includes a sumptuous antipasto buffet. The wine list is heavy on Italian imports.

Grand Millennium Plaza (look for the advertising screen), 181 Queen's Rd. Central, Central. © **852/2167 8200.** www.gaiaristorante.com. Reservations necessary. Pizza and pasta HK$158–HK$268; main dishes HK$238–HK$368; set lunch HK$248. AE, DC, MC, V. Daily noon–3pm and 6:30–11pm. MTR: Sheung Wan.

Va Bene ★★ ITALIAN   This stylish Italian restaurant, in the middle of Central's Lan Kwai Fong nightlife district, strives for elegant simplicity in both food and decor, making it a good choice for a romantic meal away from the surrounding hubbub. The long, dimly lit dining room's most eye-catching features are a wine cellar that extends the length of one wall and a sky-blue ceiling etched with floating clouds. Serving consistently creative and excellent trattoria cuisine from across Italy, it has been popular with Hong Kong's well-heeled expat community for more than 2 decades. Perhaps you'll want to start with super-thin carpaccio, followed by one of the home-made pastas like fresh pasta pockets filled with meat ragout in sage, butter, bacon, and black truffle. As a main course, you can choose from a number of veal, beef, and seafood dishes cooked to draw out natural flavors, including black cod with red bell pepper sauce and fennel-flavored zucchini. Good Italian wines, great desserts, and attentive service round out the meal.

17-22 Lan Kwai Fong, Central. © **852/2845 5577.** www.vabeneristorante.com. Reservations recommended. Main courses HK$238–HK$338; set lunch HK$198. AE, DC, MC, V. Mon–Sat noon–2:30pm; Sun–Thurs 6:30–11:30pm; Fri–Sat 6:30pm–midnight. MTR: Central.

Zuma ★★★ JAPANESE Located in the upscale Landmark shopping center, Zuma is a contemporary twist on the casual Japanese *izakaya* style of eating and drinking, in which dishes are shared and ordered in no particular order (you can, for example, order a couple dishes to start with and then add a few as you wish). A seductive spiraling staircase joins the main dining room and outdoor terrace to the lounge and sake bar (where you should order the Rubabu, a rhubarb-infused sake with vodka and passion fruit). The menu also offers contemporary interpretations of authentic Japanese cuisine, including a wide range of sushi, sashimi, and maki rolls (like the salmon, *hamachi,* and sea bass with avocado and sesame-lime sauce); grilled foods (like Hokkaido scallops with grated apple, wasabi, and sweet soy sauce; or Japanese Wagyu beef with ponzu and wasabi); and signature dishes like miso-marinated black cod wrapped in *hoba* (magnolia) leaf. Tasting menus require a two-person minimum order and must be ordered by the whole table. In short, this is a fun, sophisticated place for a meal, snack, or a drink.

The Landmark, levels 5 and 6, 15 Queen's Rd. Central, Central. © **852/3657 6388.** www.zumarestaurant. com. Reservations recommended. Main dishes HK$180–HK$1,200; tasting set menu HK$870–HK$1,280; set lunches HK$290–HK$480; Sun brunch HK$428. AE, DC, MC, V. Mon–Sat noon–3pm; Sun 11:30am–3pm; daily 6–11pm. MTR: Central.

Moderate

Several moderately priced restaurants already covered in the Tsim Sha Tsui section have branches in Central: **Dan Ryan's Chicago Grill** (p. 126), located in Pacific Place and offering American classics; **Peking Garden** (p. 127), serving food from Beijing; **Super Star Seafood Restaurant** (p. 128), known for its Cantonese seafood and dim sum; **Tsui Hang Village Restaurant** (p. 129), serving Cantonese fare; and **Wooloomooloo Steakhouse** (p. 130), an Australian import.

Bistecca Italian Steak House ★ ✔ ITALIAN/STEAK Given the local love for Italian cuisine and, more recently, beef, how could this place serving both go wrong? It has an unlikely home in Lan Kwai Fong on the second floor of a small building (where the rent is cheaper), making for a crowded but convivial atmosphere as waiters dash to bring orders from the bustling open kitchen to diners from around the globe. You'll want your rib-eye, T-bone, sirloin, or filet—carefully aged, rubbed with sea salt and peppercorns, charcoal grilled, and drizzled with Tuscan olive oil and lemon—as rare as you can stand it and served with your choice of sauce (from Chianti mustard to Gorgonzola cream). A few nonbeef entrees, from chicken to grilled tiger prawns, as well as pasta and sides like creamed spinach and mashed potatoes, round out the menu.

15–16 Lan Kwai Fong, Central. ℂ **852/2525 1308.** www.diningconcepts.com.hk. Reservations recommended. Main dishes HK$258–HK$488; set lunches HK$118–HK$168. AE, DC, MC, V. Daily noon–3pm and 6–11pm. MTR: Central.

café TOO ★★★ 🏮 INTERNATIONAL/BUFFET   Leave it to the Island Shangri-La to have taken a common dining concept and turn it into a feasting extravaganza. Light and airy, with windows overlooking the lush greenery of Hong Kong Park, this restaurant features open kitchens and seven "stations" of food presentations spread throughout the room, thereby dispelling the assembly-line atmosphere of most buffets and giving it a theatrical touch. Browse the appetizer-and-salad table, a cold seafood counter with sushi, fresh oysters, crab, and other delights, a Chinese section with dim sum and main courses, Western hot entrees, noodles that are prepared to order and run the gamut from Chinese to Italian, and Asian dishes from Thai curries to Indian tandoori. But don't fill up, because the dessert table is the crowning glory. Although there's an a la carte menu, too, I can't imagine forgoing the buffet. Come here after shopping in Pacific Place or visiting the park's Flagstaff House Museum of Tea Ware.

In the Island Shangri-La Hong Kong, Pacific Place, Supreme Court Rd., Central. ℂ **852/2820 8571.** www.shangri-la.com. Reservations recommended. Lunch buffet HK$298 Mon–Fri, HK$348 Sat–Sun and holidays; dinner buffet HK$438 Mon–Thurs, HK$478 Fri–Sun and holidays. AE, DC, MC, V. Mon–Fri noon–2:30pm; Sat–Sun and holidays noon–3pm; Mon–Thurs 6:30–10pm; Fri–Sun and holidays 6–11pm. MTR: Admiralty.

Chiuchow Garden 🍴 CHIU CHOW   Chandeliers and a multitude of round tables draped in tablecloths greet hungry diners at this popular Central eatery, renowned for its classic and original Chiu Chow dishes. While shark's fin, abalone, and bird's nest are the obvious stars of the show here, seafood dishes are also plentiful, such as steamed or boiled Mandarin fish or steamed scallops and bean curd in a black bean sauce. Surprises on the menu include pie stuffed with shredded chicken in a Portuguese sauce, foie gras served three ways (pan seared, terrine, and crème brûlée), and the bird's nest with mango dessert.

Hutchinson House, 2nd floor, Murray Rd., Central. ℂ **852/2536 0833.** www.maxims.com.hk/en. Main dishes HK$88–HK$198; set lunches for 2 people HK$396–HK$576. AE, DC, MC, V. Daily 11:30am–3pm and 6–11:30pm. MTR: Central.

Dot Cod Seafood Restaurant & Oyster Bar SEAFOOD   The Hong Kong Cricket Club owns this basement restaurant (members get a 30% discount), its location chosen for nostalgic reasons: Until the 1970s, the club practiced in nearby Chater Garden. Decorated in a nautical theme and popular for power breakfasts and lunches (though tables placed too close together rule out secretive deals), it takes its name from the popular choice of cod in its menu but is also a play on the dot.com era. Service is prompt and polished. You might start with the prawn cocktail, followed by such signature dishes as the cod fish and chips, rack of lamb, or one of the sustainable seafood selections cooked to your specifications; alternatively, you can eat more cheaply at the bar, which also serves light snacks and bar food. In any case, I always feel a bit like Alice in yesteryear when I eat lunch in the netherworld here, surrounded by business suits and hardly another woman in sight.

Prince's Building, 10 Chater (entrance on Statue Sq.), Central. ℂ **852/2810 6988.** www.dotcod.com. Reservations recommended. Main dishes HK$188–HK$348; set lunches HK$198–HK$228. AE, DC, MC, V. Mon–Sat 7:30am–10:30pm (last order). MTR: Central.

Grappa's Ristorante ★ ITALIAN   If you like to eat pizza or pasta to the accompaniment of noise, commotion, and lots of people parading past, this is the place for you. With its big glass windows overlooking the shops of Pacific Place, you can't escape the fact that this place is in a mall; the open kitchen, while providing some diversion, adds to the noise. Still, this is certainly the best place for moderately priced Italian food anywhere in the area, despite its strictly standard fare, because all the bread (served with olive oil and fresh Parmesan and brought swiftly to each table), sauces, pasta, sausages, and desserts are made in the restaurant's own kitchen. The salads are good here, as are the dozen or so authentic Italian pizzas and the even larger selection of pastas. The entrees lean toward the tried and true, from veal-shank stew in a Barolo wine sauce to roasted lamb chops with rosemary.

For more atmospheric dining, head to Grappa's Cellar in the basement of Jardine House, Connaught Road Central (**℗ 852/2521 2322;** MTR: Central), open daily 10am to 11pm and offering live jazz several nights a month.

Pacific Place, 88 Queensway, Central. **℗ 852/2868 0086.** www.elgrande.com.hk. Reservations recommended. Pizza and pasta HK$98–HK$210; main courses HK$130–HK$270; set lunches Mon–Fri HK$165–HK$195. AE, DC, MC, V. Daily 11:30am–11pm. MTR: Admiralty.

Hunan Garden ★★ 🍴 HUNANESE   Although the chili-rich cuisine of Hunan province is quite popular in Taiwan, this has long been one of the few Hunan restaurants in Hong Kong. It's puzzling, because Hunanese food is very spicy, and one would think that with the booming popularity of Thai and Sichuan food in the SAR Hunanese food would eventually catch on. In any case, this restaurant does a thriving business, especially for lunch due to its location next to Hong Kong Station and ifc mall. It's a great restaurant, both in decor and food, and even has live Chinese classical music from 7 to 9pm nightly. Start your meal with one of the soups like the Hunan minced-chicken soup, a clear soup base with ginger and mousse of chicken. If you like hot-and-spicy foods, you'll love the braised bean curd with shredded pork and chili, developed by one of Hunan province's most famous chefs. Other recommended dishes include the honey-glazed Hunan ham served in pancakes, deep-fried chicken with chili and garlic, and filet of fish with minced yellow bean. As a special treat, try one of the Hunanese wines or the tea with longan (an Asian fruit) and pear.

A second branch is on the 13th floor of Times Square's Food Forum, Causeway Bay (**℗ 852/2506 9288;** MTR: Causeway Bay), open daily 11:30am to 3pm, Monday to Saturday 6:30 to 11:30pm, and Sunday and holidays 5:30 to 11:30pm.

The Forum (3rd floor), Exchange Square, Central. **℗ 852/2868 2880.** Reservations required, especially for lunch. Main dishes HK$88–HK$188. AE, DC, MC, V. Daily 11:30am–3pm and 5:30–11:30pm. MTR: Central.

Indochine 1929 ★★ VIETNAMESE   This Lan Kwai Fong eatery serves delicious Indochinese cuisine to a consciously trendy crowd. Start with the signature spring rolls stuffed with shrimp, pork, and herbs or the hot-and-sour fish soup. Other specialties are the fish prepared Hanoi-style, with dill, turmeric, and vermicelli; the salt-and-pepper soft-shell crabs; and the beef tenderloin with tomato. If you've never had Vietnamese food, this restaurant with a knowledgeable staff and laid-back atmosphere should make you an instant convert.

The Plaza (2nd Floor), 21 D'Aguilar, Central. **℗ 852/2869 7399.** www.lankwaifong.com. Reservations recommended. Main dishes HK$128–HK$280; set lunches HK$106–HK$162. AE, DC, MC, V. Mon–Sat noon–2:30pm; daily 6:30–11pm. MTR: Central.

Isola ★★ 🏛 ITALIAN   This restaurant bills itself as Hong Kong's most stunning waterfront restaurant—quite a tall order. But while other properties can compete with the views, what sets Isola apart is its extensive outdoor terrace, along with a popular bar with views and a balcony. Even in inclement weather, the restaurant's crisp white interior with a glass facade is an inviting venue. But don't expect a quiet tête-à-tête, because this bustling place, with an open kitchen, does a roaring business. The pasta is handmade; the large, stone-baked, thin-crust pizzas can be ordered with different ingredients on each half (making them good for two to share); and all the meat and fish arrive fresh at the restaurant instead of frozen. Main dishes may include oven-broiled black cod with lemon, basil, and sautéed vegetables, and roasted veal chop with a gravy wine sauce. Lunch is a good time for grazers, who can browse the antipasti buffet and add one of seven main dishes for a satisfying set meal.

Level 3, ifc mall, Central. 🖊 **852/2383 8765.** www.isolabarandgrill.com. Reservations required. Pizza and pasta HK$138–HK$228; main courses HK$178–HK$368; set lunch HK$248 Mon–Fri, HK$288 Sat–Sun and holidays. AE, DC, MC, V. Daily noon–2:30pm; Sun–Thurs 6:30–11pm; Fri–Sat 6:30–11:30pm. MTR: Central.

Jimmy's Kitchen ★ CONTINENTAL   This restaurant opened in 1928, a replica of a similar American-owned restaurant in Shanghai. Now one of Hong Kong's oldest Western restaurants, Jimmy's Kitchen has had several homes before moving to its present site in the 1960s. The clubby atmosphere reminds me of an American steakhouse, with white tablecloths, dark-wood paneling, and elevator music, but it's a favorite with older foreigners living in Hong Kong and serves dependably good, unpretentious European comfort food. An extensive a la carte menu offers salads and soups, steaks, chicken, Indian curries, and a seafood selection that includes sole, scallops, and the local garoupa. It's also a good place for corned beef and cabbage, beef stroganoff, and hearty German fare, including Wiener schnitzel (breaded veal) and pig's knuckle.

A branch of Jimmy's Kitchen is located at 29 Ashley Rd., Tsim Sha Tsui (🖊 **852/2376 0327;** MTR: Tsim Sha Tsui), open the same hours.

1 Wyndham St., Central. 🖊 **852/2526 5293.** www.jimmys.com. Main courses HK$148–HK$370. AE, DC, MC, V. Daily 11:30am–3pm and 6–11pm. MTR: Central.

Kiku JAPANESE   Its location in the basement of the Landmark explains the high prices of this traditionally decorated restaurant (somebody has to pay the rent). Still, it offers a wide range of Japan's best-known dishes, including sushi, sashimi, *shabu-shabu* and *sukiyaki* (sliced beef cooked in a broth at your table), grilled fish, and stone-grilled *teppanyaki* beef, with prawn tempura and obento lunch boxes offered for lunch. Lattices and paper lanterns set the mood and help divide the dining area into smaller areas, but try to get a booth for more intimate dining or opt for the sushi counter. Service is a bit slow, so come only if you want to relax over your meal.

The Landmark, basement, 15 Queen's Rd. Central, Central. 🖊 **852/2521 3344.** Main courses HK$150–HK$330; set dinners HK$280–HK$360; set lunches HK$150–HK$350. AE, DC, MC, V. Mon–Sat 11:30am–3pm; Sun noon–3pm; daily 6–10:30pm. MTR: Central.

Post 97 ★ 🍴 CONTINENTAL   This is one of the old-timers in Lan Kwai Fong, opened in 1982 (its name is a cheeky reference to the handover, which seemed far in the future at the time), but it's every bit as popular as it was before all the surrounding competition moved in. That proves it must be doing something right, which it is:

down-to-earth good food, reasonable prices, cheerful staff, an inviting bar with daily happy hour (3–8pm), and a comfortable, laid-back atmosphere where diners feel at home. Catering to area businesspeople during the day and to revelers in the evening, it offers an all-day/all-night menu that includes breakfast items like eggs Benedict, salads, sandwiches and burgers, pastas, fish and chips, and bangers and mash, as well as a weekday lunch salad buffet (HK$115 just for the buffet; HK$30 extra to add a main course). A relaxing spot in hectic Lan Kwai Fong.

9 Lan Kwai Fong, Central. ℂ 852/2186 1817. www.ninetysevengroup.com. Main dishes HK$90–HK$208; lunch buffet Mon–Fri HK$115–HK$145. AE, DC, MC, V. Sun–Thurs 9:30am–1am; Fri–Sat 9:30am–2am. MTR: Central.

Posto Pubblico ★ 🍴 ITALIAN It was a long time coming, but restaurants with an ecological nod towards mother earth have finally arrived in Hong Kong, and this one leads the pack when it comes to sourcing organic foods from local farmers. Evoking a slight warehouse feel with its brick walls, tiled floor, and tall ceiling with exposed pipes, this open-fronted SoHo neighborhood restaurant serves homemade bread, mozzarella made from scratch, and a limited menu of pasta and hormone-free meats, including grass-fed New York strip and chicken Milanese. The lunch menu adds sandwiches (like veal-meatball Parmigiana), while pizza and drinks are available daily from 3 to 6pm. Also setting a new trend is its no service charge policy, leaving diners to tip what they think their service was worth.

28 Elgin St., Central. ℂ 852/2577 7160. www.postopubblico.com. Main dishes HK$180–HK$220; set lunch HK$120. AE, DC, MC, V. Mon–Fri 11:30am–11pm; Sat–Sun and holidays 11am–11pm. MTR: Central.

The Press Room ★★ 🍷 FRENCH Occupying a site once held in the 1920s by *Hua Qiao Daily* newspaper (hence the restaurant's name), near the famous Man Mo Temple in what is otherwise a fairly traditional Chinese neighborhood, this is yet more proof of the relentless westward gentrification along Hollywood Road. Still, there's little to reproach in this bustling brasserie that would look right at home in Paris or New York with its huge blackboards scribbled with the daily specials, open kitchen, artwork, and tables packed closely together. Although the emphasis is on French cuisine—with the likes of classic beef bourguignon, as well as a huge selection of oysters from around the world and French desserts—it also serves Italian bistro food and burgers. The wine list is impressive for an independent restaurant, as is the walk-in cheese room in Classified, the restaurant's adjacent shop selling gourmet foods, wine, and artisanal cheeses imported directly from producers in France, Switzerland, Ireland, and elsewhere.

108 Hollywood Rd., Central. ℂ 852/2525 3444. Reservations required. www.thepressroom.com.hk. Main dishes HK$202–HK$310; set dinner HK$260; set lunch Mon–Fri HK$132. AE, DC, MC, V. Mon–Fri noon–11pm; Sat–Sun 10am–11pm. MTR: Central.

Shanghai Garden SHANGHAINESE This upscale restaurant (part of the Maxim's group of restaurants) does a good job in presentation and cuisine. Since Shanghai does not have its own cuisine, the dishes served here are from Peking, Nanking, Sichuan, Hangchow, and Wuxi. The menu is extensive, including bird's nest and chicken soup or shark's-fin soup, such cold dishes as sautéed eel, and such main courses as sautéed prawns, chicken in rice wine sauce (drunken chicken), beggar's chicken (which costs HK$350 and must be ordered in advance), fried Shanghai noodles with spare ribs, and Peking duck (HK$320). This place, pleasantly and soothingly decorated, does a roaring business, especially for lunch, when it also serves dim sum.

Hutchinson House (1st floor), Murray Rd., Central. ✆ **852/2524 8181.** Reservations recommended. Main dishes HK$80–HK$168; dim sum HK$30–HK$64. AE, DC, MC, V. Daily 11:30am–3pm and 5:30–11:30pm. MTR: Central.

Shui Hu Ju SICHUAN   Its name is written only in Chinese, but look for the large antique Chinese door on the left side of the uphill climb from Elgin Street. Inside is a small, dark, and simple dining room, looking somehow a bit mysterious and other-worldly, but it serves good honest cuisine, mostly Sichuan but also from other regions of China. Recommended dishes include the deep-fried black chicken with Sichuan chili, crispy mutton in Peking style, and stewed beef ribs wrapped with lotus leaf. Tables are too close together for real intimacy, yet somehow you don't think about it once the feast begins.

68 Peel St., Central. ✆ **852/2869 6927.** Reservations recommended. Main dishes HK$108–HK$368. AE, DC, MC, V. Daily 6–11pm. MTR: Central.

The Square ★ CANTONESE   This smartly decorated restaurant in a building next to Hong Kong Station features flowers on each table and cabinets filled with Chinese antiques. In the evening a trio performs live music of popular tunes. The menu includes both traditional dishes and original creations, with an emphasis on presentation. You might wish to try the pan-fried foie gras with red wine sauce and seared king prawn with Chinese pear and cinnamon flavor and ice-cream filling; the seared beef tenderloin in tangy onion and tomato sauce; homemade crispy chicken; or barbecue suckling pig with a sweet dipping sauce. Dim sum is also available for lunch on weekends and holidays, with only a limited number served on weekdays.

Exchange Square II, Central. ✆ **852/2525 1163.** www.maxims.com.hk/en. Reservations required for lunch, recommended for dinner. Main dishes HK$98–HK$298; set lunches Mon–Fri (minimum of 2 people) HK$218–HK$298. AE, DC, MC, V. Daily 11am–3pm and 6–11pm. MTR: Central.

Tokio Joe ★ JAPANESE   As its quirky name suggests, this is a hip sushi bar catering to Lan Kwai Fong's youthful nighttime revelers. Dimly lit even for lunch, it offers sushi and sashimi a la carte, as well as combination platters, prepared by Chinese sushi chefs trained in Japan. A platter of assorted sashimi large enough for two people to share as an appetizer costs HK$510; sushi combinations run from HK$185 to HK$390. Unique, however, are the California-style roll creations, like the deep-fried soft-shell crab with avocado, cucumber, crab roe, and mayonnaise, and original dishes like the rock shrimp salad or kelp-grilled sea bass. Probably the best deal is one of the set lunches, featuring sashimi, tempura, or a box lunch. As the menu states, this restaurant has a "slightly irreverent, innovative, and casual approach to the Japanese culinary experience." Luckily, it succeeds.

Nearby is sister restaurant **Kyoto Joe,** 21 D'Aguilar (✆ **852/2804 6800**), which serves *robatayaki* grilled meats and vegetables in addition to sushi, open the same hours.

16 Lan Kwai Fong, Central. ✆ **852/2525 1889.** www.lkfe.com. Main dishes HK$135–HK$165; set lunches HK$145–HK$200. AE, DC, MC, V. Mon–Sat noon–2:30pm; Sun–Thurs 6:30–11pm; Fri–Sat 6:30–11:30pm. MTR: Central.

Watermark ★★ 🍴 CONTINENTAL   Located above Central's Star Ferry pier, this establishment, with a soaring ceiling and glass panel walls that can be pushed open, provides unobstructed sweeping views of the harbor and makes you feel like you're dining alfresco even though you aren't—a great choice in any kind of weather. The menu, which offers contemporary Continental cuisine, includes such mouthwatering starters as crab cake with pickled cucumber and lime butter, but many simply go with the wonderful seafood platter. Beef aged on the premises and seafood are the house specialties, with temptations ranging from red emperor (a kind of snapper) with jalapeño salsa, pinto beans, and balsamic dressing to Boston lobster and rib-eye. Very convenient for those hopping off or on the ferries.

Central Ferry Pier 7, Central. © **852/2167 7251.** www.igors.com. Reservations required. Main dishes HK$205–HK$390; set lunches Mon–Fri HK$148–HK$188; Sun brunch HK$298. AE, DC, MC, V. Mon–Sat noon–2:30pm; Sun 11:30am–3pm; daily 7–10:30pm (last order). MTR: Central.

Yun Fu ★ NORTHERN CHINESE Beginning with Hutong (p. 124), the Aqua restaurant group has lead the way when it comes to hip Chinese eateries that blur the lines between regional Chinese cuisines, and this newest venture is no exception. Its entryway is dramatic—down a flight of stairs lined with Buddhas—which leads you straight to a round bar, where you can order a cocktail and retire to one of several cozy cubicles adorned with Chinese lanterns and Tibetan decor. Then it's on to the main dining room, dark and romantic, where you'll dine on dishes influenced by Tibet, Mongolia, and Sichuan. Marinated roasted rack of lamb with assorted herbs and tea leaves, and pan-fried prawns with Szechuan pepper are popular choices, but those who can take the heat should go for the wok-fried Mandarin fish with spicy herbs and chili. After dining in the serene netherworld here, you might find the ascension to Lan Kwai Fong's hedonism a bit jarring.

43–55 Wyndham St., Central. © **852/2116 8855.** Reservations required. Main dishes HK$168–HK$288; set dinner HK$390. AE, DC, MC, V. Daily 6–11:30pm. MTR: Central.

Yung Kee ★★ CANTONESE Yung Kee started out in 1942 as a small shop selling roast goose, which did so well that it soon expanded into this very successful Cantonese enterprise. Its specialty is still roast goose with plum sauce (you'll see specimens hanging in the window), cooked to perfection with tender meat on the inside and crispy skin on the outside; a half bird, enough for five or six people, costs HK$210, while a smaller portion for two people costs HK$130 (note that goose has been pulled from the menu any time there's an avian flu scare). Other specialties include thousand-year-old eggs and any of the fresh seafood, like braised garoupa tail. Dining is on one of the upper three floors, but if all you want is a bowl of *congee* or takeout, join the office workers who pour in for a quick meal on the informal ground floor.

32–40 Wellington St., Central. © **852/2522 1624.** www.yungkee.com.hk. Main dishes HK$102–HK$180. AE, DC, MC, V. Daily 11am–11:30pm. MTR: Central.

Zen ★★ CANTONESE Both its name and its appearance leave no doubt that this is no ordinary Cantonese restaurant. Indeed, it became an instant trendsetter when it opened in 1989, eschewing the traditional flashy decor favored by most Chinese restaurants in favor of an austere Zen Buddhist style, with an open dining hall that allowed customers to see and be seen. Nowadays, of course, there are many imitators, but Zen remains on the cutting edge, with glass prisms, suspended from the ceiling and glistening with trickling water, making a swirl the length of the restaurant. As for the food, the wide variety of Cantonese specialties border on the nouvelle. Try the sautéed prawns with dried chili and walnuts, sautéed crab in an earthen pot with XO chili sauce, or the baked spareribs with Chin-Kiang vinegar. Lunch is also highly recommended for the large selection of dim sum.

Shop 001, Pacific Place, 88 Queensway, Central. © **852/2845 4555.** Reservations recommended. Main dishes HK$105–HK$208. AE, DC, MC, V. Mon–Sat 11:30am–3:30pm; Sun 10:30am–3:30pm; daily 5:30–10:30pm. MTR: Admiralty.

Inexpensive

Several inexpensive restaurants reviewed in the previous Tsim Sha Tsui section have branches in Central: **Fat Angelo's** (p. 131) is renowned for its massive portions of American-style Italian food; **Genki Sushi** (p. 132) offers conveyor-belt sushi at low prices; **Koh-I-Noor** (p. 132) is recommended for Indian curries; and **Spaghetti House** (p. 133) is a popular family restaurant. In addition, **Café O** (p. 153) in Wan Chai is popular for sandwiches, pizzas, and other fare, while **Tsui Wah** (p. 153), with a location in Causeway Bay, serves Chinese comfort food and international fare.

Keep in mind that many restaurants in the moderate category earlier offer lunches that even the budget-conscious can afford. Be sure, too, to check the section on "Dim Sum," later in this chapter, and bars in the nightlife chapter.

Finally, another good place for a casual, inexpensive meal is the **Great Food Hall,** in the basement food department of Seibu department store, Pacific Place, 88 Queensway, in Central (take the MTR to Admiralty), where various counters offer Chinese, Thai, Japanese, Indian, and other international fare and snacks Monday to Friday from 8am to 10pm and Saturday and Sunday from 10am to 10pm.

¡Caramba! MEXICAN   Located in the heart of Hong Kong's popular SoHo dining-and-nightlife district and easily accessible via the Central–Mid-Levels Escalator, this very narrow Mexican restaurant opened in 1997 as one of the first ethnic eateries on the street. ¡Caramba! offers hearty dishes of tacos, burritos, enchiladas, chimichangas, fajitas, and fresh fish of the day, all served with side dishes of black beans and rice. Of all the Mexican restaurants in Hong Kong, this is one of the best. Tables are too close together for intimate discussions, but after a few margaritas, who cares? On weekends and holidays, brunch is offered until 6pm for HK$118, including one drink.

26–30 Elgin St., Central. ✆ **852/2530 9963.** www.caramba.com.hk. Reservations recommended. Platters with side dishes HK$128–HK$148; lunch buffet Mon–Fri HK$78. AE, DC, MC, V. Mon–Sat noon–midnight; Sun 11am–11pm. MTR: Central.

Chilli Fagara ★ SICHUAN   This restaurant's menu suggests that you should start your meal with an appetizer (*tang*) dish to "awaken your taste buds"; progress to "numbing" (*ma*) dishes that will "turn your taste sensations upside down with flavors that were previously dormant exploding in spectacular fireworks"; and finish with "burning" (*la*) dishes that will provide an "exciting and fulfilling climax to a wonderful dining experience that you will not forget for a long time." I can't say that my meal here was that orgasmic, but I like both the food and the ambience—a Lilliputian spot so small you immediately feel like a local insider just by being here. What the menu does not tell you is that your server will bring a trio of *tang, ma,* and *la* appetizers (and charge you HK$30 for it), so be sure not to overorder. Popular la dishes include the red-hot chili prawns and the shredded chicken in spicy peanut sauce. The food is hot without being deadly, though you might decide otherwise if you accidentally bite into one of the dried red chilies that adorn many dishes.

51A Graham St., Central. ✆ **852/2893 3330.** www.chillifagara.com. Reservations required. Main dishes HK$118–HK$168; set lunch Mon–Fri HK$78. AE, DC, MC, V. Daily 11:30am–2:30pm and 5–11:30pm. MTR: Central.

The Flying Pan ☺ AMERICAN   Breakfast 24 hours a day is the forte of this homey, casual eatery, located uphill from Hollywood Road in the SoHo district. Everything from hearty omelets and eggs Benedict to Belgian waffles, cheese blintzes, biscuits and gravy, and even British breakfasts (two eggs, bacon, black pudding, and grilled tomato) are available from the lengthy menu, all with side dishes and juice. The children's menu includes such favorites as French toast, waffles, and grilled cheese sandwiches, but thank goodness no little ones are present at 5am, when this is the last stop for partiers who should also be in bed.

Another branch is located at 81–85 Lockhart Rd. on the third floor, Wan Chai (✆ **852/2528 9997;** MTR: Wan Chai), also open 24 hours.

9 Old Bailey St., Central. ✆ **852/2140 6333.** www.the-flying-pan.com. Breakfast platters HK$50–HK$105. No credit cards. Daily 24 hr. MTR: Central.

Heaven on Earth VARIED CHINESE   Twenty years ago you'd be hard-pressed to find a Hong Kong restaurant outside of a hotel that offered different regional Chinese cuisines under one roof, but the concept has taken hold with Hongkongers today. This basement establishment near the Lan Kwai Fong nightlife district, decorated in dark red with coiled lampshades that resemble the huge incense coils you see at temples, offers an assortment of dishes, with spicy dishes marked on the picture menu (you'll have to ask them to turn up the heat, however, as even the so-called hot dishes seem only mildly spicy to my palate). You might start with the hot- and-sour mushroom soup, dim sum, or the marinated beef and tendon with chili peppers, followed by marinated spareribs in black vinegar sauce, stir-fried clams with basil and chili, or stir-fried prawns with hot chili sauce on a sizzling platter. Chinese wines, sake, and cocktails are also available.

A second location is on the other side of the harbor, at 6 Knutsford Terrace, Tsim Sha Tsui (✆ **852/2367 8428;** MTR: Tsim Sha Tsui), open Monday to Thursday noon to 1:30am, Friday to Sunday and holidays 4pm to 1am.

1–13 D'Aguilar St., Central. ✆ **852/2537 8083.** www.kingparrot.com. Main dishes HK$68–HK$138. AE, DC, MC, V. Daily noon–midnight. MTR: Central.

Life ★ 🍴 VEGETARIAN   Located beside the Central–Mid-Levels Escalator in SoHo, Life is a godsend to travelers seeking vegetarian and vegan alternatives, with dishes made from natural and organic ingredients and utilizing fresh vegetables, whole grains, nuts, seeds, soy products, legumes, and other healthy fare. On request, they will also prepare dishes that are free of yeast, gluten, garlic, onion, or wheat. Occupying the second story above a health-food store, this simple, down-to-earth venue serves salads, whole-wheat pizzas, quiche, noodles, and daily specials (like chargrilled portobello mushroom served with roasted new potatoes, shallots, and grilled seasonal vegetables), along with juices, power and protein shakes, teas, fair-trade coffee, and organic wine and beer; rooftop dining is available in the evenings. Fitting the restaurant's earth-friendly philosophy, Life uses biodegradable packaging and nontoxic cleaning agents; plus, 10% of its profits go to charity. Service, however, can be slow.

10 Shelley St., Central. ✆ **852/2810 9777.** Main dishes HK$95–HK$110. AE, MC, V. Mon–Fri noon–11pm; Sat–Sun 9am–11pm. MTR: Central.

Nepal NEPALESE   One of many small ethnic eateries in SoHo, this one draws the crowds with its friendly waitresses, open facade, soothing ambience, and honest renditions of Nepal's best-known dishes. Fried eggplants are a good starter, followed, perhaps, by boneless lamb cooked with onions or barbecued chicken breast marinated in a cashew nut paste, saffron, and spices.

14 Staunton St., Central. ✆ **852/2869 6212.** www.nepalrestaurant.com.hk. Main dishes HK$98–HK$160; set lunch HK$98. AE, DC, MC, V. Daily noon–2:30pm and 6–11pm. MTR: Central.

PizzaExpress PIZZA   This glass-walled eatery, located on a busy intersection where Lynhurst Terrace, Cochrane, and Gage streets all converge (and in the shadow of the Central–Mid-Levels Escalator), is a terrific, if noisy (choose seating on the upper floor) pizza stop. Choices range from the ordinary (such as the American Pizza with pepperoni, mozzarella, jalapeño, and tomato) to the unusual (like the Peking Duck Pizza with duck, hoisin sauce, chili, spring onion, and mozzarella). Pasta and salads are also available.

Other branches are in Tsim Sha Tsui at 35 Ashley Rd. (**☎ 852/2317 7432;** MTR: Tsim Sha Tsui), Wan Chai at 10 Wing Fung St. (**☎ 852/3528 0541;** MTR: Wan Chai), and—my favorite location—on the waterfront in Stanley at 90 Stanley Main St. (**☎ 852/2813 7363;** bus: 6, 6A, 6X, 260, or 973).

21 Lyndhurst Terrace, Central. **☎ 852/2850 7898.** www.pizzaexpress.com.hk. Pizza HK$99–HK$130. AE, DC, MC, V. Daily noon–midnight. MTR: Central.

Pret A Manger LIGHT FARE   Located in the ifc mall at Hong Kong Station, this London import has met with resounding success, providing ready-made soups, salads, juices, cakes, wraps, and sandwiches to busy office workers. All food is made fresh daily without the use of chemicals, additives, and preservatives. What doesn't sell by the end of the day is given away to charities. Sandwiches include familiars like BLTs and clubs, as well as more exotic offerings like Thai chicken and tandoori fish. Although it's mainly for takeout, there are a few tables for dining in.

Other branches are located in the Central MTR Station (**☎ 852/2537 9230**); in the Admiralty MTR Station (**☎ 852/2537 9230**); Citibank Plaza, 3 Garden Rd., Central (**☎ 852/2521 5199;** MTR: Central); the Lippo Center, 89 Queensway, Central (**☎ 852/2537 4200;** MTR: Admiralty); Three Pacific Place, Level B3, 1 Queen's Rd. E., Central (**☎ 852/2516 9594;** MTR: Admiralty); and Harbour Centre, 25 Harbour Rd., Wan Chai (**☎ 852/2877 3686;** MTR: Wan Chai).

Shop 1015, Level 1, ifc mall, 1 Harbour View St., Central. **☎ 852/2295 0405.** www.pret.com.hk. Sandwiches and wraps HK$20–HK$38. No credit cards. Mon–Fri 7am–8:30pm; Sat 8am–8:30pm; Sun 8:30am–8:30pm. MTR: Central.

Three Sixty ★ 🛍 INTERNATIONAL/LIGHT FARE   What's not to like about this health-food store and cafeteria specializing in earth-friendly products and organic foods? Self-service counters offer a wide variety of dishes, including salads (you get to pick your own meat and ingredients), Indian curries (including both vegetarian and vegan choices), pasta (choose your sauce and pasta), pizza, sandwiches, wraps, burritos, stir-fries, noodles, and daily specials like chicken roast or lasagna, as well as desserts, gelato, and smoothies. There's ample seating (avoid the lunchtime rush), or order it to go and have a picnic in nearby Chater Garden.

There's a large branch in the Elements shopping mall, shop 1090, 1 Austin Rd. W., Kowloon (**☎ 852/2196 8066;** MTR: Kowloon), open daily from 8am to 10pm.

The Landmark (4th floor), 15 Queen's Rd., Central. **☎ 852/2111 4880.** www.threesixtyhk.com. Main dishes HK$25–HK$98. AE, DC, MC, V. Daily 8am–9pm. MTR: Central.

CAUSEWAY BAY & WAN CHAI

Very Expensive

Bo Innovation ★★ MODERN CHINESE   Born in London and raised in Toronto, self-taught chef Alvin Leung offers his own unique brand of experimental, molecular Chinese cuisine using innovative cooking techniques and incorporating non-Chinese ingredients from around the world into centuries-old recipes. The menu, therefore, changes constantly, with set dinners ranging from tasting menus to full-blown multicourse feasts, including vegetarian options (some set menus require that the entire table order it). Signature dishes include molecular *xiao long bao* (Shanghainese dumplings) and Sex on the Beach, a condom-shaped sweet offered for a supplemental charge, with proceeds going to a Hong Kong AIDS organization. Lunch offers dim sum and a limited a la carte menu (like pan-fried foie gras and white miso in a lettuce wrap) in addition to a set lunch and an eight-course chef's menu. Hidden on a side street on the second floor, the restaurant is casual and modern, with outdoor terrace seating available for dinner.

J Residence, 60 Johnston Rd. (entrance on Ship St.), Wan Chai. 𝄞 **852/2850 8371.** www.boinnovation. com. Reservations required. Set dinners HK$680–HK$1,380; set lunches HK$198–HK$680. AE, DC, MC, V. Mon–Fri noon–2pm; Mon–Sat 7–10pm (last order). MTR: Wan Chai.

Grissini ★★★ ITALIAN   This stylish, airy Italian restaurant, offering some of the best northern Italian fare in town, echoes its palatial setting of the Grand Hyatt Hotel, with a tall ceiling, Philippe Starck–designed chairs, and floor-to-ceiling windows offering a spectacular view of the harbor—day or night. Dining is on two levels, giving everyone a ringside seat; it's a perfect spot for lunch or a romantic dinner. The aroma of homemade Grissini breadsticks greets you as soon as you enter the restaurant, whetting your appetite, perhaps, for the *antipasto misto*, a selection of appetizers, or the homemade chestnut pasta with basil pesto and vegetables. Main dishes on the changing menu have included the likes of roasted garoupa with wine, thyme, Italian fennel, and saffron, and Barolo-braised veal cheek with polenta. The 1,000-bottle wine cellar is exclusively Italian. The lunch menu is lighter, with additional offerings of pasta and risotto.

In the Grand Hyatt Hong Kong, 1 Harbour Rd., Wan Chai. 𝄞 **852/2584 7722.** www.hongkong.grand. hyatt.com. Reservations recommended. Main courses HK$350–HK$400; set dinner HK$850; set lunches Mon–Fri HK$285–HK$315; Sun brunch HK$455. AE, DC, MC, V. Sun–Fri noon–2:30pm and 7–10:30pm; Sat 6:30–10:30pm (last order). MTR: Wan Chai.

Expensive

Fook Lam Moon (p. 158), famous for its exotic Cantonese fare and already covered in the earlier Kowloon section that includes Tsim Sha Tsui, also has a branch in Wan Chai.

One Harbour Road ★★ CANTONESE   For elegant Chinese dining in Wan Chai, head to the lobby of the Grand Hyatt Hotel, where a glass bubble elevator will deliver you directly to this eighth-floor restaurant designed to resemble the terrace of an elegant 1930s *taipan* mansion. A profusion of plants, a large lotus pond, and the sound of running water give the illusion of dining outdoors, while split-level dining with tables spread far apart provide both privacy and views of the harbor. The extensive menu offers straightforward, traditional Cantonese fare, with no nouvelle nuances or foreign influences. Choose from the usual abalone, bird's nest, Peking duck (HK$580; order in advance), and roast goose, all of which cost substantially more than the prices given below. Other specialties include crispy Loong Kong chicken and simmered garoupa with hot chili and vegetables. The set lunch and dinner menus, unfortunately for lone diners, require a minimum order for two people, but dim sum is served at lunchtime for HK$44 to HK$68.

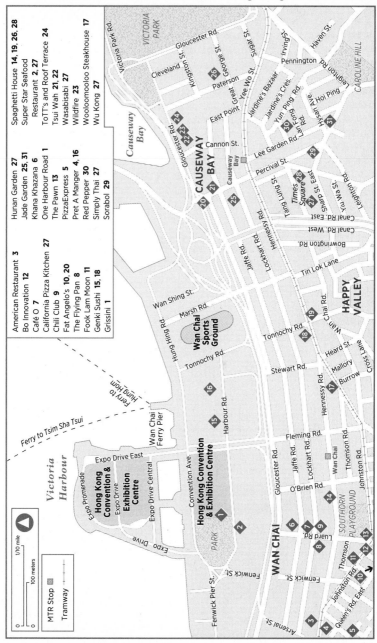

American Restaurant **3**
Bo Innovation **12**
Café O **7**
California Pizza Kitchen **27**
Chili Club **9**
Fat Angelo's **10, 20**
The Flying Pan **8**
Fook Lam Moon **11**
Genki Sushi **15, 18**
Grissini **1**

Hunan Garden **27**
Jade Garden **25, 31**
Khana Khazana **6**
One Harbour Road **1**
The Pawn **13**
PizzaExpress **5**
Pret A Manger **4, 16**
Red Pepper **30**
Simply Thai **27**
Sorabol **29**

Spaghetti House **14, 19, 26, 28**
Super Star Seafood
Restaurant **2, 27**
ToTT's and Roof Terrace **24**
Tsui Wah **21, 22**
Wasabisabi **27**
Wildfire **23**
Wooloomooloo Steakhouse **17**
Wu Kong **27**

In the Grand Hyatt Hong Kong, 1 Harbour Rd., Wan Chai. ℂ **852/2584 7722.** www.hongkong.grand. hyatt.com. Reservations recommended. Main dishes HK$180–HK$330; set dinner HK$770; set lunches HK$400–HK$500. AE, DC, MC, V. Mon–Sat noon–2:30pm; Sun 11:30am–2:30pm; daily 6:30–10:30pm (last order). MTR: Wan Chai.

ToTT's and Roof Terrace ★★★ INTERNATIONAL/FUSION   ToTT's stands for "Talk of The Town," and it certainly achieves that with its fabulous harbor views from its 34th-floor perch and eye-catching electric-blue decor. Sofas and plush seats give it a loungelike atmosphere, especially after 10pm Monday to Saturday, when there's live music—everything from rhythm and blues to pop or jazz (the cover charge is waived for hotel guests or those who dine here). Tables for two are placed mostly by the windows, making this a good choice for a fun, celebratory dinner. The contemporary cuisine is an East-meets-West culinary adventure, with spices, herbs, and ingredients from around the world brought together in creative ways, though classics like chargrilled lobster or Australian Wagyu steaks (available with a choice of sauces, from béarnaise or foie gras to shallots with red wine) are not overlooked. The alfresco Roof Terrace provides views, exotic drinks, and snacks. In short, this place is a good choice for those who want dining and entertainment in one spot, as well as for those entertaining first-time visitors to Hong Kong. Sunday brunch, featuring unlimited champagne, is so popular you should book at least 2 weeks in advance.

In the Excelsior Hong Kong, 281 Gloucester Rd., Causeway Bay. ℂ **852/2837 6786.** http://mandarin oriental.com/excelsior. Reservations recommended for dinner (request a window seat). Main courses HK$248–HK$418; lunch buffet Mon–Fri HK$198–HK$238; Sat brunch HK$318; Sun brunch HK$628 with champagne, HK$428 without. AE, DC, MC, V. Mon–Sat noon–3pm and 6:30–11pm; Sun 11:30am–3pm and 6:30–10pm. MTR: Causeway Bay.

Moderate

Several restaurants already covered in the Kowloon dining section, earlier, have branches in Wan Chai or Causeway Bay: **Jade Garden** (p. 158), good for Cantonese food and dim sum; **Super Star Seafood Restaurant** (p. 128), serving Cantonese dishes, seafood, and dim sum; **Wooloomooloo Steakhouse** (p. 130), serving Aussie steaks and fare; and **Wu Kong** (p. 130), which specializes in cuisine from Shanghai. **Hunan Garden** (p. 140), in Central, has a Causeway Bay branch dishing up the same spicy Hunanese fare.

The Pawn ★★ 🍴 MODERN BRITISH   This historic 1888 building, formerly housing a Chinese pawn shop among other tenants, has been converted by local artist and film director Stanley Wong into an "adult playground," with the first floor serving as a bar and lounge and the second-floor restaurant staying true to the building's heritage with plank wood flooring, wooden tables, white-washed walls, and balcony seating over bustling Wan Chai. Lunch and dinner menus change daily, with past starters including pork belly with green apple, spinach, red onion, and red wine vinaigrette, and main dishes ranging from chargrilled lamb chops with minted mash, roasted vegetables, and rosemary gravy to pan-roasted duck breast with sweet potato mash, roasted eggplant, and berry gravy. Kudos to the owners for breathing new life into a Wan Chai landmark.

62 Johnston Rd., Wan Chai. ℂ **852/2866 3444.** www.thepawn.com.hk. Main dishes HK$180–HK$220; set lunches Mon–Fri HK$150–HK$190. AE, DC, MC, V. Mon–Fri noon–3pm; Sat–Sun 11am–3pm; daily 6–11pm. MTR: Wan Chai.

Red Pepper ★★ SICHUAN   Open since 1970, the Red Pepper has a large following among the city's expatriates, many of whom seem to come so often that they know everyone in the place. It's a very relaxing, small restaurant, with a rather quaint decor of carved dragons on the ceiling and Chinese lanterns. Specialties include fried prawns with chili sauce on a sizzling platter, sour-pepper soup, fried garoupa with sweet-and-sour sauce, smoked duck marinated with oranges, and shredded chicken with hot garlic sauce and dry-fried string beans. Most dishes are available in two sizes, with the small dishes suitable for two people. Litchi tea is a good accompaniment.

7 Lan Fong Rd., Causeway Bay. ℂ **852/2577 3811.** Reservations recommended, especially at dinner. Small dishes HK$90–HK$240. AE, DC, MC, V. Daily 11:30am–11:15pm (last order). MTR: Causeway Bay.

Wasabisabi ★★ JAPANESE   This stunning restaurant looks like it was airlifted straight out of Tokyo, and like that huge metropolis, it's easy to get lost here. Luckily, staff is on hand to lead diners past the mirrors and corridors that make this place a confusing maze and into the dark and cozy dining room. Here, diners are faced with all the usual seafood choices (flown in daily from Tokyo's Tsukiji Fish Market) like sashimi, sushi, and *temaki* (hand-rolled sushi), the latter of which includes the Japanese chef's own creations like the avocado and barbecued-eel temaki. The extensive menu also offers grilled dishes (like grilled black cod marinated in a special miso paste from Kyoto), tempura, and rice and noodle dishes, but for a feast fit for an emperor, try the five-course tasting menu for HK$628, which changes every 2 weeks. The restaurant's bar, open until midnight, is a happening place for an after-dinner drink, but you may not have to move to enjoy it: The restaurant's C-shaped sofas can swivel to face the bar.

Times Square (13th floor), 1 Matheson St., Causeway Bay. ℂ **852/2506 0009.** www.aqua.com.hk. Main dishes HK$118–HK$228; set lunches HK$118–HK$298. AE, DC, MC, V. Daily noon–2:45pm and 6–11pm (last order). MTR: Causeway Bay.

Inexpensive

California Pizza Kitchen, Fat Angelo's, Genki Sushi, and **Spaghetti House,** reviewed in the Tsim Sha Tsui section, all have branches in Wan Chai and/or Causeway Bay (p. 131, 131, 132, and 133). **The Flying Pan, PizzaExpress,** and **Pret A Manger,** described in the Central section, also have branches here (p. 145, 147, and 147). Finally, **Wildfire,** specializing in handcrafted pizzas, is in Stanley, with a branch in Causeway Bay (p. 156).

In addition to the recommendations below, be sure to go through the moderate section above for inexpensive buffets and set lunches.

American Restaurant PEKINGESE   Despite its name, the American Restaurant has served hearty Pekingese food since it opened right after World War II. Little changed over the decades and often filled with noisy, celebratory patrons, it has an English menu listing almost 200 dishes (the small-size dishes are good for two or three people), but the perennial favorites have always been barbecued Peking duck (HK$295 and good for two or more people), beggar's chicken (which must be ordered a day in advance and costs HK$398), sizzling prawns, and the sizzling beef hot plate. Otherwise, the staff is happy to make recommendations.

20 Lockhart Rd., Wan Chai. ℂ **852/2527 1000** or 852/2527 7277. Small dishes HK$62–HK$188. AE, DC, MC, V. Daily 11am–11pm (last order). MTR: Wan Chai.

Café O ★ PIZZA/LIGHT FARE   This informal eatery does a roaring business with area office workers on lunch break, night revelers, and everyone in between looking for healthy fast food free of additives and preservatives and prepared with virgin olive oil. It serves an all-day breakfast (from organic muesli to the heart-stopping Triple O, which comes with three eggs, toast, grilled tomatoes and mushrooms, bacon, and sausages); sandwiches (from the classic BLT but with melted mozzarella cheese to smoked salmon with pesto, capers, mint, and sun-dried tomatoes, all served on house-made bread); pizzas, including create-your-own; pasta; salads; and freshly squeezed juices and smoothies. The food is available for takeout, but the dining area for those who wish to consume on the spot, is complete with free Wi-Fi.

A second location, at 2 Arbuthnot Rd. in Central (☏ **852/2868 0450;** MTR: Central), is open the same hours.

18 Luard Rd. (entrance on Jaffe Rd.), Wan Chai. ☏ **852/3543 0224.** www.cafeo.hk. Main dishes HK$50–HK$98. AE, DC, MC, V. Mon–Thurs 7am–midnight; Fri–Sat 7am–1am; Sun 10am–midnight. MTR: Wan Chai.

Chili Club 🗲 THAI   This simple upstairs restaurant wastes little money on decor, with the only nod to fine dining apparent in its white tablecloths. But the seafood, curries, and noodles, which include all the Thai favorites, are as spicy as this national cuisine should be. What's more, the price is right, making this one of Hong Kong's best dining values. Try to get a seat near the window, where you can watch the action on the street below, and, if possible, avoid the lunchtime rush.

88 Lockhart Rd., Wan Chai. ☏ **852/2527 2872.** Main dishes HK$68–HK$150. AE, MC, V. Daily noon–3pm and 6–10:30pm. MTR: Wan Chai.

Khana Khazana INDIAN/VEGETARIAN   Head up to the first floor, where you'll find this modestly decorated restaurant packed with tables close together in order to satisfy Wan Chai's hungry crowd. Serving strictly vegetarian fare from north and south India, it offers a wide range of tandoori and curries, from *Kashmiri dum aloo* (stuffed potatoes in Mughalai-style gravy) and *paneer makhani* (cottage cheese cooked in a rich gravy of butter and tomato topped with fresh cream) to fresh minced vegetables oven-baked on skewers. Most people, however, opt for the *thali* (set meal), which gives them a sampling of several dishes.

20 Luard Rd., Wan Chai. ☏ **852/2520 5308.** www.khanakhazana.hk. Main dishes HK$58–HK$88; Thali HK$138; lunch buffet Mon–Fri HK$88. AE, MC, V. Daily 11am–3pm and 6–10:45pm. MTR: Wan Chai.

Simply Thai 🗲 THAI   The fact that this restaurant is located in Times Square should be a tip-off that this is no simple eatery. Indeed, it's surprisingly elegant for its price range and offers diners a relaxed atmosphere in which to kick back, down a few Singha beers, and enjoy good Thai food. The usual Thai soups like *tom yum goong,* Thai spicy beef salad, and pad Thai noodles get the meal started, but otherwise the menu covers both classics and modern renditions, from baked seasonal fish with basil, lemon grass, chili, and coriander to betal leaves and lettuce with spicy minced chicken.

Simply Thai has two other branches: in shop 533, Grand Century Place, 193 Prince Edward Rd W., Mong Kok (☏ **852/2386 6569;** MTR: Mong Kok), and in the New Territories in the New Town Plaza in Sha Tin (☏ **852/3523 1638;** MTR: Sha Tin).

Times Square (11th floor), 1 Matheson St., Causeway Bay. ☏ **852/2506 1212.** Main dishes HK$76–HK$168; set lunches HK$58–HK$92. AE, DC, MC, V. Mon–Fri 11:30am–3pm and 5:30–10:30pm; Sat–Sun and holidays 11:30am–10pm. MTR: Causeway Bay.

Sorabol ★ KOREAN This is the Hong Kong branch of a successful Korean chain. Popular with local Chinese and Koreans, it can be quite noisy and busy, but partitions between tables lend some privacy. My personal favorites are the Korean vegetable salad, beef strips of *bulgogi* or the *kalbi* (beef strips marinated in a spicy sauce and then barbecued at your own grill), and the sliced Korean tenderloin. Barbecued set meals come with side dishes of kimchee (spicy cabbage) and vegetables. Another popular dish is the Genghis Khan hot pot with vegetables. You'll do your own barbecuing at smokeless grills at your table, which can be great fun, somewhat like an indoor cookout. The army of knowledgeable staff keeps things running smoothly and is happy to help the novice barbecuer.

Another branch is in Tsim Sha Tsui on the fourth floor of the Miramar Shopping Centre at 132 Nathan Rd. (☏ **852/2375 2882**), open the same hours.

Lee Theatre Plaza (17th floor), 99 Percival St. (across from Times Square), Causeway Bay. ☏ **852/2881 6823.** www.sorabol.com.hk. Barbecued dishes HK$95–HK$255; set meals for 2 persons HK$460–HK$620; set lunches Mon–Sat HK$68–HK$86; Sun lunch buffet HK$118. AE, DC, MC, V. Daily 11:30am–3pm and 6–11:30pm. MTR: Wan Chai.

Tsui Wah ★ VARIED CHINESE/INTERNATIONAL It's difficult to classify this down-home chain of very popular restaurants, serving what might be described as Hong Kong comfort food and low-brow international fare prepared for the Chinese palate. Although every branch location seems to have its own character, you can count on it being crowded, especially during peak dining hours when you'll probably be asked to share a table. If you want to order like a Hongkonger, start with a milk tea and then try one of the soups or noodle or fried rice dishes, like shrimp and spinach dumplings with noodles in fish soup, prawns with noodles and XO sauce, pork ribs with vermicelli in Thai *tom yam goong* soup, or fried noodle with king prawns served on a sizzling plate. Or, go for one of the international dishes such as Japanese udon noodles, Russian borscht, Malaysian curry, spaghetti with sliced beef, hot dog, or pork sandwich. Although the food may not be memorable, your experience rubbing elbows with the locals will. In fact, it could be argued that if you haven't been to Tsui Wah, you haven't experienced Hong Kong at all.

There are more than a dozen branches throughout Hong Kong, most open from about 7am to as late as 2 or 4am, or later. Those open 24 hours daily are at 15–19 Wellington St., Central (☏ **852/2525 6338;** MTR: Central); 483–499 Jaffe Rd., Causeway Bay (☏ **852/2892 2633;** MTR: Causeway Bay); and 77–81 Parkes St., Yau Ma Tei (☏ **852/2384 8388;** MTR: Jordan). Other convenient branches are at 84–86 Des Voeux Rd. Central, Central (☏ **852/2815 3000;** MTR: Central); 2 Carnarvon Rd., Tsim Sha Tsui (☏ **852/2366 8250;** MTR: Tsim Sha Tsui); 12–13 Jubilee St., Central (☏ **852/2542 2288;** MTR: Central); and 17–19 Pak Hoi St., Yau Ma Tei (☏ **852/2780 8328;** MTR: Central or Sheung Wan).

20–22 Cannon St., Causeway Bay. ☏ **852/2573 4338.** www.tsuiwahrestaurant.com. Main dishes HK$30–HK$62; set meals HK$68–HK$78. No credit cards. Daily 24 hr. MTR: Wan Chai.

AROUND HONG KONG ISLAND

Victoria Peak

In addition to the choices here, there are many more choices in Peak Tower and Peak Galleria. Also, see Tien Yi in the "Dim Sum" section later in this chapter.

EXPENSIVE

Pearl on the Peak ★ CONTINENTAL/INTERNATIONAL   This is probably the priciest restaurant on the Peak and looks it. Boasting 270-degree views of the city through floor-to-ceiling windows and from a small outdoor terrace, it pulls in fashionable foodies with its cool design and international fare, including a popular seafood and grill weekend brunch. The menu runs the gamut from lobster linguine to pan-fried Norwegian salmon and Wagyu sirloin, complemented by both old- and new-world wines. If you've come to the Peak for some hiking, this isn't the place for you (the dress is smart casual), but if you're coming for the night view and perhaps a romantic stroll, this is the top pick—reserve a window seat.

Peak Tower, Level 1, Victoria Peak. ⓒ 852/2849 5123. www.maxconcepts.com.hk. Reservations required. Main courses HK$195–HK$580; set dinner HK$625; set lunches Mon–Fri HK$98–HK$258; weekend brunch HK$205–HK$400. AE, DC, MC, V. Daily noon–10:30pm (last order). Peak Tram.

MODERATE

Cafe Deco ★ ☺ INTERNATIONAL   No expense was spared, it seems, in designing this chic, airy restaurant with its wood inlaid floor, authentic Art Deco trimmings (many imported from the U.S. and Europe), and open kitchen serving cuisines of China, Japan, Thailand, India, the U.S., and Italy. All this is secondary, however, to the restaurant's real attraction—surreal views of Hong Kong. That alone is reason enough to dine here, though some of the view has been stolen by the Peak Tower. To assure a ringside window seat, make reservations for the second floor at least 2 weeks in advance, emphasizing that you don't want your view obstructed by the Peak Tower, or opt for one of the outdoor tables, which are often easier to get. The food, designed to appeal to visitors from around the world, is an eclectic mix of international dishes and ingredients, including tandoori kabobs and dishes, Asian noodles and curries, sushi, grilled steaks, pizzas, create-your-own pastas, an oyster bar, soups, and salads. The salads are generous enough for two to share (the house salad is exceptionally good), but main dishes occasionally fall short of expectations. I suppose what you're really paying for here is the view. A children's play corner keeps the wee ones occupied.

Peak Galleria, Victoria Peak. ⓒ 852/2849 5111. www.cafedecogroup.com. Reservations recommended for dinner. Pizza and pasta HK$145–HK$178; main courses HK$136–HK$468. AE, DC, MC, V. Mon–Thurs 11:30am–midnight; Fri–Sat 11:30am–1am; Sun 9:30am–midnight. Peak Tram.

The Peak Lookout ★★ INTERNATIONAL   Although it's on the Peak, located across the street from the Peak Tram terminus, the Peak Lookout's terrace has only limited views of the South China Sea. And yet, this former tram station is a delightful, rustic place for a meal, with exposed stone walls, tall timber-trussed ceiling, open fireplace, wooden floor, and a greenhouselike room that extends into the garden. You can also sit outdoors amid the lush growth where you can actually hear birds singing—one of the best outdoor dining opportunities in Hong Kong on a glorious day (be sure to request a table outdoors if that's what you want). The menu is eclectic, offering soups (from roast chicken soup to the classic Thai seafood soup *tom yam goong*), sandwiches, great burgers, and a combination of American, Chinese, Indian, and

Southeast Asian dishes, including tandoori chicken *tikka*, pad Thai noodles, penne with salmon, grilled steaks and salmon, and curries like Thai green chicken curry with coconut milk.

121 Peak Rd., Victoria Peak. (© **852/2849 1000.** www.peaklookout.com.hk. Reservations required for dinner and all weekend meals. Main courses HK$138–HK$328. AE, DC, MC, V. Mon–Thurs 10:30am–11:30pm; Fri 10:30am–1am; Sat 8:30am–1am; Sun 8:30am–11:30pm. Peak Tram.

Repulse Bay

EXPENSIVE

The Verandah ★★★ 📷 CONTINENTAL   Unless you're planning a trip to the beach, this wonderful, veranda-like restaurant is the only reason to venture to this destination on Hong Kong Island's south side, though you do pass it by on your way to Stanley when coming from Central. A throwback to Hong Kong's colonial days in a setting reminiscent of an exclusive private club, the Verandah boasts a stylish yet relaxed atmosphere, with tall ceilings and whirling fans, starched tablecloths and flowers, and windows open to a manicured lawn and palm trees. If you can, book a table more than a month in advance and arrive starving at its famous Sunday brunch, complete with a jazz band. Otherwise, from the regular menu, you might wish to start with the Verandah's famous Caesar salad, prepared tableside and topped with a choice of parma ham, grilled prawns, or home-smoked salmon, followed perhaps by lobster bisque. For a main course, you might choose a lobster dish or the filet of U.S. prime beef tenderloin. With its excellent service, great food, and wonderful ambience, this is a very civilized place where you'll want to linger. A piano player serenades in the evening.

109 Repulse Bay Rd., Repulse Bay. (© **852/2292 2822.** www.therepulsebay.com. Reservations required. Main courses HK$298–HK$598; set lunches HK$298–HK$328; Sun brunch HK$460. AE, DC, MC, V. Lunch Tues–Sat noon–2:30pm; dinner Tues–Sun and holidays 7–10:30pm; brunch Sun and holidays 11am–2:30pm; afternoon tea Tues–Sat 3–5:30pm, Sun and holidays 3:30–5:30pm. Bus: 6, 6A, 6X, 260, or 973.

Stanley

PizzaExpress (p. 147) offers a dreamy view of the sea from its outside terrace on Stanley Main Street, where you'll also find a row of other restaurants. In addition, the **Murray House,** Stanley Plaza, has a few restaurants serving Spanish, Vietnamese, and German food, as well as pizza and pasta.

MODERATE

Lucy's ★ 📷 INTERNATIONAL   This tiny, cozy, casual restaurant, snuggled in the ground floor of an older building just off the front of Stanley Market (look for the stairs to the right of the Delifrance bakery), is a friendly neighborhood restaurant, attracting expats who live in Stanley rather than hordes of tourists (maybe because it lacks a view of the sea). Its limited menu, which always includes some vegetarian options, changes often to reflect what's available and in season, with past entrees ranging from chargrilled lamb with eggplant, mint, chili jam, and goat's cheese tart to coconut-and-chili-marinated chicken breast with roast pumpkin, long beans, and coconut cream. Most diners, however, opt for one of the daily specials, which are almost always right on, making sure to save room for the restaurant's famed desserts. Lunches feature lighter, less expensive fare, like salmon fish cakes or spinach and feta cheese soufflé with roasted tomato sauce.

64 Stanley Main St., Stanley. ℂ **852/2813 9055.** Reservations required. Main courses HK$180–HK$250; set lunches HK$145–HK$180. AE, MC, V. Mon–Fri noon–3pm; Sat–Sun noon–4pm; Mon–Thurs 7–10pm; Fri–Sat 6:30–10pm; Sun 6:30–9:30pm. Bus: 6, 6A, 6X, 260, or 973.

INEXPENSIVE

Wildfire ☺ INTERNATIONAL/PIZZA   Located on the top floor of the historic Murray House, with views of the South China Sea from its outside terrace, this restaurant is popular with families for its children's play area and its handcrafted pizzas, salads, pastas, main dishes like barbecue pork ribs, and daily specials.

You'll find branches at 2 Knutsford Terrace, Tsim Sha Tsui (ℂ **852/3690 1598;** MTR: Tsim Sha Tsui), open Sunday to Thursday 11am to 2am and Friday and Saturday 11am to 3am; shop 1005 in Elements shopping center above Kowloon Station, 1 Austin Rd., Kowloon (ℂ **852/2196 8099;** MTR: Kowloon), open daily noon to midnight; and shop P211A in the World Trade Center, 280 Gloucester Rd., Causeway Bay (ℂ **852/2894 8844;** MTR: Causeway Bay), open Monday to Friday 6 to 10pm and Saturday, Sunday, and holidays from noon to 10pm.

Murray House, Stanley. ℂ **852/2813 6161.** Pizza HK$100–HK$136; set dinner HK$158 Mon–Fri, HK$178 Sat–Sun; set lunch HK$108 Mon–Fri, HK$138 Sat–Sun. AE, DC, MC, V. Mon–Fri noon–11pm; Sat 11:30am–11pm; Sun 10am–11pm. Bus: 6, 6A, 6X, 260, or 973.

Aberdeen

MODERATE

Jumbo Kingdom ★ CANTONESE   There are many other restaurants that are more authentic and more affordable, but this floating restaurant in Aberdeen has been in operation for more than 30 years and attracts a bustling crowd with its claims to be the largest floating restaurant in the world. Simply take the bus to Aberdeen and then board one of the Jumbo Kingdom's own free shuttle boats, with departures every few minutes from the waterfront Aberdeen Promenade (another option is to join one of the nighttime organized tours that stop here for dinner). Although the exterior of the restaurant is as ornate and—perhaps to some eyes—as gaudy as you could hope for (have your cameras ready as the boat approaches), the renovated interior is contemporary. Specializing in fresh seafood, Jumbo Kingdom also offers roasted goose, Peking duck (HK$360), and changing seasonal dishes, but my favorite meal here is dim sum, available from an English menu (from trolleys on Sun and holidays) until 4pm. Dragon Court, a smaller, more formal dining hall, offers much of the same fare, with dim sum served only off the menu; you might be able to get a table here immediately on Sunday, bypassing the first-come, first-served waiting list for the more popular—and more fun—main dining hall.

Aberdeen Harbour, Hong Kong Island. ℂ **852/2553 9111.** www.jumbo.com.hk. Main dishes HK$80–HK$439; dim sum HK$18–HK$48. Table charge HK$10 per person. AE, MC, V. Mon–Sat 11:30am–11:30pm; Sun and holidays 7am–11:30pm. Bus: 7 or 70 from Central, 72 or 77 from Causeway Bay, or 973 from Tsim Sha Tsui to Aberdeen, and then the restaurant's free shuttle boat.

Top Deck, at the Jumbo ★★ ☺ INTERNATIONAL/SEAFOOD   If Cantonese fare is not your cup of tea, this is an excellent alfresco alternative, located on the roof of Jumbo Kingdom and offering comfortable sofas and oversize chairs grouped under and around awnings and a flamboyantly ornate Chinese pavilion, where an open kitchen turns out mouthwatering seafood delights and other dishes from around the world. The menu is so extensive it's hard to know where to start. Thai, Japanese, and

Indian appetizer platters solve part of the dilemma by providing a sampler of goodies from those countries, while the seafood mountain comes with lobster, oysters, mussels, Alaskan king crab legs, prawns, and other seafood, along with dipping sauces. For a main course, choose from tiger king prawns, steak, fish and lamb chops from a tandoori oven, Asian curries, pastas, pizzas, burgers, and other options from the grill. For those who feel cheated with only one entree, try the Saturday lunch buffet or the Sunday seafood buffet (the latter with free-flowing champagne), complete with a children's play corner to accommodate the many families (the boat ride to the restaurant is a bonus, as is the children's menu). It's a great place to chill out.

Jumbo Kingdom (rooftop), Aberdeen Harbour, Hong Kong Island. ℭ **852/2553 3331.** www.cafedeco group.com. Main dishes HK$138–HK$238; Sat lunch buffet HK$198; Sun brunch HK$378. AE, DC, MC, V. Tues–Thurs 6–11:30pm; Fri 6pm–midnight; Sat 11:30am–midnight; Sun and holidays 11:30am–11:30pm. Bus: 7 or 70 from Central, 72 or 77 from Causeway Bay, or 973 from Tsim Sha Tsui to Aberdeen, and then Jumbo Kingdom's free shuttle boat.

Western District

INEXPENSIVE

Sammy's Kitchen CONTINENTAL   This simple and unpretentious place, easily recognizable by its cow-shaped sign, has been in business since 1970. Chef-owner octogenarian Sammy Yip cooked at the Peninsula and Mandarin Oriental hotels before opening this restaurant, where he is now joined by his children in the family business. Although the reasonably priced meals are rather mediocre, the service is friendly and welcoming, and it's comforting to see a place that remains virtually unchanged over the decades in such a fast-changing environment. Two different menus are available: a cheaper, quicker, all-day menu offering plain dishes like spring chicken, lamb chops, and noodle and fried rice dishes, priced from HK$60 to HK$120; and a dinner menu served in the separate, more formal Grill Room Monday to Friday, with entrees ranging from HK$100 to HK$280 for fresh seafood, imported steaks, and such specialties as chicken with special pepper sauce flaming with cognac. You can bring your own bottle of wine for a HK$70 corkage fee.

204–206 Queen's Rd. W., Sheung Wan. ℭ **852/2548 8400.** Main courses HK$60–HK$280; set lunches HK$60–HK$150. AE, DC, MC, V. Daily 10am–11pm. MTR: Sheung Wan.

DIM SUM

Everyone should try a dim sum meal at least once, as much for the atmosphere as for the food. It's eaten primarily for breakfast or lunch, or as an afternoon snack with tea. On weekends, restaurants (mostly Cantonese) offering dim sum are packed with local families. On weekdays, they're popular with shoppers and businesspeople. Prices are low and you order only as much as you want. On weekends, a few remaining restaurants bring out their trolleys, filled with steaming baskets and pushed throughout the restaurant, allowing you to choose what appeals to you. Otherwise, most restaurants nowadays offer dim sum from a menu, which may or may not be in English (hotel restaurants have English menus; otherwise, many Cantonese restaurants have at least one staff member who speaks English, or try my suggestions earlier in this chapter, in the "Cantonese Food" section of "A Taste of Hong Kong," p. 133). In most restaurants that offer dim sum, one pays by the basket, and each basket usually contains two to four items of dim sum; the average price is about HK$20 to HK$40, though at expensive restaurants they can go much higher. The prices given below, unless otherwise specified, are per basket; expect to spend HK$80 to HK$150 per person for a light meal, depending on where you eat. Some restaurants discount their prices during off-peak dining hours. You'll be charged extra for tea, usually around HK$10 to HK$20 per person.

You'll find many of the restaurants below also described earlier in this chapter, so they obviously serve more than dim sum. However, because dim sum is such a special Chinese tradition, they are emphasized again below. You may also notice that a restaurant listed in this section may have a different number of stars than was given previously in an earlier listing. This is not a mistake: A restaurant that might be ho-hum in all-round meals can be a standout in dim sum.

Because dim sum is fairly predictable, with the most common dishes covered in the cuisine section at the beginning of the chapter, I've only made specific food recommendations below when the dishes are different and/or are standouts from the usual choices. The open hours below are for serving times for dim sum.

Kowloon

City Chiuchow Restaurant CHIU CHOW   Although it's a Chiu Chow restaurant, this place serves its own dim sum, which is not too surprising if you consider that Chiu Chow food has been greatly influenced by Cantonese food. About 10 varieties are available, including steamed shrimp balls and steamed dumplings Chiu Chow style, along with noodle dishes like the fried E-Fu noodles.

East Ocean Centre, 98 Granville Rd., Tsim Sha Tsui East. ☎ **852/2723 6226.** Dim sum HK$13–HK$21. AE, DC, MC, V. Daily 11am–4pm, for dim sum. MTR: Tsim Sha Tsui.

Fook Lam Moon ★★★ CANTONESE   This is a Hong Kong old-timer, with an atmosphere reminiscent of an earlier era except without trolleys. The English menu is limited, listing only the restaurant's top choices, including the highest-priced item—steamed shark's-fin dumpling with superior soup. A second branch is at 35–45 Johnston Rd., Wan Chai (☎ **852/2866 0663**); same menu, same hours.

53-59 Kimberley Rd., Tsim Sha Tsui. ☎ **852/2366 0286.** www.fooklammoon-grp.com. Dim sum HK$40–HK$120. AE, DC, MC, V. Daily 11:30am–2:30pm, for dim sum. MTR: Tsim Sha Tsui.

Jade Garden ★★ CANTONESE   An easy place for the uninitiated, this Cantonese chain is tourist-friendly and conveniently situated across from the Star Ferry terminus, with views of the old KCR clock tower and Victoria Harbour. It has an extensive English menu for dim sum (try the deep-fried shrimp rolls with garlic if available), along with rice and noodle dishes and *congee*, while desserts are offered from a trolley. On weekdays, a handful of dim sum, like the steamed minced beef dumpling, are offered at a discount of almost half price, starting at HK$9.80. Branches are located in Mong Kok and Causeway Bay (p. 127).

Star House (4th floor), 3 Salisbury Rd., Tsim Sha Tsui. ☎ **852/2730 6888.** Dim sum HK$18–HK$38. AE, DC, MC, V. Mon-Sat 11am–4:30pm; Sun and holidays 10am–4:30pm, for dim sum. MTR: Tsim Sha Tsui.

Serenade Chinese Restaurant ★★ 🏛 CANTONESE   This is my top choice in Tsim Sha Tsui for moderately priced dim sum with a view. Located up on the first floor of the Hong Kong Cultural Centre next to the Star Ferry—you might have to look for its entrance, but it's worth it—Serenade Chinese offers views of Victoria

Harbour in a bright and cheerful setting. Its comprehensive dim sum menu (only desserts are served from trolleys) includes "figurine" dim sum, such as the steamed shrimp dumpling in the shape of a fish. My favorite is the deep-fried spring rolls with crushed garlic, which is also beautifully presented and comes with a yummy dipping sauce. Bargain hunters, take note: On weekdays (excluding public holidays) from 9am to noon and again from 2 to 4:30pm, dim sum prices are substantially cheaper than those below (HK$13–HK$20). Even more impressive is that the hostess told me about the deal, recommending that I wait 10 minutes before being seated so I could dine at the cheaper prices.

Hong Kong Cultural Centre (1st floor), Restaurant Block, Salisbury Rd., Tsim Sha Tsui. (C) **852/2722 0932.** Dim sum HK$18–HK$38. AE, DC, MC, V. Daily 9am–4:30pm, for dim sum. MTR: Tsim Sha Tsui.

Shang Palace ★★ CANTONESE   One of Kowloon's most elaborate Chinese restaurants comes complete with red-lacquered walls and Chinese lanterns hanging from the ceiling. Its dim sum is among the best in town—a bit more expensive, but worth it. Choose your dim sum from the English menu, which changes every month and always includes more than a dozen varieties. If it's available, go with the baked diced chicken and mushroom bun or the steamed shrimp and chives dumpling, though the seasonal steamed vegetarian dumpling or deep-fried spring roll is also a perennial favorite. For a splurge, order the set lunch, which comes with dim sum and a main dish for HK$238.

In the Kowloon Shangri-La, 64 Mody Rd., Tsim Sha Tsui East. (C) **852/2733 8754.** www.shangri-la.com. Dim sum HK$36–HK$45. AE, DC, MC, V. Mon–Sat noon–3pm; Sun & holidays 10:30am–3pm, for dim sum. MTR: Tsim Sha Tsui.

Spring Moon ★★★ CANTONESE   As you'd expect from a restaurant in the Peninsula Hong Kong, this is a very refined and civilized place for the humble dim sum, with an English menu that lists more than a dozen mouthwatering choices that change with the seasons. Dim sum connoisseurs believe the morsels served here are among the best in town, with a past example including deep-fried taro puff with diced abalone and chicken. Spring Moon is also famous for its more than two dozen varieties of Chinese teas and even employs professionally trained tea masters. The restaurant is decorated in an Art Deco style reminiscent of how the restaurant would have looked in 1928, the year the Peninsula opened, with stained glass, wood paneling, and Frank Lloyd Wright–inspired highlights.

In the Peninsula Hong Kong, Salisbury Rd., Tsim Sha Tsui. (C) **852/2315 3160.** www.peninsula.com. Dim sum HK$46–HK$68; dim sum set lunch HK$368. AE, DC, MC, V. Mon–Sat 11:30am–2:30pm; Sun 11am–2:30pm, for dim sum. MTR: Tsim Sha Tsui.

Super Star Seafood Restaurant CANTONESE/SEAFOOD   This lively and popular seafood restaurant, filled with locals, is one of Tsim Sha Tsui's best places for authentic dim sum in a typical Chinese setting. There's an English menu that you fill out yourself (unfortunately, no more trolleys). Prices are already reasonable, but you can save a few Hong Kong dollars by dining before noon or after 2pm, when dim starts at HK$10 on weekdays and HK$11 on weekends and holidays. See p. 128 for a list of alternate locations.

83–97 Nathan Rd., Tsim Sha Tsui. (C) **852/2628 0339.** Dim sum HK$13–HK$35 Mon–Fri, HK$14–HK$39 Sat–Sun and holidays. AE, DC, MC, V. Daily 7:30am–4:30pm, for dim sum. MTR: Tsim Sha Tsui.

T'ang Court ★★ CANTONESE   This fancy restaurant offers its own interpretations of classic Cantonese dim sum on an extensive menu and even a complete dim sum lunch.

In the Langham Hotel, 8 Peking Rd., Tsim Sha Tsui. ℭ **852/2375 1133,** ext. 2250. http://hongkong. langhamhotels.com. Dim sum HK$35–HK$50; dim sum lunch HK$255. AE, DC, MC, V. Mon–Fri noon–3pm; Sat–Sun and holidays 11am–3pm, for dim sum. MTR: Tsim Sha Tsui.

Tsui Hang Village Restaurant CANTONESE   Tsui Hang Village, a modern restaurant located in a shopping complex, offers inexpensive plates of dim sum, including traditional choices like steamed shrimp dumplings and its own creations like deep-fried shrimp in mashed taro or baked mini oyster tarts.

A branch across the harbor is on the second floor of the New World Tower, 16–18 Queen's Rd., Central (ℭ **852/2524 2012;** MTR: Central), serving dim sum daily (Mon–Fri 11am–3pm, Sat 11am–5pm, and Sun and holidays 10am–5pm).

Miramar Plaza, 1 Kimberley Rd., Tsim Sha Tsui. ℭ **852/2376 2882.** www.miramar-group.com. Dim sum HK$21–HK$42. AE, DC, MC, V. Mon–Sat 11:30am–5pm; Sun and holidays 10am–5pm, for dim sum. MTR: Tsim Sha Tsui.

Yan Toh Heen ★★★ CANTONESE   One of Hong Kong's top Cantonese eateries, this elegant restaurant with large windows treats diners to views of the harbor. A daily changing menu lists almost two dozen varieties of dim sum, with past offerings including steamed rice flour cannelloni with shredded roasted duck, *conpoy* (dried scallops), and chives, and steamed assorted mushrooms and pumpkin dumplings. It also offers an excellent selection of teas.

In the InterContinental Hong Kong, 18 Salisbury Rd., Tsim Sha Tsui. ℭ **852/2313 2323.** www.hongkong-ic.intercontinental.com. Dim sum HK$44–HK$80. AE, DC, MC, V. Mon–Sat noon–2:30pm; Sun and holidays 11:30am–3pm, for dim sum. MTR: Tsim Sha Tsui.

Yat Tung Heen ★ CANTONESE   A good choice if you're in Yau Ma Tei (visiting the Jade Market, perhaps?), this is a large, elegant dining hall, with one of the most beautifully decorated open kitchens I've seen—looking more like an art gallery than a kitchen. Still, it turns out more than 30 different kinds of dim sum, from steamed squid in XO chili sauce to baked crispy barbecued pork buns.

In the Eaton Hotel, 380 Nathan Rd., Kowloon. ℭ **852/2782 1818.** http://hongkong.eatonhotels.com. Dim sum HK$20–HK$46. AE, DC, MC, V. Mon–Sat 11am–4pm; Sun and holidays 10am–4pm, for dim sum. MTR: Jordan.

Central

City Hall Maxim's Palace CANTONESE   There's no better place in Central for dim sum with a good harbor view than this enormously popular restaurant, located on the second floor of City Hall (don't confuse it with the pricier Maxim's Restaurant on the first floor). It's a lively, noisy, humungous place, with dim sum still offered from trolleys, plus an English menu with photos and prices for other dishes like noodles. Easy ordering, but it's best to avoid the lunchtime crunch.

Low Block (2nd floor), City Hall, Connaught Rd. Central and Edinburgh Place, Central. ℭ **852/2521 1303.** Dim sum HK$28–HK$46. AE, DC, MC, V. Mon–Sat 11am–3pm; Sun and holidays 9am–3pm, for dim sum. MTR: Central.

The Grand Stage CANTONESE   On the top floor of Western Market, a handsome, 1906 brick former public market now housing souvenir shops and fabric stalls, is this airy, tall-ceilinged restaurant. An English menu lists a wide variety of dim sum, from steamed tiger prawn dumplings with Kunming wild bamboo shoot to steamed rice sheet rolls with minced beef and coriander. The restaurant is best noted, though, for nightly ballroom dancing starting at 7pm.

Western Market (2nd floor), 323 Des Voeux Rd. Central, Central. ℭ **852/815 2311.** Dim sum HK$18–HK$48. AE, DC, MC, V. Daily 11:30am–3pm, for dim sum. MTR: Central.

Lin Heung Tea House ★ ▮▮ CANTONESE   This is a throwback to another era, opened more than 80 years ago and one of the few teahouses still selling dim sum from trolleys. Walk past the ground-floor pastry shop and up the stairs, where you'll find a very simple room that's packed no matter what time of day. You're supposed to find your own seat (though a waiter may take pity and help you), and most likely you'll share a table. There's no English menu, but the women manning the trolleys are willing to show you what's inside their baskets. The house specialty is *dai bao*, or big chicken buns (fluffy dough filled with chicken, dried mushroom, and salted yolk), but only 100 or so are baked each morning and they disappear almost as soon as they arrive from the kitchen. My table mates at one lunch, a couple of elderly gentlemen who meet up here every day, took me under their wing, made recommendations, and flagged down the trolley ladies to make sure I got what I wanted, making it a far more enjoyable experience than dining alone.

160–164 Wellington St., Central. ℭ **852/2544 4556.** Dim sum HK$12–HK$16. No credit cards. Daily 6am–4:30pm and 5:30–11pm, for dim sum. MTR: Central.

Luk Yu Tea House ★★ CANTONESE   Luk Yu, first opened in 1933, is the most famous dim sum teahouse remaining in Hong Kong. In fact, unless you have a time machine, you can't get any closer to old Hong Kong than this wonderful Art Deco–era Cantonese restaurant, with its ceiling fans, spittoons, individual wooden booths for couples, marble tabletops, wood paneling, and stained-glass windows. It's also one of the best places to try a few Chinese teas, including *bo lai* (a fermented black tea, which is the most common tea in Hong Kong; also spelled *bo lay*), jasmine, *lung ching* (a green tea), and *sui sin* (narcissus or daffodil). But Luk Yu is most famous for its dim sum, offered from an English menu that changes weekly, with past offerings including steamed rice with duck meat wrapped in fresh lotus leaves, deep-fried Chinese ham-and-chicken meat pie, and jumbo-size chicken bun. Although this is a pricey venue for dim sum and service can be indifferent, those looking for a slice of a bygone era should make a point of dining here.

24–26 Stanley St., Central. ℭ **852/2523 5464.** Dim sum HK$32–HK$75. MC, V. Daily 7am–5pm, for dim sum. MTR: Central.

The Square CANTONESE   This smartly decorated restaurant, next to Hong Kong Station and the ifc mall, offers only a half-dozen or so dim sum choices on weekdays but a greatly expanded dim sum menu on weekends and holidays (reservations are a must). The restaurant is renowned for its steamed lobster dumplings and jumbo shrimp, chicken, and asparagus spring rolls, but even the humble steamed barbecued pork buns here are among the best I've had.

Exchange Square II, Central. ℭ **852/2525 1163.** www.maxims.com.hk/en. Dim sum HK$17–HK$58. AE, DC, MC, V. Daily 11am–3pm, for dim sum. MTR: Central.

Zen CANTONESE   Starkly modern and hip, this Cantonese restaurant offers dim sum daily from an English menu, with more varieties available on the weekend.

The Mall, Pacific Place, 88 Queensway, Central. 🕾 **852/2845 4555.** Dim sum HK$38–HK$58. AE, DC, MC, V. Mon–Sat 11:30am–3:30pm; Sun 10:30am–3:30pm, for dim sum. MTR: Admiralty.

Victoria Peak

Tien Yi ★ CANTONESE   For Hong Kong's best dim sum meal with a view, head to this multilevel restaurant on the Peak. Although most tables are beside the expansive windows, only a few overlook Victoria Harbour (be sure to reserve one of these), with the rest looking toward the South China Sea. More than two dozen varieties of dim sum are offered for lunch on the English menu, from the ubiquitous barbecued pork buns to baked mini egg tart with bird's nest.

Peak Tower, Level 2, Victoria Peak. 🕾 **852/2907 3888.** www.rcgastronomic.com. Dim sum HK$35–HK$50. AE, DC, MC, V. Mon–Sat 11am–5pm; Sun and holidays 10am–5pm, for dim sum. Peak Tram.

AFTERNOON TEA

Colonial days are over, but the tradition of afternoon tea lives on.

China Tee Club ★ 🎒 TEA/CAKES   Located on the first floor of the Pedder Building (home of discounted clothing stores and boutiques), this quaint dining hall with ceiling fans, palm trees, and old-fashioned decor is actually a private members' club, but you can come for afternoon tea by paying an extra HK$10 fee per person. Options include a tea or coffee set with finger sandwiches, scones, and pastries or a Chinese dim sum set, as well as a limited menu of salads, soups, and sandwiches. This is a refined, nostalgic oasis in the middle of bustling Central.

101 Pedder Building, Central. 🕾 **852/2521 0233.** www.chinateeclub.com.hk. Afternoon tea or dim sum set HK$110 for 1 person, HK$195 for 2. AE, DC, MC, V. Mon–Sat 3–5:30pm, for afternoon tea. MTR: Tsim Sha Tsui.

The Lobby ★★★ TEA/CAKES   The ornate lobby of the Peninsula hotel, built in 1928, is the most famous lobby in Hong Kong. A popular place to see and be seen, the lobby features soaring columns topped with elaborate gilded ceilings and sculpted figures of gods and angels, palm trees, a Tai Ping carpet, and classically styled furniture. As late as the 1950s, the lobby was divided into east and west wings—one for the British and one for everyone else, including, as one pamphlet put it, women "seeking dalliance." While the rules aren't as strict any more, you'll still want to look presentable (no shorts, no flip-flops). The set tea includes finger sandwiches, French pastries, and scones with Devonshire clotted cream and strawberry preserve, and tea cake. Desserts are also available from an a la carte menu. No reservations are accepted, so you may have to wait for a table. A classical string quartet serenades you from an upstairs balcony (except Mon).

In the Peninsula Hong Kong, Salisbury Rd., Tsim Sha Tsui. 🕾 **852/2315 3146.** www.peninsula.com. Afternoon tea set HK$268 for 1 person, HK$398 for 2. AE, DC, MC, V. Daily 2–7pm. MTR: Tsim Sha Tsui.

Lobby Lounge ★★ TEA/CAKES   The InterContinental takes the honors of having the most gorgeous lobby view—soaring windows provide an almost surreal panorama of Victoria Harbour and Hong Kong Island. On weekends, you're serenaded by classical musicians. Feast your eyes on the view as you sip tea and indulge in finger sandwiches, pastries, and/or scones with Devonshire clotted cream and preserves. There's also a dessert menu, but for the ultimate experience, opt for one of the afternoon sets with "Golden Dragon" or "Golden Temple" tea, a blossoming green tea that opens like a flower in your cup.

In the InterContinental Hong Kong, 18 Salisbury Rd., Tsim Sha Tsui. ℭ **852/2721 1211.** www.hongkong-ic. intercontinental.com. Afternoon tea set with pastries or scones HK$130 for 1 person; tea set with sand- wiches, pastries, and scones HK$398–HK$1,388 for 2. AE, DC, MC, V. Daily 2:30–6pm. MTR: Tsim Sha Tsui.

EXPLORING HONG KONG

7

Hong Kong is perpetually revving up its sightseeing potential, opening new attractions and revamping older ones, expanding museums or developing new ones, and redesigning organized sightseeing tours to reflect the territory's changing demographics. On the other hand, if all you want to do is hike or lie on the beach, you can do that, too.

If you really want to do Hong Kong justice, plan on staying at least a week. However, because the city is so compact and its transportation is so efficient, you can see quite a bit of the city and its outlying islands in 3 to 5 days, especially if you're on the go from dawn until past dusk. In fact, some of Hong Kong's greatest sites are seen from public transportation. To get the most out of your time, it makes sense to divide the city into sections when planning your sightseeing. Museums, parks, markets, and other attractions, therefore, are subdivided in this chapter according to area, making it easier to coordinate sightseeing and dining plans.

For specific ideas on how to spend your days in Hong Kong, be sure to read my recommended itineraries in chapter 4. In addition, you might find it useful to read over the suggested walking tours in chapter 8, since they include stops at several of Hong Kong's top attractions. For sightseeing information on the New Territories and outlying islands, see chapter 11.

HONG KONG'S TOP ATTRACTIONS

Four activities I would recommend to every visitor to the SAR are: Ride the Star Ferry across the harbor, take the Peak Tram to the top of Victoria Peak, ride one of the rickety old trams on Hong Kong Island, and take a ferry to one of the outlying islands (see chapter 11, "Side Trips from Hong Kong," for information on the islands). Nothing can beat the thrill of these four experiences, or give you a better insight into the essence of Hong Kong and its people. What's more, they're all incredibly inexpensive.

Hong Kong Ferries

The stars of the Hong Kong stage, of course, are the Star Ferries, green-and-white vessels that have been carrying passengers back and forth

Kowloon Attractions

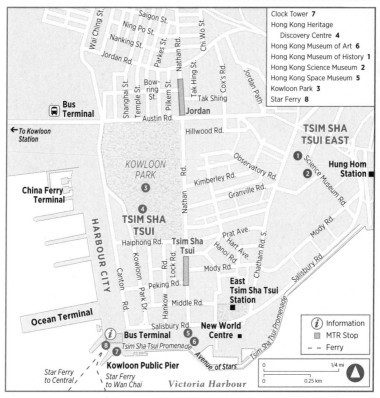

Clock Tower **7**
Hong Kong Heritage
  Discovery Centre **4**
Hong Kong Museum of Art **6**
Hong Kong Museum of History **1**
Hong Kong Science Museum **2**
Hong Kong Space Museum **5**
Kowloon Park **3**
Star Ferry **8**

between Kowloon and Hong Kong Island since 1898. At only HK$2 on weekdays for the regular, lower-deck fare, it's one of the cheapest—and yet most dramatic—harbor rides in the world. The entire ride from pier to pier takes about 5 minutes, with approximately 400 crossings a day. (For tips on using the Star Ferry, see "Getting Around" in chapter 3, beginning on p. 34.)

Because a 5-minute ride isn't nearly enough time to soak up the ambience of Victoria Harbour, another great way to relax and view the skyline is on a ferry to an outlying island. While most of Hong Kong's 260 outlying islands are uninhabited, ferry trips to the most interesting ones are described in chapter 11. These ferries, which depart from the Central Ferry Piers, are by far the cheapest way to see Hong Kong's harbor, with most trips lasting less than an hour. Some even offer an outside deck, where you can watch Hong Kong float past. In fact, part of the fun in visiting an outlying island is the ferry ride there and back.

There are also organized boat cruises of Victoria Harbour; for more information see "Organized Tours & Cultural Activities," later in this chapter.

Central District Attractions

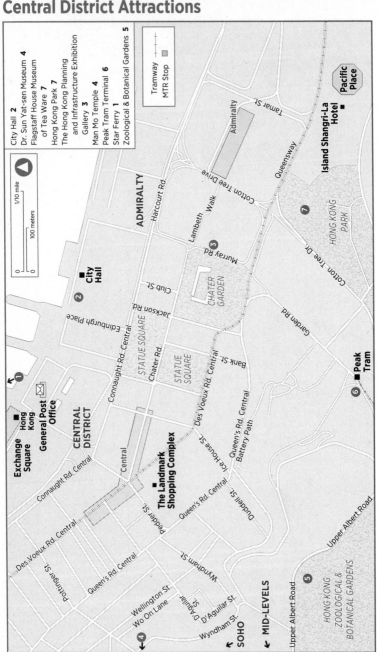

City Hall **2**
Dr. Sun Yat-sen Museum **4**
Flagstaff House Museum
  of Tea Ware **7**
Hong Kong Park **7**
The Hong Kong Planning
  and Infrastructure Exhibition
  Gallery **3**
Man Mo Temple **4**
Peak Tram Terminal **6**
Star Ferry **1**
Zoological & Botanical Gardens **5**

Tramway
MTR Stop

Attractions Elsewhere on Hong Kong Island

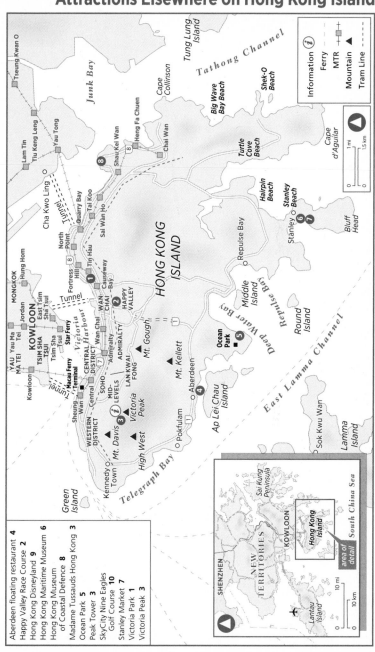

Information *i*
Ferry
MTR
Mountain ▲
Tram Line

1 mi
1.5 km

Aberdeen floating restaurant **4**
Happy Valley Race Course **9**
Hong Kong Disneyland **2**
Hong Kong Maritime Museum **6**
Hong Kong Museum
of Coastal Defence **8**
Madame Tussauds Hong Kong **3**
Ocean Park **5**
Peak Tower **3**
SkyCity Nine Eagles
Golf Course **10**
Stanley Market **7**
Victoria Park **1**
Victoria Peak **3**

Victoria Peak

At 392m (1,286 ft.), Victoria Peak is Hong Kong Island's tallest hill, which naturally makes it the best place for spectacular views of the city and surrounding areas. Be sure to bring your camera. If possible, go on a crystal-clear day, since fog—and smog—can greatly curtail vistas (in fact, I wouldn't even bother going up on a hazy day). Victoria Peak has always been one of Hong Kong's most exclusive places to live, since, in addition to the views, the Peak is typically cooler than the sweltering city below. More than 120 years ago, the rich reached the Peak after a 3-hour trip in sedan chairs, transported to the top by coolies. Then, in 1888, the **Peak Tram** began operations, cutting the journey from a grueling 3 hours to a mere 8 minutes. In 1989, the older, cast-iron green funicular cars with mahogany seats were replaced by new, modern cars imported from Switzerland, which increased the passenger load from 72 to 120 people. If you want to know more about the tram's history, stop by the **Peak Tram Historical Gallery,** ensconced in the Peak Tram Lower Terminus, which you can see for free with the purchase of a tram ticket. Filled with memorabilia and a replica of the first Peak Tram, it's open daily from 7am to midnight.

> ## The Best Peek of the Peak
>
> For the best view when riding the Peak Tram up to Victoria Peak, try to get a seat at the front, on the right side of the tram. From 1908 to 1949, the first two seats at the front were reserved—for the governor of Hong Kong.

The easiest way to reach the Peak Tram Lower Terminus, located on Garden Road, is to take the no. 15C open-top shuttle bus that operates between the tram terminus and the Star Ferry in Central. Shuttle buses cost HK$4.25 and run every 15 to 20 minutes between 10am and 11:45pm. Otherwise, it's about a 10-minute walk from Central's MTR Station to the tram terminus. Alternatively, you can take bus no. 15 from the Star Ferry terminal directly to the top of Victoria Peak for HK$9.80, but then you'd miss the tram unless you opt to take it down. Finally, you can eschew transportation altogether and walk. I have to admit I've never walked up the Peak, but the steep walk down, on shaded Old Peak Road and then Albany Road, is pleasant and brings you to the Zoological & Botanical Gardens in about 40 minutes; from there it's another 15 minutes to the MTR Central station.

As for the trams, they depart every 10 to 15 minutes between 7am and midnight. The tram climbs almost vertically for 8 minutes before reaching the top of the Peak—don't worry, there's never been an accident in its entire 100-odd years of operation. One-way tickets for the Peak Tram cost HK$25 for adults and HK$9 for seniors and children. Round-trip tickets cost HK$36 and HK$16, respectively, but there are also combination tickets for the tram and Peak attractions (see below). Or, you can use an Octopus card (p. 37).

Upon reaching the Peak, you'll find yourself at the very modern **Peak Tower** (© **852/2849 0668;** www.thepeak.com.hk), designed by British architect Terry Farrell, which looks like a Chinese cooking wok. Head straight for the rooftop **Sky Terrace** viewing deck, where you'll be privileged to view one of the world's most breathtaking 360-degree vistas, with sweeping panoramas of Hong Kong Island, the South China Sea, the skyscrapers of Central, boats plying Victoria Harbour, the ever-expanding construction on Kowloon peninsula, and the many hills of the New

Territories undulating in the background. An open-air gallery displays historic photos of old Hong Kong. It's open Monday to Friday 10am to 11pm and Saturday, Sunday, and holidays 8am to 11pm. Admission is HK$25 for adults and HK$12 for seniors and children. Slightly more economical are combination tram and Sky Terrace tickets, with one-way journeys costing HK$45 for adults and HK$19 for seniors and children, and round-trip journeys costing HK$56 and HK$26, respectively (if you don't want to spend money for the Sky Terrace, you can have good views, too, at Peak Galleria and the circular hike, described below).

Peak Tower is also home to a handful of Chinese, Western, and Japanese restaurants, as well as some fast-food outlets and a shopping arcade designed to evoke traditional Hong Kong street scenes. Also here is **Madame Tussauds Hong Kong,** Level 3, Peak Tower, 128 Peak Rd., Victoria Peak (© **852/2849 6966;** www.madame-tussauds.com.hk), with more than 100 life-size wax figures of national heroes, politicians, historical figures, Olympic medalists, movie stars, and musicians. In addition to the usual figures—Marilyn Monroe, Johnny Depp, the Beatles, Winston Churchill, President Obama—there are also local and Chinese heroes like Jackie Chan, Michelle Yeoh, Bruce Lee, Canto-pop star Andy Lau, and basketball star Yao Ming. In the scary section "Scream," live people portray psychopathic killers who are on the loose in an insane asylum (not recommended for young children). The museum is open daily from 10am to 10pm and costs HK$160 for adults and HK$90 for seniors and children; count on spending about 40 minutes here. Note that combination tickets for the Peak Tram, Sky Terrace, and Madame Tussauds are available.

Next to the Peak Tower is the **Peak Galleria,** a three-story complex with more shops, restaurants, an outdoor children's playground, and a viewing terrace. In the plaza in front of the Peak Tower is a kiosk for the **Hong Kong Tourism Board Visitor Centre,** located in a 50-year-old tram car and open daily from 9am to 9pm.

But the best thing to do atop Victoria Peak is to take a walk. One of my favorite walks in all of Hong Kong is the hour-long **circular hike ★★** on Lugard and Harlech roads, both located just a stone's throw from the Peak Tower (turn right out of the tower; both streets converge at the Peak Lookout restaurant). It's well marked, but the HKTB Visitor Centre has a map of the walk (as well as maps of other hikes from the peak to other destinations, such as Aberdeen). Mainly a footpath overhung with banyan trees and lined with lush vegetation, it snakes about 3.5km (2 miles) along the side of the peak, offering great views of the Central District below, the harbor, Kowloon, and then Aberdeen and the outlying islands on the other side. Along the path are signboards identifying flora and fauna. You will also pass several of Victoria Peak's mansions as you share the path with joggers, tourists, and locals out for a leisurely stroll. At night, the lighted path offers one of the world's most romantic views (I don't recommend walking it alone, however). Don't miss it.

Riding a Tram

Just as the Star Ferry is the best way to see the harbor, the tram is the most colorful and cheapest way to see the northern end of Hong Kong Island, including the Central District, Western District, Wan Chai, and Causeway Bay. In fact, the tram is so much a part of Hong Kong life that it was chosen for Hong Kong's exhibit at the Vancouver 1986 Expo. Dating from 1904, the tramline follows what used to be the waterfront (before the days of land reclamation). Old, narrow, double-decker affairs, the trams cut through the heart of the city, from Kennedy Town in the west to Shau Kei Wan in the east. With only one detour—off to Happy Valley—it's impossible to get lost.

In any case, if you're in Central, you can board the tram on Des Voeux Road Central. Climb to the upper deck and try to get a seat in the front row. (For more information on the fare and how to ride the tram, see "Getting Around" in chapter 3, beginning on p. 34.) I especially like to ride the tram at night, when neon signs blaze overhead and the streets buzz with activity.

7 MUSEUMS & GALLERIES

EXPLORING HONG KONG | Museums & Galleries

If you plan to visit all seven of Hong Kong's main museums—the Hong Kong Museum of Art, Hong Kong Museum of History, Hong Kong Space Museum (excluding the Space Theatre), Hong Kong Science Museum, Hong Kong Museum of Coastal Defence, Dr. Sun Yat-sen Museum, and Hong Kong Heritage Museum (located in Sha Tin in the New Territories; p. 259)—you can save money by purchasing the Museum Pass for HK$30, valid for a week and available at any of the participating museums or Hong Kong Tourism Board Visitor Centres. Note, however, that museum admissions are free on Wednesdays.

Keep in mind, too, that municipal museums are closed December 25 and 26, January 1, and the first 3 days of the Chinese New Year. Private museums are usually also closed on bank holidays.

In Kowloon

Hong Kong Heritage Discovery Centre   This museum highlighting historic preservation efforts throughout Hong Kong is itself located in a historic renovated building, former barracks built in 1910 in Hong Kong Park and used to accommodate British troops until 1967. Models, photographs, and signboards outline the history of both Western and Chinese architectural sites that have been renovated and put to new use, like Tsang Tai Uk, a walled village in the New Territories that is now a museum (p. 258). Because so many of Hong Kong's historic buildings are in the New Territories, this is a good stop before venturing outside the city. Unfortunately, displays consist mostly of text and are a bit dry, making the museum of interest mostly to architecture and history buffs. (By the way, if you have a laptop or a Wi-Fi enabled phone, you can get Wi-Fi access here for free, part of the SAR's efforts to eventually make all of Hong Kong a free wireless city.)

Kowloon Park, Haiphong and Nathan rds., Tsim Sha Tsui. © **852/2208 4400.** www.amo.gov.hk/en/discovery_center.php. Free admission. Mon–Wed and Fri–Sat 10am–6pm; Sun and holidays 10am–7pm. MTR: Tsim Sha Tsui (exit A1).

Hong Kong Museum of Art ★★★ 🏛   Because of its convenient location on the Tsim Sha Tsui waterfront, just a 2-minute walk from the Star Ferry terminus, and its manageable size, this museum is the most worthwhile if your time is limited. The museum's special exhibits and its vast collection of Chinese antiquities and fine art—shown on a rotating basis—make this one of my top picks in Hong Kong; I just love popping in to see what's on view. Feast your eyes on ceramics, bronzes, jade, cloisonné, lacquerware, bamboo carvings, and textiles, as well as paintings, wall hangings, scrolls, and calligraphy dating from the 16th century to the present. The works are arranged in five permanent galleries on three floors of exhibit space, plus two galleries devoted to changing exhibits. The Historical Pictures Gallery is especially insightful, with works in oils, watercolors, pencil drawings, and prints that provide a visual account of life in Hong Kong, Macau, and Guangzhou (Canton) in the late

18th and 19th centuries. Another gallery displays contemporary Hong Kong works by local artists. You'll want to spend at least an hour here, though art aficionados can devote more time by renting audio guides for HK$10. A bonus is the beautiful backdrop of Victoria Harbour. Outside the museum are sculptures; you can have an audio tour of the artwork and artists here if you have a cellphone by dialing ☎ **852/3696 5000** (you have to pay for the call, but the information is free).

Hong Kong Cultural Centre Complex, 10 Salisbury Rd., Tsim Sha Tsui. ☎ **852/2721 0116.** http://hk.art. museum. Admission HK$10 adults; HK$5 children, students, and seniors. Free admission Wed. Fri–Wed 10am–6pm (to 8pm Sat). MTR: Tsim Sha Tsui (exit E).

Hong Kong Museum of History ★★★ ☺

If you visit only one museum in Hong Kong and you're prepared to devote at least 2 hours, this should be it. Make it one of your first priorities, so you'll have a better understanding of what you see during the rest of your trip. The permanent exhibit, called the Hong Kong Story, is an ambitious attempt to chronicle the city's long and fascinating history, starting with the formation of its natural history and its beginnings as a Neolithic settlement and continuing through its development as a fishing village, subsequent transformation into a modern metropolis, and 1997 handover to China. Through displays that include dioramas, replicas of fishing boats, models, reconstructed traditional housing, furniture, clothing, and items from daily life, the museum introduces Hong Kong's ethnic groups and their traditional means of livelihood, customs, and beliefs. These include fishermen who lived their entire lives on boats, the Five Great Clans who settled in what is now the New Territories and built walled communities, the Hoklo (who worked the territories' salt fields), and the Hakka, primarily rice farmers.

You can peer inside a fishing junk, see what Kowloon Walled City looked like before it became a park, see the backstage of a Chinese opera, read about the arrival of European traders and the Opium Wars, study a map showing land reclamation since the 1840s, see how Hong Kong changed under Japanese occupation during World War II, and view a model of a family's flat in a public housing estate. Ten small movie theaters are spread throughout the museum depicting everything from Hong Kong's beginnings and the Opium Wars to its movie industry, though showings in English are limited. One of my favorite parts of the museum is a re-created street of old Hong Kong, complete with a pawnshop, teahouse, tailor's shop, and a Chinese herbal-medicine shop actually located in Central until 1980 and reconstructed here. Also on display are 19th- and early-20th-century photographs, poignantly showing how much Hong Kong has changed through the decades. Audio guides, providing commentaries on more than 100 exhibits, are available for HK$10.

100 Chatham Rd. S., Tsim Sha Tsui East. ☎ **852/2724 9042.** http://hk.history.museum. Admission HK$10 adults, HK$5 children and seniors. Free admission Wed. Mon and Wed–Sat 10am–6pm; Sun and holidays 10am–7pm. MTR: Tsim Sha Tsui (a 20-min. walk from exit B2). Bus: 5 or 5C from the Star Ferry bus terminus.

Hong Kong Science Museum ★★ ☺

The mysteries of science and technology come to life here, with plenty of hands-on exhibits sure to appeal to children and adults alike. More than 500 exhibits cover four floors, with sections devoted to the life sciences; light, sound, and motion; electricity and magnetism; computers; transportation and communication; occupational safety and health; energy efficiency; and food science and home technology. Children ages 3 to 7 can have free reign of an area designed especially for them. Visitors can play with different optical illusions, see themselves upside down or with a "twin" in the World of Mirrors, learn how to save energy at home, play with bubbles, navigate a flight over Hong Kong Island or Kowloon at night, drive a car simulator, put together puzzles, learn about human reproduction, and see models of embryo development in the womb. There are exhibits designed to test a visitor's fitness, such as balance, endurance, and blood pressure. The computer section has more than 30 personal computers for guests to learn about computer software and graphics production (to access the Internet, however, you'll have to go to the museum's Resource Center, where two computers are available for you to use for free until 6pm on weekdays and 7pm on weekends; Wi-Fi with your own laptop is also free). This is a great place to bring kids on a rainy or humid day; give yourself about 3 hours. However, because this museum isn't unique to Hong Kong, I think childless adults can better spend their time elsewhere.

2 Science Museum Rd., Tsim Sha Tsui East. (C) **852/2732 3232.** http://hk.science.museum. Admission HK$25 adults; HK$13 children, students, and seniors. Free admission Wed. Mon–Wed and Fri 1–9pm; Sat–Sun and holidays 10am–9pm. MTR: Tsim Sha Tsui (a 15-min. walk from exit B2). Bus: 5 or 5C from the Star Ferry bus terminus.

Hong Kong Space Museum ☺   Located across from the Peninsula Hong Kong hotel on the Tsim Sha Tsui waterfront, the Space Museum is easy to spot with its white-domed planetarium. It's divided into two parts: the Exhibition Halls containing the Hall of Space Science and the Hall of Astronomy, and the Stanley Ho Space Theatre. The Hall of Space Science explores the human journey into space, with exhibits on ancient astronomical history, science fiction, early rockets, manned space flights, and future space programs. Several interactive rides and exhibits (most with weight and height restrictions) include a virtual 3-D glider ride through the Grand Canyon, a harness that holds occupants aloft with the same approximate gravity they'd experience walking on the moon, and a multi-axis chair developed for astronaut training that gives the sensation of tumbling through space. The Hall of Astronomy presents information on the solar system, solar science, the stars, and the universe. However, I find the museum, which opened in 1980, rather dated. Come only if you have kids and extra time on your hands, in which case you'll spend about an hour here.

In addition to producing two multimedia planetarium shows each year with a projection system that can create more than 8,000 stars, the Stanley Ho Space Theatre also presents OMNIMAX screenings with an almost 360-degree panorama. Forty-minute to hour-long shows are presented several times daily. Only a few are narrated in English, but for the others free headsets are available with simultaneous English translations. You can buy Space Theatre tickets in advance at the museum or at any URBTIX outlet. In addition, telephone reservations are accepted at (C) **852/2734 9009** until 1 hour before the show commences.

Hong Kong Cultural Centre Complex, 10 Salisbury Rd., Tsim Sha Tsui. (C) **852/2721 0226.** http://hk. space.museum. Admission to Exhibition Halls HK$10 adults; HK$5 children, students, and seniors. Free admission on Wed. Space Theatre HK$24–HK$32 adults; HK$12–HK$16 children, students, and seniors. Mon and Wed–Fri 1–9pm; Sat–Sun and holidays 10am–9pm. MTR: Tsim Sha Tsui (exit E).

On Hong Kong Island

Dr. Sun Yat-sen Museum   Born in 1866 in Guangdong Province and receiving his secondary and university education in Hong Kong, Dr. Sun Yat-sen is best known for his efforts to overthrow the corrupt Qing Dynasty, thereby helping to end more than 2,000 years of the ruling monarchy. Today he is still much revered as a leader of the

Chinese revolution, and this museum, housed in a handsome Edwardian Classical building constructed in 1914 as a private residence of a local businessman, provides detailed information on Sun Yat-sen's life, including his years in Hong Kong as a secondary and university student. An 11-minute film serves as a good introduction to the Chinese revolutionary, and I also like the many photographs of Dr. Sun Yat-sen with his family and revolutionary colleagues, but most interesting to me is the museum's portrayal of Hong Kong during Dr. Sun Yat-sen's years here. You'll spend about 30 minutes here, though you'll learn decidedly more if you opt for the 90-minute spiel offered by the audio guide, which costs HK$10 extra.

7 Castle Rd., Mid-Levels, Central. ℂ **852/2367 6373.** http://hk.drsunyatsen.museum. HK$10 adults; HK$5 children, students, and seniors. Free admission on Wed. Mon–Wed and Fri–Sat 10am–6pm; Sun and holidays 10am–7pm. Bus: 3B, 12M, or 103 to Caine Rd. MTR: Central; then take the Central–Mid-Levels Escalator to Caine Rd.

Flagstaff House Museum of Tea Ware ★★ Flagstaff House, located in Hong Kong Park, is the oldest colonial building in Hong Kong—the best place to go if you want to see typical Hong Kong architecture of 165 years ago. Completed in 1846 in Greek Revival style, it served as the office and residence of the commander of the British forces until 1978. Now a museum devoted to the subject of tea culture in China, its collection includes about 600 pieces of tea ware ranging from earthenware to porcelain, primarily of Chinese origin, dating from the 7th century to the present day. However, only 150 or so pieces are on display at any one time, with exhibitions changed two or three times a year. I always find them fascinating, especially the exhibits describing the various kinds of tea and tea-making methods favored by the major dynasties and in various parts of China. Don't miss the museum shop, which sells beautifully crafted teapots as well as teas (I always buy my Pu'er tea here, which purportedly lowers cholesterol and aids in weight loss), and the K.S. Lo Gallery with its exhibits of ceramics and seals. You can see everything here in about 30 minutes, though if available (usually on Sat), you might wish to join a tea ceremony, presented on a first-come, first-served basis (check the website for the schedule).

Flagstaff House, Hong Kong Park, 10 Cotton Tree Dr., Central. ℂ **852/2869 0690.** http://hk.art. museum. Free admission. Wed–Mon 10am–5pm. MTR: Admiralty (exit C1); then follow the signs through Pacific Place to Island Shangri-La Hotel/Hong Kong Park via 2 escalators.

Hong Kong Maritime Museum Shoppers in need of a break (or their companions in need of a break from fellow shoppers) might find respite in this museum near Stanley Market. It's located in the historic 1846 Murray House, which once stood in Central but was dismantled in the early 1980s and reassembled here on the Stanley waterfront. The museum is divided into two galleries: The Ancient Gallery follows the development of Chinese vessels, from war boats and trading ships to Chinese junks, while the Modern Gallery concentrates on the evolution of Hong Kong's shipping industry and how that industry changed with the arrival of bulk carriers, tankers, and container ships. Visitors can steer a container ship in a bridge simulator, see memorabilia

> ### 💬 Did You Know?
>
> The 1,377m (4,518-ft.) Tsing Ma Bridge, the world's longest suspension bridge carrying both road and rail traffic, connects the new international airport with Kowloon. It is 97m (318 ft.) longer than San Francisco's Golden Gate Bridge and can withstand typhoon wind speeds up to 300kmph (186 mph).

from the golden age of ocean steamers, be happy they're not carting around the huge 1920s Louis Vuitton trunk on display, and listen via headphones to a former waiter describe his life working on passenger cargo lines. I was particularly captivated by the 50-some boat models on display, all wonderfully crafted down to the minutest details. Depending on your interest, you'll spend 45 to 60 minutes here.

Murray House, Stanley. © **852/2813 2322.** www.hkmaritimemuseum.org. Admission HK$20 adults; HK$10 students, seniors, and children. Tues–Sun 10am–6pm. Bus: 6, 6A, 6X, 260, or 973.

Hong Kong Museum of Coastal Defence ★   Located in Lei Yue Mun Fort, one of Hong Kong's oldest and best-preserved British coastal fortresses dating from the Victorian period, this museum explores 600 years of the territory's coastal defense. Exhibits begin with the Ming and Qing dynasties, when coastal defenses guarded southern China against the invasion of Japanese pirates and Western imperialists, and continue through the Opium Wars, Hong Kong's role as a major base for the British navy, the Japanese 1941 invasion, and the handover to the People's Liberation Army. On display are naval costumes, models of war junks, weaponry, photographs, and memorabilia. The fort itself, built by the British in 1887 to defend the eastern approaches to the harbor against possible attacks by Russia or France, retains its batteries, underground magazines, protective ditch, caponiers, and torpedo station. With its strategic location on the coast, it provides a panoramic view of the eastern approach to Victoria Harbour. You'll probably spend at least 1½ hours here.

175 Tung Hei Rd., Shau Kei Wan. © **852/2569 1500.** http://hk.coastaldefence.museum. Admission HK$10 adults; HK$5 students, seniors, and children. Free admission Wed. Fri–Wed 10am–5pm. MTR: Shau Kei Wan (exit B2 and then a 15-min. walk).

Hong Kong Museum of Medical Sciences ★ 📖   This museum charts the historical development of medical science in Hong Kong. It's located in the century-old, Edwardian-style former Pathological Institute, which was founded to combat the colony's most horrific outbreak of bubonic plague, in 1894. Back then, British patients were treated upstairs, while the Chinese were relegated to the basement rooms. Several rooms remain almost exactly as they were, including an autopsy room and a laboratory filled with old equipment, while others serve as exhibition rooms devoted to such areas as the development of dentistry and radiology (note the X-ray of the bound foot), man's attempts to relieve pain since ancient times, SARS and other infectious diseases, and the appalling living conditions in Tai Ping Shan, where the 1894 outbreak occurred (the cause of the plague was identified in Hong Kong shortly thereafter). But what makes the museum particularly fascinating is its unique comparison of traditional Chinese and Western medicine, and its funding of research into Chinese medicine. Included is a display on traditional Chinese herbs. You should spend 30 minutes here.

2 Caine Lane, Mid-Levels. ℰ **852/2549 5123.** www.hkmms.org.hk. Admission HK$10 adults; HK$5 children, students, and seniors. Tues–Sat 10am–5pm; Sun and holidays 1–5pm. Bus: 3B, 12M, or 103 to Caine Rd., or Minibus no. 8 or 22 to Ladder St. (pronounced Lau Tai Kai in Chinese).

LIFE ON THE water IN ABERDEEN

Situated on the south side of Hong Kong Island, Aberdeen is nestled around a naturally protected harbor. Famous for its colorful floating seafood restaurant and boat people who live on junks in Aberdeen Harbour, the town has undergone massive changes over the past couple decades. Originally a typhoon shelter and land base for seafarers, it used to be a charming fishing village and boat-building port, supported primarily by several thousand junks and boat people. Many of the boat people, however, have since been moved to massive housing projects, and the waterfront surrounding Aberdeen is now crowded with high-rises. At anchor are almost as many yachts as fishing boats and junks.

Still, Aberdeen continues to be popular with the tourist crowd because of its remaining boat population and floating restaurant. Women operating sampans will vie for your dollars to tour you around the harbor, which is definitely worth the price since it's about the only thing to do here and is the best way to see the junks. Although the boat population is shrinking, you'll pass huge boats that house extended families; you'll see men repairing fishing nets, women hanging out their laundry, dogs barking, children playing, and families eating. I find the ride rather voyeuristic but fascinating just the same. There was a time when a boat person could be born, live, marry, and die onboard, hardly ever setting foot on shore. Nowadays, many young people move ashore to seek more stable employment.

A 20-minute tour from a licensed operator will cost approximately HK$60 per person and is offered daily between 9am and 5:30pm from the Aberdeen Centre waterfront promenade. You will also encounter old women with wide-brimmed straw hats who will try to persuade you to board their sampan, with the price open to bargaining and depending on the numbers of tourists around at the time. On one particularly slow day, for example, I was offered, and took, a sampan tour for HK$50, and I was the only one in the boat.

Other Aberdeen attractions include the largest floating restaurant in the world—**Jumbo Kingdom,** which offers both Cantonese restaurants and a roof-top seafood restaurant (p. 156), with free shuttle service from the Aberdeen Centre promenade—and a temple built in 1851. The temple is dedicated to Tin Hau, protectress of fishing folk, and is located at the junction of Aberdeen Main and Aberdeen Reservoir roads. Short taxi rides away are the huge Ocean Park amusement park with its thrill rides and aquarium (p. 183), and Horizon Plaza, a high-rise warehouse filled with outlets and shops selling antiques, carpets, furniture, clothing, and more (p. 224 and 227).

To get to Aberdeen, take bus no. 7 from the Central Ferry Piers; bus no. 70 from the Exchange Square Bus Terminal in the Central District; bus no. 72 or 77 from Causeway Bay; or bus no. 973 from Tsim Sha Tsui.

RELIGION, myth & FOLKLORE

Most Hong Kong Chinese worship both Buddhist and Taoist deities, something they do not find at all incongruous. They also worship their family ancestors. Ancestral altars are commonplace in homes, and certain days are set aside for visiting ancestral graves. Many temples have large tablet halls, where Hong Kong families can worship the memorialized photographs of their dead. About 360 temples are scattered throughout Hong Kong; some embody a mixture of both Buddhist and Taoist principles.

While Buddhism is concerned with the afterlife, **Taoism** is a folk faith whose devotees believe in luck and in currying its favor. Fortunetellers, therefore, are usually found only at Taoist temples. Tao, essentially, is the way of the universe, the spirit of all things, and cannot be perceived. However, Taoist gods must be worshipped and Taoist spirits appeased. Most popular in Hong Kong is Tin Hau, goddess of the sea and protectress of fishermen. Hong Kong has at least 24 temples that were erected in her honor. But each profession or trade has its own god—ironically, policemen and gangsters have the same one.

If you look for them, you'll find shrines dedicated to the earth god, Tou Ti, at the entrance to almost every store or restaurant in Hong Kong. They're usually below knee level, so that everyone pays homage upon entering and departing. Restaurants also have shrines dedicated to the kitchen god, Kwan Kung, to protect workers from knives and other sharp objects.

Although not a religion as such, another guiding principle in Chinese thought is **Confucianism.** Confucius, who lived in the 5th century B.C., devised a strict set of rules designed to create the perfect human being. Kindness, selflessness, obedience, and courtesy were preached, with carefully prescribed rules of how people should interact with one another. Because the masses were largely illiterate, Confucius communicated by means of easy-to-remember proverbs.

Despite the fact that many Hong Kong Chinese are both Buddhist and Taoist, they are not a particularly religious people in the Western sense of the word. There is no special day for worship, so devotees simply visit a temple whenever they want to pay their respects or feel the need for spiritual guidance. Otherwise, religion in Hong Kong plays a subtle role and is evident

The Hong Kong Planning & Infrastructure Exhibition Gallery Its name is dry and unpromising, but anyone who has witnessed the SAR's changes over the past few decades will find this museum fascinating—Hong Kong is a never-ending work in progress and this museum gives visitors a firsthand look at the government plans for Hong Kong. Over the next few decades, the city plans to continue to develop its tourism, transportation, and urban infrastructure at what seems like breakneck speed, and the purpose of this museum is to help visitors visualize planned changes through interactive displays, sophisticated computer simulation, and high-tech models that project Hong Kong's new look 10, 20, and even 30 years from now. Future and current projects include West Kowloon, which will become one of the city's foremost cultural and entertainment centers when completed around 2015; a pedestrian promenade on Hong Kong Island stretching along the waterfront from Central to Causeway Bay; and a new cruise ship terminal where Kai Tak Airport once stood. **Note:** This museum will move into new quarters in 2012, when it will occupy the more in philosophy and action than in pious ceremony. To the Chinese, religion is a way of life and thus affects everyday living.

Almost every home has a small shrine, where lighted joss sticks are thought to bring good luck. In New Year celebrations, door gods are placed on the front door for good luck, and all lights are switched on to discourage monster spirits. On New Year's Day, homes are not swept for fear of whisking away good luck. And during a full moon or major festival, housewives may set fire to paper creations of homes, cars, or fake money to bring good luck.

But no one can ever have too much good luck; superstitions abound in Hong Kong. Certain numbers, for example, have positive or negative connotations. The most auspicious number is 8, because its pronunciation *(baht)* is similar to the word for wealth *(faht)*. Likewise, the most inauspicious number is 4, since it sounds almost exactly like the Cantonese word for death. Thirteen is also an unlucky number, so many Hong Kong buildings simply skip it in their floor-numbering scheme. License plates with lucky numbers have sold for high prices in Hong Kong. In 2007, a man paid HK$7.1 million (US$920,000) for a license plate with the number 12, which sounds like "certainly easy" in Cantonese. The most expensive so far was in 1994 for a license plate with number 9 (which sounds like "everlasting" in Cantonese)—HK$13 million (US$1.7 million). Certain foods, too, are considered auspicious. For New Year's, noodles are considered good for longevity, while fish is eaten for success. A half-eaten fish is never turned over to get to the other side, however, in the belief that doing so means a fishing boat will capsize (you're supposed to lift the spine or remove it to get to the other side). Red is considered a lucky color, making it popular for weddings and New Year celebrations. Sharp objects, such as scissors, should not be used during New Year's, because they will cut away good luck.

To be on the safe side, Hong Kong Chinese will also visit fortunetellers. Some read palms, while others study facial features, consult astrological birth charts, or let a little bird select a fortune card from a deck.

entire City Hall Annex Building (contact the museum for updated details). Until then, it is only a fraction of its future self at the address below and can be seen in a mere 10 minutes.

2 Murray Rd. (in a car park building), Central. ☏ **852/3102 1242.** www.infrastructuregallery.gov.hk. Free admission. Wed–Mon 10am–6pm. MTR: Central.

TEMPLES

For information on Po Lin Monastery and its adjacent Giant Tian Tan Buddha, see the section on Lantau Island in "The Outlying Islands," in chapter 11, p. 266.

Chi Lin Nunnery ★   Just one subway stop away from Wong Tai Sin (see below) is the Chi Lin Buddhist Nunnery, founded in the 1930s to provide religious, cultural, educational, and elderly care services to the Hong Kong community. Reconstructed in the 1990s in the style of Tang dynasty monastic architecture (A.D. 618–907), the nunnery is an amazing union of ancient building techniques and modern technology. Imported yellow cedar from Canada was carved in China by skilled artisans and craftsmen and then reconstructed here like pieces in a jigsaw puzzle; no nails were used, but rather a system of wooden doweling and brackets that is nothing short of remarkable. The main hall was modeled after the Foguang Monastery in Shanxi Province, while the double-eaved Hall of Celestial Kings is designed after the 11th-century Phoenix Hall outside Kyoto, Japan. On nunnery grounds are a lotus pond, sculpted bushes and bonsai, and statues of the goddess of mercy, god of medicine, and others. A better garden, however, the **Nan Lian Garden,** awaits across the street, styled in imitation of a famous classical garden of the Tang Dynasty and with a very good vegetarian restaurant; see p. 181 for more information. Plan on at least an hour to see the nunnery and the garden.

Chi Lin Rd., Diamond Hill. © **852/2354 1604.** Free admission. Daily 9am–4:30pm. MTR: Diamond Hill (exit C2) and then a 15-min. walk.

Man Mo Temple ★   Hong Kong Island's oldest and most important temple (Taoist) was built in the 1840s as one of the new colony's first traditional-style temples. It's named after its two principal deities: Man, the god of literature, who is dressed in red and holds a calligraphy brush; and Mo, the god of war, wearing a green robe and holding a sword. Ironically, Mo finds patronage in both the police force (shrines in his honor can be found in all Hong Kong police stations today) and the infamous triad secret societies. Two ornate sedan chairs, carved in 1862 and on display inside, were once used during festivals to carry the statues of the gods around the neighborhood. But what makes this evocative temple particularly memorable are the giant incense coils hanging from the ceiling, imparting a fragrant, smoky haze—these are purchased by patrons seeking fulfillment of their wishes, such as good health or a successful business deal, and may burn as long as 3 weeks. No flash photography is allowed inside the temple.

Hollywood Rd. and Ladder St., Western District. © **852/2803 2916.** Free admission. Daily 8am–6pm. Bus: 26 from Des Voeux Rd. Central (in front of the HSBC headquarters) to the 2nd stop on Hollywood Rd., across from the temple. Or take the Central–Mid-Levels Escalator to Hollywood Rd. and turn right.

Wong Tai Sin ★★   Located six subway stops northeast of Yau Ma Tei in the far north end of Kowloon, Wong Tai Sin is Hong Kong's most popular Taoist temple, which attracts worshippers of all three traditional Chinese guiding faiths: Taoism, Buddhism, and Confucianism. Although the temple itself is less than 100 years old, it adheres to traditional Chinese architectural principles with its red pillars, two-tiered golden roof, blue friezes, yellow latticework, and multicolored carvings. Its construction also displays the six elements dictated by geomancy (feng shui), namely bronze (the pavilion), metal (the archives hall), wood, water (a fountain), fire (Yue Heung Shrine, dedicated to the Buddha of Lighting Lamp), and earth (an earthen wall). The very popular temple attracts those seeking information about their fortunes—from advice about business or horse racing to determining which day is most auspicious for a wedding. Most worshippers make use of a bamboo container holding numbered sticks. After lighting a joss stick and kneeling before the main altar, the worshipper concentrates on a specific question and gently shakes the container until one of the sticks falls out. The number on the stick holds the answer, which is then interpreted by one of the temple's many soothsayers in the lower level, some of whom speak English. The cost of the interpretation is HK$30. If you want a more in-depth fortune, expect to pay about HK$300.

CHINESE gods

The Chinese world has many gods, each with different functions and abilities: For example, the kitchen god reigns in the household, various occupations have their own patron gods, and gods protect worshippers through certain stages of their lives; there is an earth god, goddess of pregnant women, 60 gods representing each year of the 60-year Chinese calendar, a god of riches popular with shopkeepers, and a scholar god whose favor is curried by students—to highlight a few.

Most popular in Hong Kong is **Tin Hau,** goddess of the sea and protector of seafarers (in Macau she is known as **A-Ma**). As the patron goddess of fisher folk, Tin Hau is honored by fishing communities throughout Hong Kong with more than two dozen Tin Hau temples, including those at Yau Ma Tei, Causeway Bay, Stanley, and Cheung Chau. According to popular lore, Tin Hau is the deification of a real girl who lived in Fujian Province around A.D. 900 or 1000 and who saved a group of fishermen during a storm. Her birthday is celebrated annually with gaily decorated junks and lion dances. Another popular goddess is

Kuan Yin (called Kun Iam in Macau), the goddess of mercy, capable of delivering people from suffering or misery.

Several temples in Hong Kong are devoted to **Man** (the god of literature and the patron of civil servants) and **Mo** (the god of war). Mo was a great warrior of the Han dynasty, deified not only for his integrity but also his ability to protect from the misfortunes of war. Ironically, for this reason Mo is worshipped not only by soldiers and the Hong Kong police force but also by gang members of the underworld. Hong Kong's most famous Man Mo Temple is in the Western District on Hollywood Road (p. 178).

One of the most popular gods in Hong Kong is **Wong Tai Sin,** believed to generously grant the wishes of his followers, cure sickness, and—best of all—dispense horse-racing tips. The Wong Tai Sin Temple, located in a district by the same name, is always crowded with worshippers, as well as fortunetellers, making this one of the most interesting temple destinations in Hong Kong (p. 178).

You can wander around the temple grounds, and visit the halls dedicated to the Buddhist goddess of mercy and to Confucius; the Good Wish Garden with ponds, an artificial waterfall, a replica of the famous Nine Dragons relief (the original is in Beijing's Imperial Palace), and circular, square, octagonal, and fan-shaped pavilions. Sik Sik Yuen, the religious charity organization that oversees Wong Tai Sin, provides a clinic with free traditional Chinese herbal treatments for the needy and homes for the elderly. Wong Tai Sin takes its name, in fact, from a legendary shepherd who learned the art of healing and pledged his life to help others. A visit to this temple, surrounded by vast, government housing estates, provides insight into Chinese religious practices of today and is well worth a stop despite its out-of-the-way location.

2 Chuk Yuen, Wong Tai Sin Estate. ℂ **852/2327 8141.** www.siksikyuen.org.hk. Free admission to temple, though donations of about HK$2 per person are expected at the entrance to the Good Wish Garden. Temple daily 7am–5:30pm; garden daily 9am–5pm. MTR: Wong Tai Sin (exit B2) and then a 3-min. walk (follow the signs).

PARKS & GARDENS

In Kowloon

Kowloon Park ☺ Occupying the site of an old British military encampment established in the 1860s, Kowloon Park (**℃ 852/2724 3344;** www.lcsd.gov.hk/parks/kp) is Tsim Sha Tsui's largest recreational and sports facility (13.4 hectares/33 acres), boasting an indoor heated Olympic-size swimming pool, three outdoor leisure pools linked by a series of waterfalls, an open-air sculpture garden featuring works by local and overseas sculptors, a Chinese garden, a fitness trail, an aviary, a hedge maze, two children's playgrounds, and a bird lake with flamingos and other waterfowl. Located in old army barracks is the Hong Kong Heritage Discovery Centre, with free admission to its displays relating to the historic preservation of Hong Kong's oldest structures (p. 170) and with free Wi-Fi for those with laptops or wireless-enabled phones. On Sundays free kung fu demonstrations take place at the Sculpture Walk from 2:30 to 4:30pm and a small arts fair runs from 1 to 7pm at the Loggia.

Not far from the Tsim Sha Tsui MTR station (take the A1 exit for Kowloon Park), it's easily accessible from Nathan, Haiphong, and Austin roads and is open daily from 5am to midnight, with free admission. The swimming pools (**℃ 852/2724 4522**) are open daily from 6:30am to noon, 1 to 5pm, and 6 to 10pm, and charge HK$19 for adults and HK$9 for children, seniors, and students.

Kowloon Walled City Park ★★ 👪 This park is one of Hong Kong's finest. Although it doesn't boast the varied attractions of the city's other parks, this park, on Tung Tau Tsuen Road (**℃ 852/2716 9962;** www.lcsd.gov.hk/parks/kwcp), was designed to re-create the style of a classical Southern Chinese garden and is the largest such garden outside China. Beautifully landscaped with man-made hills, ponds, streams, pines, boulders, bonsai, bamboo, and shrubs, it features winding paths through a Chinese zodiac sculpture garden, flower gardens, and pavilions.

Even more fascinating to me, however, is the site's history, described through photographs and a handful of interactive exhibition rooms in a former almshouse, known as the Yamen. More than 160 years ago, the site was on the seashore, making it perfect in 1847 for the construction of a Chinese fort to defend Kowloon after the British takeover of Hong Kong Island. Occupying 2.6 hectares (6½ acres) and surrounded by strong, stone walls (which were carted off during the Japanese occupation for an extension of Kai Tak airport), the garrison had four gates and six watchtowers. After 1898, when the British took over the New Territories, the 500 soldiers and officials occupying the fort were expelled. But China did not consider the site part of the leased territories, and for most of the next century, the Kowloon Walled City remained in sovereign limbo, ignored by British authorities and home to a growing number of squatters and misfits. It developed a lifestyle of its own, with its own set of laws. An enclave of tenements and secret societies that flouted Hong Kong's building regulations and health standards, it served as a haven for refugees, criminals, gangs, prostitutes, drug addicts, and the poor. Densely packed and infested with rats, many parts of the warrenlike slum never saw the light of day, making rooftops the place where children played and grownups socialized. Hong Kong police ventured inside only in pairs. Following a special Sino-British agreement and years of lengthy negotiations over new housing for the Walled City's 30,000 residents, the enclave was demolished in 1994.

The Yamen pays tribute to the Walled City's history with photographs and touch-screens, where you can listen to former residents describe their lives there (you'll learn, for example, that because there was no public water supply, residents had to carry in their own drinking water). Behind the Yamen are a handful of small exhibition rooms, where life-size photographs and audio re-create the Walled City, including its narrow alleyways, roof tops, and cottage industries (there were many unlicensed dentists here). In addition to the almshouse, a few other historic structures remain, including the Old South Gate entrance, wall foundations, and flagstone paths.

To reach the park, take the MTR to Lok Fu station (exit B) and then walk 15 minutes on Junction Road to Tung Tau Tsuen Road or take green minibus 39M; or take bus no. 1 from the Star Ferry in Tsim Sha Tsui to the stop opposite the park. It's open daily from 6:30am to 11pm (the exhibition rooms behind the Yamen are open Thurs–Tues 10am–6pm), and admission is free.

Nan Lian Garden ★   Across the street from Chi Lin Nunnery (discussed earlier) is Nan Lian Garden, 60 Fung Tak Rd., Diamond Hill (✆ **852/2329 8811;** www.nanliangarden.org), which was built in the classical style of the Tang Dynasty (A.D. 618–907) using the blueprint of China's Jiangshoujiu, the only Tang landscape garden remaining with its original layout. Using traditional Chinese landscaping techniques such as "borrowed scenery" (incorporating surrounding scenery, such as a hill or range of mountains, into the overall garden design) and employing artificial hillocks, ornamental rocks, water features, wooden buildings, and trees to create both natural and artificial beauty, the garden is designed to be toured in a one-way circular route, with each step bringing different vistas and scenery. Other highlights include the Chinese Timber Architecture Gallery, where you can see close-up examples of how the nunnery was made and models of pagodas and other structures made with ancient construction techniques; the souvenir shop in the Tang Gallery selling Chinese traditional handicrafts and vegetarian food, including the nunnery's own citrus peels (good for energy flow) and mature ginger (thought to cure colds and chronic coughs); and the Chi Lin Vegetarian restaurant (✆ **852/3658 9388**), set beneath a waterfall and famous for its braised supreme assorted vegetable casserole and set lunches starting at HK$85; set dinners for two people go for HK$380.

To reach the garden, take exit C2 from the Diamond Hill MTR Station, from which it's a 15-minute walk. Admission is free. The garden is open daily from 7am to 9pm; the Chi Lin Vegetarian restaurant is open Monday to Friday 11:30am to 9pm, and Saturday and Sunday from 11am to 9pm.

Yuen Po Street Bird Garden ★★   While in Hong Kong, you may notice wooden bird cages hanging outside shops or from apartment balconies, or perhaps even see someone walking down the street with a cage. Birds are favorite pets in Chinese households, and the price of a bird is determined not by its plumage but by its singing talents. To see more of these prized songbirds, visit the fascinating Yuen Po Street Bird Garden, Prince Edward Road West (✆ **852/2302 1762;** www.lcsd.gov.hk/parks/ypsbg), which consists of a series of Chinese-style moon gates and courtyards lined with stalls selling songbirds, beautifully crafted wood and bamboo cages, live crickets and mealy worms, and tiny porcelain food bowls. Nothing, it seems, is too expensive for these tiny creatures. In addition to people buying and selling birds, you will also notice people just taking their birds for an outing. This garden is very Chinese and a lot of fun to see. (**Note:** Because of concerns about avian flu, signs warning against touching bird droppings are posted at the garden, along with hand sanitizers.) Incidentally, next door is **Flower Market Road,** lined with flower shops, while on nearby Tung Choi Street is the **Goldfish Market** with exotic fish.

To reach the Bird Garden, open daily from 7am to 8pm, take the MTR to Prince Edward Road station (exit B1) and walk 10 minutes east on Prince Edward Road West, turning left at the overhead railway onto Yuen Po Street. Or take bus no. 1 from the Star Ferry in Tsim Sha Tsui. Admission is free.

On Hong Kong Island

Hong Kong Park ★★ ☺ Opened in 1991 and stretching 8 hectares (20 acres) along Supreme Court Road and Cotton Tree Drive in Central, Hong Kong Park (© 852/2521 5041; www.lcsd.gov.hk/parks/hkp) features a dancing fountain at its entrance; one of Southeast Asia's largest greenhouses, with more than 2,000 rare plant species, including desert and tropical jungle varieties; an aviary housing 600 exotic birds in a tropical rainforest setting with an elevated walkway; various gardens with ponds, streams, and waterfalls; a large children's playground; and a viewing platform reached by climbing 105 stairs. The most famous building on park grounds is the **Flagstaff House Museum of Tea Ware** housed in a historic building (p. 173). An open-air restaurant, the L16 Café & Bar (© 852/2522 6333), serves modern Thai and Italian cuisine daily 11am to 11pm. Because the marriage registry is located on an edge of the park, the gardens are a favorite venue for wedding photographs, especially on weekends and auspicious days of the Chinese calendar.

The park is open daily from 6am to 11pm, the greenhouse and aviary are open daily 9am to 5pm, and the Flagstaff House Museum of Tea Ware is open Wednesday through Monday from 10am to 5pm. Admission to all is free. To reach the park, take the MTR to Admiralty Station (exit C1), and then follow the signs through Pacific Place and up the set of escalators.

Hong Kong Zoological and Botanical Gardens ★ ☺ Established in 1864, the Zoological and Botanical Gardens, Upper Albert Road, Central (© 852/2530 0154; www.lcsd.gov.hk/parks/hkzbg), are spread over 5.6 hectares (almost 14 acres) on the slope of Victoria Peak, making it a popular respite for Hong Kong residents. Come here early, around 7am, and you'll see Chinese residents going through the slow motions of tai chi. In the gardens themselves, which retain some of their Victorian charm, flowers are almost always in bloom, from azaleas in the spring to wisteria and bauhinia in the summer and fall. More than 1,000 species of plants, most of them indigenous to tropical and subtropical regions and planted throughout the grounds, include Burmese rosewood trees, varieties of bamboo, Indian rubber trees, camphor trees, a variety of camellia, herbs, and, in a greenhouse, orchids (Hong Kong is home to about 120 native orchids). The small zoo houses 400 birds, 70 mammals, and 50 reptiles, including orangutans, tamarins, flamingos, a Burmese python, Palawan peacocks, birds of paradise from Papua New Guinea, cranes, and Mandarin ducks. The zoo is well known for its success in breeding birds on the verge of extinction and for supplying zoos around the world with new stock.

If you're tired of Central and its traffic, this is a pleasant place to regain your perspective. Also on-site is a good children's playground. Admission is free. The eastern part of the park, called Fountain Terrace and containing most of the botanical gardens and the aviaries, is open daily from 6am to 10pm, while the western half, with its reptiles and mammals, is open daily from 6am to 7pm. To reach it, take the MTR to Central and then walk 15 minutes up Garden Road to the corner of Upper Albert

Road. Or take bus no. 3B from Connaught Road Central or 12 from Queen's Road Central, both in Central.

Victoria Park   The 19-hectare (46-acre) Victoria Park (✆ **852/2890 5824;** www.lcsd.gov.hk/parks/vp) is Hong Kong Island's largest, located on Causeway and Gloucester roads in Causeway Bay and serving as the green lungs of the city. Constructed on reclaimed land formerly used for a typhoon shelter, it has tennis courts, a 50m outdoor swimming pool and a wading pool, soccer fields, basketball courts, playgrounds, a jogging and fitness trail, and—my favorite—a pebble path for massaging the bottom of your feet. It is also popular in early morning for those practicing tai chi, a disciplined physical routine of more than 200 individual movements, designed to exercise every muscle of the body and bring a sense of peace and balance to its practitioners. The Mid-Autumn Festival is held here, as is a flower market a few days around Chinese New Year. The park is open 24 hours and admission is free. To reach it, take the MTR or tram to Causeway Bay.

AMUSEMENT PARKS

Hong Kong Disneyland ★★ ☺   Opened in 2005 on Lantau Island, just a 10-minute ride from the airport, this Disney venture was Asia's second (the first was Tokyo Disneyland; the third will be in Shanghai). Re-creating many of the exact features of the original Disneyland in California but on a much smaller scale, the 22.4 hectare (55-acre) theme park contains the usual four Disney themed lands—namely, Main Street U.S.A., Fantasyland, Adventureland, and Tomorrowland—along with such classic rides and attractions as Space Mountain, Buzz Lightyear Astro Blasters, Tarzan's Treehouse, and the Jungle River Cruise, as well as high-caliber performances and shows, parades, and an evening fireworks extravaganza. Unique to the park is the world's only Fantasy Gardens, where Disney characters hang out to meet their fans. An expansion of the park, scheduled for completion in 2014, will add 30 more shows and attractions and enlarge the park by almost 25%. You can purchase tickets at the gate, in advance online, at Circle K convenience stores in Hong Kong, Peak Tower on Victoria Peak, and at the Hong Kong Disneyland Ticket Express counter at Hong Kong Station (Tung Chung Concourse) in Central.

Lantau Island. ✆ **852/1 830 830.** www.hongkongdisneyland.com. Admission HK$350 adults, HK$170 seniors, HK$250 children. Hours vary; in summer, usually 10:30am–8pm daily. MTR: From the Tung Chung Line, transfer at Sunny Bay for the Disneyland Resort Line.

Ocean Park ★★★ ☺   If you're a kid—or a kid at heart—you'll love Ocean Park, a combination aquarium and amusement park. Situated along a dramatic rocky coastline on the island's southern shore, the park is divided into two areas: the lowland Waterfront and the headland Summit, connected by cable car and underground funicular. Because of the wide range of attractions, Ocean Park is both educational and fun, making it interesting for children and adults alike. This is Asia's first accredited member of the American Zoo and Aquarium Association, and its facilities are first class.

The Waterfront is subdivided into several areas and attractions. Whiskers Harbour features rides and shows geared toward younger kids, while at SkyStar you can soar up to 100m (328 ft.) in the air in a huge helium balloon. The most popular residents are the four giant pandas, but there are also red pandas and Chinese alligators. My favorite attraction is the Goldfish Treasures exhibit, with more varieties of goldfish than you ever imagined possible, most of them from China. The pom pom fish, for example, so-named for the "nasal bouquets" protruding prominently from their heads, are truly unique, while the huge fluid-filled sacs beneath the eyes of the bubble fish look like they could burst at any moment—really too bizarre for words. From the Waterfront, visitors can board cable cars for a spectacular 8-minute ride over a hill to the Summit while being treated to great views of the coastline and the South China Sea along the way, or take the Ocean Express, an underground funicular that simulates a voyage through the ocean's depths and shuttles passengers in 3 minutes.

The action-packed Summit, situated on a peninsula that juts into the sea, is home to marine life exhibits and to most of the thrill rides. The marine life section includes an artificial wave cove that is home to sea lions; an aquarium housing more than 1,000 jellyfish and complete with theatrical lighting, multimedia sound, and visual special effects; a Chinese sturgeon aquarium; Aqua City with sharks and rays and an end-of-the-day special effects show featuring a 360-degree water screen; and Ocean Theatre, featuring shows by talented dolphins and sea lions. Swimming with the dolphins is available at Dolphin Encounter (online applications must be made 5 days in advance or at the main entrance on a first-come, first-served basis). But my favorite is the Atoll Reef, one of the world's largest aquariums, with 2,000 fish of 250 different species. The observation passageway circles the aquarium on four levels, enabling you to view the sea life—everything from giant octopi to schools of tropical fish—from various depths and from different angles. Thrill rides include a Ferris wheel, a roller coaster that turns upside down three times, a 20-story vertical drop in the Abyss, and a rather wet ride on a "raging river" (in July and Aug, there are also water slides and other water attractions). Other exhibits include a Japanese Garden; the 69m-high (226-ft.) Ocean Park Tower offering revolving, panoramic views of Aberdeen and outlying islands; and an aviary with 750 birds.

After touring the headland, you can take the long escalator down to the Tai Shue Wan Entrance, from which it's a short taxi ride to Aberdeen with its sampan rides and floating restaurant. At any rate, to do Ocean Park justice, plan on spending a minimum of 5 hours here, but with kids you'll probably stay the whole day.

Aberdeen, Hong Kong Island. ✆ **852/2552 0291.** www.oceanpark.com.hk. Admission HK$250 adults, HK$125 children. Daily 10am–6pm. Bus: Ocean Park Citybus 629 from the Central Ferry Pier no. 7 or Admiralty MTR station every 10 to 20 min.; you can buy round-trip tickets that include park admission. Or take 70 from Exchange Square in Central, 72 from Causeway Bay, or 973 from Tsim Sha Tsui (get off at the 1st stop after the tunnel and then walk 20 min.).

ESPECIALLY FOR KIDS

On the Kowloon side, the **Space Museum** (p. 172) is very much oriented to children, with buttons to push, telescopes to look through, and computer quizzes to test what they've learned, not to mention the OMNIMAX films featured in the Stanley Ho Space Theatre. In the **Science Museum** (p. 171), approximately 70% of its 500-some displays are hands on, and there's also a special play area for younger children. Across the Plaza is the **Museum of History** (p. 171), with life-size replicas and models that bring the history of Hong Kong to life. And don't forget **Kowloon Park** (p. 180), right on Nathan Road, which has two playgrounds for children (including one with restored fortifications and cannon emplacements), a pond with flamingos and other waterfowl, an aviary, swimming pools, and lots of space to run.

On Hong Kong Island, the biggest draw for kids of all ages is **Ocean Park** (see above), which boasts a wide mix of things to do and see, including white-knuckle thrill rides; aquariums; animal performances; and a children's section with kiddie rides, a playground, and shows. Of all the things unique to Hong Kong, this is probably the one kids will enjoy most. For free entertainment, visit the **Zoological and Botanical Gardens** (p. 182) with its monkeys, birds, snakes, and other animals, and **Hong Kong Park** (p. 182) with its greenhouse, aviary, children's playground, and climbing tower. Older kids will like **Victoria Peak** (p. 183), not only for the fantastic views but also Madame Tussauds Hong Kong, as well as the **Hong Kong Maritime Museum** (p. 173) with its bridge simulator and boat models.

Farther afield, in the New Territories, are the **Hong Kong Wetland Park** with its visitor center and boardwalks through wetland habitats (p. 265) and the **Hong Kong Heritage Museum** with its cultural displays, including a hands-on children's discovery gallery (p. 259). Hong Kong also abounds in beaches, especially on Hong Kong Island and the outlying islands (p. 190).

The SAR's most famous attraction, however, is **Hong Kong Disneyland** on Lantau Island (p. 183), which duplicates the Disney experience with the usual rides, attractions, shows, and fireworks.

ORGANIZED TOURS & CULTURAL ACTIVITIES

Hong Kong offers lots of organized tours, so if you're pressed for time this may be the best way to go. The vast majority of hotels have a tour desk where you can make bookings for city tours. In addition, I heartily recommend participating in one or more of the Hong Kong Tourism Board's **Meet the People** cultural activities, which are free 1-hour tours, classes, or lectures given by local specialists covering everything from Chinese antiques to tai chi. See "Special-Interest Tours & Classes," below, for more information.

Land Tours

For general sightseeing, **Gray Line** offers a variety of tours, with bookings available through most Hong Kong hotels, by calling ✆ **852/2368 7111,** or searching www.grayline.com.hk. The Deluxe Hong Kong Island Tour is a daily 5-hour trip that includes stops at Man Mo Temple, Victoria Peak (including the Peak Tram rice), Aberdeen, and Stanley. It costs HK$350 for adults and HK$250 for children. There's also a 7-hour tour for HK$490 and HK$390, respectively, which covers the above attractions plus a dim sum lunch at Jumbo Kingdom floating restaurant in Aberdeen.

Other Gray Line tours take in the Po Lin Monastery, Giant Buddha, and cable-car ride from Ngong Ping Village on Lantau Island or the New Territories; sunset cruises are also available (for information about organized evening tours, see the "Night Tours" section of chapter 10, p. 254). Most useful, in my opinion, are Gray Line's tours to the New Territories, because they cover large areas that would be very difficult, if not impossible, to reach in 1 day on your own. The "Land Between Tour" is a 6½-hour excursion that enables visitors to see how much this once-rural region has changed in the past couple decades, with traditional villages now overshadowed by huge government housing estates that house half of Hong Kong's population. Passing satellite towns with high-rise apartment buildings, farms, and villages, the bus stops at the Yuen Yuen Institute (a religious institute with Buddhist, Taoist, and Confucianist influences), a lookout point on Hong Kong's tallest mountain, and a fishing village to see how fisher folk breed fish in submerged cages, and a Cantonese restaurant for lunch. The price of this daily tour is HK$450 for adults and HK$400 for children and seniors.

Gray Line's "Heritage Tour" also takes in the New Territories but emphasizes Hong Kong's past rather than its present; the tour makes stops at historic Chinese sites that even Hong Kong residents seldom see. It's a must for those who are interested in local historic architecture; it also gives insight into clan life in the New Territories long before the region became part of colonial Hong Kong. Lasting approximately 5 hours, tours make stops at Tai Fu Tai, a Chinese-style ornate mansion built in 1865 by a high-ranking official, fascinating for its insight into how the rich lived; Tang Chung Ling, an ancestral hall belonging to one of the Five Great Clans; Lo Wai, a walled village built by the Tang clan; and the Man Mo Temple in Tai Po with its fascinating street market. Tours depart every Monday, Wednesday, Friday, and Saturday (except some public holidays), and cost HK$350 for adults and HK$300 for children and seniors.

Splendid Tours & Travel (📞 852/2316 2151; www.splendidtours.com) may be booked with the company directly or through your hotels. In addition to tours similar to those above, it also offers a "Sai Kung Coastal Treasures" tour, which takes in the natural beauty of this northeast area of the New Territories, including the new Hong Kong National Geopark, for HK$520 per person.

Walking & Hiking Tours

For those who prefer to see Hong Kong via their own two feet but under the guidance of an expert, **Walk Hong Kong** (📞 852/9187 8641; www.walkhongkong.com) offers two 3-hour walking tours of city sights: The "Kowloon Markets" tour takes in the Flower Market, Yuen Po Street Bird Garden, Fa Yuen Street Market, Goldfish Market, Ladies' Market, and Jade Market, while the "Hong Kong Heritage" walk covers some of Central's historic buildings like St. John's Cathedral. Cost of either tour is HK$400. Personally, I think you can see the sights of these two tours easily on your own (many are included in my walking tours in chapter 8), but the company also offers treks in rural areas that come highly recommended, especially if you're traveling alone. These include two hikes on Hong Kong Island, from Victoria Peak to Aberdeen, and along the Dragon's Back trail, both of which cost HK$450. Hikes are also offered on Lantau Island and in the New Territories for HK$750, including those to deserted beaches in East Sai Kung Country Park, to the pristine Plover Cove Country Park, and to Sai Kung with its National Geopark.

Boat Tours

Because so many of Hong Kong's attractions are on or near the water, a variety of boat tours are available, including those given by Gray Line (see above). Although the cheapest way to see some of the harbor is on a ferry to an outlying island (see chapter 11 for information on Hong Kong's most popular destinations), one advantage of a boat tour is that it usually covers a different part of the harbor, toward Causeway Bay and beyond.

One of the most popular boat tours is the 1-hour **Star Ferry's "Harbour Tour"** (📞 852/2118 6201; www.starferry.com.hk/tour), with boarding available at Tsim Sha Tsui, Central, Wan Chai, and Hung Hom ferry piers, with departures three to four times daily. Cost of these cruises, which have on-board commentary, is HK$55 for adults and HK$50 for children and seniors. One-hour Star Ferry evening cruises,

The most unique cruise in town is aboard the *Duk Ling,* an authentic Chinese junk built in Macau a half-century ago as a fishing boat. One-hour cruises, costing HK$50, are offered 2 afternoons a week (Thurs and Sat, though days are subject to change; call ahead). I find the cruise interesting not only because *Duk Ling* is powered by the wind, but also because it sails in the opposite direction from ferries to the outlying islands, providing different vistas of the Hong Kong skyline as it cruises toward North Point and Kai Tak. Preregistration is required beforehand at the Hong Kong Tourism Board Visitor Centre in Tsim Sha Tsui; visitors must show their passports and must be 3 to 75 years of age. For more information or the latest sailing schedule, contact HKTB at © 852/2508 1234 or go to www.discoverhongkong.com. Alternatively, *aqualuna* (© 852/2116 8821; www.aqualuna.com.hk), managed by the Aqua restaurant group, is a new junk, built using traditional designs and materials by an 80-year-old local craftsman. It offers 45-minute cruises departing from Tsim Sha Tsui and Central six to eight times daily, at a cost of HK$150 for adults and HK$120 for children for afternoon trips, HK$180 and HK$150, respectively, for evening sailings, and HK$220 and HK$180, respectively, for the cruise that takes in the "Symphony of Lights."

which include refreshments, cost HK$110 and HK$99, respectively, while 2-hour cruises that include views of the nightly "Symphony of Lights" multimedia show cost HK$150 and HK$135.

Watertours (© 852/2926 3868; www.watertours.com.hk), Hong Kong's largest tour operator of boat cruises, offers a 2-hour cruise that includes a trip to a typhoon shelter and its junks and the firing of the Noon Day Gun in Causeway Bay (a traditional holdover from colonial days) by Jardine Matheson & Co., Hong Kong's oldest trading company. The cost of this tour, which departs at 10:15am from the Kowloon public pier and 10:30am from Central Ferry Pier no. 9 and includes refreshments, is HK$230 for adults and HK$140 for children. Watertours also offers evening cruises, including a cruise to Lei Yue Mun for a seafood dinner and cruises that take in the "Symphony of Lights" (for evening cruises, see the "Night Tours" section of chapter 10, "Hong Kong After Dark," p. 254). You can pick up a Watertours pamphlet at HKTB Visitor Centres and in many hotels.

Special-Interest Tours & Classes

Several of the tour companies described above offer trips that will appeal especially to history or architectural buffs, including Gray Line's "Heritage Tour." In addition, Walk Hong Kong (see above) offers a couple of special-interest tours in addition to its hikes and walks, including a bird-watching hike and photography tours to Sai Kung. Check its website for details.

"Meet the People" Through this unique program of free 1-hour tours, lectures, classes, and seminars, visitors can meet local specialists and gain in-depth knowledge of Hong Kong's traditions. Programs are updated and revised annually; past offerings have covered such subjects as Chinese antiques, Cantonese opera, pearls, feng shui (geomancy), Chinese tea, Chinese medicine, guided museum tours, and tai chi, with something going on every day of the week. Reservations are not necessary (except for the junk cruise on the *Duk Ling,* above) but they're open only to bona fide visitors staying in Hong Kong no more than 90 days. For details on what, when, and where, pick up a *Cultural Kaleidoscope* brochure at an HKTB Visitor Centre or go to HKTB's website, www.discoverhongkong.com, and click on "Things to Do" and then "Cultural Kaleidoscope."

"Nature Kaleidoscope" During the cooler winter months (Oct–Mar), the HKTB arranges complimentary guided excursions for bona fide visitors (in Hong Kong no more than 90 days). The programs change annually, with past tours lasting approximately 3 hours and taking in the Mai Po Wetland bird refuge, the Kadoorie Farm & Botanic Garden, Tai O on Lantau Island, and Long Valley in the New Territories. For details on the current schedule, pick up a *Hong Kong Nature Kaleidoscope* brochure at an HKTB Visitor Centre or go to HKTB's website, www.discoverhong kong.com, and click on "Things to Do" and then "Nature Lovers."

"Come Horse Racing" Tour This tour, offered by Gray Line and Splendid Tours & Travel (see "Land Tours," above), allows visitors to experience the excitement of the races, at either Happy Valley or Sha Tin (where the 2008 Summer Olympic Games dressage and jumping events were held), an excitement that grows proportionally according to how much you bet. Tours are naturally scheduled only during the horse-racing season—September to mid-July—usually on Wednesday evenings and on Saturday and/or Sunday afternoons. The tour includes transportation; a prerace international buffet; beer, wine, or soft drinks; personal entry badge to the Visitors' Box in the Hong Kong Jockey Club's Members' Enclosure; a HK$30 betting voucher; guide services; and even hints to help you place your bets. Tours cost HK$690, except during special races, when they cost more. Tours are limited to tourists 18 years of age and older (bring your passport with you when booking and participating in this tour) and the dress is smart casual (no shorts, blue jeans, flip-flops, or T-shirts).

OUTDOOR ACTIVITIES

Despite the fact that the SAR is densely populated, there's enough open space to pursue everything from golf to hiking to windsurfing. For the hardworking Chinese and expatriates, recreation and leisure are essential for relaxing and winding down. With that in mind, try to schedule your golfing, swimming, or hiking trips on weekdays unless you enjoy jostling elbows with the crowds.

Golf

Golf courses can be crowded, so it's best to contact clubs beforehand to check whether they're open and to make a reservation for a tee-off time. For more information on courses in Hong Kong, as well as driving ranges, contact the Hong Kong Golf Association (© 852/2504 8659; www.hkga.com).

The **Kau Sai Chau** (© 852/2791 3388; www.kscgolf.org.hk), was created by funds donated by the Hong Kong Jockey Club and is the only public golf course in Hong Kong. Carved out of an island formerly used by the British army for shelling practice, it offers great panoramic vistas of Sai Kung Peninsula and is considered one of the world's finest public golfing facilities. There are two 18-hole and one 9-hole courses. Greens fees for 18 holes start at HK$700 on weekdays and HK$1,050 weekends and holidays (Hong Kong residents receive a discount). The 9-hole course costs HK$410 and HK$605, respectively. Note, however, that overseas visitors cannot make advance bookings for weekends and holidays unless accompanied by a Hong

Kong resident. To reach it, take the MTR to Diamond Hill Station and then board bus no. 92 to Sai Kung Bus Terminus, followed by the special 15-minute "golfer's ferry" to Kau Sai Chau (ferry fee: HK$60).

The **SkyCity Nine Eagles Golf Course** (✆ 852/3760 6688; www.nine-eagles. com), located on Lantau Island near Terminal 2 of Hong Kong International Airport, is a 9-hole course open only to airport employees and airport passengers within 7 days of their arrival or departure dates, as well as members of frequent-flier clubs and those attending events at Asia World Expo. Tee times are available daily from 7am to 10pm, with greens fees starting at HK$400 on weekdays and HK$550 weekends and holidays; tee times from 7 to 10pm cost more. A shuttle service to the golf course operates from both Terminal 2 (Coach Station, Gate 18) and from Exit D of MTR Tung Chung Station.

Hong Kong has several private golf clubs that admit nonmembers on weekdays only. Most charge HK$1,800 to HK$2,000 for greens fees on 18-hole courses. The **Hong Kong Golf Club** (www.hkgolfclub.org) maintains three 18-hole courses in **Fanling** (✆ 852/2670 1211) and a 9-hole course in **Deep Water Bay** (✆ 852/2812 7070). To reach Fanling, take the KCR railway to Sheung Shui, followed by a 5-minute taxi ride. To reach Deep Water Bay, take bus no. 6A, 6X, or 260 from Exchange Square in Central.

The **Discovery Bay Golf Club,** on Lantau Island (✆ 852/2987 7273), has a beautiful 18-hole course developed by Robert Trent Jones, Jr., offering great views of Hong Kong and the harbor. To reach it, take the 20-minute ferry ride from Central to Discovery Bay, followed by a ride in a special shuttle bus. Another scenic 18-hole course and a 9-hole course, operated by the **Clearwater Bay Golf and Country Club** (✆ 852/2335 3888; www.cwbgolf.org), is located in Sai Kung in the New Territories, on a picturesque headland overlooking the South China Sea. To reach it, take the KCR railway to Sheung Shui, and then take a taxi.

Hiking

Hong Kong's 23 country parks—amounting to more than 40% of Hong Kong's space—are laced with trails of varying levels of difficulty, including hiking trails, nature trails, and family trails. Serious hikers may want to consider the famous **MacLehose Trail** in the New Territories, which stretches about 100km (62 miles) through eight country parks, from the Sai Kung Peninsula in the east to Tuen Mun in the west. The strenuous **Lantau Trail** is a 70km (43-mile) circular trail on Lantau Island that begins and ends at Mui Wo (also called Silvermine Bay), passing several popular scenic spots and campsites along the way and including a 2½-hour trek to the top of Lantau Peak. Both the MacLehose and Lantau trails are divided into smaller sections of varying difficulty, which means that you can tailor your hike to suit your own abilities and time constraints. I also like the short Heritage Trails in the New Territories which take in historic architectural gems along the way (see "The New Territories" in chapter 11).

Easier to reach is the 50km (31-mile) **Hong Kong Trail,** which spans Hong Kong Island's five country parks, from Victoria Peak to Big Wave Bay. Another favorite trail on Hong Kong Island is the scenic **Dragon's Back,** a 3-hour hike along the spine of a ridge on D'Aguilar Peninsula, located in the southeastern end of the island. Shorter, easily accessible hikes on Hong Kong Island include the circular, hour-long hike on **Victoria Peak** (p. 168), as well as a 2½-hour hike from Victoria Peak to Aberdeen that follows part of the Hong Kong Trail. The Hong Kong Tourism Board Visitor Centre on Victoria Peak has maps outlining these last two hikes.

Hikers are advised not to hike alone and to check weather reports before departing; from May to October, irregular thunderstorms, typhoons, and heavy showers can cause flooding and landslides. The best hiking season is considered November through February. The Hong Kong Tourism Board has some trail maps and a hiking and wildlife guidebook called *Exploring Hong Kong's Countryside: A Visitor's Companion,* which provides suggested day hikes throughout the territory. HKTB also lists recommended hikes on its website, www.discoverhongkong.com, and in a nifty booklet called *Discover Hong Kong Nature,* with hikes and maps throughout the New Territories and the Outlying Islands.

Jogging

The best places to jog on Hong Kong Island without dodging traffic are **Victoria Park's jogging track** in Causeway Bay (p. 168), **Harlech Road** on Victoria Peak (p. 169), and **Bowen Road,** which stretches 2.5km (1½ miles) from Stubbs Road to Magazine Gap Road in the Mid-Levels and offers great views over the harbor. In addition, an inside track at the Happy Valley racecourse is open for runners when the horses aren't using the field. On the other side of the harbor is **Kowloon Park,** as well as the waterfront promenade along Tsim Sha Tsui and Tsim Sha Tsui East.

Remember that it can be quite hot and humid during the summer months, so try to jog in the early morning or in the evening.

Swimming

In addition to the many outdoor and indoor swimming pools at Hong Kong's hotels that are available to their hotel guests, the city has numerous public swimming pools, including those at **Kowloon Park** (p. 180), with both indoor and outdoor pools, and **Victoria Park** (p. 168), only with outdoor pools. Outdoor pools are open April through October. Prices are HK$19 for adults and HK$9 for children and seniors (you can also use your Octopus transportation card to pay admission). Avoid hot weekends, when the pools can become quite crowded.

The SAR has about 40 free public **beaches;** most of them have lifeguards on duty April through October, changing rooms, and snack stands or restaurants. Even on Hong Kong Island itself you can find a number of beaches, including Big Wave Bay and Shek O on the east coast, and Stanley, Deep Water Bay, South Beach (popular with the gay crowd), and Repulse Bay on the southern coast. Repulse Bay, by far the most popular beach, becomes unbelievably crowded on summer weekends.

The outlying islands have prettier beaches, including Hung Shing Ye and Lo So Shing on Lamma, Tung Wan on Cheung Chau, and Cheung Sha on Lantau. It is, however, advisable to check on water pollution before plunging in, especially on the islands. Check the website of the Hong Kong Environmental Protection Department (www.epd.gov.hk) for updates on water quality. Furthermore, I wouldn't recommend the waters around Sai Kung Peninsula. There seem to be fatal shark attacks here every couple of years, due to fish migration, though most of the public beaches have shark nets and guards patrolling the water.

Tai Chi

Tai chi is an ancient Chinese regimen designed to balance body and soul and thereby release energy from within. Originally a martial art developed about 1,000 years ago, tai chi today is a form of exercise that restores harmony in the body through 200 individual movements designed to use every muscle in the body. By strengthening both the mind and the body through seemingly fluid, slow movements that mask the strength and control required to perform the balletlike exercise, tai chi fosters a sense of well-being and nurtures self-discipline. It also helps develop balance, improves muscle tone and breathing, and aids in digestion.

In Hong Kong, both young and old practitioners gather every morning in downtown parks and open public spaces to perform tai chi. Good places to observe the art include Kowloon Park in Tsim Sha Tsui, as well as Victoria Park, Hong Kong Park, and the Zoological and Botanical Gardens on Hong Kong Island. Visitors can join complimentary 1-hour **lessons** in English, offered by the Hong Kong Tourism Board's "Meet the People Cultural Kaleidoscope" program. They're held every Monday, Wednesday, and Friday at 8am in front of the Hong Kong Museum of Art in the Sculpture Court near the Tsim Sha Tsui waterfront promenade (MTR: Tsim Sha Tsui, Exit E). No registration is necessary. Simply show up; you'll be led through the exercises by a tai chi master. Participants are advised to wear casual clothing and comfortable sports shoes with rubber soles. For information, contact the **Hong Kong Tourism Board** (© 852/2508 1234) or check its website at www.discoverhong kong.com.

SPECTATOR SPORTS

The **Hong Kong Marathon** (www.hkmarathon.com), run every February, breaks participation records every year since the marathon began in 1997. The **Hong Kong Sevens** (www.hksevens.com; p. 31), an international rugby tournament held in March or April, is also quite popular. Other annual sporting highlights include the **Tennis Classic** (www.hongkongtennisclassic.com) and the **Hong Kong Open Golf Championships** (www.hkga.com).

Without a doubt, **horse racing** is by far the most popular sporting event in Hong Kong. It's not, perhaps, the sport itself that draws so much enthusiasm, but rather the fact that, aside from the local lottery, racing is the only legal form of gambling in Hong Kong—there are more than 100 off-course betting centers throughout Hong Kong—and winnings are tax-free.

If you're here anytime from September to mid-June, join the rest of Hong Kong at the races. Horse racing got its start in the colony in Happy Valley more than 165 years ago, when British settlers introduced the sport, making the Happy Valley track the oldest racecourse in Asia outside China. A newer, modern track is in Sha Tin (the New Territories), which can accommodate 90,000 spectators.

Races are held Wednesday evenings and some Saturday and Sunday afternoons, and both tracks feature giant color screens that get you up close and personal. It's fun and easy to get in on the betting action, and you don't have to bet much—the minimum wager of HK$10 is enough.

The lowest admission price is HK$10, which is for the general Public Enclosure and is standing-room only. If you want to watch from the more exclusive Hong Kong Jockey Club (www.hkjc.com) members' enclosure (with benches so you can sit down), are at least 18 years old, and are a bona fide tourist, you can purchase a temporary member's badge for HK$100 on regular race days and HK$150 on rare special race days. Show your passport at either the Badge Enquiry Office at the main entrance to the members' private enclosure (at either track) or at designated off-course betting centers up to 10 days before the race, including those at 10–12 Stanley St. in Central and 2–4 Prat Ave. in Tsim Sha Tsui. Tickets are sold on a first-come, first-served basis. Note that shorts and flip-flops are not allowed in the members' enclosure.

To reach Happy Valley Racecourse, take the tram to Happy Valley or the MTR to Causeway Bay (take the Times Square exit and walk toward Wong Nai Chung Rd.). To reach Sha Tin Racecourse, take the MTR to the Sha Tin Racecourse Station.

You can also join a guided tour to the tracks, described in "Organized Tours & Cultural Activities," earlier in this chapter. For information on current sporting events and future dates, contact the Hong Kong Tourism Board (© **852/2508 1234**) or check its website at www.discoverhongkong.com.

HONG KONG STROLLS

S urprisingly compact, Hong Kong is an easy city to explore on foot. If it weren't for the harbor, you could walk everywhere. If, for example, you're in the Central District and want to have dinner in Causeway Bay, you can walk there in less than an hour, passing through colorful Wan Chai on the way. Causeway Bay is good for exploring thanks to its many shops patronized by locals, a street market, a Japanese department store, Times Square shopping complex, and restaurants. Another great place for walking is Sheung Wan in the Western District just west of Central, fascinating because it encompasses a wide spectrum of traditional Chinese shops, from chop makers to ginseng wholesalers. If you like panoramic views, nothing can beat the hour-long circular walk on Victoria Peak.

On the other side of the harbor, a walk up Nathan Road from the harbor to the Yau Ma Tei subway station takes less than 30 minutes, although you might want to browse in some of the shops and department stores along the way. For easy strolling with great views of the harbor, walk along the waterfront promenade that stretches from the Star Ferry all the way through Tsim Sha Tsui East.

Be forewarned that sidewalks and streets can be crowded at the end of the work day as people rush to buses and subway stations for trips back to the suburbs.

What follows are four recommended strolls. If you're interested in additional self-guided walks throughout Hong Kong, be sure to pick up the free HKTB pamphlet called *Hong Kong Walks,* which covers points of interest in Central, the Western District, Wan Chai, Shau Kei Wan (location of the Hong Kong Museum of Coastal Defence), Tsim Sha Tsui, Yau Ma Tei, Mong Kok, and Wong Tai Sin and Kowloon City districts. For more information, contact the Hong Kong Tourism Board (HKTB; ⓒ **852/2508 1234**). You can also download the pamphlet at HKTB's website, www.discoverhongkong.com.

START:	**Statue Square, Chater Road, Central District.**
FINISH:	**Pacific Place, 88 Queensway, Central.**
TIME:	**About 2 hours; add 1 to 2 hours if you include Victoria Peak.**
BEST TIMES:	**Weekdays, when shops and restaurants are in full swing.**
WORST TIMES:	**Tuesday, when the Flagstaff House Museum of Tea Ware is closed; Sunday and public holidays, when some stores in the Central District are closed and the Peak Tram is at its most crowded.**

The birthplace of modern Hong Kong, the Central District used to be called "Victoria," after Queen Victoria. It boasted elegant colonial-style buildings with sweeping verandas and narrow streets filled with pigtailed men pulling rickshaws. That's hard to imagine nowadays. With Central's gleaming glass-and-steel skyscrapers, little is left of its colonial beginnings. Still, this is the logical starting place for a tour of Hong Kong. The handful of historic buildings scattered among towering monoliths symbolize both the past and the future of this ever-changing city. Yet, surprisingly, Central has several city parks, good for relaxation and sightseeing. If you have time and the weather is clear, you might also consider taking a trip to Victoria Peak during this walk, from the Peak Tram Lower Terminus in Central.

Take the MTR or Star Ferry to Central, where, between Connaught Road Central and Des Voeux Road Central, lies:

1 Statue Square

Divided by Chater Road, this historic square once held a statue of Queen Victoria, which has since been moved to the park in Causeway Bay that bears her name. On weekends, Statue Square and surrounding Central become the domain of Filipino housemaids, nannies, and waitresses, thousands of whom work in the SAR and send most of what they earn back home to their families. On their day off, they meet friends here, sitting on blankets spread on the concrete and sharing food, photographs, news from home, and laughter, infusing the staid business district with a certain vitality and festivity. The only statue remaining in Statue Square today is of a banker, Sir Thomas Jackson, former manager of the Hongkong and Shanghai Bank (HSBC). He stands facing the:

2 Legislative Council Building

Formerly the Supreme Court and looking curiously out of place in modern Central, the Legislative Council Building was built in the early 1900s by architect Aston Webb, who later redesigned Buckingham Palace, and now houses Hong Kong's lawmaking body, popularly known as "LegCo." With its local pink-and-gray granite, Ionic columns, and Chinese roof, this neoclassical structure is typical of late-Victorian colonial architecture and boasts a carved-stone figure above the main portico of the goddess of justice holding scales. The building has two flags, one with the red star emblem of China and the other with the bauhinia flower of Hong Kong. By the end of 2011, LegCo will move to new government headquarters at Tamar in nearby Admiralty and the Court of Final Appeal (see below) will move here.

Walking Tour 1: The Central District

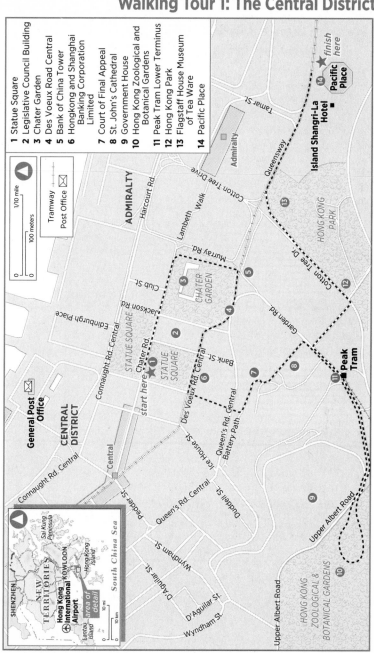

1 Statue Square
2 Legislative Council Building
3 Chater Garden
4 Des Voeux Road Central
5 Bank of China Tower
6 Hongkong and Shanghai
  Banking Corporation
  Limited
7 Court of Final Appeal
8 St. John's Cathedral
9 Government House
10 Hong Kong Zoological and
   Botanical Gardens
11 Peak Tram Lower Terminus
12 Hong Kong Park
13 Flagstaff House Museum
   of Tea Ware
14 Pacific Place

Tramway
Post Office

1/10 mile
100 meters

The most convenient place for a meal in this area is Dot Cod Seafood Restaurant & Oyster Bar, in the Prince's Building with an entrance right on Statue Square (℡ 852/2810 6988; p. 139). It's owned by the Hong Kong Cricket Club but is open to anyone.

On the other side of the LegCo building, to the east, is:

3 Chater Garden

This was the site of the Hong Kong Cricket Club from 1851 to 1975. Today, it's the only spot of green in the very heart of Central. With water fountains masking the din of passing traffic, it's popular with those who practice tai chi in the early morning and among office workers on lunch break.

Running alongside the south edge of the garden is:

4 Des Voeux Road Central

This road is easily recognizable by the tramlines snaking along it. What a contrast the quaint double-decker trams make when viewed against the high-rise banks on the other side of the street. Established in 1904 and now the city's oldest form of land transportation, trams are the most colorful way to travel from the Western and Central districts to Causeway Bay, especially at night when Hong Kong is afire in neon. Des Voeux Road itself was constructed as part of an early 1800s land reclamation project; before that the waterfront was situated farther inland, at Queen's Road. Land reclamation has proceeded continuously throughout Hong Kong's history, slowly encroaching on the harbor itself. A resident once joked with me that so much land was being reclaimed it wouldn't be long before you could walk across the harbor. With Central's most recent reclamation project—which extended the ferry piers for outlying islands and a relocated Star Ferry far into the water—the joke no longer seems quite so funny.

Across from Chater Garden, on the other side of Des Voeux Road Central, is the:

5 Bank of China Tower

This tower, the tallest building outside the United States when completed in 1990, rises like a glass finger pointing into the sky. Designed by I. M. Pei, this 70-story futuristic building, with its crisscross pattern reminiscent of bamboo, also observes the principles of feng shui, as do all modern structures in Hong Kong in an effort to maintain harmony with their natural environment. Otherwise, disaster would surely strike—something no builder in Hong Kong wants to risk (see the "Feng Shui: In Balance with Nature" box on p. 23 for more information about this). The Murray House, built on this site in 1846 as officers' quarters, was dismantled in the 1980s and rebuilt on the Stanley waterfront.

The most conspicuous building on Des Voeux Road Central, however, is farther west (to the right if facing the banks). It's the SAR headquarters of:

6 HSBC

This company, at 1 Queen's Rd. Central, formerly known as the Hongkong and Shanghai Banking Corporation, is Hong Kong's largest bank, and it maintains offices around the world. Hong Kong's first city hall once stood on this site, but the bank has been in this spot since 1865, and it's from here that it issued the colony's first bank notes in 1881. The present building, designed in the mid-1980s by renowned British architect Sir Norman Foster and reputedly one of the most expensive buildings in the world at the time (almost US$1 billion), attracts visiting architects the world over for its innovative external structure, rather than a central core. It was constructed from prefabricated components manufactured all over the world; the glass, aluminum cladding, and flooring came from the United States. Internal walls are removable, allowing for office reconfiguration. Walk underneath the bank's open ground plaza, where escalators (once the world's longest freely supported moving staircases) take customers to and from the first floor, for a look up into this unique structure. Much care was given to the angle of these escalators—62 in all, more than in any other office building in the world—as well as to many other aspects of construction, in order not to disturb the spirits who reside here. Note, too, the two bronze lions you see at the entrance, which have been "guarding" the bank since 1935. You can rub their paws for good luck.

Take HSBC's escalator up to the cavernous first floor, then turn around, and head to the opposite end of the huge hall, where you'll see the entrance to the Standard Chartered Bank. Turn left after the entrance and follow the sign for Battery Path, where you should turn left again. If HSBC is closed, you'll have to cross Queen's Road Central at the crosswalk and then take the stone steps leading up to the tree-shaded Battery Path, where you should turn left. On Battery Path, straight ahead, is a handsome brick building, the:

7 Court of Final Appeal

This neoclassical-style dates from 1917 and was formerly the French Mission Building. From 1843 to 1846 it served as the residence of the Governor of Hong Kong, and since 1977 has been home of the Court of Final Appeal. It will be vacated at the end of 2011, when the court moves into the Old Supreme Court Building presently occupied by LegCo; no word yet what will become of the historic building.

Just beyond this building is the cream-and-white-colored, Gothic-style:

8 St. John's Cathedral

Inaugurated in 1849 and the oldest ecclesiastical building in Hong Kong, this church was used for Japanese social functions during the Japanese occupation. You can enter the diminutive church and take a look inside. It underwent extensive renovations following World War II but still retains quaint tropical characteristics like the ceiling fans. It's open daily from 7am to 6pm.

Behind the church is busy Garden Road, where you should turn right and walk uphill. After passing the U.S. Consulate, you'll come to Upper Albert Road, where you should turn right. You'll soon see, on your right, the:

9 Government House

Completed in 1855, this building served as the official residence of 25 British governors until 1997. During the World War II Japanese occupation, it also served as the headquarters of Lieutenant General Isogai, who ordered some extensive building renovations, a curious mix of Asian and Western architecture, including ceramic tile roofs and a tower reminiscent of Shinto shrines. Since the 1997 handover, the grand, whitewashed edifice has served as the residence of Hong Kong's Chief Executive (the head of the Hong Kong government) and is also used for official functions.

Across the street, on the corner of Upper Albert Road and Garden Road, is a staircase leading up to the main entrance of the:

10 Hong Kong Zoological & Botanical Gardens

This wonderful oasis of plants and animals was established in 1864. It still imparts a Victorian atmosphere with its wrought-iron bandstand and greenhouse. Entrance is free, and the grounds are not too extensive, so it's worth taking the time to wander through to see its tropical botanical gardens, trees and plants, aviaries and birds, reptiles, and mammals such as apes. It opens daily at 6am, with the eastern half closing at 7pm and the western part at 10pm.

Exiting the same way you came in, cross to the other side of Garden Road and walk downhill, taking a right after passing the modern St. John's Building. Here, to your right, is the:

11 Peak Tram Lower Terminus

When this station opened in 1888, the travel time to the top of Victoria Peak was reduced from 3 hours (by sedan chair) to 8 minutes. Today the tram is the steepest funicular railway in the world (for you funicular buffs, it rises from 28m/92 ft. to 396m/1,299 ft. on a 1.4km [1-mile] track, with a gradient of between 4 to 27 degrees; a museum of the tram's history can be seen free with purchase of a tram ticket), and the view from the Peak is the best in Hong Kong. I suggest you visit the Peak twice during your stay: during the day for the great panoramic view of the city, and again at night for its romantic atmosphere. At the top is a great, 1-hour walk that circles the Peak, as well as attractions and restaurants. In all, you'll probably want to spend at least an hour or two on the Peak, so if time is limited or the weather is foggy or hazy, save it for another day.

On the other side of the tram station, on Cotton Tree Drive, is:

12 Hong Kong Park

Before opening as a park in 1991, this was once the grounds of Victoria Barracks, a housing area for soldiers. In the park is the pink Rawlinson House, built in the early 20th century as the private residence of the Deputy Commander of the British forces and now serving as a marriage registry. If it's a weekend or an auspicious day in the Chinese calendar, you'll find many newlyweds posing for pictures in the park. There's also a greenhouse, a great aviary with 600 birds, a playground, and an open-air restaurant serving modern Thai and Italian food.

Follow the signs to the park's most important attraction, and Hong Kong's oldest surviving Western building, the:

13 Flagstaff House

Built in 1846, the historic building now houses the Flagstaff House Museum of Tea Ware (© **852/2869 0690**), with a small collection of tea utensils and descriptions of tea making through the various Chinese dynasties. It's open Wednesday through Monday from 10am to 5pm. Like everything else in the park, it's free.

From the Flagstaff House, walk past the fountain (a favorite backdrop for picture taking) to the escalators downhill to:

14 Pacific Place

This large complex is filled with department stores, clothing boutiques, restaurants, and hotels. The nearest subway station from here is Admiralty Station, which you can reach without having to venture outside; just follow the signs via the air-conditioned walkway.

WINDING DOWN

Pacific Place has many eating and drinking establishments. Dan Ryan's Chicago Grill (✆ 852/2845 4600; p. 126) is a casual bar and grill that remains open throughout the day for drinks, burgers, and other American favorites. Zen (✆ 852/2845 4555; p. 144) is the ultimate in Chinese hip dining, with a modern decor and specialties that border on Cantonese nouvelle. Grappa's (✆ 852/2868 0086; p. 140) is a moderately priced trattoria with an open kitchen and good food. For all-you-can eat dining, café TOO (✆ 852/2820 8571; p. 139), in the Island Shangri-La hotel, is an upscale buffet restaurant offering views of Hong Kong Park's greenery and beautifully presented international lunches and dinners. For a cocktail with a killer view, head to Café Gray Bar (✆ 852/2918 1838) on the 49th floor of the Upper House deluxe hotel.

WALKING TOUR 2: **THE WESTERN DISTRICT**

START:	**Pedder Street, Central District.**
FINISH:	**SoHo nightlife district, Central.**
TIME:	**About 4 to 5 hours.**
BEST TIMES:	**Monday through Friday afternoons, when markets are in full swing.**
WORST TIMES:	**Sunday, when some antiques shops and Man Wa Lane are closed; Monday, when the Museum of Medical Sciences is closed.**

Whereas the Central District was developed as the colonial financial center of Hong Kong and is dominated by Western-style architecture, the Western District has always served as the commercial center for Chinese businesses. Today, especially in the Sheung Wan neighborhood, it remains a fascinating area of family-owned shops and businesses, including those dealing in traditional herbs, ginseng, antiques, preserved fish, name chops, coffins, and funeral items. Hong Kong's oldest temple; a market dealing in curios, fakes, and antiques; and an interesting museum comparing traditional Chinese and Western medicine are just some of the things you'll see in my favorite area of Hong Kong.

Named after Lieutenant William Pedder, Hong Kong's first harbor master, Pedder Street connects two of Central's major thoroughfares: Des Voeux Road Central (with its tram tracks) and Queen's Road Central. It is most well known to visitors, however, for its shopping, including:

1 The Landmark

This high-end shopping complex has brand-name boutiques, including Gucci, Tiffany & Co., Vivienne Tam, Manolo Blahnik, and a Harvey Nichols department store.

Walking Tour 2: The Western District

1 The Landmark
2 Pedder Building
3 Shanghai Tang
4 Li Yuen Street East and
  Li Yuen Street West
5 Tak Wing Pawn Shop
6 Central-Mid-Levels Escalator
7 Wing Kut Street
8 Man Wa Lane
9 She Wong Lam snake shop
10 Geow Yong Tea Hong
11 Western Market
12 Urban Council Sheung
   Wan Complex
13 Ginseng and Bird's Nest Street
14 Shops selling preserved foods
15 Herbal Medicine Street
16 Funeral and incense shops
17 Hollywood Road
18 Hollywood Road Park
19 Possession Street
20 Dragon Culture
21 Cat Street
22 Ladder Street
23 Wing Lee Street
24 Hong Kong Museum of
   Medical Sciences
25 Man Mo Temple
26 True Arts & Curios
27 Graham Street
28 Central Police Station
29 SoHo

■ Airport Express
  Hong Kong Station

⊠ General
  Post Office

■ Bus
  Terminal

■ Exchange
  Square

Across Pedder Street is a nondescript building, the:

2 Pedder Building

At 12 Pedder St., the Pedder Building has been a shopping center since 1926. It is now famous for its dozens of small factory outlets and clothing boutiques; look for the small elevator that services the first to seventh floors. I usually take the elevator up to the sixth floor (there are no shops on the seventh floor) and then work my way down. Be aware, however, that just a handful of shops here are true factory outlets. The rest are simply taking advantage of the location to set up boutiques to sell their usual goods at regular prices; some secondhand shops sell used designerwear. If you have the time, you might want to hunt for some bargains here.

Also located in the Pedder Building, but with its own entrance to the right of the one leading to the factory outlets, is the not-to-be-missed (yet easily overlooked due to its modest size):

3 Shanghai Tang

This small, chic shop (© **852/2525 7333;** p. 228) is a reproduction of a Shanghai clothing department store as it might have looked in the 1930s. It offers two floors of clothing, home decor, and accessories, including traditional Chinese clothing with a contemporary twist, jewelry, pillowcases, photo albums, beach towels, stationery, and more. The store also employs Shanghainese tailors who offer made-to-measure clothing.

Exit Shanghai Tang from its lowest level, where you'll find yourself on a narrow lane with makeshift stalls offering the services of locksmiths and shoe repairmen. Turn left here and then the next right (at Theatre Lane) to reach Des Voeux Road Central (the one with the tram tracks), where you should turn left. In about 2 minutes you will come to:

4 Li Yuen Street East & Li Yuen Street West

These two parallel pedestrian lanes, which rise steeply to your left, are packed with stalls that sell clothing and accessories, including costume jewelry, Chinese jackets, handbags, belts, and even bras, daily from noon to 7pm. If you see something you like, be sure to bargain for it. Walk up Li Yuen Street East, take a right, and then head back down Li Yuen Street West.

After walking down Li Yuen Street West, turn left back onto Des Voeux Road Central and continue walking west, keeping your eyes peeled for the:

5 Tak Wing Pawn Shop

Located at 72 Des Voeux Rd. Central, this is one of Hong Kong's many pawnshops, but it's easy to overlook and walk on by. Unlike pawnshops in other parts of the world, which double as stores selling unclaimed personal belongings after a prescribed length of time, in Hong Kong pawnshops simply hold items in storage, selling them to another store if the owner is unable to pay. Hong Kong pawnshops, therefore, look like secretive affairs, with walls shielding customers from casual and curious street observers.

One block farther west on Des Voeux Road Central you'll see the entrance to the:

6 Central–Mid-Levels Escalator

Opened in 1994 as the world's longest covered escalator system, this escalator stretches 800m (2,600 ft.) from Central to the Mid-Levels on Victoria Peak. Contrary to its name, however, it is not one long continuous escalator but rather a series of escalators and moving sidewalks, with 29 entrances and exits. Designed to accommodate commuters who live in the Mid-Levels but work in Central and beyond, the escalators operate downhill from 6 to 10am and then reverse their direction and go uphill from 10:20am to midnight (after this time, you have to walk down the hill—stairs are set beside the escalators). It takes about 20 minutes to go from one end to the other. Because of the foot traffic, the escalator has spawned a number of easily accessible new restaurants and bars along its length, most in an area dubbed SoHo (more on this later). The building in front of you housing the entrance to the escalator served as the Central Market until 2003; plans call for its eventual conversion into a shopping and dining complex.

Continue walking west on Des Voeux Road Central for a couple minutes and then turn left onto:

7 Wing Kut Street

This street, the border between the Central and Western Districts, is lined with shops specializing in costume jewelry in a wide range of styles and prices. Some shops sell only wholesale, but others will sell to individual shoppers as well.

After walking through Wing Kut Street, take a right onto Queen's Road Central.

TAKE A BREAK
Instead of turning right onto Queen's Road Central, cross it and continue straight. You will soon come to Wellington Street, where you'll see Lin Heung Tea House, 160–164 Wellington St. (② 852/2544 4556; p. 161). This old-fashioned dim sum restaurant, open more than 80 years, still sells dim sum from trolleys and is packed with locals. With no English menu, you make your selection from the steaming baskets. Or, if you backtrack in the direction of the Central–Mid-Levels Escalator, you'll find a branch of Tsui Wah on the corner of Des Voeux Road Central and Jubilee at 12–13 Jubilee St. (② 852/2542 2288; p. 153), a very popular local chain selling Chinese comfort food at very reasonable prices (closed Sun). Located in the palatial-looking Grand Millennium Plaza, the upscale Gaia Ristorante, 181 Queen's Rd. Central (② 852/2167 8200; p. 137), has a wonderful garden terrace, a contemporary interior, and very good Italian fare for lunch or dinner.

Queen's Road Central will soon curve off to the left, but you'll want to keep walking straight westward onto Bonham Strand. Soon, to your right, just after the Hongkong Bank, you'll see an interesting street:

8 Man Wa Lane

Since the 1920s this street has been the home of one of China's oldest trades—"chop," or seal, making. Sadly, the recent construction of many high-rises makes the stalls look out of place. Made from stone, ivory, jade, clay, marble, bronze, porcelain, bamboo, wood, soapstone, and even plastic, these seals or stamps can be carved with a name and are used by the Chinese much like a written signature.

You can have your own chop made at one of the several booths here, with your name translated into Chinese characters. It takes about an hour for a chop to be completed, so stop by again later after you've finished your walk. Calligraphy brushes are also for sale, and you can even have business cards made here with both English and Chinese characters; orders for that take about a day. Most stalls are open Monday through Saturday from 10am to 6pm.

Back on Bonham Strand, continue west for 2 blocks. Just a few years ago, this area was known for its many snake shops, which did a roaring business from October to February, when snake was in high demand to combat the cold. Now only a few remain, easily identifiable by cages of pythons, cobras, and banded kraits piled on the sidewalk, or by the wooden drawers lining the walls of the shop. Just past Mercer Street is Hillier Street (which is unmarked; it's the second street after Man Wa Lane, just past the corner fruit shop), where you should turn left for the 100-year-old:

9 She Wong Lam Snake Shop

You can recognize this open-fronted shop, at 13 Hillier St., by the many drawers lining its wall. Eaten as protection against the winter cold, snakes are often served in soup. They are also favored for their gallbladders, which are mixed with Chinese wine as cures for rheumatism. Who knows, you might see a shop-keeper fill a customer's order by deftly grabbing a snake out of one of the drawers, extracting the gallbladder, and mixing it in yellow wine. The snake survives the operation, but who knows what other fate it awaits. The more poisonous the snake, so they say, the better the cure. The mixture is also believed to be an aphrodisiac.

Backtrack to Bonham Strand and turn left, where you'll pass medicinal shops selling dried organic products such as mushrooms and roots, as well as the:

10 Geow Yong Tea Hong

Founded in 1886 in a tea-growing village in China and established here at this location in 1936, this tea shop at 70 Bonham Strand (© **852/2544 0025**) offers a wide range of high-quality teas from around China, including a wide variety of oolong and green tea.

Continuing on Bonham Strand, you will soon come to Morrison Street, where a rattan shop on the corner to the left has handmade wares spilling out onto the sidewalks and hanging from hooks outside the shop. It takes an apprentice 3 years to learn the skills necessary to become a master rattan maker; the rattan itself comes from a climbing vine found throughout Asia. As a sign of the times, the shop has branched into plastic housewares. At any rate, take a right here onto Morrison Street and walk to the end where, on the left, you'll find the handsome red brick:

11 Western Market

At 323 Des Voeux Rd., this market was built in 1906 as the waterfront Harbour Office and was then used as a public market until 1988; it escaped demolition when the decision was made to renovate the imposing Edwardian/Victorian landmark into a bazaar for shops and artisans. On the ground floor are a handful of souvenir and gift shops that sell everything from Chinese seals to jade jewelry, with most shops open daily from 10am to 7pm. Up on the first floor, retailers sell bolts of colorful cloth, buttons, clasps, and other sewing accessories. On the top floor is the Grand Stage, noted for its Cantonese fare and dim sum, as well as ballroom dancing nightly from 7pm.

From Western Market, backtrack on Morrison Street to Bonham Strand, where across the street you'll see the large:

12 Urban Council Sheung Wan Complex

One of Hong Kong's largest neighborhood markets, this complex, also called the Sheung Wan Civic Centre, open from 6am to 8pm Monday to Saturday, features fish and poultry on the ground floor, meats and vegetables on the first floor, and a large dining hall (Cooked Food Centre) with stalls selling cheap, cooked meals on the second floor. Early morning is the best time to come, when women buy the day's food for their families and chefs purchase ingredients for their daily specials. Until recently, the Chinese penchant for freshness called for chickens to be killed on the spot, boiled, and then thrown into machines that plucked them, but live chickens are now banned from most Hong Kong wet markets. Still, this is not a stop for the fainthearted, as every part of every animal is for sale, including the liver, heart, and intestines.

Exit the market building back onto Bonham Strand, turn left, and continue straight ahead on Wing Lok Street. This street is nicknamed:

13 Ginseng & Bird's Nest Street

Shops here specialize in ginseng and bird's nest, both valued for their aid in longevity, energy, and a fair complexion. The kings of trade in this wholesale trading area are clearly ginseng, with more than 30 varieties on offer. The most prized are the red ginseng from North Korea, white ginseng from North America, and a very rare ginseng that grows wild in the mountains of northeastern China. Red ginseng is supposed to aid male virility, while the white variety helps cure hangovers. Bird's nests are actually nests, created with the glutinous secretions of small swifts or swallows. Be on the lookout also for window displays of deer products and shark's fin.

By the way, this area has long had an exotic atmosphere—150 years ago it buzzed with activity as merchants from Shanghai, Canton (Guangzhou), Fujian, and other Chinese provinces and cities set up shop here, selling products from their native regions.

At the end of Wing Lok Street, turn left on Des Voeux Road West. Along this road you'll see:

14 Shops Selling Preserved Foods

Dried and salted fish, flattened squid, oysters, scallops, abalone, sea slugs, fish bladders, starfish, shrimp, and many other kinds of seafood have been dried and preserved for sale here. You can buy bird's nest here, as well as shark's fin, and in winter pressed duck and Chinese sausages made from pork and liver are also for sale.

Continue west on Des Voeux Road, keeping your eyes peeled for a Citibank and Princeton Tower apartments on your left. Just past it is Sutherland Street, where you should turn left. Almost immediately you will come to a somewhat larger street, Ko Shing Street. This street is nicknamed:

15 Herbal Medicine Street

Based on the Asian concept of maintaining a healthy balance between the yin and yang forces in the body, the range of medicinal herbs in the shops along this street is startling: roots, twigs, bark, dried leaves, seeds, pods, flowers, grasses, insects (such as discarded cicada shells), deer antlers, dried sea horses, dried fish bladders, snake gall bladders, and rhinoceros horns are just the beginning. The herbalist, after learning about the customer's symptoms and checking the pulses in both wrists, will prescribe an appropriate remedy, using perhaps a bit of bark here and a seed there, based on wisdom passed down over thousands of years. A typical prescription might include up to 20 ingredients, which are often boiled to produce a medicinal tea. Because most herbalists are not likely to speak English, you'll mainly be window-shopping here.

Continue on Sutherland heading south (toward the playground). A few years back, this neighborhood was renovated and the Li Sing Street Playground was built in its midst, displacing some of the narrow alleys favored by one of Hong Kong's oldest professions—street-side barbers. Once plentiful, street-side barbers have now gone the way of the rickshaw. At the top of Sutherland Street, on busy Queen's Road West, I used to see an elderly woman who set up shop on the sidewalk, using only a couple of stools and some thread. She used the thread to remove the facial hairs of her customers, an ancient method that some salons still perform. But like much of old Hong Kong, she and her sidewalk business have vanished.

TAKE A BREAK

There's no better place for Western food in this immediate vicinity than Sammy's Kitchen, 204–206 Queen's Rd. W. (reached from Sutherland St. by turning right and walking about 2 min.; © 852/2548 8400; p. 157). A landmark for almost 4 decades, it's owned by the gregarious and friendly Sammy Yip and his family. It's a good place for inexpensive lunchtime fare, an afternoon snack, a soda or ice-cream sundae, or, in the evenings, fresh seafood, steaks, chicken, and house specialties.

At the top of Sutherland Street, cross Queen's Road West and turn left, heading east. Here you'll pass several open-fronted:

16 Funeral & Incense Shops

Note the paper replicas of household goods and other items (such as houses, cars, running shoes, handbags, and even computers and cellphones) hanging from the shops' eaves and ceilings. At funerals, these paper effigies are burned to accompany the deceased into the afterlife.

After the funeral shops, follow the sidewalk up and down a small hill. Shortly thereafter you will see a road leading uphill to the right. It's the famous:

17 Hollywood Road

This long road, which runs all the way to Central, is a strange mixture of shops selling coffins, funeral items, furniture, antiques, and artwork. In fact, more antiques shops are concentrated along this rather long road than anywhere else in Hong Kong. You'll find everything from woodblock prints and rosewood tables to Neolithic pots, Ming dynasty ceramic figures, silk carpets, snuff bottles, porcelain, round-bellied smiling Buddhas, and plenty of fakes and replicas. Built in 1844 to accommodate stationed British troops, the road takes its name from the woods of holly that used to adorn the area.

Before hitting all the stores just mentioned, to your left will be:

18 Hollywood Road Park

A pleasant garden oasis with a children's playground, a pond with goldfish, and Chinese pagodas, this park makes a nice stop for a few moments of relaxation before continuing on.

Just past the playground, to your left, you'll soon pass a historic landmark:

19 Possession Street

You need not enter, but you might be interested to know that the British first landed in 1841 and planted the Union Jack to claim the island for Britain here. At the time, of course, this was part of the waterfront. The street has a less glorious name in Chinese—Shui Hang Hau—named for a big puddle that used to be here.

Continue along Hollywood Road, past Possession Street. One of the first antiques shops you'll come to is:

20 Dragon Culture

One of Hong Kong's largest and most respected shops, Dragon Culture is owned by Victor Choi, who once gave lectures on Chinese antiques for the HKTB's "Meet the People" program but is now semi-retired, concentrating his efforts on educational charities. Browse his shop, at 231 Hollywood Rd. (✆ **852/2545 8098;** p. 225), for everything from Tang pottery to Ming porcelain. If you want to learn more about antiques, buy Choi's *Collecting Chinese Antiques in Hong Kong,* which answers frequently asked questions about antiques, including important information on how to ship them home. All proceeds from Choi's *Horses for Eternity* book go to charity.

After Dragon Culture, turn left at Lok Ku Road and then right onto Upper Lascar Row, better known as:

21 Cat Street

For almost a century, Cat Street was famous for its antiques, which could be bought for a pittance; with a growing global interest in Chinese antiques and the pricey antiques shops on Hollywood Road, Cat Street vendors now offer a fantastic mix of curios, replicas, and junk. Pleasantly dotted with potted palms, this pedestrian lane is worth a browse for jade, snuff bottles, watches, pictures, copper and brass kettles, old eyeglasses, bird cages, replica Mao souvenirs, and odds and ends. You should bargain with the vendors who have laid their wares on the sidewalk; most of them do business Monday through Saturday from 11am to about 5pm. You can also bargain at the surrounding antiques shops, where prices are rather high to begin with. If you're not an expert, be wary of purchasing anything of value. During one visit, it seemed that every shop was offering fossilized "dinosaur eggs" for sale. How many can there be?

At the end of Cat Street, turn right and go up the stairs. Across the street you'll see unmistakable:

22 Ladder Street

The extremely steep flight of stairs was once a common sight on precipitous Hong Kong Island. Now, of course, Hong Kong Island has escalators and the Peak Tram, but you're going to find out exactly how steep and tiring these stairs are by heading up them, keeping a lookout for the YMCA on your right and Bridges Street.

Just past the YMCA and Bridges Street, a bit farther up Ladder Street on your left, you will soon see an unmarked flight of stairs leading up to the shady Wing Lee Street sitting area. Walk past the benches and a school to:

23 Wing Lee Street

This narrow street, lined on one side with a dozen tenements once ubiquitous in Hong Kong but now long gone, offers a window into life here in the 1950s. The tenements were slated for the wrecking ball until conservationists—spurred by the success at the Berlin Film Festival of *Echoes of the Rainbow,* which was partly filmed here—lobbied for its preservation. The street's future is now in limbo, as development plans are revised. Although some occupants have moved out, the street now attracts a steady stream of camera-toting visitors.

Back on Ladder Street, continue your trudge uphill almost to the top before turning right and following the sign down the short flight of steps to the:

24 Hong Kong Museum of Medical Sciences

This museum is housed in a stately, 1905 Edwardian-style brick building, at 2 Caine Lane (✆ **852/2549 5123;** p. 174), that once served as the Pathological Institute, founded to combat Hong Kong's worst outbreak of bubonic plague, which eventually claimed 20,000 lives. With most rooms left intact and devoted to various aspects of early medicine practiced in colonial Hong Kong, it is the only museum in the world to compare traditional Chinese and Western medicines. You'll see acupuncture needles, an autopsy room, an X-ray of a bound foot (once considered a sign of beauty for Chinese women), Chinese medicinal herbs, and the Halvo Pelvic Distraction Apparatus, a Hong Kong invention for treating humped backs. Fascinating. It's open Tuesday through Saturday from 10am to 5pm and Sunday from 1 to 5pm.

Head back down Ladder Street and turn right onto Hollywood Road, where you'll immediately see the:

25 Man Mo Temple

This is Hong Kong Island's oldest and most well-known temple. Scenes from *The World of Suzie Wong* were filmed in the surrounding neighborhood. The temple, which dates back to the 1840s, is open daily from 8am to 6pm and is dedicated to two deities: the god of literature (Man) and the god of war (Mo). Mo is popular with the police force and members of the underworld. From the ceiling hang huge incense coils, which burn as long as 3 weeks, purchased by patrons seeking the fulfillment of their wishes; the aromatic smoke is said to carry prayers to the spirit world. Historic relics on display include an 1847 bronze bell and imperial sedan chairs made in 1862. In a room to the right of the main hall is a small souvenir shop and an English-speaking fortuneteller.

Return to Hollywood Road and turn right to continue walking toward its eastern end. Here you'll find more chic and upscale antiques shops selling furniture, blue-and-white porcelain, and goods from other countries, including Korean chests and Japanese hibachi. One of my favorites is:

26 True Arts & Curios

Located at 89–91 Hollywood Rd. (© **852/2559 1485;** p. 226), this tiny shop is packed with all kinds of surprises, from antique children's pointed shoes to porcelain, jewelry, and snuff bottles. It also carries about 2,000 temple woodcarvings, most of which are about 100 years old and small enough to carry with you on the plane.

TAKE A BREAK

Just a stone's throw from Man Mo Temple, the Press Room, 108 Hollywood Rd. (© 852/2525 3444; p. 142), is a bustling brasserie offering French cuisine, Italian bistro food, burgers, and, from its adjacent gourmet shop, wine and artisanal cheeses.

Farther along Hollywood Road, turn left onto:

27 Graham Street

This is part of the Central Street Market, with sidewalk hawkers selling fruit, vegetables, slabs of meat hanging from hooks, and flowers. It's been in operation since 1841, but the city has plans to raze it for high-rise development, setting off local protests despite promises to retain a more upscale version of the market. I'm with the protestors: Too much of the Western District has already suffered mindless redevelopment, and Graham Street is a great slice of old Hong Kong that deserves protection.

Return to Hollywood Road. Farther down, just before the Central–Mid-Levels Escalator, are a couple of ancient-looking hole-in-the-wall shops selling brick-a-brac, old photographs and postcards of Hong Kong (including portraits of women engaged in that ageless profession), snuff bottles, and other interesting stuff. Walk under the elevated people mover, and just a bit beyond, to the right, on Old Bailey and Hollywood Road, is the former:

28 Central Police Station

Originally built in 1864 and expanded in 1919 and 1925, this is one of Hong Kong's largest clusters of Victorian-era buildings, built in the classical style. Plans call for the building's eventual renovation into a contemporary visual arts center.

Return to the Central–Mid-Levels Escalator. Here, on the steep lanes flanking the escalator and on narrow side alleys, is Hong Kong's newest nightlife and dining district:

29 SoHo

Though SoHo stands for "south of Hollywood," the popularity of this area has made it blossom into side streets on both sides of Hollywood Road, including NoHo to the north. Most establishments are tiny affairs, serving a great variety of ethnic cuisines at reasonable prices.

If you wish to return to Central, walk downhill on Cochrane Street (which runs underneath the escalator) to Queen's Road Central, where you should turn right.

WINDING DOWN

Because establishments are opening up in SoHo literally overnight, I suggest you simply walk along Shelley and Elgin streets and their side streets until something catches your fancy. Otherwise, at 10 Shelley St., is Life (℃ 852/2810 9777; p. 146), a vegetarian restaurant with a relaxed, casual atmosphere. Uphill from Hollywood Road, on the corner of Shelley and Staunton streets, is Staunton's Bar & Café (℃ 852/2973 6611; p. 251), one of the first venues to open in SoHo. If you walk up Shelley Street and make a right on Elgin Street, you will find many ethnic eateries, including ¡Caramba!, 26–30 Elgin St. (℃ 852/2530 9963; p. 145), serving Mexican fare, and Posto Pubblico, 28 Elgin St. (℃ 852/2577 7160; p. 142), an Italian restaurant specializing in locally sourced organic food.

WALKING TOUR 3: TSIM SHA TSUI & YAU MA TEI

START:	Star Ferry Terminus, Tsim Sha Tsui.
FINISH:	Temple Street Night Market.
TIME:	About 2 hours, not including museum stops.
BEST TIMES:	Sunday afternoon, when there are free kung fu performances in Kowloon Park and the Jade Market is likely to stay open as late as 6pm, allowing you to see nearby Temple Street Night Market as well.
WORST TIME:	Thursday, when the Hong Kong Museum of Art and Hong Kong Heritage Discovery Centre are closed. Mornings, before the Temple Street Night Market is open.

A stroll up Nathan Road through Tsim Sha Tsui and Yau Ma Tei will take you through the heart of Kowloon, past its famous hotels, restaurants, and shops, and on to the fascinating Chinese shops and markets in Yau Ma Tei. You do, however, have to make a decision before embarking on this tour. The Jade Market generally closes around 4pm, while the nearby Temple Street Night Market isn't in full swing until 7pm. However, more and more Temple Street vendors are setting up shop early, from about 4pm, so you can hit both the Jade Market and Temple Street Night Market if you time your walk just right and don't mind walking through Temple Street when it's not at its liveliest. Another possibility is to walk this tour on Sunday, when the Jade Market stays open later because of increased crowds. Otherwise, because the MTR is so efficient, you can easily return to the night market later in the evening. Whatever you choose, a logical tour of Tsim Sha Tsui begins with the Star Ferry since, for more than a century, it served as the only link with Hong Kong Island.

Within the Star Ferry terminus itself is a Hong Kong Tourism Board Visitor Centre, where you can pick up free pamphlets and maps. In front of the Star Ferry concourse is Kowloon's main bus terminal. Straight ahead to the left is Ocean Terminal, the port of call for cruise liners docking in Hong Kong. It's probably no accident that it is immediately adjacent to:

1 Harbour City

This is Hong Kong's largest interconnected shopping mall and one of the largest shopping complexes in the world. Stretching more than .8km (½ mile) along Canton Road, it contains more than 700 shops and receives up to 200,000 shoppers on a weekend. Enter it and you might not escape during this lifetime;

Walking Tour 3: Tsim Sha Tsui & Yau Ma Tei

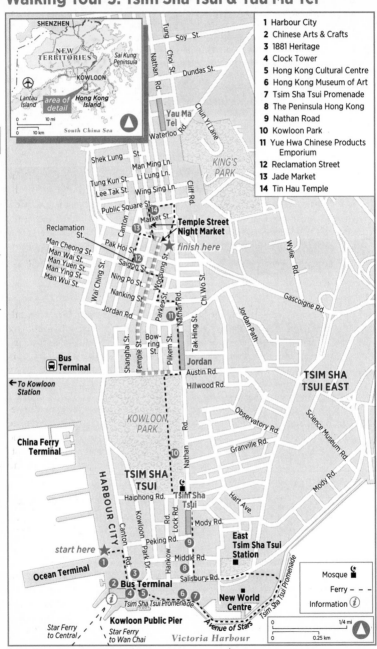

1 Harbour City
2 Chinese Arts & Crafts
3 1881 Heritage
4 Clock Tower
5 Hong Kong Cultural Centre
6 Hong Kong Museum of Art
7 Tsim Sha Tsui Promenade
8 The Peninsula Hong Kong
9 Nathan Road
10 Kowloon Park
11 Yue Hwa Chinese Products Emporium
12 Reclamation Street
13 Jade Market
14 Tin Hau Temple

better save shopping here for another day. Instead, for one-stop shopping for high-quality (but pricey) Chinese products and gifts, head to the large, nondescript building to the right of Ocean Terminal, Star House, which contains mostly offices but also some restaurants and shops, including:

2 Chinese Arts & Crafts

Located on the ground floor of Star House, 3 Salisbury Rd. (© **852/2735 4061**), this two-story store is open daily from 10am to 9:30pm and is the most upscale emporium specializing in Chinese products, including embroidered tablecloths, jewelry, ceramics, furniture, carpets, arts and crafts, and beautifully tailored clothing. It's also one of the most reliable places to buy jade.

Past Star House, across Canton Road, is the new:

3 1881 Heritage

Now an upscale shopping and dining complex, this was the former site of the Hong Kong Marine Police headquarters from the 1880s to 1996. Several of the old buildings, as well as some ancient trees, have been preserved. If you follow the escalator to the top level of Hullett House (now housing an all-suite luxury hotel, restaurants, and bars), you can see that the police stationed here once had a sweeping view of the harbor.

Cross over Salisbury Road back toward the harbor, where in front of you is the hard-to-miss:

4 Clock Tower

Completed in 1921 and now dwarfed by the buildings around it, this is the only structure remaining from Hong Kong's old train station, once the final stop for those traveling overland from London on the Orient Express. In 1975, the Kowloon-Canton Railway terminus moved to Hung Hom. Occupying the train station's former site is the modern, salmon-colored:

5 Hong Kong Cultural Centre

Opened in 1989 as the city's largest arena for the performing arts, this saddle-shaped structure, in my opinion, is terribly misplaced. After all, why situate concert and theater halls that have no windows on waterfront property with one of the world's most stunning views? Still, the Cultural Centre does offer first-rate concerts of both Western and Chinese music, as well as free shows and events several times a month on Thursdays and Saturdays.

Enter the Cultural Centre's ground floor and stop at the Enquiries counter to pick up a brochure detailing concerts and free events (there are also public toilets here). Exit the other side, where to the east you will soon come upon one of my favorite museums in Hong Kong, the:

6 Hong Kong Museum of Art

Located at 10 Salisbury Rd. (© **852/2721 0116;** p. 170), this museum contains an excellent collection of Chinese porcelain, bronzes, jade, lacquerware, bamboo carvings, and paintings of old Hong Kong and Macau, as well as works by contemporary Hong Kong artists. It even has windows overlooking the harbor. Don't miss it. It's open Friday through Wednesday, 10am to 6pm (Sat to 8pm).

Circle around behind the art museum, to the:

7 Tsim Sha Tsui Promenade

Hugging the shoreline all the way from the Star Ferry to Hung Hom, the promenade offers a great vantage point of the harbor with its boat traffic, Hong Kong Island, and the Peak. It's also a good place for a romantic stroll at night, when the dazzling lights of Hong Kong Island burn bright across the harbor. Nightly from 8 to 8:18pm, Hong Kong stages its "Symphony of Lights," an impressive laser-and-light show projected from more than 40 buildings on both sides of the harbor. Just a couple of minutes' stroll along the waterfront will bring you to the promenade's Avenue of Stars, with embedded plaques and handprints and a few statues honoring Hong Kong's most famous movie personalities, including Jackie Chan and Bruce Lee.

At the end of Avenue of Stars, turn left into the New World Centre, a shopping mall, and walk straight through to its front entrance, beyond which is a pedestrian subway. Follow signs through the pedestrian subway to Tsim Sha Tsui's most famous landmark:

8 The Peninsula Hong Kong

Built in 1928 to serve guests disembarking at the old train station and guarded by one of the largest Rolls-Royce fleets in the world, the venerable Peninsula is Hong Kong's grandest old hotel, with a newer tower that offers great harbor views from its front-facing rooms and top-floor restaurant. Its lobby, reminiscent of a Parisian palace with high gilded ceilings, pillars, and ferns, has long been a favorite spot for a cup of coffee and people-watching.

TAKE A BREAK

Many visitors feel that their Hong Kong stay would not be complete without dropping by The Lobby of the Peninsula Hong Kong (☏ 852/2315 3146). Classical music serenades guests throughout the afternoon and evening, but the best time to stop by is between 2 and 7pm daily, when an English-style afternoon tea is served for HK$268 for one person and HK$398 for two. Another great place for afternoon tea is across the street in the Lobby Lounge of the InterContinental Hong Kong, 18 Salisbury Rd. (☏ 852/2721 1211), which offers fantastic views of the harbor and Hong Kong Island, along with its delicate finger sandwiches and tea daily from 2:30 to 6pm. See the "Afternoon Tea" section at the end of chapter 6, on p. 162, for more information.

Walk to the busy road running alongside the east side of the Peninsula hotel:

9 Nathan Road

This is Kowloon's most famous street. It is also one of Hong Kong's widest and runs almost 4km (2½ miles) straight up the spine of Kowloon all the way to Boundary Road, the official border of the New Territories. Nathan Road is named after Sir Matthew Nathan, who served as governor at the time the road was constructed. After it was completed, it was nicknamed "Nathan's Folly." After all, why build such a wide road, seemingly leading to nowhere? Kowloon had very few people back then and even less traffic. Now, of course, Nathan Road is known as the "golden mile of shopping" because of all the boutiques and shops lining both sides.

You'll pass jewelry stores, electronics shops, optical shops, clothing boutiques, and many other establishments as you head north on Nathan Road. The side streets are also good hunting grounds for inexpensive casual wear, especially Granville Road for its trendy, fun fashions for the young and young at heart. You'll want to return here to explore this area at leisure; shops are open until 9 or 10pm or later. After about 10 minutes (assuming you don't stop to shop along the way), you'll see Hong Kong's largest mosque on your left, built in 1984 to replace an older mosque built in the late 19th century for Muslim Indian troops belonging to the British army. Today, about 80,000 Muslims live in Hong Kong; the mosque can accommodate 3,000 worshippers.

Just past the mosque, take the first steps you see on the left, leading up to:

10 Kowloon Park

Kowloon Park is a good place to bring children for a romp through playgrounds and open spaces. The park features a water garden, Chinese garden, sculpture garden (with Scotland's Sir Eduardo Paolozzi's bronze version of William Blake's *Concept of Newton*), aviary, woodland trail, hedge maze, Hong Kong Heritage Discovery Centre with displays of Hong Kong's historic buildings and ongoing preservation efforts, and both indoor and outdoor swimming pools. Best for visitors, however, are the free kung fu Chinese martial arts performances held every Sunday from 2:30 to 4:30pm featuring children and adult practitioners; follow the signs KUNG FU CORNER to the Sculpture Walk. A small arts fair is also held on Sundays from 1 to 7pm at the Loggia.

Walk through the park northward, past the indoor/outdoor public swimming pools, to Austin Road. To the left you can see Elements, an upscale shopping complex attached to Kowloon Station with service to the airport. You, however, should turn right and walk to Nathan Road again, where you should turn left. Be on the lookout to the left for:

11 Yue Hwa Chinese Products Emporium

On the corner of Jordan Road at 301–309 Nathan Rd. (© **852/3511 2222**), this emporium caters primarily to local and visiting Chinese with traditional Chinese products, including silk, porcelain, jade, clothing, furniture, medicinal herbs, and everyday household goods. Be sure to hit the food floor in the basement and the tea department on the fifth floor. Hours here are 10am to 10pm daily.

Yue Hwa marks the beginning of the Yau Ma Tei District. Its name translates roughly as "the place for growing sesame plants," but you won't see any such cultivation today. Rather, like the Western District on Hong Kong Island, Yau Ma Tei offers a look at traditional Chinese life, with shops that sell tea, chopping blocks, baked goods, embroidery, herbs, and dried seafood.

Just past the Yue Hwa store, take the first left onto Nanking Street and the second right onto Woosung Street, where you'll pass restaurants with live seafood in tanks and glazed ducks hanging from windows, as well as other family businesses. After 2 blocks, take a left on Saigon Street and continue 2 blocks (you'll pass Temple Street, site of the famous night market, but more of that later) to:

12 Reclamation Street

This street, along with the adjacent Yau Ma Tei Market, is an interesting stroll if you haven't yet visited a city market. You'll pass butcher shops and stalls selling fish, fruits, and vegetables.

TEMPLE STREET night MARKET

The Temple Street Night Market, with more and more stalls now open from 4pm but busiest from 7 to 10pm, is an entertaining place to spend an evening. Countless stalls sell clothing, watches, lighters, imitation designer handbags, sunglasses, sweaters, Chinese souvenirs, CDs, and more. The name of the game is bargaining. Be sure to follow Temple Street to its northern end past the overpass and around the carpark; in the vicinity of the Tin Hau Temple, you'll find palm readers, musicians, and street singers (who favor Cantonese operas and pop songs). Several of the palm readers speak English.

The edge of the market is also famous for its *dai pai dong* (Cantonese for "big rows of food stalls") that specialize in seafood. Fifty years ago, *dai pai dong* were where most Hong Kong families dined on an evening out, and they were found almost everywhere. Now the government has moved most food stalls into covered markets. The *dai pai dong* at this market are among the few that retain their original ambience. You'll find several under one roof at the Temple Street Food Store at the intersection of Temple Street and Public Square Street, where you can dine inexpensively on clams, shrimp, mussels, and crab, sitting at simple tables in the middle of the action.

At the end of Reclamation Street, straight ahead past the elevated highway, is a small red building with "Welcome" written in many languages. It's the:

13 Jade Market

This fascinating covered market consists of some 400 stalls selling jade, pearls, and collectibles and is open daily from about 10am to approximately 4pm, though vendors stay open until 6pm or so if business warrants it (especially Sun). The jade on sale here comes in a bewildering range of quality. The highest quality should be cold to the touch and translucent; that said, it's possible to infuse jade with color so that inferior stones acquire the brightness and translucence associated with more expensive stones. Therefore, unless you know your jade, you're better off just coming here for a look or limiting your purchases to pendants or bangles that cost only a few dollars. Chinese believe that jade helps protect against evil spirits. Freshwater pearls are also good buys. Although the Chinese used to bargain secretly here by using hand signals concealed underneath a newspaper so that none of the onlookers would know the final price, it appears that calculators have gained more popularity these days. If jade is your thing, a couple blocks east of Reclamation Street, on Canton Road south of Kansu Street, is so-called Jade Street, where shops sell high-quality jade.

From the Jade Market, go east 1 block to Shanghai Street and turn left, where you will soon see:

14 Tin Hau Temple

Shaded by banyan trees, this is one of many temples in Hong Kong dedicated to Tin Hau, the goddess of the sea. It's hard to imagine now, but this temple, with sections dating back more than a century, used to be on the waterfront; land reclamation has left it high and dry. No one seems to mind, however, as this popular community temple bustles with activity. Its park is popular with retirees resting on benches and people playing Chinese games, while the inner recesses are filled with people asking favors or giving thanks. It's open daily 8am to 6pm.

From here, you'll probably want to visit Yau Ma Tei's most famous attraction, the **Temple Street Night Market** (see the "Temple Street Night Market" box, below). The market is in full swing after 7pm, though more and more vendors now start setting up stalls at around 4pm.

WINDING DOWN

Mido Cafe, 63 Temple St. (© 852/2384 6402; p. 133), across from the Tin Hau Temple to the north, has changed little since it opened in 1950 and was one of the first cafes to add soy sauce to its Western dishes. Head upstairs for the best views.

On the other side of Nathan Road, between the Eaton and Nathan hotels, is a branch of Tsui Wah, 17–19 Pak Hoi St. (© 852/2780 8328; p. 153), a very popular chain offering Chinese comfort food. Nearby is Bali Bar, a pleasant rooftop oasis in the Nathan Hotel, 378 Nathan Rd. (its entrance is on Pak Hoi St.; © 852/2388 5141), with sofas and a retractable roof; it's open daily from 5pm to 2am.

WALKING TOUR 4: **MONG KOK**

START:	**Flower Market, Mong Kok.**
FINISH:	**Ladies' Market, Mong Kok.**
TIME:	**About 3 hours, including the markets.**
BEST TIMES:	**Afternoon, when all the markets are in full swing.**
WORST TIME:	**There is no worst time for this walk.**

On Kowloon Peninsula north of Yau Ma Tei, Mong Kok is a residential and industrial area, home to thousands of family businesses and a string of local markets catering largely to Chinese, making it a fascinating place for a stroll. If you start this stroll in early afternoon and you love markets, you can easily add the Temple Street Night Market (see above), just a 10-minute walk from Ladies' Market. Alternatively, you could walk this recommended stroll in reverse as a continuation of Walking Tour 3 (that's how I usually walk it), but note that combining both walks makes for a very full day.

From Prince Edward MTR Station, take exit B1 and walk east on Prince Edward Road West to Sai Yee Street, where you should turn left and then take the next right for:

1 Flower Market Road

Open-fronted shops at Hong Kong's major wholesale and retail floral hub sell potted plants, orchids, roses, and other wonderfully aromatic flowers, at prices so inexpensive you'll wish you could take some home (a nice bouquet for your hotel room will set you back about HK$10). More transportable but not nearly as appealing are the fake flowers. Shops are open daily from around 7am to 7pm.

At the end of Flower Market Road is the equally famous:

2 Yuen Po Street Bird Garden

This is an attractive series of Chinese-style open courtyards lined with shops selling songbirds, intricately fashioned bird cages, live crickets, and tiny porcelain water bowls. Note, too, the men who bring their pet birds here for an outing. This place is very Chinese and makes for some great photographs, but

Walking Tour 4: Mong Kok

start here

1 Flower Market Road
2 Yuen Po Street Bird Garden
3 Fa Yuen Market
4 Goldfish Market
5 Fa Yuen Street Market
6 Ladies' Market

Flower Market Rd.

Prince Edward Rd. West

Prince Edward

Bute St.

Mong Kok Rd.

Fife St.

Argyle St.

Mong Kok

MONG KOK

Nelson St.

Shantung St.

Shantung St.

Portland St.

Shanghai St.

Tung Choi St.

Soy St.

Soy St.

6 **finish here**

Nathan Rd.

Dundas St.

Yau Ma Tei

Pitt St.

Chun Yi Lane

Waterloo Rd.

Shek Lung St.

Man Ming Ln.

Tung Kun St.

Li Lung Ln.

Lee Tak St.

Wing Sing Ln.

KING'S PARK

Cliff Rd.

Public Square St.

Market St.

← **Temple Street Night Market** ↙

Canton

Pak Hoi St.

Woosung St.

Man Cheong St.

Man Wai St.

Man Yuen St.

Man Ying St.

Man Wui St.

Wai Ching St.

Saigon St.

Ning Po St.

Nanking St.

Parkes St.

Nathan Rd.

Chi Wo St.

Wylie Rd.

Jordan Rd.

Gascoigne Rd.

Shanghai St.

Temple St.

Bow-ring St.

Pilkem St.

Tak Hing St.

Jordan Path

To Kowloon Station ↙

Bus Terminal

Jordan

Austin Rd.

TSIM SHA TSUI EAST

0 — 1/4 mi
0 — 0.25 km

visitors are reminded to avoid direct contact with the birds. It's open daily from 7am until 8pm.

After walking through the bird market, exit onto Yuen Po Street (which translates as "Vegetable Patch Street," indicative of how much this area has changed) and turn right onto Prince Edward Street West, where you will pass more flower, plant, and garden shops. Just past Sai Yee Street, cross Prince Edward Street West at the crosswalk, where straight ahead of you is:

3 Fa Yuen Street

This is a local market with stalls selling more T-shirts, cheap toys, bags, bras, underwear, jeans, and children's clothing. There aren't as many tourists here as there are at the Ladies' and Temple Street markets, and you may pick up some bargains to boot. It's open daily from 9am to 9pm; don't neglect the inexpensive stores behind the stalls.

Turn right at Bute Street and then the next left onto Tung Choi, the heart of the:

4 Goldfish Market

You'll recognize the Goldfish Market from the shop after shop selling exotic fish as well as other pets; most are open daily from about 10:30am to 10pm. Aquariums are considered to bring good luck and are excellent for feng shui.

Cross Mong Kok Rd. and turn left, where on your right will be the:

5 Fa Yuen Street Market

This lively, covered wet market is where surrounding restaurants and families shop for seafood, poultry, and vegetables. On the third floor is the Cooked Food Centre selling cheap Chinese fare.

Exit the market onto Fa Yuen Street and continue south, taking a right at Argyle to until you come to its crosswalk, cross it, and turn left onto Tung Choi, home of the:

6 Ladies' Market

This is where street vendors sell women's clothing and accessories, including handbags, Chinese jackets, sunglasses, watches, jewelry, and shoes, as well as men's and children's clothing and toys at low prices, from about 1 to 11pm daily. Although this market used to be geared to local tastes (with smaller sizes), an increasing number of tourists have turned it into a thriving market rivaling Temple Street Night Market. The Ladies' Market, in the heart of Mong Kok, extends from Argyle Street south to Dundas Street. From Dundas Street you can either walk south on Nathan Road to Yau Ma Tei MTR station in about 5 minutes, or keep walking another 5 minutes to the Temple Street Night Market.

WINDING DOWN

At the end of Ladies' Market, across Dundas Street to the right, is a branch of California Pizza Kitchen, 56 Dundas St. (✆ 852/2374 0032; p. 131), with soups, salads, and pastas in addition to pizza.

SHOPPING

N
o doubt about it: One of the main reasons people come to Hong Kong is to shop. According to the Hong Kong Tourism Board (HKTB), visitors here spend on average 25% to 50% of their money on shopping.

In fact, the Hong Kong Special Administrative Region (SAR) is such a popular shopping destination that many luxury cruise ships dock here longer than they do anywhere else on their tours. I doubt that there's ever been a visitor to Hong Kong who left empty-handed. What I love most about shopping in Hong Kong is its sheer variety, from upscale malls to funky street markets.

Of course, Hongkongers love to shop, too, but because most homes are small, they spend much of their dispensable income on clothing. In fact, Hongkongers now spend more on name-brand designer clothing and accessories per capita than the Japanese.

THE SHOPPING SCENE
Best Buys
Hong Kong is a duty-free port, which means that imported goods are not taxed in the SAR, with the exception of only a few luxury goods like tobacco and alcohol. What's more, Hong Kong has no sales tax. Thus, you can buy some goods in the SAR at a cheaper price than in the country where they were made. It's less expensive, for example, to buy Japanese products such as designer clothing, cameras, electronic goods, and pearls in Hong Kong than in Japan itself. In fact, many of my friends who live in Japan try to visit the SAR at least once a year to buy their business clothes, cosmetics, and other accessories.

Although not as cheap as it once was, clothing is probably one of the best buys in Hong Kong, simply because of the sheer quantity and variety. It should come as no surprise that when you look at the labels of clothes sold in your own local shops, many say MADE IN CHINA or even MADE IN HONG KONG. While international designer garments and custom-made clothing are comparable to what you'd pay in high-end shops around the world (except in mainland China, where designer goods cost about 20% more than in Hong Kong), cheaper options abound, including factory outlets, discount shops that sell season's-end merchandise, street markets, and small stores where you can pick up inexpensive fashions for a song. But even when I end up paying as much for an outfit as I would back home, I'm satisfied that I've purchased unique clothing in Hong Kong that's impossible to find in homogenized shopping malls.

CAVEAT emptor

Hong Kong is a buyer-beware market. Name brands are sometimes fakes; that cheap jade you bought may actually be glass; and electronic goods may not work. To make things worse, the general practice is that goods are usually not returnable, and deposits paid are not refundable.

On a personal note, I decided to buy a digital Sony camcorder and checked approximately 10 electronics stores, where I received price quotes ranging from HK$3,500 to HK$12,000 for the exact same model. When I returned to the cheapest stores and asked to see the camcorder, however, I was told it was suddenly "out of stock," but the salesmen said they would be happy to show me a similar model for a slightly higher price. The problem is that there are so *many* models—including many that never make it to Western markets—that it's difficult to know exactly what you're getting and what constitutes a fair price. In the end, I fell for the old bait-and-switch and bought a discontinued Sony camcorder at a higher price than what I would have paid for a newer model at home in the United States. I didn't do my homework *before* departing home (even checking the Sony website while in Hong Kong would have been a smart move), and I ended up paying for my mistake.

To be on the safe side, try to make your major purchases at HKTB member stores, which display the HKTB logo (a gold circle with black Chinese calligraphy in the middle and the words "Quality Tourism Services," QTS) on their storefronts. All of the hundreds of member stores are listed at www.discover hongkong.com/qts, where you can also download the list to a PDA. The website provides the names, addresses, and phone numbers of shops that sell everything from audio-video equipment to jewelry, clothing, optical goods, antiques, and custom-made clothing. QTS-accredited shops must pass stringent assessments each year, are required to give accurate information on the products they sell, and should respond promptly to justified complaints. Of course, prices are often higher than at nonmember stores, but the payoff should be peace of mind and reassurance that you are paying a fair price. If you do have a complaint against a member store, make sure you have the receipt and then contact either the **Travel Industry Council of Hong Kong** (© 852/2807 0707; www.tichk.org) or the **Consumer Council Hotline** (© 852/ 2929 2222; www.consumer.org.hk). In case of a serious dispute you can also call the **Hong Kong Police** (© 999) 24 hours a day.

Hong Kong is also a great place to shop for other Chinese products, including porcelain (from vases to darling tea cups with lids), tableware, jade, cloisonné, silk, handicrafts, embroidery, Chinese herbs, chopsticks, Chinese traditional dresses (the cheongsam) and jackets, exotic teas from China's many provinces, snuff bottles, antiques, and artwork. While Hong Kong prices are higher than what you'd pay in mainland China, the quality and quantity are quite good.

Other good buys include shoes, gold jewelry, pearls, opals, furniture, carpets, leather goods, luggage (you'll probably need a new bag just to lug your purchases home), handbags, briefcases, cosmetics, and eyeglasses. Hong Kong is also one of the world's largest exporters of watches and toys. As for electronic goods and cameras, they are not the bargains they once were. Make sure, therefore, to check prices on goods at home before you come to the SAR so that you can accurately assess a bargain. The best deals are on recently discontinued models.

If you're interested in fake name-brand watches, handbags, or clothing to impress the folks back home, you've come to the right place. Although illegal, fake name-brand goods can still be found at Hong Kong's night markets, sold by vendors ready to flee at the first sight of an official (even cheaper prices are offered for fake designer handbags and watches just across the border in mainland China; see chapter 11, "Side Trips from Hong Kong"). Of course, if Customs officials spot these fake goods in your bags when you return home, they'll be confiscated and you could be fined. Approximately half the fake goods seized by U.S. Customs agents come from mainland China. Note, too, that goods containing tortoise shell, ivory, and precious coral are also prohibited in the United States, United Kingdom, Australia, and New Zealand. In my mind, imitation designer goods and endangered products should not be on your shopping list.

When to Shop

Because shopping is such big business in Hong Kong, most stores open 7 days a week, closing only for 2 or 3 days during the Chinese New Year. Most stores open around 10am and remain open until about 6:30 or 7:30pm in Central (some stores are closed on Sun; stores in malls stay open later), 9 or 10pm or even later in Tsim Sha Tsui and Yau Ma Tei, and 9:30pm in Causeway Bay. Street markets are open every day.

The biggest and best seasonal sale takes place around the Chinese New Year, generally in February. All the major department stores as well as shops in many of the huge shopping complexes hold sales at this time, with prices discounted about 40%. Look also for a summer sale, usually in June or July, as well as end-of-season sales in the early spring and early autumn.

Guarantees & Receipts

It's always a good idea to obtain a receipt from the shopkeeper for your purchases, if for no other reason than as proof of value when going through Customs upon returning home. You'll also need a receipt if the product you've purchased is defective. A receipt should give the full name and address of the retailer, a description of your purchase, including the brand name, model number, serial number, and price for electronic and photographic equipment; for jewelry and gold watches, there should be a description of the precious stones and the metal content. If you're making a purchase using a credit card, ask for the customer's copy of the credit card slip, and make sure "HK$" appears before the monetary total.

If you're interested in a camera, electronic goods, or any other expensive product, be sure to inspect the product carefully and make sure its voltage is compatible with that of your home country. Before purchasing, make sure that all parts, accessories, and the warranty card of your purchase are included in the box. Ask the shopkeeper for a manufacturer's guarantee, which should include the name and/or symbol of the sole agent in the SAR, a description of the model and serial number, date of purchase, name and address of the shop where you bought it, and the shop's official "chop," or stamp. Different products and models of the same brand may carry different warranties—some valid worldwide, others only in Hong Kong. Worldwide guarantees (which is what you'll want) must carry the name and/or symbol of the sole agent in Hong Kong for the given product. Be aware of parallel imports, items brought into Hong Kong by someone other than the official import agent and which may be cheaper but offer a restricted guarantee and after-sale services. If you're in doubt, check with the relevant Hong Kong sole agent (information on sole agents for Sony, Rolex, and others can be obtained by calling the **Consumer Council Hotline** at ✆ **852/2929 2222**).

Comparison Shopping & Bargaining

The cardinal rule of shopping in Hong Kong is to shop around. Unless you're planning to buy antiques or art, you'll probably see the same items in many different shops on both sides of the harbor. If you've decided to buy a washable silk blouse for that favorite niece, for example, check a few stores to get an idea of quality, color, and style. With the exception of department stores and designer boutiques, you may be able to bargain for your purchase, though I've noticed that some shopkeepers are less willing to bargain than they once were. Still, at some of the smaller, family-owned stores, a good strategy is to ask what the "best" price might be. You should also ask for a discount if you're buying several items from the same store, and generally speaking, you can get a better price if you pay with cash rather than by credit card. How much you pay will depend on your bargaining skills and how many items you intend to purchase. As for street markets, you most certainly must try to bargain, though nowadays some vendors will just shake their heads and say their prices are fixed. If vendors are willing to bargain, sometimes just saying the item is too expensive and walking away will suddenly get you that "special price."

In any case, begin your comparison shopping as soon as you arrive in Hong Kong, so that you can get an idea of the differences in prices. Or, if you already know what you want to buy in Hong Kong, check local prices before departing home. I checked two stores in Hong Kong for the price of a 4.2-ounce jar of my favorite moisturizer and found a price difference of HK$39 for the same product; yet even the cheaper price was US$10 more than what I'd pay for the exact product back home.

Shipping

Many stores, especially the larger ones, will pack and ship your purchases home for you. Because basic insurance usually insures only against loss, it's a good idea to buy an all-risk insurance for valuable or fragile goods, available at the store. However, because these policies can be expensive, find out whether using your credit card to make your purchase will provide automatic insurance.

In addition, all upper-bracket and most medium-range hotels offer a parcel-wrapping and mailing service. If you decide to ship your purchases home yourself, the easiest thing to do is to stop by the post office and buy ready-made boxes, which come with everything you need to ship goods home. Packages sent to the United States, Europe, or Australia generally take 6 to 8 weeks by surface mail and 1 week by airmail. For major purchases, you can also buy postal insurance covering damage or loss in transit.

GREAT SHOPPING AREAS

Hong Kong is so filled with shops, boutiques, street markets, department stores, and malls, it's hard to think of places where you *can't* shop. Still, there are specific hunting grounds for various products, as well as areas that have more shops than elsewhere.

Shopping in Tsim Sha Tsui

Chinese Arts and Crafts Ltd **12**
Chinese Carpet Centre **22**
city'super **11**
Chow Tai Fook **17**
Elements **7**
Fortress **11, 15**
Harbour City **11**
iSquare **16**
Jade Market **3**
Joyce **10**
K11 **18**
Langham Place **1**
Ladies' Market **2**
Lane Crawford Ltd **11**
LCX **11**
Marks & Spencer **11**
Opal Mine **9**
The Peninsula Hong Kong **14**
Sam's Tailor **9**
Seibu **1**
Shanghai Tang **7, 13, 21**
Sogo **20**
Star Computer City **12**
The Swank **11**
Temple Street Night Market **4**
Three Sixty **7**
Vivienne Tam **11**
W.W. Chan & Sons Tailor Ltd **9**
Wing On **5, 19**
Yue Hwa Chinese Products **6, 8**

To reduce the use of plastic bags, Hong Kong supermarkets, convenience stores, and stores selling personal health and beauty products charge HK$0.50 for each bag provided to customers. Save the environment and your money by bringing your own bag to these stores.

Tsim Sha Tsui has the greatest concentration of shops in Hong Kong. Nathan Road, which runs through Kowloon for 4km (2½ miles) from the harbor to the border of the New Territories, is lined with stores selling clothing, jewelry, eyeglasses, cameras, electronic goods, crafts from China, shoes, handbags, luggage, watches, and more. You will also find tailors, tattoo artists, and even shops that will carve your name into a wooden chop (a stamp used in place of a signature for official documents). Be sure to explore the side streets radiating off Nathan Road, especially Granville Road, for shops specializing in washable silk and casual clothing and for export overruns of fun, youth-oriented fashions at modest prices. Department stores, Chinese emporiums, and shopping arcades, as well as several huge shopping malls, are also located in this neighborhood. Harbour City, on Canton Road, for example, is the largest shopping center in Hong Kong, while Elements, attached to Kowloon Station, is one of the newest. Many international designers have boutiques on Canton Road. Farther north, in Yau Ma Tei, is Hong Kong's most famous outdoor market, the Temple Street Night Market, with vendors selling clothing, sunglasses, watches, toys, mobile phones, Chinese souvenirs, and accessories. The nearby Ladies' Market is also great for inexpensive clothing and accessories. Specialized markets in Yau Ma Tei and Mong Kok sell everything from clothing and flowers to goldfish, songbirds, and jade.

For upscale shopping, **Central** is where you'll find international designer labels. The Landmark, Prince's Building, Alexandra House, Chater House, and ifc mall boast designer boutiques selling jewelry, clothing, leather goods, and more, with names ranging from Armani, Cartier, and Chanel to Gucci, Louis Vuitton, and Tiffany & Co. Pacific Place is an upscale shopping mall selling everything from clothing to electronics, while ifc mall sells high-end clothing and accessories. Hip Shanghai Tang is a good place to shop for upscale Chinese clothing and souvenirs, while the adjacent six floors in the Pedder Building boast dozens of clothing boutiques and factory outlet stores. Li Yuen Street East and West street markets are a slice of old Hong Kong, offering inexpensive Chinese jackets, watches, children's clothing, and accessories.

Another happy hunting ground is **Causeway Bay** on Hong Kong Island. In contrast to Tsim Sha Tsui, it caters more to locals than to tourists, with often lower prices. It's always packed with shoppers, giving it a lively, festival-like atmosphere every day of the week. In addition to small shops selling everything from shoes and clothing to Chinese herbs, there's a Japanese department store and a large shopping complex called Times Square specializing in clothing, electronics, and housewares. Jardine's Crescent is an open-air market with cheap clothing and produce. For shoes, get on the tram and head for Happy Valley, where on Leighton and Wong Nai Chung roads (near the racecourse) you'll find rows of shoe and handbag shops.

One of my favorite places to shop for inexpensive fashions is **Stanley Market** on the southern end of Hong Kong Island, where vendors sell silk clothing and business and casual wear. In recent years, shops specializing in Chinese crafts and products have also opened in Stanley Market (and, of course, I can't resist a leisurely lunch on Stanley's quaint waterfront promenade). Another great shopping destination on

9

SHOPPING | Great Shopping Areas

southern Hong Kong Island is **Ap Lei Chau** (an island connected to Aberdeen by bridge), where at Horizon Plaza you'll find discount outlets for pricey downtown clothing stores, as well as many antiques and furniture stores.

Antiques and curio lovers also head for **Hollywood Road** and **Cat Street** in the Western District on Hong Kong Island, where everything from snuff bottles to jade carvings and Ming vases is for sale. Chinese handicrafts, including porcelain, furniture, silk clothing, and embroidery, are sold in Chinese-product department stores and Chinese arts-and-crafts shops located on both sides of the harbor. Several deluxe hotels boast arcades housing designer boutiques, most notably the Peninsula Hong Kong and InterContinental Hong Kong.

SHOPPING A TO Z

The stores listed below are just a few of the thousands upon thousands in the SAR. For more listings, check HKTB's website, www.discoverhongkong.com/qts, for a list of its member shops. You might also want to look at *Suzy Gershman's Born to Shop Hong Kong, Shanghai & Beijing* (Wiley, 2010).

Antiques & Collectibles

Several of the Chinese-product stores, listed below under "Chinese Craft Emporiums," also stock antiques, especially porcelain. Additionally, some hotel shopping arcades have shops specializing in antiques, as does Harbour City shopping mall. Antiques buffs should also inquire at HKTB whether international auctioneers Christie's or Sotheby's are holding sales for antiques in Hong Kong.

The most famous area for antiques and chinoiserie, however, is around **Hollywood Road** and **Cat Street,** both above the Central District on Hong Kong Island. This area gained fame in the 1950s following the 1949 revolution in China (which flooded the market with family possessions). Hollywood Road twists along for a little more than .8km (½ mile), with shops selling original and reproduction Qing and Ming dynasty Chinese furniture, original prints, scrolls, porcelain, clay figurines, silver, and rosewood and black-wood furniture, as well as fakes, reproductions, and curios. Near the western end is Upper Lascar Row, popularly known as Cat Street, where sidewalk vendors sell snuff bottles, curios, and odds and ends, as well as reproductions and souvenir items (Mao watches, alarm clocks, and statues are perennial favorites). At the eastern end of Hollywood Road, near Pottinger Street, is a cluster of chic antiques shops displaying furniture and blue-and-white porcelain, including goods from neighboring Asian countries such as Korean chests and Japanese hibachi. If you're a real antiques collector, I suggest you simply walk through the dozens of shops on and around Hollywood Road. Most are open Monday to Saturday from 10am to 5 or 6pm; some are open Sunday as well.

Another good shopping stop is **Horizon Plaza,** 2 Lee Wing St., Ap Lei Chau, an island connected to Aberdeen by bridge. This huge warehouse has more than a dozen shops selling antiques, including furniture, trays, baskets, and decorative art (take bus no. 590 from Exchange Square in Central to Ap Lei Chau).

Don't expect cheap prices, however. In the past few years, suddenly wealthy mainlanders have flooded the buying market, pushing prices for antiques through the roof, while dealers have been holding back supplies in the hopes of even higher prices in the future. But the main thing to keep in mind when buying antiques in Hong Kong is that they may not be antique at all. In many instances, it's obvious you're buying a reproduction, simply because of the price or because 20 items just like it are sitting in the stall next door, and you may not care simply because you like it. For serious shopping, however, if you cannot tell the difference between originals and reproductions, you're better off shopping for the real thing at one of the HKTB member stores, which display HKTB's gold circle and calligraphy logo. Be sure to ask whether an antique has been repaired or restored, as this can affect its value. An antique Chinese chair, for example, may be repaired so much that only half its original wood remains.

If the piece is quite expensive, ask that it be tested. (The most important rule is to shop with reputable dealers when buying expensive pieces. And make sure that if the test turns out negative, the shop will pay for the test. As you can see, this process takes time, money, and effort.) Wood, for example, can be tested using carbon-14 dating, while ceramics can be tested with the Oxford Test. The authenticity of bronze, jade, glass, and stone can also be determined through testing. If you're purchasing anything more than 100 years old, request a Certificate of Antiquity detailing its age and origin, along with a receipt detailing your purchase. Although it's illegal to smuggle antiques out of mainland China, many smuggled items do in fact end up in Hong Kong, where it is legal to then sell, buy, and own them. Needless to say, this has caused friction between China and Hong Kong, especially when international auction houses have sold well-documented smuggled Chinese antiques.

Arch Angel Antiques ★   Established in 1988 by an American and Dutch couple, this is one of Hollywood Road's largest and most reputable shops for Asian antiques and art, including museum-quality ceramics, furniture, Ming dynasty figurines, terracotta animals, boxes, and collectibles. In addition to this three-story main shop, nearby galleries (which the owners will show you on request) showcase ancient ceramics, bronze Buddhas, terra-cotta figures, stone sculptures, and contemporary Vietnamese art. Every antique item for sale is accompanied by a detailed certificate of authenticity. The main shop is open daily from 9:30am to 6:30pm. 53-55 Hollywood Rd., Central. © **852/2851 6848.** MTR: Central.

Dragon Culture ★★ 📖   All serious fans of Chinese antiques eventually end up here. One of the largest and most knowledgeable purveyors of antiques in Hong Kong, owner Victor Choi began collecting Chinese antiques in the 1970s, traveling throughout China from province to province and to all the major cities. He shares his expertise in three books: *Collecting Chinese Antiquities in Hong Kong* (a must for both the novice and the experienced buyer), *Horses for Eternity* (proceeds from this go to charity), and *Antiquities through the Ages,* all of which you can purchase in his shop. Choi has also lectured about Chinese antiques in the HKTB's "Meet the People" program, but you should make an appointment if you want to meet specifically with him, as his efforts nowadays go largely to charity work. He carries Neolithic pottery, three-color glazed pottery horses from the Tang dynasty, Ming porcelains, bronzes, jade, woodcarvings, snuff bottles, calligraphy, paintings, brush pots, stone carvings, and more, and also guarantees authenticity for all items he sells. He's open Monday through Saturday from 10:30am to 6pm. 231 Hollywood Rd., Sheung Wan. © **852/2545 8098.** www.dragonculture.com.hk. MTR: Sheung Wan. Bus: 26 from Des Voeux Rd. Central (in front of the HSBC headquarters) to the 2nd stop on Hollywood Rd., at Man Mo Temple. Or take the Central–Mid-Levels Escalator to Hollywood Rd. and turn right.

Teresa Coleman Fine Arts   Established in 1982, this gallery is best known for its collection of antique embroidered costumes and textiles from the Chinese imperial court, with approximately 2,000 pieces dating from the Qing Dynasty (1644–1912).

Complementing the collection are costume accessories and ornaments, including fans and paintings created in China during the 18th and 19th centuries expressly for the Western export market. Teresa Coleman also owns the nearby Tibetan Gallery, 55 Wyndham St., Central (**℄ 852/2530 4863**). Teresa Coleman Fine Arts is open Monday through Saturday from 9:30am to 6pm. 79 Wyndham St., Central. **℄ 852/2526 2450.** www.teresacoleman.com. MTR: Central.

True Arts & Curios 🎁 This tiny shop is so packed with antiques and curios that there's barely room for customers. Although everything from snuff bottles, porcelain, antique silver, earrings, hair pins, and children's shoes (impractical but darling, with curled toes) are in stock, the true finds here are some 2,000 intricate woodcarvings, pried from the doors and windows of dismantled temples and homes. You'll find them hanging from the ceiling and in bins, many of them dusty and grimy from years of neglect. The best ones are carved from a single piece of wood, masterpieces in workmanship and available at modest prices. It's open Monday through Saturday from 10:30am to 6:30pm, Sunday 2 to 6pm. 89–91 Hollywood Rd., Central. **℄ 852/2559 1485.** MTR: Sheung Wan.

Wing Tei It's not unusual to find (and hear) a vigorous game of mah-jongg being played at the back of this family-owned shop, which claims to be the biggest whole-saler of porcelain in Hong Kong. Wing Tei offers much in the lower to medium price range, making it a good bet for casual collectors looking for antique home decor. Antique furniture, woodcarvings, curios, and other objects are also for sale. It's open Monday through Saturday from 10am to 5pm. 190 Hollywood Rd., Central. **℄ 852/2547 4755.** MTR: Sheung Wan. Bus: 26 from Des Voeux Rd. Central (in front of the HSBC headquarters) to the 2nd stop on Hollywood Rd., at Man Mo Temple. Or take the Central–Mid-Levels Escalator to Hollywood Rd. and turn right.

Art Galleries

A global mania for art from mainland China has led to a gallery boom in Hong Kong; and many of these galleries also include contemporary work from other Asian countries in their collections. For art lovers with not such deep pockets, **Picture This** (www.picturethiscollection.com), with two locations in Central at 9 Queen's Rd. Central, on the sixth floor (**℄ 852/2525 2820**), and shop 212 of the Prince's Building at 10 Chater Rd. (**℄ 852/2525 2803**), sells vintage posters (including original travel and movie posters), antique maps, photographs of old Hong Kong and China, contemporary photography, and other memorabilia from both China and the West. Below are some pricier options.

Grotto Fine Art Under the direction of chief curator Henry Au-yeung, a specialist in 20th-century Chinese art history, this gallery focuses exclusively on local Chinese artists, with an emphasis on the newest and most avant-garde paintings, sculptures, prints, photography, mixed media, and conceptual installations. It's open Monday through Saturday from 11am to 7pm. 31 C-D Wyndham St., 2nd floor, Central. **℄ 852/2121 2270.** www.grottofineart.com. MTR: Central.

Hanart TZ Gallery This tiny gallery has been exhibiting, promoting, and selling experimental and contemporary art from mainland China, Hong Kong, and Taiwan since 1983. Its owner/curator, Chang Tsong-zung, has lectured on the contemporary local art scene for HKTB's "Meet the People" program. Exhibition space is small, so be sure to ask for recent catalogs. It's open Monday through Friday from 10am to

6:30pm and Saturday from 10am to 6pm. 202 Henley Building, 2nd floor, 5 Queen's Rd., Central. © **852/2526 9019.** www.hanart.com. MTR: Central.

Schoeni Art Gallery ★   This 465-sq.-m (5,000-sq.-ft.) gallery shows contemporary Chinese oil paintings by both up-and-coming and established artists, and has exhibited pioneers in Chinese avant-garde, neorealism, and pop art. A smaller gallery at nearby 27 Hollywood Rd. (© **852/2542 3143**) specializes in contemporary works by European and Asian artists. Both are open Monday through Saturday from 10:30am to 6:30pm. 21–31 Old Bailey St., Central. © **852/2869 8802.** www.schoeni.com.hk. MTR: Central.

Carpets

Hong Kong is a good place to shop for Chinese, Indian, Persian, and other types of carpets and rugs. Additionally, the locally made Tai Ping carpets are famous the world over, produced with virgin wool imported from New Zealand.

For imported carpets from India and the Middle East, several specialty shops are in the **Hollywood Road** and **Wyndham Street** areas in Central. For hand-knotted wool or silk Chinese carpets, see "Chinese Craft Emporiums," below.

The **Chinese Carpet Centre,** in Shop LO21 on the ground floor of the New World Centre at 18–24 Salisbury Rd., Tsim Sha Tsui (© **852/2730 7230;** www.cccrugs.com.hk; MTR: Tsim Sha Tsui), stocks more than 100,000 Chinese carpets, mostly handmade of silk, wool, or cotton but also machine-made acrylic, from modern to classical designs.

For **Tai Ping** carpets, a conveniently located showroom is in Shop 213 of the Prince's Building, a small high-end mall next to the Mandarin Hotel at 10 Chater Rd., Central (© **852/2522 7138;** www.taipingcarpets.com; MTR: Central). If you don't see what you like, you can have one custom-designed, specifying the color, thickness, and direction of the weave. It takes about 3 months to make a carpet; the company will ship it to you.

For one-stop shopping, head to **Horizon Plaza,** 2 Lee Wing St., Ap Lei Chau, warehouse of mostly furniture and accessory shops, including more than a dozen stores selling Persian, hand-knotted Oriental, and other rugs (bus: M590 from Exchange Square in Central to Ap Lei Chau, on the south side of Hong Kong Island, near Aberdeen). Most shops are open daily from about 10am to 6 or 7pm.

China (Porcelain)

Chinaware, a fine, translucent earthenware, was first brought from China to Europe by the Portuguese in the 16th century. Its name was subsequently shortened to "china," and Hong Kong remains one of the best places in the world to shop for both antique (mainly from the Manchu/Qing dynasty, 1644–1912) and contemporary Chinese porcelain. Traditional motifs include bamboo, flowers, dragons, carp, and cranes, which adorn everything from dinner plates to vases, lamps, and jars. Also popular is translucent porcelain with a rice grain design. And, of course, European and Japanese china is also available in Hong Kong, including Meissen, Wedgwood, and Noritake.

Probably the best place to begin looking for Chinese porcelain is at one of the Chinese-product stores, listed below under "Chinese Craft Emporiums." In addition, malls and shopping centers like Pacific Place in Admiralty, Times Square in Causeway Bay, and Harbour City in Tsim Sha Tsui also have porcelain shops (see "Megamalls &

Shopping Centers," later in this chapter). Nowadays, contemporary china is generally both dishwasher- and microwave-safe.

Wah Tung China Company ★ Established in China in 1863 to cater to both the Chinese and foreign market and moving to Hong Kong in 1976, this is reputedly the largest company specializing in hand-painted antique porcelain reproductions, especially huge pieces like vases and garden stools. Its vast collection covers all Chinese artistic periods, including Song dynasty celadons, Canton Rose, Chinoiserie, Chinese Imari, and 17th- and 18th-century Chinese export porcelain, as well as a more contemporary European look to entice the mainland nouveau riche. An additional small showroom is on the seventh floor of the Lee Roy Commercial Building, 57–59 Hollywood Rd. (✆ **852/2543 2823**), but serious shoppers will want to make the trek to the main showroom. Both locations are open Monday to Friday from 9am to 6pm and Saturday from 9am to 5pm. 16th Floor, Cheung Fat Building, 7–9 Hill Rd., Western District. ✆ **852/2873 2272.** www.wahtungchina.com. Tram: Des Voeux Rd. West (Hill Road). Bus: 1, 5B, or 18.

Chinese Craft Emporiums

In addition to the shops listed here, which specialize in traditional and contemporary arts, crafts, clothing, souvenirs, and gift items from China, many souvenir shops in Stanley Market (located on the southern end of Hong Kong Island) carry china, embroidered linens, figurines, chopsticks, and other Chinese imports. Other markets with Chinese souvenirs include Li Yuen Street East and West in Central and the Temple Street Night Market in Kowloon; see "Markets" later in this chapter.

Chinese Arts & Crafts ★★ In business for more than 50 years, this is the best upscale chain for Chinese arts and crafts and is one of the safest places to purchase jade. Prices are high, but so is the quality. You can also buy elegant silk dresses and blouses, beautiful Chinese jackets, arts and crafts, antiques, jewelry, watches, carpets, cloisonné, porcelain, stone carvings, Chinese herbs and medicine, rosewood furniture, Chinese teas, and embroidered tablecloths or pillowcases here—in short, virtually all the upmarket items that China produces. It's a great place for gifts in all price ranges. The main shop, spread on two floors and located in Star House near the Star Ferry, is open daily from 10am to 9:30pm. Branches are located in the Asia Standard Tower, 59 Queen's Rd. Central, Central (✆ **852/2901 0338**; MTR: Central); Shop 220 in Pacific Place, 88 Queensway, Central (✆ **852/2523 3933**; MTR: Admiralty); and in the China Resources Building, 26 Harbour Rd., Wan Chai (✆ **852/2827 6667**; MTR: Wan Chai). 3 Salisbury Rd., Tsim Sha Tsui. ✆ **852/2735 4061.** www.crcretail.com. MTR: Tsim Sha Tsui.

Shanghai Tang ★★★ You are stepping back into the Shanghai of the 1930s when you enter this small but upscale two-level store with its gleaming wooden and tiled floors, raised cashier cubicles, ceiling fans, and helpful clerks wearing classical Chinese jackets. This is Chinese chic at its best, with neatly stacked rows of updated versions of traditional Chinese clothing, ranging from cheongsams and silk pajamas to padded jackets, caps, and shoes—all in bright, contemporary colors and styles. If you're looking for a lime-green or shocking pink padded jacket, this is the place. Shanghai tailors are on hand to custom-make something for you. You will also find children's clothing and funky accessories and home furnishings, such as silk-covered photo albums, funky clutch purses, and silver chopsticks.

In addition to branches around the world, including New York, Paris, and London, tiny outlets are also in the InterContinental Hong Kong, 18 Salisbury Rd., Tsim Sha

SHOPPING FOR souvenir FOODSTUFFS & TEAS

Both Chinese Arts and Crafts and Yue Hwa sell Chinese teas and herbs, but for a bigger selection, head to **city'super,** which can only be described as a giant food department store, filled with every foodstuff you can imagine (and many more you cannot). Not only does it have the usual food items, drinks, and condiments, but it also imports foodstuffs found nowhere else in Hong Kong, like packages of Japanese curry rice, dried squid, and biscuits from England. It also has a good selection of Chinese teas, including so-called blossom teas,

with buds that open like a flower when you pour hot water over them (a great gift for tea drinkers back home). You'll find the largest city'super in Harbour City, Tsim Sha Tsui (🕾 **852/2375 8222;** MTR: Tsim Sha Tsui), with smaller outlets at Times Square, Causeway Bay (🕾 **852/2506 2888;** MTR: Causeway Bay), and ifc mall, Central (🕾 **852/ 2234 7128;** MTR: Central or Hong Kong). For international foodstuffs as well as organic and fair trade products, head to **Three Sixty** (p. 147 in chapter 6).

Tsui (🕾 **852/2723 1012;** MTR: Tsim Sha Tsui); 1881 Heritage, 2A Canton Rd., Tsim Sha Tsui (🕾 **852/2368 2932;** MTR: Tsim Sha Tsui); Shop 1022 in Elements, 1 Austin Rd. W., Kowloon (🕾 **852/2196 8200;** MTR: Kowloon); Shop 237 in Pacific Place (🕾 **852/2918 1505;** MTR: Admiralty), and both east and west halls of Hong Kong International Airport (🕾 **852/2261 0606** and 🕾 **852/2261 0318,** respectively), but the flagship Central shop has the largest selection. Its sign is hidden under the eaves of the Pedder Building, so you may have to search for it. It's open Monday through Saturday 10am to 8pm and Sunday 11am to 7pm. Pedder Building., 12 Pedder St., Central. 🕾 **852/2525 7333.** www.shanghaitang.com. MTR: Central.

Yue Hwa Chinese Products ★ Whereas Chinese Arts & Crafts (see above) caters to an upmarket international clientele with wide, spacious aisles and pricey goods, Yue Hwa is decidedly more for the local market, a bit disorderly, and always packed with customers shopping for both traditional Chinese and everyday products. The main shop in Yau Ma Tei stocks a wild assortment of wares, from household goods to clothing, shoes, jade jewelry, arts and crafts, china, embroidered linens, furniture, foodstuffs (in the basement), and medicinal products like Tiger Balm and dried sea horses. Don't miss the fifth-floor tea department, where you can sample products before you buy. I also love to browse its clothing department, especially the sales racks. In fact, I simply love this store! It's open daily from 10am to 10pm.

Yue Hwa branch stores, specializing primarily in Chinese medicine, are located at Park Lane Shopper's Boulevard, 143–161 Nathan Rd., Tsim Sha Tsui (🕾 **852/2739 3888;** MTR: Tsim Sha Tsui); 678 Nathan Rd., Mong Kok (🕾 **852/2395 7951;** MTR: Mong Kok); 151–155 Queen's Rd. Central, Central (🕾 **852/2522 2333;** MTR: Central); and 188 Hennessy Rd., Wan Chai (🕾 **852/2836 0355;** MTR: Wan Chai). 301-309 Nathan Rd., Yau Ma Tei, Kowloon. 🕾 **852/3511 2222.** www.yuehwa.com. MTR: Jordan.

Department Stores

It probably comes as no surprise to learn that the SAR has a great many department stores. Wing On and Lane Crawford, two upmarket local chains, offer a nice selection of clothing, accessories, and local and imported designer fashions, gift items, and cosmetics. Japanese and English department stores are also quite popular.

LOCAL DEPARTMENT STORES

Lane Crawford Ltd ★ This upscale department store, founded in 1850, is a hometown favorite for its large clothing and accessory departments for the whole family, including shoes, handbags, lingerie, jewelry, silver, crystal, and cosmetics. It has branches on both sides of the harbor and is similar to established chain stores in England and the United States, with all the usual top-name brands. The main store, with 7,618 sq. m (82,000 sq. ft.) of designer goods and consignment art that make it look more like a gallery than a store, is open daily from 10am to 9pm. Branches can be found at: Pacific Place, 88 Queensway, Central (✆ 852/2118 3668; MTR: Admiralty), which carries edgier designer fashion, as well as designer collections of furniture, linens, lighting, chinaware, and decorative accessories, all arranged as though it were in a luxury apartment; Times Square, 1 Matheson St., Causeway Bay (✆ 852/2118 3638; MTR: Causeway Bay); and Shop 100, Ocean Terminal, Harbour City, 3 Canton Rd., Tsim Sha Tsui (✆ 852/2118 3428; MTR: Tsim Sha Tsui). Bargain hunters should head to the Lane Crawford Warehouse, on the 25th floor of Horizon Plaza, 2 Lee Wing St., Ap Lei Chau (✆ 852/2118 3403), where last-season's clothing, accessories, and home decor are sold at deeply discounted prices. Podium 3, ifc mall, Central. ✆ **852/2118 3388.** www.lanecrawford.com. MTR: Central.

Wing On Founded in Shanghai more than a century ago and one of Hong Kong's oldest department stores, this main shop offers a wide selection of clothing, jewelry, accessories, and household items, with conveniently located branches at Wing On Kowloon Center across from the Nathan Hotel, 345 Nathan Rd., Kowloon (✆ 852/2710 6288; MTR: Jordan), and at Wing On Plaza, 62 Mody Rd., in Tsim Sha Tsui East (✆ 852/2196 1388; MTR: Tsim Sha Tsui). The main branch is open daily from 10am to 7:30pm. 211 Des Voeux Rd., Sheung Wan. ✆ **852/2852 1888.** www.wingonet. com. MTR: Sheung Wan.

OTHER DEPARTMENT STORES

Harvey Nichols This department store got its start in 1813, when Mr. Harvey opened a linen shop in London; Mr. Nichols joined the store in 1820. No doubt the two gentlemen would have difficulty recognizing their namesake today, especially in this very posh setting on the other side of the world. It has all the usual suspects in designer names, as well as some exclusives, not available elsewhere in Hong Kong, giving it a leg up in the city's very competitive fashion and accessories market. It's open Monday to Saturday 10am to 9pm, Sunday 10am to 7pm. The Landmark, 15 Queen's Rd. Central, Central District. ✆ **852/3695 3388.** www.harveynichols.com. MTR: Central.

Marks & Spencer Known in Britain for its great prices on clothing and affectionately nicknamed "Marks & Sparks," this import from the United Kingdom is open daily from 10am to 8pm. You might be able to find larger, Western sizes here for clothing and shoes, though many of the fashions are in smaller, Asian sizes. It also has a couple branches on the Hong Kong side, including Times Square, 1 Matheson St., Causeway Bay (✆ 852/2923 7972; MTR: Causeway Bay), and Central Tower, 22–28 Queen's Rd. Central, Central (✆ 852/2921 8323; MTR: Central). Ocean Centre, Harbour City, 5 Canton Rd., Tsim Sha Tsui. ✆ **852/2926 3344.** www.marksandspencer.com. MTR: Tsim Sha Tsui.

Seibu One of the largest department-store chains in Japan, this was Seibu's first store to open outside Japan. Targeting Hong Kong's affluent yuppie population, it's the epitome of chic, from its Art Deco Italian furnishings to fashions from the world's top design houses. More than 65% of its merchandise is European; 25% is from Japan. The Loft department carries well-designed housewares and gifts, while Seed offers the latest fashions. The basement supermarket is stocked with imported goods. It's open Sunday to Wednesday from 10:30am to 8pm, Thursday to Saturday until 9pm. Also at Langham Place, Portland Street, Mong Kok (© **852/2269 1888;** MTR: Mong Kok). Pacific Place, 88 Queensway, Central. © **852/2971 3888.** MTR: Admiralty.

Sogo Sogo is much larger and more egalitarian than the other Japanese department stores listed above; its goods are cheaper and its prices lower. Consequently, the 12-story store is often packed (particularly on Sun) with families shopping for clothing, toys, furniture, household goods, and electrical appliances. In the second basement is a large supermarket. A small, classier subterranean branch is located across the harbor, at 12 Salisbury Rd. in front of the InterContinental Hong Kong, Tsim Sha Tsui (© **852/3556 1212**). Both are open Sunday to Thursday from 10am to 10pm and Friday and Saturday from 10am to 10:30pm. 555 Hennessy Rd., Causeway Bay. © **852/ 2833 8338.** www.sogo.com.hk. MTR: Causeway Bay.

Electronics

Because Hong Kong has no import duty or sales tax and because the latest models are often on sale here months before they're available in other countries, shopping for electronic goods has long been a popular tourist pastime. Prices, however, have increased for electronic products in recent years, so if you're interested in buying a digital camera, camcorder, MP3 player, computer, mobile phone, or other electronic product, do your homework first. Check prices at home before coming to Hong Kong to make sure that what you want to buy here is really a bargain. Then, head to Tsim Sha Tsui for the many shops along Nathan Road and surrounding streets, to malls, and to dedicated electronics shopping centers. Compare prices first, and to be on the safe side, shop only in stores that are members of HKTB and skip those that do not have price tags. Otherwise, you may end up buying a discontinued model at inflated prices (see "Caveat Emptor," p. 219). **Fortress** (www.fortress.com.hk) is a big-name chain offering cameras, computers, cellphones, home appliances, and other electronic and electric goods, with locations throughout Hong Kong, including major shopping malls and tourist areas. Convenient outlets are Shop no. 333A, Harbour City (© **852/3101 1413;** MTR: Tsim Sha Tsui); 14–16 Hankow Rd. (© **852/2311 2318;** MTR: Tsim Sha Tsui); Melbourne Plaza, 33 Queen's Rd. Central, Central (© **852/2121 1077;** MTR: Central); and Times Square, 1 Matheson St., Causeway Bay (© **852/2506 0031;** MTR: Causeway Bay).

For computers and software, try dedicated malls such as **Star Computer City,** which has a handful of stores on the second floor of the Star House across from the Tsim Sha Tsui Star Ferry terminal at 3 Salisbury Rd., or the **Computer & Digital Mall,** located on the 10th and 11th floors of the Windsor House, 311 Gloucester Rd. in Causeway Bay, with more than a dozen shops. **Times Square,** a mall in Causeway Bay, has computer and camera stores on its seventh and eighth floors, including Fortress (see above) and **Broadway,** another chain you can trust. In any case, whatever you buy, be sure to inspect every piece of equipment before leaving the store (do not assume what's inside a box matches the picture on the outside and check to make sure instructions are in English), make sure equipment works and that its voltage is compatible with yours at home, and obtain warranties and receipts. For computers, look for complete packages that offer computer, printer, scanner, and software at competitive prices, and be sure that the loaded software is in English.

A fun place for adventuresome shoppers and browsers is **Apliu Street** (beside Cheung Sha Wan MTR Station and parallel to Cheung Sha Wan Rd.), which functions as a street market for secondhand electronic goods and a hodgepodge of junk, including fishing poles, pots and pans, walking sticks, flashlights, and more. The market, which caters almost exclusively to locals with nary a tourist in sight, is open Monday to Friday from about 11am to 8pm, Saturday and Sunday from 11am to 11pm. You need to know your goods here and must bargain fiercely. Don't neglect the many stores behind the vendors, selling new and used cellphones, watches, and more.

Fashion

Ever since Hong Kong received a large influx of Shanghainese tailors following the revolution in China in 1949, Hong Kong has been a center for the fashion industry. Today, clothing remains one of Hong Kong's best buys, and many major international design houses have boutiques here; several have nearby factories as well, mostly across the border in mainland China. Look for a number of Hong Kong designers, including Vivienne Tam, Walter Ma, Lu Lu Cheung, and William Tang.

For a wide range in prices, the department stores listed above are best for one-stop shopping for the entire family, as are Hong Kong's many malls and shopping centers. Otherwise, small, family-owned shops abound in both Tsim Sha Tsui, Causeway Bay, and Stanley Market, offering casual wear, washable silk outfits, and other clothing at very affordable prices.

If you're looking for international designer brands and don't care about price, several arcades and shopping centers are known for their brand names. **The Landmark,** located on Des Voeux Road Central in Central, is an ultrachic shopping complex boasting the highest concentration of international brand names in Hong Kong, including Gucci, Tiffany & Co., Polo/Ralph Lauren, Marc Jacobs, Manolo Blahnik, Sonia Rykiel, Jimmy Choo, Lu Lu Cheung, Paul Smith, Vivienne Tam, and Dior, as well as British luxury import Harvey Nichols, restaurants, and other shops. (Though for mainland Chinese these brands will be priced cheaper, Westerners will not find any particular bargains.) The shops here are generally open daily from 10:30am to 7:30pm. Other nearby fashion centers known for their international designer boutiques (and linked to the Landmark via elevated walkways) include the **Prince's Building,** next to the Mandarin Hotel, with boutiques for a. testoni, Chanel, Cartier, Ralph Lauren, and others; **Alexandra House,** with outlets for Prada and Dolce & Gabbana among others; and **Chater House,** with several Armani shops that sell everything from household items to clothing and cosmetics.

Across the harbor, the **Peninsula Hong Kong,** on Salisbury Road in Tsim Sha Tsui, has concessions for Hermès, Louis Vuitton, Chanel, Dior, and Prada, to name only a few of the 80-some shops, while nearby **K11,** on Hanoi Road, claims to be the world's first "art mall" as it intersperses sculpture and paintings with boutiques like Y-3. Tsim Sha Tsui's **Canton Road,** with a growing number of designer shops, has emerged as Hong Kong's Champs-Elysees, with Dior, Salvatore Ferragamo, Chanel, Louis Vuitton (the world's largest), Hermès, Gucci, Prada, Hugo Boss, Armani, and other stores lining the street.

For trendier designs catering to an upwardly mobile younger crowd, check out the **Joyce** (www.joyce.com) chain ★, established in the 1970s by Joyce Ma to satisfy Hong Kong women's cravings for European designs. Today her stores carry clothing by Galliano, Vera Wang, Stella McCartney, Rei Kawakubo (Comme des Garçons), Rodarte, and others on the cutting edge of fashion. You'll find Joyce shops at 18 Queen's Rd. Central, Central (© 852/2810 1120; MTR: Central); Shop 232 in Pacific Place, 88 Queensway, Central (© 852/2523 5944; MTR: Admiralty); and Shop G106 in the Gateway, Canton Road, Tsim Sha Tsui (© 852/2367 8128; MTR: Tsim Sha Tsui). Bargain hunters in the know head also to the **Joyce Warehouse,** located on the south end of Hong Kong Island near Aberdeen, on the 21st floor of Horizon Plaza, 2 Lee Wing St., Ap Lei Chau (© 852/2814 8313; bus: M590 from Exchange Square in Central to Ap Lei Chau). You never know what you may find among the discounted, off-season designer wear, but discounts run 30% to 70% off the original prices; I have found some delightful bargains here. It's open daily 10am to 7pm. **The Swank** (www.swank.com.hk) began importing European designer labels to Hong Kong in 1955 and today carries the latest fashions from established and up-and-coming international designers in its stores in the Landmark (© 852/2868 6990; see above) and Shop 230 of Pacific Place (© 852/2736 8567; MTR: Admiral), both in Central, as well as Shop 103B of Ocean Centre, Harbour City, Tsim Sha Tsui (© 852/2175 4228; MTR: Tsim Sha Tsui).

For young, fun fashion, **Granville Road,** east of Nathan Road, attracts teenagers and 20-somethings looking for clothing, lingerie, accessories, and cosmetics at bargain prices. Otherwise, Tsim Sha Tsui's number-one draw for young shoppers is **LCX,** which occupies most of Level 3 of Ocean Terminal, Harbour City, Tsim Sha Tsui (© 852/3102 3668). Cutting-edge fashions and accessories here include those by Fossil, agnès b., Bauhaus, and Swatch, as well as many names I'm too old to recognize. It's open Sunday to Thursday 10:30am to 9:30pm and Friday and Saturday 10:30am to 10:30pm.

For Chinese clothing, best bets include Chinese department stores (see "Chinese Craft Emporiums," earlier in this chapter), Shanghai Tang (p. 228), and Hong Kong's many markets (see "Markets," below). Another, albeit pricey, alternative is **Blanc de Chine** (www.blancdechine.com), with locations on the second floor of the Pedder Building, 12 Pedder St., Central (© 852/2524 7875; MTR: Central), and in the Landmark, Des Voeux Road Central (© 852/2104 7934; MTR: Central). In addition to both Western and Chinese clothing, these classy stores also produce their own chic line of Chinese clothing. You'll find **Vivienne Tam's** Chinese designs with a Western twist at Shop 309, the Landmark, Des Voeux Road Central, Central (© 852/2868 2826; MTR: Central); Shop 209, Pacific Place, 88 Queensway, Central (© 852/2918 0238; MTR: Admiralty); Shop 408, Times Square, Causeway Bay (© 852/2506 0098; MTR: Causeway Bay); and Shop 215 of Ocean Centre, Harbour City, Tsim Sha Tsui (© 852/2117 0028; MTR: Tsim Sha Tsui). She also has an outlet store in Citygate, Shop 245 (© 852/2265 8808; MTR: Tung Chung), with discounted prices.

FACTORY OUTLETS & DISCOUNT STORES

Savvy shoppers head for Hong Kong's factory outlets to buy at least some of their clothes. These outlets sell excess stock, overruns, and quality-control rejects; because these items have been made for the export market, the sizes are Western. Bargains include clothes made of silk, cashmere, cotton, linen, knitwear, and wool, and some outlets have men's and children's clothing as well. Some manufacturers even produce clothing for famous designer labels, though it's not unusual to find labels cut out.

However, there are a few caveats about shopping in factory outlets. For one thing, you never know in advance what will be on sale, and sometimes the selection is disappointing. Some outlets do not have fitting rooms, and it's important to carefully examine garments inside and out for tears and stains. What's more, some outlets are indistinguishable from upmarket boutiques, with prices to match. In fact, it seems that some shops simply call themselves "factory outlets" because that's what tourists are looking for.

Popular hunting grounds include street markets—notably Ladies' Market in Mong Kok (see "Markets," below)—which often serve as outlets for mainland factories, as do many stores on and around Granville Road in Tsim Sha Tsui. Otherwise, the best-known building that houses factory-outlet showrooms is the **Pedder Building,** 12 Pedder St., Central. Approximately 30 shops are located on five floors, though many of these shops are not factory outlets—they're simply regular boutiques with the same merchandise at the same prices found at their other branches. In addition, a new trend seems to be shops selling used designerwear, shoes, and handbags, making it good for bargains in last season's fashions. The Pedder Building also has shops selling jewelry, accessories, and home decor. In any case, it's convenient to have so many shops in one building and it's fun to just poke around here.

Probably the best place for one-stop discount shopping is **Citygate,** located at the end of Tung Chung MTR Line on Lantau Island (© **852/2109 2933;** www.city gateoutlets.com.hk; MTR: Tung Chung). Hong Kong's only outlet mall, it offers discounts of 30% to 70% off international brand names, including Bally, Burberry, Benetton, Levi's, Rockport, Vivienne Tam, Timberland, adidas, Nike, and more. Note, however, that not all the shops at Citygate are outlets. Because of its late hours, you can cap off a trip to the Giant Buddha (p. 268 in chapter 11) with a shopping expedition here. Open hours differ depending on the shop, but all are open daily, most of them from about 11am to 9:30 or 10pm.

Jewelry

According to the HKTB, Hong Kong has more jewelry stores per square mile than any other city in the world. Gems are imported duty-free from all over the world, and Hong Kong is reputedly the world's fourth-largest trading center for diamonds. Gold jewelry, both imported and locally made, is required by law to carry a stamp stating the accurate gold content.

Jade, of course, remains the most popular item of jewelry for both visitors and Chinese. It's believed to protect wearers against illness and ward off bad luck. The two categories of jade are jadeite and nephrite. Jadeite (also called Burmese jade) is generally white to apple green in color, although it also comes in hues of brown, red, orange, yellow, and even lavender. It may be mottled, but the most expensive variety is a translucent emerald green. Nephrite, which is less expensive, is usually a dark green or off-white. True jade is so hard that supposedly even a knife leaves no scratch; inferior jade is often injected with artificial coloring. Unless you know your jade, your best bet is to shop in one of the Chinese-product stores, listed earlier in this chapter under "Chinese Craft Emporiums," or at one of 30-some **Chow Tai Fook** shops, one of Hong Kong's best-known purveyors of jade, gold, and diamond jewelry, including one at 64 Nathan Rd., Tsim Sha Tsui (© **852/2368 8232;** www.chowtaifook.com;

MTR: Tsim Sha Tsui). For less expensive pieces and souvenirs, visit the Jade Market (see "Markets," below).

Pearls, almost all of which are cultured, are also popular among shoppers in Hong Kong. Both sea- and freshwater pearls in all shapes, sizes, colors, and lusters can be found for sale in Hong Kong. For inexpensive strands, check the vendors at the Jade Market. Many shops along Nathan Road in Tsim Sha Tsui also retail pearls.

Opals, most of which are mined in Australia but cut in Hong Kong, are also popular buys. Prices vary depending on quality, with black opals the most expensive and white the most common. To get an idea of prices, stop by the **Opal Mine,** 92 Nathan Rd., Tsim Sha Tsui (© **852/2721 9933;** MTR: Tsim Sha Tsui), which operates its own mine in Australia and sells both jewelry and loose stones.

Markets

Markets offer the best deals in Hong Kong, though a lot depends on how well you can bargain. Be sure to scrutinize the items that interest you carefully, since you won't be able to return them. Check clothing for faults, tears, cuts, marks, and uneven seams and hemlines. Make sure electronic gadgets work; the cute but cheap alarm clock I bought my son lasted only a week.

HONG KONG ISLAND

Jardine's Crescent The open-air market that spreads along this narrow street in Causeway Bay is a traditional Chinese market for cheap clothing and accessories, including hosiery, bras, underwear, costume jewelry, handbags, hair accessories, and cosmetics. Though you may not find something worth taking home at this very local market, it's fun just to walk around; at its far end is a wet market and flower stalls. The nearest MTR station is Causeway Bay (take exit F), but you can also reach this area easily by tram. It's open daily from 11am to 9pm.

Li Yuen Street East & West These two steep alleys are parallel pedestrian lanes in the heart of the Central District, very narrow, and often congested with human traffic. Stalls are packed with Chinese jackets, handbags, clothes, sweaters, toys, baby clothes, watches, shoes, bolts of cloth, makeup, umbrellas, knickknacks, and on and on. Bargaining is the name of the game here. Don't neglect the open-fronted shops behind the stalls; some of these are boutiques selling fashionable but cheap clothing, as well as shoes, purses, and accessories. These two streets are located just a couple of minutes' walk from the Central MTR station (take exit C), between Des Voeux Road Central and Queen's Road Central. Vendors open daily noon to 7pm.

Stanley ★★ Stanley Market, rather small and easily navigated, is probably the most popular and best-known market in Hong Kong. Located on the southern coast of Hong Kong Island on a small peninsula, it's a great place to buy inexpensive clothing, especially sportswear, cashmere sweaters, silk blouses and dresses, and even linen blazers and outfits suitable for work. Men's, women's, and children's clothing is available. Shopkeepers are not keen about bargaining unless you're buying several pieces, no doubt because tourists come here by the busload. In fact, Stanley is not as cheap as it once was, many shops have remodeled into chic boutiques, and old-timers complain that Stanley has become a tourist trap. Still, you're bound to find at least something you're wild about, especially if you like cheap, fun fashions. The inventory changes continuously—one year it seems everyone is selling tie-dyed shirts, the next it's linen suits, washable silk, Chinese traditional jackets, or Gore-Tex coats. I usually walk through the market first, taking note of things I like and which stores they're in, comparing prices along the way. Most stores carry the same products, so it pays to comparison-shop. In addition to clothing, there are also many souvenir shops selling Chinese art, embroidered linen, beaded purses, handicrafts, curios, and jewelry. And, of course, no trip to Stanley would be complete without a meal in one of its laid-back restaurants (check out the section on Stanley dining, beginning on p. 155).

To reach Stanley, take bus no. 6, 6A, 6X, or 260 from Central's Exchange Square bus terminal or from Queensway Plaza in front of Pacific Place, or take Minibus no. 40 from Causeway Bay. The bus ride to Stanley, a trip in itself due to hair-raising curves and coastal vistas, takes approximately 30 heart-stopping minutes. From Kowloon, take bus no. 973 from Mody Road in Tsim Sha Tsui East or from Canton Road in Tsim Sha Tsui. Shops are open daily from 10 or 10:30am to about 6:30pm.

KOWLOON

Jade Market　Jade, believed by the Chinese to hold mystical powers and to protect its wearer, is available in all sizes, colors, and prices at the Jade Market, located at the junction of Kansu and Battery streets in two temporary, tentlike structures in the Yau Ma Tei District. The jade comes from Burma, China, Australia, and Taiwan, and is sold here by licensed merchants. Still, unless you know your jade, you won't want to make any expensive purchases here. Rather, come for inexpensive jade bangles, pendants, earrings, figurines, cellphone charms, and gifts. This market is also recommended for pearls, especially inexpensive freshwater pearls from China. Otherwise, this market is fun just for its unique atmosphere. The Jade Market is open daily from 10am to about 4pm (mornings are best), though vendors stay until 6pm on busy days like Sunday. It's located halfway between the Yau Ma Tei and Jordan MTR stations or is less than a 30-minute walk from the Star Ferry.

Ladies' Market ★　If you want to shop at a market on the Kowloon side in the daytime, this very large market is your best bet. Stretching along Tung Choi Street (between Argyle and Dundas sts.) in Mong Kok, it serves as a lively market for inexpensive women's and children's fashions, shoes, socks, hosiery, jewelry, sunglasses, watches, handbags (including fake designer handbags), and other accessories. Some men's clothing is also sold. Although many of the products are geared more to local tastes and sizes, the increasing number of tourists has brought more fashionable clothing and T-shirts in larger sizes, and you may find some great bargains here. The atmosphere is fun and festive, especially at night when it seems to be a popular destination for young people on dates. The nearest MTR station is Mong Kok (take the E2 exit). Vendors are open daily from about 1 to 11pm.

Temple Street Night Market ★★　Temple Street, in the Yau Ma Tei District of Kowloon, is a night market that comes to life when the sun goes down. It offers the usual products sold by street vendors, including T-shirts, jeans, menswear, watches, lighters, pens, sunglasses, jewelry, CDs, mobile phones, electronic gadgets, alarm clocks, luggage, Chinese souvenirs, and imitation designer watches and handbags. Bargain fiercely, and check the products carefully to make sure they're not faulty or poorly made. The night market is great entertainment, a must during your visit to Hong Kong, though the surge of shoppers can be overwhelming. If you follow the market north around the left side of the car park (the wares here get decidedly more racy—sex toys, and so on), you'll come to the Tin Hau Temple, to the right of which are fortunetellers and sometimes even street-side performers singing Chinese opera.

Although the market is open daily from 4pm to midnight, it's at its busiest from 7 to 10pm and is located near Jordan MTR station (exit A).

Megamalls & Shopping Centers

Hong Kong boasts shopping complexes that are so huge I call them "megamalls." Aside from the more convenient ones listed below, other Hong Kong megamalls include **Festival Walk** (located above Kowloon Tong MTR Station), the **New Town Plaza** in Sha Tin in the New Territories, **Plaza Hollywood** in Diamond Hill, and the **Taikoo Shing City Plaza,** located at the Taikoo MTR station on Hong Kong Island. **Citygate,** located at Tung Chung MTR station on Lantau Island, is Hong Kong's only outlet mall (p. 234).

Elements   Connected to Kowloon Station, making it a convenient stop en route to the airport, this shopping complex in West Kowloon is divided into five themed areas—metal, wood, water, fire, and earth—each focusing on different products or experiences. The Wood Zone, for example, decorated with timber and oriental plants, houses health, beauty, and lifestyle stores, while the Fire Zone is devoted to entertainment, including Hong Kong's largest cinema complex and an ice skating rink. Otherwise, you'll find the usual boutiques like Vivienne Westwood and Prada, along with my personal faves Karen Millen, Vivienne Tam, ThreeSixty, and Shanghai Tang. Most shops are open daily 11am to 9pm. 1 Austin Rd. W., Kowloon. ✆ **852/2735 5234.** www. elementshk.com. MTR: Kowloon. Or take the free shuttle departing every 20 min. daily 12:30–9:30pm from Peking Road Tsim Sha Tsui.

Harbour City ★   This is the largest of the megamalls and certainly one of the largest in Asia. Conveniently located right next to the dock that disgorges passengers from cruise liners and just east of the Star Ferry, it stretches more than .8km (½ mile) along Canton Road and contains more than 700 outlets, with shops selling absolutely everything. It's divided into four zones (color coded on the Harbour City map): Ocean Terminal with its shops relating to kids and sportswear, including LCX (a shopping destination for teenagers, p. 233), Toys "R" Us (the largest one in Asia), and Jumpin Gym (a game arcade); Ocean Centre, anchored by Marks & Spencer department store and the flagship store of Louis Vuitton; the Marco Polo Hongkong Hotel Arcade, consisting mostly of the Lane Crawford department store and restaurants; and the Gateway Arcade at its northernmost end. If you're searching for a specific shop, stores and restaurants often give their zone as their address. To most people, however, this is like one huge mall, and the zones are meaningless. It's open daily 10 or 11am to 8 or 9pm, though some shops close on Sunday. Canton Rd., Tsim Sha Tsui. ✆ **852/2118 8601.** www.harbourcity.com.hk. MTR: Tsim Sha Tsui.

ifc mall ★★   The ifc mall is one of Hong Kong's classiest and part of a massive redevelopment beside Hong Kong Station, terminus of the Airport Express. It's a three-level complex housing more than 200 high-end shops (like Lane Crawford, Ferragamo, and Prada) and restaurants, as well as a five-screen cinema, a city'super food store, and open-air terraces with views of the harbor. While a bit confusing to navigate and not nearly as large as the other malls mentioned here, its location, just minutes from the Central Ferry Piers and practically on top of Hong Kong Station, is convenient, and some of its restaurants boast great views. Most shops are open daily from 10am to 8pm. 8 Finance St., Central. ✆ **852/2295 3308.** www.ifc.com.hk. MTR: Central.

isquare   For what it's worth, this new, 31-story mall in Tsim Sha Tsui claims to be the tallest vertical mall in the world. It offers the usual clothing and accessory boutiques, jewelry stores, audiovisual stores (including Panasonic's Ninki Denki flagship), health and beauty shops, and restaurants. It's open daily from 11am to 10pm. 63 Nathan Rd., Tsim Sha Tsui. © 852/3665 3333. www.isquare.hk. MTR: Tsim Sha Tsui.

Langham Place   I was shocked when this spiffy mall opened in 2004 in Mong Kok, traditionally an area with narrow streets packed with tiny family businesses, a poor cousin to Tsim Sha Tsui—but I guess it's just a glimpse of things to come. Boasting some 300 shops, including a Seibu Japanese department store, it's packed with both locals and mainland Chinese rather than tourists, making it an interesting stop for those who don't mind not recognizing many of the brand names sold here. It's open daily from 11am to 11pm. 8 Argyle St., Mong Kok. © 852/3520 2800. www.langhamplace. com.hk. MTR: Mong Kok.

Pacific Place   Pacific Place was the largest and most ambitious commercial project to hit Central when it opened more than 20 years ago; in fact, it shifted the city center toward the east. With the opening of Hong Kong Station and the ifc mall to the west, however, Pacific Place is no longer the center of attention. In fact, I find it rather dull, no different from the generic malls you encounter all over the world and certainly less compelling than Hong Kong's swankier, newer malls. If you're staying in one of Pacific Place's four hotels, however, you'll definitely want to take a spin through here, with approximately 200 shops selling every well-known brand and two major department stores (Lane Crawford and Seibu). Most shops are open daily from about 10:30am to 8pm. 88 Queensway, Central. © 852/2844 8988. www.pacificplace.com.hk. MTR: Admiralty.

Times Square   This popular mall offers 16 floors of shopping and dining. In the basement are fast-food outlets, a city'super food store, and shops selling health and beauty products, while the next six floors offer clothing, shoes, handbags, jewelry, watches, and other accessories. Shops dealing in computers, electronics, and home appliances dominate the seventh and eighth floors (both Fortress and Broadway, two large chains, have stores here), and the ninth floor is the place for children's clothing and toys. Marks & Spencer and Lane Crawford are also here, but one of Times Square's major draws is its Food Forum on the top four floors, home to more than a dozen top-grade restaurants. Most shops are open daily from 10am to 10pm. 1 Matheson St., Causeway Bay. © 852/2118 8900. www.timessquare.com.hk. MTR: Causeway Bay.

Tailors

The 24-hour suit is a thing of the past, but you can still have clothes custom-made here in a few days. Tailoring in Hong Kong really began in the 1950s, when tailor families from Shanghai fled China and set up shop in Hong Kong. Today, prices are no longer cheap, but they're often about what you'd pay for a ready-made, top-quality garment in the West; the difference, of course, is that a tailor-made garment should fit you perfectly. The standards of the better, established shops rival even those of London's Savile Row—at less than half the price.

Tailors in Hong Kong will make anything you want, from business suits and evening gowns to wedding dresses, leather jackets, and monogrammed shirts. Some stores will allow you to provide your own fabric, while others require that you buy theirs. Many tailors offer a variety of fabrics, however, including linen, fine wools, cashmere, and silk. Hong Kong tailors are excellent at copying fashions, including famous designerwear, even if all you have is a picture or drawing of what you want.

On average, allow 3 to 5 days to have a garment custom-made, including two or three fittings. For a suit, expect three fittings and a minimum of 6 days. Be specific about details such as lining, tightness of fit, buttons, and length. If you aren't satisfied during the fittings, speak up. Alterations should be included in the original price (ask about this during your first negotiations). If, in the end, you still don't like the finished product, you don't have to accept it, but you'll forfeit the deposit you are required to pay before the tailor begins working, about 50% of the total cost.

Hong Kong boasts more than 2,500 tailoring establishments. Some of the most famous are located in hotel shopping arcades and shopping complexes, but the more upscale the location, the higher the prices. Though touts both persistent and annoying along Nathan Road will try to get you into their shop, some of Hong Kong's most well known shops are here, too. Your best bet is to deal only with HKTB member shops, listed online (www.discoverhongkong.com/qts) and mentioned earlier in this chapter.

Once you've had something custom-made and your tailor has your measurements, you will more than likely be able to order additional clothing later, even from home.

A-Man Hing Cheong Co., LTD.   This shop was established in 1898 on Queen's Road Central but is now ensconced in the Mandarin Oriental, Hong Kong, shopping arcade, with correspondingly high prices. About 70% of its customers are from overseas, many of whom are repeat customers even after they return home. Most of its fabrics are British imports, and most suits are a classic English style. Suits require a minimum of 3 sittings and 6 days (the shop can ship your purchase), and cost HK$8,500 to HK$20,000, depending on the fabric. It's open Monday to Saturday 9:30am to 7pm, Sunday until 6pm. Mandarian Oriental, Hong Kong, 5 Connaught Rd., Central. © **852/2522 3336.** MTR: Central.

Sam's Tailor   This is one of the most well-known tailor shops on Nathan Road, with clients that have included Bill Clinton, Margaret Thatcher, and Armani. Tailor-made, two-piece suits for men and women start at HK$2,300. Shirts, starting at around HK$300, can be completed in 24 hours (except weekends). It's open Monday to Saturday 10:30am to 7:30pm and Sunday 10am to 12:30pm. 94 Nathan Rd., Tsim Sha Tsui. © **852/2367 9432.** www.samstailor.com. MTR: Tsim Sha Tsui.

W.W. Chan & Sons Tailor Ltd   Established in 1952, this is one of Hong Kong's most famous tailors, with sections for both men and women. Expect to pay about HK$9,380 for a men's two-piece suit, which takes about a week to make. Women's fashions range from HK$1,330 for a pair of slacks to HK$5,270 for an evening coat, plus the cost of fabric. It's open Monday to Saturday 9am to 6pm. 94 Nathan Rd., 2nd floor, Tsim Sha Tsui. © **852/2366 9738** for the men's department, © **852/2367 5588** for the women's. MTR: Tsim Sha Tsui.

HONG KONG AFTER DARK

Nightlife in Hong Kong seems pretty tame when compared to Tokyo or Bangkok. With the world of Suzie Wong in Wan Chai now a shadow of its former wicked self, Hong Kong today seems somewhat reserved and, perhaps to some minds, yawningly dull. For the upper crust who live here, exclusive membership clubs are popular for socializing and entertaining guests, while the vast majority of Chinese are likely to spend their free evenings at one of those huge lively restaurants.

Yet it would be wrong to assume that the SAR has nothing to offer in the way of nightlife—it's just that you probably won't get into any trouble enjoying yourself. To liven things up, Hong Kong stages several annual events, including the Hong Kong Arts Festival in February/March, and the Hong Kong International Film Festival in March/April. Other cultural events are presented throughout the year, including theater productions, pop concerts, and Chinese opera and dance performances.

Most of Hong Kong's bars and clubs are concentrated in just a handful of nightlife districts. In the Central District, most popular is Lan Kwai Fong, in the vicinity of Lan Kwai Fong and D'Aguilar streets, where a multitude of bars and restaurants have long added a spark to Hong Kong's financial district. Nearby, SoHo, along the Central–Mid-Levels Escalator south of Hollywood Road, boasts an ever-growing number of ethnic restaurants and bars. Wan Chai has also witnessed a revival with a spate of new bars, restaurants, and strip joints, while Knutsford Terrace, a small alley on the north end of Tsim Sha Tsui, is popular for its open-fronted bars and restaurants. You can party until dawn; indeed, some bars and discos don't take off until after midnight.

Remember that a 10% service charge will be added to your food/drinks bill. If you're watching your Hong Kong dollars, take advantage of happy hour. (Actually, "happy hours" would be more appropriate, since the period is generally from 5–8pm and often even longer than that.) Furthermore, many pubs, bars, and lounges offer live entertainment, which you can enjoy simply for the price of a beer. Plus, you can enjoy many of the city's finest nighttime charms—strolling along the Tsim Sha Tsui harbor waterfront or around Victoria Peak, watching the nightly "Symphony of Lights" outdoor laser and light show, or browsing at the Temple Street Night Market—for free.

INFORMATION, please

To find out what's going on during your stay in the SAR, you can pick up a number of free magazines around town.

- *What's On—Hong Kong* is a Hong Kong Tourism Board (HKTB) leaflet published weekly that lists events in theater, music, and the arts, including concerts and Chinese opera (you can also access it at **www.discoverhongkong. com**). Pick up a copy at any HKTB Visitor Centre (p. 330).

- Hong Kong's Leisure and Cultural Services Department (www.lcsd. gov.hk) also publishes its own monthly *Event Calendar,* which features events taking place in City Hall and at the Cultural Centre—from Cantonese opera to the Hong Kong Philharmonic Orchestra. The guide is available at both featured venues.

- *HK Magazine* (http://hk.asia-city. com), distributed free at restaurants, bars, and other outlets around town and aimed at a young readership, is a weekly that lists goings-on at the city's theaters and other venues, including plays, concerts, the cinema, and events in Hong Kong's alternative scene.

- *Where Hong Kong, CityLife* (www.citylifehk.com), and *bc* (www.bcmagazine.net) are three other free monthlies with nightlife information and special events. Find them in hotels, restaurants, and bookstores.

- A useful online navigational tool to find out about club events, drink specials, and special happenings is **www.hkclubbing.com**.

- For virtually everything happening in Hong Kong, from Chinese opera to pop concerts, film festivals, and family entertainment, check out **www.urbtix.hk**, Hong Kong's official ticketing agent.

THE PERFORMING ARTS

The busiest time of the year for the performing arts is during the **Hong Kong Arts Festival,** held annually in February and March. This international 3-week affair features artists from around the world performing with orchestras, dance troupes, opera companies, and chamber ensembles. For information about the Hong Kong Arts Festival programs, tickets (HK$60–HK$650), and future dates, call ✆ **852/2824 2430** or visit www.hk.artsfestival.org.

To obtain tickets for the Hong Kong Arts Festival, as well as tickets throughout the year for classical-music performances (including the Hong Kong Philharmonic Orchestra and the Hong Kong Chinese Orchestra), Chinese opera, rock and pop concerts, theatrical productions, dance, and other major events, contact the **Urban Council Ticketing Office (URBTIX),** the ticketing system run by the government's Leisure and Cultural Services Department. Convenient URBTIX outlets are in City Hall (Low Block, 7 Edinburgh Place, in Central) and the Hong Kong Cultural Centre (10 Salisbury Rd., Tsim Sha Tsui); both offices are open daily 10am to 9:30pm. Drop by one of the outlets, or reserve a ticket in advance by calling URBTIX at ✆ **852/2734 9009.** You can also book tickets before arriving in Hong Kong, either by calling the Credit Card Hotline at ✆ **852/2111 5999,** daily from 10am to 8pm Hong Kong time, or buying online at **www.urbtix.hk**.

Another agency, **HK Ticketing** (📞 852/3128 8288; www.hkticketing.com), sells tickets for major concerts, musicals, dramas, sport events, and more.

Note: Full-time students and senior citizens are often eligible for half-price tickets, so be sure to ask when making reservations.

Performing Arts Companies

CHINESE OPERA

Of the various Chinese performing arts, Chinese opera is the most popular and widely loved. Dating back to the Mongol period, Chinese opera predates the first Western opera by about 600 years, although it wasn't until the 13th and 14th centuries that performances began to develop a structured operatic form, with rules of composition and fixed role characterization. Distinct regional styles also developed, and even today marked differences are visible among the operas performed in, say, Peking, Canton, Shanghai, Fukien, Chiu Chow, and Sichuan.

Most popular in Hong Kong are Beijing (or Peking) opera, with its spectacular costumes, elaborate makeup, and feats of acrobatics and swordsmanship; and the less flamboyant but more readily understood Cantonese-style opera. Plots usually dramatize legends and historical events and extol such virtues as loyalty, filial piety, and righteousness, with virtue, corruption, violence, and lust serving as common themes. Performances feature elaborate costumes and makeup, haunting tonal orchestrations, and crashing cymbals. Accompanied by seven or eight musicians, the actor-singers sing in shrill, high-pitched falsetto, a sound Westerners sometimes do not initially appreciate. Although lyrics are in Chinese, body language helps translate the stories and costumes are chosen to signify specific stage personalities; yellow is reserved for emperors, while purple is the color worn by barbarians.

Another aspect of Chinese opera that surprises Westerners is its informality. Unlike Western performances, Chinese operas are noisy affairs. No one minds if spectators arrive late or leave early; in fact, no one even minds if a spectator, upon spotting friends or relatives, makes his or her way through the auditorium for a chat.

For visitors, the easiest way to see a Chinese opera is during the **Hong Kong Arts Festival** (see above), held from about mid-February to mid-March each year. In 2010, the Leisure and Cultural Services Department staged its first **Chinese Opera Festival** featuring Chinese opera from all over China, with plans to make it an annual event every June and July; for updates, call 📞 852/2268 7325 or visit www.lcsd.gov. hk/cp. Alternatively, Cantonese opera is a common feature of important Chinese festivals, such as the birthday of Tin Hau or the annual Bun Festival on Cheung Chau island, when temporary bamboo theaters are erected.

Otherwise, Cantonese opera is performed fairly regularly at town halls in the New Territories, as well as in City Hall in Central and the Hong Kong Cultural Centre in Tsim Sha Tsui. However, Chinese opera is immensely popular in Hong Kong, so much so that tickets for these shows often sell out well in advance, making it difficult for tourists to attend performances. If you're still determined to try, call URBTIX in advance of your arrival in Hong Kong or book online (see above), or, once in the SAR, contact the HKTB or check with one of the tourist publications for information on what's playing and then call or drop by URBTIX. Alternatively, the concierge of your hotel may be able to secure seats. Prices range from about HK$100 to HK$300.

CLASSICAL MUSIC

Hong Kong Chinese Orchestra ★★ Established in 1977, the Hong Kong Chinese Orchestra is the world's largest professional Chinese-instrument orchestra.

It features more than 80 full-time musicians who perform both traditional folk music and full-scale contemporary works, including commissioned pieces, in approximately 30 concerts annually. Musicians play a wide range of traditional and modern Chinese instruments (mainly stringed Chinese instruments, which are completely different from Western violins, cellos, and so on), as well as suitable Western instruments, combining them with Western orchestrations or Chinese music. Guest musicians, like Yo-Yo Ma, sometimes perform with the orchestra. Performing at the Hong Kong Cultural Centre and City Hall (see "Major Concert Halls," below, for more information). ℂ **852/3185 1600**. www.hkco.org. Tickets for most concerts HK$120–HK$260.

Hong Kong Philharmonic Orchestra   The Hong Kong Philharmonic, founded in 1975, is the city's largest (Western-style) orchestra. It performs regularly from September to July and at other scheduled events throughout the year, such as providing live accompaniment to the Hong Kong Ballet. Its conductor is Edo de Waart; guest conductors and soloists appear during the concert season. In addition to Western classical pieces, its repertoire is enriched by works commissioned from Chinese composers. Performance are held at the Hong Kong Cultural Centre and occasionally at City Hall (see "Major Concert Halls," below). ℂ **852/2721 2030**. www.hkpo.com. Tickets HK$100–HK$280.

DANCE

Both the **Hong Kong Ballet Company** and the **Hong Kong Dance Company** have extensive repertoires. The Hong Kong Ballet Company (ℂ **852/2573 7398;** www.hkballet.com), founded in 1979, performs both classical works and modern pieces, usually at the Hong Kong Cultural Centre. The Hong Kong Dance Company (ℂ **852/3103 1888;** www.hkdance.com) specializes in traditional Chinese dance and the development of Chinese dance in modern forms, with about five major productions each year.

THEATER

Most plays presented in the SAR are performed in Cantonese. Hong Kong's leading local troupes are the **Chung Ying Theatre Company** (ℂ **852/2521 6628**), a nonprofit community ensemble that plays in a wide range of venues, from schools and seniors' homes to Hong Kong's main theaters, often performing works by local writers, and the **Hong Kong Repertory Theatre** (ℂ **852/3103 5930;** www.hkrep. com), which performs original Chinese works and Western classics. Both perform in Cantonese at various venues, including City Hall in Central and the Hong Kong Cultural Centre in Tsim Sha Tsui. Prices range from about HK$100 to HK$160.

Otherwise, your best bet for English-language performances is at the **Fringe Club ★★**, 2 Lower Albert Rd., Central (ℂ **852/2521 7251;** www.hkfringeclub.com; MTR: Central), a venue for experimental drama (in English and Cantonese), poetry readings, live music, comedy, art exhibitions, and other happenings, from mime to magic shows. The Fringe Club occupies a former dairy-farm depot built in 1813 and consists of two theaters, exhibition space, a restaurant, and a rooftop bar.

> ### Impressions
>
> *Hong Kong illuminated . . . is wonderful. Imagine a giant Monte Carlo with a hundred times as many lights!*
> —Alfred Viscount Northcliffe, *My Journey Round the World*, 1923

10

HONG KONG AFTER DARK

The Performing Arts

Major Concert Halls

City Hall Located near the Central District's waterfront, City Hall's Low Block has a 1,500-seat balconied concert hall, plus a 470-seat theater used for plays and chamber music. Exhibitions are frequently held in the foyer; you can pick up a schedule of upcoming events in the lobby. Its URBTIX box office is open daily 10am to 9:30pm. Connaught Rd. and Edinburgh Place, Central. ℂ **852/2921 2840.** www.cityhall.gov.hk. MTR: Central.

Hong Kong Academy for Performing Arts Located across the street from the Arts Centre (see below), this is Hong Kong's institution for vocational training in the performing arts. It also features regular performances in theater and dance, by both local and international playwrights and choreographers. Its Theatre Block comprises six venues, including the Lyric Theatre, Drama Theatre, Concert Hall, and Recital Hall. The box office is open Monday to Saturday noon to 6pm; tickets are also available through www.hkticketing.com. 1 Gloucester Rd., Wan Chai. ℂ **852/2584 8633.** www.hkapa.edu. MTR: Wan Chai.

Hong Kong Arts Centre Built on Wan Chai's waterfront, this is host to the Hong Kong Arts Festival and other international presentations, as well as performances by Hong Kong's own amateur and professional companies. It offers a regular schedule of plays or dances, exhibition galleries, and foreign film screenings. There are three auditoriums: Shouson Theatre, McAulay Studio Theatre, and Agnès b. Cinema! The box office is open daily 10am to 6pm; tickets available also through URBTIX. 2 Harbour Rd., Wan Chai. ℂ **852/2582 0200.** www.hkac.org.hk. MTR: Wan Chai.

Hong Kong Cultural Centre Sandwiched between the Hong Kong Museum of Art and the Star Ferry concourse, this is the territory's largest arena for the arts. Opened in 1989, this complex is a good bet for free music and events, including family shows two Saturdays a month (usually the second and fourth Sat) from 3 to 4:30pm that may include Chinese dance, a magic show, or music. Thursday Happy Hour, held once a month from 6 to 7pm, features Chinese classical music, Western music, and other free shows by local performance groups. There are also occasional free outdoor concerts in the Piazza. Pick up a monthly leaflet of events at the center or call the number below for program inquiries.

Otherwise, the pride of the Cultural Centre is its 2,100-seat Concert Hall, home of the Hong Kong Philharmonic Orchestra. It features a 93-stop, 8,000-pipe Austrian Rieger organ—one of the world's largest. Two levels of seating surround the stage, which is set near the center of the oval hall. The center has two additional theaters: the Grand Theatre, used for musicals, large-scale drama, dance, film shows, and Chinese opera; and the smaller Studio Theatre, designed for experimental theater and dance. The URBTIX box office is open daily 10am to 9:30pm. 10 Salisbury Rd., Tsim Sha Tsui. ℂ **852/2734 2009.** www.hkculturalcentre.gov.hk. MTR: Tsim Sha Tsui.

THE CLUB & MUSIC SCENE

Live Music

Hong Kong does not have the kind of jazz-, rock-, or blues-club scenes that many other cities do. On the other hand, live music is such a standard feature of many hotel cocktail lounges and bars, it would be hard *not* to hear live music in the SAR. A few places levy a cover charge, but most charge absolutely nothing.

MAD ABOUT mah-jongg

You don't have to be in Hong Kong long before you hear it: the clack-clack of mah-jongg, almost deafening if it's emanating from a large mah-jongg parlor. You can hear it at large restaurants (mah-jongg parlors are usually tucked into side rooms), at wedding celebrations, in the middle of the day, and long into the night. In a land where gambling is illegal except at the horse races, mah-jongg provides the opportunity for skillful gambling. Many hard-core players confess to an addiction.

Although mah-jongg originated during the Sung dynasty almost 1,000 years ago, today's game is very different, more difficult, and played with amazing speed. Essentially, mah-jongg is played by four people, using tiles that resemble dominoes and bear Chinese characters and designs. Tiles are drawn and discarded (by slamming them on the table), until one player wins with a hand of four combinations of three tiles and a pair of matching tiles. But the real excitement comes with betting chips that each player receives and which are awarded to the winner based on his or her combination of winning tiles. Excitement is also heightened by the speed of the game—the faster tiles are slammed against the table and swooped up, the better. Technically, the mah-jongg game is over when a player runs out of chips, though it's not unusual to borrow chips to continue playing. Hong Kong stories abound of fortunes made and lost in a game of mah-jongg.

Bars, lounges, and clubs listed in "The Bar, Pub & Lounge Scene" below offering live music most or every night of the week include **All Night Long, Dada Bar + Lounge, Lobby Lounge** (in the InterContinental Hong Kong), **Ned Kelly's Last Stand, Salon de Ning,** and **Sticky Fingers,** all in Kowloon; the **Captain's Bar, the Cavern, Insomnia, Joyce Is Not Here Artists' Bar & Café, Peel Fresco Music Lounge,** and **Q88 Wine Bar,** in Central; **Rockschool** and **the Wanch** in Wan Chai; and **ToTT's and Roof Terrace** in Causeway Bay.

Otherwise, the **Fringe Club,** 2 Lower Albert Rd., Central (*©* **852/2521 7251;** www.hkfringeclub.com; MTR: Central), Hong Kong's best-known venue for alternative events, offers live music most Fridays and Saturdays from 10:30pm at its Fringe Gallery, including jazz, funk, classic rock, folk, Canto-pop, alternative, and blues, as well as other musical programs other days of the week. The cover for Friday and Saturday night music is usually HK$100 to HK$120 in advance (add HK$20–HK$30 the day of the show) and includes one drink. Note that atop the Fringe is an open-air bar, decked out with Astroturf and palm trees, serving weekend brunch for HK$99, a weekday vegetarian lunch for HK$90, tapas Monday to Saturday from 4pm, and happy hour Monday to Thursday from 3 to 9pm; it's open Monday to Thursday noon to midnight, and Friday and Saturday noon to 2am. Call for an updated listing, visit its website, or pick up the Fringe Club's monthly calendar.

Dance Clubs

With only a couple of exceptions, most dance clubs in Hong Kong are small, simple bars that morph into miniature discos late at night or on weekends, as well as trendy clubs that cater mostly to their in-crowd members but may occasionally allow non-members on slow nights. (The best plan of action to get into a membership club is to dress smartly, come on a weeknight or early in the evening, and be nice to the doorman.) But many clubs are "member" clubs in name only, giving them license to turn away those who don't fit their image. Discos and dance clubs in Hong Kong generally charge more on weekend nights, but the admission price usually includes one or two drinks. After that, beer and mixed drinks are often priced the same. Bars, whether with DJs or live music, only rarely charge cover.

Establishments listed in "The Bar, Pub & Lounge Scene" section below that offer a dance floor or transform into a place people dance—either to live bands or a DJ—are: **Aqua Spirit, Bahama Mama's, Delaney's, Salon de Ning,** and **Sticky Fingers** in Kowloon; **Al's Diner, The Cavern, Club 97, Dragon-i, FINDS, Insomnia, Propaganda, Red, Solas, Yumla,** and **Zinc** in Central; **Carnegies, Joe Bananas,** and **Rockschool** in Wan Chai; and **ToTT's and Roof Terrace** in Causeway Bay.

BARS, PUBS & LOUNGES
Kowloon

For concentrated nightlife in Tsim Sha Tsui, head to Knutsford Terrace, a narrow, alleylike pedestrian lane just north of Kimberley Road and east of Nathan Road, where you'll find a row of open-fronted bars and restaurants with outdoor seating.

All Night Long   This open-fronted bar is classier than the others on Knutsford Terrace, with a backlit bar at the far end of a tall-ceilinged room and modern art on the walls. Free live music, provided nightly starting at 9:30 or 10pm by in-house bands that rotate among sister bars in both Hong Kong and Singapore, ranges from rock-'n'-roll oldies to the Top 40. It's open daily 4pm to 6am; happy hour is from 4 to 9pm. 9 Knutsford Terrace, Tsim Sha Tsui. ℂ **852/2367 9487.** www.liverockmusic247.com. MTR: Tsim Sha Tsui.

Aqua Spirit ★★★   This glam venue is one of Hong Kong's hottest bars, due in no small part to its unbeatable location on the 30th floor of a Tsim Sha Tsui high-rise, where slanted, soaring windows give an incredible bird's-eye view of the city. Circular booths shrouded behind strung beads, designer drinks, and a voyeur's dream location on an open mezzanine overlooking diners at the 29th-floor Aqua (which serves passable Italian and Japanese fare) make this one of Kowloon's most talked-about venues. Note the minimum drink charge of HK$150, but since drinks are pricey, you won't have trouble meeting your quota. Check the website for resident and international DJ events (like progressive house music Fri from 11pm), some of which charge admission for the right to groove on the small dance floor. Entrance to both Aqua and Aqua Spirit is on the 29th floor. The bar is open Sunday through Thursday from 5pm to 2am, Friday and Saturday until 3am. 1 Peking Rd., Tsim Sha Tsui. ℂ **852/3427 2288.** www.aqua.com.hk. MTR: Tsim Sha Tsui.

Bahama Mama's   One of many bars lining Knutsford Terrace, this one is decorated in a kitschy Caribbean theme and offers lots of tables outside from which to watch the passing parade, as well as a small dance floor for the weekend DJ crowd. Happy hour is daily from 4 to 9pm, as well as Sunday through Thursday from midnight to closing. Drink specialties include fruit cocktails, frozen margaritas, and shooters. It's open Monday through Thursday from 4pm to 3am, Friday and Saturday from 4pm to 4am, and Sunday from 4pm to 2am. 4-5 Knutsford Terrace, Tsim Sha Tsui. ℂ **852/2368 2121.** MTR: Tsim Sha Tsui.

Dada Bar + Lounge   Fanciful decor and a wild mix of mismatched chandeliers and furniture (including day beds) are just what you'd expect from this second-floor bar in a hotel that prides itself in creating a surreal atmosphere. Live jazz is the main draw Thursday to Saturday nights from 10:15pm (HK$220 minimum charge Fri–Sat night), with DJs the rest of the week. Happy hour is from 2:30 to 9pm. Dada is open Sunday, Tuesday, and Wednesday 2:30pm to 1am and Thursday to Saturday from 2:30pm to 2am. The Luxe Manor, 39 Kimberley Rd., Tsim Sha Tsui. ✆ **852/3763 8778.** www.dada lounge.com.hk. MTR: Tsim Sha Tsui.

Delaney's   This very successful, upmarket Irish pub was founded by two traveling Irishmen who, disappointed to discover there were no Irish pubs in Hong Kong (let alone a fresh pint of Guinness), opened their first Delaney's in the 1990s in Wan Chai at 18 Luard Rd. (✆ **852/2804 2880**), followed 9 months later by this location in the heart of Tsim Sha Tsui. Decorated in old-world style with vintage-looking posters and photographs, its convivial atmosphere gets an extra boost from free weekly events, such as Tuesday quiz night with prizes and a DJ on Thursday and Friday nights. The great selection of draft beer and whiskey, as well as big soccer and rugby events shown on three big screens, also doesn't hurt. Happy hour is daily 5 to 9pm; Delaney's is open every day from 8am to 2am. 71-77 Peking Rd., Tsim Sha Tsui. ✆ **852/2301 3980.** www.delaneys.com.hk. MTR: Tsim Sha Tsui.

Lobby Lounge ★★★ ✦   This comfortable cocktail lounge boasts gorgeous water-level views of Victoria Harbour and Hong Kong Island. You'll fall in love all over again (with Hong Kong, your companion, or both) as you take in one of the world's most famous views (this is a very civilized place for watching the nightly "Symphony of Lights" laser show), listen to live music (6pm–12:45am), and imbibe in one of the bar's famous martinis or one of its signature Nine Dragons cocktails. Note that after 9pm, nonhotel guests are charged a HK$160 cover. It's open daily from 7am to 1am. In the InterContinental Hong Kong, 18 Salisbury Rd., Tsim Sha Tsui. ✆ **852/2721 1211.** www.hongkong-ic. intercontinental.com. MTR: Tsim Sha Tsui.

Ned Kelly's Last Stand   Named after one of down under's most famous outlaws, this lively Aussie saloon has been attracting a largely middle-aged crowd since 1972 with free live Dixieland jazz nightly from 9:30pm to 1am. It serves Australian chow and pub grub, including the Ploughman's Lunch, beef stew, fish and chips, Australian sirloin steak, Irish stew, hamburgers, and cottage pie (a baked bowl of minced beef, onions, vegetables, and mashed potatoes). Happy hour is from 11:30am to 9pm. It's open daily from 11:30am to 2am (to 2:30am Fri–Sat). 11A Ashley Rd., Tsim Sha Tsui. ✆ **852/ 2376 0562.** MTR: Tsim Sha Tsui.

The Parlour ★   Hullett House, occupying former marine police headquarters built in 1881, is the crowning glory of the new 1881 Heritage complex on the corner of Salisbury and Canton roads. In addition to a 10-suite luxury hotel, restaurants, and bars, there's this chinoiserie-decorated lounge, elaborately outfitted with an ornate bar and red-tassled lanterns and providing views toward Victoria Harbour. Be sure to take a peek at the side rooms with their hand-painted murals of Victoria Harbour at the turn of the 19th century and of Brighton's Royal Pavilion. Hours are Sunday to Thursday from 8am to 1am, and Friday and Saturday from 8am to 2am. Hullett House, 1881 Heritage, 2A Canton Rd., Tsim Sha Tsui. ✆ **852/3988 0101.** www.hulletthouse.com. MTR: Tsim Sha Tsui.

PJ Murphy's Irish Country Pub   Seven TV screens beaming in sports also draw in the guys, making this pub a lively place indeed during testosterone-high sporting

HONG KONG AFTER DARK | Bars, Pubs & Lounges

events. Otherwise, it's a decent place for pub grub (cottage pie, chili con carne, Irish lamb-shank stew, porter pie) or the weekend carvery lunch. It also has one computer where you can check e-mail for HK$20 an hour. It's open daily from 7:30am to 2am; happy hour runs daily from 5 to 8pm. The Imperial Hotel Hong Kong, 32 Nathan Rd., Tsim Sha Tsui. © **852/2782 3383.** www.murphyspj.com. MTR: Tsim Sha Tsui.

Salon de Ning You have to ring the doorbell, and only after someone ogles you through the slit in the mail drop will you be let in to this boudoirlike venue, decorated with the personal keepsakes of Madame Ning, a Shanghainese socialite of the 1930s. Get there early to claim one of the themed nooks, where you can gaze upon the madame's Chinese dresses, jewelry, perfume bottles, or travel souvenirs (Madame Ning loved African safaris and skiing). Kick back a few signature cocktails (like the Ning Sling with vodka, lychee liqueur, orange juice, passion-fruit purée, and fresh mint), listen to the live music hits of the '80s and '90s, shuffle around the small dance floor, and consider this: Madame Ning never existed—she is a figment of the designer's imagination. This being the Peninsula, keep in mind the dress code (no flip-flops; no shorts for men). It's open Monday to Saturday from 6pm to 2am. The Peninsula Hong Kong, basement, Salisbury Rd., Tsim Sha Tsui. © **852/2315 3355.** www.peninsula. com. MTR: Tsim Sha Tsui.

Sky Lounge This plush and comfortable lounge is on the top floor of the Sheraton, affording one of the most romantic views of the harbor and glittering Hong Kong Island. Note that from 8pm onward a minimum drink charge of HK$118 per person is enforced Sunday through Thursday, HK$138 Friday and Saturday. Or come earlier for the afternoon tea buffet, available Sunday from 2 to 6pm and weekdays from 4 to 6pm. It's open Monday through Thursday from 4pm to 1am, Friday from 4pm to 2am, Saturday from 2pm to 2am, and Sunday from 2pm to 1am. In the Sheraton Hotel and Towers, 20 Nathan Rd., Tsim Sha Tsui. © **852/2369 1111.** www.sheraton.com/hongkong. MTR: Tsim Sha Tsui.

Sticky Fingers Tsim Sha Tsui East is a wasteland when it comes to nightlife, so if you find yourself staying in one of the many hotels here, this bar with live music nightly from 10:15pm could be a godsend—if you don't mind the "professional" women who hang out here (and to be fair, at many other Hong Kong bars as well). A talented Filipino band plays rock-'n'-roll hits for the tiny dance floor. It's open daily from 7am to 5am, with happy hour lasting from 9am to 10pm. 66 Mody Rd. (just east of the Shangri-La Hotel), Tsim Sha Tsui East. © **852/2369 8981.** MTR: Tsim Sha Tsui.

Tapas Bar For a more sophisticated setting in Tsim Sha Tsui East than Sticky Fingers (above), step inside this small but popular hotel bar with its own streetside entry. In addition to a changing tapas menu that might offer the likes of sizzling prawns flavored with garlic and parsley, marinated tuna with a soy and mirin dip, roasted eggplant and black olive croquettes, and artisanal cheeses, it also offers more than 50 wines by the glass. Happy hour (5–8pm daily) is a great deal, with two glasses of wine for the price of one. The bar is open daily 3:30pm to 1am. Kowloon Shangri-La Hotel, 64 Mody Rd., Tsim Sha Tsui East. © **852/2733 8756.** www.shangri-la.com. MTR: Tsim Sha Tsui.

Central District

Central's nightlife is focused on **Lan Kwai Fong,** a square block lined with restaurants and bars. It's everyman's watering hole, from bankers in suits dropping by for a pint to camera-toting tourists to Western and Chinese gays. The fuel, of course, is happy hour, and the busiest night of the week is Friday or the night before a holiday. By midnight the streets are packed; some people don't even bother with the bars, buying beer instead from a convenience store and drinking it outside (if there's an ordinance against it, I've never seen it enforced). LKF, as it's often referred to, is so popular, bars and restaurants now extend down Wyndham and Hollywood all the way to **SoHo,** a smaller entertainment district known for its ethnic eateries and hole-in-the-wall bars.

Agave Fans of Mexico's most famous spirit should make a point of visiting this showcase for tequila (or its branch in Wan Chai at 93–107 Lockhart Rd.; ℭ **852/ 2866 3228**), with approximately 150 brands of 100% agave tequila on offer, as well as 30 different margaritas and a range of Mexican food from tacos and fajitas to burritos. An open-fronted, noisy bar in Lan Kwai Fong, it has a daily happy hour from 5 to 9pm. Agave is open Sunday through Thursday from 5pm to 2am, and Friday and Saturday from 5pm to 4am. 33 D'Aguilar St., Central. ℭ **852/2521 2010.** MTR: Central.

Al's Diner Rather innocent-looking during the day, this informal diner, decorated in 1950s Americana style and offering decent burgers, meatloaf, and breakfast served anytime, transforms into one of Lan Kwai Fong's most extroverted party scenes on weekend nights, no doubt fueled by the house specialty—Jell-O shots—and music supplied by a DJ. A few shots, and you may find yourself joining the others dancing on the tables. It opens daily at 11am, closing at 1am on Sunday, 2am Monday to Thursday, and 5am Friday and Saturday, with happy hour Monday to Friday from 4 to 8pm. 39 D'Aguilar St., Central. ℭ **852/2869 1869.** MTR: Central.

Bulldog's Bar & Grill Live broadcasts of Australian, English, and American sporting events on five large screens make this one of Lan Kwai Fong's most successful bars, especially among American navy personnel, who are welcomed by a large U.S. flag hung outside its doors whenever they're docked in town. But it's the balcony with a bird's-eye view of the never-ending parade of revelers that does it for me. Happy hour runs daily 4 to 8pm. Bulldog's is open 11:30am to 2am Sunday through Thursday, and until 4am Friday and Saturday. There's a branch at 66 Mody Rd., Tsim Sha Tsui East (ℭ **852/2311 6993**). 17 Lan Kwai Fong, Central. ℭ **852/2523 3528.** www.grtvision. com.hk. MTR: Central.

Café Gray Bar ★★ This is where I'd head if I wanted a drink with views at Pacific Place. Located on the 49th floor of the Upper House, a hip, deluxe hotel, this swank venue boasts great views and Hong Kong's longest bar (14m/46 ft.). Candles at night lend a romantic air. Adjoining Café Gray Deluxe, a casual restaurant serving modern European cuisine, the bar is open daily from 11am to 1am. The Upper House, Pacific Place, 88 Queensway, Central. ℭ **852/2918 1838.** www.upperhouse.com. MTR: Central.

Captain's Bar ★ This refined bar is so popular with Hong Kong's professional crowd, especially at the end of the working day, that the Mandarin Oriental's recent overhaul left it virtually unchanged. Well known for its expertly made martinis and pints of beer served in aluminum and silver tankards (regulars even have their own, with their name engraved), it's a small, intimate place, with seating at the bar or on couches and live music of popular tunes Monday to Saturday from 9pm. Hours are Monday through Saturday from 11am to 2am and Sunday 11am to 1am. In Mandarin Oriental, Hong Kong, 5 Connaught Rd., Central. ℭ **852/2825 4006.** www.mandarinoriental.com. MTR: Central.

The Cavern ★ Located at the top end of Lan Kwai Fong, this classy live-music venue attracts a slightly older crowd with its casual-chic dress code, large outdoor seating area, and sexy interior bathed in red lights. The three house bands, silhouetted on stage, play a wide range of music starting at 8:15pm, from classic rock and rhythm and blues to alternative. A HK$100 admission, which includes one drink, is charged Friday and Saturday from 11pm. Happy hour is daily from 6 to 9pm. The Cavern is open Sunday through Tuesday from 6pm to 4am and Wednesday to Saturday from 6pm to 5am or later. Lan Kwai Fong Tower, ground floor, 55 D'Aguilar St., Central. ✆ **852/2121 8969.** www.igors.com. MTR: Central.

Club 97 ★★   Opened about 30 years and still one of Lan Kwai Fong's most revered nightlife establishments, this open-fronted club packs 'em in with a small dance floor and a string of popular weekly events, including Salsa Wednesdays, Thursday Ladies' Night with drink specials, Friday Gay Happy Hour (6–10pm) complete with drag shows, and Sunday Reggae Night, which draws a huge crowd. It's open Monday through Thursday from 6pm to 2am (happy hour 6–9pm), Friday 6pm to 4am (happy hour 6–10pm), Saturday 8pm to 4am (happy hour 8–9pm), and Sunday 8pm to 3am (happy hour 8–9pm). 9 Lan Kwai Fong, Central. ✆ **852/2816 1897.** www.ninetysevengroup.com. MTR: Central.

Dragon-i   This is one of Hong Kong's most talked-about bars; the fact that it lures models with promises of free drinks is obviously good for business, since it also brings in those who like to ogle models. Its interior is bathed in red from the glow of lanterns, while the outdoor patio, decorated with huge bird cages filled with live birds, provides some relief from the crowds, especially when things start hopping from 11:30pm when top-rated DJs stir action on the dance floor. Located on a hill above Lan Kwai Fong and open all day, it closes Monday, Tuesday, and Thursday at 3am and Wednesday, Friday, and Saturday at 5am—but you'll never get in on Wednesday, Friday, or Saturday unless you're a dead ringer for Uma Thurman. The Centurium, 60 Wyndham St., Central. ✆ **852/3110 1222.** www.dragon-i.com.hk. MTR: Central.

Insomnia   One of Lan Kwai Fong's most popular bars, Insomnia is at its most crowded in the wee hours of the morning, when there's no room to spare on the packed dance floor. Live music, provided by bands that rotate venues in Hong Kong and Singapore, begins at 7pm nightly. Both the kitchen and the bar are open 24 hours, though they'll close the place down if the number of patrons dwindles by dawn, leaving true insomniacs with nowhere to go until things kick up again at 8am, when the bar reopens with a 13-hour happy hour, lasting until 9pm. 38-44 D'Aguilar St., Central. ✆ **852/2525 0957.** MTR: Central.

Joyce Is Not Here Artists' Bar & Café ★★ 💼   This tiny establishment, with a Bohemian atmosphere not unlike what you'd find in a college town, attracts artistic intellectuals whose idea of entertainment is more than just drinking beer. Wednesday is poetry reading night, Thursday is jam night, Friday and Saturday feature live music from mostly local talents (string music, classical, blues, vocal jazz, fusion, urban folk, and so on), and Sunday is movie night with international films. Tuesday nights, photographers and designers can present their work. Admission is free, but there is a two-drink minimum. Opening hours, according to its quirky owners, are Tuesday to Friday from 4:33pm and Saturday and Sunday from 1:22pm "until we get tired." 38-44 Peel St., Central. ✆ **852/2851 2999.** www.joycebakerdesign.com. MTR: Central.

Lei Dou ★ 💼   Its name translates as "Right Here," which for the longest time seemed like a cruel joke since there was no outdoor sign to alert passersby exactly where right here might be. That's been remedied with a *huge* sign, so there's no mistaking this place as you walk up Lan Kwai Fong. Inside, the decor is old-world-boudoir-meets-edgy-contemporary, with sofas and easy chairs spread through several cozy rooms, palm trees, fanciful decorations, and artwork spotlit on the walls. It's open daily 5pm to 3am, with happy hour Monday to Friday 5 until 8pm. 20-22 D'Aguilar St., Central. ☏ **852/2525 6628.** MTR: Central.

Peel Fresco Music Lounge ★★ 👔 Across the street from Joyce Is Not Here (and managed by Joyce's husband) is this similarly tiny place, decorated with Renaissance-style paintings and featuring live music (mostly jazz but also sometimes rhythm and blues) nightly from 9:30 or 10pm. There's no cover, but there is a two-drink minimum. It's open daily from 5pm to 3am; happy hour is from 5 to 9pm. 49 Peel St., Central. ☏ **852/2540 2046.** MTR: Central.

Pier 7 Café & Bar If you find yourself waiting for a ferry to the outlying islands (or even if you don't), this is a pleasant stop for a drink or light meal, and a convenient one to boot, right on top of the Star Ferry pier. Although it offers both indoor and alfresco seating, you can't see the harbor from here, but the Central skyline isn't bad to look at as you down a few (happy hour is Mon–Fri 6–9pm) or indulge in the lunch buffet offered daily from noon to 2:30pm, starting at HK$98. Pier 7 is open daily from 6am to midnight. Central Ferry Pier 7, Central. ☏ **852/2167 8377.** www.igors.com. MTR: Central.

Red Bar & Restaurant Those in search of a drink outside Lan Kwai Fong should head to this hip bar on the fourth floor of ifc mall, with an outdoor patio and panoramic views of Central's skyscrapers and Victoria Harbour. Popular with bankers and other working professionals from surrounding Central, Red offers healthy Californian cuisine (entrance, in fact, is through health club Pure), happy hour from 6 to 9pm daily, and a DJ Thursday to Saturday nights from 7pm. Opening daily at 11:30am, it closes Monday through Wednesday at midnight, Thursday at 1am, Friday and Saturday at 3am, and Sunday and holidays at 10pm. ifc mall, 8 Finance St., Central. ☏ **852/8129 8882.** www.pure-red.com. MTR: Central.

Sevva I prefer to spend my money elsewhere (and if you look like you don't have any, you're apt to be treated indifferently at best), but there's no denying that the open-air rooftop bar, with panoramic views of Central and the harbor, can be worth the pricey drinks and is a great place to watch the nightly "Symphony of Lights" laser show. It's open Monday to Thursday from noon to midnight and Friday and Saturday from noon to 2am. Prince's Building, 25th floor, 10 Chater Rd., Central. ☏ **852/2537 1388.** www.sevva.hk. MTR: Central.

Solas Bar & Lounge If you don't have what it takes to get into Dragon-i (see above), take solace in Solas, just a short walk downhill. The roomy, Irish-owned lounge bar, with dramatic red lighting and Celtish-themed accents, has a daily happy hour from 4 to 9pm and a DJ Wednesday to Saturday from 10pm playing everything from funk and Latin to underground disco. It's open Sunday through Thursday from 4pm to 3am and Friday and Saturday from 5pm to 4am. 60 Wyndham St., Central. ☏ **852/3162 3710.** www.solas.com.hk. MTR: Central.

Staunton's Bar & Café Located on the corner of Staunton and Shelley streets, beside the Central–Mid-Levels Escalator, this open-fronted bar, with views of commuters traveling on the escalator, was one of the first of many bars and restaurants that now give the SoHo district its unique, homey atmosphere. It offers more than 30 wines by the glass, as well as Wi-Fi. Happy hour is from 4 to 8pm daily. It's open Monday through Friday from 10am to 2am, and Saturday and Sunday from 8am to 2am. 10-12 Staunton St., Central. ☏ **852/2973 6611.** MTR: Central.

10

HONG KONG AFTER DARK

Bars, Pubs & Lounges

The gay scene in Hong Kong is fairly low key, but it's a lot more visible now than it used to be. Hong Kong's longest-standing and most popular gay disco is **Propaganda**, 1 Hollywood Rd., Central (© 852/2868 1316; MTR: Central), with a discreet entrance in a back alley (it's a bit hard to find; look for the alley off Pottinger St.). Only about 5% of the people who come through the doors are straight, but everyone is welcome; cover ranges from HK$100 to HK$240, and it's open Tuesday through Saturday. Other popular gay venues include **Zoo**, 33 Jervois St., Sheung Wan (© 852/3583 1200; MTR: Sheung Wan); **T:ME**, 65 Hollywood Rd., Central (© 852/2332 6565; www.time-bar.com); **Volume**, 83–85 Hollywood Rd., Central (© 852/2857 7683; www.volume.com.hk; MTR: Central); and **Déjà Vu**, 41 Staunton, Central (© 852/3481 9996; MTR: Central). In addition, several bars have dedicated gay nights, including Club 97 on Friday nights (p. 250). For a list of gay events and bars, pick up *DS*, a gay lifestyle magazine distributed free at bars, or check its website at www.dimsum-hk.com. Another useful website is www.utopia-asia.com/hkbars.htm.

Yumla This is a small bar with a big heart and is very much loved by its regulars. It claims to host music no one else loves, though the crowds that surge in to listen to resident and visiting DJs spin everything from techno and funky house to hip-hop clearly dispel that claim. On weekends you'll want to get here early: if Yumla gets too full, it becomes a member's only bar after 11pm Friday and Saturday and charges HK$180 admission (including one drink) to nonmembers in an effort at crowd control. It's open Monday to Thursday from 5pm to 2am, Friday from 6pm to 4am, and Saturday from 7pm to 4am or later. Happy hour is until 9pm, except on Friday and Saturday when it goes until 10pm. Located off Pottinger just down from Wyndam Street, look for its artsy facade, which serves as a canvas for changing murals painted by resident and traveling artists. 79 Wyndham St., Central. © **852/2147 2382.** www.yumla.com. MTR: Central.

Zinc I like this bar for several reasons. For one, it's independently owned rather than part of a restaurant/bar conglomerate, which is as rare in Lan Kwai Fong these days as late-night sobriety. Also, it's classier than most of the bars here, with a Zen-like decor and a statue of Buddha at the entrance. Finally, it's a great place for people-watching, with outdoor spectator seating for the never-ending pedestrian parade. But what would the Buddha say if he could comment on the pole dancing that takes place here some nights? And when the DJ starts livening things up Monday to Saturday nights, this bar ends up being not much different from its competitors. Happy hour is from 5 to 10pm daily; Thursday is ladies' night. Zinc is open daily from 5pm to 5am. 35 D'Aguilar St., Central. © **852/2868 3446.** MTR: Central.

Causeway Bay & Wan Chai

Back in the 1950s and 1960s, Wan Chai was where the action was, buzzing with sailors fresh off their ships and soldiers on leave from Vietnam. It was a world of two-bit hotels, raunchy bars, narrow streets, and dark alleyways where men came to drink and brawl and spend money on women. Nowadays, most of Wan Chai has become

10

Bars, Pubs & Lounges

HONG KONG AFTER DARK

respectable (and a bit boring)—an area full of office buildings, mushrooming high-rises, and Hong Kong's expansive convention center. A small pocket of depravity, however, is concentrated mostly on Lockhart and Luard roads and consists of bars catering to young revelers and shows of erotic female dancers.

In addition to the listings below, **Agave** and **Delaney's** (p. 249 and 247) have branches in Wan Chai.

Carnegie's　Named after the Scotsman who made it big in the United States and gave millions to charity, this bar, decorated with rock memorabilia, offers a good selection of wines and spirits but is best known as the place where everyone dances on the bar. Wednesday is Ladies' Night, when women get free sparkling wine from 9pm to closing. Otherwise, happy hour is until 9pm daily. Carnegie's is open daily from 11am to 3am (to 5am Fri–Sat). 53-55 Lockhart Rd., Wan Chai. ℂ **852/2866 6289.** www.carnegies.net. MTR: Wan Chai.

Inn Side Out　Causeway Bay isn't known for nightlife, making this bar/American bistro even more of a standout. It's one of the few places selling the local Hong Kong beer, along with an impressive list of mostly Belgian microbrews and free peanuts, *and* has large patio seating complete with palm trees between its two glass-enclosed bar areas, where big screens broadcast major sporting events. It's a bit hard to find, behind Sunning Plaza and off Sunning and Hoi Ping roads. Happy hour is from 2:30 to 8:30pm daily. It's open daily from 11:30am, and closes at 1am Sunday to Thursday, 1:30am Friday and Saturday. 10 Hysan Ave., Causeway Bay. ℂ **852/2895 2900.** www.elgrande. com.hk. MTR: Wan Chai.

Joe Bananas　This has long been one of the most popular hangouts in Wan Chai, maybe because it's reportedly also one of Hong Kong's best pickup bars. Still, it attracts a wide range of people during its various incarnations throughout the day, from area office workers of all ages for its popular weekday lunch buffet (HK$73) and after-work drinks, to a more youthful crowd that begins to loosen up when a DJ starts spinning electro, funky house, hip-hop, and retro at 10pm. Wednesday is Ladies' Night, with free drinks for women from 9pm to 2am. Happy hour is until 10pm nightly. It's open Monday to Thursday from noon to 4am, Friday from noon to 5am, Saturday from 4pm to 6am, and Sunday from 3pm to 5am. 23 Luard Rd., Wan Chai. ℂ **852/2529 1811.** www.joebananas.com. MTR: Wan Chai.

Old China Hand　Surrounded by girlie bars, this is an old-timer in Wan Chai (since 1977), an informal British pub popular with older expats but welcoming to tourists as well with its open facade good for people-watching. Happy hour is daily from noon to 10pm, with even cheaper drinks during "crazy hour" Monday through Friday from 5 to 7pm. Live music is Sundays from 5pm to midnight; Wednesday brings the popular quiz night. It's open 24 hours on Friday and Saturday; the rest of the week from 10am to 4am. 104 Lockhart Rd., Wan Chai. ℂ **852/2865 4378.** www.oldchina hand.com. MTR: Wan Chai.

Rockschool ★　This is my top pick for dancing in Wan Chai. It offers live (and loud) music every night of the week starting at 10pm, either for free or for HK$100 to HK$250, which includes one drink. With its large stage, varied acts (from the house band to guest gigs), and cheap drinks, this is one of Hong Kong's best party scenes, but don't expect to carry on a conversation. It's open daily at noon until 3am or later; happy hour is Monday to Friday from 4 to 7pm. 21-25 Lockhart Rd., Wan Chai. ℂ **852/2510 7339.** MTR: Wan Chai.

Bars, Pubs & Lounges

ToTT's and Roof Terrace ★★   This striking venue, with an eye-catching oval bar accented with electric-blue lights and spiraling blue pendants, offers fabulous views of Victoria Harbour and Kowloon from its 34th-floor perch and outdoor terrace. Live music and dancing begins at 10pm Monday through Saturday, with a minimum drink/snack charge of HK$168 Monday to Thursday and HK$188 Friday and Saturday (the minimum charge is waived for hotel guests or diners who eat here; see p. 150 for the restaurant's review). The bar opens at 6pm daily and closes Sunday at 10pm, Monday through Thursday at 1am, and Friday and Saturday at 2am. Excelsior Hotel, 281 Gloucester Rd., Causeway Bay. ✆ **852/2837 6786.** http://mandarinoriental.com/excelsior. MTR: Causeway Bay.

The Wanch ★★★   Established in 1987 and claiming to be Hong Kong's oldest bar in its original state (not relocated or renovated), this small and intimate unpretentious bar is one of Hong Kong's best for live music, offering free live music nightly. With a long history of nuturing local and international talent, the Wanch supports all genres of music, from blues and folk to jazz and rock. Monday is jam night, Tuesday is acoustic night, and every other Sunday there's a singalong. In contrast to many other Wan Chai bars, this is not a pickup bar, making it a good bet not only for music lovers but also couples and women traveling solo. Live music begins at 9pm Monday through Saturday and at 3pm Sunday. It's open Monday through Saturday 5pm to 2am and Sunday 3pm to 2am; happy hour is 9 to 10pm Monday through Saturday. 54 Jaffe Rd., Wan Chai. ✆ **852/2861 1621.** MTR: Wan Chai.

ONLY IN HONG KONG

Night Tours

If you have only 1 or 2 nights in Hong Kong and you're uncomfortable roaming around on your own, I recommend taking an organized night tour. **Watertours** (✆ 852/2926 3868; www.watertours.com.hk), **Gray Line** (✆ 852/2368 7111; www.grayline.com.hk), and **Splendid Tours & Travel** (✆ 852/2316 2151; www.splendidtours.com) all offer evening tours. Gray Line's Aberdeen and Harbour Night tour, for example, includes dinner aboard the Jumbo Kingdom floating restaurant in Aberdeen and the Sky Terrace on top of Victoria Peak, while its Highlight of the Night tour takes you to the Temple Street Night Market, on a ride on an open-top bus, and a harbor cruise with a buffet dinner, live music, and the Symphony of Lights laser-and-light show (see "Night Strolls," below). Both tours last about 5 hours and cost HK$680 and HK$580, respectively. Similarly, the Splendid Night of Delights tour for HK$580 takes in the Temple Street Night Market, dinner aboard Jumbo Kingdom, and a stop at a scenic overlook midway up Victoria Peak.

Watertours, an old Hong Kong company that specializes in boat tours, offers a 2-hour Lei Yue Mun Seafood Village Dinner Cruise for HK$400, which includes a junk cruise with an open bar and dinner at one of the many seafood restaurants in the village of Lei Yue Mun, while the 1 1/2-hour Symphony of Lights Cruise offers complimentary drinks while you watch the night light and laser show (HK$310 adults; HK$210 children). In addition, the **Star Ferry** (✆ 852/2118 6201; www.starferry.com.hk/harbourtour) has 2-hour cruises that include the Symphony of Lights for HK$150.

Night Strolls

One of the most beautiful and romantic sights in the world is surely from **Victoria Peak** at night. The Peak Tram, which costs HK$36 round-trip and runs daily until midnight, deposits passengers at the Peak Tower terminal. From the terminal, turn right, and then turn right again onto a pedestrian footpath. This path, which is lit at night and which follows Lugard and Harlech roads, circles the Peak, offering great views of glittering Hong Kong. This is definitely the best stroll in Hong Kong, and it only takes about an hour.

On the other side of the harbor, a promenade lines the **Tsim Sha Tsui waterfront**. It stretches from the Star Ferry terminus all the way through Tsim Sha Tsui East, with romantic views of lit-up Hong Kong Island across the choppy waters. Best of all is the nightly **Symphony of Lights**, from 8 to 8:18pm, an impressive laser-and-light show projected from more than 40 buildings on both sides of the harbor. The Guinness World Records says this is the "World's Largest Permanent Light and Sound Show." The best vantage point: between the Avenue of Stars and the Cultural Centre, where music and English narration is played Monday, Wednesday, and Friday nights; another top viewing spot is Bauhinia Square in front of the Convention Centre in Wan Chai.

The Tsim Sha Tsui waterfront is very safe at night, as it has lots of people. As for Victoria Peak, I have walked it alone several times at night, but to be honest, it's probably best with someone else.

Night Markets

If you're looking for colorful atmosphere, head for the **Temple Street Night Market** (p. 236), near the Jordan MTR station in Kowloon. Extending for several blocks, it has stalls offering clothing, accessories, toys, watches, sunglasses, household items, crafts, and more. Be sure to bargain fiercely and look over merchandise to make sure it isn't going to fall apart in 2 weeks. This is also a good place for an inexpensive meal at one of the *dai pai dong* (roadside food stalls), which specialize in seafood.

The most wonderful part of the market, however, is its northern end, to the right, around the parking garage. Here, near the Tin Hau temple, are palm readers and fortunetellers, some of whom speak English, as well as street musicians and singers. You'll have to hunt for the tiny alleyway of musicians, where groups set up their own stages and are surrounded by an appreciative audience. Get there before 9pm to see the musicians. Otherwise, although vendors set up shop as early as 4pm, the market is in full swing from about 7 to 10pm daily.

Farther north, near the Mong Kok MTR station, is the **Ladies' Market** (p. 236), which stretches along Tung Choi Street between Argyle and Dundas streets. It's a great place to shop for inexpensive women's, men's, and children's fashions and accessories, including watches, handbags, T-shirts, and other goods. It's not quite as touristy as the Temple Street Night Market, and the atmosphere is fun and festive. It's open daily from about 1 to 11pm.

11

SIDE TRIPS FROM HONG KONG

Mention Hong Kong and most people think of Hong Kong Island's Central District, Victoria Peak, the shops and neon of Tsim Sha Tsui, and the Star Ferry crossing Victoria Harbour. What they don't realize is that Hong Kong Island and Kowloon total only 10% of the entire territory—the New Territories and the outlying islands make up the other whopping 90%.

If you have a day or two to spare, or even just an afternoon, I suggest you spend it in one of the SAR's rural areas. Escape the bustle and chaos of the city in one of the region's small villages or on a hiking trail in the countryside or on the islands, and you'll have the chance to glimpse an older, slower way of life, where traditions still reign supreme and where life follows a rhythm all its own.

THE NEW TERRITORIES

Before the 1980s, the New Territories were made up of peaceful countryside, with duck farms, fields, and old villages. No more. A vast 1,008-sq.-km (389-sq.-mile) region that stretches from Kowloon to the border of mainland China, the New Territories have long been Hong Kong's answer to its growing population. Huge government housing projects mushroomed throughout the New Territories, especially in towns along the railway and subway lines. Once-sleepy villages became concrete jungles virtually overnight.

Close to one-half of Hong Kong's population—about 3.5 million people—lives in the New Territories, many in subsidized housing. The New Territories, therefore, are vitally important to the SAR's well-being and its future. For visitors to ignore the area completely would be shortsighted; many find the housing projects, in some suburbs stretching as far as the eye can see, nothing short of astounding. If, on the other hand, it's peace and quiet you're searching for, don't despair. The New Territories are so large and so mountainous that not all the land has been turned into housing, especially along the deserted eastern coast. In fact, the region is so different from the city itself that it's almost like visiting an entirely different country.

Traveling in the New Territories, you may notice women wearing wide-brimmed hats with a black fringe. These women are Hakka, as are most of the farmers of the New Territories. During the Ming dynasty (1368–1644), some of the Hakka clans built walls around their homes to protect themselves against roving bandits and invaders. A handful of these walled villages still exist today, along with ancestral halls and other ancient, traditional buildings. One of my favorite things to do in the New Territories is to walk two heritage trails, both of which highlight village life in the New Territories and take you past significant historic buildings and walled villages. Both trails are described in more detail later, but be sure to pick up the Hong Kong Tourism Board's (HKTB's) two pamphlets, the *Lung Yeuk Tau Heritage Trail* and the *Ping Shan Heritage Trail*. I also suggest that before visiting any walled village, try to see the Sam Tung Uk Museum in Tsuen Wan (also described later), since it will greatly enrich your visit to a lived-in walled village.

Visitor Information & Tours

All MTR train stations in the New Territories offer free maps in English of their immediate surroundings, complete with descriptions of buses that serve the area. Simply stop by the MTR ticket or customer-service counter at your destination and ask for the *Station Information* location map. Other useful pamphlets, which you should pick up at an HKTB Visitor Centre before heading to the New Territories, are *Major Bus Routes in the New Territories*, which tells you which bus to take, the fare, and the frequency of buses along the route; *Discover Hong Kong by Rail*, which describes attractions at MTR stations and provides maps; *Discover Hong Kong Nature*, with detailed maps and recommended hiking trails in the New Territories; and pamphlets for the Lung Yeuk Tau and Ping Shan heritage trails.

If your time is limited, a good tactic for seeing the New Territories is to leave the driving to someone else and opt for an organized tour. The "Land Between" Tour by Gray Line emphasizes both the rural side of Hong Kong and its urban development, enabling visitors to learn about the lifestyle, customs, and beliefs of the local people. The "Heritage Tour," a must for architectural buffs, covers historic Chinese architectural sites spread throughout Kowloon and the New Territories, including a restored 18th-century walled village, a Man Mo temple, an ancestral hall, and Tai Fu Tai, a stately country mansion. For more information on these and other tours, see "Organized Tours & Cultural Activities" in chapter 7, beginning on p. 185.

Getting Around the New Territories

Two major MTR lines, the East Rail Line and the West Rail Line, provide the fastest and most convenient way to reach major destinations. Subway lines also serve some satellite towns in the New Territories.

For years, every visitor to the New Territories took the train to the border for a look into forbidden and mysterious China. Now, of course, it's easy to get permission to enter China, and the border lookout was never very exciting anyway. Still, you might want to take the train up into the New Territories just for the experience, as well as for the interesting stops you can make on the way.

The East Rail, in operation since 1910, is Hong Kong's primary north-south transportation link. Departing from Hung Hom in Kowloon, the East Rail connects 12 stations along its main route, passing through such budding satellite towns as Sha Tin, University, Tai Po Market, Tai Wo, and Fanling before reaching Sheung Shui— your last stop unless you have a visa to enter China. The entire trip from Hung Hom to Sheung Shui takes just 38 minutes and costs only HK$8.50 one-way for ordinary class and HK$17 for first class. Trains depart every 3 to 8 minutes. There are two offshoot lines from the East Rail; the Ma On Shan Rail from Tai Wai Station (convenient for visiting Che Kung Temple, below) and a small spur line running from Sheung Shui to Lok Ma Chau, another border crossing into mainland China.

Along the East Rail

I've arranged the towns below in the order you'll reach them when traveling north from Kowloon. Be sure you have the *Discover Hong Kong by Rail* booklet, available at any HKTB Visitor Centre. For a map of the New Territories, see the "Hong Kong Region" map on p. 2.

SHA TIN

Fewer than 13km (8 miles) north of Tsim Sha Tsui, Sha Tin is Hong Kong's prime example of a budding satellite town, with a population of more than 700,000. It's so huge that it has swallowed what were once surrounding villages, including Tai Wai, the first stop on the East Rail after passing into the New Territories. Change trains here for the Ma On Shan Rail and go one stop to Che Kung Temple Station (ask for the *Station Information* brochure with a map of the surrounding area at the station). Take Exit B from Che Kung Temple Station, walk through the pedestrian tunnel, and then turn right for **Che Kung Temple,** 7 Che Kung Miu Rd. (📞 **852/2603 4049**). This modern Taoist temple, built in 1993 on the site of a previous temple established long ago, honors Che Kung, a general from the Song dynasty (A.D. 960–1279) credited with suppressing a revolt in southern China, controlling floods, and safeguarding villagers from a plague. You'll find a giant statue of Che Kung inside, holding his sword, but the temple is popular mainly because of Che Kung's reputation for granting good fortune. Many visitors bring food offerings and burn incense to ask for blessings, and many fortunetellers are on hand. Admission is free; it's open daily from 7am to 6pm.

Just a 15-minute walk east of the temple, on the other side of Lion Rock Tunnel Road on Sha Kok Street, is **Tsang Tai Uk** (also called Shan Ha Wai, which means Walled Village at the Mountain Foot), a tiny, walled village built in the 1840s for members of the Tsang clan, who made their fortune as stonemasons. (Tsang Tai Uk translates as "Mr. Tsang's Big House".) With its high, thick walls, four parallel rows, two side columns of houses, and central courtyard with ancestral halls housing a painting of the clan founder and photographs of the family, it's typical of Hakka settlements in Guangdong Province (formerly Canton Province) but unusual for Hong Kong. Still occupied by about 300 members of the Tsang clan, it is a vision of communal life from Hong Kong's not-so-distant past, with seniors sitting in doorways and women drawing water from courtyard wells and hanging up laundry. Although neither as old nor as famous as other walled villages, Tsang Tai Uk is, in my opinion, more intriguing and interesting because it has been spared the intrusion of the modern apartments that now plague most villages (the new Ma On Shan Rail, however, passes right outside Tsang Tai Uk, destroying some of its former pastoral peacefulness). The recent addition of public toilets has made life easier, as most of the 99 apartments are without private facilities and residents formerly relied on chamber pots. Because Tsang Tai Uk is off the tourist pathway and serves as home to a number of families, visitors should be respectful of the inhabitants' privacy when visiting the compound.

Tsang Tai Uk is about a 15-minute walk from Che Kung Temple. To reach it, turn right out of the temple onto Che Kung Miu Road and then follow signs through the pedestrian tunnels to Tsang Tai Uk. After exiting the last tunnel, you'll pass a tennis court to your left before seeing Tsan Tai Uk. Because getting there is confusing despite a few small signs, it's best to have the concierge of your hotel write out the name in Chinese so you can show it to people when asking for directions.

The **Hong Kong Heritage Museum ★★**, 1 Man Lam Rd. (© **852/2180 8188;** http://hk.heritage.museum), across the river from Che Kung Temple and Tsang Tai Uk (walk back to the pedestrian tunnels and follow signs to the museum, crossing Lion Bridge; the walk takes about 15 min.), is in my opinion the main reason for a visit to the area. It presents both the history and culture of the New Territories in a series of themed exhibitions, foremost of which is the New Territories Heritage Hall with displays, photographs, and videos relating to the customs, religions, and lifestyle of the early fishermen and settlers and how they have changed over the centuries. A barge loaded for market, an ancestral hall, a Chinese medicine shop, traditional clothing, and other items are also on display. Particularly stunning are the models showing the growth of Sha Tin since the 1930s. I also like the Cantonese Opera Heritage Hall, a must for anyone wishing to gain insight into the history and characteristics of this unique form of entertainment, with musical instruments, elaborate costumes and headgear, a typical backstage scene, and touch screens for viewing actual Cantonese operas. The Chao Shao-an Gallery shows the works of Chao Shao-an (1905–98), a Hong Kong artist famous for his bird-and-flower paintings, while the T. T. Tsui Gallery of Chinese Art contains porcelain, bronze, furniture, jade, and other works of Chinese art dating from the Neolithic period to the 20th century. Kids will especially enjoy the toy museum with games they can play and the hands-on Children's Discovery Gallery, where they can practice being an archaeologist, wear traditional costumes, and learn about marshes. A teahouse off the lobby offers an extensive range of Chinese teas. Allow at least 2 hours for the museum. It's open Monday and Wednesday through Saturday from 10am to 6pm and Sunday and holidays from 10am to 7pm. Admission is HK$10 for adults and HK$5 for children, students, and seniors (free admission to all on Wed). It's located about halfway between Tai Wai and Sha Tin stations, about a 15-minute walk from each.

On a hill west of Sha Tin Station is the **Monastery of 10,000 Buddhas ★** (© **852/2691 1067**). Annoyingly, it's not shown on any HKTB maps nor mentioned in any of its literature, but there are two ascents that begin just west of the station (if you're arriving at Sha Tin Station, take exit B for Pai Tau Village, walk through the village, and then look for the sign). In any case, it takes about a half-hour's energetic walk to reach the actual monastery; first you have to climb more than 400 twisting steps, flanked by life-size gold-colored statues, an impressive sight themselves. The temple was established in the 1950s by a monk named Yuet Kai, who wrote 98 books on Buddhism. He's still at the temple—well, actually, his body is still there. He's been embalmed and covered in gold leaf and sits behind a glass case in the main hall. In attendance are more Buddha images than you've probably ever seen gathered in one place. In fact, despite the monastery's name, almost 13,000 of the tiny statuettes line the walls, and no two are exactly alike. Also on the expansive grounds are a nine-story pink pagoda you can climb to the top, statues galore (including those of animals painted a riot of colors), numerous mausoleums where ashes are interred for a steep fee (this is how the monastery earns its money), and a very simple vegetarian cafeteria.

The temple affords a good view of Sha Tin's high-rise housing estates and the sur-rounding mountains. Admission is free, and it's open daily from 9am to 5:30pm.

Where to Dine

The **Monastery of 10,000 Buddhas** has a very simple dining hall (© **852/2699 4144**) serving vegetarian dishes from an English menu, including deep-fried taro fish (not real fish, of course), fried bean curd, E-Fu noodles with vegetables, and other choices. All dishes cost HK$45 Monday to Friday, HK$50 weekends and holidays. No credit cards are accepted and it's open daily from 11:30am to 5pm.

Otherwise, the massive shopping mall **New Town Plaza** (© **852/2684 9175;** www.newtownplaza.com.hk), located beside Sha Tin MTR station with more than 400 shops and restaurants, is a good place for a snack or meal, with cafeterias, fast-food outlets, and restaurants serving both Western and Asian fare, including Indone-sian, Thai, Korean, Vietnamese, Japanese, and Chinese food. Restaurants with branches here that were described in chapter 6 are **Simply Thai,** Shop 703 (© **852/ 3523 1638;** p. 152), serving Thai specialties; the **Spaghetti House,** Shop 153 (© **852/2697 9009;** p. 133), one in a chain of successful American-style spaghetti-and-pizza parlors; and **Genki Sushi,** Shop A197a (© **852/2608 9322;** p. 132), with conveyor-belt sushi.

TAI PO ★★

Another satellite town in the New Territories, Tai Po was first settled by Tanka boat people more than 1,000 years ago because of its strategic location on a river that flows into Tolo Harbour. Today, many Hakka farmers and residents—more than 300,000 of them—call it home. Yet it retains its rural atmosphere, especially the vicinity around its traditional market, one of the most colorful in Hong Kong and one of my favorites.

To reach it, take the East Rail to Tai Wo Station, surrounded by housing estates built in the last few decades and now part of the Tai Po satellite town (ask for the *Tai Wo Station* street map and information pamphlet at the station). Exit the station onto Po Nga Road (in the direction of McDonald's), cross the Tai Wo Bridge over the Lam Tsuen River, turn left on Pak Shing Street and then right onto **Fu Shin Street ★★★**, a pedestrian lane that has been serving as Tai Po's market since 1892. It bustles with activity from 7am to 6pm as housewives shop here twice daily to secure the freshest produce, fish, meat, dried herbs, and other ingredients for the day's meals. Big chunks of meat hang from hooks; butcher shops sell virtually every part of the pig; hardware stores are packed to the rafters with pots, bamboo steam-ers, and other goods; and fish swim in tanks. I love this market.

Near the middle of Fu Shin Street is a small **Man Mo Temple,** built in 1892 to commemorate the founding of Tai Po's market. Dedicated to the Taoist gods of war and literature, it could accommodate overnight guests to the market in its ladder-accessible upper floor, while side halls were used by market administrators to settle disputes between merchants and to store records. Today it's a popular spot for older residents to gather and play mah-jongg or simply pass the time. As at the Man Mo Temple on Hong Kong Island (p. 178), huge incense coils suspended from the tem-ple's ceiling are purchased by worshippers and burn for more than 2 weeks. Behind the temple is the tiny Town Earthgod Shrine, where townspeople burn offerings for dead relatives. A nearby shop sells paper offerings in the shapes of cars, gold bars, clothing, and other luxury goods that might prove useful for the dead in their afterlife.

At the end of Fu Shin Street, turn right and walk uphill 1 block to the small **Hong Kong Railway Museum,** 13 Shung Tak St. (*C* **852/2653 3455;** http://hk.heritage. museum), occupying what was formerly the very tiny Tai Po Market railway station, built in 1913 in traditional Chinese style with ceramic figurines cresting its gabled roof. Besides the station's original waiting hall and ticket office, the museum displays a few model trains (including those from other countries, like the Shinkansen bullet train from Japan and the ICE from Germany) and fascinating historical photographs showing Tai Po, Yau Ma Tei during construction of its station approximately 100 years ago (completely void of buildings, almost impossible to visualize today), and the former Tsim Sha Tsui Station rail station, completed in 1916 for passengers arriving overland from London. Outside the station are a narrow-gauge steam locomotive, six vintage railway coaches dating from the early 1900s, and an outdoor model train set for children. This museum will appeal mainly to railway buffs, who will probably spend about 20 minutes here. It is open (and free) Wednesday to Monday 9am to 5pm.

FANLING

A small farming settlement for several centuries, Fanling is now a huge satellite town with more than 350,000 inhabitants. However, the **Lung Yeuk Tau Heritage Trail ★★** takes you through the traditional part of Fanling with its rural atmosphere. Many of the historic buildings along the trail are legacies of the Tang clan, the first and largest of the Five Great Clans to settle in the New Territories, back in the 12th century. Royal descendants of the eldest son of the princess of the Southern Song dynasty (1127–1279), they established five *wais* (walled villages) and six *tsuen* (villages) in the area around Luk Yeuk Tau, which takes its name from the nearby Mountain of the Leaping Dragon. The trail, which stretches about 2.3km (1.4 miles) and takes approximately 1 hour to complete, passes more than a dozen historic structures along the way, including four walled villages (Lo Wai, the first walled village built by the Tang clan, is my favorite, but only the entrance tower is open to the public), a study hall, a Tin Hau temple, and one of Hong Kong's largest ancestral halls, built in the 16th century to honor the founding Tang ancestor and noted for its elaborate woodcarvings and central chamber housing the soul tablets of the Song princess and her husband (Wed–Mon 9am–1pm and 2–5pm). Admission to all sights is free. The Tangs of the area still practice traditional village customs, including the Tin Hau Festival (usually in Apr) and a special lantern lighting ceremony held the 15th day of the first lunar month to honor baby boys. This is a great walk, but I'm saddened by modern housing that has encroached upon what was once pastoral farmland just a few years back; instead of the chirping of birds, the most common sound nowadays comes from buzz saws (luckily, the Ping Shan Heritage Trail in the West New Territories has remained largely untouched, but it doesn't have the walled villages this walk has; see p. 265).

To reach the Lung Yeuk Tau Heritage Trail, take minibus no. 54K from the east exit of Fanling Station to Lo Wai walled village (it's not the beginning of the trail, but it gets most interesting from here onward). Near the end of the trail, at the San Wai walled village, take bus no. 56K back to Fanling Station. Be sure to pick up the free brochure *Lung Yeuk Tau Heritage Trail,* which contains a map and information on historic buildings, at an HKTB Visitor Centre.

Where to Dine

The most memorable place to dine in Fanling is at **Fung Ying Seen Koon,** 66 Pak Wo Rd. (*C* **852/2669 9186**), Hong Kong's largest Taoist temple, established in

1929 by refugees fleeing Canton (Guangzhou). It offers vegetarian food daily from 11am to 5pm in a simple dining room to the left of the main hall. Main dishes on the English menu, ranging in price from HK$40 to HK$65, include hot and spicy bean curd, deep-fried crispy taro rolls, and fried elm fungus with three kinds of mushroom; get rice and *congee* at the self-service station. Set meals for two people are HK$105, though the menu for this is in Chinese only (you can't go wrong, as all the food is good). MasterCard and Visa are accepted. To reach Fung Ying Seen Koon, visible from the Fanling Station platform, take the west exit and go through the pedestrian underpass.

SHEUNG SHUI

Once its own market town, Sheung Shui, the last stop before the China border, has been swallowed up in the budding satellite town that now spreads out from Fanling. Although much of Sheung Shui's charm has been lost due to the construction of modern buildings, it's still more peaceful than other old villages closer to the beaten path. Of all the historic, traditional Chinese buildings in the New Territories, few impress me as much as **Tai Fu Tai ★★**, built in 1865 and the only Mandarin mansion restored and remaining in Hong Kong. It belonged to Man Chung-luen, the 21st generation of the Man clan (another of the Five Great Clans), a merchant and scholar who attained the highest grade in the Imperial Chinese Civil Service Examinations. Constructed of granite and bricks and adorned with colorful ceramic figurines, fine plaster moldings, woodcarvings, and murals, it is striking for its simplicity, a stark contrast to mansions built by the Western gentry class during the same period. Resembling a miniature fort, without windows but with an inner courtyard to let in light, it contains a main hall, side chambers, bedrooms, study, kitchen, servants' quarters, and lavatory. In the back of the main hall is a portrait of Man Chung-luen, flanked by pictures of his two wives and two sons. Not shown are his eight daughters. Remarkably, the mansion was occupied by members of the Man clan until the 1980s. Nearby is the **Man Lun Fung Ancestral Hall,** built to honor the eighth member of the Man clan.

Both Tai Fu Tai and the ancestral hall are free to the public and open Wednesday through Monday 9am to 1pm and 2 to 5pm. To reach them, take bus no. 76K from Sheung Shui Station traveling in the direction of Yuen Long (west) about 30 minutes to San Tin (near the post office), followed by a 5-minute walk back along Castle Peak Road to the signposted entrance. Because it's a bit difficult and time consuming to visit on your own, you might want to take Gray Line's guided "Heritage Tour" (p. 186), which takes in this site, as well as a few stops of the Lung Yeuk Tau Heritage Trail and the Man Mo Temple in Tai Po, described above.

Sai Kung

Located on the eastern coast of the New Territories, Sai Kung is the second largest yet least populated of Hong Kong's 18 districts and boasts Hong Kong's longest coastline and its most numerous outlying islands. It's popular for its stunning scenery, country parks, rock formations, nature trails, deserted beaches, remote islands, Hong Kong Geopark with its unique geological features, and Sai Kung Town with its harborfront seafood restaurants.

To reach Sai Kung Town, the main transportation hub of the area, take the MTR to Diamond Hill Station and then board bus no. 92 to Sai Kung Town. The bus will deposit you at the bus terminal near the waterfront, where you can turn right and walk along the harbor to the local fish market. Around 5pm each evening, sampans docked at the public pier sell live fish to tourists and residents alike. Here, too, are many seafood restaurants with outside tanks holding live prawns, crabs, lobster, abalone, garoupa, and other creatures of the sea. Behind the waterfront restaurants, on Sai Kung Tai Kai Street, is Sai Kung Old Town with its narrow, twisting lanes lined with shops selling incense, dried seafood, herbs, and provisions.

HONG KONG GEOPARK

Covering 50 sq. km (19 sq. miles) of mostly coastline and islands in Sai Kung Peninsula and the northeast New Territories, **Geopark ★★** preserves a variety of significant geological features, accessible from hiking trails and boat tours. Most famous, and most rare, are the hexagonal volcanic rock columns, exposed after construction of a reservoir and the East Dam in the 1970s. Measuring 30m (98 ft.) in height and an average 1.2m (3.9 ft.) in diameter, the formations cover more than 100 sq. km (39 sq. miles) on land and underwater. They're the highlight of the **High Island Geo Trail,** which you can reach by taking bus no. 94 for 25 minutes from Sai Kung Town (or no. 96R from Diamond Hill Station on weekends and holidays) to Pak Tam Chung and then walking 9km (5½ miles) to the 1-km (.6 mile) High Island Trail. Better yet, take a taxi from Sai Kung Town directly to the east dam (Ton Pa) which takes about 30 minutes and costs HK$100. If you pack a lunch, you might wish to hike farther along the connecting Macleose Trail to Long Ke Wan, a beautiful bay with a beach and calm water.

Another interesting destination is **Sharp Island** (Kiu Tsui Chau), 2.5km (1½ miles) long but only a half km (⅓ mile) wide. It's part of Hong Kong's smallest island country park and is popular for its 1-km (.6 mile) Sharp Island Geo Trail with its volcanic rocks from various periods (agglomerate, eutaxite, and rhyolite, in case you're interested) and a 250m (820-ft.) natural sand levee (called a tombolo) connecting Sharp Island with neighboring Kiu Tau, visible only in low tide. Most people come, however, for its beaches, of which Kiu Tsui Beach and Hap Mun Bay Beach, both with full facilities, are the best. To reach Kiu Tsui Chau, hire a *kaido* (private boat for hire) from Sai Kung Town public pier for about HK$35 round-trip.

For more information on Geopark, including seven other hiking trails and recommended boat tours, stop by an HKTB Visitor Centre or the Geopark Visitor Centre near the Sai Kung Town bus terminal (Sat–Sun 9:30am–5:30pm), or check www.geopark.gov.hk.

HIKING

For more hiking, board bus no. 94 (going in the direction of Wong Shek Pier) from Sai Kung Town's bus terminal and ride 25 minutes to Pak Tam Chung. Here you'll find the **Sai Kung Country Park Visitor Center** (© **852/2792 7365**), open Wednesday to Monday from 9am to 4:30pm, where you can pick up a hiking map. Beside the visitor center is a barrier gate, restricting vehicular access to Tai Mong Tsai Road. If you follow this road to its junction with Pak Tam Road, you'll find the starting point of the 100km-long (62-mile) **MacLehose Trail,** which winds through eight country parks and ends at Tuen Mun in the western part of the New Territories. It's divided into 10 stages of varying difficulty; the beginning stage, which runs along the High Island Reservoir, is one of the easiest. For a shorter hike, I recommend the **Sheung Yiu Family Walk ★**, just a 5-minute walk from the visitor center (or get off bus no. 94 at the Sheung Yui Family Walk). This 1km (.6 mile) walk takes you past mangroves, signboards identifying trees (such as the incense tree that gave Hong Kong its name), an abandoned kiln used in the 1800s to extract lime from coral and shells, and—the highlight—the **Sheung Yiu Folk Museum** (© **852/2792 6365**), a former Hakka enclave settled in the late 1800s and abandoned in the 1960s. An English pamphlet highlights its history; its handful of rooms are filled with furnishings and implements (I like the double-sided jar with water to discourage ants and the hole in the wall created so dogs and cats could pass through). It's open Wednesday to Monday from 9am to 4pm; admission is free.

Where to Dine

No trip to Sai Kung Town would be complete without dining on fresh seafood at one of the town's waterfront seafood restaurants. I suggest simply wandering from tank to tank of live fish, shellfish, and other delectables until something catches your fancy, but for specific recommendations, try **Chuen Kee Seafood Restaurant,** 51 Hoi Pong St. (© **852/2791 1195**), or **Hung Kee Seafood Restaurant,** 4–8 Hoi Pong St. (© **852/2792 1348**), both on the Sai Kung Town waterfront and open daily. After selecting your lobster, prawns, or fish from their live tanks and having it weighed by the catty (one catty is about 1½ lb.), your selections will be sent directly to the kitchen, along with your directions for cooking. My favorite: crab sautéed with ginger and shallots, though most seafood is steamed. Prices depend on market price, with most meals costing about HK$350 per person (MasterCard and Visa accepted).

West New Territories

If I were to choose only one quick destination in the New Territories, it would be Tsuen Wan with its excellent walled-village museum. It's easily reached by taking the MTR Tsuen Wan Line, which runs from Central through Tsim Sha Tsui and Kowloon, to the last stop. Tsuen Wan was a small market town just 100 years ago, with a population of about 3,000 Hakkas and a thriving incense powder–producing industry. The first of many designated satellite towns in the New Territories, it has grown to a population of more than 300,000 residents, living mostly in high-rise housing estates.

The main reason for visiting Tsuen Wan is its excellent **Sam Tung Uk Museum ★★★**, 2 Kwu Uk Lane, Tsuen Wan (© **852/2411 2001**; http://hk. heritage.museum), located just a few minutes' walk from Tsuen Wan MTR station by taking exit B2. The museum is actually a restored Hakka walled village, built in the 18th century by members of the farming Chan clan and consisting of miniscule lanes lined with tiny tile-roofed homes. Once the home of as many as 300 clan members, the village was abandoned in 1980 and today serves as an oasis in the midst of modern high-rise housing projects. Four of the homes, all windowless, have been restored to their original condition and are furnished much as they would have been when occupied long ago, with traditional Chinese pieces (including some created from elegant black wood), and contain farm implements, kitchens, and lavatories. In the middle of the village is the ancestral hall, while other rooms contain exhibits dedicated to Hakka traditions and customs such as rice cultivation (rice, no longer produced in Hong Kong, is all imported) and to Tsuen Wan's history, complete with photographs of Sam Tung Uk before and during its restoration. At reception ask to see the 8-minute video, played on request, that describes the walled village's restoration into a folk museum and the purpose of its many rooms, including the ancestral hall. Be sure to take a look at the landscaped garden adjacent to the village. The museum is open Wednesday to Monday from 9am to 5pm; admission is free.

A free minibus, no. 95K, makes runs between MTR Tsuen Wan Station and Tsuen Wan West Station, a stop on the West Rail Line. Or, you can walk between the two stations in about 20 minutes via Tai Ho Road (be sure to stop by the customer service counter at MTR Tsuen Wan Station to pick up the *Station Information* brochure, which contains a map showing the location of both stations).

From Tsuen Wan West Station, take the West Rail four stops to Tin Shui Wai Station. At Tin Shui Wai Station, take exit E for the **Ping Shan Heritage Trail ★★**, the start of which is easy to spot by its ancient pagoda (get the free *Ping Shan Heritage Trail* brochure at HKTB). This wonderful walking trail is only 1km (.6 miles) long and takes 30 minutes to complete, yet it passes a wealth of traditional Chinese structures along the way, most relating to the powerful Tang clan, who settled the Ping Shan area in the 12th century as one of the Five Great Clans of the New Territories. Although it lacks the wow factor of walled villages that the Lung Yeuk Tau Heritage Trail boasts (see above), I prefer this walk because of its rural, traditional surroundings, which make for a fascinating stroll.

The three-story Tsui Sing Lau Pagoda (Wed–Mon 9am–1pm and 2–5pm) is the only ancient pagoda in Hong Kong, constructed more than 600 years ago to improve the area's feng shui and ward off evil spirits. Other highlights are a walled village (not open to the public), two temples, and two study halls built for members of the Tang clan studying for the Imperial Civil Service Examination (those who passed could become officials in the Qing government, thereby enhancing the social status of the Tang family). But the main attraction is the 700-year-old Tang Ancestral Hall (daily 9am–1pm and 2–5pm), still used by the Tang clan for ancestral worship, ceremonies, and festivals. Be sure, too, to take a peek in the village surrounding the ancestral hall, with its impossibly narrow lanes that hark back to earlier centuries. The trail culminates at the Old Ping Shan Police Station, built in 1899 atop a hill and now serving as the Ping Shan Tang Clan Gallery (© **852/2617 1959**), a visitor center that introduces local folk customs and history. In addition to historic items like furniture, a wedding dress, implements used for cricket fights (forbidden today), and old photographs, videos throughout cover everything from traditional marriage ceremonies to the Tang educational system. The gallery is open Tuesday to Sunday from 10am to 5pm. Admission to this and other sights along the trail is free.

If you have more time to spare, following the map on the *Ping Shan Heritage Trail* brochure, walk 5 minutes to the Ping Shan Light Rail Station (which is so small it looks like a tram stop). Take light rail Rte. 761 to Tin Yat Station and then transfer to Rte. 706 for Wetland Park Station, from which it's a 5-minute walk to the new **Hong Kong Wetland Park,** Tin Shui Wai (© **852/3152 2666;** www.wetlandpark.com). This 61-hectare (150-acre) park was created to replace lost habitat due to construction of the Tin Shui Wai satellite town. A visitor center, overlooking the wetland reserve, introduces the importance of wetlands, from tundras to tropical swamps, with plenty of touch screens to engage kids. Outside, boardwalks and pathways lead past freshwater marshes, fish ponds, woodlands, grasslands, mudflats, and mangroves, which serve as habitats for 150 species of birds that live here or pass through (including the winter habitat of the endangered black-faced spoonbill; the prime time for bird-watching is Nov–Mar), as well as fish, reptiles, mammals, and butterflies. Unfortunately, surrounding high-rise housing estates detract from what would otherwise be a great outdoor experience. In any case, avoid weekends and holidays, as this is a very popular family attraction. It's open Wednesday through Monday from 10am to 5pm; admission is HK$30 for adults and HK$15 for children, students, and seniors.

THE OUTLYING ISLANDS

Hong Kong is surrounded by some 260 outlying islands, most of them uninhabited. Those that are inhabited offer the easiest opportunity to see something of rural Chinese life—just hop on a ferry in Central and then sit back and enjoy the view. In fact, taking a ferry to an outlying island is the cheapest harbor cruise there is, making getting there part of the fun.

> ## The Best Seat on Board
>
> **The best view aboard ferries to the outlying islands is on the left side of the boat, as Central, the Western District, and Hong Kong Island glide past in all their glory.**

Three of the most accessible and popular islands are **Lantau, Cheung Chau,** and **Lamma.** Each offers something different: Lantau, which can also be reached by MTR and then cable car, is famous for its giant outdoor Buddha—one of Hong Kong's major attractions—and Po Lin Monastery with its vegetarian meals; Cheung Chau, with its beach, boat population, and thriving fishing community, is a popular destination for families and is the best choice for immersion into village life; and Lamma, known for its open-air seafood restaurants, hiking trail, and beaches, is best for getting away from it all.

Getting to the Islands

Ferries to all three islands depart approximately every hour or two from Hong Kong Island's Central Ferry Piers, also home of the Star Ferry. You can purchase your ticket at the piers just prior to departure or use the magnetic Octopus transportation card, but avoid going on Sunday or holidays when the ferries are packed with city folks on family outings. There are two kinds of ferries: ordinary ferries and quicker hover-ferry service (called Fast Ferries). The Fast Ferries to Lantau, Cheung Chau, and Lamma are used mostly by commuters. I personally prefer the slower, ordinary ferries because the view is better, especially if you're headed for Lantau or Cheung Chau: These have the bonus of deluxe class, which is on the upper deck and has an open deck out back—a great place to watch the harbor float past when the weather is nice (ferries to Lamma are only one class and have no outside deck). In addition, deluxe cabins are the only ones that are air-conditioned, a plus when humidity is at its peak. In any case, you might wish to head out to an island via regular ferry and then return via Fast Ferry. On Saturday afternoon and Sunday, there is additional infrequent ferry service from Tsim Sha Tsui's Star Ferry concourse to Lantau and Cheung Chau, but it may not offer deluxe class.

Fares to the islands are a bargain. Monday to Saturday, tickets for ordinary ferries cost just HK$12 to HK$18 for ordinary class and HK$18 to HK$22 for deluxe, depending on the destination. Fares are slightly higher on Sunday and public holidays: HK$17 to HK$20 for ordinary class and HK$26 to HK$32 for a deluxe ticket. Fast Ferries range from HK$23 to HK$37, depending on the destination and the day of the week. Children and seniors pay half price.

In any case, by ordinary ferry it takes only 35 minutes to reach Lamma, 55 minutes to reach Cheung Chau, and 50 minutes to reach Lantau. Fast Ferry reduces travel time to 20 minutes for Lamma, 35 minutes for Cheung Chau, and 40 minutes for Lantau.

For information on ferry schedules and prices, drop by an HKTB Visitor Centre. You can also obtain information on schedules to Cheung Chau and Lantau at ☎ **852/2131 8181** and www.nwff.com.hk; for Lamma, call ☎ **852/2815 6063** or visit www.hkkf.com.hk.

Lantau ★★★

Inhabited since Neolithic times and twice the size of Hong Kong Island, Lantau is Hong Kong's largest island. But while Hong Kong Island has a population of 1.3 million, **Lantau** has only about 100,000. Much of its population growth has occurred only recently, first with the founding of Discovery Bay, a large and expensive settlement of condominiums popular with expats and chuppies (the local term used to identify Chinese yuppies), then with Hong Kong's new airport (which brought with it the creation of a new satellite town at Tung Chung), and finally with the 2006 opening of Hong Kong Disneyland (p. 183). But one of its biggest draws is the Giant Tian Tan Buddha, the largest seated outdoor Buddha in the world. Accessible by ferry or via MTR and then cable car, Lantau is by far Hong Kong's most popular outlying island.

Yet much of Lantau remains mountainous and lush. Country parks make up more than half of the island, with 70km (43 miles) of marked hiking trails. Lantau is an island of high peaks, remote and isolated beaches, small villages, temples, and monasteries. To do the island justice, I suggest arriving the old-fashioned way, by ordinary ferry, followed by a bus to the Giant Buddha and then returning to the city by cable car and subway. You should allow at least 5 hours for the entire trip.

Ordinary ferries, with both ordinary and deluxe class, depart from Central Ferry Pier no. 6 in Central approximately every 2 hours between 6:10am and 10:30pm and arrive about 50 minutes later at Silvermine Bay, known as Mui Wo in Chinese. Hoverferry service departs more frequently from the same pier, and gets you there in about 40 minutes, but it doesn't provide panoramic views from an outside deck in deluxe class. In Mui Wo, as soon as you exit the ferry pier, you'll see a bus terminal with buses going to other parts of the island, with departures coinciding with the arrival of the ferries. For the Giant Buddha and Po Lin Monastery, take bus no. 2 bound for Ngong Ping (Po Lin Monastery). The exact fare of HK$17 Monday through Saturday and HK$27 on Sunday and public holidays is required, so come with lots of change or use the handy Octopus transportation card. The bus from Silvermine Bay to Po Lin Monastery takes about 45 minutes as it hurtles around hair-raising curves and up and down through lush countryside—not for the faint of heart. I always enjoy every minute of it. For the most panoramic views, sit on the left side of the bus.

Lantau is also accessible by taking the Tung Chung MTR Line, which departs from Hong Kong Station in Central and travels to Tung Chung, the end terminus, in about 30 minutes. In Tung Chung, you can board a 17-passenger cable car that travels 5.7km (3½ miles) directly to Ngong Ping in about 25 minutes, with fantastic views of the surrounding countryside, the airport, and the South China Sea. The round-trip fare of the Ngong Ping Cable Car is HK$107 for adults and HK$54 for children; one-way fares are HK$74 and HK$38, respectively. Packages that bundle cable car rides with attractions at Ngong Ping Village (see below) are also available. If you like spending money, you can even spring for cable cars with glass floors or private cars. Otherwise, bus no. 23 also travels between Tung Chung and Ngong Ping in about 50 minutes; the fare is the same as from Mui Wo and the ride is no less hair-raising.

A TAI O excursion

I used to love going to Tai O, a small fishing village once famous for its salt-making industry on the northwestern end of Lantau. It wasn't so much for the stilt houses here, which were never very attractive anyway, but for the slow pace of life; the only way to cross the creek dividing the village was on a boat that was hand-pulled along a rope. A draw-bridge now spans the creek and Tai O has grown. But travelers in search of sustainable tourism might want to make a detour here to stay overnight in one of the stilt homes or to visit its protected mangroves. Most people combine Tai O with a trip to Po Lin Monastery (p. 268).

Visitors can experience life in Tai O through several programs, including an overnight homestay in one of the stilt houses (HK$120) or a boat trip along the Tai O River, all of which provide local residents with jobs. Tai O is interesting also for its protected mangroves and migratory birds. For more information, contact the **Tai O Cultural and Ecological Integrated Resource Center,** 61–63 Wing On St. (an address it shares with the Hong Kong YWCA), Tai O (© **852/2985 6310**).

EXPLORING LANTAU

The most famous attractions on Lantau (in addition to Disneyland, p. 183) are the **Giant Tian Tan Buddha** and **Po Lin Monastery,** both situated on the plateau of Ngong Ping at an elevation of 738m (2,421 ft.). The Buddha is so huge that you'll have your first glimpses of it en route. More than 30m (98 ft.) tall and weighing 250 tons, it was erected in 1993 as the world's largest seated outdoor bronze Buddha and can be seen as far away as Macau (or so it is claimed) on clear days. Some 260 steps lead up to the Buddha itself, but first you should stop at the ticket office at the bottom of the steps to purchase a meal ticket, since the other reason people come to Po Lin is to eat. The monastery is famous for its vegetarian lunches, served in a big dining hall (see "Where to Dine," below). Your meal ticket doubles as your admission ticket to a small museum inside the base of the statue, but there isn't much to see here. Rather, the best part is the view of the surrounding countryside from the statue's platform, which is free. The Giant Buddha is open daily from 10am to 5:30pm.

It's a couple minutes' walk onward to the colorful Po Lin Monastery, largest and best known of the dozens of Buddhist monasteries on Lantau. Po Lin (which means "precious lotus") was first established more than 100 years ago by reclusive monks; the present buildings date from 1921 and 1970. The ornate main temple houses three bronze statues of Buddha, representing the past, present, and future; it also has a brightly painted vermilion interior with dragons and other Chinese mythical figures on the ceiling. You'll probably want to spend about a half-hour wandering through the grounds here, but the best thing to do is dine on vegetarian cuisine (see below).

As for other things to do on Ngong Ping, about a 15-minute walk from the Giant Buddha, at the foot of Lantau Peak, is the **Wisdom Path,** designed in a figure eight to symbolize infinity and marked by 38 towering wooden pillars, each bearing a portion of the centuries-old Heart Sutra in Chinese characters. If you're truly adventurous or energetic, you can continue the climb to the top of Lantau Peak, the second-tallest peak in Hong Kong (1,000m/3,281 ft.); plan on 3 hours for the hike up and back.

Just a couple minutes' walk from the Buddha is also **Ngong Ping Village** (✆ 852/3666 0606; www.np360.com.hk), a Disneyesque interpretation of a traditional Chinese village with white-washed walls and landscaping. It's home to the Ngong Ping Cable Car as well as souvenir shops (my favorite is the Chopstick Gallery) and restaurants. There are also two minor attractions: **Walking with Buddha,** a multimedia museum that describes the life of Siddhartha Gautama (who lived 2,500 years ago in Nepal and became Buddha), his path to enlightenment, the origin of Buddhism, and the religion's subsequent expansion around the world; and **Monkey's Tale Theatre,** which presents a computer-animated comical story with a moral twist about a selfish monkey who, with the help of the Monkey King, learns about greed, humility, friendship, and kindness. Admission to either is HK$36 for adults and HK$18 for children; tickets that bundle attractions with the cable car are also available. Ngong Ping Village is open Monday through Friday from 10am to 6pm, and Saturday and Sunday from 9am to 6:30pm (also the operational hours of the cable car).

From Po Lin, you can take the cable car to Tung Chung's MTR station; or you can board buses that will take you back to Mui Wo (Silvermine Bay) or Tung Chung (I always check departure times upon arrival at Po Lin, so I don't have to sit around after a just-missed bus). Energetic travelers can even opt to hike down to Tung Chung in about 3 hours. In Tung Chung, shoppers might want to check out Citygate, Hong Kong's only outlet mall and located right next to the MTR station (p. 234).

Where to Dine

Po Lin Monastery ★★ VEGETARIAN   Po Lin Monastery, offering fixed-price vegetarian meals, is the most famous place to eat on the island. Buy your lunch ticket from the counter at the base of the Giant Buddha or at the monastery; during busy times, your ticket is for a specific time, at an assigned table. Otherwise, set meals are served every half-hour. Two different meals of soup, vegetarian dishes, and rice are available. The HK$60 meal is served in an unadorned dining hall and the procedure is rather unceremonious, with huge dishes of vegetables, rice, and soup brought to communal tables. Grab a bowl and chopsticks and help yourself. Packed with Chinese families, the dining hall here is certainly colorful, and the food, though mediocre, is plentiful. The HK$100 "deluxe" meal, served on china plates in a smaller adjacent "VIP Room" and popular mostly with foreign visitors, is a notch above the cheaper meal. There's also a snack menu available at an open-air counter at the monastery; it consists of fried noodles and bean curd—skip it.

Ngong Ping. ✆ **852/2985 5248.** Fixed-price lunch HK$60 or HK$100. No credit cards. Daily 11:30am–4:30pm.

Cheung Chau

If you have only 3 or 4 hours to spare and don't want to worry about catching buses and finding your way around, Cheung Chau is your best bet. In fact, if I were forced to select only one island to show visiting friends on a limited time schedule, Cheung Chau would be it. Only 12km (7½ miles) from Hong Kong Island, it's a 55-minute ride by ordinary ferry from outlying ferry pier no. 5 in Central, with ferries leaving approximately every hour and offering scenic harbor views from the outdoor deluxe-class deck. Even quicker are the Fast Ferries, also departing every hour or so and making the trip in 30 minutes (but these don't have outdoor decks). Despite its name (Cheung Chau means "Long Island"), Cheung Chau is a tiny, dumbbell-shaped island (only 2.5 sq. km/1 sq. mile), with more than 25,000 residents concentrated in a thriving fishing village. There are no cars on the island, making it a delightful place for walking around and exploring rural village life. The island is especially popular with Chinese families for its rental bicycles, beach (you might want to bring your bathing suit), and basic rooms and apartments for rent, but my favorite thing to do here is to walk the tiny, narrow lanes of Cheung Chau village.

Inhabited for at least 2,500 years by fisher folk and serving as a haven for smugglers and pirates until the 1920s, Cheung Chau still supports a small population of fishing families, with fishing and tourism the island's main industries. The waterfront where the ferry lands, known as the Praya, buzzes with activity as vendors sell fish, lobster, and vegetables. The village itself is a fascinating warren of narrow alleyways, food stalls, and open-fronted shops selling everything from medicinal herbs and incense to dried fish, rice, haircuts, and—a reflection of the island's tourist trade—sun hats, sunglasses, and beach toys.

EXPLORING CHEUNG CHAU

To see Cheung Chau village, begin with a stroll along the **Praya,** the waterfront promenade right in front of the ferry pier. It's a good place from which to observe the many junks and fishing boats in the harbor. Although there seem to be fewer and fewer junks in Cheung Chau's harbor each time I visit, a small group of fishermen and their families still live on their junks here. I like this harbor more than Aberdeen because boats are moored right next to the waterfront, and I find it amazing how many families keep dogs aboard their boats (not to mention radar systems and computers). To the right as you exit the ferry pier are several open-air restaurants (and, as a sign of the times, a McDonald's), as well as the unimaginative-looking Regional Council Cheung Chau Complex, which houses a library, post office, and city market (daily 6am–8pm) with more than 200 stalls that sell everything from fresh seafood to vegetables.

On the opposite end of the Praya (to the left as you exit the ferry) are more waterfront restaurants, shops with bicycles to rent, staffed kiosks with photos of holiday rental flats, and souvenir shops. After about a 4-minute walk, take a right at the playground onto Pak She Fourth, at the end of which is the **Pak Tai Temple** (daily 7am–5pm), guarded by stone lions. Built in 1783, it's dedicated to the Supreme Emperor of the Dark Heaven, long worshipped as a Taoist god of the sea. Before the altar are also statues of two formidable generals, Thousand Miles Eye and Favourable Wind Ear, who together can see and hear everything. Beside the temple, on a shaded terrace, old villagers are almost always engaged in games of mah-jongg. But the most important event here is the Bun Festival, held in late April or May. It originated a century ago following a terrible plague and is famous throughout Hong Kong. It features 15m-tall (50-ft.) towers of buns (yes, they're edible) and a parade of children who "float" through the streets suspended by hidden wires and rods.

Leaving the Pak Tai Temple, take a left onto Pak She Street, which later becomes San Hing Street. As you walk back to the center of the village, you'll pass open-fronted shops that sell incense, paper funeral objects such as cars (cremated with the deceased to accompany them to the next life), medicinal herbs, lotus-seed cakes, pungent shrimp paste, vegetables, jade, rattan, cheap toys, and souvenirs. You'll also pass people's homes with the living rooms that hold the family altar opening onto the street. This is the traditional Chinese home, with the family business and communal

ACCOMMODATIONS ■
B&B Cheung Chau 5

ATTRACTIONS ●
Cheung Chau
  Windsurfing Centre 6
Kwun Yam Beach 7
Pak Tai Temple 2
Tung Wan Beach 3

DINING ◆
Hometown Teahouse 4
New Baccarat Seafood
  Restaurant 1

rooms on the ground floor and the bedrooms up above. All day long you can hear people playing mah-jongg.

At the end of San Hing Street, at a square, take a left to Tung Wan Road, which cuts across the thinnest part of the island from the Praya with its ferry to Tung Wan Beach. Here, just past the square, is a gnarled old banyan tree, considered to be the dwelling place of the spirit of health and fertility. At the end of Tung Wan Road is **Tung Wan Beach,** the most popular beach on the island, with lifeguards and shark nets. Nearby, past the playground and Warwick Hotel, is a smaller public beach, **Kwun Yam Beach,** and the **Cheung Chau Windsurfing Centre** (✆ 852/ 2981 2772; www.ccwindc.com.hk) with a pleasant outdoor cafe (daily 10am–7pm), windsurfing classes, and rental windsurfing boards (HK$90–HK$150 per hour, depending on the board size) and kayaks (HK$60 per hour for a one-seater, HK$100 for a two-seater). Unfortunately, views from both beaches are marred by the sight of the Lamma power plant and Hong Kong Island's high-rises.

From Tung Wan Beach, it's only a few minutes' walk via Tung Wan Road back to the Praya and ferry pier.

WHERE TO DINE

Hometown Teahouse ★★ TEA/SUSHI   This is a quirky teahouse, a laid-back and pleasant oasis just off the village's main passageway between the Praya and Tung Wan Beach. It's owned and managed by a bubbly Japanese woman, Takahiko-san, and her artist husband. Only a few items—sushi rolls with crab or sausage and herbal teas like *ganoderma* tea (which is thought to boost energy levels)—are available. Most people order the sushi set, which comes with tea, sushi, and a cookie, and dine on the outdoor terrace with a few tables and chairs. I always enjoy stopping here.

Cheung Chau Church Rd. 17 (on the corner of Tung Wan Rd, near the beach). **Ⓒ 852/2981 5038.** Rolled sushi HK$11–HK$17; sushi sets HK$21–HK$24. No credit cards. Daily noon–10pm.

New Baccarat Seafood Restaurant ★ CANTONESE   On the Praya, one of many open-air restaurants now crowding the waterfront but also one of the oldest (located near the Pak Tai Temple on the corner of Pak She Praya St. beside a playground), this simple spot offers outdoor seating under a canopy with a view of the harbor. Sporting tanks of live sea creatures, it specializes in fresh seafood, including crab, lobster, squid, scallop, shrimp, and various fish. Try the steamed fresh fish, deep-fried crispy shrimp, or—my favorite—the steamed fresh scallops with minced garlic. Alternatively, you can buy your own fresh seafood from one of the many vendors on the Praya and have it cooked here for HK$30 to HK$40.

9A Pak She Praya St. **Ⓒ 852/2981 0606.** Main dishes HK$48–HK$100. No credit cards. Daily 11am–10:30pm. Turn left from the ferry and walk along the Praya about 4 min.

Lamma

Lamma is the island to visit if you want to escape city life, do some pleasant hiking, swim, or dine alfresco on fresh seafood with views of a peaceful waterfront. The closest of the outlying islands, only 35 minutes by ordinary ferry and 20 minutes by Fast Ferry from Central Ferry Piers no. 4 in Central, Lamma is Hong Kong's third-largest island, has a population of about 8,000, and is still largely undeveloped. The island has no cars, and a 1½-hour hiking trail connects Lamma's two main villages—Yung Shue Wan and Sok Kwu Wan—both served by ferries from Hong Kong Island. Yung Shue Wan, with a large and youthful expat population, has a decidedly bohemian laid-back atmosphere, while much smaller Sok Kwu Wan is popular for its open-air seafood restaurants. If it's summer, don't forget to bring your bathing suit, since there are several beaches along the trails. You'd be smart, too, to buy bottled water from one of the many stores in either Sok Kwu Wan or Yung Shue Wan before setting out on the trail. In addition, try to avoid Sundays, when the trail is crowded with families, seniors walking dogs, and even mountain bikers. For an insider's perspective on Lamma, check out www.lamma.com.hk.

EXPLORING LAMMA

Although ferries from Central will deposit you at either Yung Shue Wan or Sok Kwu Wan, I personally prefer to land at Sok Kwu Wan for a light seafood meal, hike to a beach for some R & R, and then continue onward to Yung Shue Wan for drinks or dinner before heading back to Central. The advantage of this route is that ferry service is more frequent from Yung Shue Wan, which means you're not constricted to a limited departure schedule. If you choose to hike the trail in reverse from my description below, you'll have to time your arrival and departure with precision because ferries from Sok Kwu Wan are less frequent (or, if you dine at Rainbow Seafood Restaurant, described below, you can take advantage of the restaurant's free shuttle boat to Central and Tsim Sha Tsui by making advance reservations). The hike between the two villages along a marked, concrete footpath takes about 1½ hours and is a true delight, with great views of the surrounding sea and, in the distance, even Ocean Park and Aberdeen on Hong Kong Island.

Tiny **Sok Kwu Wan** is famous for its open-air seafood restaurants and is a popular destination for those lucky enough to own pleasure boats. The restaurants are aligned along the small waterfront, extended over the water on stilts and shaded by canopies; they offer views of the harbor (and, unfortunately, of denuded hills belonging to a defunct cement factory across the harbor; there is talk of eventual landscaping, but only time will tell). All restaurants here have tanks filled with fresh seafood, available by the catty (one catty is about 1½ lb.), with prices that vary daily depending on supply and demand. One catty of prawns costs approximately HK$160 to HK$200, with half a catty usually enough for two people. A catty of lobster will cost about HK$350 to HK$450, though small lobsters for one person are also listed on English menus for around HK$140, along with a variety of other seafood, poultry, and vegetable dishes.

Incidentally, as you dine, you'll notice Hong Kong's largest fleet of fish-breeding rafts in the harbor, some also supporting family homes. Also in the harbor is **Lamma Fisherfolk's Village** (© 852/2982 8585; www.fisherfolks.com.hk), which you can visit if you're looking for something to do or simply want to support a worthwhile local endeavor. Reached by shuttle from Sok Kwu Wan's public pier (the same pier where the ferry docks), the floating "village" consists of moorings, fish-breeding rafts, and displays relating to local fisher-folk culture, including fishing tools, implements used to craft traditional junks, model boats, clothing, and more. Most interesting is the authentic 60-year-old junk, which you can explore at leisure, peeking into the boat's tiny sleeping quarters, the kitchen with its wood-burning stove, and even the "outhouse" toilet. It's open daily from 10am to 6pm; admission, including the shuttle boat, is HK$60 for adults and HK$50 for children and seniors.

Turning right from the public pier and walking past the many seafood restaurants, you will soon come to a newly renovated Tin Hau temple on the edge of town, first founded more than 150 years ago. Tin Hau temples are common near the sea, since the goddess Tin Hau is believed to protect fishermen. Continue on the concrete path that hugs the harbor about 10 minutes to Lo So Shing School, where, if you want to swim, you should turn left. Soon you'll see the turnoff for **Lo So Shing Beach,** which you can reach in about 5 minutes (there are also public latrines along this path). Prettily situated in a small bay, this is the island's nicest and least crowded beach, offering changing rooms and lifeguards on duty April through October daily from 9am to 6pm.

Otherwise, continuing on the main pathway takes you through lush and verdant valleys and banana groves, with butterflies flitting across the path and roosters crowing from the distance, before ascending to a hillside pavilion overlooking the scandalous former cement factory. From this point, the path climbs higher onto barren and windswept hills. About halfway along the trail, on the top of a peak, is a pagoda where you can take a rest and enjoy the view of the South China Sea. After that, the barren hills give way to valleys and trees and then **Hung Shing Yeh Beach,** which also has changing facilities, showers, toilets, and lifeguards on duty in the summer. If it's hot, it may be hard to resist joining the throngs of families and taking another dip in the water. Regrettably, however, the beach is overshadowed by an unsightly power station.

The hiking path resumes on the other side of the beach. In less than 20 minutes, you'll reach Lamma's main town, **Yung Shue Wan,** which translates as "Banyan Tree Bay," but it takes awhile to walk past new development before reaching Yung Shue Wan Main Street and the center of town. It used to be small and undeveloped, with old houses and little garden plots, but new apartment buildings and shops have sprung up on its hillsides in the past couple decades, and the town is unfortunately blighted by that unsightly power station. What's more, small motorized wagons carrying building supplies zip around as if they can't get to construction sites soon enough. Compared to how the village looked in the early 1980s, I can barely recognize the place. Still, the village has a laid-back, tropical-island atmosphere, with a sizable population of expatriates drawn by low rents and the slow pace of life. With Yung Shue Wan's narrow streets, funky eateries, and shops selling Southeast Asian crafts, jewelry, and clothing, Hong Kong's bustling city life seems more than a short boat ride away.

WHERE TO DINE

Bookworm Café ★★ 🍴 VEGETARIAN   Lined with shelves of used books and serving as an informal resource and meeting center for Yung Shue Wan's expat residents, with occasional video nights and other happenings, this casual restaurant is a great alternative to seafood and a godsend for those seeking organic vegetarian and vegan food. The interesting menu includes breakfasts, sandwiches, veggie pizza, tofu burgers, spinach lasagna, and salads like the "veg-out" salad plate with roasted eggplant, feta, and black olives on a bed of mixed greens and herbs with Lebanese bread. There are also various teas, fresh juices, and power shakes. Dining is either in a small, air-conditioned room or across the street on an open terrace. In addition to free Wi-Fi, the cafe has one computer with free Internet access.

79 Yung Shue Wan Main St., Yung Shue Wan. 📞 **852/2982 4838.** www.bookwormcafe.com.hk. Main dishes HK$50–HK$85. MC, V. Fri–Wed 10am–9pm.

Concerto Inn Garden Cafe ☺ LIGHT FARE   Located right on Hung Shing Yeh Beach, about a 30-minute walk from the ferry pier in Yung Shue Wan, this clean, low-key establishment offers both accommodations and a pleasant cafe, with outdoor, covered seating providing views of the beach. Though its menu is limited, the restaurant makes a comfortable stop along the hiking trail for a hamburger, sandwich, spaghetti, rice and noodle dishes, desserts, juice, or beer. There's a children's menu, and a toddlers' play area makes for a good diversion for the little ones, especially on crowded days when service can be a bit slow.

Hung Shing Yeh Beach, Yung Shue Wan. 📞 **852/2982 1668.** Main dishes HK$54–HK$78. AE, DC, MC, V. Daily 8am–10pm.

Man Fung Restaurant ★ CANTONESE/SEAFOOD   If you start your hike at Sok Kwu Wan and end up hungry for seafood on this side of the island, this is my number-one pick for a hearty meal. Located just a minute's walk from the ferry pier, it offers pleasant outdoor seating right by the water with a view of the harbor and town. Specialties are its fresh seafood straight from the tank, including lobster served with a cheese sauce; fried prawns with garlic and butter; fried crab with ginger and spring onion; and other seafood dishes available at market price (inquire first before ordering). Otherwise, the menu lists pork, beef, chicken, and pigeon dishes, as well as vegetarian choices like deep-fried bean curd with chile or braised eggplant in a hot pot. Pitchers of draft beer and bottles of wine are also available.

5 Yung Shue Wan Main St., Yung Shue Wan. 🕐 **852/2982 0719.** Main dishes HK$150–HK$250. AE, MC, V. Daily 11am–10pm.

Rainbow Seafood Restaurant ★★ CANTONESE/SEAFOOD   This is the largest open-air restaurant on Sok Kwu Wan's waterfront, easily recognizable by its whir of ceiling fans and red lanterns. Farther from the pier (and the defunct factory across the harbor) than many other restaurants, it therefore offers a better view of the harbor and rafts (don't confuse it with its smaller branch beside the ferry pier, which does nevertheless have the convenience of an air-conditioned bar). A nice touch is the water sprayed over its canopy to cool the restaurant on hot summer days. A member of the Hong Kong Tourism Board, it offers an English menu with photographs of its main dishes, including a variety of fresh seafood, with prices for lobster, prawn, and fish clearly marked. Among its specialties are steamed garoupa, lobster available several ways (baked with a cheese sauce is most popular), and fried crab with ginger and scallions. Incidentally, this restaurant offers free ferry service to and from Central Ferry Pier no. 9 in Central and Tsim Sha Tsui's public pier, with less frequent service from Aberdeen; reservations are required (check the schedule on the restaurant's website).

17 1st St., Sok Kwu Wan waterfront. 🕐 **852/2982 8100.** www.rainbowrest.com.hk. Seafood dishes HK$120–HK$200. AE, DC, MC, V. Daily 10am–11pm.

A LOCAL BAR

The Island Bar   Located next to Man Fung Restaurant on the waterfront, just a minute's walk from the ferry pier, this is a longtime bar and local *gweilo* (foreign) hangout, popular with a mostly middle-aged crowd. Owned by expats living in Yung Shue Wan, it's a comfortable place to wait for the next ferry, play darts, and meet the locals. Happy hour is from 4 to 8pm Monday to Friday.

6 Yung Shue Wan Main St., Yung Shue Wan. 🕐 **852/2982 1376.** Mon–Fri 4pm–2am; Sat–Sun and holidays noon–2am.

CHINA

Hong Kong is a major gateway to China. Many first-time visitors to China join an organized tour for excursions to the mainland, though it's certainly easy enough to do on your own. Avid shoppers with a sense of adventure may want to make a day trip across the border to Shenzhen, where fake designer watches and handbags are sold for a song. Two caveats, however, for would-be shoppers: The cost of visas for some nationals, including Americans, is so high that it cancels out bargains on goods; and pirated goods are illegal in many countries, including the United States. Frankly, I've never understood the desire for fake goods, but I do love shopping for fun accessories, and there are plenty of nondesigner purses, watches, and other goods as well.

Organized Tours

Virtually all hotels in Hong Kong work with tour agencies that offer a variety of excursions to China, ranging from 1-day trips to Guangzhou or Shenzhen to longer trips that include Guangzhou, Beijing, and other major destinations. Most of these trips follow identical itineraries at similar prices. When I took a 1-day guided tour of Shenzhen (Shekou) and Guangzhou, we were shown a small, musty museum containing a few terra-cotta figures taken from the tomb of China's first emperor near the city of Xi'an, a local market, Six Banyan Temple, and the outside of a concert hall built in 1931 as a memorial to Sun Yat-sen (on weekdays, tours also take in a local kindergarten). While the sites themselves were uninteresting and not worth seeing, what I most enjoyed about the trip was the journey by hover ferry to Shenzhen, the bus trip to Guangzhou, and the trip back by KCR railway, as these provided good vistas of the surrounding countryside with its duck and fish farms, rice fields, banana groves, and simple living conditions. But probably the most compelling reasons for joining a group tour are to see more than you could accomplish in a limited time on your own and to save money through the tour's group visa, which may be cheaper than applying for a visa on your own depending on your nationality. If the cost of your visa is inexpensive, however (see below), you can save money going on your own.

Companies offering organized trips into China (including day trips to Shenzhen's largest shopping mall, Splendid China, and China Folk Culture Villages, all described below) include **Splendid Tours** (② 852/2316 2151; www.splendidtours.com), **Gray Line Tours** (② 852/2368 7111; www.grayline.com.hk), and **China Travel Service** (see "Visas," below), the official travel agency of the People's Republic of China. Unsurprisingly, CTS offers the most extensive list of tours, with trips that include Beijing, Guilin, Shanghai, Xi'an, Lijiang, and other major cities. CTS's 11-day trip, for example, includes train and plane travel from Hong Kong to Guangzhou, Guilin, Beijing, Xian, and Shanghai before returning to Hong Kong. The cost of this trip runs HK$17,140 to HK$17,790, depending on the season.

Visas

If you join an organized tour of China lasting 1 or 2 days, your visa for China will be taken care of by the tour agency, with the price of tour group visas (which cost less than individual visas) included in the tour price. You can book tours up to the day before departure if there's room, but most charge more if you book later than 11:30am the day before departure because the company will have to apply for an individual rush visa rather than submitting your passport along with the others for a group visa. For longer tours in China, however, or if you wish to visit China on your own, you'll need to obtain a visa yourself. Your hotel or a travel agency may be able to arrange this for you. Having your hotel's concierge or tour desk do the work certainly saves time, but prices are higher. Travel agencies are cheaper, but you'll have to first apply and then return to pick up the visa. You can also save money by planning ahead, as rush orders for visas add to the price.

One of the most popular places to apply for a visa is at a **China Travel Service** (**CTS;** ② 852/2851 1700; www.ctshk.com), the official travel agency of the PRC. Hong Kong has several branches, including 78 Connaught Rd., Central District (② 852/2853 3533: MTR: Central); 138 Hennessey Rd., Wan Chai (② 852/2832 3888; MTR: Wan Chai); and 27–33 Nathan Rd., Tsim Sha Tsui (② 852/2315 7171; MTR: Tsim Sha Tsui), which is the most convenient with the most convenient hours: Monday through Friday from 9am to 7pm, Saturday from 9am to 5pm, and Sunday and holidays from 9am to 12:30pm and 2 to 5pm. Although a CTS is also located at the Lo Wu border crossing, residents of the United States and United Kingdom cannot obtain visas here.

To fill out an application for your visa, you will need your passport (with an expiration date of not less than 6 months away) and one passport photograph (you can have your portrait taken at Tsim Sha Tsui's CTS office for HK$35; otherwise, the nearby YMCA Salisbury on Salisbury Road and the Tsim Sha Tsui MTR station have portrait machines). Prices for a visa, unfortunately, vary depending on nationality and are subject to change, but it's always cheapest to turn in your visa application at least 4 business days prior to departure. At the time this book was going to press, Americans applying for a visa 4 days in advance at CTS, which is cheaper than most places (especially hotel tour desks), were required to pay HK$1,180 for a single- or double-entry visa valid for 6 months. Americans in a hurry can obtain a visa more quickly by paying more: HK$1,530 for visa applications made 3 days in advance and HK$2,470 for same-day applications made before 9:30am. The cost of applying for a visa from the Chinese embassy in the United States is US$140 (www.china-embassy.org).

U.K. residents fare better: HK$600 for a single-entry visa (valid for 30 days) applied for 4 days in advance, HK$900 3 days in advance, HK$1,350 for next-day service, and HK$1,950 for same-day visa pickup. Otherwise, the regular price of a single-entry visa for many other nationalities, including Canadians, Australians, and New Zealanders, is HK$210 for applications made 3 days in advance, and HK$480 for same-day pickup. In any case, visa requirements and prices can change overnight; call your embassy for updated information.

Shenzhen

If you're planning a 1-day trip to China, your destination will be either Shenzhen or Guangzhou (see below). **Shenzhen** (www.shenzhentour.com), located across the Hong Kong–China border, was established in the 1980s as one of China's first Special Economic Zones. Today, this experiment with capitalism looks almost like Hong Kong with its 14 million people, concrete high-rises, traffic, industries, pollution, and relative prosperity. It's a shopping mecca for day-trippers who come for fake designer handbags, watches, and other goods at prices much cheaper than in Hong Kong. However, the HK$1,180 minimum Americans now pay for a visa makes shopping in Shenzhen no longer a bargain. Shenzhen is also known for its many theme parks.

You can travel to Shenzhen via the MTR East Rail, with trains departing Kowloon's Hung Hom Station every 6 to 8 minutes. The trip to Lo Wu, the border crossing (daily 6:30am–midnight), takes about 42 minutes and costs HK$33 for ordinary class and HK$66 for first class. Prices are slightly cheaper if you have an Octopus card, but if you're traveling first class, you'll have to swipe your card again at the First Class Processor located on the train platform in front of the first-class compartment. The Lo Wu Border Control is one of the busiest border crossings in the world. Avoid traveling on weekends and holidays, if possible, when crowds can make the wait to cross over very long. Or, you can change trains in Sheung Shui for a 6-minute ride to Lok Ma Chau, a new border crossing into Shenzhen, also with shopping and connection via the Shenzhen Metro to other destinations in Shenzhen.

After going through Customs, you can walk across the border into Shenzhen. Just across the border from Lo Wu is a huge shopping mall called Luohu Commercial City (also called Lo Wu Shopping Mall by tour agencies), with five floors of tiny shops selling a bewildering amount of inexpensively priced handbags, shoes, watches, jewelry, clothing (including Chinese padded jackets), and bolts of cloth. As for imitation designer bags and pirated DVDs, Chinese officials have cracked down on counterfeit goods (half the fake goods seized by U.S. Customs agents come from China, which should give would-be purchasers pause as well). That is not to say that such goods are unavailable. When I agreed, at a shopkeeper's insistence, to look at imitation handbags, I was whisked to a concealed backroom closet with rows and rows of bags. In a tiny electronics shop, the owner closed all his doors and sent his assistant scurrying up a concealed hole in the drop ceiling to retrieve pirated DVDs (don't bother buying DVDs—most of the time they aren't fully copied or they don't work). Several salons offer combination manicures and pedicures for as little as HK$40, but lack of hygienic conditions may discourage most tourists from giving them a whirl. In any case, bargaining is the name of the game, and because there are no ATMs around, bring plenty of HK dollars. You should also guard your belongings against pickpockets. Shops are open daily from 10am to 10pm.

As for tourist attractions, theme parks are big in Shenzhen, including Splendid China, a theme park with more than 80 miniatures of China's most historic buildings, sites, and scenic wonders, including the Great Wall and the Imperial Palace; China Folk Culture Villages, which presents the art and cultures of China's various ethnic groups with life-size villages and people dressed in native dress; and Window of the World, which re-creates famous buildings, monuments, and scenic spots from around the world, including the Taj Mahal, Eiffel Tower, and Grand Canyon. All three are clustered together about 13km (8 miles) west of the border crossing; take the very efficient Shenzhen Metro subway from Lo Wu to Window of the World/Shijiezhichuang Station (otherwise, Splendid China and China Folk Culture Villages are often included in 1-day tours offered by tour companies listed above). Farther afield are Happy Valley, a large sophisticated theme park with a variety of thrill rides, and Minsk World, a military theme park with the Soviet aircraft carrier *Minsk*. Most visitors to Shenzhen, however, come for the shopping.

Farther Afield

Farther afield is **Guangzhou (Canton),** capital of Guangdong Province with a population approaching 12 million. A commercial city, Guangzhou is famous for its markets, including Haizhu Square with vendors selling electronics, toys, and souvenirs at great prices. Otherwise, the sights are confined to a Buddhist temple and the monuments and statues in the city's largest park, Yuexiu Yuan, that include a memorial to Sun Yat-sen. You can reach Guangzhou by rail in 2 hours or less from Hung Hom Station in Kowloon; cost of this trip is HK$230 for "premium" class and HK$190 for first class. At last check, through-train service to Guangzhou departed Hung Hom every hour or so from 7:25am to 7:24pm.

Be forewarned, however, that because tourist attractions in Shenzhen and Guangzhou are extremely limited, if you're really interested in a trip to China you should plan on traveling to Shanghai, Beijing, and beyond. For more information on visiting China, see *Frommer's China.*

MACAU

H anging from China's gigantic underbelly on its south-eastern coast, Macau covers all of 29.2 sq. km (11.4 sq. miles). About 64km (40 miles) west of Hong Kong across the Pearl River Estuary, it served as Portugal's last holdout in Asia until 1999, when it was handed back to China. Portugal's other former Asian strongholds, Goa and Malacca, had long before been claimed by neighboring powers.

With its unique mixture of Portuguese and Chinese cultures, Macau makes an interesting day trip or overnight stay if you want to get away from the bustle of Hong Kong. Although Macau's rising reputation as a gambling and shopping mecca—spurred by the grand openings of ever larger and grander casinos with equally ostentatious shopping malls—is a major attraction for many, the city also has its fair share of beaches, fortresses, churches, temples, gardens, and excellent museums to explore. What's more, even though prices have risen sharply the past few years, Macau is still a bargain compared to Hong Kong, especially when it comes to dining and accommodations (you can bask in luxury in Macau for a fraction of what you'd pay in the former British colony). And finally, Macanese cuisine, unique to Macau and combining ingredients from former Portuguese trading ports from around the world, is both inexpensive and delicious, especially when accompanied with Portuguese wine. If you're looking for a vacation from your vacation, I heartily recommend Macau.

MACAU TODAY

Macau is no longer off the tourist radar, in large part because it is now touted as the Las Vegas of the East. Whereas only 7.4 million tourists visited Macau in 1999, 21.7 million tourists crossed its borders in 2009, a number fast approaching the number of tourists entering Hong Kong during the same year (29.5 million). More than 90% of visitors are from mainland China (which relaxed travel restrictions in 2003 and where gambling is illegal), Hong Kong, and Taiwan. Casinos were always a part of Macau's draw, especially for Hong Kong Chinese, but deregulation of the gaming industry in 2002 paved the way to an explosion of ritzier, more conspicuous casinos, including big-name imports from the United States like the Venetian and MGM Grand. The former Portuguese territory's transformation into Asia's Las Vegas has played nicely with Macau's vigorous policy of land reclamation, which has more than doubled its size over the last 2 decades and added high-rises, superhighways, housing complexes, and huge entertainment and shopping complexes. Compared to the real Las Vegas, however, Macau seems underdeveloped, with only

19,600 hotel rooms compared to Las Vegas's 148,000. And yet, Macau's annual gaming revenue now exceeds that of Las Vegas (in 2009, Macau's gambling revenues were about twice as high as those of Las Vegas), and it doesn't take a rocket scientist to recognize Macau's huge potential market just across the border. There are so many hotels coming onto the Macau scene, it's hard to say who is *not* scooping up property here, with Four Seasons, Hyatt, Hard Rock, and Mandarin Oriental recently opening their doors and Sheraton, Shangri-La, St. Regis, and Ritz-Carlton soon to follow. Although growth has slowed the past couple of years due to the global economy, Macau has fared better than many other Asian destinations.

Macau bears almost no resemblance to the laid-back town I first laid eyes on in the 1980s. A sleepy backwater just 2 decades ago—when the local populace got from place to place unhurriedly by pedicab and the road from the ferry to downtown was a lonely stretch of potholes—Macau is changing so rapidly that old-timers are right when they complain that the place isn't what it used to be. In fact, Macau is *more* than it used to be, with land reclamation and new construction dramatically altering the city's skyline in just 20 short years, with no end in sight. The small downtown, built in the era of pedicabs with its narrow lanes, is ill equipped to deal with Macau's ever-increasing traffic. Indeed, city planners seem so intent on expansion, I fear that much of Macau's unique architectural legacy and charm will be lost in an ever-growing concrete jungle.

Needless to say, the influx of new capital, new businesses, and new jobs has dramatically altered the lives of local residents. A labor shortage has brought intense competition, with many employees poached from existing Macau businesses or the service industry in Hong Kong, the Philippines, and other Asian countries. Small, family-owned establishments, unable to compete with salaries offered by the big casinos and rising real-estate prices, are especially feeling the economic squeeze. With more and more workers moving to Macau, housing prices have exploded. To assuage public resentment, the Macau government has given cash handouts to residents the past few years so that they could share in the wealth the casinos have created.

Macau's development as a tourist mecca has, of course, brought some positive changes. When I first came to Macau, its downtown was crumbling and neglected, and there were few attractions beyond its casinos, churches, a couple of ruined forts, and a lone museum (the Maritime Museum). In the 1990s, however, the small downtown underwent a major renovation, with the restoration of its main plaza and its Mediterranean-influenced, colonial-era buildings with their arched, shuttered windows. In 2005, Macau's historic center was declared a UNESCO World Heritage Site, encompassing 8 squares and 22 temples, churches, mansions, fortresses, and other historic buildings and monuments. The restaurant scene has exploded, offering a variety of international cuisines. There are now more attractions than you could ever visit in a day.

But the things that drew me to Macau in the first place—the unique blend of Chinese and Portuguese culture, architecture, and food—remain irresistibly in place. It's as though two Macaus now exist: the sterile new developments and glitzy casinos on reclaimed land; and the old downtown of candy-colored colonial buildings, banyan trees, narrow hilly streets, and low-key neighborhood restaurants.

The only pedicabs driven today are after the tourists' dollar, but Macau still possesses a lifestyle that is way less frenetic than that of Hong Kong. In fact, compared to the former British colony, Macau is downright Lilliputian, and, with its mixture of

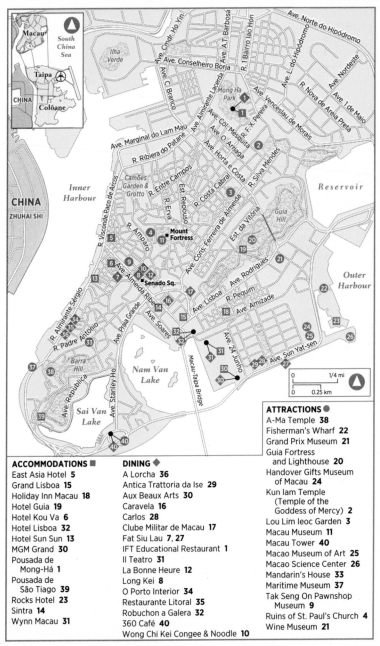

Portuguese and Chinese elements, feels different from Hong Kong, different from China—different from anywhere else. Maybe it's the jumble of Chinese signs and stores mixed in with freshly painted colonial-style buildings, or the Buddhist and Taoist temples alongside Catholic churches. Maybe it's because people smile here more readily than they do in Hong Kong, seem more relaxed, and friendlier. It's an attractive mix—Portuguese flair blended with Chinese practicality—all in a setting found nowhere else in the world.

There is no doubt in my mind that the world will be hearing more about Macau. It has clearly set its sights to become Asia's top gambling, conference, resort, and shopping destination, making it a fascinating study if you want to see what the new China is all about. Though I'm not sure whether Macau will be able to retain its historic charm as it strives to become Asia's major leisure destination, that's a gamble this former Portuguese enclave is clearly willing to take.

FROMMER'S FAVORITE MACAU EXPERIENCES

○ **Following the Mosaic Pathway to St. Paul's Church:** From Largo do Senado, Macau's main, colonial-era square, follow one of the wavy-patterned mosaic tiled streets through the old city uphill to the ruins of St. Paul's Church, Macau's most photographed facade. See p. 308.

○ **Exploring Macau's Historic Center:** I love Macau's old, twisting, narrow streets that lead past historic churches, temples, forts, stately squares, and mansions. If you don't take at least a few hours to roam its historic center, you haven't really seen Macau. See my recommended strolls (p. 315 and 319).

○ **Dining on Local Macanese and Portuguese Specialties:** African chicken, spicy prawns, sole, and codfish are just some of the culinary treats for the visitor to Macau, all available at very reasonable prices. Portuguese wine, the perfect accompaniment to both Macanese and Portuguese food, is also a bargain. See the "Where to Dine" section, later in this chapter.

○ **Splurging for a Room at a Resort Hotel:** After the traffic and crowds of Hong Kong, there's nothing more relaxing than gazing at the sea from your hotel room, sunning at an outdoor pool surrounded by greenery, and feeling tension and aches melt away under the expert care of a massage therapist. See the "Where to Stay" section, later in this chapter.

○ **Learning About Macau's History:** The Museum of Macau is a delight, built into the ruins of a fortress and highlighting not only the history of Macau but also unique Macanese traditions, culture, architecture, and cuisine. See p. 307.

○ **Visiting Lou Lim Leoc Garden Early in the Morning:** Get to this Chinese garden early in the morning, when you're apt to see locals practicing tai chi, playing traditional Chinese music, and taking birds for walks in cages. See p. 312.

○ **Swimming on Colôane Island:** Two public beaches, Cheoc Van and Hac Sa (p. 314), feature lifeguards on duty, dining facilities, and public swimming pools. Afterward, retire for a drink or a Portuguese meal at Fernando's (p. 303), a beach shack on Hac Sa.

○ **Gambling on a Stroke of Luck at a Casino:** Even if you don't gamble, it's a jaw-dropping experience to wander through Macau's big casinos, packed with Chinese visitors and with gaming tables and slot machines designed specifically for the Asian market. The biggest to date? The Venetian Macao-Resort-Hotel in Cotai

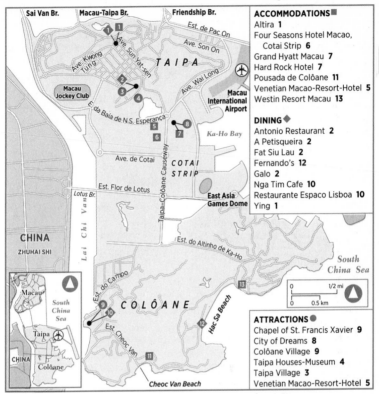

Taipa & Colôane

ACCOMMODATIONS ■
Altira **1**
Four Seasons Hotel Macao,
    Cotai Strip **6**
Grand Hyatt Macau **7**
Hard Rock Hotel **7**
Pousada de Colôane **11**
Venetian Macao-Resort-Hotel **5**
Westin Resort Macau **13**

DINING ◆
Antonio Restaurant **2**
A Petisqueira **2**
Fat Siu Lau **2**
Fernando's **12**
Galo **2**
Nga Tim Cafe **10**
Restaurante Espaco Lisboa **10**
Ying **1**

ATTRACTIONS ●
Chapel of St. Francis Xavier **9**
City of Dreams **8**
Colôane Village **9**
Taipa Houses-Museum **4**
Taipa Village **3**
Venetian Macao-Resort-Hotel **5**

with 3,400 slot machines and 800 tables, which together with its 3,000-suite hotel, Grand Canal Shoppes, convention facilities, and huge arena, comprise the second-largest building in the world. See p. 323.

○ **Watching the Sun Set from Macau Tower:** This 220m-high (722-ft.) Space Needle wannabe looks out of place in tiny Macau, but you can't beat it for its views: 360 degrees and 55km (34 miles) on clear days. Come for dinner in its revolving restaurant. Or, for the truly daring, there are adventure tours *outside* the tower, including a climb up its mast. See p. 308 and 305.

○ **People-Watching After Midnight:** After the sun goes down, Macau's nighttime revelers head to the Docks, a string of bars and discos with sidewalk seating. But the action doesn't really start hopping until after midnight. See p. 324.

ESSENTIALS & ORIENTATION
Entry Requirements

Entry procedures into Macau are very simple. If you are American, Canadian, Australian, or New Zealander, you do not need a visa for Macau for stays of up to 30

A BRIEF HISTORY OF MACAU: A blending OF CULTURES

Macau (also spelled Macao) was born centuries before Hong Kong was even conceived. The first settlers were farmers from Guangdong and fishermen from Fujian, but even in ancient times, its strategic location at the mouth of the Pearl River, downriver from Guangzhou (Canton), made it a port of call for ships laden with goods from the Silk Road on their way to Rome.

Portuguese ships first landed in southern China in 1513; in 1557, Portugal acquired Macau from China with permission from Guangdong's mandarins. The Portuguese adopted the name for their new city from the Chinese *A-Ma Gao,* which translates as the "Place of A-Ma" and refers to the temple honoring the goddess of seafarers, which still stands at the entrance to the sheltered Inner Harbour (p. 290). Before long, Macau had achieved a virtual monopoly on trade among China, Japan, India, and Europe, making it Portugal's most important trading center in Asia and the East's greatest port by the early 1600s.

As the only Europeans engaged in trade in Asia, the Portuguese made a fortune acting as middlemen. Every spring, Portuguese ships laden with Indian goods and European crystal and wines sailed out of Goa, anchored in Malacca to trade for spices, stopped in Macau for silk brought down from China,

and then traveled on to Nagasaki to trade the silk for silver, swords, and lacquerware. Using the monsoon winds, the ships returned to Macau to trade silver for more silk and porcelain, and then sailed back to Goa where the exotic Asian goods were shipped to eager customers in Europe. The complete circuit from Goa and back took several years.

As Macau grew and prospered, it also served as an important base for the attempt to introduce Christianity to China and Japan, becoming a springboard for Jesuit missionaries to China and a refuge for Asian Christians, including Japanese Christians who faced persecution and death at home. Many churches dotted Macau's hills (many of which still stand), and a Christian college was built beside what is now the ruins of St. Paul's. Many Portuguese married local Chinese, creating a new community of Macanese (Eurasian) families with a blend of the two cultures. This blending is still evident today in the Macanese population, cuisine, and architecture.

Needless to say, because of Macau's obvious prosperity, it attracted jealous attention from other European nations. Dutch invasions were repelled several times in the first decades of the 1600s. In response to the threat of invasion, the Portuguese built a series of forts,

days—all you need is your passport. Residents of the United Kingdom and Ireland can stay up to 90 days without a visa.

Visitor Information

ONLINE   Visitor information is available on the **Macau Government Tourist Office's (MGTO's)** website at **www.macautourism.gov.mo**.

OVERSEAS   The **Macau Government Tourist Office** maintains the following tourist offices:

○ **United States:** 501 5th Ave., Ste. 1101, New York, NY 10017 (✆ **646/227-0690;** fax 646/366-8170; macau@myriadmarketing.com), and 1334 Parkview, Ste.

foundations of which, like Guia Fortress and Monte Fortress, still exist. Despite growing competition from the Dutch and British, Macau survived as a trading center thanks to its preferred status with the Chinese, prompting many large trading houses, like the British East India Company, to set up shop in Macau and rent elegant mansions like the Casa Garden (p. 318). European merchants working in Guangzhou often traveled to Macau for recreation and leisure.

In the 1630s, Japan closed its doors to foreign trade, granting a limited admittance only to the Dutch. This was a great blow for Macau, but the coup de grace came in 1841 when the British established their own colony on Hong Kong Island, only 64km (40 miles) away. As Hong Kong's deep natural harbor attracted trading ships, Macau lost its importance as a base for trade and slowly sank into obscurity.

It wasn't until the 1970s that Macau gained a new foothold in the world of trade by producing electronics, clothing, toys, and other items for export. At the same time, tourism began to grow, and with the establishment of casinos, Macau attracted a large number of Chinese gamblers from Hong Kong. In 1995, Macau opened an airport, making the colony easily accessible for the first time in its history.

On December 20, 1999, Portugal's 442 years of rule came to an end, with Macau's transition to a Special Administrative Region of China. Like Hong Kong, Macau is permitted its own internal government and economic system for another 50 years. In addition, after the handover two independent developments came together that would radically change Macau's outlook for the future: the liberalization of its gaming industry, thus ending gaming operator Stanley Ho's 40-year monopoly, and mainland China's 2003 implementation of its Individual Visit Scheme, thereby allowing mainlanders to visit Hong Kong and Macau on their own in addition to group tours. Several mega-developments have opened since then, including Fisherman's Wharf, the Venetian Macao-Hotel-Resort, and City of Dreams, with more scheduled to open in the coming years.

Today, 94% of Macau's population of 542,400 are Chinese (almost half of whom were born in China). There are about 2,500 Portuguese and an additional 20,000 Macanese, of mixed Chinese and Portuguese heritage. Tourism and gambling are the economic mainstays of the economy, with visitors from mainland China accounting for almost half of Macau's tourists.

300, Manhattan Beach, CA 90266 (✆ **866/OK-MACAU** [656-2228] or 310/545-3464; fax 310/545-4221; macau@myriadmarketing.com).

- **United Kingdom:** Parkshot House, 5 Kew Rd., Surrey TW9 2PR (✆ **20/8334-8325;** fax 20/8334-8100; macau@humewhitehead.co.uk).
- **Australia:** Level 11, 99; Bathurst St., Sydney NSW 2000 (✆ **02/9264-1488;** fax 02/9267-7717; macau@worldtradetravel.com).
- **New Zealand:** Level 10, 120 Albert St., Auckland Central (✆ **09/308-5206;** fax 09/308-5207; macau@aviationandtourism.co.nz).

IN HONG KONG   Your first stop for information about Macau should be as soon as you arrive in Hong Kong, at the Hong Kong International Airport. In the arrivals lobby, at counter A06, you'll find the **Macau Government Tourist Office (MGTO)** information office (✆ 852/2769 7970), open daily from 9am to 10pm (closed for lunch 1–1:45pm and dinner 6–6:45pm). Stop here for a wealth of printed material about hotels and sightseeing in Macau. Another MGTO information bureau is located in Hong Kong's Macau Ferry Terminal, the departure pier for most jetfoils and other craft bound for Macau. You'll find it on the third-floor Departure Floor, in room 336 of the Shun Tak Centre, 200 Connaught Rd., in Central (✆ 852/2857 2287). It's open daily from 9am to 10pm. Be sure to pick up a map of Macau; the hefty *Macau Guide Book,* with useful information on attractions; and *What's On,* a monthly leaflet with information on festivals, exhibitions, and events.

IN MACAU   Once in Macau, you'll find an **MGTO** at the Macau Ferry Terminal, located just outside Customs, and in the arrivals hall of Macau International Airport, both open daily 9am to 10pm. In town, there's the main office, the **Macau Business Tourism Centre,** Largo do Senado (Senado Sq.), located on the main plaza just across from the water fountain; it's open daily from 9am to 6pm. Other MGTO counters are located at Fisherman's Wharf, open daily from 10am to 1pm and 2 to 6pm; at Guia Fortress and Lighthouse, open daily from 9am to 1pm and 2:15 to 5:30pm; the Border Gate (also called Barrier Gate and serving visitors from mainland China), open daily from 9:15am to 1pm and 2:30 to 6pm; and the Taipa Ferry Terminal, open daily 9:30am to 1pm and 2:30 to 6:15pm. For information by telephone, call the Tourist Hotline at ✆ 853/2833 3000 24 hours a day. Finally, a number of publications are distributed free to hotel rooms, restaurants, and tourist locales, including *Macau Talk* (www.talkmagazines.cn), a bimonthly with restaurant reviews, a calendar of events, and other useful information. Look also for *Destination Macau Magazine* (www.macauignite.com), a glossy bimonthly magazine placed in high-end hotel rooms with information on shopping, dining, sightseeing, and nightlife. Two free English-language tabloids, the *Macau Post Daily* and *the Macau Daily Times* (www.macaudaily times.com.mo), are also available.

Getting There

BY BOAT   Located only 64km (40 miles) from Hong Kong across the mouth of the Pearl River, Macau is most easily accessible from Hong Kong by high-speed jetfoil, with most departures from the **Macau Ferry Terminal,** located just west of the Central District in the Shun Tak Centre, 200 Connaught Rd., on Hong Kong Island. Situated above the Sheung Wan MTR station, the Shun Tak Centre houses booking offices for all forms of transportation to Macau, as well as the Macau Government Tourist Office (Room 336, on the same floor as boats departing for Macau). If you're staying in a hotel on the Kowloon side, the **China Ferry Terminal** on Canton Road, Tsim Sha Tsui, also provides limited service to Macau, as well as to other parts of China. The nearest MTR station for this terminal is Tsim Sha Tsui. If you plan to travel on a weekend or holiday, it's wise to buy round-trip tickets well in advance.

From the Macau Ferry Terminal on Hong Kong Island, the fastest, most convenient way to travel to Macau is via **TurboJET** (✆ 852/2859 3333 in Hong Kong, 853/790 7039 in Macau; www.turbojet.com.hk). Jetfoils depart every 15 minutes, 24 hours a day, with the trip to Macau taking approximately 1 hour. One-way fares Monday through Friday are HK$236 for super class and HK$134 for economy class; fares on Saturday, Sunday, and holidays are HK$252 in super class and HK$146 in economy. Fares for night service (6:10pm–6:30am) are HK$267 and HK$168, respectively. Fares from Macau to Hong Kong are an additional HK$8, a reflection of a higher departure tax, included in the price of the ticket. Seniors 60 and older and children 11 and under receive a HK$15 discount. Super class provides wider, more comfortable seats, better views from an upper deck (though there isn't much to see), drinks, and a snack. But if you really wish to travel in style, TurboJET offers eight daily sailings of the **Premier Jetfoil,** which includes use of a VIP waiting lounge at the departure hall, free onboard Wi-Fi service, reclinable leather seats, one free check-in baggage up to 20 kilograms (44 lbs.), and, for Premier Grand Class seats, a hot meal and free wine. The Premier Jetfoil costs HK$212 for a regular seat and HK$312 for Premier Grand Class; night sailings cost HK$262 and HK$362.

TurboJET tickets can be purchased at either the Macau Ferry Terminal on Hong Kong Island or the China Ferry Terminal in Kowloon, as well as at all China Travel Service branches in Hong Kong (p. 276). Credit-card bookings may be made by phone or online (see contact information, above). All tickets are for a specific time and cannot be changed. If, however, you've purchased your ticket in advance and then decide you'd like to leave at an earlier time, head for the special queue for standby passengers. There's a good chance you can get a seat, except during peak periods.

If you're staying at a hotel in Kowloon, you might find it more convenient to take a **First Ferry Macau** (© 852/2131 8181 in Hong Kong; 853/2872 7676 in Macau; www.nwff.com.hk) from Tsim Sha Tsui's China Ferry Terminal. Departures are about every 60 minutes from 7am to 10:30pm. Fares run HK$133 to $168 for ordinary class, depending on the day of the week and time, while deluxe class runs HK$238 to HK$268.

If your destination is Taipa, Cotai, or Colôane, you can travel from the Macau Ferry Terminal directly to Taipa via **Cotai Waterjets** (© 852/2359 9990 in Hong Kong, or 853/2885 0595 in Macau; www.cotaijet.com.mo). Ferries depart every 15 or 30 minutes between 7am and 1am; there are also a few morning departures from Tsim Sha Tsui's China Ferry Terminal. One-way fares Monday through Friday are HK$236 for first class and HK$134 for economy class; fares on Saturday, Sunday, and holidays are HK$252 and HK$146, while night sailings (6pm–1am) are HK$267 and HK$168. Tickets can be purchased online or at Hong Kong's Macau Ferry Terminal, the China Ferry Terminal, or the Venetian Macao-Resort-Hotel.

If you plan to spend only 1 or 2 nights in Macau, consider leaving most of your luggage at your Hong Kong hotel, or in computer-monitored lockers located at both the Hong Kong Island and Kowloon Macau ferry terminals. Then travel to Macau with only a small, hand-carried bag. Otherwise, you could end up paying an extra charge. Passengers traveling on a TurboJET are officially allowed one piece of luggage, not to exceed 20 kilograms (44 lb.). Additional baggage must be checked, with charges ranging from HK$20 to HK$40 depending upon weight; in my experience, though, authorities are somewhat lax about this rule and I've often traveled with two bags. In any case, baggage must be at the check-in counter, located just before Customs, 30 minutes before the jetfoil's departure. Obviously, your life will be easier if you leave heavy luggage in Hong Kong.

If you're arriving at Hong Kong International Airport and wish to travel directly to Macau, you can do so via TurboJET's **Sea Express** service (www.turbojetseaexpress.com.hk) without passing through Hong Kong Customs and immigration formalities (if you do pass through Customs, you will not be allowed to take the Sea Express). Upon exiting your arrival gate, look for the FERRIES TO MAINLAND/MACAU signs. At the Sea Express counter, you can purchase your Sea Express ticket and produce your baggage identification tag for baggage reclaim (your luggage will be retrieved from baggage claim by a TurboJET employee). You will then board a bus for the 7-minute shuttle to the SkyPier, take the TurboJET directly to Macau, and go through Customs there. Baggage is limited to 20 kilograms (44 lb.) in economy class and 30 kilograms (66 lb.) in super class, except for passengers from or to North America, who are allowed two pieces of baggage, with each piece not to exceed 32 kilograms (71 lb.). There are 13 sailings daily approximately every hour between 10am and 10pm (check-in 1 hr. before sailings), with fares costing HK$215 for economy class and HK$315 for super class. Note that if you're returning from Macau to Hong Kong International Airport, you will pay HK$20 extra to account for Macau's departure tax. On the plus side, because your departure point is considered Macau rather than Hong Kong, you will be refunded the HK$120 you paid for the Hong Kong airport departure, which was included in the price of your plane ticket.

BY PLANE   Macau's **International Airport** (✆ **853/2886 1111;** www.macau-airport.gov.mo) opened in 1995, heralding the birth of **Air Macau** (✆ **853/8396 5555;** http://en.airmacau.com.mo), the territory's fledgling carrier. The airport is located on reclaimed land on Taipa Island and is conveniently connected to the peninsula by a bridge and bus service. The airport serves flights from China, including Beijing, Xiamen, and Shanghai, as well as from several other Asian cities, including Taipei, Singapore, Manila, Seoul, Tokyo, and Bangkok. Contact your travel agent or the Macau Government Tourist Office for more information.

Arriving in Macau

Passengers traveling by boat arrive at either the Macau Ferry Terminal, located on the main peninsula, or at the Taipa Ferry Terminal near the International Airport. After going through Customs (which can take 30 min. or more, depending on the crowds), stop by the Macau Government Tourist Office for a map and brochures, including the useful *Macau Guide Book.* In the arrivals hall of the Macau Ferry Terminal, there's also a counter for hotel reservations, open daily 10am to 2am, where you can book rooms free of charge after paying a deposit. Outside the Macau Ferry Terminal are hotel shuttle buses. Most expensive and moderately priced hotels operate **free shuttle** services, including the Altira, Four Seasons, Grand Hyatt, Grand Lisboa, Hard Rock Hotel, Holiday Inn, Hotel Guia, Lisboa, MGM Grand, Pousada de São Tiago, Rocks Hotel, Sintra, Venetian Macao-Resort-Hotel, Westin Resort Macau, and Wynn. Otherwise, **city bus** nos. 3, 3A, 10, and 10A travel from the terminal to Avenida Almeida Ribeiro, the main downtown street. The fare is MOP$3.20.

From the Taipa Ferry Terminal, free shuttles operate to Taipa hotels, including the Four Seasons, Grand Hyatt, Hard Rock Hotel, and Venetian Macao-Resort-Hotel. From the airport, there are complimentary shuttle buses to major hotels. Otherwise, the **airport bus,** AP1, travels to the Macau Ferry Terminal, Holiday Inn, Lisboa Hotel, and the Border Gate. The fare for this is MOP$4.20. A **taxi** from the airport to the Lisboa costs approximately MOP$47.

Currency

Macau's currency is the **pataca,** composed of 100 *avos.* Coins come in 10, 20, and 50 avos and 1, 2, and 5 patacas. Banknotes are issued for 10, 20, 50, 100, 500, and 1,000 patacas. Even though the pataca (ptc; also referred to as MOP$) is Macau's official currency, you can use your Hong Kong dollars everywhere, even on buses and for taxis (though you are likely to receive change in patacas). The pataca is pegged to the Hong Kong dollar at the rate of MOP$103.20=HK$100; however, on the street and in hotels and shops, the Macau pataca and Hong Kong dollar are treated as having equal value. I suppose, therefore, that you could save a minuscule amount by exchanging your money for patacas, but I rarely have done so and don't consider it worth the hassle for short stays in Macau. You may wish to exchange a small amount—say, HK$20, but keep in mind that the pataca is *not* accepted in Hong Kong. If you do exchange U.S. dollars or U.K. pounds (which you can do at banks, generally open weekdays 9am–5pm; at hotels; or at ATMs throughout the city), you'll receive approximately MOP$8 for each US$1, or MOP$15.4 for each £1. You can find money exchange counters at seemingly every corner, plus exchange counters at the airport and Hotel Lisboa are open 24 hours. The bank will give you a better exchange rate but exchange counters usually don't charge a commission.

In addition, most Macau hotels and their restaurants, as well as restaurants catering largely to tourists, list room rates and menu items in Hong Kong dollars. For the sake of simplicity, the hotel rates given later are quoted in HK$, but this could just as well read "patacas." Outside of hotels, restaurants are more likely to give prices in MOP$, but sometimes they use HK$, too. Attractions, however, always use patacas. To mirror the most common pricing practices in Macau, I use HK$ for hotels but patacas (MOP$) for restaurants and attractions listed later. ATMs are located at the ferry terminal, airport, and throughout the city and accept American Express, MasterCard, Visa, and cards operating on the PLUS and Cirrus systems.

Getting Around

Because the peninsula is only 9.3 sq. km (about 3½ sq. miles), you can walk to most of the major sights (be sure to get a free map from MGTO). If you get tired, you can always jump into one of the licensed metered **taxis,** all painted black and beige and quite inexpensive. To overcome the language barrier, MGTO has supplied most taxis with a destination guide listing most destinations in both English and Chinese. The charge is MOP$13 at flag fall for the first 1.6km (1 mile) and then MOP$1.50 for each subsequent 230m (754 ft.). A taxi from the peninsula all the way to Hac Sa Beach on Colôane Island costs about MOP$90. Luggage costs MOP$3 per piece, and there's a surcharge of MOP$5 if you board a taxi at the airport. There's also a MOP$5 surcharge if you take a taxi from Macau peninsula to Colôane, or MOP$2 if you travel between Taipa and Colôane; there is no surcharge, however, for the return journey to Macau. To order a taxi by phone, call © **853/2893 9939** or 853/2851 9519.

Public buses run daily 7am to midnight, with fares costing MOP$3.20 for travel within the Macau peninsula, MOP$4.20 for travel to Taipa, and MOP$5 to MOP$6.40 for travel to Colôane. Bus nos. 3, 3A, 10, and 10A travel from the ferry terminal past the Lisboa Hotel to the main street, Avenida Almeida Ribeiro, in the city center and then continue to the Inner Harbour. Buses going to Taipa and Colôane islands stop for passengers at the bus stop in front of the Hotel Lisboa, located on the mainland near the Macau-Taipa Bridge. Bus nos. 11, 21A, 25, 26A, 28A, 33, MT1, and MT2, as well as the airport bus no. AP1, travel between Macau and Taipa or Cotai; bus nos. 21A, 25, and 26A continue onward to Colôane. The MGTO has a free map with bus routes.

For my hotel recommendations below, I provide a list of buses that travel only from the Macau Ferry Terminal to each individual hotel (most likely you'll be able to take the free shuttle bus), but for restaurants and attractions, I list all the buses from throughout the city that travel to each destination.

Incidentally, you might come across people offering rides in a **pedicab,** a tricycle with seating for two passengers. As late as the early 1980s, this used to be one of the most common forms of transportation in Macau for the locals. But increased traffic and rising affluence have rendered pedicabs almost obsolete, and I suppose they will eventually vanish from the city scene much like the Hong Kong rickshaw. Today, pedicab drivers vie mostly for the tourist dollar, charging about MOP$150 for an hour of sightseeing, but keep in mind that there are many hilly sights you can't see by pedicab. The most popular route is along the Praia Grande Bay around the tip of the peninsula, and back via Rue do Almirante Sérgio. Be sure to settle on the fare, the route, and the length of the journey before climbing in. You'll find them parked outside the Hotel Lisboa and downtown tourist sites.

City Layout

Macau comprises a small peninsula and Taipa and Colôane, two former islands that are now merged due to a massive land reclamation called Cotai and are linked to the mainland by bridges. The peninsula—referred to simply as Macau—is where you'll find the city of Macau, as well as the main ferry terminal and most hotels, shops, and attractions. The Macau Ferry Terminal is located on what is called the Outer Harbour, which faces Taipa and connects to the South China Sea. On the opposite side of the peninsula is the Inner Harbour, which faces China. Although I used to love the Outer Harbour for its dreamy view of boats plying the Pearl River waterway and the tree-shaded Avenida da República, which ran along the waterfront, land reclamation (including new highways, high-rises, the Macau Tower, megacasinos, hotels, and Fisherman's Wharf) has rendered the Outer Harbour a horror zone. I advise fleeing this side of the peninsula as hastily as possible for downtown and the more colorful Inner Harbour. Walking along the Inner Harbour from Avenida Almeida Ribeiro to the Maritime Museum, you will see an unchanged Macau, with decaying buildings, small family businesses, and, occasionally, fish laid out on sidewalks to dry. The side streets on either side of Almeida Ribeiro and running downhill from the ruins of St. Paul's are also gold mines for atmosphere. In the evening, however, you may want to return to the Outer Harbour, where Macau's nightlife district, called the Docks, spreads along the waterfront near the Statue of Kun Iam.

Near the middle of the peninsula is Guia Hill, the highest natural point of Macau. Because of its strategic location, a fort was constructed atop the hill in the 1630s, followed in 1865 by a lighthouse, the first of its kind on the China coast. Also on the grounds of Guia Fortress are a small chapel, a tourist information counter, and a jogging path, complete with exercise stations, circling the top of the hill. Although there's not much to do on Guia Hill, it does provide a good overview of Macau. You can reach it by taking bus nos. 2, 9, 12, 17, 18, 28C, or 32 to Flora Garden and then boarding what must be the world's shortest ropeway to the top of the hill.

Connecting the two harbors is Macau's main road, Avenida Almeida Ribeiro (nicknamed San Ma Lo by locals), remarkably with only a few traffic lights despite nightmarish traffic. About halfway down its length is the attractive Senado Square (Largo do Senado), Macau's main plaza. Lined with colonial-style buildings painted in hues of yellows and pinks, it is paved in a wavy pattern of black and white tiles, which lead from the square through the neighborhood and to the ruins of St. Paul's Church crowning the crest of a hill. On the other side of the square is Leal Senado, Macau's

CAR RACES & FIREWORKS—THE heat IS ON!

Of Macau's several annual events, none are as popular or draw as many crowds as the Macau Grand Prix, held the last weekend in November, and the Macau International Fireworks Display Contest, held every Saturday in September.

The **Macau Grand Prix,** first staged in 1954, features motorcycle and Formula Three races, and attracts drivers from all over the world. Very similar to the famous circuit in Monaco, the 6.2km (3¾-mile) Guia Circuit, which snakes through town near the ferry terminal and is lined with grandstands along the way, includes the winding roads of Guia Hill, hard corners around the waterfront, and the straightaway along the Outer Harbour. Champion drivers can complete a lap in as little as 2 minutes, 20 seconds. Tickets for stands during the 2 practice days cost MOP$50 each day, while race-day tickets range from MOP$200 for standing room on the first day of races to MOP$900 for the best seats the second day. For ticket inquiries, call ✆ **853/2879 62268** or visit www.macau.grandprix.gov.mo. Note that ferry tickets and hotel accommodations in Macau are tight during the races.

Macau's other major competition, the **Macau International Fireworks Display Contest,** has a more universal appeal with its dazzling displays of fireworks spread over Saturday nights in September. Established in 1989, it is now the world's biggest fireworks contest, with more than 100 international teams competing. Displays are judged using criteria such as the height reached by the fireworks, the explosive bang and spread of each firework, color and variety, and the overall choreographic effect of each display. Best viewing spot: along the waterfront near Macau Tower.

most outstanding example of Portuguese colonial architecture. Radiating from Avenida Almeida Ribeiro is old Macau, a fascinating warren of narrow streets, street markets, open-fronted family shops, and a cacophony of sounds, sights, and smells.

Taipa, closest to the mainland and connected by three bridges, has witnessed a construction boom over the past decades, with the addition of high-rise apartments and Macau's airport. In its midst, now enveloped by surrounding development, is the picturesque Taipa Village with its many restaurants. Connected to Taipa by reclaimed land (called Cotai) is Colôane, largely undeveloped and the site of Macau's best beaches. Although Taipa and Colôane are still referred to as individual islands, in reality Cotai is so extensive (5.8 sq. km/more than 2 sq. miles) that the two are now one fused island. Cotai is being developed as a resort and entertainment destination, with the Venetian Macao-Resort-Hotel as the biggest player. Once completed, which is still several years down the road, Cotai will boast more than a half-dozen resorts, convention space, and a light rail that will whisk visitors from the airport through downtown Macau to the Border Gate with China by 2014.

[FastFACTS] MACAU

For more information on Macau, see "Fast Facts: Hong Kong & Macau," in chapter 13.

Area Code The international telephone country code for Macau is 853.

From Hong Kong, dial **001/853** before the number. When dialing an international number from Macau, you must first dial **00,** followed by the country code. However, when calling Hong Kong from Macau, you need only dial the prefix **01.**

Emergencies Dial ✆ **999** for medical emergencies and ✆ **110** or 112 for the police's special 24-hour tourist hot line, all free calls. For the fire department, dial ✆ **853/ 2857 2222;** for nonemergencies you can also reach the police at ✆ **853/2857 3333,** both toll calls. However, you can also just call ✆ **999** and the operator will transfer you to the police or fire departments.

Hospitals If you need to go to a hospital, contact the S. Januario Hospital, Estrada do Visconde de S. Januario (✆ **853/ 2831 3731**), or Kiang Wu Hospital, Estrada Coelho do Amaral (✆ **853/2837 1333**), both with 24-hour emergency service. For nonemergencies, Metro International Clinic, Av. Da Praia Grande 405 (✆ **853/ 2835 5522;** www.metro clinic.com.mo), has English-speaking staff.

Internet The Macao Museum of Art (p. 309) has a Media Library on the ground floor, with 37 computers you can use for free Tuesday to Friday from 2 to 7pm and Saturday and Sunday from 11am to 7pm.

Otherwise, several public libraries offer free Internet facilities, including the Macao Central Library, 89 A–B Av. Conselheiro Ferreira da Almeida (✆ **853/ 2856 7567**), open daily 10am to 8pm (closed holidays). If all you want is to check e-mail, there are two computers at the main MGTO office, Largo do Senado, which you can use free for 30 minutes from 9am to 6pm.

Language Both Portuguese and Chinese are official languages, with Cantonese the most widely spoken language. However, hotel and restaurant staffs usually understand English.

Mail Mailboxes are red in Macau. The main post office (✆ **853/2832 3666**), located in the city center on Largo do Senado, is open Monday through Friday from 9am to 6pm and Saturday from 9am to 1pm. It costs MOP$5 to send a postcard or letter weighing up to 10 grams via airmail to the United States. Macau is famous for its themed series of stamps, including the "Chinese Zodiac" and "Legends and Myths," which you can purchase at philately counters at all post offices.

Telephone For local calls made from public phone booths, it costs MOP$1 for every 5 minutes.

Most local telephone numbers in Macau are eight digits, now that *28* has been added to the beginning of most—but not all—numbers. The additional *28* may not be reflected in old pamphlets listing six-digit phone numbers. Telephones in Macau also offer international direct dialing, though in your hotel room you may have to go through the hotel operator. For calls to the United States, it costs about MOP$10 for every 3 minutes from a public phone. In the busy tourist sections of town there are also phones that accept credit cards. If you think you'll be making a lot of international calls, purchase a prepaid phone card for MOP$50, $100, or $150 at **Edificio CTM,** 25 Rua Pedro Coutinho (✆ **853/1000**), where you can also check whether your own mobile phone will work in Macau and buy a SIM card starting at MOP$50. Otherwise, vending machines at the Macau Ferry Terminal sell CTM prepaid phone cards starting at MOP$100 and SmarTone SIM cards for MOP$120. For international directory assistance, dial ✆ **101;** for local directory inquiries, dial ✆ **181.**

Weather For weather information, call ✆ **853/ 8898 6276** or go online to www.smg.gov.mo.

WHERE TO STAY

Most of Macau's hotels are located in the city of Macau on the peninsula, providing convenient access to most of Macau's sights, though Cotai, reclaimed land between Taipa and Colôane, will eventually overtake it as a slew of hotels open over the next few years. For a more relaxed getaway, seek out the resort hotels on Colôane.

Big spenders will have many new options over the next few years in addition to the hotel recommendations below. Muscling in on the action will be a Sheraton, Shangri-La, St. Regis, and Ritz-Carlton, among others. In all, the Macau government expects the current 19,600 rooms now available to increase over the next decade by some 40,000 more rooms in more than 40 new hotels. For updated information on the rapidly changing hotel scene, contact the Macau Government Tourist Office.

In addition to the room rates given below (which are the same whether you pay in Hong Kong dollars or in patacas), you will also be charged a 10% hotel service charge and a 5% government tax. Except for some of the moderate and inexpensive hotels, most charge the same price for single or double occupancy. However, as in Hong Kong, the prices given below are rack rates; you should be able to find a better rate, especially in the off season or on the Internet. Weekends are busier than weekdays, not to mention more expensive, as many hotels have higher weekend rates. If you plan on visiting Macau during Chinese New Year, Easter, summer holidays (July–Aug), the two major holidays for mainland Chinese (the so-called Golden Week following May 1 and in autumn for up to 10 days from Oct 1), or Macau's Grand Prix in November, you should book in advance and expect to pay top dollar. Otherwise, you shouldn't have difficulty securing a room even on short notice. (A hotel reservations desk is located in the Macau Ferry Terminal, where you can book rooms for free by paying a deposit toward your room rate).

Very Expensive

Altira ★★★   This sophisticated, Australian-owned property occupies the top floors of Taipa's tallest building (at least for now), providing great views of the Macau skyline, especially wonderful at night when many hotels and casinos display dazzling lights. Guest rooms boast floor-to-ceiling windows and are thoughtfully designed into sleeping and living quarters separated by a built-in desk and L-shaped sofa; they feature walk-in closets, 42-inch plasma TVs with Internet capabilities, free beer and soft drinks in the fridge, and spacious bathrooms with double sinks, circular stone-crafted tubs, and LCD TVs built right into the mirror. For diversions, there's a casino with natural lighting, a top-floor lounge with outdoor seating, an interesting array of restaurants, and an indoor infinity pool, complete with sound system so you can listen to music while swimming laps. This is a stylish property, but unless you look out the window, you may forget you're in Macau.

Avenida de Kwong Tung, Taipa, Macau. © **853/2886 8888.** Fax 853/2886 8666. www.altiramacau. com. 216 units. HK$5,380 single or double; from HK$8,880 suite. AE, DC, MC, V. Free shuttle bus from Macau Ferry Terminal or bus no. 28A from Macau Ferry Terminal. **Amenities:** 4 restaurants, including Cantonese restaurant Ying (p. 302); lounge; 2 bars; 24-hr. casino; concierge; health club and spa; 25m indoor pool; room service. *In room:* A/C, TV w/keyboard for Internet access, hair dryer, minibar, MP3 docking station, free Wi-Fi.

Venetian Macao-Resort-Hotel ★ ☺   This is Macau's biggest development, twice as big as its Las Vegas sister property and further distinguished as being the second-largest building in the world. The Venice-themed resort, complete with replicas of famous landmarks like St. Mark's and indoor canals navigated by singing gondoliers, is such a tourist draw (more than 66,000 people pass through its doors daily) its lobby resembles Hong Kong Central Station during rush hour; be sure to pick up a map at the concierge, because you're going to need it. Although its Renaissance-style rooms are billed as suites, most are actually 70-sq.-m. (753-sq.-ft.) split-levels with all the amenities you'd expect and then some, including canopied beds and bathrooms with sit-down vanities, two sinks, and separate tub and shower areas. In addition to the world's largest casino, the property boasts 300-plus specialty shops, a dizzying array of dining options (including a 1,000-seat food court), a 15,000-seat arena with big-name acts, and a Cirque du Soleil theater. Entertainment for kids ranges from an 18-hole minigolf course and children's activity center complete with climbing structures and video games to four outdoor pools, including a wave pool and wading pools. Clearly, this is a destination in itself; some guests check in and go nowhere else.

Estrada da Baia de N. Senhora da Esperanca, Cotai, Macau. ✆ **853/2882 8877.** Fax 853/2882 8822. www.venetianmacao.com. 3,000 units. HK$5,500 single or double; from HK$8,000 suite. AE, DC, MC, V. Free shuttle bus from both ferry terminals. **Amenities:** 19 restaurants; 2 bars; lounge; 24-hr. casino; children's play center; concierge; gym; Jacuzzi; minigolf (fee charged); 4 outdoor pools; room service; spa. *In room:* A/C, TV, fax/scanner/printer, hair dryer, minibar, Wi-Fi (HK$160 for 24 hr.).

Expensive

Four Seasons Hotel Macao, Cotai Strip ★★ 🔥 Upon entering the lobby of this refined property, with its sweeping staircase and opulent Portuguese and Chinese decor, you may feel as if you're walking into a Macau mansion of yore. The rest of the hotel, opened in 2008, doesn't disappoint either, from its bright and airy guest rooms that combine neoclassical elegance with Oriental accents to its lushly landscaped gardens, complete with five outdoor pools and private cabanas equipped with TVs. I also like the spa, where hotel guests can unwind in the hot tub, steam room, and sauna for free. Owned by the Venetian but managed by Four Seasons, the hotel provides direct access to the Venetian complex via a three-story shopping arcade touting top international brands. While not as polished as the Four Seasons Hotel Hong Kong, it is also much cheaper. My only real quibble: long waits at the taxi stand, but if you're like most guests, you're probably here to stay.

Estrada da Baia de N. Senhora da Esperança, Cotai, Macau. ✆ **800/819-5053** in the U.S. and Canada, or 853/2881 8888. Fax 853/2881 8899. www.fourseasons.com/macau. 360 units. HK$2,700–HK$3,800 single or double weekdays, HK$3,100–HK$4,200 Sat–Sun; from HK$4,100 suite. Children 12 and under stay free in parent's room. AE, DC, MC, V. Free shuttle bus from both ferry terminals. **Amenities:** 3 restaurants; bar; lounge; 24-hr. casino; concierge; gym; outdoor Jacuzzi; 5 outdoor pools (including 1 heated pool open year-round and 2 children's pools); room service; spa. *In room:* A/C, TV, hair dryer, minibar, Wi-Fi (MOP$160 for 24 hr.).

Grand Lisboa 🥄 Stanley Ho may have lost his gaming monopoly, but he's back with a vengeance with this 50-story monolith, dominating the Macau landscape with what is said to resemble a lotus flower but to me looks like a marooned starship. The cavernous lobby, too, is meant to put mere mortals in their place, with lots of marble, crystal, and brass, as well as priceless Chinese antiques from Ho's private collection. Facilities run the gamut from Asia's longest buffet spread to a strip show featuring Japanese performers. Guests wishing to recover from the rigors of the casino can do so in comfortable and well-planned rooms and luxurious bathrooms, complete with steam shower rooms (some even have saunas), whirlpool tubs, and two TVs. This flashy hotel was clearly built to impress a high-rolling Chinese market, but those looking for a quaint Macau stay will want to stay elsewhere.

Avenida de Lisboa, Macau. © **853/2828 3838.** Fax 853/2871 6360. www.grandlisboa.com. 431 units. HK$3,000–HK$4,200 single or double; HK$4,200–HK$5,000 executive floors; from HK$6,800 suite. Children 12 and under stay free in parent's room. AE, DC, MC, V. Free shuttle bus from Macau Ferry Terminal or bus no. 3, 3A, 10, 10A, 10B, 12, 28A, or 32. **Amenities:** 7 restaurants; bar; 2 nightclubs; 24-hr. casino; concierge; executive-level rooms; gym; outdoor heated pool (open year-round); room service; spa. *In room:* A/C, TV, hair dryer, minibar, free Wi-Fi.

MGM Grand ★★★ Of all the big casino-hotels to open the past couple years, this collaboration between MGM Mirage and Pansy Ho (daughter of Stanley Ho) is probably my favorite. The otherwise spartan lobby features glass art by Dale Chihuly—clearly all it needs—but the real attention grabber lies beyond, in a huge glass-ceilinged conservatory modeled after a Portuguese square, complete with a replica facade of a Lisbon train station, restaurants that spill onto terraces, fountains, and trees. Pluses include top-notch dining options, champagne and vodka/caviar bars, a classy shopping center, extensive recreational facilities, and smart-looking rooms that have all the expected features. This hotel is much more than its casino, making it a good choice even if you don't care to hit the gaming tables.

Avenida Dr. Sun Yat-sen, Nape, Macau. © **853/8802 8888.** Fax 853/8802 3333. www.mgmgrand macau.com. 600 units. HK$3,680–HK$4,370 single or double. AE, DC, MC, V. Free shuttle bus from Macau Ferry Terminal or bus no. 3A or 12. **Amenities:** 5 restaurants, including Aux Beaux Arts (p. 301); 4 bars; lounge; 24-hr. casino; concierge; gym; outdoor pool/children's pool; room service; spa. *In room:* A/C, TV, hair dryer, minibar, Wi-Fi (MOP$160 for 24 hr.).

Pousada de São Tiago ★★ 🏨 Built around the ruins of the Portuguese Fortress da Barra (dating from 1629), this intimate inn on the tip of the peninsula is perfect for travelers looking for a romantic getaway. The entrance is dramatic: A flight of stone stairs leads through a cavelike tunnel that was once part of the fort (there is no elevator). Once inside, guests are treated to the hospitality of a Portuguese inn, with a delightful Spanish restaurant complete with a terrace shaded by banyan trees, a great place to while away an afternoon, as is the nearby outdoor swimming pool. Rooms, however, all of which are two-room suites, don't live up to expectations (the crocodile-skin-covered desk can only be described as odd), but most have balconies facing the Inner Harbour and all have spa-like bathrooms with steam-room showers, Jacuzzi tubs, and bidets. Although lacking the resort facilities or attentive staff of other deluxe hotels, this is a slice of life in old Macau. The Maritime Museum and A-Ma Temple are nearby; a stroll through historic neighborhoods brings you to the city center in about a half-hour.

Avenida da República, Fortaleza de São Tiago da Barra, Macau. © **853/2837 8111.** Fax 853/2855 2170. www.saotiago.com.mo. 12 units. HK$3,000 single or double weekdays, HK$3,600 Sat–Sun. AE, DC, MC, V. Free shuttle bus (on request) or bus no. 28B from Macau Ferry Terminal. **Amenities:** Restaurant; lounge; outdoor pool; room service. *In room:* A/C, TV/DVD w/DVDs, hair dryer, minibar, free Wi-Fi.

Wynn Macau ★ Opened in 2006 as Macau's first Las Vegas–style casino resort, the Wynn is much more low key than the Grand Lisboa across the street but lacks the design pizzazz of the MGM. Still, it's free attractions really wow the crowds: Performance Lake with its synchronized dancing fountains, colored lights, and music (chosen by Wynn himself); and the Tree of Prosperity, which rises out of the floor to meet a descending chandelier. The Wynn is best known, however, for its upscale shopping esplanade—a Who's Who of designer names—and its landscaped courtyard pool, visible from the small lobby through a glass wall and from many public areas, making it an exhibitionist's dream. Rooms have views toward the sea (that rival MGM) or city lights (better), and large bathrooms sport sit-down vanities separating the double sinks. This is a solid choice, but to keep up with competition, Wynn opened an adjacent all-suite boutique tower, Encore, in 2010 (same phone number and website as below).

Rua Cidade de Sintra, Nape, Macau. ✆ 853/2888 9966. Fax 853/2832 9966. www.wynnmacau.com. 600 units. HK$3,000–HK$3,700 single or double; from HK$7,800 suite. Children 12 and under stay free in parent's room. AE, DC, MC, V. Free shuttle bus from Macau Ferry Terminal or bus no. 3, 3A, 10, 10A, 10B, 12, 28A, 28B, 28BX, or 32. **Amenities:** 6 restaurants, including Il Teatro (p. 301); bar; lounge; 24-hr casino; concierge; gym (fee charged); outdoor pool; room service; spa. *In room:* A/C, TV, hair dryer, minibar, MP3 docking station, Wi-Fi (MOP$160 for 24 hr.).

Moderate

Grand Hyatt Macau ★ ☺ Located in the City of Dreams, an aquatic-themed entertainment resort that rivals the nearby Venetian complex, this new property has set its sights on being the leading MICE (meetings, incentives, conferences, and exhibitions) destination in the region. As such, it's more subdued than neighboring Hard Rock Hotel (below), more down to earth than the Venetian, and less pretentious than the Four Seasons. Large contemporary rooms, decorated with photographs of local heritage sites, provide all the creature comforts and then some, including TV hookups for your iPod, camera, and laptop. A rarity in Macau these days, the Grand Hyatt doesn't have its own casino (though there is one in City of Dreams), but it does offer diversions for adults and children alike, including a 40m outdoor pool and a toddler pool, plus access to City of Dreams attractions: Kid's City (MOP$90 for 2 hr.), complete with climbers, slides, video games, and other activities; the free "Dragon's Treasure" 10-minute show; and the high-powered "House of Dancing Water," which combines water with acrobats, dancers, and musicians (see p. 314 for ticket info).

City of Dreams, Estrada do Istmo, Cotai, Macau. ✆ 853/8868 1234. Fax 853/8867 1234. www.macau. grand.hyatt.com. 791 units. HK$1,788–HK$1,988 single or double; HK$2,188–HK$2,388 club floors; from HK$6,888 suite. Children 12 and under stay free in parent's room. AE, DC, MC, V. Free shuttle bus from both ferry terminals. **Amenities:** 2 restaurants; bar; lounge; free shuttle bus to downtown Macau; concierge; executive-level rooms; fitness center; access to Kid's City in City of Dreams for 12 and under (MOP$90 for 2 hr.); 2 pools, including outdoor heated pool open year-round and toddler pool; room service; spa. *In room:* A/C, TV, hair dryer, minibar, MP3 docking station, free Wi-Fi.

Hard Rock Hotel ☺ You gotta love rock music to stay here, because it's broadcast almost everywhere—in the elevators, lobby, poolside, even in the casino. This is a hotel with attitude, where bellboys are likely to be decked out in mock leather jackets and Converse sneakers; a quote from the Doors, "Hello, I love you. Won't you tell me your name?" hangs above reception. Memorabilia once belonging to Michael Jackson, Elton John, and others decorates the lobby and public areas. Rooms, too, are fun and edgy, decorated with retro furnishings in bold colors and outfitted with home theater systems and complimentary music-streaming channels. Combined with the entertainment options in City of Dreams, this is a teenager's dream come true, but for my money I'd prefer a hotel with local character.

City of Dreams, Estrada do Istmo, Macau. ✆ 853/8868 3338. Fax 853/8867 3338. www.hardrock hotelmacau.com. 326 units. HK$2,088–HK$2,188 single or double; from HK$4,300 suite. AE, DC, MC, V. Free shuttle bus from both ferry terminals. **Amenities:** Restaurant; 3 bars; 24-hr. casino; gym; access to Kid's City in City of Dreams for 12 and under (MOP$90 for 2 hr.); outdoor pool w/artificial sand beach and volleyball net; room service; spa. *In room:* A/C, TV, hair dryer, minibar, MP3 docking station, free Wi-Fi.

Hotel Lisboa ★ 🏨

Although overshadowed by newer properties, the Hotel Lisboa, not to be confused with the Grand Lisboa across the street, remains in a class by itself. Built in 1969, it's a Chinese version of '60s Las Vegas on acid: big, flashy (check out the peacocklike decoration on its roof), and with a bewildering array of facilities. I always get lost in this hotel. The property has numerous restaurants (even the front-desk staff is unsure how many), shops, display cases of owner Stanley Ho's private art collection, and nighttime diversions, including, you might say, the countless women roaming the shopping complex's halls, hoping for some short-term business from a lucky gambler. Ah, the Lisboa. Guest rooms are located in an older east wing and a 1993 tower, the latter of which offers the best—and priciest—harbor views, especially Royal Tower deluxe rooms with either traditional Chinese architecture or Western decor. Otherwise, small standard rooms have some recommendable perks, including Jacuzzi tubs, free in-house movies, and free drinks in the fridge. In short, this is a unique, retro choice in the thick of it (though don't expect any personal time with the busy staff). Buses to the outlying islands stop nearby, and downtown Macau is less than a 5-minute walk away.

2-4 Av. de Lisboa, Macau. ✆ 853/2888 3888. Fax 853/2888 3838. www.hotelisboa.com. 927 units. HK$1,850–HK$3,400 single or double; from HK$4,400 suite. Children 12 and under stay free in parent's room. AE, DC, MC, V. Free shuttle bus from Macau Ferry Terminal or bus no. 3, 3A, 10, 10A, 10B, 12, 28A, or 32. **Amenities:** 18 restaurants, including Robuchon a Galera (p. 301); bar; lounge; 24-hr. casino; room service. *In room:* A/C, TV, hair dryer, free Internet, minibar.

Rocks Hotel ★ 🏨

Macau's fabricated village known as Fisherman's Wharf is pure fantasy, so a Victorian-style boutique hotel doesn't seem out of place here. In fact, because it's located on a spit of land with water on most sides, it has a breezy, resort-like feel, far from Macau's density just a short walk away. All the rooms take advantage of this location with balconies (the priciest directly face the sea), and, keeping in character, boast claw-foot tubs and period furniture. The rooftop lounge is nice and the ground-floor restaurant, specializing in seafood and Australian beef, has an outdoor terrace. Those searching for a relaxed, convenient 1-night getaway from Hong Kong can find refuge here, but for longer stays the Westin offers more facilities at a slightly higher price.

Fisherman's Wharf, Macau. ✆ 853/2878 2782. Fax 853/2872 8800. www.rockshotel.com.mo. 72 units. HK$1,880–HK$2,580 single or double; from HK$4,080 suite. Children 11 and under stay free in parent's room. AE, DC, MC, V. Free shuttle from Macau Ferry Terminal or a 10-min. walk. **Amenities:** Restaurant; lounge; babysitting; small gym; room service. *In room:* A/C, TV, hair dryer, minibar, free Wi-Fi.

Sintra

With a prime spot in the heart of Macau, the Sintra, under the Lisboa group, is within easy walking distance of Avenida de Almeida Ribeiro (Macau's main street) and Senado Square, the heart of the city. Built in 1975 but completely overhauled in the 1990s, it looks good for its age and the staff is friendly. Though the standard rooms are large, most face another building. Even roomier are the higher-priced rooms occupying higher floors; individual bookings (not through a travel agency) are often upgraded to one of these rooms if space is available. Of note for night owls is the hotel's coffee shop, open 24 hours and offering free Wi-Fi to those ordering a meal.

Av. de D. João IV, Macau. ✆ 853/2871 0111. Fax 853/2851 0527. www.hotelsintra.com. 240 units. HK$1,480–HK$2,480 single or double; HK$2,280–HK$3,280 executive floor; from HK$3,680 suite.

Children 12 and under stay free in parent's room. AE, DC, MC, V. Free shuttle bus from Macau Ferry Terminal or bus no. 3, 3A, 10A, from the ferry terminal. **Amenities:** 2 restaurants; executive-level rooms; room service. *In room:* A/C, TV, hair dryer, Internet (MOP$120 for 24 hr.), minibar.

Westin Resort Macau ★★★ ☺   Located on Colôane Island near Hac Sa Beach (with its popular Fernando's restaurant, p. 303), this Mediterranean-style hotel is a bit far from the center of town (about a 20-min. ride from the Macau Ferry Terminal via the hotel's complimentary shuttle bus, with departures every 30 min.), but management is betting that most prospective guests are those who want to get away from it all. It offers beautifully landscaped grounds, indoor and outdoor swimming pools, a health club with free yoga and aerobics classes, Macau's first golf course (accessed from the resort's top floor), and facilities geared toward families, including a child-care center and Westin Kids' Club with a multitude of activities. Each of the eight-storied hotel's very spacious, vibrantly colored rooms faces either the South China Sea or the beach (sea views are better, with higher floors costing more) and features glass sliding doors opening onto—I love this—a huge 25-sq.-m (269-sq.-ft.) private terrace with plants and patio furniture.

1918 Estrada de Hac Sa, Colôane, Macau. ✆ **800/WESTIN-1** (937-8461) in the U.S. and Canada, or 853/2887 1111. Fax 853/28871122. www.westin.com/macau. 208 units. HK$2,200–HK$2,700 single or double; from HK$5,000 suite. Children 18 and under stay free in parent's room. AE, DC, MC, V. Free shuttle bus from Macau Ferry Terminal. **Amenities:** 3 restaurants; bar; lounge; babysitting; basketball court; free shuttle bus to City of Dreams and Taipa; children's day-care center (MOP$40 per hr.) and Westin's Kids Club (ages 3–12); concierge; croquet; 18-hole golf course; health club and spa; indoor and outdoor Jacuzzi; jogging lanes; outdoor swimming pool year-round; outdoor children's pool; indoor pool; room service; 8 outdoor floodlit tennis courts. *In room:* A/C, TV, hair dryer, Internet (MOP$120 for 24 hr.), minibar.

Inexpensive

Best Western Hotel Sun Sun ★★ 🎁   With a charming location near the Inner Harbour, across from a small square complete with fountain and exercise equipment, this Best Western offers nondescript motel-like rooms with tired decor and is often abuzz with tour groups. However, the highest-priced rooms have views of the Inner Harbour with its boat traffic, and executive floor rooms have been redone in modern chic. Although pricey, a beach package is available for HK$550, which provides transportation to Colôane beaches, towels, chairs, and drinks. What I love most about this hotel is its location in Old Macau, making it highly recommendable despite its modest rooms.

14-16 Praca Ponte E. Horta, Macau. ✆ **800/780-7234** in the U.S. or Canada, or 853/2893 9393. Fax 853/2893 8822. www.bestwestern.com. 175 units. HK$1,200–HK$1,650 single or double; HK$1,800 executive floor; HK$2,680 suite. 1 child 12 and under stays free in parent's room. AE, DC, MC, V. Bus: 3A, 10, or 10A from Macau Ferry Terminal. **Amenities:** Bar; executive-level rooms; room service. *In room:* A/C, TV w/DVD player and rental DVDs, hair dryer, minibar, free Wi-Fi.

East Asia Hotel   This is one of Macau's better choices for backpacker accommodations in the heart of the city (I've seen some pretty grim hotels and guesthouses in this category), located near the Inner Harbour just off Avenida de Almeida Ribeiro in an area filled with local color and atmosphere. Some of that local color extends to a room just off the lobby where I sometimes see a bevy of beauties awaiting phone calls or customers, which may admittedly be a bit too atmospheric for some (maybe that's why the hotel brochure promises that "your nights with us will be the most enjoyable"). Still, the 70-some-year-old hotel features a polite staff and large, perfectly fine rooms with clean, tiled bathrooms and complimentary Chinese tea. The least expensive rooms are windowless and a bit depressing. Best are rooms on top floors offering good views, including some of the Inner Harbour.

1 Rua da Madeira (corner of Rua Cinco de Outubro), Macau. © **853/2892 2433.** Fax 853/2892 2431. 98 units. HK$330–HK$400 single; HK$580 twin. MC, V. Bus: 3, 3A, 10, or 10A from the Macau Ferry Terminal. **Amenities:** Restaurant. *In room:* A/C, TV.

Holiday Inn Macau   Situated in a drab area of high-rises between the Macau Ferry Terminal and downtown (only a 10-min. walk away), this well-known chain will be familiar to North American guests, except like most moderately priced Macau hotels, it caters largely to gamblers and tour groups, especially because of its on-site casino. Rooms, all with two double beds or queen- or king-size beds, are simple and unimaginative and are tiny compared to their U.S. counterparts. Steer clear of the standard rooms, which are on lower floors and face another building. Splurge instead on a renovated deluxe room on a higher floor, with duvet-covered beds, ergonomic chairs at long desks, and the popular glass partition between the bedroom and bathroom. Like most Macau hotels, rates depend on availability and day of the week—the cheapest rate listed below is for Sunday through Thursday.

82–86 Rua de Pequim, Macau. © **800/465-4329** in the U.S. and Canada, or 853/2878 3333. Fax 853/2878 2321. www.macau.holiday-inn.com. 323 units. HK$850–HK$1,980 single or double; HK$1,580–HK$2,080 executive floor. Children 11 and under stay free in parent's room. AE, DC, MC, V. Free shuttle bus from Macau Ferry Terminal or bus no. 3, 3A, 10, 10A, 10B, 28A, 28B, or 32. **Amenities:** Restaurant; bar; babysitting; 24-hr. casino; executive-level rooms; exercise room; small indoor pool; room service; spa. *In room:* A/C, TV, hair dryer, minibar, Wi-Fi (MOP$160 for 24 hr.).

Hotel Guia ★   Located on the slope of Guia Hill, below Guia Fortress and Lighthouse (with a park popular with joggers) and surrounded by traditional colonial architecture, this is one of Macau's more secluded inexpensively priced hotels. It's small with a friendly staff, though tour groups from the mainland can disrupt the tranquillity and I don't even want to know what goes on in PlayMate's nightclub. Spotless rooms range from those facing inland to those with little balconies facing the distant sea. By far the best are those with a view of Guia Lighthouse and the harbor in the background—request a room with a balcony on the highest (fifth) floor, where you also have a ringside view of the annual Grand Prix. The main drawback is that it's a bit far from the action, but a free shuttle bus makes runs every half-hour or so to and from the Macau Ferry Terminal, where you can then catch a bus to downtown Macau.

1–5 Estrada do Engenheiro Trigo, Macau. © **853/2851 3888.** Fax 853/2855 9822. www.hotelguia macau.com. 90 units. HK$650–HK$1,100 single or double; from HK$1,680 suite. AE, DC, MC, V. Free shuttle bus from Macau Ferry Terminal. **Amenities:** Restaurant; nightclub/disco; room service. *In room:* A/C, TV, hair dryer, minibar.

Hotel Kou Va 🍴   Despite its name, this seems more like a guesthouse, and while many guesthouses around the Inner Harbour, Macau's oldest district, are of very low standard, this one on picturesque Rua da Felicidade is better than most, though staff can be gruff. Some of the rooms have windows, others don't, but all have the basics including tiled bathrooms. If all you're looking for is cheap accommodations in the heart of Macau's most colorful old town, this fits the bill.

71 Rua da Felicidade, Macau. © **853/2893 0755.** 27 units. HK$300–HK$350 single; HK$350–HK$450 double. No credit cards. Bus: 3, 3A, 10, or 10A from Macau Ferry Terminal. *In room:* A/C, TV.

Pousada de Colôane ★★★ 🏨 This small, family-owned gem, perched on a hill above Colôane's Cheoc Van Beach with views of the sea, is a great place for couples and families in search of a reasonably priced isolated retreat. Opened in 1977 as Macau's first beach property, it's a relaxing, rather rustic place (no elevator), with modestly furnished rooms, nothing fancy but all with Portuguese-style furnishings, Jacuzzi bathtubs, two sinks, and balconies facing the sea and a popular public beach. For some visitors it awakens memories of beachside vacations from childhood. The outdoor terrace is perfect for relaxing with a view of the sunset and a drink; the inn's Portuguese restaurant is especially popular for its Sunday lunch buffet offered during peak season. The main drawback is one of access, but buses pass by frequently; when arriving at the Macau Ferry Terminal, you're best off traveling to the hotel by taxi (fares average MOP$115).

Praia de Cheoc Van, Colôane, Macau. © **853/2888 2143.** Fax 853/2888 2251. www.hotelpcoloane.com. mo. 30 units. HK$750–HK$880 single or double. MC, V. Bus: 21A, 25, or 26A from Lisboa Hotel (tell the bus driver you want to get off at the hotel). **Amenities:** Restaurant; bar; lobby computer w/free Internet; outdoor pool; children's pool. *In room:* A/C, TV, hair dryer, minibar, free Wi-Fi (superior rooms only).

Pousada de Mong-Há ★★ 🏨 You're performing a good deed by staying here, since this hostelry is run by students attending the adjacent Institute for Tourism Studies, but you're by no means sacrificing comfort. Located above the old town on a hill once dominated by a fortress, this *pousada* offers simple but traditionally decorated rooms (all nonsmoking), with carved wooden headboards and all the usual amenities. After breakfast (included in hotel rates, which do not have a tax or service charge since this is a government-owned facility), be sure to roam through campus grounds with an herb garden used by the Institute's student-run restaurant (p. 306) and the adjacent park on old fortress grounds. Although a bit far from the usual action (you should take a taxi from the ferry terminal since it's an uphill climb from the bus stop), Kun Iam Temple and Red Market are within walking distance. This is surely one of Macau's best-kept secrets.

Instituto de Formacao Turistica, Colina de Mong-Há, Macau. © **853/2851 5222.** Fax 853/2855 6925. www.ift.edu.mo/pousada. 20 units. HK$480–HK$680 single; HK$640–HK$960 double; HK$960–HK$1,360 suite. Long-staying packages available. Rates include breakfast. AE, MC, V. Bus: 12 from the Macau Ferry Terminal. **Amenities:** Restaurant (p. 306); bar; gym. *In room:* A/C, TV, hair dryer, minibar, free Wi-Fi.

WHERE TO DINE

As a former trading center for spices and a melting pot for Portuguese and Chinese cultures, it's little wonder that Macau developed its own very fine cuisine. The Portuguese settlers brought with them sweet potatoes, peanuts, and kidney beans from Brazil, piri-piri peppers from Africa, chilies from India, and codfish, coffee, and vegetables from Europe. In turn, the Chinese introduced rhubarb, celery, ginger, soy sauce, lychees, and other Asian foods. The result is Macanese cuisine. One of the most popular dishes is African chicken, grilled or baked with chilies and piri-piri peppers, but I also love *minchi*, a Macanese dish of minced beef prepared with fried potatoes, onion, and garlic. Other favorites include Portuguese chicken (chicken baked with potatoes, tomatoes, olive oil, curry, coconut, saffron, and black olives), Macau sole, *caldeirada* (seafood stew), spicy giant shrimp, baked quail and pigeon, curried crab, and *feijoada* (a Brazilian stew of pork, black beans, cabbage, and spicy sausage). Several restaurants also specialize in traditional Portuguese cuisine—don't pass up the Portuguese sausage, clams, green vegetable soup, or *bacalhau* (codfish, served hundreds of ways). Of course, Macau also has countless Chinese restaurants, and in recent years fine dining has burst onto the scene in the form of mostly Italian, French, and Japanese restaurants, thanks largely to the gaming industry (which supplements the high costs of running a restaurant with casino profits). Many restaurants have extensive wine cellars, but for a bargain, try one of the inexpensive Portuguese imports. Most famous is the *vinho verde,* a young wine served very cold that is refreshing on hot summer days and goes great with seafood. For a tasty snack, be sure to sample a Portuguese egg tart, yolk-filled pastries topped with caramelized sugar.

Restaurants will add a 10% service charge to your bill, but as you'll discover, even the "moderate" restaurants in Macau would be a bargain in Hong Kong.

Very Expensive

Robuchon a Galera ★★ FRENCH   Despite stiff competition, this remains one of Macau's most exclusive—and expensive—restaurants, with an elegant decor and a knowledgeable staff. Although it seemed odd when renowned French chef Joel Robuchon chose Macau in 2001 to showcase his talents, the subsequent explosion of resort casinos in this Asian boomtown now makes Robuchon's choice almost prophetic. Robuchon flies in four times a year to supervise the seasonal menu, which in the past has included such offerings as pan-seared Kagoshima beef with green asparagus stuffed with black truffles and soufflés potatoes; or crispy papillotes of scampi with basil, poached in saffron bouillon with aromatic garnishes, scampi ravioli, and cabbage and truffle. Beautifully presented, main courses sometimes fall short, but other times they're a foodie's dream. The cheese, dessert, and after-dinner drink trolleys are hard to pass up, and the wine list is probably the best in town. Save money by coming for the set lunch, unless, of course, you strike it big at the casino.

Hotel Lisboa, 3rd floor of Lisboa Tower, Avenida da Amizade. ✆ **853/8803 7878.** www.hotelisboa.com. Reservations recommended. Main dishes MOP$460–MOP$1,080; 10- to 12-course tasting menus MOP$1,488–MOP$2,088; set lunch MOP$398–MOP$638. AE, DC, MC, V. Daily noon–2:30pm and 6:30–10:30pm (last order). Bus: 3, 3A, 8, 10, 10A, 10B, 12, 21A, 25, 26A, 28A, 32, 33, or AP1.

Expensive

Aux Beaux Arts ★★ FRENCH   Sadly, Macau never really developed a sidewalk cafe culture, but you can pretend otherwise while dining on the terrace here, which overlooks MGM Grand's faux Lisbon square and is protected from the elements by a glass ceiling. A quartet serenades from a corner of the square in the evenings, but I think the interior of the restaurant is more romantic, done up in 1930s Art Deco brasserie style. Start with the seafood platter, which includes lobster, prawns, mussels, and oysters served on a bed of ice, followed by the wild lobster bisque or traditional French onion soup and a main course like grilled salmon with béarnaise sauce or U.S. prime beef tenderloin with black pepper and cognac sauce. Before or after dinner, stop by the dramatically lit ABA Bar or, for caviar and vodka, the Russian Room.

MGM Grand, Av. Dr. Sun Yat-sen, Nape. ✆ **853/8802 8888.** www.mgmgrandmacau.com. Reservations recommended. Main courses MOP$160–MOP$440. AE, DC, MC, V. Tues–Fri 6pm–midnight; Sat–Sun and holidays 11am–midnight. Bus: 1A, 3A, 8, 10A, or 17.

Il Teatro ★★★ SOUTHERN ITALIAN   This restaurant lives up to its name, with theatrics supplied by an open kitchen and dancing fountains in the Wynn Macau's outdoor Performance Lake. Although there are three balcony tables bringing you closer to the choreographed action on the lake (which include balls of fire), you'll get more bang for your buck if you book one of the comfy, elegant ringside tables inside. Everything is wonderful, from the handmade pastas and gourmet pizzas to artichoke-crusted black cod or prime beef tenderloin with porcini cannelloni. The dessert sampler is a great choice for those who want it all.

Wynn Macau, Rua Cidade de Sintra, Nape. © **853/8986 3663.** www.wynnmacau.com. Reservations required. Pizza and pasta MOP$118-MOP$218; main courses MOP$288-MOP$448. AE, DC, MC, V. Tues-Sun 5:30-11:30pm. Bus: 1A, 3, 3A, 8, 10A, 12, 28A, 28C, or 32.

Ying ★★ CANTONESE You don't have to spend a fortune to enjoy great Chinese food in Macau, but in case you want to this is one of the best. Perched on the 11th floor of one of Macau's most expensive hotels, with views toward the Macau skyline, this small venue caters to the well-heeled with a menu that emphasizes healthy and organic foods in the creation of both modern and traditional interpretations of Canton-ese cuisine. Past dishes I've enjoyed are the stir-fried Wagyu beef escalope with green apple in brown sauce; traditional oven-baked sesame chicken; and braised pumpkin with wild mushroom. Or, come for lunch, when in addition to pricey set meals there's an a la carte menu for dim sum and the views of Macau are at their best (reflection from the restaurant's interior on glass windows detract from evening views).

Altira, Avenida de Kwong Tung, Taipa. © **853/2886 8868.** www.altiramacau.com. Reservations recom-mended. Main dishes MOP$88-MOP$168; set lunches MOP$450-MOP$750; dim sum MOP$22-MOP$38. AE, DC, MC, V. Daily 11:30am-4pm and 6-10:30pm. Bus: 11, 21A, 25, 26A, 28A, 33, MT1, or MT2.

Moderate

A Lorcha ★ PORTUGUESE Just a stone's throw from the Maritime Museum and A-Ma Temple, this is the best choice if you find yourself hungering for Portu-guese food in the area. Look for its whitewashed walls, an architectural feature repeated in the interior with an arched, low ceiling. Casual yet often filled with busi-nesspeople, it offers *feijoada*, codfish in a cream sauce, chargrilled king prawns, clams prepared in garlic and olive oil, grilled pork chops, baked minced beef potato pie, and other traditional dishes that are consistently good. Its name, by the way, refers to a type of Portuguese boat, which is appropriate for a colony founded by seafaring explorers.

289 Rua do Almirante Sérgio. © **853/2831 3193.** Reservations recommended. Main courses MOP$90-MOP$165. AE, DC, MC, V. Wed-Mon 12:30-3pm and 6:30-11pm. Bus: 2, 5, 9, 10, 10A, 11, 18, 21A, or 28B.

António ★ ⬛ PORTUGUESE People in the know head to this small, tradition-ally styled restaurant in Taipa Village, done up with blue-and-white-tiled walls and under the direction of chef António Coelho. Because it seats only 24 diners on the main floor and another dozen on the rooftop terrace, reservations are a must. You might want to start with the roasted homemade Portuguese sausage, assorted Portu-guese cheeses, Portuguese green cabbage soup, or the yummy stuffed crab meat, followed by African chicken, black pork imported from Portugal, monkfish and prawns served with rice in a ceramic pot, or tenderloin steak Portuguese style (fried with garlic and white wine) and served with Portuguese smoked ham, fried egg, pota-toes, and pickles. You'll want to linger here, inspired, perhaps, by the Spumanti sparkling wine or chef António's engaging personality.

3 Rua dos Negociantes, Taipa Village. © **853/2899 9998.** www.antoniomacau.com. Reservations required. Main courses MOP$150-MOP$250. AE, MC, V. Mon-Fri noon-3pm and 6-10:30pm (last order); Sat-Sun noon-10:30pm. Bus: 11, 15, 28A, or 33.

A Petisqueira PORTUGUESE A small, unpretentious restaurant just off Taipa Village's main road, on the corner of Rua de S. João and Rua das Virtudes, A Petisqueira is popular with the locals for its typical Portuguese fare, including charcoal grilled, roasted, or boiled codfish; grilled sole with lemon-butter sauce; grilled king prawns; paella; fried tenderloin steak Portuguese style; grilled sea bass; and curried crab. The fresh cheeses are especially recommended. Of course, everything tastes better with Portuguese wine.

15 Rua de S. João, Taipa Village. © **853/2882 5354.** Main courses MOP$100–MOP$185. AE, MC, V. Tues–Fri noon–2:15pm; Sat–Sun and holidays noon–2:45pm; Tues–Sun 7–10:15pm. Bus: 11, 15, 28A, or 33.

Clube Militar de Macau ★★ 📖 MACANESE/PORTUGUESE This is certainly one of Macau's most atmospheric and historic dining halls, located in the Macau Military Club, built in 1870 as a private cultural and recreation center for military officers. Painted bright pink, this striking colonial building behind the Hotel Lisboa opened its restaurant to the public in 1995, offering nonmembers the chance to dine in style in its old-fashioned dining hall with its tall ceilings, whirring ceiling fans, arched windows, wood floor, and displays of antique Chinese dishware. As for the food, it's best to stick to the classics, such as roasted codfish in a crust of olives and herbs, chickpeas purée, and emulsion of roasted tomato. The lunch buffet, which gives a choice of a main course along with a buffet for appetizers and desserts, is a downtown favorite, and the list of Portuguese wines is among the best in town.

795 Av. da Praia Grande. © **853/2871 4009.** www.clubemilitardemacau.net. Reservations recommended for lunch. Main courses MOP$123–MOP$198; set lunch or dinner MOP$128. AE, DC, MC, V. Daily noon–3pm and 7–11pm. Bus: 3, 3A, 8, 9, 10, 10A, 10B, 11, 26A, 28A, 28B, 32, or 33.

Fat Siu Lau MACANESE This is Macau's oldest restaurant (dating from 1903), but its three floors of dining have been renovated in upbeat modern Art Deco. Its exterior matches all the other storefronts on this renovated street—whitewashed walls and red shutters and doors—which used to serve as Macau's red-light district. The Macanese cuisine here includes roast pigeon marinated according to a 108-year-old secret recipe; spicy African chicken; curried crab; garoupa stewed with tomatoes, bell pepper, onion, and potatoes; and grilled king prawns. Branches are located at the Docks nightlife district, Avenida Dr. Sun Yat-sen (© **853/2872 2922**), open daily noon to 3pm and 6 to 11:30pm; and Rua do Regedor 181–185, Taipa Village (© **853/2882 5257**), open daily noon to 10:30pm.

64 Rua da Felicidade. © **853/2857 3580.** www.fatsiulau.com.mo. Main courses MOP$85–MOP$180. MC, V. Daily noon–11pm. Bus: 2, 3, 3A, 5, 10, 10A, 11, 18, 21A, 26A, or 33.

Fernando's ★★ 📖 PORTUGUESE Although outwardly there is nothing to distinguish this from the other shacks on Hac Sa Beach (it's the brick one closest to the beach, below the vines), Fernando's, with a pavilion out back and an adjacent open-air bar with outdoor seating, is *the* place to dine on the beach and a destination in itself. Everyone knows Fernando's, and even the lack of air-conditioning (that goes for the kitchen as well) doesn't seem to deter the faithful who pilgrimage here, especially on weekends, when you'll probably have to wait for a table. Outspoken Fernando is usually on hand, holding court. The menu is strictly Portuguese and includes Portuguese chorizo, clams, crabs, fried prawns, codfish, *feijoada,* chargrilled chicken, pork ribs, suckling pig, stewed beef, and salads. The bread all comes from the restaurant's own bakery, and the vegetables are grown on the restaurant's own garden plot across the border in China. Only Portuguese wine is served, stocked on a shelf for customer perusal (there is no wine list). It's all very informal, and not for those who demand pristine conditions.

9 Praia de Hac Sa, Colôane. © **853/2888 2531.** Reservations not accepted. Main courses MOP$80-MOP$180. No credit cards. Daily noon-9:30pm (last order). Bus: 15, 21A, 25, or 26A.

La Bonne Heure ★ 🍴 FRENCH With the exception of Portuguese restaurants, most of Macau's Western eateries are ensconced in casino/hotel complexes, so it's nice to find an independent establishment centrally located in Old Macau. Near Senado Square, on a small side street catty-corner from S. Domingos Church, La Bonne Heure offers a cozy ambience, with low, arched ceilings and candles on the tables of its split-level dining area. The food, prepared by a former chef at Robuchon, eschews fancy preparations in favor of simple yet delicious creations, such as crunchy roasted lamb in sesame crust served with mashed potatoes, or duck's leg confit with braised cabbage and sherry vinegar dressing. This hideaway is a great place for a romantic dinner or a relaxed evening with friends.

12AB Travessa de S. Domingos. © **853/2833 1209.** Reservations recommended. Main courses MOP$98-MOP$298. AE, MC, V. Mon-Sat noon-3pm; Mon-Thurs 6-10pm; Fri-Sat 6-11pm. Bus: 2, 3, 3A, 5, 10, 10A, 11, 18, 21A, 26A, or 33.

O Porto Interior ★ 🍴 MACANESE/PORTUGUESE Located on the Inner Harbour not far from the Maritime Museum and A-Ma Temple, this comfortable, classy restaurant decorated in colonial style with woodwork carvings, a brick floor, and decorative bird cages offers surprisingly inexpensive fare. You might start with the codfish cakes, stuffed crab Macau style, or seafood supreme soup, served inside a bread bowl. Main dishes range from Macau curry crab and Macanese garlic king prawns to African chicken, black pepper steak, and *minchi*.

259B Rua do Almirante Sérgio. © **853/2896 7770.** Main courses MOP$80-MOP$158. AE, DC, MC, V. Daily noon-11pm. Bus: 2, 5, 9, 10, 10A, 11, 18, 21A, or 28B.

Restaurante Espaco Lisboa ★★ 🍴 PORTUGUESE This tiny two-story restaurant, located in a traditional Chinese village house just off the main square of Colôane Village (Vila Colôane), is popular with the locals for its country-style Portuguese food. It offers so many great choices it's hard to know where to start. Fried codfish cakes, an assortment of Portuguese sausages, or the sautéed clams with garlic and coriander are a good launch to a feast here, followed, perhaps, by the traditional Portuguese cabbage soup. For the main course, which comes with side dishes, you might opt for the African chicken with garlic, onions, chili, ginger, and coconut milk sauce served with gratinéed potatoes and mixed salad, or the tenderloin steak Portuguese style, fried with garlic and white wine and served with Portuguese honey ham, fried egg, and potatoes. And to top it all off? How about banana ice cream, served with rum *au flambé?* In nice weather, you may want to sit at one of the three tables outside on the tiny balcony, where you can look upon ancient tiled roofs and listen to the click of mah-jongg tiles.

8 Rua das Gaivotas, Colôane Village. © **853/2888 2226.** Reservations recommended Sat-Sun. Main courses MOP$115-MOP$320. AE, MC, V. Mon-Fri noon-3pm and 6:30-10pm; Sat-Sun noon-10:30pm. Bus: 15, 21, 21A, 25, or 26A.

Restaurante Litoral ★★ MACANESE Exactly which restaurant serves the most "authentic" Macanese food in town is a hotly contested subject, but I think this attractive entrant, with its dark-gleaming woods, whitewashed walls, and stone floor, can easily lay claim to the title. All the traditional favorites are here, including curry crab, African chicken, *feijoada,* and *minchi,* but Portuguese specialties like codfish baked with potato and garlic, roast Portuguese sausage, and Portuguese green soup are not overlooked. Wash it all down with Portuguese wine or beer. It's located along the covered sidewalk not far from the Maritime Museum and A-Ma Temple.

261A Rua do Almirante Sérgio. ℂ 853/2896 7878. www.restaurante-litoral.com. Main courses MOP$148–MOP$200. AE, MC, V. Daily noon–3pm and 5:30–10:30pm. Bus: 2, 5, 9, 10, 10A, 11, 18, 21A, or 28B.

360 Café INTERNATIONAL   This is Macau's most conspicuous restaurant, more than 220m (722 ft.) above reclaimed ground in the soaring Macau Tower. Although there's an observation deck in the tower with an admission of MOP$100, head instead to the tower's revolving restaurant, where for the price of a buffet meal you'll get an equally good view. It takes 1½ hours for a complete spin, giving you ample time to sample the various Portuguese, Southeast Asian, Indian, Chinese, Macanese, and Continental dishes as you soak in the view. Note that there are two sittings for lunch. Safety precautions make this Macau's only nonsmoking restaurant.

In the Macau Tower, Lago Sai Van. ℂ 853/8988 8622. www.macautower.com.mo. Reservations recommended Sat–Sun. Buffet lunch MOP$198; teatime buffet MOP$138; buffet dinner MOP$288. Daily 11:30am–1pm and 1:30–3pm for lunch; 3:30–5pm for teatime; 6:30–10pm for dinner. AE, DC, MC, V. Bus: 18 or 32.

Inexpensive

Antica Trattoria da Ise ITALIAN   This casual, second-story restaurant, located near the Docks nightlife district, is always crowded. Simply decorated with cast-iron chandeliers, plants, and palm trees, it offers 18 different kinds of pizza in two sizes (the small size is good for two people) and more than 30 pasta dishes, as well as main courses like T-bone steak with garlic and lemon sauce, along with Portuguese and Italian wines to wash it all down.

40–46 Av. Sir Anders Ljungstedt, Edificio Vista Magnifica Court. ℂ 853/2875 5102. Reservations recommended. Small pizzas MOP$115–MOP$130; main dishes MOP$126–MOP$185. AE, DC, MC, V. Mon–Fri noon–3:30pm and 6:30–11:30pm; Sat–Sun noon–11:30pm. Closed 2nd Tues of every month. Bus: 1A, 3A. 8, 10A, or 17.

Caravela 🏮 PORTUGUESE   This local Portuguese hangout serves as a bakery, cafe, restaurant, and informal gathering spot for friends, with both sidewalk seating and a small dining room. Professionals stop by for breakfast on their way to work, old men peruse newspapers over cups of Portuguese coffee, and office workers take advantage of the MOP$58 breakfast or the daily set meal for MOP$75 which includes soup, a main dish, and dessert. The menu itself is limited, offering a few dishes like oven-roasted codfish with potatoes, barbecued chicken, and sandwiches, but the bread is homemade, the pastries are irresistible (a typical Christmas dessert that resembles French toast is always on offer), and the atmosphere is a slice of Portugal in the heart of Asia. It's located in downtown Macau but is a bit hard to find, on an alley 1 block northeast of the intersection of Avenida Do Infante D. Henrique and Avenida de D. João IV.

7 Mata e Oliveira. ℂ 853/2871 2080. Main dishes MOP$69–MOP$120. No credit cards. Mon–Sat 8am–8pm; Sun 9:30–1:30pm. Bus: 2, 3, 3A, 5, 9, 10, 10A, 11, 21A, 26A, 28B, or 33.

Carlos PORTUGUESE   Just a block inland from the Docks nightlife district, this bare room with a tall ceiling offers no-nonsense, home-cooked Portuguese food at very reasonable prices, assuring a faithful clientele. The menu is extensive and includes all the classics, but standouts include the shrimp in garlic sauce, the clams and pork stewed in white wine and herbs, and the *bacalhau à bras* (fried codfish, potatoes, onions, and egg).

Rua Cidade de Braga. © **853/2875 1838.** Main dishes MOP$75–MOP$100. MC, V. Tues–Sun 11am–3pm and 6–11pm. Bus: 1A, 3A, 8, 10A, or 17.

Galo PORTUGUESE/MACANESE A delightful, two-story house on the main street in Taipa Village was converted long ago into this informal and festively decorated restaurant specializing in local cuisines and unique creations. *Galo* means rooster in Portuguese; look for the picture of the rooster outside the restaurant, on a corner of the main pedestrian street. Its menu, which includes photographs of each dish, offers such house specialties as Macau crabs, prepared with a mixture of Shanghainese and Macanese ingredients rather than curry (be sure to ask for the market price). You might also want to try African chicken, fried codfish, or stewed lamb. In any case, be sure to start out with the *sopa da casa* (house soup), made from potatoes, red beans, onions, and vegetables simmered in broth from boiled beef and sausages. Delicious! Unfortunately, service is indifferent.

45 Rua dos Clérigos, Taipa Village. © **853/2882 7423** or 853/2882 7318. Main courses MOP$60–MOP$100. MC, V. Mon–Fri 11:30am–3pm and 6–10:30pm; Sat–Sun 11:30am–10:30pm. Bus: 11, 15, 28A, or 33.

IFT Educational Restaurant ★★ 🍴 MACANESE/PORTUGUESE Its name is uninspiring, but this is a unique restaurant, run by students receiving hands-on training in the restaurant and hotel business while attending the adjoining Institute for Tourism Studies (Instituto de Formacao Turistica, or IFT). Even better, it looks like a real restaurant, with contemporary furnishings and candles on the tables (though it can be a bit noisy). The changing menu, which pairs entrees with wine recommendations, offers Macanese and international fare, as well as IFT originals, with past dishes like grilled sole with a red-wine, Portuguese bacon, mushroom, and parsley sauce, and beef filet with a gratin of wild mushrooms and cream potatoes. The only drawback is you'll probably want to take a taxi here (it's located on a hill, site of former Mong-Ha Fortress), but inexpensive prices make this a bargain nonetheless and it's heartwarming to watch the students try their darndest to make your meal a success.

Colina de Mong-Ha. © **853/8598 3077.** www.ift.edu.mo/restaurant. Main courses MOP$80–MOP160; Fri dinner buffet MOP$180; set lunch MOP$140. AE, MC, V. Mon–Fri 12:30–3pm and 7–10:30pm. Bus: 12, 17, 18, or 28C.

Long Kei CANTONESE Located on Senado Square near the tourist office, this is one of Macau's oldest Cantonese restaurants, open since 1945. It's nothing fancy, filled with loyal patrons and serving a long list of local favorites, including grilled pigeon, roasted chicken, grilled prawn, fried garoupa, and sweet and sour pork.

7B Largo do Seal Senado. © **853/2857 3970.** Main dishes MOP$60–MOP$120. AE, DC, MC, V. Daily 11:30am–3pm and 6–11pm. Bus: 2, 3, 3A, 5, 10, 10A, 11, 18, 21A, 26A, or 33.

Nga Tim Cafe ★ 🏛 CANTONESE/MACANESE/PORTUGUESE This lively, open-air, pavilion restaurant is on the tiny main square of Colôane Village, dominated by the charming Chapel of St. Francis Xavier. Its popularity with the locals on weekends and holidays lends it a festive, community-affair atmosphere; it's a great place for relaxing and people-watching. The food, which combines Chinese, Macanese, and Portuguese styles of cooking and ingredients, is in a category all its own, with many unique dishes not available elsewhere. Try the salt-and-pepper prawns or crab, *feijoada,* baked perch Portuguese style, or the barbecued chicken in a fresh coconut, accompanied by Portuguese wine or fresh fruit juice. This is a good place to rub elbows with the natives, and when the weather is perfect, there's no finer place in Macau.

8 Rua Caetano, Colôane Village. © **853/2888 2086.** Main courses MOP$48–MOP$128. MC, V. Daily 11:30am–12:30am. Bus: 15, 21, 21A, 25, or 26A.

Wong Chi Kei Congee & Noodle 🍴 CANTONESE   Opening its first shop in mainland China in 1946, this inexpensive eatery on Senado Square has been a Macau mainstay for more than 40 years. It's a noisy, busy place, with several floors of dining for people pouring in to sample wonton in noodle soup, barbecue duck in noodle soup, fried noodle with shrimp, fried noodle with shredded chicken, and *congee.* It doesn't get more local than this.

17 Largo do Seal Senado. © **853/2833 1313.** Main dishes MOP$23–MOP$48. AE, DC, MC, V. Daily 8am–11pm. Bus: 2, 3, 3A, 5, 10, 10A, 11, 18, 21A, 26A, or 33.

EXPLORING MACAU

You'll need a minimum of 2 days to see most of what Macau offers, spending 1 day in the historic center and the next on Taipa, Cotai, and Colôane. Although it's easy enough to get around on your own, if you're pressed for time, **Gray Line** (© **853/2833 6611**), in conjunction with MGTO, offers a 6-hour Macau Highlights Tour, with pickup and drop-off at the Macau Ferry Terminal. It costs MOP$118 for adults, MOP$108 for children and seniors, and takes in the ruins of St. Paul's Church, Senado Square, A-Ma Temple, Macau Tower, Taipa Houses-Museum, and Fisherman's Wharf, among other places. Other Gray Line tours concentrate on historic sites, Taipa and Colôane, cuisine, and shopping. For more information, contact Gray Line or MGTO (© **853/2833 3000;** www.macautourism.gov.mo).

The Top Attractions

Macau Museum ★★★   Located in the bowels of ancient Monte Fortress, this ambitious museum provides an excellent overview of Macau's history, local traditions, and arts and crafts. If you see only one museum in Macau, make it this one. Entrance is via an escalator located next to St. Paul's Church. Arranged chronologically, the first floor depicts the beginnings of Macau and the arrival of Portuguese traders and Jesuit missionaries. Particularly interesting is the room comparing Chinese and European civilizations at the time of their encounter in the 16th century, including descriptions of their different writing systems, philosophies, and religions. The second floor deals with the daily life and traditions of old Macau, including festivals, wedding ceremonies, and industries ranging from fishing to fireworks factories. Displays include paintings and photographs of Macau through the centuries, traditional games and toys, an explanation of Macanese cuisine and architecture, and a re-created Macanese street lined with colonial and Chinese facades and containing tea, pastry, and traditional Chinese pharmacy shops. The top floor, the only one above ground, is of contemporary Macau and its plans for the future. From here you can exit to the wall ramparts of the fort, which was built by the Jesuits about the same time as St. Paul's and largely destroyed by the same fire. You'll want to spend at least an hour here.

112 Praceta do Museu de Macau (St. Paul Monte Fortress, next to St. Paul's). © **853/2835 7911.** www.macaumuseum.gov.mo. Admission MOP$15 adults, MOP$8 seniors and children; free admission on 15th

of every month. Tues–Sun 10am–6pm. Bus: 2, 3, 3A, 5, 10, 10A, 11, 18, 21A, 26A, or 33 to Senado Sq. (off Av. Almeida Ribeiro) and then a 10-min. walk.

Macau Tower ♨ Does the world really need more towers? Local authorities apparently thought so, opening the Macau Tower Convention & Entertainment Centre in 2001. In addition to exhibition and convention space, it contains restaurants and shops, but the crowning glory is the 330m (1,083-ft.) tower, with an observatory about 223m (731 ft.) high—the equivalent of 61 stories. Because admission to the outdoor observation deck and indoor lounge is exorbitant by Macau standards, I personally think you are best off coming for a meal in the revolving **360 Café** (p. 305). However, thrill seekers take note: The indoor observation lounge has a glass-floored section that gives the illusion of standing on thin air. But real daredevils will want to tour the observation deck's *outside* ramparts with the safety of harnesses and ropes, which costs MOP$588, including a CD of your adventure and a T-shirt. Other ways to have fun with Macau Tower: climbing the mast (a 2-hr. ordeal) or bungee jumping 233m (764 ft., listed in the Guinness World Records as the "highest commercial bungy jump").

Lago Sai Van. ℭ **853/8988 8895.** www.macautower.com.mo. Admission to observatory MOP$100 adults, MOP$50 children and seniors. Mon–Fri 10am–9pm; Sat–Sun and holidays 9am–9pm. Bus: 18 or 32.

Ruins of St. Paul's Church ★★ The most famous structure in Macau is what's left of St. Paul's Church. Crowning the top of a hill in the center of the city and approached by a grand sweep of stairs, only its ornate facade and some excavated sites remain. It was designed by an Italian Jesuit and built in 1602 with the help of Japanese Christians who had fled persecution in Nagasaki. In 1835, during a typhoon, the church caught fire and burned to the ground, leaving only its now-famous facade. The facade is adorned with carvings and statues depicting Christianity in Asia, a rather intriguing mix of images: a Virgin Mary flanked by a peony (representing China) and a chrysanthemum (representing Japan), and a Chinese dragon, a Portuguese ship, and a demon. Beyond the facade is the excavated crypt, where in glass-fronted cases are the bones of 17th-century Christian martyrs from Japan and Vietnam. Here, too, is the tomb of Father Allesandro Valignano, founder of the Church of St. Paul and instrumental in establishing Christianity in Japan. Next to the crypt is the underground Museum of Sacred Art, which contains religious works of art produced in Macau from the 17th to 20th centuries. Included are intriguing 17th-century oil paintings by exiled Japanese Christian artists, crucifixes of filigree silver, carved wooden saints, and other sacred objects. To the left of the church's ruins are tiny Na Tcha Temple and a remnant of Macau's old city wall, which, along with St. Paul's Church, are among the 20-some historic structures protected collectively as a World Heritage Site.

Rua de São Paulo. ℭ **853/2835 8444.** Free admission. Grounds open daily 24 hr.; museum daily 9am–6pm. Bus: 2, 3, 3A, 5, 10, 10A, 11, 18, 21A, 26A, or 33 to Senado Sq. (off Av. Almeida Ribeiro) and then a 10-min. walk.

More Museums & Attractions

Grand Prix Museum One of two museums located in the Tourism Activities Centre (see the Wine Museum, below), a 10-minute walk from the Macau Ferry Terminal, the Grand Prix Museum opened in 1993 to celebrate the 40th anniversary of the Macau Grand Prix. Its display hall is filled mainly with cars and motorcycles that have competed in the race through the years. There are also simulator games, which cost MOP$10 and give visitors the thrill of "experiencing" high speeds down a racetrack (participants must be at least 150cm/59 in. tall). Together with the Wine Museum, it takes less than an hour to explore.

Centro de Actividades Turisticas Macau, 431 Rua Luis Gonzaga Gomes. © **853/8798 4108.** Free admission. Wed–Mon 10am–6pm. Bus: 1A, 3, 3A, 10, 10B, 12, 28A, 28B, 28C, or 32.

Handover Gifts Museum of Macao ★★ 🎁 Its name doesn't promise much, but this is actually an astonishing museum if you like decorative art and an absolute must if you love Chinese art. Located on the site of Macau's 1999 handover to China, next to the Macao Museum of Art (see below), it contains superbly crafted gifts presented to Macau for the occasion from all over China. The provincial government of Heilongjiang, for example, gave two vases made from walnut shells selected from 10,000 hickories grown in Xiao Xingan Forest, while Henan gave a sundial encircled by nine flying dragons and carved from an 800kg (1,763-lb.) piece of Dushan jade. You can easily spend a half-hour of wonderment here.

Av. Xian Xing Hai, Nape. © **853/8504 1800.** http://handovermuseum.iacm.gov.mo. Free admission. Tues–Sun 10am–7pm. Bus: 1A, 3A, 8, 10A, 12, or 17.

Macao Museum of Art ★ Located in the Macao Cultural Centre on reclaimed land near the Outer Harbour, this small but interesting museum displays historical paintings, Chinese calligraphy, pottery, and works by contemporary local artists. Particularly fascinating are paintings by Western artists such as British painter George Chinnery and others, who painted scenes, people, and customs of Macau and Guangdong, including depictions of the port town as it looked long ago. Their works were often copied and then sold to visiting foreigners as souvenirs. Also impressive is the collection of Shiwan ceramic figurines. There are also temporary exhibitions. Depending upon your interest, you'll spend anywhere from 30 to 60 minutes here. Incidentally, on the ground floor is the Media Library, with computers you can use for free from 2 to 7pm Tuesday to Friday and 11am to 7pm Saturday and Sunday.

Centro Cultural de Macau, Av. Xian Xing Hai, Nape. © **853/8791 9814.** www.artmuseum.gov.mo. Admission MOP$5 adults, MOP$2 students and children 11 and over, free for seniors and children 10 and under; free admission Sun. Tues–Sun 10am–7pm. Bus: 1A, 3A, 8, 10A, 12, or 17.

Macao Science Center ★★ ☺ On the Outer Harbour waterfront not far from the Macao Museum of Art (see above), this cone-shaped museum that to me resembles a giant snail was designed by Chinese-American architect I. M. Pei and contains 14 galleries related to technology, science, and our daily lives, including space science, earth science, robotics, health, sports, and food science. It also contains a planetarium that boasts the world's first digital system equipped with both ultrahigh definition (8,000 x 8,000 pixel screen) and 3D. Several galleries are geared specifically to children, including a Fun Science Gallery where kids 2 to 7 years old can work a crane, climb, and explore other age-related exhibits, while the Children Science Gallery is designed for slightly older kids to let them experiment with electricity, communicate as in days of yore (remember the telex?), and learn about hydrodynamics in a large water play area. The Robotic Gallery features robot shows several times daily and lets you build your own robot. Other galleries highlight ways to protect the environment, let you test your physical strength, and teach about nutrition. Although this is a great learning center for local families, I personally think you should see Macau before venturing here, unless, of course, you have kids.

Avenida Dr. Sun Yat-sen, Nape. © **853/2888 0822.** www.msc.org.mo. Admission to exhibits MOP$25 adults, MOP$15 students, seniors, and children; planetarium MOP$35–MOP$45 adults, MOP$20–MOP$30 students, seniors, and children. Fri–Wed 10am–6pm. Bus: 3A, 8, 10A, 12, and 17.

Mandarin's House ★★★ 👔 This recently restored mansion, part of the World Heritage Site's Historic Centre of Macao (p. 312), is my new favorite sightseeing destination in town, a must-see for anyone interested in history or architecture. Constructed around 1860 by the Zheng family, it's a magnificent home, occupying a 4,000-sq.-m (43,055-sq.-ft.) compound of more than 60 rooms and a series of courtyards. Although it retains the essential characteristics of a traditional Guangdong residence, including an Earthgod shrine at the entrance, moon gates (circular garden passageways), and plaster ornamentation, it incorporates architectural details from other cultures as well, such as arched doorways and French windows. A small museum displays photographs before and after its restoration; an English pamphlet thoroughly describes what you'll see. Not only is a private residence of this scale rare in Macau, but it also remains Macau's largest mansion. Plan on 30 minutes here.

10 Travessa António da Silva. © **853/2896 8820.** www.wh.mo/mandarinhouse. Free admission. Fri–Tues 10am–6pm. Bus: 18, 28B.

Maritime Museum ★ 😊 Macau's oldest museum, ideally situated on the waterfront of the Inner Harbour where visitors can observe barges and other boats passing by, does an excellent job of tracing the history of Macau's lifelong relationship with the sea. It's located at the tip of the peninsula, across from the A-Ma Temple, in approximately the same spot where the Portuguese first landed. The museum begins with dioramas depicting the legend of A-Ma, protectress of seafarers and Macau's namesake, and continues with displays of sea-related festivals (like the A-Ma Festival in Apr, similar to Hong Kong's Tin Hau Festival, and the Dragon Boat Festival in May/June). Peruse models of various boats, including trawlers, Chinese junks, Portuguese sailing boats, and even modern jetfoils, as well as life-size original boats from the sampan to an ornate festival boat. Various fishing methods are detailed, from trawling and gill netting to purse seining, as well as various voyages of discovery around the world. The museum also has a model of Macau in the 17th century, nautical equipment, navigation instruments used by the Portuguese and Chinese, and—a hit with small children—a one-room aquarium. You'll spend about 45 minutes here.

1 Largo do Pagode da Barra. © **853/2859 5481.** www.museumaritimo.gov.mo. Admission MOP$10 adults, MOP$5 children 10–17, free for seniors and children 9 and under; Sun half price. Wed–Mon 10am–6pm. Bus: 2, 5, 9, 10, 10A, 11, 18, 21A, or 28B.

Tak Seng On Pawnshop Museum Located on Macau's main street between Senado Square and the Inner Harbour (look for the sign CLUBE CULTURAL), this historic building opened as a traditional pawnshop in 1917 and today serves as a museum outlining the pawnshop business in Macau. Unlike pawnshops in the West, this pawnshop held personal possessions for up to 3 years, safeguarded against fires, floods, and theft in a thick-walled tower in the back. A screen at the entrance to the shop shielded customers pawning their belongings from curious glances of passersby. There isn't a lot to see here (you can tour the entire building in about 10 min.), so be sure to stop by the adjoining shop selling local souvenirs, some antiques, and reproductions and stop for refreshment at the third-floor tearoom.

Clube Cultural, 396 Av. Almeida Ribeiro. © **853/2892 1811.** Admission MOP$5. Daily 10:30am–7pm. Closed 1st Mon of every month. Bus: 2, 3, 3A, 5, 10, 10A, 11, 18, 21A, 26A, or 33.

Wine Museum Located in the same building as the Grand Prix Museum (see above), this is Asia's first museum dedicated to wine. Modeled like a wine cellar, it begins with a brief history of winemaking, starting with its discovery by Egyptians and Phoenicians in 6000 to 4000 B.C. and its spread from Greece through the rest of Europe, reaching Portugal around A.D. 1100. On display are wines (the oldest is an 1815 Madeira), wine presses, storage barrels, harvesting tools, and other winemaking equipment, as well as descriptions of every winegrowing region in Portugal. Wine production in China is also presented. A museum highlight is the wine tasting of red, white, or verde wine; bottles of wine are available for purchase.

Centro de Actividades Turisticas Macau, Rua Luis Gonzaga Gomes. *C* **853/8798 4188.** Free admission; wine tasting MOP$10. Wed–Mon 10am–6pm. Bus: 1A, 3, 3A, 10, 10B, 12, 28A, 28B, 28C, or 32.

Temples

A-Ma Temple ★★ Macau's oldest Chinese temple—and the longest surviving building in Macau—is situated at the bottom of Barra Hill at the entrance to the Inner Harbour, across from the Maritime Museum. Parts of this temple, dedicated to A-Ma, goddess of seafarers, date back more than 600 years. According to legend, a poor village girl sought free passage on a boat but was refused until a small fishing boat came along and took her onboard. Once the boat was at sea, a typhoon blew in, destroying all boats except hers. Upon landing at what is now Barra Hill, the young girl revealed herself as A-Ma, and the fishermen repaid their gratitude by building this temple on the spot where they came ashore. The temple was already here when the Portuguese arrived; they named their city A-Ma-Gao (Place of A-Ma) after this temple, now shortened, of course, to Macau.

At the entrance is a large rock, with a picture of a traditional sailing junk engraved more than 400 years ago to commemorate the Chinese fishing boat that carried A-Ma to Macau. The temple, spreading along the steep slope of a hill with views of the water, has good feng shui. Several shrines set in the rocky hillside are linked by winding paths through moon gates. The uppermost shrine honors Kun Iam, the goddess of mercy, and affords good views of the Inner Harbour. If you happen to be here on the 23rd day of the Third Moon (Apr or May), you'll be treated to the A-Ma Festival (similar to the Tin Hau Festival in Hong Kong), with its throngs of worshippers and Cantonese opera performed on a temporary stage in front of the temple. At the very least, your visit may coincide with an explosion of fireworks, traditionally set off to scare away evil spirits and now a popular demonstration for visiting tour groups (avoid mornings, however, when most tour buses come here).

Rua de S. Tiago da Barra. Free admission. Daily 7am–6pm. Bus: 2, 5, 9, 10, 10A, 11, 18, 21A, or 28B.

Kun Iam Tong (Temple of the Goddess of Mercy) ★★ Of the many temples in Macau, one of the most important is the Temple of Kun Iam Tong, founded in the 13th century. Its present buildings, with ornate porcelain figurines adorning its roofs, date from 1627. The most significant historical event that took place at this largest and wealthiest of Macau's Buddhist temples was the 1844 signing of the first treaty of trade and friendship between the United States and China; the round granite table where the treaty was signed is still here, in the back garden. The temple houses images of Buddha, representing the past, present, and future, as well as the goddess of mercy (Kun Iam) dressed in the costume of a Chinese bride. She is attended by 18 gold-lacquered figures lining the walls that represent the 18 wise men of China. Curiously enough, the figure on the left with bulging eyes and mustache is

EAST meets WEST

The Historic Centre of Macao, a World Heritage Site, celebrates more than 400 years of cultural exchange between the East and the West. Encompassing most of the historic old town, it ensures the preservation of both traditional Chinese architecture and the oldest Western structures on Chinese soil, with forts, temples, churches, mansions, squares, a library, cemetery, and a garden among 30 protected sites. Several of the most famous attractions are described above and in my walking tours below, but for a complete list of protected structures and a map, stop by the Macau Government Tourist Office for its *Macau World Heritage* pamphlet. Among my favorites: the A-Ma Temple, Moorish Barracks, Mandarin's House, Leal Senado Building, Senado Square, Lou Kau Mansion, the Protestant Cemetery, and Guia Fortress.

At the other end of the spectrum is another "town," **Fisherman's Wharf** (✆ **853/2899 3300;** www.fishermans wharf.com.mo), a fabricated village on reclaimed land in the Outer Harbour just a few minutes' walk from the Macau Ferry Terminal. It's divided into three zones: Tang Dynasty, with architecture and decor typical of the era; East Meets West, a fairy-tale rendition of history, with a man-made "active" volcano, an underground game center (daily noon–2am), and a 2,000-seat Roman amphitheater for concerts and performances; and Legend Wharf, with replica European, North American, and South African historic architecture. Mostly, Fisherman's Wharf is an excuse to shop and eat, with plenty of upscale opportunities for both. With regularly scheduled street performances and other events, it makes for an interesting stroll.

identified here as Marco Polo, who, having embraced Buddhism, came to be viewed as one of China's 18 wise men. Behind the temple to the right is a landscaped Chinese garden; it has four banyan trees with intertwined branches, popularly known as the Lovers' Tree and considered symbols of marital fidelity. According to local legend, the trees grew from the burial site of two lovers who committed suicide when they were forbidden to marry. Although the original trees have died, new ones have taken their place.

As you wander through the various buildings on the temple grounds, you will notice small funeral rooms with altars dedicated to the newly deceased, complete with photographs, offerings of fruit and other food, and paper money to assist the departed in the afterlife. You may even chance upon a funeral service, in which participants are dressed in white. Please show respect by being quiet, and refrain from taking photographs. It is also considered bad manners—not to mention bad luck—to take a picture of a monk without his permission. In any case, a visit to this temple is like going back in time; allow 20 minutes in this time capsule.

Avenida do Coronel Mesquita. Free admission. Daily 7am–6pm. Bus: 12, 17, 18, or 28C.

A Garden

Lou Lim Ieoc Garden 🎁   Macau's most flamboyant Chinese garden was built in the 19th century by a wealthy Chinese merchant and modeled after the famous gardens in Suzhou, China. Tiny, with narrow winding paths, bamboo groves, rock grottoes, a nine-turn zigzag bridge (believed to deter evil spirits), and ponds filled with carp, it's a nice escape from the city. If possible, come in the morning, when the garden is filled with Chinese doing tai chi exercises, musicians practicing traditional Chinese music, and bird lovers strolling with their birds in ornate wooden cages.

Estrada de Adolfo Loureiro. © **853/2835 6622.** Free admission. Daily 6am–9pm. Bus: 2, 5, 9, 12, 25, or 28C.

Taipa

Closest to the mainland, Taipa once served as a protected anchorage for clipper ships and was accessible only by ferry until 1974, when the Macau-Taipa Bridge was finally completed. Two additional bridges have led to increased development on Taipa, including unsightly apartment blocks and booming suburbs that have pushed the population on this small, 6.8-sq.-km (2½-sq.-mile) island to more than 50,000. Still, Taipa is worth a visit for quaint Taipa Village with its popular restaurants and colonial architecture. Taipa is also home of the United Chinese Cemetery with its blend of Confucianist, Taoist, and Buddhist influences, a university, Macau Stadium, Macau's airport, and the Macau Jockey Club for horse racing.

For architecture buffs and those looking for atmospheric restaurants, the first stop should be **Taipa Village ★**, a small traditional community of narrow lanes, alleys, squares, and two-story colonial buildings painted in hues of yellow, blue, and green. Although now almost completely engulfed by nearby housing projects, village life remains in full view here, with children playing and older residents sunning themselves on benches. On or near Rua do Cunha, the picturesque pedestrian-only main street, are a number of fine, inexpensive restaurants, making dining reason enough to come (see "Where to Dine," earlier in this chapter).

But for sightseeing, the best place to visit is the nearby **Taipa Houses-Museum,** on Avenida da Praia (© **853/2882 7088**), where five colonial-style buildings that once belonged to Macanese families in the early 1900s are now open to the public. They line the banyan-shaded Praia, which used to be on the shoreline but now faces unsightly reclaimed land (Cotai). Still, with their large verandas facing what was formerly a sea filled with clipper ships, they reflect the fact that most entertaining in this small colonial outpost—a boat ride from Macau—took place at home. Probably most interesting is the Macanese House, which combines both European and Chinese design as a reflection of the families' Eurasian heritage. It has a dining and living room, study, kitchen, and upstairs bedrooms, all filled with period furniture, paintings, art, and personal artifacts reflective of a dual heritage. Three other houses contain displays relating to the history of Taipa and Colôane, traditional regional costumes of Portugal, and special exhibitions (a fourth house is used for special functions). The Taipa Houses-Museum is open Tuesday through Sunday from 10am to 6pm; admission is MOP$5 for adults, MOP$3 for students, and free for seniors and children 11 and younger. Next to the buildings, on a hill, is Our Lady of Carmel Church, built in the 19th century for the devout Macanese Catholics.

The easiest way to reach Taipa Village is to board one of the buses that stops in front of the Hotel Lisboa near the bridge on the mainland. Bus nos. 11, 15, 28A, or 33 all go to Taipa Village.

Colôane

Farther away and connected to Taipa via a huge added strip of reclaimed land (called Cotai, which has essentially made the two islands one), Colôane once served as a haven for pirates who preyed upon the rich trading ships passing by. The last pirate raid was as late as 1910, when bandits kidnapped 18 children and demanded ransom. Government forces eventually overpowered the pirates, freeing all the children. Colôane today, measuring 7.8 sq. km (3 sq. miles) but with a population of only 4,000, is far less developed than Taipa and is known for its beaches, pine trees, eight marked hiking trails, golf course, and traditional village. The trails are accessible from Seac Pai Van Park, from various picnic parks on the island, and from both Cheoc Van and Hac Sa beaches. Trail maps are available at the information booth at the entrance to Seac Pai Van Park (bus: 15, 21A, 25, or 26A) and at the trail heads. At its center, on Colôane Hill and visible from miles away, is a 20m (65-ft.) white marble statue of A-Ma. Two of the most popular **beaches** are Cheoc Van and Hac Sa (which means "black sand"). Both beaches have lifeguards on duty in the summer, and nearby you'll find restaurants and public swimming pools that are open until 10pm. To reach them, take bus no. 21A or 26A from Avenida de Almeida Ribeiro in the city center or from the Hotel Lisboa; additionally, bus no. 25 also runs from the Lisboa to both beaches. Bus no. 15 connects the beaches with Taipa Village.

Now that Taipa Village has suffered so much surrounding development, I find **Colôane Village ★★** much more picturesque and a worthy destination if exploring the islands. Located on the southwestern tip of the island, it is so close to China that it almost seems like you can reach out and touch it. Boats headed to and from the mainland pass through the narrow waterway. The social center of the village revolves around a small, tiled square, which is lined on two sides with cloistered cafes. In its center is a monument erected in 1928 to commemorate those who fought in the 1910 battle against the pirates. At its end is the small but sweet **Chapel of St. Francis Xavier,** built in 1928 and dedicated to Asia's most important and well-known Catholic missionary. The church, built in classic Portuguese style, would seem rather plain if it weren't for its exuberant Asian artwork. For a snack, head to **Lord Stow's Bakery,** Colôane Town Square (✆ **853/2888 2534**), serving what some contend are Macau's best Portuguese egg tarts, best when eaten fresh from the oven, as well as sandwiches and bread.

Cotai

Connecting the former islands of Taipa and Colôane is a strip of reclaimed land called Cotai. It's home to Macau's growing convention trade, the Macau East Asian Games Dome used for international events, a go-cart track, a golf course, and the 15,000-seat Cotai Arena used for big events. Here, too, is the **Venetian Macao-Resort-Hotel** (✆ **853/2882 8888;** www.venetianmacao.com) and **City of Dreams** (✆ **853/8868 6688;** www.cityofdreamsmacau.com), complexes containing hotels, restaurants, shops, casinos, and other entertainment. City of Dreams, for example, offers the Bubble, a dome-shaped standing theater that presents a 10-minute visual extravaganza about four dragons, free on a first-come, first-served basis; the House of Dancing Water, the world's largest water-based show, with performances by acrobats, stuntmen, and musicians (http://thehouseofdancingwater.com; tickets from MOP$380 for adults, MOP$340 for students and seniors, MOP$270 for children); and Kids' City, with climbers, a bouncy tent, princess dress-up clothes, and arts and crafts geared toward 2- to 12-year-olds (daily 10:30am–9:30pm; admission MOP$90 for 2 hr.).

HISTORIC CITY STROLLS

Two walks are described below, but because they connect at Senado Square, they can easily be combined into one stroll. Together, they take in more than half of the World Heritage Site's 30 historic structures and squares.

WALKING TOUR 1 **AROUND ST. PAUL'S**

START:	**Senado Square (Largo do Senado).**
FINISH:	**Senado Square.**
TIME:	**Allow approximately 3 hours, including museum stops.**
BEST TIMES:	**Weekends and holidays, when the second floor of Lou Kau Mansion is open.**
WORST TIMES:	**Monday, when the Macau Museum and Lou Kau Mansion are closed.**

If anything remains of old Macau, this is it. Declared a World Heritage Site in 2005, the Historic Centre of Macao celebrates Macau's dual heritage with architectural treasures ranging from temples and Chinese mansions to churches and plazas. With their narrow, hilly streets, diminutive squares shaded by ancient banyan trees, family-owned shops, and unique buildings, the slopes and neighborhoods below the ruins of St. Paul's offer colorful snapshots of Macau's long past. This is also the vibrant heart of the city, with children's laughter drifting from schoolyards, shopkeepers gossiping in the street, worshippers filing in for Mass, and friends playing mah-jongg right in the middle of a store. And don't worry if you get lost—Macau is too small to be truly lost for long, and the back streets and alleys make for fascinating exploring.

1 Senado Square (Largo do Senado)

This large plaza, paved with a wavy pattern of black and white cobblestones, dominated by a fountain, and encircled by pastel-colored neoclassical buildings from the 19th and 20th centuries, has been the center of Macau's commercial life for centuries. It's always packed with tourists, families, and passersby, giving it a festive atmosphere even when no public events—and there are plenty—are staged. If you haven't already done so, stop off at the MGTO tourist office on Senado Square to pick up a map and the *Macau World Heritage* brochure.

Following the wavy-patterned paving uphill, at the top of Senado Square, to the left, is:

2 St. Dominic's Church (Igreja de São Domingos)

Founded in 1587 by three Spanish Dominican priests from Mexico, the present yellow-and-white church with green shutters dates from the early 17th century. Its baroque altar, with a statue of the Virgin Mary and Jesus, is the picture of serenity today, belying an act of violence that occurred in 1644 during Mass: A military officer sympathetic to the Spanish rushed inside to escape a street mob but was murdered at the altar. If you take the stairs at the end of a side corridor, you'll arrive at the free Treasure of the Sacred Heart museum, open daily 10am to 6pm, with three floors of woodcarvings, vestments, and other religious artifacts (the top floor is especially interesting, since its soaring ceiling allows you to see something of the building's architecture).

Upon exiting the church, head for the small side street catty-corner across the square to the right (beside McDonald's), called Travessa de S. Domingos. It leads uphill, where, to the right, it opens onto:

3 Largo da Sé (Cathedral Square)

This handsome square, boasting a big cross at its center, is most famous for the Cathedral (Igreja da Sé), which has stood here in various forms since 1622. Once serving as the mother church of a diocese that stretched from China and Korea to Japan, it was last rebuilt in 1937 and boasts fine stained-glass windows. If time permits, soak up the local atmosphere from one of the square's benches, where you have a front-row seat of Macau's laid-back urban life and the parade of people walking by.

Head back downhill to the right of the cross, on Travessa da Sé, where almost immediately on the right, at no. 7, you'll come to a highlight of this stroll, the:

4 Lou Kau Mansion

Built in 1889 by a prominent Chinese merchant, this handsome two-story house centered on a courtyard, is one of only a few Chinese mansions remaining in Macau. Before the mansion was renovated in 2002, however, it had fallen into acute neglect, with as many as 20 families living here at one time. It's open Tuesday to Sunday from 9am to 7pm, but the second floor is open only weekends and holidays. Admission is free.

Continuing on Travessa da Sé, you'll find yourself back at St. Dominic's. To the right of the church is Rua da Palha, which you should follow shortly before veering uphill on Rua da S. Pāolo. This is one of Macau's liveliest old streets, with open-fronted shops selling souvenirs and local foodstuffs, including slices of barbecued beef jerky. You'll also see a few stores specializing in reproduction Chinese furniture, some of which is so good that many visitors commission pieces to be shipped back home. In fact, this area has long been famous for its craftsmen; centuries ago, many from this neighborhood helped build St. Paul's Church. At the top of Rua da S. Pāolo is a grand flight of stairs, always packed with tourists and leading to Macau's most famous landmark, the Ruins of St. Paul's. First, however, at the top of the stairs, turn right for the:

5 Macau Museum

Occupying the foundations of a former fortress, the Macau Museum does a good job depicting Macau's colorful history, traditions, and architecture, making it well worth a spin (p. 307). After touring the museum, be sure to exit from the top floor, which takes you to the fortress ramparts with its cannons and good views of the Inner Harbour with its busy boat traffic.

Exit the ramparts by following the sign for the SNACK BAR and continuing on around to the right, which will bring you back to Macau's most famous landmark, the:

6 Ruins of St. Paul's (Ruinas de São Paulo)

Constructed in 1602 but destroyed by fire in 1835, leaving only its facade punctuated by reliefs and statues, this is Macau's top tourist attraction. Its facade, carved by Japanese Christian exiles and local craftsmen and with a curious mix of Asian and Western symbols, has been called a "sermon in stone." Its grounds contain a viewing platform behind the facade, archaeological pits, a crypt containing bones of Japanese and Vietnamese martyrs, and a museum of sacred art (p. 308).

1 Senado Square
(Largo do Senado)

2 St. Dominic's Church
(Igreja de São Domingos)

3 Largo da Sé
(Cathedral Square)

4 Lou Kau Mansion

5 Macau Museum

6 Ruins of St. Paul's
(Ruinas de São Paulo)

7 Na Tcha Temple

8 Section of Old City Walls

9 St. Anthony's Church
(Igreja de Santo António)

10 Protestant Cemetery
(Cemitério Protestante)

11 Casa Garden

12 Camões Garden
(Jardim Luís de Camões)

13 Tercena neighborhood

14 Mercado de São
Domingos

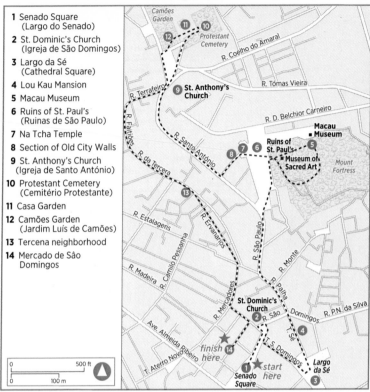

On the other side of St. Paul's is:

7 Na Tcha Temple

Another protected structure of the World Heritage Site, this tiny temple was built in 1888 to honor Na Tcha, the patron saint of children and—well, this is Macau—of lotteries and gambling. It stands next to a:

8 Section of the Old City Walls

The Portuguese invariably constructed walls around their port settlements, including those in India and Africa. Built of clay, soil, sand, rice straw, crushed rocks, and oyster shells, the chunk you see today was once part of a defensive wall first built by the Portuguese in 1569.

Follow the wall onto Calçada de S. Francisco Xavier, turning right on Rua de S. Paulo and continuing on Rua de Santo António, where you'll find more shops selling antiques, reproduction furniture, and pottery. After a 5-minute walk or so, following signs for CAMOES SQUARE, you'll come to:

9 St. Anthony's Church (Igreja de Santo António)

Macau's first church, made of wood and bamboo, was built here in 1558. After many fires and reconstructions, this latest reincarnation dates from 1930. It's dedicated to St. Anthony, a military saint and a captain in the Portuguese army.

Take a right out of the church, where, across the small square with its minibus station, is the old:

10 Protestant Cemetery (Cemitério Protestante)

A good illustration of Macau's religious diversity, this picturesque graveyard with about 160 graves provides a visual record of Macau's earliest Protestant community, with many prominent citizens buried here, including artist George Chinnery (buried in the upper row at the end; you can see his works in the Macao Museum of Art), Robert Morrison (who wrote the first Chinese-English dictionary and translated the Bible into Chinese), Joseph Adams (grandson of George Washington), and—they were considered respectable at the time—opium traders. It's open daily from 8:30am to 5:30pm.

Upon exiting the cemetery, you'll see a gate to the right with the sign FUNDACAO ORIENTE. Headquarters of the Oriental Foundation, this attractive pink and white building is the old:

11 Casa Garden

Built in 1770 as the private mansion of a wealthy Portuguese merchant, it was later rented out to officials of the East India Company, which maintained an office in Macau. You're welcome to enter the small gallery, which holds changing exhibitions Monday to Friday from 9:30am to 6pm.

Next to Casa Garden is:

12 Camoes Garden (Jardim Luís De Camões)

Once part of Casa Garden's private estate, this public park is dedicated to Portugal's most famous poet, often referred to as Portugal's Shakespeare and thought to have lived in Macau in 1557. A natural grotto contains a bust of Camões, but I like walking beyond the grotto to the end of the park, where there's a good view of the Inner Harbour and tables where men play Chinese games. If you come in early morning, you may also see men walking their pet birds in cages and people going through their daily exercise regimen. The garden is open daily from 6am to 10pm.

Walking back toward St. Anthony's Church, turn right onto Calçada do Botelho, which turns into Rua do Tarrafeiro, and then left at the bottom of the hill onto Rua dos Faitiôes. This soon turns into Rua da Tercena, heart of the:

13 Tercena Neighborhood

A typical old Macau street, Rua da Tercena is noted for its shops selling everything from antiques to coconut products. At the end of Rua da Tercena, take the tiled street to the right, Rua dos Ervanarios. This is a wonderful, narrow pedestrian lane, where you'll see small ma-and-pa shops, some with back tables where women are busy in that favorite pastime, mah-jongg. Yet towering above the lane, in the far distance, is modern Macau's new landmark, the 50-story Grand Lisboa.

After Rua dos Ervanarios ends, continue on Rua dos Mercados, turning left on a tiled street called Travessa do Soriano and the first right onto Rua Oeste do Mercado de São Domingos, site of the:

14 Mercado de São Domingos

This street market, with stalls and open-fronted shops, sells inexpensive casual attire, mostly overruns and seconds from Macau's many garment factories. You'll find inexpensive children's clothing, knitwear, jeans, and Chinese jackets, at prices much cheaper than Hong Kong's, making it fun to browse. At the end of the lane, turn left and you'll end up back at Senado Square.

WINDING DOWN

If you're hungering for Chinese, two of Macau's oldest Cantonese restaurants are Long Kei (✆ 853/2857 3970; p. 306), which has been offering inexpensive fare since 1945; and Wong Chi Kei (✆ 853/2833 1313; p. 307), always packed with patrons enjoying its noodles and *congee*. For French fare, head to La Bonne Heure (✆ 853/2833 1209; p. 304), serving lunch and dinner in a cozy setting.

WALKING TOUR 2 **PENHA PENINSULA**

START:	**Leal Senado, across from Senado Square.**
FINISH:	**A-Ma Temple.**
TIME:	**Allow approximately 2 hours.**
BEST TIMES:	**You can do this walk any day of the week.**
WORST TIMES:	**Tuesday, when the Maritime Museum is closed; Wednesday and Thursday, when the Mandarin House is closed.**

In contrast to the commercial neighborhoods around Senado Square and St. Paul's with their many shops and restaurants, Penha Peninsula is more residential, sprinkled with many fine churches, squares, and other architectural treasures that are part of the World Heritage Site's Historic Centre of Macao (the highlight is the Mandarin House). Still, it's off the beaten path for most tourists, despite the fact that Penha Peninsula boasts Macau's grandest examples of Portuguese colonial architecture.

1 Leal Senado

This neoclassical masterpiece, Macau's most striking example of Portuguese colonial architecture, was built in 1784 and renovated following a typhoon in 1875. Since its founding, this building has housed Macau's municipal chamber. Its name means "Loyal Senate," derived from a title Portuguese King Dom John IV bestowed in 1654: "City of Our Name of God Macao, There is None More Loyal." Inside the foyer to the right is a small gallery with changing exhibitions, often mounted without much advance notice but interesting since they relate to Macau and are free (Tues–Sun 9am–9pm). Up the stairs is a pretty inner courtyard, lined with blue and white tiles typical of Macau's Portuguese buildings and with a bust of poet Camoes.

In front of Leal Senado is busy:

2 Avenida Almeida Ribeiro

Called San Ma Lo by the Chinese, this has long been Macau's main thorough-fare. Many old buildings from the early 20th century, with decorated facades on the upper floors and shops below, remain, though modern architecture is slowly encroaching. There are many shops selling jewelry here, with prices dependent on the daily market price for gold.

Cross to the other side of Avenida Almeida Ribeiro at the crosswalk and turn left toward the Inner Harbour, looking for a sign on the right that reads CLUBE CULTURAL, at no. 396. It's home of the small:

3 Tak Seng On Pawnshop Museum

This museum provides an interesting insight into the Chinese pawnshop business, which operates under different principles than pawnshops in the West (p. 310). Be sure, too, to take a spin through the adjoining shop selling antiques and souvenirs.

TAKE A BREAK

On the third floor of the pawnshop museum is a traditional teahouse, the Water Teahouse, offering various types of tea and tea ware for purchase. Or, you can choose to drink it here in a private booth where the waitress will prepare the tea at your table. It's open daily 10:30am to 8pm.

Cross Avenida Almeida Ribeiro at the crosswalk to the right and continue walking dead ahead on Travessa Do Mastro 2 short blocks to a lively street with open-fronted shops selling sheets of barbecued beef jerky, pastries, and other foodstuffs. This is the beginning of picturesque:

4 Rua da Felicidade

It's aptly named, since the Street of Happiness once served as the nightlife district. Most of it was renovated some years back so that the traditional buildings all have the same whitewashed walls and red shutters and doors. Today they house a few shops, restaurants, and other businesses.

Walk all the way up Rua da Felicidade to where it ends, turning right onto Rua da Alfandaga, where you'll pass Pac Cheong Tong, a traditional Chinese medicinal shop at no. 114. Turn left at the next street, Calçada Do Gamboa and walk uphill, at the top of which is Largo de Santo Agostinho (St. Augustine's Square). This is one of Macau's loveliest squares, so architecturally intact that it's one of the World Heritage Site's eight protected squares. Immediately in front of you is:

5 St. Augustine's Church (Igreja de Santo Agostinho)

This pretty yellow church with green shutters was first established by Spanish Augustinians in 1591 and remains one of the city's most popular, with Sunday Mass celebrated in Tagalog at 10:30am for Macau's large Filipino population and in English at 4:30pm. It also holds a very popular Easter Procession, with thousands of devotees.

1 Leal Senado
2 Avenida Almeida Ribeiro
3 Talk Seng On Pawnshop Museum
4 Rua da Felicidade
5 St. Augustine's Church
   (Igreja de Santo Agostinho)
6 Sir Robert Ho Tung Library
7 Dom Pedro V Theatre
8 Lilau Square (Largo do Lilau)
9 Mandarin's House
10 Moorish Barracks
   (Quartel dos Mouros)
11 A-Ma Temple
12 Maritime Museum

Also on St. Augustine's Square, behind the yellow gate, is the:

6 Sir Robert Ho Tung Library

Built in 1894 as a residence, this building has since been donated to the city and now serves as a public library. There's a small open courtyard out back, good for a short break.

The other important building here, across the street, is the light green:

7 Dom Pedro V Theatre

China's first Western-style theater was built in 1860 and attracted many international touring companies, making it a cultural centerpiece for the Macanese community. It's still used for concerts and public events, but otherwise isn't open to the public.

Take Calçada Do Teatro, the downhill slope curving to the right around Dom Pedro V Theater, and continue straight on to Rua Central, which in succession becomes de S. Lorenço and then Rua Do Padre António. After about 10 minutes, to your left will be:

8 Lilau Square (Largo do Lilau)

Shaded by a large banyan tree and bordered by colorful old houses, this little square is probably my favorite in Macau. Because of a natural spring found here, this was the center of one of Macau's first residential areas. A local saying promises anyone who drinks from Lilau's spring will never forget Macau. The fountain became a popular drinking spot for visitors, who hoped that drinking the spring water would ensure their return. Nowadays, due to health reasons, the fountain is dry, but you can whet your thirst with a drink purchased at the square's kiosk. As you relax on a bench, you can almost picture how lively this part of Macau used to be, with housewives coming to fetch water and children playing in the square.

The interwoven quality of the lives of the Chinese, Macanese, and Portuguese in old Macau is reflected by the imposing building across from Lilau Square, the:

9 Mandarin's House

This magnificent traditional Chinese mansion, first built in 1860 and expanded in the 1880s, is the highlight of this stroll (p. 310). The former home of Zheng Guangying, a forward thinker who wrote *Words of Warning in Times of Prosperity*, it had fallen on hard times, with more than 300 tenants packed inside the 60-room complex, before 8 years of renovation restored it as a masterpiece of the World Heritage Site's Historic Centre of Macao.

Turn right onto Rua da Barra and continue on Calçada da Barra, where soon to your left you'll see the handsome:

10 Moorish Barracks (Quartel dos Mouros)

This brick and stone neoclassical structure, with distinct Mughal embellishments, was built in 1874 to house an Indian regiment brought in from Goa (which was also under Portuguese rule). Today it serves as headquarters of the Maritime Administration and is not open to the public.

Continue on Calçada da Barra to its end, which brings you to Macau's namesake:

11 A-Ma Temple

Already here when the Portuguese arrived, A-Ma Temple has grown over the years, with various pavilions and halls built along a steep slope (p. 311). The fact that so many deities are worshiped in a single complex is testimony to how much Chinese culture has been influenced by Confucianism, Taoism, and Buddhism.

Across the square from A-Ma Temple is the:

12 Maritime Museum

Macau's long relationship with the sea is the focus of this small museum, with displays that cover both Portuguese and Chinese seafaring vessels (p. 310).

WINDING DOWN

Across from the Moorish Barracks is Pizzeria Toscana, 2A Calçada da Barra (© 853/2872 6637), offering inexpensive pizzas and pastas daily 11:30am to 3:30pm and 6:30 to 11:30pm. Not far from A-Ma Temple is a succession of restaurants on Rua do Almirante Sergio: A Lorcha (© 853/2831 3193; p. 302), serving Portuguese fare; Restaurante Litoral (© 853/2896 7878; p. 304), specializing in Macanese cuisine; and O Porto Interior (© 853/2896 7770; p. 304), which serves both.

GAMBLING, SHOPPING & NIGHTLIFE

Gambling

The Chinese so love gambling that it's often said that if two flies are walking on the wall, the Chinese will bet on which one will walk faster. It's not surprising, therefore, that mainland and Hong Kong Chinese together with Taiwanese make up more than 90% of the 20-some million annual visitors to Macau.

In 2002, a 40-year monopoly on gambling ended, paving the way for grander casinos and an upsurge in Las Vegas–style entertainment. The number of casinos quickly grew from 11 in 2002 to more than 30 today, approximately half of them owned by foreign investors. Many are located in hotels or large resort complexes. Some are fancy, others not so, but none allow photographs to be taken, and shorts may not be worn. Admission is free, but you may be required to show a passport to enter. All are open 24 hours.

Macau's casinos, designed mostly for the Asian market, offer blackjack, baccarat, roulette, and slot machines (known, appropriately enough, as "hungry tigers"), but Chinese games like fan tan and sic bo dominate. If you're interested in seeing the largest casino in the world, head to the casino at **Venetian Macao-Resort-Hotel** on Cotai (© **853/2882 8888;** www.venetianmacao.com), a 50,725-sq.-m (546,000-sq.-ft.) space with more than 3,400 slot machines and 800 table games. Nearby in the **City of Dreams** is another casino with 378 tables and more than 1,000 machines (© **853/8868 6688;** www.cityofdreamsmacau.com). More centrally located is the **MGM Grand Macau,** Avenida Dr. Sun Yat-sen (© **853/8802 8888;** www.mgmgrandmacau.com), with 386 table games and 1,000 slot machines. Nearby, the **Wynn Macau,** Rua Cidade de Sintra (© **853/2888 9966;** www.wynnmacau.com), attracts crowds not only to its casinos but also to Performance Lake with its choreographed dancing fountains. Here also is the **Grand Lisboa,** Avenida de Lisboa (© **853/2828 3838;** www.grandlisboa.com), the first to add Texas Hold'em in its casino. Other hotels with casinos include **Holiday Inn, Hotel Lisboa, Hard Rock Hotel,** and **Altira,** with more slated to open in the next few years.

Shopping

A duty-free port, Macau has long been famous for its jewelry stores, especially those offering gold jewelry along Avenida Horta e Costa, Avenida do Infante D. Henrique, and Avenida de Almeida Ribeiro. Many Chinese consider buying gold as an investment. Market prices per tael (1.2 oz.) of gold are set daily. When buying gold or jewelry, always request a certificate of guarantee.

After gold, Portuguese wines are another good bargain, as are Chinese antiques and leather garments. In recent years, a number of fashionable clothing boutiques have opened in the center of town, similar to what you'd find in Hong Kong. More colorful are the clothing stalls near Largo do Senado square (circling the building that houses the MGTO), many of which sell overruns and seconds from regional garment factories, as well as Chinese jackets much cheaper than at markets in Hong Kong. Another colorful local shopping experience is the **Red Market,** on the corner of Avenida Almirante Lacerda and Avenida Horta e Costa, built in 1936 in Art Deco style and housing a lively food market daily from 7:30am to 7:30pm. A street market extends from the Red Market to Rotunda de Carlos Maia, a district popularly dubbed the Three Lamps District and a fun place to browse for cheap clothing. To reach the Red Market, take bus no. 3, 5, 8, 9, 17, 25, 26A, 32, or 33 to Mercado Vermelho.

The **Taipa Flea Market** is held Sundays from 11am to 8pm in Taipa Village, with booths selling traditional crafts, souvenirs, clothing, toys, and food. In Colôane Village, check out **Asian Artefacts,** 9 Rua dos Negociantes (© **853/2888 1210**), which sells restored antique furniture from north China, including trunks, chests, tables, chairs, and more, as well as handicrafts from Thailand, India, and other Asian countries. It's open daily from 10am to 6:30pm and can arrange shipping.

Macau, which didn't have one department store when I first visited in the 1980s, let alone boutiques or malls, is on the verge of a shopping explosion, with most new developments tied to its gaming industry. These glitzy new shopping malls are filled with international designer names, making Macau a mecca for mainland Chinese who can window-shop in Beijing or Shanghai but purchase the same goods in Macau at cheaper prices. The first large-scale addition to Macau's shopping and entertainment scene was **Fisherman's Wharf** (© **853/2899 3300;** www.fishermanswharf. com.mo), just a few minutes' walk from the ferry terminal. In Cotai, the **Shoppes at Four Seasons** (© **853/8117 7992;** www.shoppesatfourseasons.com) is a luxury mall connected to the Four Seasons Hotel with more than 160 designer brands, including Chanel, Dior, Prada, and Ferragamo, but it's the nearby Venetian Macao-Resort-Hotel's **Grand Canal Shoppes** (© **853/2882 8888;** www.venetianmacao. com) that boasts Macau's most ambitious mall to date, with a million square feet of retail space housing 350 designer shops, designed around a Venetian theme complete with canals and gondoliers. It's just the start of many more retail complexes planned for Cotai.

Nightlife

For many years, Macau's only nighttime entertainment outside gambling centered on hotel bars and lounges. While these are still recommendable for a drink and live entertainment, one of the few benefits to have arisen from the otherwise hideously sterile reclaimed-land development on the Outer Harbour is the **Docks,** a string of sidewalk cafes and bars lining Avenida Dr. Sun Yat-sen near the Kun Iam Statue (locals also refer to it as Lan Kwai Fong, after Hong Kong's famous nightlife district). It's a great place for a drink and watching the parade of people file past. True to Macau's Mediterranean roots, the action doesn't start until after 10pm and is at its most frenetic after 1am. For a suggestion, try **Moonwalker** (© **853/2875 1326**), open daily from 4pm to 4am (to 5am Fri–Sat) and offering happy hour daily until 9pm, free Wi-Fi, and live music Wednesday through Monday nights from 10pm.

If you've had dinner in Taipa Village, consider ambling over to the **Old Taipa Tavern,** 21 Rua dos Negociantes (© **853/2882 5221**), popular with the expat crowd. Open to the street with sidewalk seating, it offers a good selection of draft beers and cocktails. It's open daily from noon to midnight, with happy hour from 5 to 8pm.

FAST FACTS

FAST FACTS: HONG KONG & MACAU

Your hotel concierge or guest relations manager is usually a valuable source of information. The Hong Kong Tourism Board (HKTB) is also well equipped and eager to help visitors and answer their questions.

For additional information on Macau not covered here, see "Fast Facts: Macau," p. 291.

Area Codes   The area code for Hong Kong is 852. The area code for Macau is 853.

Business Hours   Although open hours can vary, banking hours are generally Monday through Friday from 9am to 4:30pm and Saturday from 9am to 12:30pm. Keep in mind, however, that some banks stop their transactions—including foreign currency exchange—an hour before closing time.

Most business offices are open Monday through Friday from 9am to 5pm, with lunch hour from 1 to 2pm; for those that have them (civil servants adopted a 5-day work week in 2006), Saturday business hours are generally 9am to 1pm.

Most shops are open 7 days a week. Shops in the Central District in Hong Kong are generally open from 10am to 7:30pm; in Causeway Bay and Wan Chai, 10am to 9:30pm; and in Tsim Sha Tsui, 10am to 9 or 10pm (and some even later than that). As for bars, most stay open until at least 2am; some stay open until the crack of dawn.

Cellphones (Mobile Phones)   See "Staying Connected," p. 53.

Dentists & Doctors   Many first-class hotels have medical clinics with registered nurses, as well as doctors, on duty at specified hours or on call 24 hours for emergencies. Otherwise, the concierge can refer you to a doctor or dentist. The U.S. consulate (see "Embassies & Consulates," below) can also provide information on English-speaking doctors. If it's an emergency, dial 𝄐 **999** (a free call) in both Hong Kong and Macau, or contact one of the recommendations under "Hospitals," below. For Macau, see "Hospitals," in "Fast Facts: Macau," p. 291.

Drinking Laws   The legal age for purchase and consumption of alcoholic beverages (and tobacco) in Hong Kong and Macau is 18. Open hours for bars vary according to the district, though those around Lan Kwai Fong and Tsim Sha Tsui in Hong Kong stay open the longest, often until dawn. In Macau, most every casino has at least one bar that is open 24 hours. Beer is available at convenience stores, including 7-Eleven, while a larger selection of beer, wine, and liquor is available from the basement food emporiums of department stores.

Drugstores   Hong Kong does not have any 24-hour drugstores, so if you need something urgently in the middle of the night, you should contact one of the hospitals listed below. One of the best-known pharmacies in Hong

Kong is **Watson's,** which dates back to the 1880s. Today, more than 100 Watson's are spread throughout Hong Kong, most of them open from 9am to 10pm. Ask the concierge at your hotel for the location of a Watson's or drugstore nearest you (only about half the Watson's dispense medicine; the rest deal only in cosmetics and toiletries). Note, however, that prescriptions can be filled only when ordered by a local doctor.

Macau also does not have 24-hour drugstores. Look for signs that say DROGARIA or FARMÁCIA, or ask your concierge for the location of the nearest drugstore.

Electricity   The electricity used in both Hong Kong and Macau is 220 volts, alternating current (AC), 50 cycles (in the U.S. and Canada it's 110 volts and 60 cycles). Most laptop computers nowadays are equipped to deal with both 110 and 220 volts. Outlets are the British-style three-pin, rectangular plugs. Most hotels are equipped to fit shavers of different plugs and voltages, and higher-end hotels also have outlets with built-in plug adapters to fit foreign prongs. For cheaper hotels, ask your hotel whether it has a plug adapter you can use—many often do, for free—or bring your own.

Embassies & Consulates   The following consulates are in Hong Kong. If you need to contact a consulate about an application for a visa, a lost passport, tourist information, or an emergency, telephone first to find out the hours of the various sections. The visa section, for example, may be open only during certain hours of the day. In addition, consulates are usually closed for their own national holidays and often for Hong Kong holidays as well.

The **American Consulate,** 26 Garden Rd., Central District (© **852/2523 9011;** 852/2841 2211 for the American Citizens Service; http://hongkong.usconsulate.gov), is open Monday through Friday from 8:30am to 12:30pm and 1:30 to 5:30pm; its hours of service for American citizens is Monday to Friday 8:30am to noon and 1:30 to 4pm (closed Wed afternoon).

The **Canadian Consulate,** 12th–14th floors of Tower One, Exchange Square, 8 Connaught Place, Central District (© **852/3719 4700;** www.canadainternational.gc.ca/hong_kong), is open Monday through Friday from 8:30am to 1:30pm.

The **British Consulate,** at 1 Supreme Court Rd., Central District (© **852/2901 3000;** http://ukinhongkong.fco.gov.uk/en), is open Monday through Friday from 8:30am to 5:15pm.

The **Australian Consulate** is on the 23rd floor of Harbour Centre, 25 Harbour Rd., Wan Chai (© **852/2827 8881;** www.hongkong.china.embassy.gov.au), and is open Monday through Friday from 9am to 5pm.

The **New Zealand Consulate** is on the 65th floor of Central Plaza, 18 Harbour Rd., Wan Chai (© **852/2525 5044;** www.nzembassy.com/hong-kong), and is open Monday through Friday from 8:30am to 1pm and 2 to 5pm.

For information on visa applications to mainland **China,** contact a tour operator such as China Travel Service (see "China," in chapter 11).

Emergencies   All emergency calls in Hong Kong and Macau are free—just dial © **999** for police, fire, or ambulance.

Holidays   Most Chinese festival holidays are determined by the lunar calendar, which changes each year, while national and Christian religious holidays, such as Labour Day, Easter, or National Day, are the same each year. Note, however, that if a public holiday falls on a Sunday, Monday becomes a holiday. For detailed information on specific holidays and the way they're celebrated, see "Hong Kong Calendar of Events" in chapter 3.

Public holidays for 2011 are New Year's Day (Jan 1); Lunar New Year (Feb 3–5); Ching Ming Festival (Apr 5); Easter (Good Friday through Easter Monday, Apr 22–25); Labour Day (May 2); Buddha's Birthday (May 10); Tuen Ng Festival (Dragon Boat

Festival, June 6); Hong Kong Special Administrative Region Establishment Day (Hong Kong's return to China, July 1); Chinese Mid-Autumn Festival (Sept 13); National Day (Oct 1); Chung Yeung Festival (Oct 5); and Christmas (Dec 25–27). For 2012 lunar holidays, which had not yet been announced at press time, go to www.info.gov.hk/about/abouthk/holiday.

Hospitals   Hong Kong has more than 40 public hospitals. The following can help you round the clock: **Queen Mary Hospital,** 102 Pokfulam Rd., Hong Kong Island (© **852/2855 3838;** www3.ha.org.hk/qmh/index.htm); and **Queen Elizabeth Hospital,** 30 Gascoigne Rd., Kowloon (© **852/2958 8888;** www3.ha.org.hk/qeh/index.htm). For Macau hospitals, see "Fast Facts: Macau," p. 291.

Insurance   For information on traveler's insurance, trip cancelation insurance, and medical insurance while traveling, please visit www.frommers.com/tips.

Internet Access   See "Staying Connected," p. 53.

Languages   Before the 1997 handover, English and Cantonese were Hong Kong's two official languages. Now, however, English and "Chinese" are listed as the two official languages. However, there is no one Chinese language. Most Hong Kong and Macau Chinese speak Cantonese, but in Beijing, where the official language is Mandarin (Putonghua), Cantonese is a foreign language. In reality, Mandarin has also become the official language of the SAR and is being taught in Hong Kong schools. At any rate, while Mandarin and Cantonese differ widely, they use the same characters for writing. Therefore, while a Hong Kong Chinese and a mainland Chinese may not be able to communicate orally, they can read each other's newspapers. Chinese characters number in the tens of thousands; knowledge of at least 2,500 characters is necessary to read a newspaper. Chinese is difficult to learn primarily because of the tonal variations. Western ears may find these differences in pronunciation almost impossible to detect, but a slight change in tone changes the whole meaning. One thing you'll notice, however, is that Chinese is spoken loudly—whispering does not seem to be part of the language.

Despite the fact that English is an official language and is spoken in hotels and tourist shops, few Chinese outside these areas understand it. Bus drivers, taxi drivers, and waiters in many Chinese restaurants do not speak English and will simply shrug their shoulders to your query. To avoid confusion, have someone in your hotel write out your destination in Chinese so that you can show it to your taxi or bus driver (and don't forget to pick up your hotel's card in case you need to show it to a taxi driver for your return). Most Chinese restaurants in tourist areas—and almost all those listed in this book—have English menus. If you need assistance, try asking younger Chinese, since it's more likely that they will have studied English in school.

If you'd like to learn some basic Cantonese before your trip, good choices are *Conversational Cantonese Chinese* (Pimsleur, 2006) and *Berlitz Cantonese Chinese CD Travel Pack* (Berlitz, 2003), since both include a CD so you can listen to the tonal differences. Or, to listen to a few key Cantonese phrases, go to HKTB's website at www.discoverhongkong.com and click "Plan Your Trip," then "About Hong Kong," and then "Languages."

Laundromats   Hotels provide laundry service, though it's expensive. Only a few modestly priced accommodations catering to families have coin-operated washers and dryers (see individual hotel listings in chapters 5 and 12). Otherwise, laundromats in Hong Kong and Macau are generally not self-service. Rather, you drop off your laundry and come back a few hours later to fetch your clothes neatly folded. If that's what you need, ask the concierge for the closest one. Clean Living (© **852/2333 0141;** www.cleanliving.com.hk) is Hong Kong's largest laundry-service provider, with more than 30 branches open daily.

Legal Aid Contact your embassy if you find yourself in legal trouble. If you can't afford a solicitor (attorney), contact the Hong Kong government's **Legal Aid Department,** 24th to 27th floors of the Queensway Government Offices, 66 Queensway (✆ **852/2537 7677;** www.lad.gov.hk), which provides legal aid to both residents and nonresidents who become involved in court proceedings, with fees based on a sliding scale according to the client's ability to pay. In addition, the **Community Legal Information Centre** provides useful information and legal advice on its website, www.hkclic.org, from how to obtain free legal advice to how to find a lawyer.

Lost & Found To report stolen or lost property, call the **police:** ✆ **852/2527 7177** in Hong Kong; ✆ **853/2857 3333** in Macau, or go to the nearest police station. If you've lost your passport, make a police report at the nearest station and then contact your embassy or consulate for a replacement. The minute you discover your wallet has been lost or stolen, alert all of your credit card companies and file a report at the nearest police station. Your credit card company or insurer may require a police report number or record of the loss. Most credit card companies have an emergency toll-free number to call if your card is lost or stolen; they may be able to wire you a cash advance immediately or deliver an emergency credit card in a day or two. Visa's Hong Kong emergency number is ✆ **800/900 782.** American Express cardholders and traveler's check holders should call ✆ **852/2811 6122.** MasterCard holders should call ✆ **800/966 677.**

Luggage & Storage Lockers The best and most convenient place to store luggage is at your hotel, even if you plan on traveling to Macau or China for a couple of days. Otherwise, there are luggage-checking services ("left-luggage") at Hong Kong International Airport, Hong Kong Station, Kowloon Station, the Macau Ferry Terminal on Hong Kong Island, and the China Hong Kong Terminal on Canton Road, Tsim Sha Tsui.

Mail Postal service is cheap and reliable. Most hotels have stamps and can mail your letters for you. Otherwise, there are plenty of post offices throughout the SAR. Most are open Monday through Friday from 9:30am to 5pm and Saturday from 9:30am to 1pm. The main post office is on Hong Kong Island at 2 Connaught Place, in the Central District (✆ **852/2921 2222**), where you'll find stamps sold on the first floor (what those from the U.S. would call the second floor). If you don't know where you'll be staying in Hong Kong, you can have your mail sent to the main post office above as "Poste Restante," where it will be held for 2 months; when you come to collect it, be sure to bring your passport for identification. On the Kowloon side, the main post office is at 10 Middle Rd., which is 1 block north of Salisbury Road (✆ **852/2366 4111**). Both are open Monday through Saturday from 8am to 6pm; in addition, the Central post office is open Sunday and holidays from 9am to 5pm, while the Tsim Sha Tsui post office is open Sunday from 9am to 2pm (closed holidays).

Mailboxes are green in Hong Kong. Airmail letters up to 20 grams and postcards cost HK$3 to the United States, Europe, or Australia. You can count on airmail letters to take about 5 to 7 days, sometimes longer, to reach the United States.

Prices for mailing packages vary as follows: Australia surface 5kg HK$181, 10kg HK$213, air 5kg HK$355, 10kg HK$645; U.K. surface 5kg HK$233, 10kg HK$271, air 5kg HK$454, 10kg HK$784; U.S. surface 5kg (11 lb.) HK$251, 10kg (22 lb.) HK$441, air 5kg HK$419, 10kg HK$799. For general inquiries, call ✆ **852/2921 2222** or check www.hongkongpost.com/eng/index.htm.

For information on mail in Macau, see p. 292.

Newspapers & Magazines See "Staying Connected," p. 53.

Passports   For information on obtaining passports, please contact the following agencies:

For Residents of Australia   Contact the **Australian Passport Information Service** at ✆ **131-232,** or visit www.passports.gov.au.

For Residents of Canada   Contact the central **Passport Office,** Department of Foreign Affairs and International Trade, Ottawa, ON K1A 0G3 (✆ **800/567-6868;** www.ppt.gc.ca).

For Residents of Ireland   Contact the **Passport Office,** Setanta Centre, Molesworth Street, Dublin 2 (✆ **01/671-1633;** www.foreignaffairs.gov.ie).

For Residents of New Zealand   Contact the **Passports Office,** Department of Internal Affairs, 47 Boulcott St., Wellington, 6011 (✆ **0800/225-050** in New Zealand or 04/474-8100; www.passports.govt.nz).

For Residents of the United Kingdom   Visit your nearest passport office, major post office, or travel agency or contact the **Identity and Passport Service (IPS),** 89 Eccleston Square, London, SW1V 1PN (✆ **0300/222-0000;** www.ips.gov.uk).

For Residents of the United States   To find your regional passport office, check the U.S. State Department website (http://travel.state.gov/passport) or call the **National Passport Information Center** (✆ **877/487-2778**) for automated information.

Police   You can reach the police for an emergency by dialing ✆ **999,** the same number as for a fire or an ambulance in Hong Kong and Macau. This is a free call. There's also a 24-hour crime hot line in Hong Kong (✆ **852/2527 7177**).

Smoking   Hong Kong is mostly smoke-free, rare in Asia. Smoking is prohibited in virtually all public places, including restaurants, bars, nightclubs, workplaces, shopping malls, and most outdoor areas like public beaches and large swaths of public parks. The fine if you're caught smoking is HK$1,500.

Though there's movement underfoot to ban smoking in Macau, it's currently permitted in public places.

Taxes   Hong Kong is a duty-free port. In addition, since 2008 the 3% government tax has been waived for hotels and restaurants. A 10% service charge, however, is automatically added to bills for hotels, restaurants, and bars.

In Macau, also a duty-free port, hotels levy a 5% government tax and a 10% service charge on room rates. Restaurants also levy a 10% service charge, but government tax has been waived on the consumption of food and beverages.

Telephones   See "Staying Connected," p. 53.

Time   Hong Kong and Macau are 8 hours ahead of Greenwich Mean Time, 13 hours ahead of New York, 14 hours ahead of Chicago, 16 hours ahead of Los Angeles, and 2 hours ahead of Sydney. Because Hong Kong does not have a daylight saving time, subtract 1 hour from the above times if you're calling the United States in the summer. Because Hong Kong is on the other side of the international date line, you lose 1 day when traveling from North America to Asia. Don't worry—you gain it back when you return, which means that you arrive back home the same day you left Hong Kong.

Tipping   Even though restaurants and bars will automatically add a 10% service charge to your bill, you're still expected to leave small change for the waiter (who may never see any of that automatic 10% service charge). A general rule of thumb is to leave 5%, but in most Chinese restaurants where meals are usually inexpensive (less than HK$100), it's acceptable to leave change up to HK$5. In the finest restaurants, you should leave 10%. If you're paying by credit card, pay a cash tip, because a gratuity put on a credit card is likely to go to the restaurant and not the staff.

You're also expected to tip taxi drivers, bellhops, barbers, and beauticians. For taxi drivers, add up to the nearest HK$1, or, for longer hauls, round up to the nearest

HK$5; for a HK$23 fare, for example, round up to HK$25. Tip people who cut your hair 5% or 10%, and give bellhops HK$10 to HK$20, depending on the number of your bags. Chambermaids and room attendants are usually given about 2% of the room charge.

Toilets   The best places to track down public facilities in Hong Kong and Macau are its many hotels, fast-food restaurants, and shopping malls. Attendants on duty nowadays rarely expect tips, but if you encounter one who does, HK$2 is sufficient. Note that the MTR subway stations do not have public facilities. Hotels and tourist sites usually have Western toilets, but you may encounter Chinese toilets on ferries and in rural areas. To use them, squat facing the hood. Since some public facilities may not have toilet paper, be sure to carry tissue (in rural areas, a communal roll of toilet paper may be hanging outside the stalls).

Useful Phone Numbers & Websites   The Hong Kong Tourism Board's hot line is ✆ **852/2508 1234**, with service available daily from 9am to 6pm. The Police Crime Hotline is ✆ **852/2527 7177**. Other useful numbers and websites are:

- Hong Kong's Department of Health ✆ **852/2961 8989**; www.dh.gov.hk
- Hong Kong Telephone Directory Enquiries ✆ **1081** for local numbers, ✆ **10013** for international numbers
- Hong Kong Special Administrative Region Government www.gov.hk

Visas   No visas are required for citizens of the United States, Canada, United Kingdom, New Zealand, or Australia. For more information, go to www.gov.hk/en/nonresidents.

Visitor Information   The **Hong Kong Tourism Board (HKTB)** offers a wealth of free information for travelers.

HKTB Online: You can have a virtual visit to Hong Kong at HKTB's home page, **www.discoverhongkong.com**. The site provides a comprehensive overview of Hong Kong—maps of the region, major attractions, a detailed weekly calendar of performing arts and festivals, listings for hotels and restaurants, suggested itineraries, and guided tours. It also provides links to e-ticketing services so you can book shows, events, and concerts online before your arrival.

HKTB Overseas: Although the information stocked by HKTB offices abroad is sometimes not as up-to-date or as thorough as that available in Hong Kong itself or through the Internet (see above), it's worth contacting a local HKTB office before leaving home for general information and a map.

In the United States: General information can be obtained by calling ✆ **800/282-4582**. HKTB offices are located at 115 E. 54th St., 2nd floor, New York, NY 10022-4512 (✆ **212/421-3382**; fax 212/421-8428; nycwwo@hktb.com); and 5670 Wilshire Blvd., Ste. 1230, Los Angeles, CA 90036 (✆ **323/938-4582**; fax 323/938-4583; laxwwo@hktb.com).

In Canada: 9 Temperance St., Toronto, ON, Canada M5H 1Y6 (✆ **416/366-2389**; fax 416/366-1098; yyzwwo@hktb.com).

In the United Kingdom: Mutual House, 6th House, 70 Conduit St., London W1S 2GF, England (✆ **207/432-7700**; fax 207/432-7701; lonwwo@hktb.com).

In Australia: Hong Kong House, Level 4, 80 Druitt St., Sydney, NSW 2000, Australia (✆ **02/9283-3083**; fax 02/9283-3383; sydwwo@hktb.com).

HKTB in Hong Kong: Three **HKTB** counters are located in the arrival halls of the Hong Kong International Airport, all open daily from 7am to 11pm. In town, two **HKTB Visitor Centres** are on both sides of the harbor. On the Kowloon side, a convenient office in Tsim Sha Tsui is right in the Star Ferry concourse, open daily from 8am to 8pm. On Hong Kong

Island, you'll find a convenient office if you're going to Victoria Peak (and who isn't?), occupying a vintage tram car on the plaza outside the Peak Tower, that's open daily 9am to 9pm.

If you have a question about Hong Kong, you can also call the **HKTB Visitor Hotline** (*© **852/2508 1234**) daily from 9am to 6pm. After hours, a telephone-answering device will take your call and a member of HKTB will contact you the next day at your hotel.

In addition to HKTB's free map, HKTB publishes a wealth of free, excellent literature about Hong Kong. *Visitor's Kit* is a booklet that gives a brief rundown of Hong Kong's major tourist attractions and information on shopping and dining, while *Hong Kong Kaleidoscope* outlines HKTB's current free classes and seminars in its excellent "Meet the People" program. *Discover Hong Kong by Rail* is useful for trips to the New Territories, while *Hong Kong Walks* is designed for those who like to explore on foot. For families, the *Hong Kong Family Fun Guide* highlights children's sights and activities. In addition, invaluable leaflets are available showing the major bus routes throughout Hong Kong, including Hong Kong Island, Kowloon, and the New Territories, and for current ferry schedules to the outlying islands.

If you're traveling with a Wi-Fi–enabled phone or laptop and want to know more about a landmark you're passing or a good spot for lunch, you can surf HKTB's website for free at more than 7,000 PCCW Wi-Fi hot spots around town, including most MTR platforms, Starbucks and Pacific Coffee outlets, 7-Eleven and Circle K convenience stores, and PCCW phone booths (browsing does not include hyperlinks to third-party websites). Through the service you can also download free tourist apps, such as the *Hong Kong Mobile Travel Guide,* with information on sightseeing, dining, and shopping.

To find out what's going on during your stay in Hong Kong, pick up HKTB's free weekly leaflet *What's On—Hong Kong,* which tells what's happening in theater, music, and the arts, including concerts and special exhibitions in museums (you can also access HKTB's event calendar at www.discoverhongkong.com). Hong Kong's Leisure and Cultural Services Department (www.lcsd.gov.hk) also puts out its own monthly *Event Calendar.* The *South China Morning Post,* a local newspaper, carries an events and exhibition section in its Sunday edition. *HK Magazine,* aimed at a young expat readership and distributed free at restaurants, bars, and other outlets around town, is a weekly that lists what's going on at the city's theaters and other venues, including plays, concerts, exhibitions, the cinema, and events in Hong Kong's alternative scene. *Where Hong Kong, CityLife,* and *bc* are other free magazines published monthly with information on Hong Kong. *Where Hong Kong* and *CityLife* are distributed to guest rooms in major hotels and are also available at HKTB offices; *bc* is distributed to bookstores and restaurants.

Water   It's considered safe to drink urban tap water in Hong Kong and Macau, though most people prefer bottled water, which is widely available. In summer it's wise to carry bottled water with you. Some hotels have their own purification systems; many more provide a free bottle of water in their rooms. I always drink the water and have never gotten ill. If you travel into rural Hong Kong or China, however, drink only bottled water.

Weather   If you want to check the day's temperature and humidity level in Hong Kong or the 2-day forecast, dial *© **187 8200** for a free weather report in English. Otherwise, if a storm is brewing and you're worried about a typhoon, tune in to one of Hong Kong's English-language TV channels, either TVB Pearl or ATV World, or go to the Hong Kong Observatory's website at www.hko.gov.hk.

AIRLINE WEBSITES

AIRLINES FLYING TO HONG KONG

Air Canada
www.aircanada.com

Air France
www.airfrance.com

Air India
www.airindia.com

Air New Zealand
www.airnewzealand.com

All Nippon Airways
www.anaskyweb.com

British Airways
www.british-airways.com

Cathay Pacific
www.cathaypacific.com

China Airlines
www.china-airlines.com

Continental Airlines
www.continental.com

Delta Air Lines
www.delta.com

Dragonair
www.dragonair.com

El Al Airlines
www.elal.co.il

Emirates Airlines
www.emirates.com

Finnair
www.finnair.com

Hong Kong Airlines
www.hkairlines.com

Hong Kong Express
www.hongkongexpress.com

Japan Airlines
www.jal.co.jp

Jetstar Asia Airways
www.jetstar.com

KLM Royal Dutch Airlines
www.klm.com.hk

Korean Air
www.koreanair.com

Lufthansa
www.lufthansa.com

Philippine Airlines
www.philippineairlines.com

Qantas Airways
www.qantas.com.au

Singapore Airlines
www.singaporeair.com

South African Airways
www.flysaa.com

Swiss Air
www.swiss.com

Thai Airways International
www.thaiair.com

United Airlines
www.united.com

Virgin Atlantic Airways
www.virgin-atlantic.com

Index

See also Accommodations and Restaurant indexes, below.

General Index

A

Aberdeen, 62, 175
restaurants, 156–157
Accommodations, 70–105. *See also* Accommodations Index
best, 4–6, 72, 74, 76
Causeway Bay & Wan Chai
expensive, 88
inexpensive, 102–103
moderate, 96–98
very expensive, 83–84
Central District
expensive, 87–88
inexpensive, 102
moderate, 95
very expensive, 81–83
family-friendly, 85
guesthouses, 104–105
Kowloon
expensive, 84–86
inexpensive, 99–102
moderate, 89–95
very expensive, 80–81
Macau, 293–300
Mid-Levels, 95–96
money-saving tips, 78–79
price categories, 80
with rock-bottom rates, 103–105
selecting, 77–80
youth hostels and dormitory beds, 105
Acupuncture, 13
Addresses, finding, 58, 60
Admiralty, 61
Afternoon tea, 162–163
Agave, 249
Airline websites, 332
Air Macau, 288
Air pollution, 48
Airport Express Line, 35
Airport Hotelink, 35
Air travel, 34–35
Macau, 288
Alexandra House, 232
All Night Long, 246
Al's Diner, 249
A-Ma, 179
A-Man Hing Cheong Co., LTD., 239
A-Ma Temple (Macau), 311, 322
American citizens
Consulate, 326
customs regulations, 33
Macau Tourist Office, 284–285

passports, 329
visitor information in, 330
Amusement parks, 183–184
Antiques and collectibles, 224–226
Ap Lei Chau, 224
Apliu Street, 232
Aqualuna, 187
Aqua Spirit, 246
Arch Angel Antiques, 225
Architecture, 22–25
Area codes, 325
Macau, 291–292
Art galleries, 226–227
Art museums
Handover Gifts Museum of Macao (Macau), 309
Hong Kong Museum of Art, 170–171, 211
Macao Museum of Art, 309
Asian Artefacts (Macau), 324
ATMs (automated-teller machines), 46
Attractions, 164–217
Aberdeen, 175
Hong Kong Island, 172–175, 182–183
museums and galleries. *See* Museums and galleries
organized tours and cultural activities, 185–188
parks and gardens, 180–183
Camoes Garden (Jardim Luís De Camoes; Macau), 318
Hong Kong Park, 182
Hong Kong Zoological and Botanical Gardens, 182–183
Kowloon Park, 180
Kowloon Walled City Park, 180–181
Lou Lim Ieoc Garden (Macau), 312–313
Nan Lian Garden, 181
Victoria Park, 183
Yuen Po Street Bird Garden, 181–182
temples, 177–179
Che Kung Temple (Sha Tin), 258
Macau, 311–312
Man Mo Temple, 178, 207
Man Mo Temple (Tai Po), 260
Na Tcha Temple (Macau), 317
Pak Tai Temple (Cheung Chau), 270
Tsui Sing Lau Pagoda, 265
Wong Tai Sin, 178–179
top attractions, 164–170

Australia
Consulate, 326
customs regulations, 33
Macau Tourist Office, 285
passports, 329
visitor information in, 330
Avenida Almeida Ribeiro (Macau), 320
Avian flu, 21, 47

B

Bahama Mama's, 246
Ballet, 243
Bank of China Tower, 196
Bargaining, 221
Bars, pubs and lounges
Central District, 248–252
Kowloon, 246–248
Beaches, 190
Cheung Chau, 271
Lamma, 273–274
Macau, 314
Beer, 117
Big Bus Company, 40
Bird Garden, Yuen Po Street, 181–182
Blanc de, 233
Boat travel and tours, 186–187
Aberdeen, 175
from the airport, 36
Macau, 286–288
Books, recommended, 25–26
Botanical Gardens, Hong Kong Zoological and, 182–183
Bowen Road, 190
British citizens
Consulate, 326
customs regulations, 33
Macau Tourist Office, 285
passports, 329
visitor information in, 330
Broadway, 231–232
Buddha's Birthday, 31
Buddhism, 176
Bulldog's Bar & Grill, 249
Business attire, 50
Business cards, 50
Business hours, 325
Business travelers, tips for, 50
Bus travel, 39–40
from the airport, 37
Macau, 289–290

C

Café Gray Bar, 199, 249
Calendar of events, 30–32
Camoes Garden (Jardim Luís De Camoes; Macau), 318
Canada
Consulate, 326
customs regulations, 33
passports, 329
visitor information in, 330

Accommodations

Restaurants